THE ROUTLEDGE BOOK OF
WORLD PROVERBS

A good book, a good friend. (Italian)

Neither love nor a cough can be hidden. (Roman)

Knowledge is a treasure, but practice is the key to it. (Arabian)

One enemy is too many, one hundred friends is not enough. (Indian)

The Routledge Book of World Proverbs invites the reader to travel the globe in search of the origins of such words of wisdom, experiencing the rich cultural traditions reflected in each nation's proverbs. This collection contains over 16,000 gems of humor and pathos that draw upon themes from our shared experiences of life. And we are not just invited to learn about other cultures; proverbs are 'bits of ancient wisdom' and thus teach us about our shared histories.

This book draws together proverbs that transcend culture, time and space to offer a collection that is both useful and enjoyable, making this book one of enduring interest.

Professor Jon R. Stone specializes in Theories and Methods in the Study of Religion. He is author or editor of nine books, including *The Essential Max Müller* (2002), *Expecting Armageddon: Essential Readings in Failed Prophecy* (Routledge, 2000), *The Craft of Religious Studies* (1998), and *Latin for the Illiterati* (Routledge, 1996), which was named '1997 Outstanding Reference Source' by the American Library Association.

THE ROUTLEDGE BOOK OF WORLD PROVERBS

Jon R. Stone

Routledge
Taylor & Francis Group

LONDON AND NEW YORK

First published 2006 by Routledge

2 Park Square, Milton Park, Abingdon, Oxfordshire OX14 4RN
52 Vanderbilt Avenue, New York, NY 10017

Routledge is an imprint of the Taylor & Francis Group, an informa business

First issued in paperback 2018

Typeset in Bembo by RefineCatch Limited, Bungay, Suffolk

Library of Congress Cataloging in Publication Data
Stone, Jon R., 1959–
The Routledge book of world proverbs / Jon R. Stone.
    p. cm.
Includes bibliographical references and index.
1. Proverbs. I. Title.
PN6405.S85 2006
398.9—dc22
2006008640

British Library Cataloguing in Publication Data
A catalogue record for this book is available from the British Library

ISBN13: 978–0–415–97423–3 (hbk)
ISBN13: 978–0–415–97424–0 (pbk)

Also available from Routledge

Language: the Basics (Second edition)
R.L. Trask
0–415–34019–5

Semiotics: the Basics (Second edition)
Daniel Chandler
0–415–36375–6

Psycholinguistics: the Key Concepts
John Field
0–415–25891–X

Key Concepts in Language and Linguistics
R.L. Trask
0–415–15742–0

The Routledge Companion to Semiotics and Linguistics
Paul Cobley
0–415–24314–9

The Routledge Dictionary of English Language Studies
Michael Pearce
0–415–35172–3

The Routledge Dictionary of Egyptian Gods and Goddesses
George Hart
0–415–34495–6

The Routledge Dictionary of Gods, Goddesses, Devils and Demons
Manfred Lurker
0–415–34018–7

British Folk Tales and Legends
Katharine Briggs
0–415–28602–6

Also by Jon R. Stone

Latin for the Illiterati (1996)
More Latin for the Illiterati (1999)
The Routledge Dictionary of Latin Quotations (2005)

and

The Craft of Religious Studies (1998)
The Essential Max Müller: On Language, Mythology, and Religion (2002)
Expecting Armageddon: Essential Readings in Failed Prophecy (2000)
A Guide to the End of the World (1993)
On the Boundaries of American Evangelicalism (1997)
Prime-Time Religion: An Encyclopedia of Religious Broadcasting (1997)

In honor of Dr William P. Germano

The dean of academic editors —

with deepest appreciation

CONTENTS

PREFACE

'Wisdom is learned through the wisdom of others.' – Yoruban

In his small book of Persian proverbs, Lawrence Elwell-Sutton relates the fable of a sparrow into whose nest the wind chances to blow a cotton seed. Not knowing what it was, the sparrow inquired of his neighbor and learned that, at length, the seed, if planted, would grow to produce cotton, which could be spun into thread, which could be woven into cloth, which could be dyed and sewn into fine coats, which then could be sold at the bazaar. Delighted by the prospect of gain, the sparrow thereupon took the seed to a peasant farmer, saying, 'Sow this seed! Half for me, half for you.' The farmer agreed. After a time, the seed produced a plant whose ripened cotton bolls the farmer divided with the sparrow. Next, the sparrow took his share of cotton to the spinner, saying, 'Spin this cotton! Half for me, half for you.' The spinner agreed, and when the thread was spun, he divided it with the sparrow. The sparrow then took the thread to the weaver, saying, 'Weave this thread! Half for me, half for you.' The weaver agreed and gave the sparrow half of what he had woven. Next, the sparrow took the cloth to the dyer, saying: 'Dye this cloth! Half for me, half for you.' The dyer agreed and dyed the cloth a brilliant blue. But when the sparrow saw the cloth drying on the line, he marveled at the color and thought to himself, 'What a pity to divide such a fine piece of cloth.' So, the sparrow swooped down, snatched the cloth, and took it to the tailor, saying, 'Sew this cloth into coats! One for me, one for you.' The tailor made two fine coats and hung them on a peg. But, seeing the coats, the sparrow marveled at the stitching and thought to himself. 'What a pity to share them with the tailor.' So, the sparrow swooped down, snatched the coats, and took them to the mullah to keep until the weather grew cold and they could be sold at the bazaar. But after the sparrow had flown away, the mullah thought to himself, 'What need has a sparrow for a coat,' and decided to keep them for himself. When winter approached, the sparrow came for his coats, but the mullah pretended to know nothing and offered instead to pray for the sparrow. Angry at being cheated, the sparrow flew off, but from a distance he saw the mullah washing the two coats and hanging them up to dry. When the mullah had gone off to pray, the sparrow swooped down, snatched both coats, and took them to the bazaar to sell. But on the way, a great wind blew and carried the two coats away, dropping one coat before the dyer and the other coat before the tailor. In this way justice was done. Hence the proverb, 'What is brought by the wind will be carried away by the wind' (see Elwell-Sutton 1954: 33–4).

This fable, reminiscent of those told by Aesop, offers an apt example of how a simple tale can teach a profound lesson. Not only is justice served, even to double-dealing sparrows and mullahs, but one learns that the wind, in bestowing her gifts, can be just as capricious as a bird. Indeed, one can almost hear the sparrow's neighbor – perchance having witnessed the whole affair from afar – sigh and then recite quietly to himself this very proverb, 'What is brought by the wind . . .,' his voice trailing off into a faint laugh. In this instance, 'recite' is perhaps the best word to use. For just as this sparrow's misadventure brought to mind the proverb cited above, who among us has not greeted the day by glancing out the window while reciting the line, 'Red sky in the morning, sailor take warning . . .,' or greeted someone with a handshake and not instinctively said to ourselves, 'Cold hand, warm heart,' or has not recited any of a number of proverbs hoping to 'snatch opportunity from the passing day'? Proverbs guide our thoughts and actions, and warn us of the hidden dangers along life's way. For, as Archbishop Richard Trench had counseled, 'There is hardly a mistake which in the course of our lives we have committed, but some proverb, had we known and attended to its lesson, might have saved us from it' (see Champion 1938: 3).

When hearing the word 'proverb,' one most often thinks of the wisdom imparted by King Solomon in the Bible or of the clever analects of the sagely Confucius. But proverbs are common to nearly all cultures, both ancient and modern, literate and non-literate. Generally speaking, proverbs are popular sayings that express commonly held truths, with their chief ingredients, according to James Howell, being 'sense, shortness, and salt.' They are, to quote Lord Russell, 'the wit of one and the wisdom of many.' And, as Sir Francis Bacon had pointed out, 'the genius, wit, and spirit of a nation are discovered in its proverbs.' But such observations are not limited to the English. Some 2,000 years before Bacon's time, Aristotle had gathered his own collection of 'ancient' proverbs, referring to them as 'fragments of an elder wisdom' whose 'brevity and aptness' had preserved them 'amidst wreck and ruin' (see Westermarck 1930: 1 and Champion 1938: xvii).

Proverbs are indeed bits of ancient wisdom that, as Max Müller had argued, bear 'the impress of the early days of mankind.' But their charm is not simply to be found in their being artifacts of an earlier day, or in their brevity and wit, but in the way they draw upon, and reflect, the common human experiences that are shared across time and space. The Spanish, after Cervantes, described the proverb as 'a short sentence based on long experience,' while the Dutch called it 'the daughter of daily experience.' To the Germans, proverbs can be compared to butterflies in that 'some are caught and some fly away.' Or, for the Arab, 'a proverb is to speech what salt is to food.' What is even more intriguing about the proverb is its freshness, applicability, and continued relevance to every age, including our own. Its is an ancient voice that appeals to every generation. For, when King Solomon compared a gold ring in a pig's snout to a beautiful woman who lacks discretion, he gave both a word of caution to his time and a knowing wink to our own. A similar observation is made by Elwell-Sutton: 'In East and West alike people "bury the hatchet," they "lay the axe to the root," they ask "who will bell the cat," they observe that "dog does not eat dog," and they laugh at "the pot for calling the kettle black" ' (1954: 4–5). Even a cursory glance at vintage collections of proverbs, such as those by Burton Stevenson and S.G. Champion, or the more recent ones by Rosalind Fergusson and Wolfgang Mieder, gives evidence of shared human concepts and experiences, if not borrowed turns of phrase. The similarities are certainly remarkable.

But, lest we see only a broad river with no rivulets flowing into it, Elwell-Sutton goes on to remind us that 'There may be a common stream of ideas, but as they pass through each cultural area they become changed and transmuted through contact with and absorption by local character, tradition and custom' (1954: 8). This comment calls to mind the old Latin proverb: 'Si duo dicunt idem non est idem'; that is, 'If two languages say the same thing, it is not the same thing.' And so, as Elwell-Sutton writes further, 'a loaf of bread means one thing to us, another thing to a Persian.' And again, 'in Persia . . . the sun is generally a torment from which one is glad to escape, [but] in Britain it is a rare and welcome visitor' (1954: 9).

The value and importance, then, of a collection of ancient and modern proverbs from peoples around the world, lies in what we can learn about customs and cultures different from ours. Proverbs can also teach us something about the character of our own. As Elwell-Sutton puts it, 'A study of their proverbs and folk-lore attached to them will not only give us an idea of outside influences to which they have been subjected in the past, but will also illumine their ways of thought and their national characteristics to an extent that perhaps no other medium can do' (1954: 8). In this way, by presenting a treasury of ancient and modern proverbs, *The Routledge Book of World Proverbs* seeks to provide its readers with a collection of wise sayings drawn from humanity's shared experiences in the world as well as miniature portraits of humankind's likewise distinct cultural characteristics.

But, while the aim throughout has been to compile as comprehensive a treasury of world proverbs as possible, it did not seem desirable, or even prudent, to heap proverb upon proverb without some way to 'separate the wheat from the chaff.' In preparing his comprehensive book of world proverbs, S.G. Champion expressed frustration over the careless way by which others before him had classified proverbs. He was determined to define more precisely the kinds of sayings that would belong more properly in a collection of proverbs. He writes: 'I can conceive of no greater mental punishment than to be compelled to wade through a collection of so-called proverbs which almost invariably consists of a heterogeneous conglomeration of sayings, colloquialisms, idioms, slang, bon mots, rhymes, riddles, and a mass of stupid, silly, commonplace proverbs, producing in my unfortunate translators and myself a boredom verging on tears' (1938: xiii). To Champion's complaint, I would add that a great number of the proverbs that I have encountered in standard works were little more than statements of obvious facts, insults, similes, hackneyed phrases, or humorous asides. Some examples include: 'Go and wake up your luck' (Persian); 'Don't teach your grandmother to suck eggs' (French); 'He has too many lice to feel an itch' (Chinese); 'Let the big dog eat' (American); 'Either a man or a mouse' (Scottish); 'He cannot find water in the sea' (Spanish); 'You have hit the nail on the head' (Roman); and 'He goes as willingly as a thief to the gallows' (German). Thus, in this present collection, I have endeavored to include only those proverbs which most folklorists and paremiologists would recognize as such.

Beside the initial problem of defining the difference between the proverb and simple idiomatic expressions, there were also nagging problems posed in attempting to attribute proverbs to their respective languages or rightful countries of origin. For instance, one discovers English proverbs in India, China, and America, French and Dutch proverbs in Asia and Africa, Spanish and Portuguese proverbs in the Philippines and the New World, and, of course, Greek and Roman proverbs throughout Europe, North Africa, and the Middle East. What is more, many Japanese, Vietnamese, and Korean proverbs appear to be derived from older Chinese proverbs. Added to this problem is the difficulty of determining in which direction these cultural influences flowed. Chinese merchants and European explorers were doubtlessly influenced by the cultures they sought to trade with or dominate. And no doubt, emigrants traveling to the United States in the nineteenth and twentieth centuries brought with them their peculiar customs as well as their folk wisdom. For instance, the proverb 'Every man hath a fool in his sleeve,' is found in Italian as well as American collections. Additionally, in Anand Prahlad's *Reggae Wisdom*, one finds in reggae lyrics such well-known proverbs as 'Birds of a feather flock together,' 'An ounce of prevention is worth a pound of cure,' and 'Jah [i.e., God] helps those who help themselves,' among scores of others.

Related to the issue of the proper attribution of proverbs was the problem of multiple versions of the same proverb. As an example, the Italian proverb 'Good wine needs no bush' is also found in Spanish as 'Good wine needs no crier,' in French as 'Good wine needs no sign,' in Dutch as 'Good wine praises itself,' and in German as 'Good wine sells itself.' The same types of variations occur in 'Faint heart never won fair lady,' 'Every cock is proud on its own dung hill,' and other such proverbs. With so many versions of one proverb, not only is it difficult to decide which version is the original one, but it makes for far too much repetition in a book of proverbs, as is the case with Wolfgang Mieder's text. The repetition of the same basic proverb in all its variations evokes the witty Yiddish saying: 'Once gets a cheer, twice a deaf ear, thrice a kick in the rear.'

Last of all, during the years that I have been working on this project, and even beginning with my first Latin book, I have encountered within nearly all cultures many – too many – racist and sexist proverbs, proverbs that would no doubt offend modern readers. Some of the more mild examples include 'Lilies are whitest in a black Moor's hand' (Italian), 'He that would cheat a Jew, must be a Jew' (German), 'Biting and scratching is Scots folk's wooing' (English), and 'Beat your wife on the wedding day, and your married life will be happy' (Japanese). While, for a variety of cultural and historical reasons, some editors might wish to include these types of proverbs, I have chosen otherwise and have tried my very best to keep offensive and belittling proverbs out of this collection.

Notwithstanding these and other minor imperfections, it is hoped that readers will be charmed and edified by the selection of proverbs in this collection, and will delight in sharing them with their families and friends. Perchance a seed or two of the world's wisdom will blow into a neighboring sparrow's nest.

Humani Nihil Alienum.

Jon R. Stone
California State University, Long Beach
August 2005

REFERENCES AND SOURCES

Apperson, George L. *English Proverbs and Proverbial Phrases*. London: J.M. Dent; New York: Dutton, 1929.

Aquilina, Joseph. *A Comparative Dictionary of Maltese Proverbs*. Msida: The Royal University of Malta, 1972.

Ayalti, Hanan J. *Yiddish Proverbs* (trans. by Isidore Goldstick). New York: Schocken Books, 1949.

Ballesteros, Octavio A. *Mexican Proverbs: The Philosophy, Wisdom, and Humor of a People*. Burnet, TX: Eakin Press, 1979.

Bartlett, John R. *Dictionary of Americanisms* (4th edn, enlarged). Boston: Little, Brown & Co., 1896.

Beilenson, Peter. *Chinese Proverbs from Olden Times*. Mt. Vernon, NY: Peter Pauper Press, 1956.

Benham, W. Gurney. *Benham's Book of Quotations, Proverbs, and Household Words* (new & rev. edn). London: G.G. Harrap, 1948.

Berrey, Lester V. *A Treasury of Biblical Quotations*. Garden City, NY: Doubleday, 1948.

Bohn, Henry G. *A Hand-book of Proverbs; Comprising an Entire Republication of Ray's Collection of English Proverbs with His Additions from Foreign Languages*. London: H.G. Bohn, 1855.

———. *A Polyglot of Foreign Proverbs . . ., with English Translations*. London: H.G. Bohn, 1857.

Brougham, Aileen E. and A.W. Reed. *Maori Proverbs*. Wellington, NZ: A.H. & A.W. Reed Ltd, 1963.

Brown, Brian. *The Wisdom of the Chinese: Their Philosophy in Sayings and Proverbs*. New York: Garden City Publishing Company, 1938.

Browning, David C. *Everyman's Dictionary of Quotations and Proverbs*. London: Dent; New York: Dutton, 1952.

Buchanan, Daniel C. *Japanese Proverbs and Sayings*. Norman, OK: University of Oklahoma Press, 1965.

Burckhardt, John Lewis. *Arabic Proverbs; or the Manner and Customs of the Modern Egyptians, Illustrated from their Proverbial Sayings Current at Cairo*. London: Curzon Press, 1984 (originally published in 1830).

Champion, Selwyn Gurney. *Racial Proverbs* (2nd edn). London: Routledge & Kegan Paul, 1938.

Christy, Robert. *Proverbs, Maxims, and Phrases of All Ages*. New York and London, G.P. Putnam's Sons, 1888.

Coffin, Tristram P. and Hennig Cohen (eds). *Folklore in America*. Garden City, NY: Doubleday & Co., 1966.

Davidoff, Henry. *A World Treasury of Proverbs from Twenty-Five Languages*. New York: Random House, 1946.

Davis, Sir John Francis. *Chinese Novels, Translated from the Originals; to which are added Proverbs and Moral Maxims, Collected from their Classical Books and Other Sources* . . . London: J. Murray, 1822.

Dawson-Gröne, Herman. *Ming Hsien Chi: Being a Collection of Proverbs and Maxims in the Chinese Language*. Shanghai: Kelly & Walsh Ltd, 1911.

Delano, Isaac O. *Owe L'esin Oro: Yoruba Proverbs – Their Meaning and Usage*. Ibadan, Nigeria: Oxford University Press, 1966.

Denham, M.A. *Collection of Proverbs and Popular Sayings Relating to the Seasons, the Weather, and Agricultural Pursuits*. London: T. Richards, 1846.

Elwell-Sutton, Lawrence P. *Persian Proverbs*. London: John Murray, 1954.

Farsi, S.S. *Swahili Sayings from Zanzibar*. Nairobi: Kenya Literature Bureau, 1958.

Fergusson, Rosalind. *The Penguin Dictionary of Proverbs*. London: Penguin/Allen Lane, 1983.

Franklin, Benjamin. *Benjamin Franklin: Autobiography, Poor Richard, and Later Writings* (edited by J.A. Leo Lemay). New York: Library of America, 2005.

————. *Sayings from Poor Richard's Almanack*. Old Tappan, NJ: Fleming H. Revell, 1960.

Gordon, Edmund I. *Sumerian Proverbs*. Philadelphia: University of Pennsylvania Press, 1959.

Griffis, William E. *Proverbs of Japan: A Little Picture of the Japanese Philosophy of Life as Mirrored in Their Proverbs*. New York: Japan Society, 1924.

Ha, Tae Hung. *Maxims and Proverbs of Old Korea*. Seoul: Yonsei University Press, 1970.

Haig, Kerest. *Dictionary of Turkish–English Proverbial Idioms*. Amsterdam: Philo Press, 1969 (reprint of 1951 edition).

Hamilton, A.W. *Malay Proverbs – Bidal Mélayu* (3rd edn). Sydney: Australasian Publishing Co., 1947.

Hart, Henry H. (trans.). *Seven Hundred Chinese Proverbs*. Palo Alto, CA: Stanford University Press, 1937.

Hazlitt, William C. *English Proverbs and Proverbial Phrases* (2nd edn). London: Reeves & Turner, 1882.

Henderson, Andrew. *Scottish Proverbs* (new edn). Glasgow: Thomas D. Morrison, 1881.

Kremer, Edmund P. *German Proverbs*. Stanford, CA: Stanford University Press, 1955.

Lean, Vincent Stucky. *Lean's Collectanea* (4 vols.). Bristol: J.W. Arrowsmith, 1902–04 (reprinted by Gale Research Co., 1969).

Leslau, Charlotte and Wolf Leslau. *African Proverbs*. Mt. Vernon, NY: Peter Pauper Press, 1962.

Long, James. *Eastern Proverbs and Emblems Illustrating Old Truths*. London: Routledge, 2000 (reprint of 1881 edition).

Lunde, Paul and Justin Wintle. *A Dictionary of Arabic and Islamic Proverbs*. London: Routledge & Kegan Paul, 1984.

Mac Con Iomaire, Liam. *Ireland of the Proverb*. Grand Rapids, MI: Master Press, 1988.

MacDonald, T.D. *Gaelic Proverbs and Proverbial Sayings*. Stirling, Scotland: E. Mackay, 1926.

Merrick, Captain G[eorge]. *Hausa Proverbs*. London: Kegan Paul, Trench, Trübner & Co., 1905.

Mieder, Wolfgang. *The Prentice-Hall Encyclopedia of World Proverbs*. Englewood Cliffs, NJ: Prentice-Hall, 1986.

Mieder, Wolfgang, Stewart A. Kingsbury, and Kelsie B. Harder (eds). *A Dictionary of American Proverbs*. New York: Oxford University Press, 1992.

Mizukami, Hitoshi. *A Collection of Japanese Proverbs and Sayings, with Their English Parallels*. Tokyo: Kairyudo Press, 1940.

Okada, Rokuo. *Japanese Proverbs and Proverbial Phrases* (2nd edn). Tokyo: Japan Travel Bureau, 1958.

O'Rahilly, Thomas F. *A Miscellany of Irish Proverbs*. Dublin: Talbot Press, 1922.

Pahk, Induk. *The Wisdom of the Dragon: Asian Proverbs*. New York: Harper & Row, 1970.

Plopper, Clifford H. *Chinese Proverbs*. Peking: North China Union Language School, 1932.

——— . *Chinese Religion Seen through the Proverb* (2nd edn). New York: Paragon Reprint Corporation, 1969 (reprint of 1935 edition).

Pe, Hla. *Burmese Proverbs*. London: John Murray, 1962.

Plotkin, David (a.k.a., David Kin). *Dictionary of American Proverbs*. New York: Philosophical Library, 1955.

Prahlad, Sw. Anand. *Reggae Wisdom: Proverbs in Jamaican Music*. Jackson, MS: University of Mississippi Press, 2001.

Rattray, R.S. *Ashanti Proverbs*. Oxford: Clarendon Press, 1969 (reprint of 1916 edition).

Rovira, Luis Iscla. *Spanish Proverbs*. Lanham, MD: University Press of America, 1984.

Scarborough, William. *A Collection of Chinese Proverbs* (rev. and enl. by C. Wilfrid Allan). New York: Paragon Reprint Corporation, 1964.

Simpson, J.A. (ed.). *The Concise Oxford Dictionary of Proverbs*. New York: Oxford University Press, 1982.

Smith, Arthur H. *Proverbs and Common Sayings from the Chinese*. New York: Paragon Reprint Corp, 1965 (reprint of 1902 edition).

Stevenson, Burton G. *The Home-Book of Proverbs, Maxims, and Famous Phrases*. New York: Macmillan, 1948.

Stone, Jon R. *The Essential Max Müller: On Language, Mythology, and Religion*. New York: Palgrave, 2002.

————. *Latin for the Illiterati*. New York & London: Routledge, 1996.

————. *More Latin for the Illiterati*. New York & London: Routledge, 1999.

————. *The Routledge Dictionary of Latin Quotations*. New York & London: Routledge, 2005.

Taylor, Archer. *The Proverb*. Cambridge, MA: Harvard University Press, 1931.

Taylor, Archer and Bartlett J. Whiting. *Dictionary of American Proverbs and Proverbial Phrases, 1820–1880*. Cambridge, MA: Belknap Press of Harvard University Press, 1958.

Tilley, Morris P. *A Dictionary of the Proverbs in England in the Sixteenth and Seventeenth Centuries*. Ann Arbor, MI: University of Michigan Press, 1950.

Trench, Richard C. *Proverbs and Their Lessons*. London: George Routledge; New York: E.P. Dutton, 1905.

Westermarck, Edward. *Wit and Wisdom in Morocco: A Study of Native Proverbs*. London: George Routledge & Sons, 1930.

Whiting, Bartlett J. *Early American Proverbs and Proverbial Phrases*. Cambridge, MA: Harvard University Press, 1977.

————. *Modern Proverbs and Proverbial Sayings*. Cambridge, MA: Harvard University Press, 1989.

Wilson, F.P. (ed.). *Oxford Dictionary of English Proverbs* (3rd edn). New York: Oxford University Press, 1970.

Winstedt, Richard. *Malay Proverbs*. London: John Murray, 1950.

Yoo, Young H. *Wisdom of the Far East*. Washington, D.C.: Far Eastern Research & Publications Center, 1972.

World Proverbs

A

Abbot

An abbot who has been an altar boy knows well who drinks the altar wine. (Spanish)

Ability, Able

A bird can roost but on one branch, a mouse can drink no more than its fill from a river.
   (Chinese)
He who is unable is always willing. (Italian)

Above and Below

Those above are going down, those below are going up. (Polynesian)

Absence, Absent

A little absence does much good. (French)
Absence, and a friendly neighbor, washeth away love. (English)
Absence makes the heart grow fonder. (English)
Absence makes the heart grow fonder – for someone else. (American)
Absence sharpens love; presence strengthens it. (English)
Absent, none without blame; present, none without excuse. (Spanish)
After ten years' absence, even the mountains and rivers have changed. (Korean)
He is guilty who is not at home. (Ukrainian)
He who is absent is always in the wrong. (German)
Long absence changes friends. (French)
Long absent, soon forgotten. (English)
The absent are always to blame. (Yiddish)
The absent get further off every day. (Japanese)
The absent one always loses. (Spanish)

Absent-minded

Absent-mindedness is searching for the horse you are riding. (Russian)

Abstain, Abstinence

Abstinence and fasting cure many a complaint. (Danish)
Abstinence is the best medicine. (Tamil)
Abstinence makes the heart grow fonder. (the Editor)
It is easier to abstain than to restrain. (French)
To many, total abstinence is easier than perfect moderation. (St Augustine)

Abundance

Abundance begets indifference. (German)
Abundance does not spread; famine does. (Zulu)
Abundance is from activity. (Turkish)
Abundance will make cotton pull a stone. (Hausan)
Abundance, like want, ruins many. (Rumanian)
From abundance comes boredom. (Roman)
The abundance of money is a trial for man. (Moroccan)
The abundance of money ruins youth. (English)

Abuse, Abuses

A man who is not spoken of is not abused. (Danish)
Abuse does not take away use. (Roman)
Abuse doesn't hang on the collar. (Russian)
Abuse is like a god that destroys his master. (Hawaiian)
Abuses are the result of seeing one another too often. (Swahili)
He who abuses others must not be particular about the answer he gets. (Danish)
If you utter abuse, you must expect to receive it. (Roman)
The abuse of a thing is no argument against its use. (Roman)
What you can't have, abuse. (Italian)

Accept

Who accepts from another sells his freedom. (German)
Who accepts nothing has nothing to return. (German)
Who accepts, sells himself. (Italian)

Accident

A ridiculous accident has often been the making of many. (Roman)
Accidents will happen. (American)
Accidents will happen even in the best regulated families. (English)

Accommodate

As men are, so must you humor them. (Roman)
If you accommodate others, you will be accommodating yourself. (Chinese)

Accomplice

Accomplices in evil actions are always regarded as approaching the deed. (Roman)
The accomplice is as bad as the thief. (Portuguese)

Accomplish, Accomplishment

Accomplishment of purpose is better than making a profit. (Hausan)
Accomplishments are lifelong benefits to those who possess them. (Japanese)
An accomplishment sticks to a person. (Japanese)
If you wish a thing done, go; if not, send. (Danish)

Accuse, Accusation

Accusing the times is but excusing ourselves. (English)

It is just so much easier to accuse than to defend, as it is easier to inflict than to heal a wound. (Roman)

No one is bound to accuse himself. (Roman)

One against whom accusations when made are easily believed. (Roman)

Accustom

Accustom yourself to that which you bear ill, and you will bear it well. (Roman)

One soon gets used to good things. (Yiddish)

We can accustom ourselves to anything. (Roman)

Ache

The worst ache is the present ache. (Lebanese)

Acid

Sharp acids corrode their own containers. (Albanian)

Acquaintance

A person is known by the company he keeps. (English)

Come live with me and you'll know me. (Spanish)

The more acquaintance, the more danger. (English)

You should know a man seven years before you stir his fire. (Roman)

Act, Acts

A stupid act entails doing the work twice over. (Burmese)

Act according to your age. (German)

Act according to your strength. (Roman)

Act honestly, and answer boldly. (Danish)

Act in the valley so that you need not fear those who stand on the hill. (Danish)

Act quickly, think slowly. (Greek)

Act uprightly, and despise calumny; dirt may stick to a mud wall, but not to polish'd marble. (Poor Richard)

Act your office. (Roman)

An act done against my will is not my act. (Roman)

It is not the name but the act that counts. (American)

Judge acts by the intention of the one who acts. (Roman)

That an act is not prohibited, it does not follow that it is permitted. (Roman)

When we cannot act as we wish, we must act as we can. (Roman)

Acting, Actor

All the world practices the art of acting. (Roman)

All the world's a stage and we are merely actors. (English)

Action, Actions

A good action is better than a bad action. (African)
Action and reaction are equal. (American)
Action is the proper fruit of knowledge. (English)
Actions speak louder than words. (English)
For the sake of one good action, a hundred evil ones should be forgotten. (Chinese)
Good actions are never lost. (Turkish)
Great actions come from great ability. (Unknown)
Innocent actions carry their warrant with them. (English)
It is a bad action that success cannot justify. (Roman)
Let us be judged by our actions. (Roman)
Never repent a good action. (Danish)
Our outward actions reveal our hidden intentions. (Roman)
Poor in speech, swift in action. (Japanese)
Postpone not a good action. (Irish)
To every action there is an equal and opposite reaction. (German)
Words may show a man's wit, but actions his meaning. (Poor Richard)

Acts of God

Acts of God do injury to no one. (Roman)

Add

It is easy to add to what has already been invented. (Roman)
The more you add, the worse it gets. (Yiddish)

Admire

He who esteems none but himself is as happy as a king. (Italian)
The more a woman admires her face, the more she ruins her house. (Spanish)

Adultery

The tears of an adulteress are ever ready. (Egyptian)
Were all adulterers to wear gray coats, gray cloth would be dear. (German)

Advance

He who does not advance recedes. (Roman)

Advantage

A single advantage is worth a thousand sorceries. (Turkish)
Advantage is a better soldier than rashness. (English)
An inch in a sword, or a palm in a lance, is a great advantage. (Spanish)
Every advantage has its disadvantage. (Roman)

Adventure

Adventures are to the adventurous. (English)

Adversity
A dose of adversity is often as needful as a dose of medicine. (American)
Adversity borne with patience opens the door to Heaven. (Spanish)
Adversity brings knowledge, and knowledge wisdom. (Welsh)
Adversity brings out a man's virtue. (American)
Adversity comes with instruction in his hand. (Welsh)
Adversity flatters no man. (English)
Adversity is a better teacher than prosperity. (Spanish)
Adversity is easier borne than prosperity forgot. (English)
Adversity is the foundation of virtue. (Japanese)
Adversity is the parent of virtue. (Japanese)
Adversity makes a great man. (Japanese)
Adversity makes a man wise. (French)
Adversity makes a man wise, not rich. (Rumanian)
Adversity makes strange bedfellows. (French)
Adversity often leads to prosperity. (American)
Adversity reminds men of religion. (Roman)
Adversity reveals genius, and prosperity conceals it. (Roman)
Adversity tries men. (Roman)
Fire tests gold, adversity brave men. (Roman)
Fire tests gold, adversity good men. (German)
He who does not tire, tires adversity. (French)

Advice
A son should treasure his father's advice. (Spanish)
A wife's advice is not worth much, but woe to the husband who refuses to take it.
    (Welsh)
Advice after injury is like medicine after death. (Danish)
Advice is least heeded when most needed. (English)
Advice should be viewed from behind. (Swedish)
Advice should precede the act. (German)
Advice to all, security for none. (English)
Ask advice of your equals, help of your superiors. (Danish)
Bad advice is often fatal to the advisor. (Roman)
Crafty advice is often got from a fool. (Irish)
Don't offer me advice; give me money. (Spanish)
Fools need advice most, but wise men only are the better for it. (Poor Richard)
Give advice; if people don't listen, let adversity teach them. (Ethiopian)
Good advice is seldom welcome. (Unknown)
Good medicine is bitter to the taste, but will heal illness; sincere advice is harsh to the ear,
    but will benefit one's conduct. (Korean)
Good medicine may taste bitter to the mouth; good advice may sound unpleasant to the
    ear. (Japanese)
Good medicine tastes bitter; good advice is seldom welcome. (Unknown)
He asks advice in vain who will not follow it. (French)

He tells me my way, and knows not his own. (Roman)

He who builds according to every man's advice will have a crooked house. (Danish)

He who seeks advice seldom errs. (Filipino)

He who will not take cheap advice, will have to buy dear repentance. (Danish)

He who won't be advised, can't be helped. (German)

If advice will not improve him, neither will the rod. (Greek)

If time comes, advice comes. (German)

If you are wise, take advice. (Irish)

If you wish good advice, consult an old man. (Rumanian)

It is bad not to take advice, but worse to take every advice. (Irish)

It is easy to give advice when all goes well. (Italian)

It's a bad child who does not take advice. (African)

Less advice and more hands. (German)

Let him who will not have advice have conflict. (Irish)

Never give advice in a crowd. (Arabian)

Never give advice unasked. (German)

Never trust the advice of a man in difficulty. (Japanese)

Nothing is so liberally given as advice. (French)

One piece of good advice is better than a bag full. (Danish)

Take a woman's first advice and not her second. (French)

Take help of many, advice of few. (Danish)

The advice of the aged will not mislead you. (Welsh)

The best advice is found on the pillow. (Danish)

There is no price for good advice. (Spanish)

We may give advice, but we cannot give conduct. (Poor Richard)

We receive nothing with so much reluctance as advice. (Roman)

When a thing is done, advice comes too late. (French)

Worthless is the advice of fools. (Roman)

Write down the advice of those who love you, though you like it not at present. (English)

You can give a piece of advice, but not good luck along with it. (Norwegian)

Advise, Advisor

A friend advises in his interest, not yours. (Arabian)

A man is often a good advisor to others and a bad advisor to himself. (Irish)

Advise me well in this matter, but don't advise me against it. (Yiddish)

Advising is easier than helping. (German)

Advising is often better than fighting. (German)

Advisors are not givers. (Dutch)

Advisors are not the payers. (French)

He that builds next to the highway will have many advisors. (Dutch)

Never advise a man to go to war, or to marry. (Spanish)

No one is wise enough to advise himself. (German)

When things go well it is easy to advise. (Dutch)

Who won't be advised can't be helped. (German)

Afar

Things coming from afar are most esteemed. (Roman)

Affair

A great affair covers up a small matter. (Yoruban)
A great affair grows out of a small matter. (Japanese)
No one is wise in his own affairs. (Dutch)

Affection

Affection is a bad judge. (Italian)

Affinity

A bird may be ever so small, but it always seeks a nest of its own. (Danish)
A blade won't cut another blade; a cheat won't cheat another cheat. (German)
Affinity is a mysterious thing, but it is spicy! (Japanese)
Jackdaw always perches by jackdaw. (Roman)
Like associates more easily with like. (Roman)
Like attracts like. (Japanese)
Like will to like, be they poor or rich. (Dutch)
Likeness is the mother of love. (Italian)
People of the same stock and trade are friendly. (Irish)

Affliction

Affliction shows forth true character. (Spanish)
The bitterest part of a person's affliction is to remember that he was once happy.
   (Roman)
We benefit by affliction. (Roman)

Africa

Out of Africa there is always something new. (Roman)

After, Afterthought

After losing the sheep, he repairs the pen. (Korean)
After me, the deluge! (French)
After meat comes mustard. (German)
After mischance, everyone is wise. (French)
After nine months the secret comes out. (Yiddish)
After one that earns comes one that wastes. (Danish)
After pleasant scratching comes unpleasant smarting. (Danish)
After shaving there is nothing to shear. (French)
After sorrow, joy. (Unknown)
After the act wishing is in vain. (French)
After the daughter is married, then come sons-in-law in plenty. (French)
After the horse is stolen, the stable door is shut. (Unknown)
After the house is finished, he deserts it. (Spanish)

After the sour comes the sweet. (Dutch)

After the war, aid. (Greek)

He builds the dam after the flood. (Burmese)

He digs a well to put out a house fire. (Unknown)

When the calf is drowned they cover the well. (Dutch)

When the calf is stolen, the peasant mends the stall. (German)

When the war is over then comes help. (Roman)

Age, Aged

A prodigy at ten, a genius at twenty, an ordinary man at thirty. (Japanese)

Age and wedlock tame man and beast. (English)

Age brings aches. (German)

Age carries everything away, even the mind. (Roman)

Age is a sorry traveling companion. (Danish)

Age is honorable and youth is noble. (Irish)

Age makes many a man whiter, but not better. (Danish)

Age may wrinkle the face, but lack of enthusiasm wrinkles the soul. (Danish)

An aged willow is difficult to bend. (Irish)

As you are at seven so are you at seventy. (Yiddish)

At twenty years of age the will reigns; at thirty the wit; at forty the judgment. (Poor Richard)

At seventy, a candle in the wind; at eighty, frost on the tiles. (Chinese)

Every age has its own care: each one thinks his own time of life is disagreeable. (Roman)

Everyone is the age of his heart. (Guatemalan)

He who at twenty understands nothing, at thirty knows nothing, and at forty has nothing, will lead a wretched old age. (Spanish)

It's not the years that age, but the sorrow. (Russian)

Often a man has no evidence to prove that he has lived a long life other than his age. (Roman)

Sense comes with age. (Spanish)

Teeth lie, gray hair deceives, but wrinkles tell one's true age. (Spanish)

What age destroys no art can restore. (Spanish)

Aggregate

A little and a little, collected together, becomes a great deal. (Arabian)

The heap in the barn consists of single grains, and drop and drop makes an inundation. (Arabian)

Agree, Agreement

Agreement with two people, lamentation with three. (Kashmiri)

Rare is agreement between beauty and modesty. (Roman)

When cat and mouse agree, the farmer has no chance. (Danish)

When the cat and mouse agree, the grocer is ruined. (Persian)

When two agree in their desire, one spark will set them both on fire. (English)

Aim, Aiming

A man does not always aim at what he means to hit. (Danish)
Aim at a certain end. (Roman)
Aim at a sure thing. (American)
Aim at what you can accomplish. (Roman)
Aiming isn't hitting. (Swahili)
Before shooting, one must aim. (African)
Do not aim at lofty things. (Roman)
It is not enough to aim, you must hit. (Italian)
Who aims at things beyond his reach, the greater will be his fall. (Roman)

Ale

Ale in, wit out. (English)
Better good sale than good ale. (Scottish)
Plenty know good ale but many know little else. (English)

Alert

No occasion to be alert is to be overlooked. (Roman)

All

Do not all you can; spend not all you have; believe not all you hear; and tell not all you
    know. (Chinese)
We cannot all do all things. (Roman)

Allah

Allah gives to each according to the measure of his heart. (Persian)
Allah is nearer to you than your jugular vein. (Arabian)
Allah is the one who knows everything, not man. (Hausan)
Allah provides, but he needs a nudge. (Persian)
Allah will give water to the wheat on a rock. (Hausan)
He who puffs at the lamp of Allah will singe his beard. (Persian)

Alligator

Don't call the alligator a big-mouth till you have crossed the river. (Honduran)
No call alligator long mouth till you pass him. (Jamaican)

Almost

All but saves many a man. (Danish)
Almost is not eaten. (Zulu)
Almost kills no man. (Danish)
Almost never killed a fly. (German)

Alms, Almsgiving

Alms are the golden key that opens the gate of Heaven. (German)
Alms do not empty the purse, and a mass does not exhaust the day's duty. (German)

Alms given openly will be rewarded in secret. (Chinese)
Alms never make one poor. (English)
Better to give nothing than stolen alms. (German)
Do not trumpet your almsgiving. (English, after Jesus)
Giving alms never lessens the purse. (Spanish)
He who gives alms to the poor faces Heaven. (Filipino)
More alms are at hand for a cripple than for a scholar. (Yiddish)
No one ever became poor through giving alms. (Italian)

Alone

Better to be alone than in bad company. (German)
He who eats alone chokes alone. (Spanish)
He who eats alone, coughs alone. (Egyptian)
He who falls alone cries alone. (Unknown)
He who sleeps alone keeps long cold, two soon warm each other. (German)
It is not good to be alone, even in Paradise. (Yiddish)
Man cannot live in this world alone. (American)
Never less alone than when alone. (Roman)
One man alone is no man. (Roman)
Who eats his fowl alone, must saddle his horse alone. (Portuguese)

Altar

He that serves at the altar ought to live by the altar. (English)

Ambassador

An ambassador bears no blame. (Italian)

Ambition, Ambitious

Ambition and fleas both jump high. (German)
Ambition will tear your coat. (Mexican)
Every ambitious man is a captive and every covetous one a pauper. (Arabian)
False ambition leads to perdition. (Egyptian)
He who sacrifices his conscience to ambition burns a picture to obtain the ashes. (Chinese)
If you would be pope, you must think of nothing else. (Spanish)
Nothing humbler than ambition, when it is about to climb. (Poor Richard)

Ambush

At an ambush of villains a man does better with his feet than his hands. (Spanish)

Ancestor, Ancestry

If a man falls he blames his ancestors. (Korean)
They brag most of their ancestors who are unworthy of them. (Danish)
We can scarcely call birth and ancestry, and what we have not ourselves done, our own.
  (Roman)

Anchor

He is like the anchor that is always in the sea, yet does not learn to swim. (Italian)
It is better to lose the anchor than the whole ship. (Dutch)

Angel, Angels

A young angel, an old devil. (French)
Nowadays you must go to Heaven to meet an angel. (Polish)
Time was when angels walked the earth, now they are not even in Heaven. (Yiddish)
When an angel turns bad, it is worse than the Devil. (German)
When the angels present themselves, the devils abscond. (Egyptian)

Anger, Angry

A lover's anger is short-lived. (Italian)
A man is only as big as the things that make him mad. (American)
A man, when angry, is beside himself. (Roman)
An angry lover tells himself many lies. (Roman)
An angry man heeds no counsel. (Portuguese)
An angry man is not fit to pray. (Yiddish)
Anger and haste hinder good counsel. (English)
Anger assists hands however weak. (Roman)
Anger can be an expensive luxury. (Italian)
Anger can't stand, without a strong hand. (German)
Anger dies quickly with a good man. (English)
Anger does not accomplish anything; patience is the chief virtue. (Yoruban)
Anger edges valor. (English)
Anger ends in cruelty. (Indian)
Anger has no eyes. (Indian)
Anger hears no counsel. (German)
Anger increases love. (Italian)
Anger is a bad counselor. (French)
Anger is a brief madness. (Roman)
Anger is a stone cast into a wasp's nest. (Indian)
Anger is more hurtful than the injury that caused it. (English)
Anger is never without a reason, but seldom with a good one. (Poor Richard)
Anger is not appeased by anger. (Roman)
Anger is short-lived in a good man. (English)
Anger manages everything badly. (Roman)
Anger so clouds the mind that it cannot perceive the truth. (Roman)
Anger without power is folly. (German)
Anger without power receives the blow. (Egyptian)
Anger, though concealed, is betrayed by the countenance. (Roman)
Better to cross an angry man than a fasting man. (Danish)
By getting angry, you show you are wrong. (Madagascan)
Do not trust an angry man with a sword. (Roman)
Give way to your anger for an instant and you may rue it for a lifetime. (Chinese)

He that can reply to an angry man is too strong for him. (Dutch)
He who conquers his anger has conquered an enemy. (German)
Hunger and delay stir up one's bile in the nostrils. (Roman)
Kick a stone in anger and you will hurt your own foot. (Korean)
Let not the sun set on your anger. (the Bible)
Like fragile ice, anger passes away in time. (Roman)
Never answer a letter while you are angry. (Chinese)
Never let the sun go down on your anger. (Italian)
Never write a letter while you are angry. (Chinese)
So long as a man is angry he cannot be in the right. (Chinese)
The anger of the prudent never shows. (Burmese)
The best answer to anger is silence. (German)
The best remedy for anger is delay. (Roman)
The force of anger is broken by a soft answer. (Roman)
The one who subdues his anger, conquers his greatest enemy. (Roman)
The physician of anger is reason. (Greek)
When against any your anger grows, be sure you never come to blows. (Chinese)
When an angry man returns to himself, he is angry with himself. (Roman)
When anger blinds the eyes, truth disappears. (Danish)
When anger comes, wisdom goes. (Hindi)

Animal
Even wild animals, if you keep them in confinement, forget their fierceness. (Roman)
Every animal loves itself. (Roman)

Answer
It is a good answer which knows when to stop. (Italian)
Let the superior answer for the actions of his agent. (Roman)
No answer is also an answer. (Danish)
Not every word requires an answer. (Italian)
To a civil question, a civil answer. (Danish)
Who answers for another pays. (French)

Ant, Ants
Ants do not visit empty barns. (Roman)
Even the ant has its anger. (Roman)
Even the ant has its bite. (Turkish)
Every ant has its ire. (Portuguese)
Many ants together can carry a beetle. (Spanish)
None preaches better than the ant, and she says nothing. (Poor Richard)

Anticipate
Better anticipate than be anticipated. (Portuguese)
His mouth waters before the soup is ready. (Burmese)

Anvil

A great anvil fears not noise. (Roman)
Either an anvil or a hammer. (French)
The anvil is used to noise. (German)
The anvil fears no blows. (Rumanian)

Anxiety, Anxious

Anxious about the shoe, but careless about the foot. (Roman)
Dreadful is the state of that mind that is anxious about the future. (Roman)
The tiger and the leopard are likewise anxious. (Chinese)

Apart

Mouth and heart are wide apart. (German)

Ape, Apes

An ape, a priest, and a louse, are three devils in one house. (Dutch)
An ape is an ape, though clad in purple. (English)
An ape is an ape, though decked with gold. (Roman)
An ape's an ape, a varlet's a varlet, though they be clad in silk and scarlet. (Roman)
An ape's an ape, though he wear a gold ring. (Dutch)
An old ape hath an old eye. (Roman)
An old ape never made a pretty grimace. (French)
Apes remain apes, though you clothe them in velvet. (German)
No ape but swears he has the handsomest children. (German)
When apes climb high, they show their naked bottoms. (Dutch)

Appearance, Appearances

A pleasing countenance is no small advantage. (Roman)
A pretty face costs money. (Yiddish)
A smart coat is a good letter of introduction. (Dutch)
An open countenance often conceals closed thoughts. (Portuguese)
Appearances are deceiving. (German)
As a man dresses so is he esteemed. (Danish)
As is the face so is the mind. (Roman)
As you look at a man, so he appears. (Yiddish)
Be as you would seem to be. (German)
Be what you seem to be. (Roman)
Good clothes open all doors. (German)
I should wish to be rather than to seem. (Roman)
Neglect of appearance becomes men. (Roman)
The appearances of things are deceptive. (Roman)
The first appearance deceives many. (Roman)

Appetite

A good appetite needs no sauce. (Polish)

A waiting appetite kindles many a spite. (Italian)
All things require skill except an appetite. (German)
Appetite comes after eating. (Italian)
Appetite comes with eating. (French)
Excess of delight palls the appetite. (Roman)
For a good appetite there is no hard bread. (Dutch)
He who restrains his appetite avoids debt. (Chinese)
Let us go where our appetite prompts us. (Roman)
No sauce like appetite. (French)
The death that will kill a man begins as an appetite. (Nigerian)
The less one eats, the greater the appetite. (Vietnamese)

Applaud, Applause
Applause is the beginning of abuse. (Japanese)
Applause is the reward of virtue. (Roman)
Men seek less to be instructed than applauded. (American)
The applause of the people is a blast of air. (Italian)
The people boo me, but I applaud myself. (Roman)

Apple
An apple a day keeps the doctor away. (English)
An apple that ripens late keeps longest. (Serbian)
An apple thrown into the air will turn a thousand times before it reaches the ground.
    (Persian)
Bite into a bitter apple first, and the good one will taste all the sweeter. (German)
Don't look for apples under poplar trees. (Slavic)
Everything round isn't an apple. (Armenian)
Handsome apples are sometimes sour. (Dutch)
How could the apple be but as the apple tree? (Irish)
Never look for a worm in the apple of your eye. (French)
One bad apple will spoil the whole barrel. (English)
Sometimes it is better to give your apple away, than to eat it yourself. (Italian)
The apple does not fall far from the tree. (German)
The apple never falls far from the tree. (English)
The attractive apple sometimes hides a worm within. (German)
The bad apple floats on top. (Yiddish)
The rotten apple spoils his companion. (Poor Richard)
Who has tasted a sour apple, will have the more relish for a sweet one. (Dutch)

Appreciate
No one appreciates what he has until it is gone. (American)
No one is appreciated until he is gone. (German)
One never appreciates what he has until he has lost it. (English)

Approach
Firmly in the matter, and gently in the manner. (Roman)

Approve
Approve not of him who commends all you say. (Poor Richard)
The one who does not disapprove, approves. (Roman)

Archer
The archer that shoots badly has a lie ready. (Spanish)

Argue, Argument
He argues in vain who argues without means. (Roman)
Lower your voice and strengthen your argument. (Lebanese)
Never argue with a man who buys ink by the barrel. (Chinese)
Prepare your proof before you argue. (Yiddish)
The arguments of the strongest have always the most weight. (French)
There's no argument like that of the stick. (Spanish)
To argue stubbornly is to stray from the truth. (Spanish)

Armor
Armor is lighter putting on than taking off. (German)
The best armor is to keep out of range. (Italian)

Arms
Arms and money require good hands. (Spanish)
Arms are of little service abroad unless directed by the wisdom of counselors at home.
    (Roman)
Arms carry peace. (Italian)
Arms cause laws to be respected. (Roman)
Arms, women, and books should be looked at daily. (Dutch)

Army
An army marches on its stomach. (French)
An army of deer commanded by a lion is more formidable than one of lions
    commanded by a deer. (Roman)
An army of sheep led by a lion would defeat an army of lions led by a sheep. (Arabian)
If it moves, salute it; if it doesn't move, pick it up; and if you can't pick it up, paint it.
    (American Army)
It is easier to recruit ten thousand privates than one general. (Japanese)
It is the blood of the soldier that makes the general great. (Italian)

Around
What comes around, goes around. (German)

Arrogance

Arrogance diminishes wisdom. (Arabian)

Arrogance is a weed that grows mostly on a dunghill. (Arabian)

Arrow, Arrows

Do not shoot the arrow that will return against you. (Kurdish)

Draw not thy bow before thy arrow be fixed. (Persian)

If you have no arrows in your quiver, go not with archers. (German)

If you sow arrows, you will reap arrows. (Filipino)

Not every sort of wood is fit to make an arrow. (French)

The arrow that has left the bow cannot be recalled. (German)

The arrow will not always hit the object which it threatens. (Roman)

Art, Arts

All art is an imitation of nature. (Roman)

Apelles was not a master painter the first day. (Irish)

Art holds fast when all else is lost. (German)

Art improves upon nature. (English)

Art is art, despite its success. (Danish)

Art is born of the observation and investigation of nature. (Roman)

Art is improved by practice. (Roman)

Art is long, life is short. (Roman)

Art knows no nationality. (Korean)

Every art requires the whole person. (French)

It is a sign of nobility to patronize the arts. (Irish)

It is easier to criticize art than to create it. (Spanish)

It is the perfection of art when no trace of the artist appears. (Roman)

Nature without an effort surpasses art. (Roman)

That which achieves its effect by accident is not art. (Roman)

The learned understand the principles of art, the unlearned feel its pleasure. (Roman)

Where art is displayed truth does not appear. (Roman)

Artisan, Artist

A good painter need not give a name to his picture, a bad one must. (Polish)

A skilled artisan doesn't fuss about his material. (Japanese)

Every land supports the artisan. (Roman)

Knowledge without practice makes but half an artist. (West African)

Musicians, poets, painters are half crazy. (Spanish)

Painters and poets have leave to lie. (Roman)

The artist never dies. (German)

Ashamed

He that is ashamed to eat is ashamed to live. (French)

Ashes
Ashes fly back into the face of him who throws them. (African)
Under white ashes lie glowing embers. (Danish)

Ask, Asking
Ask a lot, but take what is offered. (Russian)
Ask and you shall receive. (English)
Ask for much to receive a little. (German)
Ask no more of others than of yourself. (Chinese)
Ask the experienced rather than the learned. (Arabian)
Ask the way even if you know the way. (Korean)
Ask too much to get enough. (Spanish)
Asking costs little. (Italian)
Better to ask than go astray. (Italian)
Better to ask twice than to lose your way once. (Danish)
By asking for the impossible, obtain the best possible. (Italian)
Courteous asking breaks even city walls. (Russian)
Handsomely asked, handsomely refused. (French)
He that asks faintly begs for denial. (German)
He that cannot ask cannot live. (Yiddish)
He that does not ask will never get a bargain. (French)
He who asks does not go wrong, but his secret is known. (Hausan)
He who asks questions cannot avoid the answers. (West African)
In the asking is the receiving. (Mexican)
It costs us nothing to ask. (American)
Never ask of him who has, but of him who wishes you well. (Spanish)
The one who asks timidly courts denial. (Roman)
The person who asks for little deserves nothing. (Mexican)
To have a calf, ask for an ox. (German)
What we obtain merely by asking is not really our own. (Roman)
You ought to obtain what you ask, as you only ask for what is fair. (Roman)

Asleep
Not all are asleep who have their eyes shut. (Italian)

Ass, Asses
A braying ass eats little hay. (Italian)
A contented ass enjoys a long life. (Portuguese)
A goaded ass must trot. (Italian)
A hungry ass eats any straw. (Italian)
An ass does not appreciate fruit compote. (Turkish)
An ass does not hit himself twice against the same stone. (Dutch)
An ass does not stumble twice over the same stone. (French)
An ass is but an ass, though laden with gold. (Rumanian)
An ass to an ass is a beauty. (Roman)

An ass with her colt goes not straight to the mill. (Spanish)

An ass's tail will not make a sieve. (Italian)

An ass's trot does not last long. (Italian)

Asses carry the oats and horses eat them. (Dutch)

Asses that bray most eat least. (German)

Better to be killed by robbers than by the kick of an ass. (Portuguese)

Better to have a bad ass than be your own ass. (Spanish)

Either the ass will die, or he that goads it. (Spanish)

Even an ass will not fall twice in the same quicksand. (Italian)

Even an ass will not follow someone onto the ice. (German)

Every ass loves to hear himself bray. (English)

For a stubborn ass a stubborn driver. (French)

Give me the ass that carries me in preference to the horse that throws me. (Spanish)

Give oats to an ass and he'll run after thistles. (Dutch)

He who is an ass and thinks himself a stag, finds his mistake when he comes to leap the ditch. (Italian)

If an ass goes a-traveling, he'll not come home a horse. (French)

If one person tells you that you have ass's ears, take no notice; should two tell you so, procure a saddle for yourself. (Yiddish)

If the ass had horns and the ox knew its strength, the world would be done for. (Yiddish)

If three people say you are an ass, put on a bridle. (Spanish)

If three say you are an ass, put on a tail. (Spanish)

If three say you are an ass, put on the ears. (Dutch)

It is better to strive with a stubborn ass than to carry the wood on one's back. (Spanish)

Let him be an ass who brays at an ass. (Spanish)

Make yourself an ass, and everyone will lay his sack upon you. (German)

Many asses have only two legs. (Roman)

Never went out an ass and came home a horse. (Unknown)

Not every ass has long ears. (German)

Nothing passes between asses but kicks. (Italian)

One ass among many monkeys is grinned at by all. (Spanish)

One ass nicknames the other 'Long-ears!' (German)

Out of a little grass comes a great ass. (German)

The ass and his driver do not think alike. (German)

The ass carries corn to the mill, and gets thistles. (German)

The ass embraced the thistle, and they found themselves relations. (Portuguese)

The ass is the one who cannot say no. (German)

The ass knows well in whose face it brays. (Spanish)

The ass must browse where it is tied. (German)

The ass of many owners is eaten by wolves. (Portuguese)

The ass that is common property is always the worst saddled. (French)

The ass that trespasses on a stranger's premises will leave them laden with wood. (Portuguese)

The ass well knows in whose house it brays. (Portuguese)

The ass will go into business with the lion. (German)

The ass will not lose its oats for want of braying. (French)
The ass's hide is used to the stick. (Italian)
The braying of an ass does not reach Heaven. (Italian)
The son of an ass brays twice a day. (Spanish)
There are more asses than carry sacks. (Italian)
Though an ass goes to Rome, it still comes back an ass. (French)
Though laden with gold, an ass is still an ass. (German)
When all men say you are an ass, it is high time to bray. (German)
When the ass is too happy it begins dancing on the ice. (Dutch)
Where the ass lies down, there some hair will be found. (German)
Wherever an ass is crowned to fame, both town and country bear the shame.
  (German)
Willy-nilly, the ass must go to the fair. (Portuguese)
You cannot make an ass drink if it's not thirsty. (French)

Assail, Assailed
A man assailed is half overcome. (French)

Assistance
A benefit is estimated according to the mind of the giver. (Roman)
Assist men in their extremities and bring relief to men when in danger. (Chinese)
Assistance given when it is not required, is as bad as an injury. (Roman)
Offer not assistance when you can be of no service. (Roman)

Associate, Association
He who associates with the virtuous becomes good; he who associates with the wicked
  becomes evil. (Chinese)
To associate with evil men is like sleeping among knives and swords; although you have
  not been wounded, you are constantly afraid. (Chinese)

Assurance, Assured
Assurance is two-thirds success. (Italian)
Nothing is assured to men. (Roman)

Astray
All we, like sheep, have gone astray. (the Bible)
It is better to turn back than go astray. (German)
We most often go astray on a well-beaten path and a much-traveled road. (Roman)

Atheist
There are no atheists in foxholes. (American)

Attempt
A bold attempt is half success. (Danish)
Either do not try it or go through with it. (Roman)

He who strives to do, does more than he who has the power. (Spanish)
It's better to try than to hope. (Irish)

Attraction, Attractive

An ass is beautiful in the eyes of an ass; a sow in those of a sow; and every race is attractive
to itself. (Roman)
While we attract we are attracted [i.e., we are drawn by mutual attraction]. (Roman)

Auction

At an auction keep your mouth shut. (Spanish)

Audience

If you want an audience, start a fight. (Chinese)

Authority

Authority does not depend on age. (African)
He that exceeds his commission must answer for it at his own cost. (Italian)
He who has no bread has no authority. (Turkish)

Avarice

Avarice blinds our eyes. (Japanese)
Avarice bursts the bag. (French)
Avarice increases with wealth. (French)
Gold and silver are mingled with dirt, till avarice parts them. (Chinese)
It is not want but abundance that makes avarice. (German)
Luxury is in want of many things, avarice of everything. (Roman)
Poverty craves many things, but avarice more. (German)
Poverty is in want of many things, avarice of everything. (Roman)
Poverty wants some things, luxury many things, avarice all things. (Poor Richard)
The avaricious man is kind to no person, but most unkind to himself. (Roman)
There are no limits to avarice. (Korean)
When all other sins grow old, avarice is still young. (French)

Avenge, Avenging

Noiseless is the approach of the avenging deities. (Irish)
The avenging god follows in the steps of the proud. (Roman)

Avoid, Avoidance

Avoid both the fool and the saint. (Serbian)
Avoid strife with those in power. (Roman)
Avoid the inquisitive person, for he is sure to be a talker. (Roman)
He avoided the fly and swallowed the spider. (Portuguese)
I have avoided what is censurable, not merited what is commendable. (Roman)
Man never takes sufficient and hourly care against that which he ought to avoid. (Roman)
See that in avoiding cinders you step not on burning coals. (Roman)

Three things it is best to avoid: a strange dog, a flood, and a man who thinks he is wise. (Welsh)

Ax, Axe
Don't use an axe to embroider. (Malaysian)
Little ax can cut down big tree. (Jamaican)
The ax falls first upon a straight tree. (Korean)
The ax forgets what the tree remembers. (Roman)
The ax strikes the chisel, and the chisel strikes the wood. (Chinese)
You need a sharp axe for a tough bough. (Russian)

B

Baby
Don't throw out the baby with the bath water. (English)
Kissing the baby touches the mother's cheek. (Siamese)
Throw not the baby out with the bath. (Danish)
When the baby grows, the crying changes. (African)

Bachelor, Bachelorhood
Bachelor, a peacock; betrothed, a lion; married, an ass. (Spanish)
There is no sovereignty like bachelorhood. (Turkish)

Back
'Give me a push from my back' does not mean give me a hunchback. (Nigerian)
The willing back gets all the load. (German)

Backbite
The listener makes the backbiter. (French)

Bacon
In the end, it will be known who ate the bacon. (French)

Bad
A bad cause requires many words. (German)
Bad is never good until worse happens. (Danish)
Bad tidings always come too soon. (German)
Bad ware is never cheap. (French)
Bad ware must be cried up. (German)
He keeps his road well enough who gets rid of bad company. (Portuguese)
Nothing bad is all bad. (Mexican)
Nothing so bad as not to be good for something. (German)
Nothing so bad but it finds its master. (Dutch)
Nothing so bad but it might have been worse. (Dutch)

Once bad is to be presumed always bad. (Roman)
'Tis easier to prevent bad habits than to break them. (Poor Richard)
What is bad for one is good for another. (French)

Bad Luck
All is good luck or bad luck in this world. (French)
Bad luck comes by pounds and goes away by ounces. (Italian)
Bad luck is good for something. (French)
Bad luck upon bad luck, and a stone for a pillow. (Spanish)
Even the luckless need their luck. (Yiddish)
He that has no bad luck grows weary of good luck. (Spanish)
If a black cat crosses the street, bad luck is around the corner. (Unknown)
In bad luck, hold out; in good luck, hold in. (German)
See a pin and pick it up, all the day you'll have good luck; see a pin and let it lie, bad luck
    you'll have all day. (French)
Storing milk in a sieve, you complain of bad luck? (Afghani)

Bad Name
Give a dog a bad name and it will begin to stink. (Unknown)
Give a dog a bad name and you may as well hang it. (English)

Bad News
Bad news always comes in the morning. (English)
Bad news comes apace. (German)
Bad news has wings. (French)
Bad news is always true. (Spanish)
Bad news is the first to come. (Italian)
Bad news runs a thousand miles. (Japanese)
Bad news travels fast. (American)
Bad news travels faster than good. (Unknown)
Bad news comes in threes. (American)
Before good news goes out the door, bad news is known for a thousand miles. (Chinese)
Good news knocks louder than bad. (Spanish)
He who brings bad tidings, comes soon enough. (German)
Ill tidings come soon enough. (Dutch)

Bagpipe, Bagpiper
Bring not a bagpipe to a man in trouble. (Roman)
In the bagpiper's house, all are dancers. (Spanish)
The bagpipe never utters a word till its belly is full. (French)

Bait
A little bait catches a large fish. (Greek)
He who does not bait his hook fishes in vain. (French)
It is not the hook or the rod, but the bait that lures. (Spanish)

The bait hides the hook. (English)
The fish sees the bait, not the hook. (Chinese)

Bake, Baker
As you bake, so shall you brew. (German)
As you brew, so you shall bake. (Dutch)
He is little suited to be a baker, whose head is made of butter. (Danish)
The baker's child goes hungry. (Turkish)
You must bake with the flour you have. (Danish)

Balance (Scale)
The balance in doing its job knows neither gold nor lead. (French)

Bald
A bald head is combed before dawn. (Spanish)
A bald head is soon shaven. (German)
A completely bald head is like the full moon. (Spanish)
After a hundred years we shall all be bald. (Spanish)
God made a few good heads, and put hair on the rest. (American)
Hair by hair and the head gets bald. (Danish)
No one becomes bald overnight. (Spanish)

Bale
By their bindings the bales are known. (Italian)

Ball
He that plays at racket must watch the ball. (Dutch)
Keep your eye on the ball. (American)
Take the ball as it bounces. (French)
Take the ball on the hop. (Irish)

Bamboo
You won't help bamboo shoots grow by pulling them up higher. (Chinese)
Young bamboo trees are easy to bend. (Vietnamese)

Baptize
Baptize your own child first. (Irish)

Barbarians
Set barbarians to stop barbarians. (Chinese)

Barber
A barber does not shave himself. (African)
A barber learns to shave by shaving fools. (Rumanian)
He is a very sorry barber who has but one comb. (Italian)

Never ask a barber if you need a haircut. (American)
On a fool's beard the barber learns to shave. (Italian)
On poor people's beards the young barber learns his trade. (German)
One barber shaves the other. (German)
The bad barber leaves neither hair nor skin. (Spanish)
The village barber knows the village news. (Spanish)

Barefoot
He that goes barefoot must not plant thorns. (English)
He that sows thorns, should never go barefoot. (Poor Richard)

Bargain, Bargaining
A bargain is a bargain. (German)
A good bargain is a pick-purse. (Polish)
At a good bargain pause and ponder. (Italian)
At a great pennyworth pause awhile. (English)
Bargaining has neither friends nor relations. (Poor Richard)
Bargains are costly. (German)
Don't bargain for fish which are still in the water. (Indian)
Go to a man in difficulty and you will get a bargain. (Irish)
Good bargains are ruinous. (French)
Good seems every bargain that is far away. (Irish)
Great bargains empty the purse. (Italian)
He who hunts after bargains will scratch his head. (Catalan)
It is a bad bargain, where both are losers. (Roman)
It is only good bargains that ruin. (French)
It takes two to make a bargain. (American)
It's never a bargain when you spend money to save money. (the Editor)
Let your bargain suit your purse. (Irish)
Make every bargain clear and plain, that none may afterwards complain. (Roman)
Make the best of a bad bargain. (German)
Make your bargain before beginning to plow. (Spanish)
No one gets a bargain he does not ask for. (French)
On a good bargain, think twice. (English)

Bark, Barking
His bark is worse than his bite. (English)
One barking dog sets the whole street to barking. (Unknown)
One dog barks at something, the rest bark at him. (Chinese)
The barking of a dog does not disturb the man on a camel. (Egyptian)
The barking of dogs does not reach Heaven. (Sicilian)
The dog barks and the ox feeds. (Italian)
The dog barks at the stone, not at him that throws it. (German)
The dog does not bark in its own house. (Egyptian)
The dog that barks much is never good for hunting. (Portuguese)

The dog that barks much, bites little. (Portuguese)
The dog that bites does not bark in vain. (Italian)
The dog that has no understanding barks loudly. (Japanese)
The dog's bark is not might but fright. (Madagascan)
The dogs may bark but the caravan moves on. (Arabian)
The greatest barkers bite not sorest. (English)
The lion does not turn around when a small dog barks. (African)
The smaller the dog, the hardier the bark. (the Editor)
When an old dog barks, look out. (Roman)
When dog is eating it cannot bark, lest its food run away. (Unknown)
When one dog barks, another will follow suit. (Roman)
Why keep a dog and bark yourself? (English)

Barkeeper
The barkeeper loves a drunk, but not for a son-in-law. (Yiddish)

Barn
The barn may not be beautiful but it keeps out rain. (Hausan)

Bashful, Bashfulness
A bashful dog never fattens. (German)
Bashfulness is of no use to the needy. (Dutch)
It is only the bashful that lose. (French)
Bashfulness will not avail a beggar. (Roman)

Bastard
A bastard is the son of no one. (Roman)
Don't let the bastards grind you down. (Portuguese)

Bathe
Bathe early every day and sickness will avoid you. (Indian)
One who bathes willingly with cold water doesn't feel the cold. (Tanzanian)

Battle
A bold onset is half the battle. (German)
Away from the battle all are soldiers. (German)
In the stress of battle brave men do not feel their wounds. (Roman)
Seldom is there a battle from which no one escapes. (Irish)
There is no battle unless there be two. (Roman)

Bay
Each bay has its own wind. (Fijian)

Be
Better that it be so than that it may be so. (Irish)

That which must be, will be. (Danish)
What has not been, may be. (Italian)
What must be, must be. (Spanish)
What will be, will be. (Italian)

Beak
Every hooked beak is maintained by prey. (French)

Beam
No matter how stout one beam, it cannot support a house. (Chinese)

Bean
Every bean hath its black. (English)

Bear (noun)
Bear won't bite bear. (Roman)
Call the bear 'Uncle' till you are safe across the bridge. (Turkish)
Don't play with a bear if you don't want to be bit. (Italian)
Don't sell the bear's skin before you enter the woods. (Yiddish)
Don't sell the bear skin before you have killed the bear. (German)
Even savage bears agree among themselves. (Roman)
The bear dances but the owner collects the fare. (Korean)

Bear (verb)
Bear and forbear. (English)
Easy to declare, hard to bear. (Yiddish)

Beard
A man without a beard is like a loaf without a crust. (Russian)
He who dyes his beard deceives no one but himself. (Spanish)
He who has a beard entertains himself with it. (Spanish)
If a beard were all, the goat would be the winner. (Danish)
If being well-bearded brings happiness, then a he-goat must be happier than any of us.
   (Roman)
If the beard were all, the goat might preach. (German)
It is merry in the hall when beards wag all. (French)
It's convenient to learn the barber's trade on the other fellow's beard. (Yiddish)
Little beard, little shame. (Spanish)
Long whiskers cannot take the place of brains. (Russian)
The beard does not make the philosopher. (Italian)
The brains do not reside in the beard. (German)
When a man's beard turns gray, so do his friends. (Egyptian)
When your son's beard has fully grown, it's time to shave your own. (Arabian)

Beast

Every beast roars in its own den. (African)

One beast recognizes another. (Roman)

Beat, Beating

Beat your own and others will fear you. (Russian)

Beaten, but today the beater. (Egyptian)

Better beaten than broken. (German)

Even a boy can beat a man when bound. (Roman)

The beaten pay the fine. (French)

You may as well give a good beating as a bad one. (French)

Beautiful

A beautiful bird is a caged bird. (Japanese)

A beautiful flower does not stay on the stem. (German)

A beautiful girl, though she indeed be poor, is yet abundantly dowered. (Roman)

A beautiful thing is never perfect. (Egyptian)

A beautiful woman is more beautiful undressed than were she dressed in fine purple.
    (Roman)

A beautiful woman smiling, bespeaks a purse weeping. (Italian)

A daughter is more beautiful than her beautiful mother. (Roman)

As an ass is beautiful to an ass, so a pig is to a pig. (Roman)

Beautiful things are secured with the most difficulty. (Roman)

Beautiful women have generally an evil fate; intelligent men are seldom handsome.
    (Chinese)

Everything beautiful is loveable. (Roman)

He who loves a one-eyed girl thinks that one-eyed girls are beautiful. (Roman)

It is the beautiful bird that gets caged. (Chinese)

Not that which is great is beautiful, but that which is beautiful is great. (Roman)

She who is born beautiful is born married. (Hindi)

The truly beautiful is never separated from the useful. (Roman)

Beauty

A poor beauty finds more lovers than husbands. (English)

Beauty and folly are often companions. (French)

Beauty carries its dowry in its face. (Danish)

Beauty does not ensnare men; they ensnare themselves. (Chinese)

Beauty draws with a single hair. (Danish)

Beauty is a fading flower. (Danish)

Beauty is a good letter of introduction. (German)

Beauty is a transitory blessing. (Roman)

Beauty is but dross if honesty be lost. (Dutch)

Beauty is but skin deep. (English)

Beauty is difficult to attain. (Roman)

Beauty is in the eye of the beholder. (English)

Beauty is lost soon enough. (German)
Beauty is only skin deep, but ugly goes all the way through. (American)
Beauty is short-lived. (Korean)
Beauty is ten, nine of which is dressing. (Georgian)
Beauty is the seasoning of virtue. (Polish)
Beauty will fade, but not goodness. (Filipino)
Beauty will not make the pot boil. (Irish)
Beauty will not season your soup. (Polish)
Beauty will sit and weep, fortune will sit and eat. (Indian)
Beauty without chastity, a flower without fragrance. (Indian)
Beauty without virtue is a curse. (Georgian)
Beauty without virtue is like a rose without scent. (Danish)
Beauty, unaccompanied by virtue, is as a flower without perfume. (French)
Fancy surpasses beauty. (Spanish)
He who strives after beauty, let him endure the arduous. (Roman)
Health and cheerfulness make beauty; finery and cosmetics cost money and lie. (Spanish)
Meal, not beauty, makes a porridge. (Irish)
Naked love loves not the beauty that is due to art. (Roman)
One cannot make soup out of beauty. (Estonian)
She who is born a beauty is born betrothed. (Italian)
The autumn of beauty is still beautiful. (Roman)
The one who marries beauty marries trouble. (Yoruban)
The veil that covers the face seldom covers beauty. (Russian)
To each his own beauty. (Roman)

Becoming

It more becomes a woman to be silent than to talk. (Roman)
It much becomes us to live honorably. (Roman)

Bed, Bedtime

A bed may never say all it knows. (German)
Any bed is a palace if you fancy it. (Burmese)
As a man makes his bed, so he must lie in it. (Unknown)
As you have made your bed, so must you lie in it. (Irish)
Bed is the poor man's opera. (Egyptian)
Do not strip before bedtime. (French)
Go to bed with the hen, get up with the rooster. (German)
Go to bed with the lamb and rise with the lark. (Spanish)
If a bed is too short, draw up your legs. (Spanish)
It is hard to sleep on a strange bed. (Spanish)
It is no advantage for a man in fever to change his bed. (Roman)
The one known as an early-riser can stay in bed until noon. (Irish)
The person who lies in bed with children will find himself wet in the morning.
   (Mexican)
The warmest bed is a mother's. (Yiddish)

The way you make your bed, is the way you shall lie. (Swedish)
There is no bed like one's own. (German)
Those who go to bed with babies get up damp. (Spanish)
Too much bed makes a dull head. (English)
Where a man makes his bed, there must he also sleep. (German)
You've made your bed, now lie in it. (American)

Bee, Bees

Bees do not become hornets. (French)
Bees do not sip from faded flowers. (Chinese)
Bees taste from every flower. (Spanish)
Bees that have honey in their mouths have stings in their tails. (French)
Better one bee than a host of flies. (Italian)
Every bee's honey is sweet. (English)
How hallowed the bee, which makes honey for man and wax for God. (Spanish)
No bees, no honey. (Roman)
One bee is better than a thousand flies. (Spanish)
The bee has both sweetness and a sting. (Hausan)
The bee, from her industry in the summer, eats honey all the winter. (Belgian)
When the bee comes to your house, let it have nectar; you may want to visit the bee's house some day. (African)
When you hear the bee buzzing, you know that it is making honey and wants someone to take it. (Hausan)
Where there are bees, there is honey. (Roman)

Beekeeper

The beekeeper never lacks dessert. (Spanish)

Beer

Better weak beer than an empty cask. (Danish)
Beware, froth is not beer. (Danish)
Cider on beer, never fear; beer upon cider, makes a bad rider. (English)
Froth is no beer. (Dutch)
He that drinks beer, thinks beer. (Danish)
Not all of life is beer and skittles. (German)
When the beer goes in the wits go out. (Danish)
Wine upon beer is very good cheer; beer upon wine consider with fear. (German)

Before

Think before you speak, and look before you leap. (Irish)
Thatch your roof before rainy weather; dig your well before you become parched with thirst. (Chinese)

Beg, Begging

Better to beg than steal. (Dutch)

Better to have to give than have to beg. (Portuguese)
Constant begging only meets with constant refusal. (Irish)
He buys very dear who begs. (Portuguese)
He who knows how to beg may leave his money at home. (Danish)
I had rather buy than beg. (Roman)
If begging should unfortunately be your lot, then knock only at the large gates. (Arabian)
It is better to beg than to be hanged. (Spanish)
What is got by begging is dearly bought. (Danish)
With hat in hand a man can travel the entire land. (German)

Beggar, Beggars

A beggar never becomes a giver. (Greek)
A beggar's estate lies in all lands. (Dutch)
A beggar's hand is a bottomless basket. (Dutch)
A beggar's sack is bottomless. (German)
A beggar's wallet is never full. (Portuguese)
Beggars and dogs fight for crumbs. (German)
Beggars breed and rich men feed. (German)
Beggars can never be bankrupt. (Dutch)
Beggars can't be choosers. (American)
Beggars fear no rebellion. (Dutch)
Beggars mounted ride their horses to death. (Dutch)
Give a beggar a bed and he'll repay you with a louse. (Chinese)
It is a beggar's pride that he is not a thief. (Japanese)
One beggar likes not that another has two wallets. (Danish)
One ungrateful beggar does injury to all who are wretched. (Roman)
Put a beggar into your barn and he will make himself your heir. (Spanish)
Put a beggar on horseback and he will gallop away. (Irish)
Set a beggar on horseback, and he'll ride to the Devil. (German)
The beggar is the companion of the loafer. (Hausan)
The beggar may sing before the thief. (Belgian)
The beggar's bag is bottomless. (German)
The beggar's weapon is his cough. (Hausan)
To a beggar not even his own parents show affection. (Roman)
When it rains porridge the beggar has no spoon. (Danish)

Begin and End

Good to begin well, better to end well. (English)
He who begins badly, ends badly. (Spanish)
He who begins ill, finishes worse. (Italian)
He who begins many things, finishes few. (Italian)
Take care not to begin anything of which you may repent. (Roman)
What is well begun is already half done. (Roman)
Who begins amiss ends amiss. (German)
Who begins too much, accomplishes little. (German)

Beginning, Beginnings

A bad beginning may make a good ending. (German)
A good beginning makes a good ending. (English)
A hard beginning makes a good ending. (Italian)
All beginnings are hard, said the thief, and began by stealing an anvil. (Dutch)
Bad beginnings lead to bad results. (Roman)
Beware beginnings. (German)
Every beginning is weak. (Irish)
Everything must have a beginning. (French)
Of a good beginning comes a good end. (Chinese)
The beginning hot, the middle lukewarm, the end cold. (German)
The beginning is half of the whole. (Roman)
The beginning is the half of every action. (Greek)
The beginnings of all things are small. (Roman)

Behave

To a man behave like a man, to a dog behave like a dog. (Albanian)

Behind

He who does not go forward, stays behind. (German)

Belief, Believe

Believe no man more than yourself when you are spoken of. (Roman)
Believe not all you hear. (English)
Believe not half of what you hear, nor all of what you see. (German)
Believe not your ears but your eyes. (Korean)
Believe only half of what you see, nothing of what you hear. (Roman)
Believe that, and drink some water to wash it down. (French)
Do not believe any man more than yourself about yourself. (Roman)
For him who does not believe in signs, there is no way to live in the world. (Russian)
For what a man would like to be true, that he more readily believes. (English)
If what we see is doubtful, how can we believe what is spoken behind the backs.
    (Chinese)
If you believe everything you read, it is better not to read. (Japanese)
It is better to believe too much than too little. (Chinese)
It is equally dangerous to believe and to disbelieve. (Roman)
Men are readier to believe their eyes than their ears. (Roman)
Quick to believe is quickly deceived. (Serbian)
The eyes believe themselves; the ears believe other people. (German)
The one who believes is the one who achieves. (German)
Those who readily believe are readily deceived. (the Editor)
We are slow to believe that which, if believed, would work us harm. (Roman)
What the eyes see, the heart believes. (German)
Who goes not, sees not; who proves not, believes not. (Italian)
Who neither believes Heaven or Hell, the Devil heartily wishes him well. (German)

Who sees with the eye believes with the heart. (Unknown)
You believe that easily, which you hope for earnestly. (Roman)
You might believe a good man easily, a great man with pleasure. (Roman)

Bell, Bells
A bell rings for good reason. (Spanish)
A cracked bell can never sound well. (German)
A motionless bell never rings. (Chinese)
Bells call to church but do not enter. (French)
Bells toll twice for a woman and thrice for a man. (Spanish)
Even bells tremble when they strike. (Spanish)
Nine tolls of the church bell make a man. (English)
One bell serves a parish. (Italian)
People make the bells say what they please. (French)
The bell does not go to mass, and yet it calls everyone to it. (Italian)
The bell is loud because it is empty. (Polish)
The bell never rings of itself. (Roman)
While the great bells are ringing no one hears the little ones. (Danish)

Belly
A bellyful is a bellyful. (French)
A full belly brings forth every evil. (Poor Richard)
A full belly counsels well. (French)
A full belly dances better than a fine coat. (Danish)
A full belly is neither good for flight, nor for fighting. (Spanish)
A full belly sets a man to dance. (French)
A full belly, a cheerful mind. (German)
A fat belly does not produce a refined mind. (Danish)
Don't make an oven of your cap or a garden of your belly. (French)
First the belly, then the collar. (German)
Full stomach, happy heart. (Mexican)
If it were not for the belly, the back might wear gold. (Poor Richard)
Ill befalls the belly that forgets eaten bread. (Portuguese)
Let their bellies be full, for it is they that carry the legs. (Portuguese)
Neither an ocean nor a large belly can ever be filled. (Unknown)
Ten men, ten bellies. (Japanese)
The belly gives no credit. (Danish)
The belly is a bad advisor. (German)
The belly is a pot that's difficult to fill. (Unknown)
The belly is the giver of genius [i.e., poverty inspires genius]. (Roman)
The belly overrules the head. (French)
The belly robs the back. (French)
The belly warm, the foot at rest. (Portuguese)
The epicure puts his purse into his belly. (Spanish)
The full belly does not believe in hunger. (Italian)

There may be snow on the roof, but there's fire in the belly. (Russian)
You cannot reason with a hungry belly – it has no ears. (Greek)

Beloved
The last place is meet for the best beloved. (Irish)

Bench
He who throws himself under the bench will be left to lie there. (Danish)

Bend
An iron rod bends while it is hot. (Greek)
Best to bend while it is a twig. (Swedish)
Better is the branch that bends, than the branch that breaks. (Danish)
Better to bend than break. (French)
The branch must be bent early that is to make a good crook. (Danish)
To bend bamboo, start when it is a shoot. (Malay)
We bend out of compliance and not because of force. (Roman)

Benefice, Benefit
A small benefit obtained is better than a great one in expectation. (Irish)
Horses run after benefices and asses get them. (French)
Let us derive some benefit from evil. (Roman)
Never forget benefits done you, regardless how small. (Vietnamese)
The last benefit is most remembered. (English)

Berry
The blacker the berry, the sweeter the juice. (Jamaican)

Best
Better the best of the worst than the worst of the best. (Yiddish)
Let us always strive for the best. (Roman)
Many eschew the good in search of the best. (Spanish)
Some people put the best outside, some keep the best inside. (Jamaican)
The best always goes first. (Italian)
The best becomes every person, which is more peculiarly his own. (Roman)
The best go first, the bad remain to mend. (German)
The best is he who does the best. (Roman)
The best is the enemy of the good. (German)
The best is what one has in his hand. (German)
The best of men are but men at best. (English)
The best things come in small packages. (English)
The best things in life are free. (English)
The best things in life aren't things. (American)
The biggest fish is not always the best. (German)

Bet

Win a bet of your friend, and drink it on the spot. (Portuguese)

Betray, Betrayal

If someone betrays you once, it's his fault; if he betrays you twice, it's your fault. (Italian)

Woe to the one whose betrayer sits at his table. (Irish)

Better

A better seldom comes after. (German)

Better and better knows no limit. (Yiddish)

Better is better. (German)

If better were within, better would come out. (Roman)

To be better one must first be worse. (Icelandic)

Beware

Beware of a man's shadow and a bee's sting. (Burmese)

Beware of an oak, it draws the stroke; avoid an ash, it counts the flash; creep under the thorn, it can save you from harm. (Dutch)

Beware of laughing hosts and weeping priests. (German)

Beware of men who flourish hereditary honors. (German)

Beware of people who dislike cats. (Irish)

Beware of placing your hopes in the death of others. (Roman)

Beware of silent dogs and still waters. (German)

Beware of still water, a still dog, and a still enemy. (Yiddish)

Beware of the man of two faces. (Dutch)

Beware of the one who has nothing to lose. (Italian)

Beware of your friends, not your enemies. (Yiddish)

Beware the wolf in sheep's clothing. (Jamaican)

In life beware of law court; in death beware of Hell. (Chinese)

Bible

He has the Bible on his lips, but not in his heart. (Dutch)

How many daily read the Bible, and yet from vice are not deterred. (Dutch)

How many read the Bible, and yet pursue their course of evil. (German)

Bile

One does not have black bile inside and spit out white saliva. (Yoruban)

Bird, Birds

A bird does not sing because it has an answer; it sings because it has a song. (Chinese)

A bird in the cage is worth a hundred at large. (Italian)

A bird in the hand is better than a hundred flying birds. (Spanish)

A bird in the hand is worth two in the bush. (English)

A bird is distinguished by its note. (Roman)

A bird is known by its feathers. (Yiddish)

A bird is known by its song, a man by his chatter. (Jamaican)
A bird never flew so high but it had to come to the ground for food. (Dutch)
A chattering bird builds no nest. (West African)
A small bird is betrayed by its chirp. (Spanish)
All the same birds sing the same songs. (Japanese)
As the old birds sing, the young ones twitter. (German)
Better a sparrow in the hand than two flying. (Portuguese)
Better to be a bird of the wood than a bird in the cage. (Italian)
Better when birds sing than where irons ring. (Dutch)
Birds fly not into our mouths ready roasted. (Roman)
Birds in their little nests agree. (Roman)
Birds of a feather flock together. (English)
Clumsy birds have need of early flight. (Chinese)
Do not rear a bird of a bad breed. (Portuguese)
Even a bird chooses a sturdy branch before alighting. (Korean)
Every bird feathers its own nest. (Unknown)
Every bird is as its nest. (Irish)
Every bird sings its own song. (Hausan)
Every bird thinks its own nest beautiful. (Italian)
Fine birds are commonly plucked. (French)
Full-fledged birds fly away. (Chinese)
God gives birds their food, but they must fly for it. (Dutch)
Grain by grain the hen fills her crop. (Portuguese)
He that would take the bird must not scare it. (English)
However high a bird may soar, it seeks its food on earth. (Danish)
If you cannot get the bird, get one of its feathers. (Danish)
In vain the net is spread in the sight of the bird. (Roman)
It is a foul bird that defiles its own nest. (German)
It is a lazy bird that will not build its own nest. (Danish)
Little birds may peck a dead lion. (Spanish)
Old birds are hard to pluck. (German)
Old birds are not caught with cats. (Dutch)
Old birds are not caught with chaff. (Danish)
Old birds are not caught with new nets. (Italian)
One bird in the dish is better than a hundred in the air. (German)
One bird in the hand is better than two flying. (Dutch)
One bird in the hand is better than two on the roof. (Danish)
One bird in the hand is worth four in the air. (Roman)
Sweetly sings each bird in its own grove. (Irish)
The bird once out of hand is hard to recapture. (Danish)
The mantis seizes the locust but sees not the bird behind it. (Chinese)
The owl has one note, the crow another. (Roman)
The robin and the wrens be God Almighty's friends. (English)
Throwing your cap at a bird is not the way to catch it. (Portuguese)
'Tis a fat bird that bastes itself. (Dutch)

'Tis the early bird that catches the worm. (American)
With one arrow two birds are not struck. (Turkish)
Young birds do not fly far. (Jamaican)

Birds of Prey
Birds of prey do not flock together. (Portuguese)
Birds of prey do not sing. (German)
Birds of prey fly alone. (Spanish)

Birth
At birth we bring nothing, at death we take nothing away. (Chinese)
Great birth is a poor dish at table. (German)

Birth and Death
There is a day to be born and a time to die. (Chinese)
There is a universal law which commands that we shall be born and we shall die.
   (Roman)
We are born but to die, the end hangs from the beginning. (Roman)
We are born; we die: end of story. (American)

Bishop
Golden bishop, wooden crosier; wooden bishop, golden crosier. (French)

Bite, Bitten
A sheep's bite is never more than skin deep. (Italian)
All bite the bitten dog. (Portuguese)
All do not bite that show their teeth. (Dutch)
Bite not the dog that bites. (Danish)
Don't bite off more than you can chew. (Spanish)
Don't bite the hand that feeds you. (English)
Don't bite till you know whether it is bread or a stone. (Italian)
He who has been bitten by a serpent is afraid of a lizard. (Italian)
He who has been bitten by a snake is afraid of an eel. (Danish)
He that hath been bitten by a serpent is afraid of a rope. (Dutch)
If it can lick, it can bite. (French)
It is the quiet dog that bites first. (Unknown)
Keep to the little ones, and the big ones will not bite you. (Danish)
Let the dog bark at me, so long as he doesn't bite me. (Portuguese)
Muzzled dogs cannot bite. (German)
Once bitten, twice shy. (English)
One bite brings another. (Danish)
One would rather be bitten by wolves than by sheep. (Danish)
The biter is sometimes bit. (Italian)
The same dog that bit you in the morning will bite you in the evening. (Jamaican)
Those who cannot bite should not bare their teeth. (Spanish)

Bitter, Bitterness

A bitter word comes from a bitter heart. (Swiss)

Bitter pills are gilded. (German)

Bitter pills may have blessed effects. (English)

Eat the wind and swallow bitterness. (Portuguese)

Sugar in the mouth will not make a bitter life sweet. (Yiddish)

When bitterness is exhausted, sweetness follows. (Chinese)

Bitter and Sweet

He who has not tasted bitter, knows not the sweet. (German)

If you are bitter at heart, sugar in the mouth will not help you. (Yiddish)

Sometimes sweet things become bitter. (Roman)

The man who has tasted the bitter is worthy of the sweet. (Danish)

What was bitter to endure is sweet to remember. (German)

You have to take the bitter with the sweet. (American)

Black, Blacken

Black will take no other hue. (Dutch)

By blackening another you do not whiten yourself. (Rumanian)

'Fie upon thee, how black thou art!', said the kettle to the saucepan. (Danish)

He who blackens others does not whiten himself. (German)

Blacksmith

Blacksmith's children are not afraid of sparks. (Danish)

The blacksmith was guilty, but they hanged the gypsy. (Unknown)

Blame

A bad workman always blames his tools. (English)

Adam must have an Eve, to blame for his own faults. (German)

Blame is the lazy man's wages. (Danish)

Blame yourself as you would blame others; excuse others as you would excuse yourself.
   (Chinese)

Do not lay on the multitude the blame that is due to a few. (Roman)

Even doubtful accusations leave a stain behind them. (Danish)

He must be pure who would blame another. (Danish)

It is easier to blame than do better. (German)

Neither repine against Heaven nor blame man. (Chinese)

No name, no blame. (American)

Nobody is to blame for all. (German)

The absent always bear the blame. (Dutch)

You have no one to blame but your spouse. (American)

You have nobody to blame but yourself, if you stumble more than once over the same
   stump. (Italian)

Blanket
Make sure your blanket covers your feet. (Georgian)

Bleed
According to the arm be the bleeding. (French)

Bless, Blessing
An evil may be a blessing in disguise. (English)
Blessings brighten as they take their flight. (Italian)
Blessings do not come in pairs. (German)
God's blessing gained, enough is obtained. (German)
Great blessings come from Heaven, small ones from other men. (Chinese)
Men are slower to recognize blessings than misfortunes. (Roman)
Some evils bring blessings, and some blessings evils. (Spanish)
The blessings of the present life were stored up in a previous existence. (Chinese)
There are no unmixed blessings. (Roman)
We men only realize the value of our blessings when we have lost them.
    (Roman)
With the blessed, all things are blessed. (Roman)

Blind, Blindness
A blind horse makes straight for the pit. (Yiddish)
A blind man can see his mouth. (Irish)
A blind man is no judge of colors. (Italian)
A blind man may fear no snake. (Japanese)
A blind man swallows many a fly. (German)
A blind man will not thank you for a looking-glass. (English)
A blind man's wife needs no makeup. (Spanish)
A blind person who sees is better than a seeing person who is blind. (Persian)
Among the blind, the one-eyed man is king. (Chinese)
Among the blind, the squint rules. (Indian)
Better to be one-eyed than all blind. (Portuguese)
Blind is the bookless man. (English)
Blind men should not judge of colors. (English)
Even a blind man may sometimes shoot a crow. (Japanese)
Even a blind pig finds an acorn now and then. (Russian)
For whom does the blind man's wife adorn herself? (Spanish)
He is very blind who cannot see the sun. (Italian)
He who is in hot pursuit of gain is blind to reason. (Unknown)
If a blind man leads another, they both fall together. (Swedish)
If a blind man says, 'Let's throw stones,' be assured that he has stepped on one.
    (Nigerian)
If the blind leads the blind, then both shall fall into the pit. (English, after Jesus)
In the country of the blind, the one-eyed man is king. (Italian)
It is not easy to show the way to a blind man. (Italian)

Men are blind in their own causes. (American)
Men in the game are blind to what onlookers see clearly. (Chinese)
One blind man leads another into the ditch. (French)
The blind have their eyes in their fingers. (Spanish)
The blind horse is the hardiest. (German)
The blind man blames his stick if he falls. (Korean)
The blind man blames the ditch for his fall. (Korean)
The blind man blames the stream for his fall. (Korean)
The longer the blind man lives, the more he sees. (Yiddish)
There is no one as blind as the one who does not want to see. (Mexican)
There's none so blind as those who will not see. (English)
When the blind lead the blind, both do not wander very far. (German)
When the blind man carries the banner, woe to those who follow. (French)

Blind and Deaf
The blind and the deaf are always suspicious. (Spanish)
The blind are quick at hearing; the deaf are quick at sight. (Chinese)

Blood
All blood is alike ancient. (Poor Richard)
Blood boils without fire. (Spanish)
Blood cannot be washed out with blood. (Persian)
Blood is not the remedy for thirst. (Hausan)
Blood is thicker than water. (German)
Blood will out. (English)
Blood will tell. (Afghani)
Good blood will never lie. (French)
Human blood is all of a color. (English)
No matter how thin, blood is always thicker than water. (Danish)
Noble and common blood is of the same color. (German)
One cannot draw blood from a turnip, or ask a goat for wool. (Irish)
The nobler the blood the less the pride. (Danish)
There is no getting blood from a turnip. (Italian)
When blood appears it is apt to run. (African)

Bloom, Blossom
Bloom where you are planted. (English)
Blossoms are not fruits. (Dutch)
Blossoms are the pledge of fruit. (Unknown)
From the withered tree, a flower blooms. (Chinese)
Roses and maidens soon lose their bloom. (German)
Timely blossom, timely fruit. (German)
When gorse is in bloom, my lover's in tune. (English)
You raise flowers for a year; you see them bloom for but a few days. (Chinese)

Blot
Cleaning a blot with blotted fingers makes a greater blot. (Spanish)

Blow (verb)
Better to blow hard than burn yourself. (Danish)
Blow first, and sip afterwards. (Dutch)
Blow not on dead embers. (Irish)

Blow, Blows (noun)
A blow on the back reveals the bandit. (Burmese)
Blows always strike us on our sore spots. (Spanish)
Blows are not given upon conditions. (Italian)

Blue
Blue comes of indigo and yet it is bluer than indigo. (Japanese)

Blush, Blushing
Better a blush in the face than a spot in the heart. (Dutch)
Blushing is a sign of grace. (English)

Boar
A boar is often held by a not-so-large dog. (Roman)
A boar remains a boar, though it sleep on silken bolsters. (Danish)

Boast, Boaster
A boaster and a liar are cousins. (Spanish)
All my goods are of silver and gold, even my copper kettle, says the boaster. (Dutch)
Believe a boaster as you would a liar. (Italian)
Big boast, small roast. (English)
Do not boast about tomorrow, for you know not what the day might bring. (Unknown)
Great boast, small roast. (Chinese)
Great boaster, little doer. (French)
He that boasts of himself affronts his company. (Danish)
He who boasts of his accomplishments will heap ridicule on himself. (Filipino)
If a man says he can swallow a pickaxe, hold the handle for him. (Hausan)
It ill becomes the one who boasts of giving as the one who boasts of getting. (Irish)
No one sticks a knife into his stomach and then boasts about it. (Hausan)
No one with a good catch of fish goes home by the back alley. (French)
The benefit that is boasted of is a sorry one. (Irish)
The one who boasts of his descent, boasts of what he owes to others. (Roman)
They can do least who boast loudest. (Roman)
Unworthy offspring brag the most of their worthy descent. (Danish)

Boat, Boats
Don't rock the boat. (French)

From the boat we get to the ship. (Dutch)
Little boats should keep near shore. (Poor Richard)
Show her the rudder, but don't steer her boat. (Yiddish)
The water is the same on both sides of the boat. (Finnish)
Vessels large may venture more, but little boats must keep near shore. (French)
When the boat was going well the oar broke. (Burmese)
Woe to him who burns his boat before he crosses back. (Irish)

Body, Bodies
Bodies are slow in growth, rapid in decay. (Roman)
Bury a body in the snow and soon enough it will come to light. (Chinese)
Great bodies move slowly. (English)
No one is free who is a slave to the body. (Roman)
The body, loaded with yesterday's excess, also bears down the mind. (Roman)
What your hands commit your body must bear. (Jamaican)

Bold
Every man is bold until he is at a public assembly. (Irish)
Nothing is so bold as a blind man. (Unknown)
Nothing so bold as a blind mare. (Dutch)

Bone, Bones
A bone is more valuable to a dog than a pearl. (Filipino)
Keep hold of the bone and the dog will follow you. (Irish)
No bones are broken by a mother's fist. (Russian)
The bone binds the dog. (Croatian)
You can't have meat without the bone. (Sicilian)

Book, Books
A book gives knowledge, but it is life that gives understanding. (Yiddish)
A book holds a house of gold. (Chinese)
A book is a friend. (American)
A book is like a garden carried in the pocket. (Arabian)
A book that remains shut is but a block of wood. (Arabian)
A good book, a good friend. (Italian)
A great book is a great evil. (Greek)
A library of books does not equal one good teacher. (Chinese)
A multitude of books distracts the mind. (Roman)
Beware of the man of one book. (German)
Books are preserved minds. (Japanese)
Books do not exhaust words; words do not exhaust thoughts. (Chinese)
Boys read books one way, men another, old men another. (Roman)
By night and day thumb through the pages of your Greek exemplars. (Roman)
Don't judge a book by its cover. (American)
In a long book it is allowable for sleep to steal upon us. (Roman)

It's not healthy to swallow books without chewing. (German)

Some men have only one book in them, others a library. (English)

There is no book so bad that it is not profitable in some part. (Roman)

There is no worse thief than a bad book. (Italian)

To open a book brings profit. (Chinese)

Word by word the big books are made. (French)

You can't tell a book by its cover. (English)

Boots

He that has good legs, has often bad boots. (German)

Two boots make a pair. (Russian)

Born

Everyone is born crying, not even one laughing. (Spanish)

No one is born for himself. (Roman)

One should be born either a king or a fool. (German)

The man who is born in a stable is not a horse. (English)

There are a thousand ways of dying, only one of being born. (Spanish)

Those who have come into the world are not as many as those who accompanied them.
   (Yoruban)

We are a mere cipher, and born to consume the fruits of the earth. (Italian)

We are born crying, live complaining, and die disappointed. (English)

We are but dust and shadows, born to consume the fruits of the earth.
   (Roman)

Borrow, Borrower

A borrowed cloak does not keep one warm. (Egyptian)

A borrowed horse and your own spurs make short miles. (Danish)

Borrowed garments never fit well. (Italian)

Borrowers must not be choosers. (French)

Borrowing brings care. (Dutch)

Borrowing does well only once. (German)

He that goes a-borrowing goes a-sorrowing. (Dutch)

He who borrows sells his freedom. (German)

He who is quick at borrowing, is slow in paying. (German)

He who pays well may borrow again. (German)

Long borrowed is not given. (German)

Scratching and borrowing do well enough, but not for long. (German)

The early man never borrows from the late man. (French)

The law of borrowing is to break what is borrowed. (Irish)

The person who wears borrowed clothes often loses what he wears.
   (Mexican)

To borrow is to sorrow. (Poor Richard)

Who pays soon borrows when he will. (French)

Who readily borrows, readily lies. (German)

Boss

Straw bosses are worse than bosses. (Yiddish)

The boss is not always right. (American)

Both Ways

You can't have it both ways. (English)

Bottle

A narrow neck keeps the bottle from being emptied in one swig. (Irish)

Drop after drop fills the bottle. (Spanish)

You can't put new wine in old bottles. (Persian)

Bottom

Always taking out and never putting in, soon reaches the bottom. (Spanish)

It is best to begin at the bottom. (Hungarian)

Let not the bottom of your purse or of your mind be seen. (Portuguese)

Boundary Marker

A marker is very well-placed between the fields of two brothers. (French)

Bow (noun)

A bow kept taut will quickly break, but kept loosely strung it will serve you when you
    need it. (Roman)

A bow long bent at length waxes weak. (Danish)

Have two strings to your bow. (Italian)

Strain not your bow beyond its bend, lest it break. (Dutch)

The bow that is always bent slackens or breaks. (Spanish)

You will break the bow if you keep it always bent. (Greek)

Bow (verb)

A person who bows never gets his cheek slapped. (Korean)

A respectful bow has its own reward. (Yoruban)

To bow the body is easy; to bow the will is hard. (Chinese)

When you bow, bow low. (Chinese)

Who bows to might loses his right. (German)

Whoever needs milk, bows to the animal. (Yiddish)

Boy, Boys

A boy knows not fire till it burns him. (Hausan)

A lazy boy and a warm bed are difficult to part. (Danish)

Boys will be boys and girls will be girls. (English)

Boys will become men, and then men boys. (American)

Do not entrust a sword to a boy. (Roman)

Send a boy where he wants to go and you see his best pace. (African)

The smallest boy always carries the biggest fiddle. (Cambodian)

Train a boy strictly, but a girl kindly. (Indian)

Two boys are half a boy, and three boys are no boy at all [i.e., regarding work]. (Spanish)

While the boy is young, you can see the man. (Chinese)

Brag, Braggart

Nobody takes a beating like a braggart. (Yiddish)

They brag most who can do least. (English)

Brain

A brain is worth little without a tongue. (French)

Brain is better than brawn. (English)

Half a brain is enough for him who says little. (Italian)

The brain that sows not corn, plants thistles. (Spanish)

The brains are not in the beard. (Indian)

Where brains need to prevail, mere brain will not avail. (Yiddish)

Branch, Branches

A crooked branch has a crooked shadow. (Japanese)

The highest branch is not the safest roost. (Italian)

The old branch breaks when it is bent. (Danish)

The high branches are more easily broken. (Korean)

Brave, Bravery

A brave man gets his reward. (Irish)

A cock is valiant on its own dunghill. (Dutch)

A short sword for a brave man. (French)

All are brave when the enemy flees. (Italian)

Be brave, not ferocious. (Roman)

Brave men have no need of walls. (Roman)

Brave men lived before Agamemnon. (Roman)

Brave men never warred with the dead and conquered. (Roman)

Brave sons spring from the steadfast and good. (Roman)

Difficulties embolden rather than impede the brave. (Roman)

Even brave men are alarmed by sudden terrors. (Roman)

He who acts honestly acts bravely. (Roman)

He who sees injustice and does not act is not brave. (Korean)

It little avails the unfortunate to be brave. (Spanish)

Live as brave men, and stand against adversity with stout hearts. (Roman)

Many are brave when the enemy flees. (Italian)

None but the brave deserve the fair. (Unknown)

The brave always show mercy. (Roman)

The brave man lives only as long as the coward allows him. (Mexican)

The brave man will yield to a braver man. (Roman)

The brave may die, but they never say 'die'. (American)

The brave may fall, but they cannot yield. (Roman)

The bravest men sleep the soundest. (German)
Though frightened, the brave seldom run. (Burmese)
Through bravery you win, and through bravery you lose. (Polish)

Bread
Beggar's bread has the hardest crusts. (German)
Better bread with water than cake with trouble. (Russian)
Better half a loaf than none at all. (Danish)
Bread by the color and wine by the taste. (English)
Bread is better than the song of birds. (Danish)
Bread is the staff of life. (English)
Bread is the staff of life, but beer is life itself. (English)
Don't bite till you know whether it is bread or a stone. (Italian)
Eat bread at pleasure, drink wine by measure. (French)
Every tomorrow brings its bread. (French)
Good bread is lost when given to dogs and waifs. (German)
Half a loaf is better than none. (English)
He who has loaves has dogs. (Italian)
If you have the bread, you can always find a knife. (Yiddish)
If you have two loaves of bread, sell one and buy a lily. (Chinese)
It is hard to pay for bread that has been eaten. (Danish)
Let every man look to the bread upon which he must depend. (Portuguese)
Look for the fancy bread and you lose the plain. (Yiddish)
Man cannot live by bread alone. (Jesus)
Many children, and little bread, is a painful pleasure. (German)
No food tastes good without bread. (Spanish)
No meal suffices without bread. (German)
One's own simple bread is much better than someone else's pilaf. (Georgian)
Since we have loaves let us not look for cakes. (Spanish)
Some have bread who have no teeth. (French)
Take the mouth to the bread, not the bread to the mouth. (Albanian)
The bread eaten, the company departs. (Spanish)
The bread never falls but on its buttered side. (English)
To a starving man bread is sweeter than honey. (Russian)
There is no hard bread if you are hungry. (Spanish)
When I had teeth I had no bread; now I have bread but no teeth. (Spanish)
When there is little bread at table put plenty on your plate. (Italian)
Where there is little bread, cut first. (Portuguese)
Who has no bread to spare should not keep a dog. (Spanish)
Whose bread I eat, his song I sing. (German)
You can't fill your belly painting pictures of bread. (Chinese)

Break
The best you get is an even break. (French)
Too much will soon break. (German)

Very little avails to break a bruised thing. (Roman)
You break it, you buy it. (American)

Breath

Breath is the music of life. (Indian)
No person is aware of his own foul breath. (Japanese)
One man's breath's, another man's death. (Kashmiri)
The first breath is the beginning of death. (German)

Breed, Bred

Good breeding shows in horse and man. (Unknown)
Good feeding before good breeding. (Unknown)
Like breeds like. (French)
What's bred in the bone will come out in the flesh. (English)

Brevity

Brevity is pleasing. (Roman)
Brevity is the soul of wit. (Roman)
In brevity lies delight. (German)

Bribe, Bribery

A friend that you buy with presents, will be bought from you. (Roman)
A greased mouth cannot say no. (Italian)
All offices are greasy. (Dutch)
All things at Rome may be bought for a price. (Roman)
An official never flogs the bearer of gifts. (Chinese)
Bribery can split a stone, for even a stone may be bribed. (Irish)
Bribes will enter without knocking. (Roman)
Buy the rogue, and you need have no fear of the honest man. (Irish)
Even the gods are conciliated by offerings. (Roman)
He that is won with a nut, may be lost with an apple. (Rumanian)
He who would stop every man's mouth must have a great deal of meal.
   (Italian)
If the pocket is empty, the judge is deaf. (Russian)
You can buy any man, but they won't stay bought. (Georgian)

Bride

A sad bride makes a glad wife. (Dutch)
All brides are beautiful, all the dead are holy. (Yiddish)
Always the bridesmaid, never the bride. (American)
At the wedding feast the least eater is the bride. (Spanish)
Blessed is the bride upon whom the sun shines. (English)
Choose neither bride nor linen by candlelight. (Spanish)
On her wedding day, only the bride is beautiful. (Spanish)
The weeping bride makes a laughing wife. (German)

With all the world looking for pretty brides, what becomes of the homely girls? (Yiddish)

Bridge

Cross even a stone bridge after you've tested it. (Korean)
Don't burn your bridges before they're crossed. (English)
Don't burn your bridges behind you. (American)
Don't cross the bridge till you come to it. (English)
Don't cry 'hallo!' till you're over the bridge. (Dutch)
Everyone speaks well of the bridge which carries him over. (Chinese)
If you destroy a bridge, be sure you can swim. (African)
It is better to build bridges than walls. (African)
Let every man praise the bridge he goes over. (English)
Never cross a bridge till you come to it. (French)

Bring

Fair is he that comes, but fairer he that brings. (French)
Whoever brings finds the door open for him. (Italian)

Brook

It is easier to stem the brook than the river. (Danish)
Little brooks make great rivers. (French)
The shallower the brook, the more it babbles. (Indonesian)
You cannot say hello until you have crossed the brook. (Swedish)

Broom, Brooms

A bad broom leaves a dirty room. (English)
A new broom is good for three days. (Italian)
A new broom sweeps a new way. (Russian)
A new broom sweeps clean. (Russian)
A new broom sweeps clean, but an old broom knows the corners. (Irish)
An old broom knows the corners of the house. (German)
New brooms sweep clean. (English)
The new broom sweeps the house best. (Irish)

Broth

Boil stones in butter, and you may sip the broth. (Italian)
Fox's broth: cold and scalding. (Spanish)
Much broth is sometimes made with little meat. (Danish)

Brothel

He who has one foot in a brothel, has the other in a hospital. (German)

Brother, Brothers

A brother is a treasure if good, an enemy if bad. (Korean)

A brother turned enemy is an enemy for life. (Yiddish)
At the narrow passage there is no brother and no friend. (Arabian)
Brothers and sisters are like hands and feet. (Vietnamese)
Even brothers keep careful accounts. (Chinese)
If brothers disagree, the bystander takes advantage. (Chinese)
Woe to him who lacks a dear brother. (Irish)
You should deem it a crime to hurt even an evil brother. (Roman)

Bucket
Don't throw away the old bucket until you know whether the new one holds water.
   (Yiddish)
The bucket goes so often to the well that it leaves its handle there. (Italian)

Buds
Though cut, new buds sprout out. (Korean)

Build, Building
Buildings rise by a gradual accumulation of bricks. (Chinese)
He who builds by the roadside has many surveyors. (Italian)
He who builds on another's ground loses his stone and mortar. (Italian)
He who builds on the public way, must let the people have their say. (German)
It is easier to pull down than to build up. (English)
It takes time to build a castle. (Irish)
No good building without a good foundation. (English)
Who builds upon the people, builds upon sand. (Italian)
Who builds with sweat, defends with blood. (Albanian)
You cannot build a house for last year's summer. (Ethiopian)

Bull
A mad bull is not to be tied up with packthread. (Greek)
Feign death and the bull will leave you. (Portuguese)
It is not the same thing to talk of bulls as to be in the bullring. (Spanish)
Not everyone with a cape would fight a bull. (Spanish)
Take the bull by the horns. (Russian)
Two bulls cannot live in one stable. (African)
When bulls fight, woe to the frogs. (Portuguese)

Bully
A bully is always a coward. (Spanish)

Burden, Burdensome
A lamb carried far becomes as burdensome as a ewe. (Irish)
A light burden carried far becomes a heavy one. (Irish)
A voluntary burden is no burden. (Italian)
Another man's burden is always light. (Danish)

Every man's burden is suited to his strength. (German)
Everyone feels his own burden is heavy. (French)
Everyone thinks his own pack's the heaviest. (German)
God makes the back to the burden. (Spanish)
He who carries one burden will soon carry a hundred. (French)
It is not the burden but the over-burden that kills the beast. (French)
Lay the burden on the lazy ass. (Roman)
Light burdens, borne long, grow heavy. (German)
Nothing is so burdensome as a secret. (French)

Burn, Burnt

He who burns his buttocks must sit on blisters. (Dutch)
He who burnt his mouth will blow on his salad. (Unknown)
He who has been burnt by hot broth will blow even cold water. (Korean)
Never burn your fingers to snuff another man's candle. (Irish)
Once burned by milk you will blow on cold water. (Russian)
Once burnt, twice shy. (American)
Some who mean only to warm, burn themselves. (French)
Who glows not burns not. (Italian)

Bury

By the living we bury the dead. (Dutch)

Business

A man without a smiling face should not open a shop. (Chinese)
Boldness in business is the first, second, and third thing. (Roman)
Business before pleasure. (German)
Business is easy, profit is not. (Korean)
Business is one thing, friendship another. (Mexican)
Business makes the man, and tries him. (German)
Corporations have neither bodies to be punished nor souls to be damned. (Chinese)
Do business best when the wind's in the west. (Roman)
Don't draw another's bow, don't ride another's horse, don't mind another's business.
    (Roman)
Don't open a shop unless you know how to smile. (Yiddish)
Done in by his own trade like a water merchant in the rain. (Madagascan)
Everybody's business is nobody's business. (German)
Everyone is ignorant in another person's trade. (Irish)
Exchange is no robbery. (German)
Fuel is not sold in the forest, nor fish by the lake shore. (Chinese)
He loses his market who has nothing to sell. (Spanish)
He that deals in dirt has foul fingers. (Danish)
He who cannot speak well of his trade does not understand it. (French)
He who desires small gains will hardly be able to accomplish great transactions.
    (Chinese)

He who doth his own business defiles not his fingers. (Italian)

He who is of the craft can discourse about it. (Italian)

Hold back some goods for a thousand days and you will be sure to sell at a profit. (Chinese)

If you deal in camels, make the doors high. (Afghani)

It is the seller, not the maker, who makes the goods expensive. (Yoruban)

Keep your shop and your shop will keep you. (Jamaican)

Know each other as if your were brothers; negotiate deals as if you were strangers. (Arabian)

Let every man mind his own business, and leave others to theirs. (Portuguese)

Let everyone mind his own business, and the cows will be well tended. (French)

Many buyers make higher prices. (German)

Men see better into other people's business than into their own. (Roman)

Merchant today, beggar tomorrow. (German)

Mind your own business. (German)

Prudent pauses forward business. (German)

Punctuality is the soul of business. (English)

Scholars talk books, butchers talk pigs. (Chinese)

Schoolmasters should stick to their books; farmers to their pigs. (Chinese)

Set thy expense according to thy trade. (Dutch)

Shoemaker, stick to your last. (Roman)

Take in laundry before you take in partners. (Spanish)

Tell everybody your business and the Devil will do it for you. (Italian)

The first mistake in public business, is the going into it. (Poor Richard)

To open a shop is easy, to keep it open is hard. (Chinese)

What's everybody's business is nobody's business. (Spanish)

When everyone minds his own business the work gets done. (Danish)

When selling flour the winds blows, when selling salt the sky drizzles. (Korean)

Without business, debauchery. (French)

Busy

He that hath many irons in the fire, some of them will cool. (Dutch)

None so busy as those who do nothing. (French)

Busybody

A busybody is always malevolent. (Roman)

Butcher

Better to pay the butcher than the doctor. (English)

One butcher fears not many sheep. (Roman)

The butcher is not startled by the numbers of sheep. (Egyptian)

Butter

All is not butter that comes from the cow. (Italian)

Butter is gold in the morning, silver at noon, lead at night. (English)
Butter spoils no meat, and moderation injures no cause. (Danish)

Butterfly, Butterflies
Butterflies are free. (American)
Butterflies come to pretty flowers, birds alight upon fruit trees. (Korean)
The butterfly often forgets it was a caterpillar. (Swedish)

Buy, Buyer
A buyer wants a hundred eyes, a seller none. (Dutch)
Better to buy than to be given. (Japanese)
Beware the buyer. (English)
Buy him at his own price and sell him at yours and you'll make no bargain. (Danish)
Buy by the pound and sell by the ounce. (Spanish)
Buy cheap, sell dear. (Unknown)
Buy in the cheapest market and sell in the dearest. (Danish)
Buy not what you want, but what you need; what you do not want is costly at a penny.
   (Roman)
Buy your neighbor's ox, and woo your neighbor's daughter. (German)
Buying is cheaper than asking. (German)
Do not buy a carrier's ass, or marry an innkeeper's daughter. (Spanish)
Do not buy either the moon or the news, for in the end they will both come out.
   (Arabian)
Don't buy a cat in a sack. (Dutch)
Don't buy a pig in a poke. (English)
Don't buy from enemies, and don't sell to friends. (Spanish)
Everything may be bought except day and night. (French)
For overbuying there's no help but selling again. (French)
For the buyer a hundred eyes are too few, for the seller one is enough. (Italian)
He that finds fault wants to buy. (German)
He that speaks ill of the mare, will buy her. (Poor Richard)
He who buys early buys cheaply. (Italian)
He who buys the broom can also buy the handle. (Italian)
He who buys what he cannot pay for, sells what he would rather not. (Italian)
He who buys what he doesn't want, will soon sell what he does want. (German)
He who decries, wants to buy. (Italian)
If you buy cheaply, you pay dearly. (English)
If you buy things you don't need, you'll soon be selling things you do. (Filipino)
It is good to buy when another wants to sell. (Italian)
Let the buyer beware. (Roman)
Never buy through your ears but through your eyes. (Irish)
Silver buys a prayer, gold buys a mass. (the Editor)
The buyer needs a hundred eyes, the seller none. (English)
When you buy land you buy stones, when you buy meat you buy bones. (English)
When you go out to buy, do not show your silver. (Chinese)

When you go to buy, use your eyes, not your ears. (Czech)
Who buys hath need of eyes. (Italian)

Buy and Sell
Buy low, sell high. (American)
Buying and selling is but winning and losing. (English)
Sell publicly and buy privately. (Spanish)

Buzzard, Buzzards
Where buzzards, there death. (German)

Bygones
Let bygones be bygones. (English)

Bystander
The bystander sees more than the player. (English)

C

Cabbage
He who would have good cabbage, must pay its price. (Danish)
It's no use boiling your cabbage twice. (Irish)

Cactus
People go to the cactus only when it bears fruit. (Mexican)

Caesar
Render unto Caesar the things that are Caesar's. (Jesus)

Cage
A fine cage won't feed the bird. (French)
A golden cage is still a cage. (Mexican)
When the cage is ready the bird has flown. (French)

Cake
You cannot have your cake and eat it. (English)

Calamity
Calamities look for the luckless man. (Spanish)
Calamities may come down from Heaven, but let us seek to be blameless. (Chinese)
He who sees the calamity of other people finds his own calamity light. (Arabian)
How weak are the hearts of mortals under calamity! (Roman)

Calf

Do not search for a calf under an ox. (Turkish)

Every cow licks its calf. (German)

Call, Called

Be the thing you would be called. (German)

Call me not olive before you see me gathered. (Italian)

It is not what you are called, but what you answer to. (African)

Many are called but few are chosen. (Jesus)

No one calls to do you a favor. (the Editor)

Calumny

Calumniate strongly and some of it will stick. (Roman)

Hurl calumny boldly: some of it always sticks. (English)

Nothing is so swift as calumny. (Roman)

Camel

A camel that wants fodder stretches out its neck. (Persian)

A camel with bells is not lost. (Turkish)

Even a mangy camel will carry more than a herd of asses. (Roman)

If the camel once get its nose in a tent, the body will soon follow. (Arabian)

It is the last straw that breaks the camel's back. (Danish)

Little by little, the camel gets into the couscous. (Moroccan)

One camel does not make fun of another camel's hump. (African)

The camel went seeking for horns and lost his ears. (Arabian)

The camel, begging for horns, was deprived of its ears as well. (Roman)

Trust in God, but tie your camel. (Persian)

Cancer

Cancer – schmancer! – as long as you're healthy. (Yiddish)

Candle, Candlelight

A candle lights others and consumes itself. (English)

A candle, no matter how bright it shines, cannot illumine tomorrow. (Chinese)

Burn a candle at both ends, and it will not last long. (Scottish)

By candlelight a goat looks like a lady. (French)

Choose not a woman nor linen by candlelight. (English)

Light a candle for God and another one for the Devil. (Unknown)

The best candle is understanding. (Welsh)

The candle that goes before gives the best light. (Dutch)

The candle that goes before is better than that which comes after. (French)

We are no more than candles burning in the wind. (Japanese)

You may light another's candle from your own without loss. (Danish)

Candor
Candor breeds hatred. (Roman)

Canoe
Do not kick away the canoe which helped you cross the river. (Madagascan)
Paddle your own canoe. (English)

Cap
If the cap fits, wear it. (English)
Make the cap to fit the head. (German)

Capitalism
Under capitalism man exploits man; under socialism the reverse is true. (Polish)

Cards
A pack of cards is the Devil's prayer-book. (German)

Care, Cares
Another's care hangs by a hair. (Spanish)
Care brings gray hairs. (Roman)
Care brings on gray hairs, and age without years. (German)
Care not for lost things. (German)
Care, and not fine stables, makes a good horse. (Danish)
Fretting cares make gray hairs. (English)
He who takes no care of little things, will not have the care of great ones. (German)
Want of care admits despair. (English)
We are all consumed by cares. (Roman)

Careless, Carelessness
Alert at the beginning, careless at the end. (Roman)
Carelessness is a great enemy. (Japanese)

Carpenter
A carpenter is known by his chips. (Roman)
A carpenter may lend his wife but not his tools. (Korean)
The worse the carpenter the more the chips. (Dutch)

Carry
Every man must carry his own sack to the mill. (Danish)
He can carry the ox who has carried the calf. (Roman)
He is better equipped for life, as for swimming, who has the lesser to carry. (Roman)
He who carries nothing loses nothing. (French)
He who lets the goat be laid on his shoulders is soon after forced to carry the cow. (Italian)
It takes four living men to carry one dead man out of a house. (Italian)

The man being carried doesn't notice the distance to the town. (Nigerian)
When the blind man carries the lame man, both go forward. (Swedish)

Cart
Don't upset the apple cart. (American)

Cask
A poor cask often holds good wine. (Roman)
It is easy to set a cask to rolling. (Roman)
The cask savors of the first fill. (German)
The cask smells of the wine it contains. (Spanish)
The full cask makes no noise. (Italian)
The fuller the cask, the duller its sound. (German)
The old cask tastes of what the new cask held. (Roman)
'Tis too late to spare when the cask is bare. (Dutch)

Castle
A cabin with plenty of food is better than a hungry castle. (Irish)
Better inside a cottage than outside a castle. (Welsh)
It's easy to keep a castle that's not besieged. (Irish)

Cat, Cats
A cat always knows whose meat it eats. (Russian)
A cat contained becomes a lion. (Italian)
A cat has nine lives, as the onion seven skins. (German)
A cat is a lion to mouse. (German)
A cat likes fish, but hates to wet its paws. (Roman)
A cat may go to a monastery, but she still remains a cat. (Ethiopian)
A cat that licks the spit is not to be trusted with roast meat. (Italian)
A cat that mews much catches but few mice. (Dutch)
A gloved cat catches no mice. (German)
A good cat, a good rat. (French)
A muffled cat never caught a mouse. (French)
A puss in boots catches no mice. (French)
A scalded cat is afraid of cold water. (Mexican)
A shy cat makes a proud mouse. (Scottish)
A silent cat catches mice. (Japanese)
All cats love fish but fear to wet their paws. (Chinese)
An old cat will not learn how to dance. (Moroccan)
At night, all cats are gray. (French)
Care killed the cat. (German)
Cats and kings always land on their feet. (German)
Cats don't catch mice to please God. (Afghani)
Cats hide their claws. (German)
Don't send away your cat for being a thief. (Spanish)
Even a cat may look at a king. (Yiddish)

He has a good pledge of the cat who has her skin. (French)
He who hunts with cats will catch mice. (Danish)
He who puts by for the night, puts by for the cat. (Danish)
If the cat were a hen, it too would lay eggs. (German)
In a cat's eye, all things belong to cats. (English)
It is better to feed one cat than many mice. (Norwegian)
It is for her own good that the cat purrs. (Irish)
It takes a good many mice to kill a cat. (Danish)
Keep no more cats than will catch mice. (Portuguese)
Never was a mewing cat a good mouser. (Italian)
No one likes to bell the cat. (German)
Old cats like young mice. (Mexican)
Old or young, all cats lap as much milk. (Unknown)
The cat does not give leave to the mice. (German)
The cat has nine lives: three for playing, three for straying, three for staying. (English)
The cat is friendly, but scratches. (Spanish)
The cat that is always crying catches no mice. (Egyptian)
The cat well knows whose beard she licks. (Portuguese)
The kind man feeds his cat before sitting down to dinner. (Yiddish)
The quiet cat catches the rat. (Japanese)
The scalded cat dreads cold water. (Spanish)
The stroked cat is meek. (Roman)
Those that dislike cats will be carried to the cemetery in the rain. (Dutch)
To a good cat a good rat. (French)
Wanton kittens make sober cats. (English)
What is born of a cat will catch mice. (English)
What is play to the cat is death to the mouse. (Danish)
What would a young cat do but kill a mouse? (Irish)
When cats are mousing they don't mew. (Dutch)
When the cat is gone, the mice come out to stretch. (Chinese)
When the cat's away, the mice will play. (English)
When the cat's away, the rats dance. (Italian)
Who will not feed the cats, must feed the mice and rats. (German)
You can throw a cat wherever you want, it always falls on its feet. (Yiddish)
Young cats will mouse, young apes will louse. (Dutch)

Cats and Dogs
By biting and scratching cats and dogs come together. (French)
Cats and dogs seldom make alliances. (German)

Catch, Caught
Catch as catch can. (American)
Come fish, come frog, all goes into the basket. (Spanish)
Hares are caught with hounds, fools with praise, and women with gold. (German)
He who would catch a rogue must watch behind the door. (Dutch)

He who would catch is caught. (Roman)
It is wretched to be found out. (Roman)
Let us first catch the bear and then sell its skin. (Italian)
Little by little, one catches the monkey in the jungle. (African)
No one can be caught in places he does not visit. (Danish)
One catches the hare and another eats it. (German)
One man beats the bush, another catches the bird. (Spanish)
One startles the hare, another catches it. (Italian)
Too late the bird cries out when it is caught. (French)
When we think to catch we are sometimes caught. (Spanish)
Who follows the trail catches the game. (Spanish)
Who watches not catches not. (Dutch)
You can't catch two frogs with one hand. (Chinese)
You cannot catch a flea with gloves. (Albanian)
You cannot catch a fox without bait. (Roman)
You cannot catch a mule without an ear of corn. (German)
You cannot catch old birds with chaff. (English)

Cause
All things are cause for either laughter or weeping. (Roman)
Happy is the one who understands the cause of all things. (Roman)
He who fails his own cause, supports the other's. (Yiddish)
There is a cause for all things. (Italian)

Caution, Cautious
A castle is not overthrown by precaution. (Japanese)
A cautious man is worth two. (Mexican)
Abundant caution does no harm. (Roman)
Caution is not cowardice; even the ants march armed. (Ugandan)
Caution is the parent of delicate beer-glasses. (Dutch)
Caution keeps one safe. (German)
Caution will not overthrow a castle. (Japanese)
Cautious in small matters, careless in great. (Roman)
Happy are they that learn caution from the danger of others! (Roman)
Much caution does no harm. (Portuguese)
The cautious seldom err. (Confucius)
The most cautious passes for the most chaste. (Spanish)

Cavalier
A good cavalier never lacks a lance. (Italian)

Cemetery
A cemetery never refuses the dead. (Lebanese)
The cemeteries are filled with people who thought the world couldn't get along
    without them. (American)

Censorship
A book whose sale is forbidden all men rush to see, and prohibition turns one reader into three. (Italian)

Centipede
If a centipede loses a leg, the loss does not prevent it from walking. (African)

Ceremony
Nothing is more ridiculous than mere ceremony. (French)
To stand on ceremony makes one hungry. (Japanese)

Certain, Certainty
If you forsake a certainty and depend on an uncertainty, you will lose both the certainty and the uncertainty. (Indian)
Nothing is certain but death and taxes. (American)
Nothing is certain but the unforeseen. (Unknown)
Only three things in life are certain: birth, death and change. (Arabian)
The only certainty is that nothing is certain. (Roman)

Chaff
From much chaff I have gathered little grain. (Roman)
No corn without chaff. (Dutch)
There is no wheat without chaff. (Roman)
Wheat has chaff on every grain. (Hindi)

Chain, Chains
If a link is broken, the whole chain breaks. (Yiddish)
No one likes chains, though of gold. (Unknown)

Chair, Chairs
A rickety chair will not long serve as a seat. (Danish)
Chairs sink and stools rise. (Portuguese)

Chameleon
A chameleon does not leave one tree until it is sure of another. (Arabian)
The chameleon changes color to match the earth; the earth doesn't change color to match the chameleon. (West African)
When the log was struck by lightning, the chameleon was hit too. (Burmese)

Chance
Do not entrust to an hour's chance what you have earned in a lifetime. (Spanish)
He that leaves certainty and sticks to chance, when fools pipe he may dance. (French)
How often things occur by mere chance, for which we dared not even to hope? (Roman)

Change, Changeable
A change is as good as a rest. (Arabian)
All things change, and we ourselves change with them. (Roman)
All things in the universe flow and change. (Japanese)
All things merely change, nothing perishes. (Roman)
April weather, woman's love, rose leaves, dice, and luck at cards, change every moment.
   (German)
Change yourself, and fortune will change with you. (Portuguese)
Changes are generally agreeable to the wealthy. (Roman)
Every change of place becomes a delight. (Roman)
Everything passes, everything breaks, everything wearies. (French)
Everything that rises sets, and everything that grows grows old. (Roman)
In this world nothing is permanent but change. (Unknown)
It is never too late to change. (German)
Make no rash innovations. (Roman)
Nothing is as changeable as man and the weather. (German)
Only trousers and jackets come and go. (Korean)
People often change but seldom for the better. (German)
The more things change, the more they stay the same. (English)
They change the sky, not their souls, who run across the sea. (Roman)
Time, wine, women, and fortune, are ever changing. (German)
Times change, and we change with them. (Roman)
Times change, people change. (American)
To change and change for the better are two different things. (German)
To change one's mind is rather a sign of prudence than ignorance. (Spanish)
Weather, wind, women, and fortune change like the moon. (French)
When the fence is left behind, you'll be sure to change your mind.
   (Yiddish)
Who changes his condition changes fortune. (Italian)
Why do we change for soils warmed only by another sun? (Roman)
Women, wind, and fortune soon change. (Spanish)
You may change the clothes, but you cannot change the man. (Chinese)

Character
A man shows his character by what he laughs at. (German)
A man's character reaches town before his person. (Danish)
A pretty face and fine clothes do not make character. (African)
Bring forth what is in you. (Roman)
Character and appearance remain with you until the grave. (Mexican)
Character is a god; according to the way you behave it supports you. (Yoruban)
Character is habit long continued. (Greek)
Study carefully the character of the one you recommend, lest his misdeeds bring you
   shame. (Roman)
Those who cross the seas change their climate, but not their character. (Roman)
When the character of a man is not clear to you, look at his friends. (Japanese)

You can judge a man by the company he keeps. (Danish)
You know the man by the company he keeps. (English)

Charity
Charity and pride have different aims, yet both feed the poor. (Yiddish)
Charity begins at home. (Roman)
Charity covers a multitude of sins. (Yiddish)
Charity does not excuse cheating. (Yiddish)
Charity gives itself rich, covetousness hoards itself poor. (German)
Charity is a plant whose roots are ever green. (Urdu)
Charity seasons riches. (Yiddish)
Charity sees the need, not the cause. (German)
He that feeds upon charity has a cold dinner and no supper. (Turkish)
May your charity increase as much as your wealth. (Native American)
The door of charity is hard to open and hard to shut. (Chinese)
The one who sows charity reaps friendship. (Arabian)

Charm
An object loses its charm soon after it is gotten. (Roman)
Charm is more than beauty. (Yiddish)
Charm is stronger than beauty. (Maltese)

Chase
A stern chase is a long chase. (English)
He that chases another does not sit still himself. (Dutch)
If you chase after two hares you will catch neither. (English)
The one who chases another must also run. (German)

Chaste
A chaste wife influences her husband by obeying him. (Roman)
If not chastely, then at least cautiously. (Roman)

Chastise
Chasten your son while there is hope. (Maltese)
Chastise a good child, that it may not grow bad, a bad child, that it may not grow worse.
    (Danish)
Chastise one that is worthless, and he will presently hate you. (Spanish)
Chastise the good and he will mend, chastise the bad and he will grow worse. (Italian)
He who chastises one threatens a hundred. (Italian)

Cheap
Dear is cheap, and cheap is dear. (Portuguese)
It is as cheap sitting as standing. (Danish)

Cheat, Cheater

Cheat me in the price and not in the goods. (Spanish)
Cheat the earth and the earth will cheat you. (Chinese)
Cheat your conscience and a whole life's happiness is destroyed. (Chinese)
Cheaters never prosper. (American)
Cheating is more honorable than stealing. (German)
He is most cheated who cheats himself. (Danish)
He that will cheat at play, will cheat you any way. (Dutch)
He who makes more of you than he is wont, either means to cheat you or wants to.
  (Portuguese)
He who wants to cheat the Devil must get up early. (Spanish)
He who would cheat a peasant, must take one with him. (German)
He who would cheat the fox must rise early. (Spanish)
It is fair and just to cheat the cheater. (Spanish)
One half of the world tries to cheat the other half. (Spanish)
Two cheats make an even bargain. (American)

Cheek

Learn to turn the other cheek. (Unknown)

Cheer, Cheerful

A cheerful look makes a dish a feast. (Unknown)
A light heart lives long. (Irish)
Cheerful company makes any meal a feast. (Korean)
Cheerful company shortens the miles. (German)
Cheerful for others, wise for himself. (Roman)
Cheerfulness and goodwill make labor light. (Danish)
Cheerfulness gives sweetness to life. (Filipino)
Cheerfulness is the very flower of health. (Japanese)
When good cheer is lacking, our friends go packing. (Italian)

Cheese

Cheese and bread make the cheeks red. (German)
Cheese is gold in the morning, silver at noon, and lead at night. (German)
Cheese is healthy when given with a sparing hand. (Roman)
The nearer the cow, the better the cheese. (German)

Cherry, Cherries

Cherries are bitter to the glutted blackbird. (French)
He who likes cherries soon learns to climb. (German)
Those who eat cherries with the great, are likely to have the stones and stems flung in
  their faces. (German)

Chicken

Chicken merry, hawk is near. (Jamaican)

Chickens are counted in autumn. (Russian)
Don't count your chickens before they be hatched. (English)
On Monday, not even the chickens lay eggs. (Mexican)

Chief
If the townspeople are happy, look to the chief. (Liberian)

Child
A child at twenty is an ass at twenty and one. (Yiddish)
A child is a certain worry and an uncertain joy. (Swedish)
A child may have as many clothes as his father, but not as many rags. (Yoruban)
A child may have too much of his mother's blessing. (Roman)
A child must creep until it learns to walk. (Danish)
A child thinks twenty shillings and twenty years can scarce ever be spent. (Poor Richard)
A child turns the whole household on its head. (German)
A child's hand and a pig's trough must always be full. (Swiss)
A child's life is like a piece of paper on which every passerby leaves a mark. (Chinese)
A young ewe and an old ram, every year bring forth a lamb. (Dutch)
Boil not the pap before the child is born. (Italian)
Every child is dear to its parents. (Unknown)
Every mother's child is handsome. (German)
He that loves his child chastises him. (Dutch)
He who takes the child by the hand, takes the mother by the heart. (Danish)
He who wipes the child's nose, means to kiss the mother's cheek. (German)
If a child washes his hands he could eat with kings. (Unknown)
If the child does not cry, the mother knows not its wants. (Russian)
It takes a village to raise a child. (Nigerian)
Let a child have its will, and it will not cry. (Danish)
Monday's child is fair of face, Tuesday's child is full of grace; Wednesday's child is full of woe, Thursday's child has far to go; Friday's child is loving and giving, Saturday's child works hard for its living; and a child that's born on the Sabbath day is bonnie and blithe and good and gay. (English)
No one would seek her child in an oven had she not been there first. (Irish)
Overindulgence makes a child mean. (Spanish)
Spare the rod and spoil the child. (the Bible)
The adult looks to deeds, the child to love. (Indian)
The child is the father of the man. (English)
The child says nothing, but what it heard by the fire. (Haitian)
The child tells what is in the house. (Albanian)
The child who gets a stepmother also gets a stepfather. (Danish)
The dearest child of all is the dead one. (Spanish)
The jewel of the house is a child. (Singhalese)
The greatest respect is due to a child. (Roman)
The spoilt child is an ungrateful child. (Spanish)
'Tis a wise child that knows its own father. (Dutch)

To raise a child is to amass gold. (Spanish)

What the child sees, the child does; what the child does, the child is. (Irish)

When a mother calls her child 'bastard', you can take her word for it. (Yiddish)

Who does not beat his own child will later beat his own breast. (Persian)

Who takes the child by the hand takes the mother by the heart. (German)

Children

As seed corn is from former years reserved, so children are in former lives deserved.
(Chinese)

Bad matches beget good children. (Yiddish)

Big or small, a mother's children are prodigies all. (Yiddish)

Boys will be boys and girls will be girls. (English)

Children and chickens, many are too few. (Spanish)

Children are a poor man's wealth. (Danish)

Children are certain cares but uncertain comforts. (German)

Children are certain sorrow, but uncertain joy. (Danish)

Children are children, and children occupy themselves with childish things. (Roman)

Children are sons and daughters of God and little witnesses of the Devil. (Spanish)

Children are the riches of the poor. (English)

Children are what they are made. (French)

Children aren't dogs; adults aren't gods. (Haitian)

Children at play are both angels and devils. (Spanish)

Children have wide ears and long tongues. (Haitian)

Children married, cares increased. (Portuguese)

Children pick up words, as pigeons peas, and utter them again as God shall please.
(Portuguese)

Children should be seen and not heard. (English)

Children suck the mother when they are young and the father when they are old.
(English)

Children tell in the highway what they hear by the fireside. (Portuguese)

Children: one is one, two is fun, three is a houseful. (Portuguese)

Dried trees have no buds, wicked trees have no children. (Vietnamese)

Even children of the same mother look different. (Korean)

From children you must expect childish acts. (Danish)

From the time they are seven, boys and girls should not sit together. (Japanese)

Girls will be girls and boys will be boys. (Chinese)

Give your children too much freedom and you lose your own. (Russian)

Good children are a poor man's riches. (German)

If you hate someone, place him in the hands of children. (Spanish)

Late children are early orphans. (English)

Little children, little joys; big children, big cares. (Yiddish)

Little children, little sorrows; big children, great sorrows. (Danish)

Married life without children is as the day deprived of the sun's rays. (Roman)

Other people's harvests are always better, but not their children. (Chinese)

Out of the mouths of little children comes truth. (Roman)

Pretty children sing pretty songs. (Danish)
Small children give you headache; big children heartache. (Russian)
Small children won't let you sleep, big children won't let you live. (Yiddish)
That which should feed our children ought not to be given to dogs. (Roman)
The indulgence of parents is the bane of children. (Roman)
There are no better treasures than children. (Japanese)
Twenty children will not play together for twenty years. (Yoruban)
Well-behaved children are a parents' joy. (German)
Who has no children does not know what love is. (Italian)
Wicked children, when little, tread on their mothers' aprons, when big, on their hearts.
   (German)
You can do anything with children if you only play with them. (German)

Chili
A red chili, seven fathoms under the water, will still taste hot. (Burmese)

Chimney
A sooty chimney costs many a beef-steak. (Spanish)
'Tis easier to build two chimneys, than maintain one in fuel. (Poor Richard)

Chin
Keep your chin up. (English)
Pointed chin, wicked man. (German)

Choice
He that has a choice has trouble. (Dutch)
No choice is also a choice. (Yiddish)
Who has a choice, has a problem. (German)

Choose, Choosy
Never choose your women or linen by candlelight. (French)
The choosy sometimes get the dregs. (Japanese)
The hungry person is not choosy about food, nor the shivering about clothes. (Chinese)
The more you pick and choose, the more you stand to lose. (Yiddish)

Church, Churches
A great church and little devotion. (Italian)
Big churches, little saints. (German)
Golden churches, wooden hearts. (Unknown)
He who lives by the church shall serve the church. (German)
Many bring their clothes to church rather than themselves. (Rumanian)
Near the church, far from God. (Italian)
New churches and new taverns are seldom empty. (German)
Not all who go to church are saints. (Unknown)
Old churches have dark windows. (German)

Some make conscience of wearing a hat in the church, who make none of robbing the
    altar. (Poor Richard)

The Church is an anvil that has worn out many hammers. (German)

The nearer the church, the farther from God. (English)

The poorer the church, the purer the heart. (German)

Churl

A churl knows not the work of spurs [i.e., honor]. (French)

A churl never liked a gentleman. (French)

Circumstance, Circumstances

Circumstances alter cases. (English)

Let the circumstances take care of themselves. (Filipino)

Citizen

A good citizen owes his life to his country. (Russian)

City

A great city, a great solitude. (Roman)

Good and bad make up a city. (Portuguese)

Men, not walls, make a city. (Chinese)

Civil, Civility

A civil question deserves a civil answer. (French)

Civility costs nothing. (French)

There is nothing lost by civility. (English)

Clam

The shell of a clam is free from rust. (Korean)

Cleanliness

Cleanliness is next to godliness. (American)

Cleanliness is part of glory. (Irish)

Cleanliness is the luxury of the poor. (Mexican)

Clergy

Be neither intimate nor distant with the clergy. (Irish)

Clergymen's sons always turn out badly. (Spanish)

He who has been first a novice and then an abbot, knows what the boys do behind the
    altar. (Spanish)

He who has the Pope for his cousin may soon be a cardinal. (German)

He who never budges from Paris will never be pope. (French)

He who was first an acolyte, and afterwards a priest, knows what the boys do behind the
    altar. (Portuguese)

Clever

A clever person turns great troubles into little ones and little ones into none at all.
   (Chinese)
A clever wife, a foolish husband. (Chinese)
Clever men are often the servants of fools. (Chinese)
Clever women seek stupid men. (German)
He is called clever who cheats and plunders his friend. (French)
It is the clever host that would take the Devil into his hostelry. (Danish)
Too clever by half. (English)

Climb

He that climbs high, falls low. (American)
He that climbs high, falls far. (German)
He who climbs too high is near a fall. (Italian)
He who would climb the ladder must begin at the bottom. (German)
If you climb up a tree, you must climb down the same tree. (African)
When climbing a mountain, take no step backwards. (Chinese)

Cloak

A cloak is not made for a single shower of rain. (Italian)
An old cloak makes a new jerkin. (German)
Arrange your cloak as the wind blows. (French)
Cut your cloak according to the cloth. (Scottish)
However bright the sun may shine, leave not your cloak at home. (Spanish)
No cloak is big enough to cover poverty and drunkenness. (Hungarian)
There is no better friend in winter than a warm cloak. (Spanish)
Truth's cloak is often lined with lies. (Danish)
Under a good cloak may be a bad man. (Spanish)
Under a tattered cloak you will find a heavy drinker. (Spanish)

Clock

A watched clock never tells the time. (Welsh)
Even a clock that does not work is right twice a day. (Polish)

Close, Close by

Close only counts in horseshoes and hand grenades. (American)
Close sits my shirt, but closer my skin. (Roman)

Close, Closed

Close your ears and a thief may steal even your nose. (Korean)
Don't close the barn door after the horse runs away. (American)

Cloth

A cloth is not woven from a single thread. (Chinese)
Better coarse cloth than naked thighs. (Danish)

Fine cloth is never out of fashion. (English)
New cloth is not new for long; it is old for long. (African)
The best cloth has uneven threads. (Spanish)

Clothes, Clothing
A person changing his clothing always hides while changing. (Kenyan)
Clothes make the man. (Irish)
Everyone feels the cold according as he is clad. (Spanish)
Fine and fine make but a slender doublet. (French)
Good clothes open all doors. (English)
Needle and thread are half clothing. (Spanish)
Showy clothes attract most. (Roman)
That suit is best that best fits me. (Italian)
The finest clothes are often lined with heartache and sorrow. (German)
Those of a certain height must wear clothes of a certain length. (Chinese)
Throughout life, a person changes his clothes many times. (Unknown)

Cloud, Cloudy
All clouds are not rain clouds. (Roman)
Every cloud has a silver lining. (English)
He that pries into the clouds, may be struck with a thunderbolt. (Dutch)
If it does not get cloudy, it will not get clear. (Albanian)
If there were no clouds, we should not enjoy the sun. (Roman)
The smallest cloud can eclipse the sun. (Armenian)

Clown
A clown enriched knows neither relation nor friend. (French)
No fine clothes can hide the clown. (French)

Coal, Coals
A live coal kindles the others. (German)
Glowing coals sparkle oft. (Russian)

Coalminer
Like a coalminer's sack, black without worse within. (Spanish)

Coat
Cut your coat according to the cloth. (English)
The coat makes the man. (English)

Cobbler
Cobbler, stick to your last [i.e., mind your own business]. (Roman)
If the shoe fits, let the cobbler wear it. (the Editor)
The cobbler always wears the worst shoes. (French)
The cobbler's children go barefoot. (Unknown)
There will be trouble if the cobbler starts making pies. (Russian)

Cock, Coxcomb

A barley corn is better than a diamond to a cock. (Portuguese)

A good cock was never fat. (Portuguese)

All cocks must have a comb. (Dutch)

As the old cock crows, so crows the young. (German)

Be a coxcomb rather than an ox's tail. (Korean)

Better to be the beak of a cock than the tail of an ox. (Japanese)

Encouraged by the hen, the cock announces the hour. (Japanese)

Every cock crows best on its own dunghill. (German)

Many a good cock comes out of a tattered bag. (English)

The cock cannot profit by friendship with the fox. (Georgian)

The cock is king on its own dunghill. (German)

The cock is proudest on its own dung-heap. (Roman)

The cock often crows without a victory. (Danish)

Coconut

The stone we throw at a coconut, the coconut throws back at us. (Yoruban)

Coffee

An American will go to hell for a bag of coffee. (American)

Coffee and love are best when they are hot. (German)

Coffee has two virtues, it is wet and warm. (Dutch)

Good coffee should be black like the devil, hot like hell, and sweet like a kiss.
   (Hungarian)

Coffin

Even a coffin is made to measure. (Russian)

Prepare the coffin and the man won't die. (Chinese)

Coin

For poor people small coin. (Portuguese)

One coin in the money-box makes more noise than when it is full. (Arabian)

There are two sides to every coin. (American)

Cold

As the day lengthens, so the cold strengthens. (Spanish)

Because men do not like the cold, Heaven does not cause winter to cease. (Chinese)

One hour's cold will suck out seven years' heat. (Unknown)

What keeps out the cold keeps out the heat. (Italian)

Colt

A colt is good for nothing if it does not break its halter. (French)

The ragged colt often makes a powerful horse. (Irish)

Combat

When wind and sea combat, the ships get the worst of it. (Egyptian)

Come

Come uncalled, sit unserved. (Scottish)
First come, first served. (English)
The last come is the best liked. (French)
The last comers are often the masters. (French)
The Lord will not fail to come, though he may not come on horseback. (Danish)
Who comes last closes the door. (Italian)

Comedy, Comedian

A comic matter cannot be expressed in tragic verse. (Roman)
All the world plays the comedian. (Roman)

Comet

A comet is never seen in the sky without indicating disaster. (Roman)

Comfort

A crowd of fellow-sufferers is a miserable kind of comfort. (Roman)
Comfort derived from the misery of others is slight. (Roman)
In comfort, always remember the time of illness. (Chinese)
It is a comfort to the wretched to have companions in misfortune. (Roman)
No comforter's head ever aches. (Italian)
Three comforts of the old: fire, tobacco, and tea. (Irish)

Command

He who demands does not command. (Italian)
No man commands ably unless he has himself obeyed discipline. (Roman)

Common

Common goods, no goods. (Dutch)

Common Good

The abandonment of what is for the common good is a crime against nature. (Roman)

Common Sense

Common sense is generally rare in those of high position. (Roman)
One pound of learning requires ten pounds of common sense to apply it. (Persian)
Seek advice but use your own common sense. (Yiddish)

Community

Communities begin by building their kitchen. (French)

Companion

A faithful companion is a sure anchor. (Roman)
A merry companion on the road is as good as a nag. (Japanese)
A pleasant companion on the road is as good as a vehicle. (Roman)

Choose the companion who recommends himself to you by his life as well as by his speech. (Roman)

For a good companion, good company. (Spanish)

Take a dog for a companion and a stick in your hand. (English)

Company

Better to be alone than in bad company. (German)

Choose your company before you choose your drink. (Irish)

Company in distress makes trouble less. (French)

Good company makes short miles. (Dutch)

Good company shortens the way. (German)

Keep good company and you shall become good company. (Portuguese)

No camel route is long with good company. (Turkish)

Seven is company, nine is a brawl. (American)

Tell me the company you keep, and I will tell you who you are. (Dutch)

Tell me your company and I will tell you thyself. (Irish)

'Tis the company that makes the feast. (English)

Two birds of prey do not keep each other company. (Spanish)

Two's company but three's a crowd. (American)

Who keeps company with the wolves, will learn to howl. (English)

You will be sad if you keep company with only yourself. (Roman)

Compare, Comparison

Comparison is not proof. (French)

Comparisons are odious. (Roman)

Compassion

Have pity on the orphans and be compassionate to widows; revere the aged and be tenderhearted to the young. (Chinese)

The best passion is compassion. (Jamaican)

Compete, Competition

Compete not with a friend. (Roman)

Compete, don't envy. (Arabian)

Complain, Complaint

Complain to one who can help you. (Serbian)

Go not with every ailment to the doctor, nor with every complaint to a lawyer. (Portuguese)

He drinks the ocean and then calls it salty. (American)

He who complains is never pitied. (English)

Compliment, Compliments

A soft-spoken compliment is honeyed poison. (Roman)

Compliments cost nothing, yet many pay dearly for them. (German)

Of a compliment only a third is meant. (Welsh)

Comportment

Be as hard as the world requires you to be, and as soft as the world allows you to be.
(Japanese)
Be as wise as the serpent and gentle as the dove. (English, after Jesus)
Be firm or mild as the occasion may require. (Roman)

Compose

He that can compose himself, is wiser than he that composes books. (Poor Richard)

Conceal, Concealment

It is one thing to conceal, another to be silent. (Roman)
Leave in concealment what has long been concealed. (Roman)
Love, and a cough, are not concealed. (Roman)
You are in a pitiable condition when you have to conceal what you wish to tell.
(Roman)

Conceit

Excessive politeness assuredly conceals conceit. (Chinese)
Many deem nothing right but what suits their own conceit. (Roman)

Conduct

A man conducts himself abroad as he has been taught at home. (Danish)
As a man is, so must you conduct yourself. (Roman)
If your conduct be noble, you will be a king. (Roman)
The safest haven for the penitent is a change in conduct. (Roman)

Confess, Confession

He that jokes, confesses. (Italian)
The man who sleeps does not confess. (Yoruban)
A fault confessed is half redressed. (Portuguese)
Confess and be hanged. (Portuguese)
Confessed faults are half mended. (Scottish)
Confession is as healing medicine to the one who has erred. (Roman)
Confession is good for the soul. (German)
Confession is the first step to repentance. (English)
He who denies all confesses all. (Italian)
Open confession is good for the soul. (Scottish)

Confide, Confiding

Confide a secret to a dumb man and he will speak. (Russian)
Confide your secrets to your own heart. (Yoruban)
Confiding a secret to an unworthy person is like carrying grain in a bag with a hole.
(African)
None are deceived but they that confide. (Poor Richard)

Confidence

Confidence begets confidence. (German)

Men are slow to rest their confidence in undertakings of magnitude. (Roman)

Conflict

Better conference than conflict. (Irish)

Deep-seated are the wounds dealt out in civil conflict. (Roman)

Conquer, Conquest

Conquerors are kings, the beaten are bandits. (Chinese)

Divide and conquer; divide and rule. (Roman)

He that would conquer must fight. (English)

If you have conquered your inclination, rather than your inclination you, you have
     something to rejoice at. (Roman)

It is harder, much harder, to conquer yourself than it is to conquer your enemy.
     (Roman)

The greatest conqueror is he who conquers himself. (German)

Conscience

A clear conscience is a wall of brass. (Roman)

A good conscience is a soft pillow. (German)

A good conscience is a sound sleeper. (German)

A guilty conscience needs no accuser. (Dutch)

A mind conscious of guilt is its own accuser. (Roman)

An evil conscience breaks many a man's neck. (Roman)

Cheat your conscience and a whole life's happiness is destroyed. (Chinese)

Conscience betrays guilt. (Roman)

Conscience is as a thousand witnesses. (Roman)

Conscience is the chamber of justice. (Italian)

Conscience makes cowards of us all. (Italian, after Shakespeare)

He who sacrifices his conscience to ambition burns a picture to obtain the ashes.
     (Chinese)

Let your own conscience be a check against the flattery of others. (Roman)

Put your hand in your conscience and see if it doesn't come out as black as pitch.
     (Dutch)

There is no hell like a troubled conscience. (English)

There is no pillow so soft as a clear conscience. (French)

You may often feel that heavily on your back which you took lightly on your
     conscience. (Danish)

Consensus

Consensus is the absence of leadership. (English)

Consent

If you let them put the calf on your shoulders, it will not be long before they clap on the
   cow. (Italian)

Consider

Before you begin, consider; but having considered, use dispatch. (Roman)
That should be considered long, which can be decided but once. (Roman)
While we consider when to begin, it becomes too late. (Japanese)

Consideration

A handful of consideration is better than a cartful of riches. (Egyptian)
Consideration is the parent of wisdom. (Roman)
Consideration should be shown to a novice. (Roman)
The greatest consideration should be shown to a child. (Roman)

Consistent

Let him proceed as he began, and be consistent with himself. (Roman)

Consult

Consult with your pillow [i.e., sleep on it]. (German)
Consult your friend on everything, but particularly on what concerns yourself.
   (Roman)

Contempt, Contemptible

Nobody considers himself contemptible. (Egyptian)

Content, Contentment

A contented ass enjoys a long life. (Portuguese)
A contented man is always rich. (Roman)
A contented mind is a continual feast. (Roman)
Anyone who is content to stand still should not complain when others pass him. (Italian)
Be content and you will be free. (Egyptian)
Better is a little with contentment than much with contention. (Poor Richard)
Content makes poor men rich; discontent makes rich men poor. (Poor Richard)
Content with little, content with much. (Greek)
Contentment is better than wealth. (Unknown)
Contentment is happiness. (Korean)
He has enough who is content. (French)
He has nothing who is not content with what he has. (Portuguese)
He is blessed who knows how to be satisfied; he is poor who does not feel content.
   (Japanese)
He is well constituted who grieves not for what he has not, and rejoices for what he has.
   (Italian)
He who cannot get meat, must be content with cabbage. (Danish)
Heavy purses and light hearts can sustain much. (Dutch)

If you are content, you have enough to live comfortably. (Roman)

If you are contented with your lot, you will live wisely. (Roman)

It is better to enjoy what we possess than to be desirous after other things. (Roman)

Let everyone be content with what God has given him. (Portuguese)

Let him who is well off stay where he is. (Italian)

Never be content with your lot; try for a lot more. (American)

No man is contented with his lot in this life. (Roman)

No man is so rich as to say, 'I have enough!' (Roman)

No one is content with his lot. (Portuguese)

Nothing will content the one who is not content with little. (Greek)

The fetter falls from the foot of the content. (Egyptian)

The greatest wealth is contentment with a little. (German)

To be content with what one has is the greatest and truest of riches. (Roman)

Wealth and content are not always bed-fellows. (Poor Richard)

Wealthy is he who knows how to be content. (Chinese)

Where there is content there is abundance. (Roman)

Woe to him who is not content to have God for his sustenance. (Irish)

You will live wisely if you live contented with your lot. (Roman)

Contribute

Only when all contribute their firewood can they build up a strong fire. (Chinese)

Convenience

Every convenience brings its own inconveniences along with it. (Roman)

Conversation

A man's conversation is the mirror of his thoughts. (Chinese)

Conversation ministers to a mind diseased. (Roman)

Cook, Cooks

All are not cooks who carry long knives. (German)

Every cook praises his own broth. (English)

He who cooks a bad thing eats of it. (Egyptian)

He's an ill cook that cannot lick his own fingers. (Italian)

If you want dinner, don't offend the cook. (Chinese)

It is a poor cook who will not taste the dish. (Unknown)

The choicest morsel is eaten by the cook. (Spanish)

The more cooks, the worse broth. (Danish)

Too many cooks spoil the broth. (English)

Where there are six cooks, there is nothing to eat. (American)

Who makes the dough will also cook it. (Albanian)

You may cook in small pots as well as in large ones. (Danish)

Coral

A coral reef hardens into land. (Hawaiian)

Corn

Barren corn makes bitter bread. (Dutch)
Good corn is not reaped from a bad field. (Danish)
The heaviest ear of corn bends its head lowest. (Irish)
Very good corn grows in little fields. (French)

Cornerstone

The same stone the builders rejected in the morning becomes the cornerstone.
   (Jamaican, from the Bible)

Correction

Acknowledgement is half of correction. (Russian)
Correction is good when administered in time. (Danish)

Corrupt, Corruption

All things tend to corrupt perverted minds. (Roman)
If the teacher be corrupt, the world will be corrupt. (Arabian)
The corruption of the best is the worst. (Roman)

Cost

It costs nothing to look. (Yiddish)
What costs little is little esteemed. (Italian)
What costs more is appreciated more. (Spanish)
What costs nothing is worth nothing. (Dutch)

Cough

A cough will stick longer by a horse than a peck of oats. (Roman)
A dry cough is Death's trumpeter. (German)
Love and a cough cannot be hid. (Roman)

Council

Seven brothers in a council make wrong right. (Spanish)

Counsel, Counselor

A fool sometimes gives good counsel. (Spanish)
Advise and counsel him; if he does not listen, let adversity teach him. (Ethiopian)
After-counsel is a fool's counsel. (English)
An enemy may chance to give good counsel. (French)
Anger and haste hinder good counsel. (English)
Counsel after action is like rain after harvest. (Danish)
Counsel before action. (Dutch)
Counsel is as welcome to him as a shoulder of mutton to a sick horse. (Dutch)
Counsel is irksome when the matter is past remedy. (Dutch)
Counsel is nothing against love. (Italian)
Counsel is of no effect after the fact. (Roman)

Everybody knows good counsel except the one who has need of it. (German)
Fools sometimes give wise men counsel. (Portuguese)
Give neither counsel nor salt till you are asked for it. (English)
Good counsel comes over night. (German)
Good counsel is no better than bad counsel, if it be not taken in time. (Danish)
Good counsel never comes too late. (German)
He that gives bad counsel suffers most by it. (Roman)
He that will not be counseled cannot be helped. (Irish)
In the night is counsel. (Roman)
Keep counsel of thyself first. (English)
Keep your own counsel. (Roman)
Light is the grief that can take counsel. (Roman)
Of hasty counsel take heed, for haste is very rarely speed. (Dutch)
Often has wise counsel come from a fool's head. (Irish)
Seek counsel of him who makes you weep, and not of him who makes you laugh.
    (Arabian)
Take counsel before it goes ill, lest it go worse. (Dutch)
Take counsel of your pillow [i.e., sleep on it]. (Roman)
The best counselors are the dead. (Roman)
The counsel of the aged is sound. (Roman)
The night brings counsel. (French)
They that will not be counseled cannot be helped. (Scottish)
Though you are a prudent man, do not despise counsel. (Spanish)
When a king has good counselors, his reign is peaceful. (African)
Woe to him who heeds not the counsel of a good wife. (Irish)

Count
Count in autumn the chickens hatched in spring. (Korean)
Count not what is lost but what is left. (Chinese)
Count not your chickens before they be hatched. (German)
Count your blessings. (German)
Don't count the loaves as they go into the oven. (Serbian)
Don't count your eggs before they have been laid. (German)

Counterfeit
A counterfeit coin passes current at night. (Portuguese)

Counterpart
No house without a mouse, no barn without corn, no rose without a thorn. (German)
None but himself can be his parallel. (Roman)

Country
A country may go to ruin but its mountains and streams remain. (Japanese)
He knows best the sun of his own country. (Egyptian)
It is sweet and meritorious to die for one's country. (Roman)

No one can cast off his native country. (Roman)

No one could ever meet death for his country without the hope of immortality.
(Roman)

Our country ought to be dearer to us than ourselves. (Roman)

Protect your motherland like the eagle protects its nest. (Albanian)

Sweet and seemly it is to die for one's country. (Roman)

That country will I call mine which supports me, not that which gave me birth.
(Roman)

You can take the boy out of the country, but you can't take the country out of the boy.
(Unknown)

Courage, Courageous

A courageous foe is better than a cowardly friend. (Chinese)

A courageous man never wants a weapon. (Unknown)

A stout heart overcomes ill fortune. (Spanish)

A stout heart tempers adversity. (Dutch)

Alertness and courage are life's shield. (Filipino)

Courage conquers all things; it even gives strength to the body. (Roman)

Courage is often caused by fear. (French)

Courage is ten, nine is the ability to escape. (Georgian)

Courage leads to Heaven; fear, to death. (Roman)

Courage mounts with occasion. (Georgian)

Courage should have eyes as well as arms. (English)

Courage would fight, but Discretion won't let him. (Poor Richard)

For whom strength and courage are not enough, armor and lance will not be enough.
(Spanish)

Good courage in a bad circumstance is half of the evil overcome. (Roman)

Happy is the one who dares courageously to defend what he loves. (Roman)

Here comes courage!, that seized the lion absent, and ran away from the present mouse.
(Poor Richard)

It is the courage not the weapon that vanquishes in war. (Spanish)

Even the courageous are sometimes startled by an unexpected turn of events. (Roman)

There is no lack of courage in a noble heart. (Roman)

When you have no choice, mobilize the spirit of courage. (Yiddish)

Who hath no courage must have legs. (Italian)

You cannot fathom the ocean unless you have the courage to lose sight of the shore.
(Italian)

Court of Law

He who would not go to Hell, must not go to court. (Danish)

Home is home, as the Devil said when he found himself in the law courts. (Roman)

In a court of fowls, the cockroach never wins its case. (Rwandan)

The court clerk makes more money by what he does not write. (Spanish)

The court is most merciful when the accused is most rich. (Yiddish)

You don't know what a frightful thing it is to go to court. (Roman)

Court (Royal)

A courtier should be without feeling and without honor. (French)
At court there are many hands, but few hearts. (German)
At court they sell a good deal of smoke without fire. (Danish)
At the king's court, everyone for himself. (French)
Be not an esquire where you were a page. (Spanish)
Courts grant not their favors as men are good and deserving. (Roman)
He that would rise at court, must begin by creeping. (Poor Richard)
If you care for the court, the court will bring cares for you. (Roman)
Life at court is often a shortcut to Hell. (Danish)
The court official in one life has seven rebirths as a beggar. (Chinese)
The courts of kings are full of men, empty of friends. (Roman)
The steps at court are slippery. (Danish)

Courtesy, Courteous

Who is overly nice, loses many a slice. (German)
A courtesy is a flower. (Italian)
A courtesy much entreated is half recompensed. (Chinese)
An excess of courtesy is discourtesy. (Japanese)
Courteous men learn courtesy from the discourteous. (Persian)
Courtesy costs little. (Spanish)
Courtesy does not detract from valor. (Mexican)
Courtesy is cumbersome to them that know it not. (Persian)
Courtesy is not a duty. (German)
Courtesy on one side can never last long. (Persian)
Courtesy opens all doors. (English)
Courtesy pleases much and costs little. (Italian)
Full of courtesy, full of craft. (German)
Gentility, sent to market, will not buy a peck of meal. (Dutch)
Less of your courtesy, and more of your purse. (Roman)

Courtship

A lass that has many wooers often fares the worst. (Danish)
A maid who laughs is half taken. (English)
A short courtship is the best courtship. (English)
At first shy as a maiden, at last swift as an escaping hare. (Japanese)
Belles are not for the beaux. (French)
Courting and wooing brings dallying and doing. (French)
Happy's the wooing that's not long in doing. (Roman)
He who would win the daughter must first win her mother. (English)
In courtship a man pursues a woman until she catches him. (Roman)

Cover

Stretch your legs according to your cover. (Roman)
That which covers thee discovers thee. (Spanish)

Covet, Covetous

A covetous man does nothing that he should till he dies. (Roman)

A covetous woman deserves a swindling gallant. (French)

A poor man wants some things, a covetous man all things. (German)

All covet, all lose. (German)

An abbot who covets one offering loses a hundred. (Spanish)

Covet not the property of others. (Roman)

Covet wealth, and want it; don't, and luck will grant it. (Chinese)

Covetous men's chests are rich, not they. (Chinese)

Covetousness bursts the bag. (Spanish)

Covetousness fills a bottomless vessel. (Unknown)

Covetousness is never satisfied till its mouth is filled with earth. (Dutch)

Covetousness is the father of avarice. (Yoruban)

Covetousness is the mother of mischief and ruin. (English)

If you covet, you will scheme; if you scheme, so will others. (Chinese)

That is guarded at great risk which is coveted by many. (Roman)

The covetous man is ready to die for wealth. (Chinese)

We covet what is guarded. (Roman)

What many covet is difficult to guard. (Spanish)

Cow, Cattle

A bellowing cow soon forgets its calf. (Unknown)

A cow does not know what her tail is worth until she has lost it. (French)

A cow from afar gives plenty of milk. (French)

A cow is milked by gentle hands. (Hausan)

A cow that burned its throat in the sun pants at the moon. (Korean)

A noisy cow gives little milk. (Polish)

All is not butter that comes from the cow. (Italian)

An ill cow may have a good calf. (Unknown)

Better a good cow than a cow of a good kind. (German)

Better one cow in peace than seven in trouble. (Danish)

Cow of many: well milked and badly fed. (Spanish)

Cows have no business in horseplay. (Jamaican)

Cows will give birth to calves. (Irish)

Cursed cows have short horns. (Chinese)

Far-off cows have long horns. (German)

If a fool holds the cow by the horns, a clever man can milk her. (Yiddish)

Many a cow stands in the meadow and looks wistfully at the common. (Danish)

Many a good cow has a bad calf. (German)

No cows, no cares. (English)

One cow breaks the fence, and a dozen leap over it. (Irish)

The bailiff's cow and another's cow are two different cows. (German)

The best cows are not at market. (German)

The cattle is as good as the pasture in which it grazes. (Ethiopian)

The cow gives good milk, but kicks over the pail. (Dutch)

The cow gives milk through her mouth. (German)
The cow licks no strange calf. (German)
The cow must graze where she is tied. (Sierra Leonean)
The cow that does not go in the field gets the ax. (Albanian)
The cows that moo most give the least milk. (German)
The one with cattle on the hill will not sleep easy. (Irish)
What good is the cow that gives plenty of milk and then kicks over the pail? (Yiddish)

Coward, Cowardice

A coward has no scars. (African)
A coward often deals a mortal blow to the brave. (French)
A coward's fear may make him valiant. (French)
A dishonorable flight from death is worse than any death. (Roman)
Battle, not bragging, reveals the coward. (Yoruban)
Better they should say, 'There he ran away', than 'There he died'. (Spanish)
Between two cowards, he has the advantage who first detects the other. (Italian)
Coward against coward, the assailant conquers. (Spanish)
Cowards die many times before their death. (German)
Cowards die many times, but a brave man only dies once. (English)
Cowards have no luck. (German)
Cowards win no laurels. (Roman)
Cowards' weapons neither cut nor pierce. (Italian)
Find a cruel man and you see a coward. (Roman)
It is better to be a coward for a minute than dead the rest of your life. (Irish)
Necessity and opportunity may make a coward valiant. (Italian)
Nothing was ever written about a cowardly man. (Spanish)
Of two cowards, the one who attacks conquers the other. (Portuguese)
One coward makes ten. (German)
Put a coward on his mettle and he will even fight the Devil. (Irish)
Strength avails not a coward. (Italian)
The coward calls himself cautious, the miser thrifty. (Roman)
The coward is a lion at home and a hare abroad. (Spanish)
The coward sweats in water. (Ethiopian)
The most seditious is the most cowardly. (Roman)
The mother of the coward does not grieve. (Egyptian)
The mother of the coward has no occasion to weep. (Roman)
To wish for death is a coward's part. (Roman)

Crab

A crab does not beget a bird. (African)
A lame crab walks straight. (Afghani)
Remove the claws of even a boiled crab. (Korean)
The crab that walks too far falls into the pot. (Haitian)
'Walk straight, my son', said the old crab to the young one. (Irish)

Cradle

From the cradle to the tomb, not all gladness, not all gloom. (Dutch)

The hand that rocks the cradle rules the world. (German)

What is learned in the cradle is carried to the grave. (English)

Craft

Be not ashamed of your craft. (German)

Before undertaking his craft, the artisan first sharpens his tools. (Chinese)

No man masters his craft the first day. (Roman)

No one becomes master craftsman in a day. (German)

Crave

What the eyes do not see the heart does not crave. (Spanish)

Crawl

You have to crawl before you can walk. (English)

Creak

Creaking carts last the longest. (Dutch)

Cream

Cream doesn't rise to the top, it works its way up. (Dutch)

Credit, Creditors

A pig bought on credit grunts all year long. (Spanish)

A pig on credit makes a good winter and a bad spring. (Portuguese)

Better to sell cheap than for credit. (Hausan)

Credit is better than ready money. (German)

Credit is dead; bad pay killed it. (Italian)

Credit lost is like a broken mirror. (Italian)

Creditors have better memories than debtors. (Poor Richard)

Everyone gives himself credit for more brains than he has, and less money. (Italian)

Give credit where credit is due. (Dutch)

He that has lost his credit is dead to the world. (German)

Crime, Crimes

Crime cries out for punishment. (Filipino)

Crime does not pay. (Mexican)

Crime is always fearful. (Roman)

Crime often falls back upon its author's head. (Roman)

Crime puts those on an equal footing whom it defiles. (Roman)

Crime, when it succeeds, is called virtue. (Roman)

Crimes may be secret, yet not secure. (Italian)

From the crime of one learn the nature of them all. (Roman)

He has committed the crime, who has derived the profit. (Roman)

He that carries a small crime easily, will carry it on when it comes to be an ox. (Poor Richard)

In times of trouble leniency becomes crime. (Roman)

No crime has been without a precedent. (Roman)

One crime has to be concealed by another. (Roman)

Out of adultery comes murder; out of gambling comes thieving. (Chinese)

Punishment presses hard upon the heels of crime. (Roman)

The greatest incitement to crime is the hope of sinning with impunity. (Roman)

The one who does not prevent a crime when he can, encourages it. (Roman)

The one who overlooks one crime invites the commission of another. (Roman)

The one who secretly meditates a crime bears all the guilt of the deed. (Roman)

There are always two witnesses to every crime: God and the conscience. (Unknown)

To violate the law is the same crime in the emperor as in the subject. (Chinese)

We are often deterred from crime by the disgrace of others. (Roman)

Where crime is taught from early years, it becomes a part of nature. (Roman)

While crime is punished, it yet increases. (Roman)

Crisis

A crisis is an opportunity riding the dangerous wind. (Chinese)

Criticism, Criticize

Criticism is easy, art is difficult. (Unknown)

Criticizing another's garden doesn't keep the weeds out of your own. (Italian)

'Your feet are crooked, your hair is good for nothing', said the pig to the horse. (Russian)

Crocodile

Cross in a crowd and the crocodile won't eat you. (Madagascan)

Do not insult the crocodile until you've crossed the river. (Chinese)

Don't think there are no crocodiles because the water is calm. (Malayan)

Only when you have crossed the river can you say the crocodile has a lump on its snout. (African)

Where the water recedes, there is a crocodile. (African)

You must have crossed the river before you may tell the crocodile it has bad breath. (Chinese)

Crook, Crooked

A crooked iron may be hammered straight. (Danish)

Crooked by nature is never made straight by education. (Italian)

Crooked firewood disturbs the fire; a bad man upsets the home. (Yoruban)

Crooked logs make straight fires. (German)

Crooked wood burns quite as well as straight. (German)

Crooked wood is straightened with fire. (Sicilian)

Loaves put awry into the oven come out crooked. (French)

The crook of an old stick is hard to take out. (Irish)

When the light is crooked, the shadow is crooked. (Yiddish)

Cross, Crosses

Crosses are ladders to Heaven. (English)

No cross, no crown. (Unknown)

Take your cross out to the street and you will see others whose crosses are greater than yours. (Spanish)

Crow, Crows

A crow is never the whiter for being washed. (Danish)

A crow that imitates the cormorant gets drowned. (Japanese)

A whitewashed crow soon shows black again. (Chinese)

Bad the crow, bad the egg. (American)

Crows are black the whole world over. (Chinese)

Crows bewail the dead sheep, and then eat them. (Madagascan)

Follow a crow and it will lead you to a dog's carcass. (Egyptian)

If the crow had been satisfied to eat its prey in silence, it would have had more meat and less envy and quarreling. (Roman)

Jackdaws have nothing to do with a lute. (Roman)

Old crows are hard to catch. (German)

On the first of March, the crows begin to search. (Arabian)

One crow does not peck out another crow's eyes. (German)

The carrion which the eagle has left feeds the crow. (Roman)

The crow is a pretty bird when the jackdaw is not present. (Roman)

The crow regards no egg but its own. (Burmese)

The crow thinks its own chicks fairest. (German)

The crow will find its mate. (Danish)

When you mingle with the crows, caw as they do. (Unknown)

Who can tell the sex of a crow? (Japanese)

Crowd

A crowd is not company. (Danish)

No crowd ever waited at the gates of patience. (Arabian)

Nothing is so uncertain or so inestimable as the disposition of a crowd. (Roman)

Ten constitute a crowd. (English)

Cruelty

Cruelty is the strength of the wicked. (Arabian)

Crumb, Crumbs

A crumb is also bread. (German)

A person eating must make crumbs. (Sicilian)

Cry, Crying

Avoid bawling in conversation or in play. (Roman)

Better the child cry than the old man. (Danish)

Better the child cry than the mother sigh. (Danish)

Cry and the whole world cries with you. (Russian)
Crying fattens a child. (Spanish)
Don't cry before you're hurt. (German)
He who doesn't cry, doesn't suckle. (Spanish)
It is better the child should cry than the father. (German)
Laugh and everybody sees you; cry and you cry unseen. (Yiddish)
No one cries unseen. (German)
The one who falls alone never cries. (Turkish)

Cucumber
Raw cucumber makes the churchyards prosperous. (English)

Cunning
Cunning has little honor. (Danish)
Cunning men's cloaks sometimes fall. (Italian)
Cunning surpasses strength. (German)
The most cunning are the first caught. (French)
There's cunning in a pointed chin. (German)
You may be too cunning for one, but not for all. (Poor Richard)

Cup
The last drop makes the cup to run over. (English)
When the cup is full, carry it even. (Scottish)
When the cup is fullest, it is most difficult to carry. (Irish)

Cure
A good laugh and a long sleep are the best cures in the doctor's book. (Irish)
Hunger is cured by food, ignorance by study. (Chinese)
It is a step to the cure to be willing to be cured. (Roman)
Like cures like. (English)
No cure, no pay. (Arabian)
The cure is easy if the malady be recent. (Roman)
The cure is worse than the disease. (English)
What butter or whiskey does not cure cannot be cured. (Irish)
What cannot be cured must be endured. (German)

Curiosity
A man should live if only to satisfy his curiosity. (Yiddish)
Curiosity killed the cat. (German)
Curiosity killed the cat; satisfaction brought it back. (American)

Curse, Curses
A curse returns threefold. (English)
A curse will not strike out an eye, unless the fist go with it. (Danish)
Better to hear curses than to be pitied. (Yiddish)

Curses are like processions: they return to whence they set out. (Italian)
Curses, like chickens, come home to roost. (Spanish)
If you curse a man there will be two graves. (Japanese)
If you curse anyone, first prepare two graves. (Indian)
Never beat a man on a wound nor curse him about a disgrace. (Chinese)
The curse on the hearth wounds the deepest. (Danish)

Custom, Customs

A bad custom is to be abolished. (Roman)
A cake and a bad custom ought to be broken. (French)
An ancient custom obtains the force of nature. (Roman)
Ancient custom is always held as law. (Roman)
Be a custom good or bad, a peasant will have it continue in force. (Spanish)
Custom becomes law. (Spanish)
Custom in infancy becomes nature in old age. (Spanish)
Custom is king over all. (Greek)
Custom is the fifth element of the universe. (Syrian)
Custom makes all things easy. (Spanish)
Even the wise follow custom. (Korean)
Every country has its custom. (Spanish)
Every land to its own custom, every wheel its own spindle. (Portuguese)
Every tongue, every nation, has its own vibration. (Jamaican)
How many unjust and improper things are authorized by custom! (Roman)
National customs are national honors. (Danish)
Once is not a custom. (German)
Seek neither to augment nor diminish custom. (Chinese)
That which is customary requires no excuse. (Italian)
The power of custom is most weighty. (Roman)
To each his own custom. (Roman)
What were once vices are now customs. (Roman)
When you enter a village, obey its customs. (Japanese)

Customer, Customers

An old establishment never wants for customers. (Unknown)
Charge nothing and you'll get a lot of customers. (Yiddish)
Clientele are not inherited. (German)
Customers are jade; merchandise is grass. (Chinese)
The customer is always right. (English)
The customers are known to the shopkeepers. (Kashmiri)

Cut, Cuts

Desperate cuts must have desperate cures. (German)
Never cut what can be untied. (Portuguese)

Cycle

In all things there is a kind of law of cycles. (Roman)

D

Dabble

Nothing is more foolish than to dabble in too many things. (Roman)

Dam

Raise the dam and the waters fill it. (Unknown)

Damage

Damage suffered makes you knowing, but seldom rich. (Danish)

Damned

People take more pains to be damned than to be saved. (French)

Dance, Dancer

A pair of light shoes is not all that is needed for dancing. (Danish)

A poor dancer will be disturbed even by the hem of her skirt. (Polish)

As beats the drum, so goes the dance. (Malayan)

As they pipe to me, so I will dance. (Portuguese)

Dance to the tune that is played. (Spanish)

He who dances well goes from wedding to wedding. (Spanish)

He who is unable to dance says the yard is stony. (Kenyan)

If you dance at every wedding, you will weep at every funeral. (Yiddish)

It does not become a sparrow to mix in the dance of the cranes. (Unknown)

It is no child's play when an old woman dances. (German)

It's good dancing on another man's floor. (Dutch)

No longer fiddle, no longer dance. (French)

Not everyone that dances is glad. (French)

The girl who can't dance says the band can't play. (Yiddish)

The man who can't dance says the band can't play. (German)

We're fools whether we dance or not, so we might as well dance. (Japanese)

When an old cow dances, it kicks up a lot of dust. (German)

When old couples dance, they raise a lot of dust. (Spanish)

When you go to dance, take heed whom you take by the hand. (Danish)

Danger, Dangerous

A common danger produces unity. (Roman)

All is not lost that is in danger. (Spanish)

At a dangerous passage yield precedence. (Italian)

Constant exposure to dangers will breed contempt for them. (Roman)

Danger and delight grow on one stalk. (English)

Danger is next neighbor to security. (English)
Danger past and God forgotten. (German)
Dangers come more quickly when despised. (German)
Dumb dogs and still water are dangerous. (German)
He is most free from danger, who, even when safe, is on his guard. (Roman)
He is out of danger who rings the alarm-bell. (Spanish)
He that fears danger in time seldom feels it. (Turkish)
He who turns aside avoids danger. (French)
Lasses and glasses are always in danger. (Italian)
Man is never sufficiently aware of the dangers that await him hourly. (Roman)
Nothing is so steadfast as to be free of danger from even the weakest person. (Roman)
Past dangers are present pleasures. (Unknown)
Shun danger and it will shun thee. (Irish)
The danger past, the saint cheated. (Italian)
The danger we despise comes quickest upon us. (Roman)
The humble are in danger when the powerful disagree. (Roman)
The one who loves danger shall perish in it. (Irish)
Then your property is in danger, when the neighboring house is on fire. (Roman)
Through danger, safety comes. (Unknown)
Women and glass are always in danger. (Portuguese)

Dare, Daring
Against the daring, daring is unsafe. (Roman)
He most prevails who nobly dares. (German)
He that dares not venture must not complain of ill luck. (Danish)
No one reaches a high position without daring. (Roman)

Dark, Darkness
Better to light a candle than to curse the darkness. (Danish)
Darkest is the hour before dawn. (English)
Darkness reigns at the foot of the lighthouse. (Japanese)

Daughter, Daughters
A house full of daughters is a cellar full of sour beer. (Dutch)
A lucky man's first child is a daughter. (Spanish)
A silly daughter teaches her mother how to bear children. (Ethiopian)
Daughters are brittle ware. (Dutch)
Daughters are easy to rear, but hard to marry. (German)
Daughters may be seen but not heard. (Dutch)
He who has both money and bread, may choose with whom his daughter to wed.
　　(Spanish)
He who has daughters is always a shepherd. (French)
He who has daughters to marry, let him give them silk to spin. (Spanish)
My son is my son till he gets him a wife, but my daughter's my daughter all the days of
　　her life. (English)

One daughter helps to marry the other. (Italian)
The lucky man has a daughter for his first-born. (Spanish)
When our daughter is married sons-in-law are plenty. (Spanish)
Would you know your daughter?; see her in company. (Portuguese)

Dawn

Dawn does not come twice to awaken a man. (Arabian)
Dawn doesn't hurry if you get up earlier. (Spanish)
For all one's early rising, it dawns none the sooner. (Spanish)
It is always darkest before the dawn. (American)
The darkest hour is nearest dawn. (Irish)

Day, Daylight

A bad day hath a good night. (English)
A bad day never hath a good night. (Spanish)
A day is long but a lifetime is short. (Russian)
Be the day weary or be the day long, at last it ringeth to evensong. (English)
Believe that each day that shines on you is your last. (Roman)
Daylight will come, though the cock does not crow. (Danish)
Daylight will peep through a little hole. (Scottish)
Each day succeeding is the student of the one preceding. (Roman)
Fair and softly goes far in a day. (Portuguese)
Let not a day so fair be without its white mark [i.e., a favorable rating]. (Roman)
No day in which you learn something is a complete loss. (Italian)
No day is wholly productive of evil. (Roman)
No day passes without some grief. (German)
No day should pass without something being done. (Roman)
No day so long but has its evening. (French)
No one knows what the day may bring forth. (Danish)
One day is as good as two for him who does everything in its place. (French)
One single bright day will equal the dark ones. (Roman)
Seize the day, trusting little in tomorrow. (Roman)
The days follow each other and are not alike. (French)
The end of one day is the beginning of another. (Roman)
The longest day soon comes to an end. (Roman)

Day and Night

A blustering night, a fair day. (English)
Bright enough in the dark, dull in time of day. (Roman)
Every day has it night. (Italian)
Every day hath its night, every weal its woe. (Danish)
Long as the day is, night comes. (Irish)
Many seek good nights and lose good days. (Dutch)
Merry nights make sorry days. (English)
Out before day, in before night. (Dutch)

The day has eyes, the night has ears. (Scottish)
The day without work, the night without sleep. (Albanian)
There is no day without its night. (Portuguese)
Without day, without night; no growth, no rest. (Chinese)

Dead

A dead man does not speak. (Portuguese)
A dead man has neither relations nor friends. (French)
A dead mouse feels no cold. (French)
Blessed are the dead that die in the Lord. (the Bible)
Blessed are the dead that the rain rains on. (Spanish)
Dead men do not bite. (Roman)
Dead men tell no tales. (Portuguese)
Do you think that the ashes of the dead concern themselves with our affairs?
   (Roman)
Let the dead rest. (German)
Many are dead before they die. (Spanish)
Of the dead, say nothing but good. (Roman)
Of the dead, say nothing but what is true. (Roman)
Of the great and of the dead, either speak well or say nothing. (Italian)
Stone-dead hath no fellow. (English)
The dead are free of worry. (Yoruban)
The dead are many, the living few. (Buddhist)
The dead are soon forgotten. (French)
The dead are the best counselors. (Roman)
The dead open the eyes of the living. (Italian)
The only truly dead are those who have been forgotten. (Yiddish)
When one is dead, it is for a long while. (French)

Deaf, Deafness

It is bad preaching to deaf ears. (German)
There are none so deaf as those who will not hear. (American)

Dealer

A dealer in onions is a good judge of scallions. (French)
A dealer in rubbish sings the praises of rubbish. (Roman)

Death

A good death honors a long life. (Spanish)
A good man looks upon death as a returning. (Chinese)
A man comes from the dust and in the dust he will end – and in the meantime it is good
   to drink a sip of vodka. (Yiddish)
After death no pleasure remains. (Roman)
Against the evil of death there is no remedy. (Roman)
Any death is easier than death by the sword. (Irish)

Anyone may take life from man, but no one death; a thousand gates stand open to it. (Roman)

At birth we bring nothing; at death we take nothing away. (Chinese)

At death, a bird's song becomes sad, a man's words good. (Japanese)

Be sure to send a lazy messenger for the Angel of Death. (Yiddish)

Before life has been, death has been appointed. (Chinese)

Begin thinking of death, and you are no longer sure of your life. (Yiddish)

Better an honest death than a shameful life. (German)

Death alone reveals how small are men's bodies. (Roman)

Death always comes too early or too late. (English)

Death and sorrow come but once. (Persian)

Death brings to a level spades and scepters. (Roman)

Death cancels everything but truth. (Roman)

Death claims all things; it is law, not punishment, to die. (Roman)

Death closes all doors. (English)

Death comes to young and old alike. (Unknown)

Death defies the doctor. (Roman)

Death devours lambs as well as sheep. (German)

Death does not come without a cause. (Irish)

Death does not sound a trumpet. (Danish)

Death is a black camel which kneels at every man's gate. (Arabian)

Death is a blessing to the joyless man. (Hausan)

Death is common to every age. (Roman)

Death is everywhere; God has provided well for that. (Roman)

Death is nature's way of telling you to slow down. (Dutch)

Death is never at a loss for occasions. (Greek)

Death is preferable. (Roman)

Death is repose from all our toils and miseries. (Roman)

Death is the front of an old person and the back of a young person. (Irish)

Death is the great leveler. (Roman)

Death is the last boundary of things. (Roman)

Death is the last doctor. (Swedish)

Death itself often takes flight at the presence of a man. (Roman)

Death keeps no calendar. (Dutch)

Death knocks alike at palace and cottage. (Italian)

Death levels all things. (Italian)

Death pays all debts. (Roman)

Death pursues the man as he flees from it. (Roman)

Death rides a fast camel. (Arabian)

Death said to the man with his throat cut, 'How ugly you look'. (Maltese)

Death sets everything right. (Maltese)

Death snatches away the most deserving, and leaves the wicked. (Roman)

Death spares neither Pope nor beggar. (Portuguese)

Death squares all accounts. (Portuguese)

Death takes no bribes. (Poor Richard)

Death takes the poor man's cow and the rich man's child. (French)

Death to the wolf is life to the lambs. (Roman)

Death's day is doom's day. (German)

Deliver yourself from the fear of death. (Roman)

Every man goes down to his death bearing in his hands only that which he has given away. (Persian)

Everyone must pay his debt to nature. (German)

Everything has a remedy except death. (Spanish)

Fear not death; for the sooner we die, the longer shall we be immortal. (Poor Richard)

Few have luck, all have death. (Danish)

He fears not death who has learned to despise life. (Roman)

He waits long that waits for another man's death. (Dutch)

He who is anxious for the death of another has a long rope to pull. (French)

If death be terrible, the fault is not in death, but in thee. (Nigerian)

If you want to be dead, wash your head and go to bed. (Spanish)

In flight death is disgraceful; in victory, glorious. (Roman)

Let us drink, death is certain. (Roman)

Live ever mindful of death; the hour flies. (Roman)

Neither fear nor wish for your last day. (Roman)

No birth without death. (Unknown)

No one can ever obtain from the pope a dispensation from death. (German)

One cannot tell if the skin of the old sheep or the young sheep will meet its end first. (Irish)

One night awaits us all, and the path of death must be trodden once. (Roman)

Only death is certain. (Unknown)

Our last garment is made without pockets. (Italian)

Passing from death into the next life, calamities turn into happiness. (Chinese)

The best death is that which comes on the day that fate has determined. (Roman)

The fear of death is worse than death. (Roman)

The person who desires to die can taste death. (Mexican)

There grows not the herb which can protect against the power of death. (Roman)

There is no remedy for death, but death is itself a remedy. (Spanish)

There is only one death, but many ways to reach it. (Spanish)

Until death there is no knowing what may befall. (Italian)

We are all equal before death. (Maltese)

What new thing then is it for a man to die, whose whole life is nothing else but a journey to death? (Roman)

When death comes it will not go away empty-handed. (Irish)

When death takes your friends, it is a warning to yourself. (Yoruban)

When the child cuts its teeth, death is on the watch. (Spanish)

Whoever despises death escapes it; while it overtakes the one who is afraid of it. (Roman)

Debauch, Debauchery

The market of debauch is always open. (Egyptian) [In Arabic, 'open' is a play on words with 'erect'.]

Debt, Debts

A debt is not paid with words. (Turkish)

A hundred wagons full of sorrow will not pay a handful of debt. (Danish)

A living man should not owe a dead man any debts. (Chinese)

An agreement is a kind of debt. (Moroccan)

Better old debts than old grudges. (Irish)

Better to be without than to be in debt. (German)

Better to go to bed without supper than run into debt. (German)

Debt severs love. (Afghani)

Debts are like children: the smaller they are the more noise they make. (Spanish)

Eat vegetables and fear no creditors, rather than eat duck and hide. (Yiddish)

Forgetting a debt does not pay it. (Irish)

Happy is the one who owes nothing. (Roman)

He gets a great deal of credit, who pays but a small debt. (Roman)

He is rich enough who owes nothing. (French)

He that dies pays all debts. (German)

He that spends more than he is worth spins a rope for his own neck. (French)

He who cannot pay with his purse, must pay with his hide. (German)

He who gets out of debt enriches himself. (French)

He who is surety for another, pays for him. (Dutch)

He who is without debt is without credit. (Italian)

He who pays his debts, betters his condition. (German)

He who pledges or promises runs into debt. (Spanish)

Interest on debts grows without rain. (Yiddish)

It is better to go to bed without supper than to rise in debt. (Spanish)

Loans and debts make worries and frets. (American)

No man is impatient with his creditors. (Roman)

One can pay back the loan of gold, but one dies forever in debt to those who are kind. (Malayan)

Out of debt, out of danger. (Italian)

Without debt, without care. (Italian)

You have debts, and make debts still; if you haven't lied, then lie you will. (Spanish)

Debtor

A debtor is a slave. (Korean)

A little debt makes a debtor, a great one an enemy. (Arabian)

Debtors are liars. (German)

Early to rise and late to bed, lifts again the debtor's head. (German)

Goods are better sureties than the debtor's person. (Roman)

Deceit, Deceive

A deceiver deals in generalities. (Roman)

A fair face, a foul heart. (German)

A fair skin often covers a crooked mind. (Danish)

A few things gained by fraud destroy a fortune otherwise honestly won. (Roman)

A great cry for so little wool. (Egyptian)

A mouth that praises may conceal a hand that kills. (Arabian)

A saint on the outside, but a devil on the inside. (Unknown)

An angel without, a devil within. (German)

Deceit and treachery make no man rich. (Danish)

Deceit deserves deceit. (Roman)

Deceit is in haste, but honesty can wait a fair leisure. (Danish)

Deceive not thy physician, confessor, or lawyer. (Spanish)

Deceive the rich and powerful if you will, but don't insult them. (Japanese)

Deceiving a deceiver is not deceit. (Japanese)

Dissemblers more often deceive themselves than others. (German)

Falseness often lurks beneath fair hair. (Danish)

Feigned love is worse than hatred. (Roman)

Good words and bad acts deceive both wise and simple. (Portuguese)

He falls into the pit who leads another into it. (Spanish)

He that is kinder than usual hath a design upon thee. (Italian)

He who caresses thee more than the occasion justifies, has either deceived thee or
    intends it. (French)

He who has once used deception will deceive again. (Roman)

Honey in his mouth, knives in his heart. (Chinese)

Honey on the tongue, gall in the heart. (Roman)

If a man deceive me once, shame on him; if he deceive me twice, shame on me.
    (Japanese)

In generalities lurks deception. (Roman)

It's the easiest thing in the world for a man to deceive himself. (Poor Richard)

May the man be damned and never grow fat, who wears two faces under one hat.
    (Spanish)

No one is deceived who is knowingly deceived. (Roman)

One deceit brings on another. (French)

The bad man always suspects deceit. (Spanish)

The deceitful carry a double load. (Hindi)

The one who wants to be deceived, will be deceived. (Roman)

There's none deceived but he that trusts. (Poor Richard)

To deceive a diplomat, speak the truth – he has no experience with it. (Greek)

We admire at a distance the things that deceive us. (Roman)

Who are ready to believe, are easy to deceive. (German)

Who deceives me once, shame on him; who deceives me twice, shame on me. (German)

Who has deceived thee so oft as thyself? (Dutch)

With nice appearance people want to be deceived. (German)

Women naturally deceive, weep, and spin. (Italian)

You may deceive man; you cannot deceive Heaven. (Chinese)

Decorum

Observe decorum even in play. (Roman)

Deed, Deeds

An evil deed has a witness in the bosom. (Danish)

Better a good deed that is boasted than no good deed at all. (Irish)

Between wording and working is a long road. (German)

Dark thoughts lead to dark deeds. (American)

Deeds are better than words. (Chinese)

Deeds are fruits, words are leaves. (English)

Deeds are love, and not sweet words. (Portuguese)

Deeds not words are required. (Roman)

Even a good deed may result in harm done. (Spanish)

Every good deed has its recompense. (Chinese)

Good deeds are the best prayer. (Serbian)

Good deeds may not be rewarded; even good firewood may ruin the stove. (Chinese)

Good deeds return to the house of their author. (Persian)

He has the face of a saint but the deeds of a villain. (Spanish)

Let deeds match words. (Danish)

Let your deeds speak as words. (Spanish)

No good deed goes unpunished. (American)

Nothing is more easily blotted out than a good turn. (French)

One good deed has many claimants. (Yiddish)

One's own deed returns to oneself. (Korean)

See one deed and know ten. (Korean)

Slow in word, swift in deed. (Chinese)

Swift in word, slow in deed. (Korean)

Take care not to do good deeds that appear to be bad deeds. (Mexican)

The better the day, the better the deed. (English)

The smallest good deed is better than the grandest good intention. (Japanese)

There's a great distance between the word to the deed. (Spanish)

'Twixt the word and the deed there's a long step. (French)

To do brave deeds and to suffer is Roman. (Roman)

What a difference it makes by whom the deed is done! (Roman)

Deep

He who has crossed the ford knows how deep it is. (Italian)

Defeat

A vanquished general has no word. (Korean)

Defeat isn't bitter if you don't swallow it. (Chinese)

How easy it is to defeat people who do not kindle fire for themselves. (Kenyan)

We learn little from victory, much from defeat. (Japanese)

Where defeat is inevitable, it is expedient to yield. (Roman)

Defend

Defend what you have won. (Roman)

Defendant

A client 'twixt the judge and his attorney is like a goose 'twixt two foxes. (Chinese)

Admission by the defendant is worth a hundred witnesses. (Yiddish)

Defense

A combined defense is the safest. (Roman)

Attack is the best form of defense. (Spanish)

People live in one another's defense. (Irish)

The best defense is a good offense. (American)

The defense of a just cause is easy. (Roman)

There is always more spirit in attack than in defense. (Roman)

Defer, Deferred

Defer not till tomorrow what may be done today. (Chinese)

Deferred is not annulled. (German)

That which is deferred is not abandoned. (Roman)

Defile

He who touches pitch defiles himself. (Italian)

Delay, Delayed

All delay is hateful, but it produces wisdom. (Roman)

All is not lost that is delayed. (French)

Delay and procrastination are hateful. (Roman)

Delay has always been injurious to those who are prepared. (Roman)

Delay will reach the door. (Scottish)

Delays are dangerous. (Italian)

Every delay is too long to one who is in a hurry. (Roman)

Every delay, that postpones our joys, is long. (Roman)

Good is the delay which makes sure. (Portuguese)

He that peeps into every bush will hardly get into the wood. (German)

He who delays, gathers. (Spanish)

He will never get into the wood who stops at every bush. (Danish)

No delay is too long when the life of a man is at stake. (Roman)

Put off for one day and ten days will pass. (Korean)

Tarrying takes all the thanks away. (German)

The impetuous man meets with delay. (Hausan)

The man will surely fail, who dares delay, and lose tomorrow that has lost today.
   (Chinese)

There is danger in delay. (Roman)

To deliberate about useful things is the safest delay. (Roman)

What reason could not avoid, has often been cured by delay. (Roman)

You may delay, but time will not. (Poor Richard)

Delegate
A delegate cannot delegate. (Roman)

Deliberate, Deliberation
A good dinner helps deliberation. (Roman)
Deliberation gets as many victories as rashness loses. (Roman)
Deliberate before you act. (Italian)
Deliberate slowly, execute quickly. (Roman)

Delight
Each one is drawn by his own delight. (Roman)

Demand
To a hasty demand a leisurely reply. (Spanish)

Demon
A demon is not entitled to forgiveness. (Irish)

Depend, Dependent
Expect not at another's hand what you can do by your own. (Spanish)
He who depends on another dines ill and sups worse. (German)
He who is fed by another's hand seldom gets enough. (Danish)
It is a wretched position to be dependent on others for support. (Roman)

Depraved
A depraved mind never comes to good. (Roman)

Descend, Descent
It is easier to descend than ascend. (German)
The descent to Hell is easy. (Roman)

Descendants
If a man leaves little children behind him, it is as if he did not die. (Moroccan)
Your descendants will pick your fruit. (Roman)

Desecrate
None ever took a stone out of the temple but the dust did fly in his eyes. (English)

Desert
All sunshine makes the desert. (Arabian)

Desire, Desirous
Always poor is the one who desires more. (Roman)
Desire beautifies what is ugly. (Spanish)
Desire nothing that would bring disgrace. (Roman)

Desires are nourished by delays. (Roman)
Everything goes to him who does not want it. (French)
Fancy requires much, necessity but little. (German)
First deserve then desire. (English)
Great desire obtains little. (Burmese)
He who wants a thing is blind to its faults. (Egyptian)
He will have most who desires least. (Roman)
However extravagant men's desires, they hope to see them gratified. (Roman)
If one won't another will. (Dutch)
If the eyes do not admire, the heart will not desire. (West African)
If you desire many things, many things will seem but a few. (Poor Richard)
In desire swiftness itself is delay. (Roman)
It is better to possess something than to desire it. (Spanish)
It is easier to suppress the first desire than to satisfy all that follow it. (Danish)
Let your desires be governed by reason. (Roman)
Look not upon your desires and your heart will not be confused. (Chinese)
Mad desire, when it has the most, longs for more. (Roman)
Nothing is desired that is not known. (Roman)
Seeing creates a desire. (Mexican)
Set a definite limit to your desire. (Roman)
The man who sees a saddled horse often decides that he needs to take a trip.
　　(Mexican)
The man who walks wants to ride when he sees a horse. (Korean)
There is no limit to man's desire. (Japanese)
To fill a valley is easier than to satisfy a man's desire. (Chinese)
Unbridled gratification produces unbridled desire. (Roman)
What is much desired is not believed when it comes. (Spanish)
What is permitted us we least desire. (Roman)
What is seen is desired. (Irish)

Despair
Despair doubles our strength. (English)
Despair gives courage to a coward. (English)

Desperation
A dog in desperation will leap over a wall. (Chinese)
A drowning man will grasp at straw. (German)

Despise, Despised
A man must despise himself before others will. (Chinese)
Despise not a small wound, a poor kinsman, or an humble enemy. (Danish)
Despise not the weak: the gnat stings the eyes of the lion. (Roman)
Do not despise an insignificant enemy, nor a slight wound. (German)
He that despises the little is not worthy of the great. (Dutch)
He who despises small things seldom grows rich. (Danish)

To be despised is more galling to a foolish man than to be whipped. (Roman)
What is cheaply found is despised. (Persian)

Dessert
The dessert is saved until last. (German)

Destiny
Destiny makes wishes come true. (Roman)
Fate and self-help share equally in shaping our destiny. (Indian)
He must stand high that would see the end of his own destiny. (Danish)
No matter where you go, your destiny follows you. (Kurdish)
Often one finds his destiny just where he hides to avoid it. (Chinese)
One meets his destiny often in the road he takes to avoid it. (French)

Detain
Tear yourself from all that detains you. (Roman)

Determination
A man without determination is but an untempered sword. (Chinese)

Determined
A determined heart will not be counseled. (Spanish)
To him who is determined it remains only to act. (Italian)

Devil
A dimple in the chin, a devil within. (Irish)
A young angel, an old devil. (French)
All saint without, all devil within. (Italian)
An ape, a priest, and a louse, are three devils in one house. (Dutch)
An usurer, a miller, a banker, and a barkeeper, are the four evangelists of Lucifer. (Dutch)
Be sure to keep busy, so that the Devil may always find you occupied. (Italian)
Beads about the neck, and the Devil in his heart. (Roman)
Behind the Cross stands the Devil. (Dutch)
Better the devil you know than the devil you don't know. (English)
Call not the Devil, he will come fast enough unbidden. (Danish)
Calling the Devil is not the same as seeing him come. (Puerto Rican)
Devil must drive out devil. (German)
Do not make two devils of one. (French)
Don't mention the Cross to the Devil. (Italian)
Even the Devil was handsome at eighteen. (Japanese)
Every man for himself, and the Devil take the hindmost. (Roman)
From a closed door the Devil turns away. (Portuguese)
He drives out one devil by another. (Roman)
He must be ill-favored who scares the Devil. (Danish)
He must cry aloud who would scare the Devil. (Danish)

He that would eat out of the same dish with the Devil needs a long spoon. (Danish)

He that has swallowed the Devil may swallow his horns. (Italian)

He that has the Devil on his neck must find him work. (Dutch)

He that is afraid of the Devil does not grow rich. (Italian)

He that is embarked with the Devil must sail with him. (Dutch)

He who has once invited the Devil into his house, will never be rid of him. (German)

He who is embarked with the Devil must make the passage in his company. (Italian)

He who sups with the Devil should have a long spoon. (English)

If the Devil catch a man idle he'll set him at work. (Russian)

If the Devil must take us, let it be in a handsome carriage. (Spanish)

In every church the Devil has his altar. (German)

It is easier to raise the Devil than to lay him down. (Roman)

'It is easy to work with a good comb', said the Devil, when he combed his mother's hair with a pitchfork. (Danish)

Let the Devil never find you unoccupied. (Roman)

Let the Devil take the hindmost. (Chinese)

One devil does not make hell. (Italian)

One devil drives out another. (Italian)

One devil knows another. (Italian)

One man is another's devil. (German)

One must sometimes hold a candle to the Devil. (Dutch)

One to one, and two to the Devil. (Danish)

Outside a saint, inside a devil. (Japanese)

Raise no more devils than you can lay down. (German)

Renounce the Devil, and thou shalt wear a shabby coat. (Spanish)

Sometimes even the Devil tells the truth. (Spanish)

Speak of the Devil and he appears. (Italian)

The Cross on his breast, the Devil in his heart. (Spanish)

The Devil can quote Scripture for his own ends. (English)

The Devil catches most souls in a golden net. (German)

The Devil comes to us in our hour of darkness, but we do not have to let him in. (Yiddish)

The Devil dances in an empty pocket. (German)

The Devil does not destroy his own house. (Egyptian)

The Devil finds work for idle hands to do. (German)

The Devil gets into the belfry by the vicar's skirts. (Spanish)

The Devil has his martyrs among men. (Dutch)

The Devil hides behind the Cross, deception behind courtly words. (Spanish)

The Devil is a great friend of the wealthy. (Spanish)

The Devil is bad because he is old. (Italian)

The Devil is civil when he is flattered. (German)

The devil is in the details. (German)

The Devil is never so dark as he is painted. (German)

The Devil is not always at a poor man's door. (French)

The Devil is not so ugly as he is painted. (Italian)

The Devil is subtle, yet weaves coarse webs. (Unknown)

The Devil knows the Lord but still practices evil. (Egyptian)
The Devil looks after his own. (German)
The Devil never rests. (Mexican)
The Devil often lurks behind the Cross. (Spanish)
The Devil rocks the children of the rich. (Russian)
The Devil turns away from a closed door. (Italian)
The Devil was handsome when he was young. (French)
Those who wish to eat with the Devil should use a long spoon. (Spanish)
Though the Devil rises early, God is up before him. (Yiddish)
When the Devil finds the door shut he goes away. (French)
When the Devil says his prayers he means to cheat you. (Spanish)
When the devil was sick the devil a monk would be, when the devil got well the devil a
    monk was he. (Spanish)
Where the Devil can't go himself, he sends an old woman. (German)
Where the Devil cannot put his head he puts his tail. (Italian)
Write on one of the Devil's horns, 'Good Angel', and many will believe it. (German)

Devotion
A devoted heart may move Heaven. (Korean)

Dew
Man's life is like the morning dew. (Roman)
No dew drop ever competed against the sun. (African)
Tiny drops of dew become a stream. (Yoruban)

Diamond
Better a diamond with a flaw than a pebble without. (Chinese)
Diamond cuts diamond. (French)

Dice
The best throw of the dice is not to play. (Spanish)
The best throw of the dice is to throw them away. (Roman)
The Devil leads him by the nose who the dice too often throws. (French)

Dictator
Dictators ride to and fro upon tigers which they dare not dismount. (Indian)

Die
A bad thing never dies. (Spanish)
A man can die just once. (American)
A man dies as often as those he loves die. (Roman)
A man has learned much who has learned how to die. (German)
All life must die, and in dying return to the earth. (Chinese)
All must die. (Korean)
All who meet must part; all who live must die. (Japanese)

As soon as a man is born he begins to die. (German)
As you have lived, so shall you die. (Spanish)
Both friend and enemy think that you will never die. (Irish)
Both rich and poor die empty-handed. (English)
Deep swimmers and high climbers seldom die in their beds. (Dutch)
Don't die until death comes. (Indian)
Dying young is a boon in old age. (Yiddish)
Eat, drink, and be merry, for tomorrow we shall die. (after St Paul)
Ever since dying came into fashion, life just hasn't been the same. (Yiddish)
Everyone wishes that the man whom he fears would perish. (Roman)
Everything which is born passes away. (Roman)
For dying, you always have time. (Yiddish)
From olden times all have had to die. (Chinese)
Happy is the one who dies before he must call on death. (Roman)
He dies twice who perishes by his own hand. (Roman)
He dies twice who perishes by his own weapons. (Roman)
He hath lived ill that knows not how to die well. (Chinese)
He who must die, must die in the dark, even though he sells candles. (Colombian)
If blown it will fly, if grasped it will die. (Korean)
Is it then so very wretched a thing to die? (Roman)
It is all one whether you die of sickness or of love. (Italian)
It is better to die on your feet than to live on your knees. (German)
It is better to say 'there he dismounted' than 'there he died'. (Spanish)
It is never too late to die. (Yoruban)
Let him take leave of life, as a guest satisfied with his entertainment. (Roman)
Only the good die young. (American)
The one whom the gods love dies young. (Roman)
To die is to pay all debts. (English)
To die with honor is better than to live in disgrace. (Persian)
To die without fear of death is something to be desired. (Roman)
When you die, your trumpeter will be buried. (Spanish)

Diet
Diet cures more than doctors. (English)
Diet cures more than the scalpel. (Indian)

Different, Difference
Different fields, different grasshoppers; different seas, different fish. (Indonesian)
Different pursuits suit different ages. (Roman)
Each person has his own wish, the inclinations of all cannot be the same. (Roman)
We are all Adam's children, but silk makes the difference. (English)

Difficult, Difficulty
All things at first appear difficult. (Chinese)
For a hard knot a hard tool must be sought. (Roman)

Knotty timber requires sharp wedges. (Rumanian)
To the brave and faithful, nothing is difficult. (Roman)

Dignity
Dignity increases more easily than it begins. (Roman)
He who hurries cannot walk with dignity. (Chinese)
It is easier to increase dignity than to acquire it in the first place. (Roman)
Where is dignity unless there is honesty? (Roman)

Dilemma
On one side a wolf besets you, on the other a dog. (Roman)

Diligent, Diligence
A diligent man ever finds that something remains to be done. (Roman)
Diligence is a great teacher. (Arabian)
Diligence is a very great help even to a mediocre intelligence. (Roman)
Diligence is the mother of good luck. (Arabian)
Diligence overcomes difficulties, sloth makes them. (Poor Richard)
Diligence, the one virtue that embraces in it all the rest. (Roman)
Diligent work makes a skillful workman. (Danish)
Nothing is so difficult that diligence cannot master it. (Madagascan)

Dine, Dinner
A little dinner, long expected and cold, is by no means given, but dearly sold. (French)
Better a good dinner than a fine coat. (French)
Dine rightly, sup lightly. (German)

Dirt
He that makes himself dirt is trod on by the swine. (Italian)
Never cast dirt into the fountain from which you drink. (Unknown)
The one who washes off dirt, washes off luck. (Mongolian)
Throw dirt enough, and some will stick. (Arabian)
When you throw dirt, you lose ground. (American)

Disagree, Disagreement
An itch for disputation is the mange of the Church. (English)
Reasonable people can differ. (French)
'Tis a shameful sight when children of one family fall out, chide, and fight. (Unknown)
Where two fall out, the third wins. (German)
While the dogs are growling at each other, the wolf devours the sheep. (Unknown)

Disappear
Only rivers and streams can disappear without a trace; a people cannot. (Burmese)

Disappointment

Disappointments make men prudent. (Spanish)

Discern, Discernment

Few men can discern the truly good from the reverse. (Roman)

Not everyone has the powers of discernment. (Roman)

Discipline

At the end of the rod grows deep love. (Korean)

He that corrects not youth, controls not age. (French)

He who does not whip the child does not mend the youth. (Spanish)

If you refuse to be made straight when you are green, you will not be made straight
    when you are dry. (African)

The bamboo stick makes a good child. (Chinese)

The dearer the child, the sharper must be the rod. (Danish)

Discontent

A man whose heart is not content is like a snake that tries to swallow an elephant.
    (Chinese)

A man's discontent is his worst evil. (Chinese)

Let thy discontents be secrets. (Poor Richard)

The discontented man finds no easy chair. (Poor Richard)

Discretion

A dram of discretion is worth a pound of wisdom. (German)

An ounce of discretion is better than a pound of knowledge. (Italian)

Discretion in speech is more important than eloquence. (English)

Discretion is the better part of valor. (English)

In a discreet man's mouth, a public thing is private. (Poor Richard)

You may give a man an office, but you cannot give him discretion. (Poor Richard)

Disdain

One often gets what one disdains. (Vietnamese)

One should not sniff at what one is not going to eat. (Yoruban)

Disease, Diseases

A disease known is half cured. (Irish)

A malignant sore throat is a danger; a malignant throat not sore is worse. (American)

A mind diseased cannot bear anything harsh. (Roman)

An imaginary ailment is worse than a disease. (Yiddish)

Confront disease at its onset. (Roman)

Desperate diseases must have desperate cures. (English)

Disease is soon shaken by a physic soon taken. (English)

Diseases come on horseback, but steal away on foot. (English)

Diseases enter at the mouth. (Unknown)

Every disease will have its course. (English)
He who conceals his disease cannot expect to be cured. (Ethiopian)
Many dishes many diseases, many medicines few cures. (Poor Richard)
The best of nursing may overcome the worst disease. (Irish)
The diseases of the mind are more and more destructive than those of the body.
    (Roman)
The entire flock in the field dies of the disease introduced by one. (Roman)

Disgrace, Disgraceful
Disgrace is immortal, and it lives even when one thinks it dead. (Roman)
Disgrace is the man whose own pet bites him. (Madagascan)
Disgraced once, disgraced always. (Yoruban)
I prefer death to disgrace. (Roman)
It is better to fly than to remain in disgrace. (Roman)
It is disgraceful to hate the one whom you praise. (Roman)
It is not the condemnation but the crime that disgraces a man. (Roman)
One whose life has been disgraceful is not entitled to escape a disgraceful death.
    (Roman)
That only brings disgrace on a man which he has deserved to suffer. (Roman)
The disgrace of others often deters tender minds from vice. (Roman)
What is more disgraceful than an old man just beginning to live? (Roman)

Dishonesty
No man understands dishonesty better than the abbot who has been a monk. (French)

Dishonor
A good man is never honored in his own country. (Jamaican)
A hundred years cannot repair a moment's loss of honor. (Italian)
A man may live after losing his life, but not after losing his honor. (Irish)
He who lives without restraint, will die without honor. (Danish)

Disposition
Each person has his own way of thinking, and a peculiar disposition. (Roman)
Treat a thousand dispositions in a thousand ways. (Roman)
When the disposition wins us, the features please. (Roman)

Dispute, Disputing
Great disputing repels truth. (French)
In too much disputing, truth is apt to be lost. (Roman)
No and yes cause long disputes. (Danish)
Old reckonings breed new disputes. (French)

Dissension
Dissensions among equals are the worst. (Roman)
Not yet victory, and there was already dissension. (Roman)

Distance

Distance lends enchantment to the view. (German)

From a distance, oh how pleasant things appear. (German)

Keep five yards from a carriage, ten yards from a horse, and a hundred yards from an elephant; but the distance one should keep from a wicked man cannot be measured. (Indian)

Paintings and fightings are best seen at a distance. (Poor Richard)

Things are more pleasant from a distance. (Roman)

Uninterested in things near, men pursue those which are at a distance. (Roman)

Distress

The outer dress hides the inner distress. (Yiddish)

Whenever you see a fellow-creature in distress, remember that he is a man. (Roman)

Distrust

Distrust is poison to friendship. (Danish)

If my shirt knew my design, I'd burn it. (Japanese)

Disturb

Do not disturb things at rest. (Roman)

Ditch

Better to go about than fall into the ditch. (Spanish)

Diversity

A thousand men, a thousand minds. (Chinese)

Divide, Division

A divided orange tastes just as good. (Chinese)

A house divided cannot stand. (American)

He who divides gets the worst share. (Spanish)

Something to everyone is good division. (German)

Divorce

Even the handsome are divorced. (Egyptian)

Never the bridesmaid, ever the bride. (American)

When two divorced people marry, four people get into bed. (Yiddish)

Do, Doing

As to yourself do so to another. (Roman)

As you do to others, you may expect another to do to you. (Roman)

Better to do it than wish it done. (Chinese)

Better to do well than to say well. (Japanese)

Between saying and doing there is a great distance. (Danish)

Do ill, and expect the like. (Portuguese)

Do to another as to yourself. (Italian)

Do unto others before they do it unto you. (English)

Do well and have well. (Roman)

Do well the little things now, so that great things will come to you asking to be done. (Persian)

Do what you ought, come what may. (French)

Do when ye may, or suffer ye the nay, in love 'tis the way. (English)

Doing is a mistake, not doing is a greater mistake. (Japanese)

Doing nothing is doing ill. (German)

Fear to do ill, and you need fear naught else. (Poor Richard)

For ill do well, then fear not Hell. (German)

From saying to doing is a long way. (Italian)

Give orders, and do it yourself, and you will be rid of anxiety. (Portuguese)

Give orders, and do no more, and nothing will be done. (Spanish)

He slumbers enough who does nothing. (French)

He that does amiss may do well. (English)

He that does ill never wants for excuses. (Portuguese)

He that doth most at once doth least. (Danish)

He that doth what he should not, shall feel what he would not. (Poor Richard)

He who does all he may, never does all so well. (Italian)

He who does no more than another is no better than another. (Spanish)

He who does not when he can, cannot when he will. (Italian)

He who does nothing does ill. (French)

He who is afraid of doing too much, always does too little. (German)

He who is not ashamed does whatever he likes. (Egyptian)

If a thing is worth doing, it's worth doing well. (English)

If we cannot do what we will, we must do what we can. (Yiddish)

If you cannot do what you want, do what you can. (Spanish)

If you did it, deny it. (Roman)

If you do what you've always done, you'll get what you've always gotten. (Russian)

If you do wrong, make amends. (Haitian)

If you want no one to know it, then don't do it. (Chinese)

It is better to do well than to say well. (the Editor)

It is easier to know how to do a thing than to do it. (Chinese)

It is more painful to do nothing than something. (German)

Let each man do his best. (Roman)

Men, by doing nothing, learn to do ill. (Roman)

Never do anything standing that you can do sitting, or anything sitting that you can do lying down. (Chinese)

No one can do nothing, and no one can do everything. (German)

One cannot do all things. (German)

One does it for love, another for honor, a third for money. (Dutch)

Overdoing is doing nothing to the purpose. (Roman)

Tell me with whom you are going and I will tell you what you are doing. (Irish)

The day you decide to do it is your lucky day. (Japanese)

There is happiness in doing good, and secret merit in virtuous deeds. (Chinese)
Think of many things, do one. (Portuguese)
To do good to the bad is a danger just as great as to do bad to the good. (Roman)
We cannot all do all things. (Roman)
What one likes, one does well. (Unknown)
What you do in the dark will come to the light. (Jamaican, after Jesus)
What you do, do quickly. (German)
Whatever man has done, man may do. (English)
Whatever you do, do with all your might. (Roman)
When two do the same thing, it is not the same. (Roman)
You never know what you can do till you try. (American)

Do or Die

Sink or swim; do or die. (American)

Doctor, Doctors

A clever doctor never treats himself. (Chinese)
A doctor cannot cure his own illness. (Korean)
A young doctor makes a full graveyard. (Chinese)
After death, the doctor. (French)
An apple a day keeps the doctor away. (English)
An ignorant doctor is no better than a murderer. (Chinese)
Better to go without medicine than call in an unskilled physician. (Japanese)
Bleed him, purge him, and if he dies, bury him. (Spanish)
Death is the poor man's best physician. (Irish)
Doctors cure the more serious diseases with harsh remedies. (Roman)
Doctors make the worst patients. (English)
Doctors would be poor were it not for the old. (Spanish)
God heals but the doctor receives the fee. (Spanish)
Herring in the land, the doctor at a stand. (Dutch)
If doctors fail thee, be these three thy doctors: rest, cheerfulness, and moderate diet. (Roman)
If the doctor cures, the sun sees it; but if he kills, the earth hides it. (Russian)
It is a good doctor that follows his own advice. (Unknown)
It is no time to go for the doctor when the patient is dead. (Irish)
New doctor, new churchyard. (German)
No good doctor ever takes a physic. (Italian)
No one becomes a good doctor before he fills a churchyard. (Swedish)
One doctor makes work for another. (English)
The best doctors are Dr Diet, Dr Quiet, and Dr Merriment. (Italian)
The doctor demands his fees whether he has killed the illness or the patient. (Polish)
The doctor is to be feared more than the disease. (Roman)
The doctor must heal his own bald head. (Persian)
The doctor seldom takes a physic. (Italian)
Where there are no doctors, the people die old. (Spanish)

Doctrine
There is no doctrine so false that it does not contain some mixture of truth. (Roman)

Dog, Dogs
A barking dog does not bite. (Egyptian)
A barking dog was never a good hunter. (Portuguese)
A biting dog does not bark. (Korean)
A cur's tail grows fast. (Italian)
A dog does not flee from a bone. (Irish)
A dog in a kennel barks at his fleas; a dog hunting does not notice them. (Roman)
A dog is a dog whatever its color. (Danish)
A dog is a man's best friend. (American)
A dog is never offended at being pelted with bones. (Italian)
A dog is worthy of its food. (Roman)
A dog that has once tasted the flesh cannot be kept from the skin. (Roman)
A dog that will fetch a bone will carry a bone. (Roman)
A dog with a bone knows no friend. (Dutch)
A dog with two homes is never any good. (Irish)
A dog without teeth will also attack a bone. (Yiddish)
A dog's tail never stands straight. (Egyptian)
A good dog deserves a good bone. (Roman)
A good dog does not block the road. (Chinese)
A good dog hunts by instinct. (French)
A good dog never gets a good bone. (French)
A good man indeed, but his vicious dog won't let you near him. (Yiddish)
A kitchen dog is never a good rabbit hunter. (Spanish)
A kitchen dog never was good for the chase. (Italian)
A living dog is better than a dead lion. (Italian)
A mad dog cannot live long. (French)
A man who wants to drown his dog says it is mad. (French)
A scalded dog thinks cold water hot. (Italian)
A slow-footed hound often has good qualities. (Irish)
A vicious dog must be tied short. (French)
An ill dog is not worth the whistle. (Irish)
An ill-tempered dog has a scarred nose. (Danish)
An old dog does not bark in vain. (Spanish)
An old dog does not grow used to the collar. (Italian)
An old dog will learn no tricks. (Italian)
As the hound, so the pup. (Irish)
Barking dogs do not bite. (Thai)
Barking dogs seldom bite. (English)
Beat the dog; wait for its master. (Haitian)
Before beating a dog, first find out its owner. (Chinese)
Better a dog fawn on you than bite you. (Dutch)
Better a living dog than a dead lion. (the Bible)

Better the head of a dog than the tail of a lion. (German)

Better to be the head of a dog than the tail of a lion. (French)

Better to have a dog for your friend than your enemy. (Dutch)

Better to have a dog welcome you than bark at you. (Irish)

Beware of the dog himself, his shadow does not bite. (Danish)

Beware of the dog that does not bark. (Portuguese)

Brag is a good dog, but Hold-fast is better. (Roman)

Buy your greyhound, don't rear him. (Portuguese)

By gnawing skin a dog learns to eat leather. (Danish)

By what servant is his master better loved than by his dog? (Roman)

Caress your dog and he will spoil your clothes. (Dutch)

Corner a dog in a dead-end street and it will turn and bite. (Chinese)

Cut off a dog's tail, it remains a dog. (Italian)

Dead dogs don't bite. (Dutch)

Dead dogs no longer bark. (German)

Do not call to a dog with a whip in your hand. (African)

Do not give the dog bread every time it wags its tail. (Italian)

Dog does not eat dog. (Italian)

Dogs bark at those they don't know. (Italian)

Dogs bark, but the caravan goes on. (Italian)

Dogs have teeth in all countries. (Dutch)

Dogs snap at flies. (German)

Dogs that bark at a distance bite not at hand. (Dutch)

Dogs that bark much don't bite. (German)

Even a dog knows the difference between being stumbled over and being kicked.
   (American)

Even a dog wags its tail before its owner. (Korean)

Even a wandering dog will find something to eat. (Japanese)

Even dogs eat. (Japanese)

Even the dog gets bread by wagging its tail. (Italian)

Every dog has its day. (English)

Every dog is a lion at home. (Italian)

Every dog is allowed one bite. (Italian)

Every dog is valiant at its own door. (Irish)

Fast as the hare runs, the greyhound outruns and catches it. (Spanish)

He painted a tiger, but it turned out a dog. (Chinese)

He that has not bread to spare should not keep a dog. (Chinese)

He that pelts every barking dog, must pick up a great many stones. (German)

He that wants to hang a dog, is sure to find a rope. (Danish)

He that wants to hang a dog, says that it bites the sheep. (Danish)

He that would beat his dog can easily find a stick. (Italian)

He who awakens a sleeping dog sells peace and buys noise. (Spanish)

He who gives bread to others' dogs is often barked at by his own. (Italian)

He who wants to kill his dog only has to say it is mad. (Spanish)

He who would buy sausage from a dog must give it bacon in exchange. (Danish)

How can you expect to find ivory in a dog's mouth? (Chinese)

Hunting dogs have scratched faces. (Egyptian)

'I will not bite any dog', says the shepherd's dog, 'for I must save my teeth for the wolf'. (German)

If a dog shows its teeth, show it a stick. (Albanian)

If a sane dog fights a mad dog, it's the sane dog that loses an ear. (Burmese)

If the bitch were not in haste, she would not litter blind puppies. (German)

If the dog is not at home, it barks not. (West African)

If you can't run with the big dogs, stay under the porch. (American)

If you want the dog, accept the fleas. (Spanish)

If you would have the dog follow you, give it bread. (Spanish)

If you're out to beat a dog, you're sure to find a stick. (Yiddish)

Into the mouth of a bad dog falls many a good bone. (Roman)

It is hard to catch hares with unwilling hounds. (Dutch)

Let a dog get at a dish of honey, and it will jump in with both legs. (Danish)

Let sleeping dogs lie. (English)

Many dogs kill a hare, no matter how many turns it makes. (Indian)

Modest dogs miss much meat. (German)

No one ever kicks a dead dog. (Italian)

Not every dog that barks bites. (French)

One dog bays at nothing, a hundred relay it as truth. (Chinese)

One dog growls to see another go into the kitchen. (German)

One must talk soothingly to the dog until one has passed it. (French)

Out of a dog's mouth will never come ivory tusks. (Chinese)

Show a dog a finger, and he wants the whole hand. (Yiddish)

Snarling curs never want for sore ears. (French)

Stones or bread, one must have something in hand for the dogs. (Italian)

The black dog gets the food; the white dog gets the blame. (Chinese)

The dog does not get bread every time it wags its tail. (German)

The dog gets into the mill under cover of the ass. (French)

The dog laps the river as if to finish it all. (Yoruban)

The dog returns to its vomit. (German, after the Bible)

The dog that has been beaten with a stick is afraid of its shadow. (Italian)

The dog that is forced into the woods will not hunt many deer. (Danish)

The dog that kills wolves, is killed by wolves. (Spanish)

The dog that licks ashes is not to be trusted with flour. (Italian)

The dog that means to bite doesn't bark. (Italian)

The hindmost dog may catch the hare. (Roman)

The lean dog is all fleas. (Spanish)

The mad dog bites its master. (Portuguese)

There is danger when a dog has once tasted flesh. (Roman)

Throw a dog a bone and it will return. (German)

Timid dogs bark the loudest. (English)

Wake not a sleeping dog. (German)

Wash a dog, comb a dog, still a dog remains a dog. (French)

When a dog sees a leopard's face, it will be silent. (Yoruban)
When a dog wags its tail, it is thinking of the meat not the master. (German)
When the dog is awake, the shepherd may sleep. (German)
When the dog is down, everyone is ready to bite him. (Dutch)
When the dog is drowning everyone brings it water. (French)
When the old dog barks, it gives counsel. (Spanish)
Who wants to beat a dog, soon finds a stick. (Dutch)
Young dogs have sharp teeth. (Danish)

Dog and Cat
A dog and a cat will eat from the very same plate. (Spanish)

Dog in a Manger
He is like the gardener's dog, who doesn't eat cabbage and will let no one else eat it.
    (French)
The gardener's dog neither eats greens not lets anyone else eat them. (Spanish)

Done
Begun is half done. (German)
Could everything be done twice, everything would be done better. (German)
Do not consider that anything has been done if anything is left to be done. (Roman)
Do not do what is already done. (Roman)
For what you have done yourself there is no remedy. (Persian)
He has not done who is always beginning. (French)
Ill begun, ill done. (Dutch)
Little is done when every man is master. (German)
Little is done where many command. (Dutch)
Much has been said, little has been done. (Jamaican)
Nothing is done while something remains undone. (French)
Self-done is soon done. (German)
Sooner said than done. (English)
That is done soon enough which is well done. (French)
That is idly done by many, which may be done by a few. (Roman)
That is rightly done which is honestly done. (Roman)
The greatest things are done by the help of small ones. (German)
The more said the less done. (English)
The one who has a thing done by another does it himself. (Roman)
The sooner begun, the sooner done. (Portuguese)
Those who say it can't be done shouldn't interrupt the one doing it. (Chinese)
Well begun is half done. (Roman)
Well done is better than well said. (Poor Richard)
Well done outlives death. (German)
What is done cannot be undone. (Roman)
What may be done at any time will be done at no time. (Scottish)
What you do not want done to you, do it not to others. (Chinese)

What you do yourself is well done. (Danish)
What's done is done. (Roman)
Whatever good is done for good men is never done in vain. (Roman)
When a thing is done, make the best of it. (German)

Donkey

A donkey does not make for a good racehorse. (Irish)
A donkey is known by its ears. (Roman)
Better to fight with a donkey than carry your own wood. (German)
If you marry the donkey, you must carry its load. (Persian)
No need spurring a donkey to the stable. (Spanish)
The donkey sweats so the horse can be decorated with lace. (Haitian)

Doomsday

A thousand pounds and a barrel of hay are all the same at doomsday. (English)

Door

A creaking door hangs long on its hinges. (German)
A door must either be open or shut. (French)
A man does not look behind the door unless he has stood there himself.
   (Danish)
An open door may tempt a saint. (English)
Beware of a door that has many keys. (Portuguese)
He that has a low door must stoop. (Italian)
If you have no door, why have a doorman? (Persian)
One door never shuts but another opens. (Italian)
Shut your door, and you will make your neighbor a good woman. (Spanish)
Shut your door, and you will make your neighbor good. (Portuguese)
Sweep before your own door. (English)
The back door is the one that robs the home. (Italian)
The last one closes the door. (German)
The postern door makes thief and whore. (English)
When one door shuts, another door opens. (English)
When the door is low one must stoop. (French)

Doubt, Doubtful

Doubt is the beginning, not the end, of wisdom. (English)
Doubt is the key to knowledge. (Persian)
Doubt makes the mountain which faith can move. (Persian)
Doubtful the die, and dire the cast (Persian)
He who doubts nothing knows nothing. (Spanish)
If there is room for question, something is wrong. (Yiddish)
When in doubt, do nothing. (American)
When in doubt, go without. (the Editor)
When in doubt, shoot it out. (American)

Which you doubt, then neither do. (Roman)
While the mind is in doubt, a very little can sway it one way or the other. (Roman)

Dough
Everyone is kneaded out of the same dough but not baked in the same oven. (Yiddish)

Dove
Dread the anger of the dove. (French)
He who makes himself a dove is eaten by the hawk. (Italian)
The dove finds it comfortable everywhere. (Yoruban)

Downhill
It is easy to go downhill. (German)

Dowry
A great dowry, a bed full of brambles. (Roman)
Provided she come with virtuous principles, a woman brings dowry enough. (Roman)
Quarrels often arise in marriages when the dowry is excessive. (Roman)
Strife is the dowry of a wife. (Roman)
The virtue of parents is a great dowry. (Roman)

Dragon, Dragons
A dragon stranded in shallow water provides amusement to the shrimps. (Chinese)
Better to sit all night than to go to bed with a dragon. (Chinese)
In shallow holes moles make fools of dragons. (Chinese)

Dream, Dreams
A sow is always dreaming of swill. (French)
Dream different dreams while on the same bed. (Chinese)
Dreams are froth. (German)
Dreams are lies. (French)
Dreams give wings to fools. (Yiddish)
Dreams go by contraries. (French)
Dumplings in a dream are not dumplings but a dream. (Yiddish)
Golden dreams make men wake hungry. (Yiddish)
I dreamed a thousand new paths. I woke and walked my old one. (Chinese)
If you want your dreams to come true, don't sleep. (Yiddish)
In one night's sleep, a man builds a great wall [i.e., in his dreams]. (Korean)
In the same bed, they dream differently. (Japanese)
It is better to interpret the dream than to dream it. (Korean)
Many who build castles in the air cannot build a hut on earth. (German)
Morning dreams come true. (English)
The whole world is a dream, and death the interpreter. (Yiddish)
Though they rest on the same bed, they dream of different things. (Korean)
To believe in one's dreams is to spend all of one's life asleep. (Chinese)

What we speak of by day we dream of by night. (Yiddish)

When troubles are few, dreams are few. (Chinese)

Dress

A dress not worn wears itself out. (Armenian)

Dress makes the man. (French)

Who arrays himself in other men's garments is stripped on the highway. (Spanish)

Drink

A drink is shorter than a story. (Irish)

A drink precedes a story. (Irish)

A good drink ends in thirst. (Irish)

All vices follow too much drink. (Spanish)

Always drink upstream from the herd. (American)

Better that the belly should burst than to throw away good drink. (German)

Drink is the curse of the land: it makes you fight with your neighbor; it makes you shoot
    at your landlord; and it makes you miss him. (Irish)

Drink upon salad costs the doctor a ducat; drink upon eggs costs him two. (German)

Drinking a little too much is drinking a great deal too much. (German)

For dust thou are and unto dust shalt thou return – betwixt and between, a drink comes
    in handy. (Yiddish)

Full bottles and glasses make cusses and asses. (Dutch)

Good drink drives out bad thoughts. (Dutch)

Good eating deserves good drinking. (English)

He that spills the rum, loses that only; he that drinks it, often loses both that and himself.
    (Poor Richard)

He who drinks sleeps; he who sleeps does not sin; he who does not sin goes straight to
    Heaven. (Spanish)

He who drinks well sleeps well; he who sleeps well thinks no harm. (English)

He who has drunk will drink. (French)

It is sweet to drink but bitter to pay for it. (Irish)

Long quaffing makes a short life. (German)

My money, your money, let us go to the tavern. (Portuguese)

One cannot drink and whistle at the same time. (Italian)

One drink is just right; two is too many; three are too few. (Spanish)

The church is near, but the way is icy; the tavern is far, but I will walk carefully. (Ukrainian)

The cure for a hangover is to drink again. (Irish)

The Frenchman sings well, when his throat is moistened. (Portuguese)

The intemperate youth rarely enjoys old age. (Roman)

The more they have been drinking, the more water they drink. (Roman)

The one who drinks a dollar's worth of spirits will speak at the value of half that.
    (Yoruban)

The tongue speaks best when moistened. (Croatian)

The true man comes out in drink. (American)

Thirst is the end of drinking and sorrow the end of drunkenness. (Irish)

Thousands drink themselves to death before one dies of thirst. (German)

When drink enters, wisdom departs. (Spanish)

Women do not drink liquor but it disappears when they are present. (Irish)

Drive, Driver

Drive gently over the stones. (German)

If you drive slowly, you will arrive more quickly. (Yiddish)

He is not a bad driver who knows how to turn. (Danish)

Drought

Brackish water is sweet in a drought. (Portuguese)

Drown, Drowned

A drowning man clings even to thorns. (Filipino)

A drowning man will grasp at straw. (German)

Better to go around than be drowned. (Portuguese)

Drown not yourself to save a drowning man. (Roman)

Even a river monster may sometimes drown. (Japanese)

He that is drowning shouts though he be not heard. (Italian)

He that is fated to drown will drown – even in a spoonful of water. (Yiddish)

If you wish to drown, do not wade in shallow water. (Bulgarian)

It is folly to drown on dry land. (Danish)

It is the calm and silent water that drowns a man. (African)

More are drowned in the bowl than in the sea. (German)

Pity the one drowned during the tempest, for after rain comes sunshine. (Irish)

The drowning man is not troubled by the rain. (Spanish)

The person who knows water drowns in water. (Japanese)

Those who wade in unknown waters will surely to be drowned. (German)

Drum, Drums

A big drum makes a big sound. (Korean)

A good drum does not require hard beating. (Chinese)

Beat your drum inside the house to spare the neighbors. (Chinese)

Untouched drums are silent. (African)

Drunk, Drunkard

A drunk man's words are a sober man's thoughts. (Italian)

A drunk tells everything. (Spanish)

A drunken man may soon be made to dance. (Danish)

A drunken man, when asleep, is better left alone. (Roman)

A drunken night makes a cloudy morning. (Danish)

A drunken person is lost to shame. (Irish)

A red-nosed man may not be a drunkard, but he will always be called one. (Chinese)

Deeds done drunk are paid for when sober. (German)

Ever drunk, ever dry. (Italian)

He that is drunk is gone from home. (Italian)
If drunkards had wings, the sky would always be cloudy. (Mexican)
No one is more like a madman than the one who is drunk. (Roman)
The drunkard is not a spendthrift. (Yoruban)
The drunken man speaks the truth. (Korean)
The drunken man's joy is often the sober man's sorrow. (Danish)
The drunken mouth reveals the heart's secrets. (German)
The wise drunkard is a sober fool. (German)
There are more old drunkards than old doctors. (French)
Thought when sober, said when drunk. (German)
What is said when drunk has been thought out beforehand. (Flemish)
When two say you're drunk, it's time to go to bed. (Yiddish)
When your companions get drunk and fight, tip your hat, and wish them good night.
    (Japanese)

Drunkenness
Drunkenness and anger speak truly. (Irish)
Drunkenness is nothing but voluntary madness. (Roman)
Drunkenness kills more than the sword. (Roman)
Drunkenness makes some men fools, some beasts, and some devils. (Roman)
Drunkenness reveals one's true thoughts. (Korean)
Drunkenness reveals secrets. (Irish)
Drunkenness reveals what soberness conceals. (English)
Intemperance is the doctor's wet-nurse. (German)
Little profit comes from constant drunkenness. (Irish)
Mad drunkenness discloses every secret. (Roman)
The best cure for drunkenness is to observe a drunken person whilst sober. (Chinese)
What soberness conceals drunkenness reveals. (German)

Duck, Ducks
A duck will not always dabble in the same gutter. (Danish)
Ducks quack loudly before a rain. (German)
If it walks like a duck, quacks like a duck, looks like a duck, it must be a duck. (Italian)
Some birds avoid water, the duck searches for it. (Hausan)

Due
Give the Devil his due. (English)
Let every man have his due. (Roman)

Dull, Dullness
A dull speaker always talks long. (Japanese)

Dung, Dunghill
Dung is no saint, but where it falls it works miracles. (Spanish)
Every cock crows best on its own dunghill. (German)

The cock is king on its own dunghill. (German)
The cock is proudest on its own dunghill. (Roman)
Trampling on dung only spreads it the more. (Irish)
Walls sink and dunghills rise. (Spanish)

Dust

Dust amassed will form a mountain. (Japanese)
Even a new mat, when beaten, will raise dust. (Japanese)
From that dust comes this mud. (Spanish)
Gather enough dust and it makes a high mountain. (Korean)
He who blows dust fills his eyes with it. (Italian)
Shake, and dust will rise from everybody. (Korean)
Small and bold thrusts the great into the dust. (German)

Duty

Do not desert your post. (Roman)
Honor the old, teach the young. (Danish)
If you judge, inquire; if you reign, command. (Roman)
Let the reward of duty be duty itself. (Roman)
Man is to man a god when he recognizes his duty. (Roman)
The first duty of a soldier is obedience. (Spanish)
The first duty of man is seeking after and investigating the truth. (Roman)

Dying

The dying man writes in marble. (Roman)

E

Eagle, Eagles

An eagle will not catch flies. (Italian)
Cows and sheep live together, but eagles fly alone. (German)
Eagles do not beget doves. (Roman)
Eagles don't catch flies. (German)
Eagles eat no carrion. (Unknown)
Eagles fly alone. (English)
No need to teach an eagle to fly. (Greek)
The eagle does not war against frogs. (Italian)
The eagle flies in the sky, but nests on the ground. (Albanian)
The eagle in the sky does not know that those on the ground are looking at him.
   (Yoruban)

Ear, Ears

A man with soft ears is sure to get them pulled. (Malayan)
A pair of good ears will drain dry an hundred tongues. (Poor Richard)

Even the woods have ears. (Italian)
Let the ear despise nothing, nor be too ready to believe. (Roman)
Man suffers from the plague of itching ears. (Roman)
Of listening children have your fears, for little pitchers have great ears. (Dutch)
One pair of ears would exhaust a hundred tongues. (Italian)
One should not lend an easy ear to criminal charges. (Roman)
Pull the ear and the head follows. (Bengali)
The ear is the road to the heart. (French)
The ear of the bridled horse is in the mouth. (Roman)
To a quick ear half a word. (German)
Walls and fences have ears. (Irish)
Walls have ears, pitchers have mouths. (Japanese)
Walls have mice and mice have ears. (Persian)

Early
An early riser gets through his business. (Irish)
Early rising is most conducive to health. (Roman)
Early sow, early mow. (Irish)
Early to bed and early to rise, makes a man healthy, wealthy and wise. (Poor Richard)
God helps the early riser. (Mexican)
Had you gotten up early, you wouldn't have needed to stay up late. (Yiddish)
He who gets up early is rewarded by God. (Unknown)
The early riser does not affect the sunrise. (Mexican)
The early riser is cheerful, healthy, and industrious. (French)
'Tis the early bird that gets the worm. (English)

Earn
Let him that earns the bread eat it. (Roman)

Earth
Earth is dearer than gold. (Estonian)
Earth's labors will earn you little. (German)
The earth is our womb, the earth is our tomb. (the Editor)
The earth is the mother and grave of all men. (German)
The earth now supports many bad and weak men. (Roman)
The earth produces all things, and receives all things again. (German)
We do not inherit the earth from our ancestors; we borrow it from our children.
    (African)
When man partakes of the earth, there is laughter; when the earth eats man, there is
    great wailing. (Chinese)
You are earth, and to the earth you will return. (the Bible)

Easy, Easier
Easy come, easy go. (American)
Easy does it. (American)

Easy to say is hard to do. (French)

Easy to say, hard to do. (Japanese)

If things are getting easier, maybe you're headed downhill. (West African)

Eat, Eating

A man must eat, though every tree were a gallows. (Dutch)

A man that has had his fill is no eater. (Spanish)

Eat at pleasure drink by measure. (English)

Eat bread that's light, and cheese by weight. (Dutch)

Eat to live, don't live to eat. (English)

Eat today's meat, yesterday's bread, with last year's wine. (Spanish)

Eat with him, and beware of him. (Portuguese)

Eaten bread is soon forgotten. (German)

Eating while standing makes one strong. (Indian)

He sups ill who eats up all at dinner. (French)

He who eats of the king's goose will void a feather forty years after.
    (French)

He who eats pears with his master should not choose the best. (Italian)

He who eats the king's cow lean, pays for it fat. (Spanish)

He who eats the meat let him pick the bone. (Spanish)

He who eats till he is sick must fast till he is well. (English)

He who eats with the Devil should have a long spoon. (Italian)

He who eats with you to get some advantage is like the lower jaw; if one dies in the
    morning, it will drop by the evening. (Yoruban)

In eating 'tis good to begin, one morsel helps the other in. (Dutch)

It is very savory to eat without cost. (Spanish)

Man fed by Heaven grows fair and strong; man fed by man is skin and bones ere long.
    (Chinese)

Many a man digs his grave with his teeth. (English)

One may tire of eating tarts. (French)

Sooner or later, everything is consumed. (Irish)

The fortunate eat food, the unfortunate eat bitterness. (Chinese)

The one who wishes to eat the kernel must crack the nut. (Roman)

We should eat to live, not live to eat. (Roman)

What you eat, you have. (English)

Who eats slowly eats twice. (Spanish)

You are what you eat. (German)

You can eat your fill only at your own table. (Yiddish)

Eat and Drink

Eat and drink, and let the world go to ruin. (Egyptian)

Eat when you're hungry, and drink when you're dry. (Unknown)

Eating and drinking holds body and soul together. (German)

Eating and drinking shouldn't keep us from thinking. (Italian)

Eating teaches drinking. (Italian)

Eat-well is Drink-well's brother. (German)
To good eating belongs good drinking. (German)

Eavesdrop

He who listens at doors hears more than he desires. (French)
If you listen at a keyhole, you will hear ill of yourself as well as others. (Spanish)
Listeners hear no good of themselves. (Spanish)
The walls have ears, the doors and windows have eyes. (Japanese)

Ebb

Every flood has its ebb. (Dutch)

Echo

As the call, so the echo. (Spanish)
The echo knows all languages. (Finnish)

Economy

Economy is a great revenue. (Roman)
Economy is a more certain road to wealth. (Roman)
There is no economy in going to bed early to save candles if the result is twins. (Chinese)

Education

A faithful study of the liberal arts refines the manners and corrects their harshness. (Roman)
A jade stone is useless before it is polished; a man is good-for-nothing until he is educated. (Chinese)
An easy education weakens all powers both of mind and body. (Roman)
As a field, however fertile, can yield no fruit without cultivation, so neither can the mind without education. (Roman)
Education is life not books. (African)
Education is the poor man's haven. (Roman)
If a son is uneducated, his father is to blame. (Chinese)
Instruction improves the innate powers of the mind, and good discipline strengthens the heart. (Roman)

Eel, Eels

An eel, held by the tail, is not yet caught. (Roman)
Cover up the pot, there's an eel in it. (Dutch)
Eels become accustomed to skinning. (Roman)
There is no eel so small but it hopes to become a whale. (German)
'Tis hard to hold a conger by the tail. (Irish)

Effort

Sometimes it takes a pound of effort to gain an ounce of gold. (the Editor)

Egg, Eggs
A bad egg, a bad bird. (Irish)
A chicken is hatched even from such a well-sealed thing as an egg. (Chinese)
A rotten egg cannot be spoiled. (Roman)
An egg does not fight a rock. (African)
An egg in the mouth is better than a hen in the coop. (Hausan)
An egg is dear on Easter day. (Russian)
Bad egg, bad chick. (Dutch)
Better an egg today than a hen tomorrow. (Italian)
Better half an egg than empty shells. (Dutch)
Black hen lays white egg. (Dutch)
Don't put all your eggs in one basket. (English)
Don't count your eggs before they are laid. (Italian)
Eggs and stones will not stay in the same place. (Hausan)
Eggs are put to hatch on chance. (French)
Eggs cannot teach a hen. (Russian)
Eggs have no business dancing with stones. (Italian)
Eggs must not quarrel with stones. (Chinese)
Eggs today are better than chickens tomorrow. (Roman)
He that would have eggs must endure the cackling of hens. (Italian)
He who feeds the hen should have the egg. (Danish)
He who will have eggs, must bear with the cackling. (German)
If the egg is smart, how much more the chick? (Hausan)
If you want your eggs hatched, sit on them yourself. (Haitian)
One bad egg spoils the whole basket. (German)
Out of a white egg often comes a black chick. (Italian)
Sometimes an egg is given for an ox. (Italian)
The egg laid by the duck is sometimes hatched by the hen. (Malaysian)
The egg teaches the hen how to hatch. (German)
The egg will be more knowing than the hen. (German)
The fine pullet shows its excellence from the egg. (Egyptian)
There is no making pancakes without breaking the eggs. (Italian)
They wrangle about an egg, and let the hens fly away. (German)
To get eggs there must be some cackling. (Dutch)
Unlaid eggs are uncertain chickens. (German)
You can't unscramble an egg. (American)

Egotism
Egotism is an alphabet of one letter. (Scottish)

Elder
The elder who does not share his food with the young will carry his own load.
  (Yoruban)
The elder who has no money is considered to be unwise. (Yoruban)

Elephant

An elephant does not catch mice. (Roman)
An elephant's tusks are never too heavy for it. (African)
By a sweet tongue and kindness, you can drag an elephant with a hair. (Persian)
The elephant does not feel a flea bite. (Italian)
The elephant does not get tired of its tusks. (Masai)
The great elephant of India cares not for a gnat. (Roman)
The smallest elephant is bigger than a buffalo. (Yoruban)
When elephant steps on a trap, no more trap. (African)
When elephants fight, it is the grass that suffers. (African)

Eloquence, Eloquent

An idiot's eloquence is silence. (Japanese)
In an easy cause, any person may be eloquent. (Roman)
It is the heart that makes one eloquent. (Roman)
Often there is eloquence in a silent look. (Roman)
Some men die eloquent. (English)
Whom have flowing cups not made eloquent? (Roman)

Embarrassment

Better a red face than a black heart. (Portuguese)

Ember

An ember about to blaze grows brightly. (Burmese)
An ember burns where it falls. (Turkish)
Burning embers are easily kindled. (Irish)

Embrace

The embrace at meeting is better than at parting. (Egyptian)

Emergency

In an extreme emergency all things are common. (Roman)

Emperor, Empire

Every staff of empire is truly crooked at the top. (English)
Only one can be emperor. (German)
The emperor is in the Church, not above the Church. (Italian)
The emperor is rich, but he cannot buy one extra year. (Chinese)
To serve the emperor is to sleep with a tiger. (Chinese)

Employment

Employment brings enjoyment. (German)

Empty

An empty barrel makes more noise. (Spanish)

An empty cask is easily rolled. (Roman)
An empty cellar makes an angry butler. (Danish)
An empty house is full of noise. (Swiss)
An empty purse frightens away friends. (Portuguese)
An empty purse, and a finished house, make a man wise, but too late. (Portuguese)
An empty sack can hardly stand upright. (German)
An empty vessel makes the most sound. (Roman)
Empty barrels make the most sound. (English)
Empty people think about empty things. (Greek)
Empty pitchers ring loudest. (Roman)
Empty pockets, empty promises. (Burmese)
Empty rooms make giddy housewives. (French)
Empty sacks will never stand upright. (French)
Empty wagons make most noise. (Danish)
It is hard for an empty sack to stand up straight. (Dutch)
It is hard to catch birds with an empty hand. (German)
It's the empty canister that makes the most noise. (English)
Splendid without but empty within. (Burmese)
The empty gives way to the full. (Arabian)
The empty wagon must make room for the full one. (German)

End

All's well that ends well. (English)
Call no man blessed before his end. (Greek)
Everything comes to an end, and a sausage has two. (German)
Good to begin well, better to end well. (German)
He who starts many things finishes few. (Spanish)
If the end is good everything is good. (Japanese)
It's not over till it's over. (English)
The best part comes at the end. (German)
The end crowns the work. (Roman)
The end justifies the means. (English)
The end of an ox is beef, and the end of a lie is grief. (African)
The end praises the work. (Italian)
Whatever begins, also ends. (Roman)
Woman's beauty, the forest echo, and rainbows, soon pass away. (German)

Endurance, Endure

Bear and endure to the end; one day this pain will be useful to you. (Roman)
Bear and endure to the end; you have borne much heavier misfortunes than these.
    (Roman)
Bear with others and you shall be borne with. (Roman)
Biding makes thriving. (Dutch)
By bravely enduring it, an evil which cannot be avoided is overcome. (Roman)
Endure this evil, lest a greater come upon you. (Roman)

He that can't endure the bad, will not live to see the good. (Yiddish)
He who endures with patience is a conqueror. (Roman)
Let no man refuse to endure that which is the common lot of all. (Roman)
Men can bear all things except good days. (Dutch)
To endure the unendurable is true endurance. (Japanese)
What cannot be cured must be endured. (German)

Enemy, Enemies

A friend is got for nothing, an enemy has to be paid for. (Yiddish)
A man's greatest enemy is his own opinion. (Italian)
An enemy does not sleep. (French)
An enemy's mouth seldom speaks well. (German)
An intelligent enemy is worth more than a stupid friend. (West African)
An open enemy is better than a false friend. (Greek)
An open foe may prove a curse; but a pretended friend is even worse. (American)
Be your enemy an ant?; see in him an elephant. (Turkish)
Better a wise enemy than a foolish friend. (Roman)
Better fifty enemies outside the house than one within. (Irish)
Beware of a reconciled enemy. (French)
Build a golden bridge for a flying enemy. (German)
Dangerous enemies will meet again in narrow streets. (Chinese)
Despise not your enemy. (Japanese)
Despise your enemy and you will soon be beaten. (Portuguese)
Do not speak ill of your enemy, but plan it. (Roman)
Don't rejoice when your enemy falls – but don't pick him up either. (Yiddish)
Enemies carry a report in a form different from the original. (Roman)
Every man carries an enemy in his own bosom. (Danish)
Every man is his own worst enemy. (German)
For a fleeing enemy make a silver bridge. (Dutch)
For the fleeing enemy a golden bridge. (Italian)
He cannot be a friend to any one who is his own enemy. (French)
He is nobody's enemy but his own. (Dutch)
He that dallies with his enemy gives him leave to kill him. (Danish)
He that shows his passion, tells his enemy where he may hit him. (Italian)
He who cannot agree with his enemies is controlled by them. (Chinese)
He who feeds a wolf, strengthens his enemy. (Danish)
He who has three enemies must agree with two. (German)
He who is not for me, is against me. (German)
He who makes light of his enemy dies by his hand. (Spanish)
If an enemy is annoying you by playing well, consider adopting his strategy.
    (Chinese)
In fleeing one enemy you encounter another. (Roman)
In the house of your enemy, make the wife your friend. (Spanish)
It is better for my enemy to see good in me than for me to see evil in him. (Yiddish)
It is enough to defeat an enemy, too much to destroy him. (Roman)

It is good to be taught even by an enemy. (Roman)

It is good to make a bridge of gold to a flying enemy. (Danish)

Keep your friends close, your enemies closer. (American)

Let our friends perish, provided our enemies fall along with them. (Greek)

Look with suspicion on the flight of an enemy. (Italian)

Love your enemies, for they tell you your faults. (Poor Richard)

Make a silver bridge for a flying enemy. (Portuguese)

Make no one an enemy without cause. (Turkish)

Man is his own worst enemy. (Roman)

Most wretched is the fortune of him who has no enemy. (Roman)

My friend's enemy is often my best friend. (German)

Never fight an enemy whilst it is possible to cheat him. (German)

Observe your enemies, for they first find your faults. (Greek)

One enemy can harm you more than a hundred friends can do you good. (German)

One's accomplishments may sometimes become one's enemy. (Japanese)

Only one God and so many enemies. (Yiddish)

Repay your enemy with a favor. (Japanese)

Scratch a lover and find an enemy. (German)

The dissatisfaction of the citizenry gives occasion to the enemy. (Roman)

The enemy of my enemy is my friend. (Arabian)

There is no little enemy. (Poor Richard)

Think that you may make a friend of an enemy. (Roman)

Though your enemy be a mouse, watch him like a lion. (Unknown)

Use your enemy's hand to catch a snake. (Persian)

When enemies reconcile, take heed. (German)

When our enemy flies, build him a golden bridge. (Spanish)

When there is no enemy within, the enemies outside cannot hurt you. (African)

When you are on the road speak not ill of your enemy. (Spanish)

Your enemy is to be found in your own backyard. (Yoruban)

Your enemy makes you wiser. (Italian)

Your friend lends and your enemy asks payment. (Dutch)

Your worst enemies are those whose faces are cheerful while their hearts are bitter. (Roman)

Your worst enemy could be your best friend. (Jamaican)

England, English

England is the paradise of women, the hell of horses, and the purgatory of servants. (Roman)

Turkey, heresy, hops and beer came into England all in one year. (English)

An Englishman will burn his bed to catch a flea. (Turkish)

An Englishman's home is his castle. (Turkish)

An Englishman's word is his bond. (Turkish)

Only mad dogs and Englishmen go out in the noonday sun. (Indian)

War with all the world, and peace with England. (Spanish)

127

Enjoy
Enjoy yourself, for there is nothing in the world we can call our own. (Maltese)
Enjoy yourself: it's later than you think. (Chinese)

Enlighten, Enlightenment
If a man be not enlightened within, what lamp shall he light? (Chinese)

Enough
Enough is as good as a feast. (English)
Enough is better than a sackful. (German)
Enough is better than too much. (Dutch)
Enough is enough, and too much spoils. (Italian)
Enough is great riches. (Danish)
Enough shovels of earth make a mountain, enough pails of water a river. (Chinese)
He has nothing who has not enough. (French)
He has nothing, for whom nothing is enough. (Portuguese)
He has what he desires who can limit his desires to what is enough. (Roman)
He is young enough who has health, and he is rich enough who has no debts. (Danish)
Many have too much, but none have enough. (Danish)
More than enough is too much. (Danish)
Not having enough is like not having anything. (Italian)
Not too little, not too much. (German)
The one who has enough for his share, should wish for nothing more. (Roman)
What is enough was never little. (French)
What suffices is enough. (Roman)

Entreat, Entreaty
Entreat him in jackass fashion: if he won't carry the sack, give him a whack. (German)
Entreat the churl and the bargain is broken off. (Italian)
Entreaties to get him to sing, and entreaties to leave off. (Spanish)
Entreaty and right do the deed. (Spanish)

Envy
After honor and state follow envy and hate. (Dutch)
An envious man is a squint-eyed fool. (German)
An envious man waxes lean with the fatness of his neighbor. (Dutch)
Another man's morsel tastes sweet. (Yiddish)
Another's bread costs dear. (Spanish)
Are you trying to appease envy by the abandonment of virtue? (Roman)
Better is my neighbor's hen than mine. (Portuguese)
Better envy than pity. (German)
Biting envy is more merciful to good things that are old than such that are new.
   (Roman)
Envy aims very high. (Roman)
Envy breeds hate. (Yiddish)

Envy cries of spite where honor rides. (Dutch)
Envy does not enter an empty house. (Danish)
Envy does not wane with time. (Yoruban)
Envy eats nothing but its own heart. (German)
Envy envies itself. (German)
Envy follows worth as a shadow follows a body. (Spanish)
Envy goes beyond avarice. (French)
Envy is blind. (Roman)
Envy is its own torturer. (Danish)
Envy is stronger than pity. (English)
Envy is the companion of glory. (Roman)
Envy is the foe of honor. (Roman)
Envy, like fire, always makes for the highest points. (Roman)
Envy neither the fish that swims nor the bird that flies. (Chinese)
Envy never has a holiday. (Roman)
Envy never enriched any man. (English)
Envy no man. (Roman)
Envy shoots others and wounds itself. (English)
Envy strikes high. (English)
Envy waits on boasting. (Roman)
Envy was never a good spokesman. (Danish)
Even the beggar envies the beggar. (Roman)
He who envies, suffers. (German)
If envy were a fever, all the world would be ill. (Danish)
If envy were a ringworm, we would all have scabs. (Mexican)
If envy would burn, there would be no need for wood. (Serbian)
It is better to be envied than pitied. (Spanish)
Nothing can allay the rage of biting envy. (Roman)
Nothing sharpens sight like envy. (Unknown)
Only the fortunate are able to endure envy. (Roman)
Other people's things are more pleasing to us, and ours to other people. (Roman)
Potter envies potter, and smith smith. (Roman)
Relationship produces envy. (Roman)
Rust consumes iron, and envy consumes itself. (Danish)
The envious man grows lean at the prosperity of another. (Roman)
The low envy the high; the high despise the low. (Yoruban)
The one who envies is inferior. (Roman)

Equal, Equity

A canoe does not know who is king: when it turns over, everyone gets wet.
   (Madagascan)
After the game, the king and the pawn go into the same box. (Italian)
An equal has no authority over an equal. (Roman)
Each to his equal. (Portuguese)
He who cannot cut the bread evenly cannot get on well with people. (Czech)

In all things, regard is to be given to equity. (Roman)
It is very difficult to preserve equity aiming to surpass others. (Roman)
Let the other side also have a hearing. (Roman)
Make sure to be in with your equals if you're going to fall out with your superiors. (Yiddish)
The only real equality is in the cemetery. (German)
We are not all equal. (Spanish)

Err, Error

An error that is not resisted is approved. (Roman)
An old error has more friends than a new truth. (Danish)
Begin with an error of an inch and end by being a thousand miles off the mark. (Chinese)
Better to be wrong with the many than right with the few. (Portuguese)
Erring is not cheating. (German)
Error is no payment. (Italian)
Even the wisest man makes an occasional error. (German)
Every error has its excuse. (Polish)
Greater errors are caused by defending little ones. (Spanish)
In generalities lurks error. (Roman)
One wanders to the left, another to the right: both are equally wrong, but in different directions. (Roman)
The error of one moment becomes the sorrow of a whole life. (Chinese)
The eyes do not err if the mind governs them. (Roman)
To be human is to err, but it is truly the fool who perseveres in error. (Roman)
To err is human, to forgive divine. (English)
To err is human, to repent divine, to persist devilish. (Poor Richard)
When a wise man errs, he errs very badly. (Yiddish)
While fools try to avoid one error, they fall into its opposite. (Roman)
Who errs in the tens errs in the thousands. (Italian)

Escape

Escaping from the smoke he falls into the fire. (Dutch)
He knows the roads by which he has escaped before. (Roman)

Estate

Praise a large estate, but cultivate a small one. (Roman)

Esteem

Many are esteemed, only because they are not known. (French)
No man can think well of himself who does not think well of others. (Roman)
That which we obtain too easily, we esteem too lightly. (Roman)

Eternity

Eternity gives no answer. (African)
Think on eternity. (Roman)

Etiquette
With sufficient clothing and food, one comes to observe etiquette. (Japanese)

Evening
In the evening one may praise the day. (German)
Only the evening will show what the day has been. (Russian)
The evening crowns the day. (English)
You know not what the evening may bring with it. (Roman)

Events
Coming events cast their shadows before. (English)
Events of great consequence often spring from trifling circumstances. (Roman)
Past events are as clear as a mirror; the future as obscure as varnish. (Chinese)

Everywhere
He who is everywhere is nowhere. (Danish)
He who would be everywhere will be nowhere. (German)
The man who is everywhere is never anywhere. (Roman)

Evil, Evils
A store-house of evil is a woman if she is depraved. (Roman)
A strong remedy for evils is ignorance of them. (Roman)
An evil comes from a neighboring evil. (Roman)
Avoid even the appearance of evil. (Christian)
Avoid the evil, and it will avoid thee. (Irish)
Better to hear the evil than see it. (Irish)
Better to suffer a known evil than change for an uncertain good. (Spanish)
Between evil tongues and evil ears, there is nothing to choose. (Danish)
By doing nothing men learn to do evil. (Roman)
Dig the hole of evil shallow. (Hausan)
Do not surrender to evil but go boldly against it. (Roman)
Each day has its own evil. (French)
Every evil is easily crushed at its birth; when grown old, it generally becomes more obstinate. (Roman)
Evil acts are long felt. (Irish)
Evil be to him who evil thinks. (Italian)
Evil enters like a needle and spreads like an oak tree. (Ethiopian)
Evil gotten, evil spent. (Ethiopian)
Evil is of old. (Egyptian)
Evil is soon done, but slowly mended. (Danish)
Evil knows the sleeping place of evil. (Hausan)
Evil may spring from the tiniest thing. (Irish)
Evil must be driven out by evil. (Danish)
Evil wastes itself. (Danish)
Evils follow each other. (Roman)

For evil, return kindness. (Japanese)

He prepares evil for himself who plots mischief for others. (Roman)

He who walks in evil ends in evil. (Mexican)

Hear no evil, see no evil, speak no evil. (Spanish)

How often it happens that men fall into the very evils they are striving to avoid. (Roman)

If evils come not, then our fears are vain; and if they do, fear but augments the pain. (Poor Richard)

If forced to choose between two evils, choose rather to go to the pub than the hospital. (Spanish)

In the name of the Lord every evil begins. (Roman)

It is more advantageous not to know the evils that are coming upon us. (Roman)

Let a slumbering evil rest where it is. (Roman)

Never do evil that good may come of it. (Italian)

No evil is great which is the last. (Roman)

No evil person is happy. (Roman)

No one ever became evil all at once. (Roman)

Of evil grain no good seed can come. (Kurdish)

Of evils, choose the least. (Roman)

Of two evils, always choose the lesser. (German)

One does evil enough when one does nothing good. (German)

See no evil, hear no evil, speak no evil. (English)

Such is the short sum of our evils. (Roman)

Sufficient unto the day is the evil thereof. (Jesus)

The best known evils are the easiest to bear. (Roman)

The evil is lessened when it is seen beforehand. (Roman)

The last evil hurts most. (English)

The one who commits evil, shuns the light. (Roman)

The one who does evil suspects others of the same evil. (Yoruban)

There are evils that happen for the good. (Portuguese)

There is no evil from which some good cannot come. (Spanish)

There is no evil without good. (Russian)

Those who are conscious of their own evil, suspect others. (Roman)

To do evil is to transgress the laws of Heaven. (Chinese)

To flee evil is a triumph. (Roman)

To live an evil life is a type of death. (Roman)

To return evil for evil is a praiseworthy action. (Hausan)

Who does not punish evil, invites it. (German)

Who has endured evil knows best the good. (English)

Evildoer

An evildoer abhors the light of day. (Roman)

An evil-speaker differs from an evil-doer in nothing but want of opportunity. (Roman)

Evil-doers are evil-dreaders. (Italian)

He who has done evil, expects evil. (Guinean)

The evildoer never lacks excuses. (Italian)
Those who would do evil never fail to find a reason. (Roman)

Example

A good example is the best sermon. (French)
A man profits more by the sight of an idiot than by the orations of the learned. (Arabian)
An example is no proof. (Yiddish)
Example is better than precept. (Roman)
Example is the greatest of all seducers. (French)
Nothing is more contagious than a bad example. (French)
Precepts guide, but examples drag along. (Roman)
Teaching by precept is a long road, but brief and beneficial is the way by example. (Roman)
They do more mischief by the example, than by the sin. (Roman)
Vulgar minds are more impressed by examples than by reasons. (Roman)
We live more by example than by reason. (Roman)

Excellent, Excellence

All excellent things are rare. (Roman)
Excellent people are honored wherever they go. (Tibetan)

Exception

Everything would be well were there not a 'but'. (German)
The exception proves the rule. (Roman)

Excess

Every excess develops into a vice. (Roman)
Excess mars perfection. (Greek)
Many more die of excess than of hunger. (Roman)
Nothing to excess. (Roman)
Surfeits slay more than swords. (Dutch)
The excess of mirth leads to tears. (Roman)
This consider a valuable principle in life: not to do anything in excess. (Roman)

Excrement

Shit floats to the top. (Roman)
Shit happens. (American)
Shit rolls downhill. (Roman)

Excuse, Excuses

A bad excuse is better than none. (Spanish)
Accusing the times is but excusing ourselves. (English)
Any excuse is good if it holds. (Italian)
He is a bad shot who cannot find an excuse. (German)
He who excuses, accuses himself. (Italian)

If IFs and ANDs were pots and pans, there'd be no work for tinkers' hands. (Roman)
Who excuses himself accuses himself. (Italian)
Who excuses himself without being accused makes his fault manifest. (Roman)

Executioner
The executioner is a keen shaver. (German)

Expect, Expectation
Blessed is he that expects nothing, for he shall never be disappointed. (Poor Richard)
Expect from Heaven what you have done to another. (Roman)
Expect the unexpected. (American)
He expects that larks will fall ready roasted into his mouth. (French)
He expects to find water at the first stroke of the spade. (Spanish)
He hauls at a long rope who expects another's death. (Italian)
Long foretold, long last; short notice, soon past. (German)
Long looked for comes at last. (Dutch)
Look not out for dead men's shoes. (Spanish)
The blow falls more lightly when it is anticipated. (Roman)
What one hopes for is always better than what one has. (Ethiopian)

Expense, Expenses
Allot your expenses to what you have, not what you expect. (English)
It is necessary that the one who seeks gain should incur expense. (Roman)
It is the petty expenses that empty the purse. (Italian)

Experience, Experienced
Believe him who speaks from experience. (Roman)
Better than being taught is to become experienced. (Japanese)
Experience bought with pain teaches. (Roman)
Experience is a long road. (Swedish)
Experience is the best teacher. (Roman)
Experience is the comb that nature gives us when we are bald. (Belgian)
Experience is the father of wisdom. (Belgian)
Experience is the mistress of fools. (English)
Experience is the teacher of fools. (Roman)
Experience keeps a dear school, but fools will learn in no other. (Unknown)
Experience without learning is better than learning without experience. (Roman)
Let the doctor be old and the lawyer be young. (Burmese)
The best proof by far is experience. (English)
The tongue of experience holds the most truth. (Egyptian)
To one of little experience, there are many strange things. (Chinese)
We start as fools and become wise through experience. (African)

Expert
Trust the expert. (Roman)

Extremity

Man in his extremity turns to his source. (Chinese)

Man's extremity is God's opportunity. (English)

Man's extremity is Heaven's opportunity. (Chinese)

Eye, Eyes

A servant's eye hath as high a reach as a lord's look. (English)

An evil eye can see no good. (Danish)

Away from the eye, away from the mind. (Arabian)

Bad eyes never see any good. (German)

Better one-eyed than no-eyed. (German)

Buyers want a hundred eyes, sellers only one. (German)

Do everything as in the eye of another. (Roman)

Every eye has its look. (Arabian)

Every man has one black patch, and some have two. (American)

Eye for eye, tooth for tooth, hand for hand, foot for foot. (the Bible)

Eyes that do not cry, do not see. (Swedish)

Far from the eye, far from the heart. (Italian)

Four eyes see more than two. (German)

He that cuts above himself, will get splinters in his eye. (Danish)

He that would keep his eye sound must tie up his hand. (Portuguese)

He who has one eye is always wiping it. (Unknown)

He who peeps at the neighbor's window may chance to lose his eyes.
   (Arabian)

Hew not too high, lest a chip fall in your eye. (Dutch)

If we doubt our eyes, how can we believe our ears? (Chinese)

Keep one eye on the frying pan and the other on the cat. (Spanish)

One bad eye spoils the other. (German)

One eye in the corner is keener than two eyes about the house. (Irish)

Onions, smoke, and a shrew, make a good man's eyes water. (Danish)

Some have fine eyes and can't see a jot. (French)

Sore eyes see nothing good. (Swiss)

The eye cannot rise above the eyebrow. (Arabian)

The eye is bigger than the belly. (German)

The eye is not a measure, but it knows what is small. (Hausan)

The eye is the mirror of the heart, the nose is the pivot of the mind. (Korean)

The eye shuns what it does not see. (Irish)

The eye that sees smoke looks for fire. (Hausan)

The eyes are the mirror of the soul. (Yiddish)

The eyes are the window of the soul. (English)

The eyes, like sentinels, occupy the highest place in the body. (Roman)

What fills the eye fills the heart. (Irish)

What is held in the heart seems good to the eye. (Persian)

What the eyes see, the heart believes. (German)

When the view leaves the eyes, love leaves the heart. (Irish)

Who has but one eye must take good care of it. (Dutch)
You will not see many with green eyes. (Portuguese)

Eyes and Ears
Fields have eyes and woods have ears. (Danish)
Hedges have eyes, walls have ears. (Chinese)
Woods have ears, fields have eyes. (German)

Eyewitness
Better one eyewitness than ten hearsay witnesses. (Dutch)
The eyewitness observes what the absent doesn't see. (Egyptian)

F

Face
A dress is made by measuring the body, a name is given by reading the face.
   (Korean)
A fair face may be a foul bargain. (English)
A fair face will get its praise, though the owner keep silent. (Danish)
A man's face is a lion's. (German)
Better a red face than a black heart. (Portuguese)
Do not show on your face what you feel in your heart. (African)
Human countenances, as they smile on those who smile, so they weep with those that
   weep. (Roman)
Not to every face is said 'welcome'. (Egyptian)
Often a silent face has a voice and speaks [i.e., has expression]. (Roman)
The countenance of one man brightens another. (Jamaican)
The face is the index of the soul. (Roman)
The face is the mirror of the heart. (Japanese)
The face reveals all. (German)
Unpleasing is the face that does not smile. (Roman)
You will not dare mistreat the face you see in the morning. (Arabian)
Your years are counted on your face. (Roman)

Fact, Facts
Fact is stranger than fiction. (Swedish)
Facts are stubborn things. (American)

Fail, Failure
A man never fails among his own people. (Irish)
A person who misses a chance and the monkey who misses its branch can't be saved.
   (Indian)
Failure is the source of success. (Japanese)
Failure teaches more than success. (Russian)

He that never fails never grows rich. (Italian)

If anything can go wrong, it will (American; Murphy's law).

It is more shameful not to try than to have tried and failed. (Spanish)

The great question is not whether you have failed, but whether you are content with failure. (Chinese)

The one who feared he would fail sat still. (Roman)

The same failings attach not to all. (Roman)

Fair (adjective)

All that's fair must fade. (Italian)

Fair things are soon snatched away. (French)

Fair without, foul within. (French)

Fair (noun)

Three women, three geese, and three frogs make a fair. (German)

Fair, Fairness

A fair exchange brings no quarrel. (Danish)

A fair exchange is no robbery. (Danish)

Fair play's a jewel. (Dutch)

Give and take is fair play. (Dutch)

Faith, Faithful

Faith is confirmed by the heart, confessed by the tongue, and acted upon by the body. (Unknown)

Faith must be kept even to the enemy. (Roman)

Faith will move Heaven. (Japanese)

Faith will move mountains. (American, after Jesus)

Give to faith that which belongs to faith. (Roman)

He who does not keep faith with God will not keep faith with men. (Dutch)

He who has lost his faith has lost everything. (Spanish)

In the affairs of this world men are saved, not by faith, but by the want of it. (Poor Richard)

Love demands faith, and faith firmness. (Italian)

Not long will man's faith endure when fortune is tottering. (Roman)

The faithful are certain of their reward. (Roman)

Falcon

A wise falcon hides its talons. (Danish)

Every man thinks his own owl a falcon. (Dutch)

The falcon dies, yet its eye is still on its prey. (Egyptian)

Fall, Falling

A man who falls into a well will seize even the edge of a sword. (Hausan)

Better to fall from the window than the roof. (Italian)

By falling we learn to go safely. (Dutch)

Do not look where you fell, but where you slipped. (Liberian)

Don't fall before you're pushed. (English)

Even more dangerous is a fall from high. (Roman)

Even the fall of a dancer is a somersault. (Singhalese)

Everything does not fall that totters. (French)

Falling hurts least those who fly low. (Chinese)

Falling is easier than rising. (Irish)

Fine old things have a way of falling. (German)

Had it not been for the stone, I would not have fallen. (Hausan)

He fell today, I may fall tomorrow. (Roman)

He that falls today may be up again tomorrow. (Turkish)

He that lies on the ground cannot fall. (Yiddish)

He that lies upon the ground can fall no lower. (German)

He that stands may fall. (Italian)

If a man falls, all will tread on him. (Moroccan)

If one must fall, let him meet the hazard head on. (Roman)

If you get up one more time than you fall you will make it through. (Chinese)

Let the one who stands be careful lest he fall. (St Paul)

Look high and fall low. (Italian)

Many things fall between the cup and the lip. (Roman)

Many things have fallen only to rise higher. (Roman)

No one falls low unless he attempts to climb high. (Danish)

No tree falls at the first stroke. (German)

Not all that shakes falls. (Italian)

One against all is certain to fall. (Yiddish)

The bigger they come, the harder they fall. (English)

The chips don't fall too far from the block. (Jamaican)

The fall is nobody's sire. (Kashmiri)

The harder you fall, the higher you bounce. (American)

The higher the rise the greater the fall. (French)

Those who contemplate the heights, fall. (Roman)

Those who gaze at the heights, fall. (Italian)

Though the heavens fall, there will be a hole through which to escape. (Korean)

When a man falls, the whole world walks over him. (Swedish)

When a tree falls, everybody runs to it to cut firewood. (Spanish)

When a tree falls, the monkeys scatter. (Chinese)

When the big tree falls, the goat eats its leaves. (African)

When the flight is not high, the fall is not heavy. (Chinese)

When the ox falls, there are many that will help to kill him. (Dutch)

When the sky falls we'll all catch larks. (Irish)

When the tree falls everyone runs to gather sticks. (Danish)

When the tree falls, any child can climb it. (Vietnamese)

When the tree falls, everyone runs to it with a hatchet to cut wood. (Italian)

When the tree is thrown down, anyone that wishes may gather the wood. (Roman)

Fallen

A fallen lighthouse is more dangerous than a reef. (Chinese)
A fallen tree does not yield fruit. (Korean)
From a fallen tree, all make kindling. (Spanish)

False

A false friend and a shadow attend only while the sun shines. (Poor Richard)
A false report rides post. (Unknown)
False in one thing, false in everything. (Roman)
From the false, we can obtain nothing true. (Roman)

Falsehood

Falsehood is nothing but an imitation of truth. (Roman)
Falsehood is the Devil's daughter, and speaks her father's tongue. (Danish)
Falsehood never tires of going round about. (Danish)
Falsehood often borders so nearly on the truth, that a wise man should not trust himself
　　to the precipice. (Roman)
Falsehood often goes farther than truth. (Irish)
Falsehood travels and grows. (Danish)
Falsehood, like a nettle, stings those who meddle with it. (Danish)
No one can be called happy who is living a life of falsehood. (Roman)
One falsehood leads to another. (Spanish)
One falsehood spoils a thousand truths. (West African)
Suppression of the truth is the suggestion of falsehood. (Roman)

Fame

Common fame is seldom to blame. (German)
Common fame seldom lies. (Dutch)
Consider not death but the fame that will survive you. (Irish)
Even for the wise, the desire for glory is the last of all passions to be laid aside.
　　(Roman)
Evil name is evil fame. (English)
Fame and honor sometimes fall more fitly on those who do not desire them.
　　(Roman)
Fame and repute follow a man to the door. (Danish)
Fame does not always err; sometimes it chooses well. (Roman)
Fame is a magnifying glass. (English)
Fame is longer than life. (Welsh)
Fame lasts longer than riches. (Welsh)
If you would acquire fame, let not the sun shine on you in bed. (Spanish)
It is a wretched thing to lean upon the fame of others. (Roman)
It is pleasing to be pointed at with the finger and to have it said: there he goes. (Roman)
Presence diminishes fame. (Roman)
Reality often belies the fame. (Japanese)
The fame of men of action is immortal. (Roman)

The love of fame usually spurs on the mind. (Roman)
The man who wakes up and finds himself famous hasn't been asleep. (Chinese)
The way from the earth to the stars is no soft one. (Roman)
Those who write books condemning fame inscribe their own names on the cover.
   (Roman)
Various are the roads to fame. (Italian)
Who can escape envy and blame, that speaks or writes for public fame? (Dutch)
Who lends his lips to naught but blame, has in his heart no love of fame. (German)
Wretched, indeed, is the man whose fame makes his misfortunes famous. (Roman)

Familiarity
By the familiarity of the master the servant is spoilt. (Roman)
Familiarity breeds. (the Editor)
Familiarity breeds contempt. (English)

Family
A princely mind will undo a private family. (Danish)
Better a little relationship than much acquaintance. (Irish)
Better an ounce of blood than a pound of friendship. (Spanish)
Govern a family as you would cook a small fish – very gently. (Chinese)
If the family lives in harmony, all their affairs will prosper. (Chinese)
In the family leave the family; in the world separate from the world. (Chinese)
In time of test, family is best. (Burmese)
Live together like brothers, do business like strangers. (Arabian)
To the degenerate man his good family is a disgrace. (Roman)
When a mother dies, the family disintegrates. (Spanish)
When husband and wife are at one, the ideal of a family is realized. (Chinese)
With bare hands one establishes a prominent family. (Chinese)

Famine
Even in a famine cakes are cheap if they come out in abundance. (Korean)
Famine compels a man to eat from all kinds of trees. (Yoruban)
People who have bread to eat do not appreciate the severity of a famine. (French)

Far
He who is being carried does not realize how far the town is. (African)

Farm, Farmer
A good farmer takes with force the bread from the earth. (Albanian)
A rich farmer will still carry a basket on his back. (Yiddish)
A son of the field makes the best of soldiers. (Spanish)
He is but a poor farmer, who sows in sand. (Roman)
He that by the plow would thrive, himself must either hold or drive. (Poor Richard)
If a farmer had no hope, he would not sow. (Spanish)
'I'll go myself', and 'I'll see to it', are two good servants on a farm. (Danish)

The bad plowman quarrels with his ox. (Korean)
The best manure is under the farmer's shoe. (Danish)
The lazy farmer dies with his head on the seed-grain. (Korean)
The poorer the farmer, the greater the boast. (German)
The poorest farmer has the largest potatoes. (German)
The townsfolk see the farmer in a silk shirt and think him lazy. (Unknown)

Farthing
'Tis a good farthing that saves a penny. (English)

Fashion
Better to be out of the world than out of fashion. (Portuguese)
Everyone after his fashion. (English)
Fashion is a tyrant from which there is no deliverance; all must conform to its whims.
    (French)
Fashion is more powerful than any tyrant. (Roman)
Fools invent fashions and wise men follow them. (French)
We live more by fashion than common sense. (Roman)
What's in fashion will be out of fashion. (Japanese)

Fasting
A fast day is the eve of a feast day. (Spanish)
A fast is better than a bad meal. (Irish)
After Christmas comes Lent. (German)
Every fast day has three feast days. (German)
Fasting is the best medicine. (Indian)
He who has little to eat fasts well enough. (Spanish)
Long fasting is no economy of food. (German)
Who goes fasting to bed will sleep but lightly. (Dutch)

Fat
A fat spouse is a quilt for the winter. (Punjabi)
Fat head, few brains. (Italian)
Fat hens lay few eggs. (German)
Fat pastures make fat venison. (French)
You must take the fat with the lean. (Italian)

Fate
A person born to be a flower pot will not go beyond the porch. (Mexican)
Both riches and honors are settled by fate; their time of arrival each man must await.
    (Chinese)
But one short hour will change the lot of the highest and the lowest. (Roman)
By fleeing, men often meet the very fate they seek to avoid. (Roman)
Every fate is to be overcome by enduring. (Roman)
Every pig has its San Martin's day: what goes around, comes around. (Spanish)

141

He that is born to be hanged will never be drowned. (Italian)
He that is fated to drown will drown – even in a spoonful of water. (Yiddish)
He that would be rich by nightfall will be hanged by noon. (English)
He who is meant to be a basket-carrier is born with the handle in his hand. (Italian)
He who was born to be hanged will not be drowned, unless the water go over the
    gallows. (Danish)
He who was born to pennies, will never be master of dollars. (Danish)
If a man is fated to be poor, nothing will enrich him. (Unknown)
If you can't change your fate, change your attitude. (Chinese)
It does not fall to the lot of all to smell of musk. (Roman)
It needs a light spirit to bear a heavy fate. (Danish)
Let us go where fate directs us. (Roman)
Man can cure disease but not fate. (Chinese)
One's character fashions his fate. (Roman)
Prayer and medicine won't help the man fated to die. (Hausan)
Some were born to grind, others to be ground. (Spanish)
The Fates lead the willing and drag the unwilling. (Roman)
There is no escaping fate. (Irish)
Venture all; see what fate brings. (Vietnamese)
While we flee from our fate, we like fools run into it. (English)
You often meet your fate on the road you take to avoid it. (French)

Father

A bad father has never a good son. (Roman)
A father's virtue is a child's best inheritance. (Unknown)
A good father will keep his children in check. (Spanish)
As the field, so the crops; as the father, so the sons. (German)
Father earns and son spends. (Japanese)
He follows his father, but not with equal steps. (Roman)
It is a wise father that knows his own child. (English)
Like father, like son. (Roman)
No one knows a son better than the father. (Chinese)
One father is better at caring for ten children than ten children are for one father.
    (Italian)
The cruel father raises a cruel child. (Yoruban)
Three daughters and their mother, four devils for the father. (Spanish)
When a father gives to his son, both laugh; when a son gives to his father, both cry.
    (Yiddish)
When a father helps his son, both laugh; when a son helps his father, both cry. (Spanish)

Fault, Faults

A fault confessed is half redressed. (African)
A fault once denied, is twice committed. (French)
A friend's fault should be known but not abhorred. (Portuguese)
A friend's faults may be noticed, but not blamed. (Danish)

Be not afraid to mend your fault. (Chinese)

Blaming your faults on your nature does not change the nature of your faults.
(English)

Deal with the faults of others as gently as with your own. (Chinese)

Denying a fault doubles it. (English)

Don't find fault with what you don't understand. (French)

Even a good man has his faults. (English)

Every fault is laid at the door of the hyena, but it does not steal a bale of cloth.
(Hausan)

Every fool can find fault, though it would confound him to do better. (German)

Every fool can find faults that a great many wise men can't remedy. (Danish)

Everyone finds fault with his own trade. (Italian)

Faults are thick where love is thin. (Danish)

Fear not mending your own fault. (Japanese)

For no one is born without faults; and the best is the one who has the fewest. (Roman)

Forget not little kindnesses, and remember not small faults. (Chinese)

He is lifeless that is faultless. (English)

He who suffers by his own fault is not deemed a sufferer. (Roman)

He who suspects is seldom at fault. (Italian)

He who denies his faults cannot atone for them. (Roman)

If there were no fault, there would be no pardon. (Egyptian)

If you see no reason for giving thanks, the fault lies in yourself. (Native American)

It does not depend upon the dog when the horse shall die. (Danish)

It is characteristic of folly to judge the faults of others and to forget its own. (Roman)

It is common to man to pardon all his own faults. (Roman)

It is easier to spot faults in others than virtues in oneself. (Yiddish)

It is from the little faults that sin is stored up. (Chinese)

Justifying a fault doubles it. (French)

Love him who tells you your faults in private. (Yiddish)

Men know not all their faults, oxen all their strength. (Chinese)

Men ought to be most annoyed by the sufferings which come from their own faults.
(Roman)

Neglect mending a small fault, and 'twill soon be a great one. (Poor Richard)

No one becomes guilty by fate. (Roman)

No one is able to examine his own faults: no one! (Roman)

No one is born without faults. (Italian)

No one sees his own faults. (Persian)

One man's fault is another man's lesson. (Maltese)

People count the faults of those who keep them waiting. (French)

Small faults indulged in are little thieves that let in greater ones. (Russian)

Tell me my faults, and mend your own. (Poor Richard)

The absent are never without fault, nor the present without excuse. (Poor Richard)

The fault belongs alike to the one who does as to the one who persuades. (Roman)

The fault is as great as he that commits it. (Spanish)

The fault of another is a good teacher. (German)

The faults of the true man are like the eclipses of the sun and moon. (Chinese)

The first faults are theirs that commit them, the second theirs that permit them.
　(Spanish)

The first half of the night, think of your own faults; the second half, the faults of others.
　(Chinese)

The one quick to find faults is not quick to give praise. (Irish)

The one who asks pardon for faults should grant the same to others. (Roman)

The one with ten faults sneers at him with only one. (Korean)

Those who see the faults of others, but not their own, are wise for others and fools for
　themselves. (Roman)

To justify a fault is a second fault. (Roman)

To see a man do a good deed is to forget all his faults. (Chinese)

Unless you bear with the faults of a friend, you betray your own. (Roman)

We pardon faults in youth. (Roman)

Where there's no love, all faults are seen. (German)

Who wants a thing is blind to its faults. (Egyptian)

Wink at small faults; remember thou hast great ones. (Poor Richard)

Faultless

No man is faultless. (Roman)

Who among us is faultless? (Chinese)

Faux Pas

Neither beg of him who has been a beggar, nor serve him who has been a servant.
　(Roman)

Never mention rope in the house of one who has been hanged. (Portuguese)

When with dwarfs do not talk about pygmies. (Chinese)

Favor, Favors

A favor ill placed is a great waste. (French)

A favor often costs more than what's hard-bought. (Irish)

A favor which a person cannot recall without a blush is not a favor. (Roman)

A king's favor is no inheritance. (English)

An ounce of favor goes further than a pound of justice. (French)

Favor oft avails more than justice or reason. (Portuguese)

Favors please like flowers, when they are fresh. (Roman)

For the smallest favor you become a debtor. (Yiddish)

Force not favors on the unwilling. (Roman)

Forget the favors you have given; remember those received. (Chinese)

He receives the most favors who knows how to return them. (Roman)

He who asks the fewest favors is the best received. (Spanish)

Let him who has given a favor be silent; let he who has received it tell it. (Roman)

Most people return small favors, acknowledge middling ones, and repay great ones with
　ingratitude. (Poor Richard)

No one comes calling who does not also seek a favor. (the Editor)

The favor of the great is not lasting. (Roman)

The first time a favor, the second time a rule. (Chinese)

There are private favors even in public affairs. (Korean)

Thundershowers and great men's favor are always partial. (Danish)

To accept a favor is to sell one's liberty. (Roman)

To refuse a favor quickly is to grant one. (Roman)

To refuse graciously is to confer a favor. (Italian)

When out of favor, none know thee; when in, thou dost not know thyself. (Poor Richard)

Where you confer a benefit on those worthy of it, you confer a favor on all. (Roman)

Fear, Fearful

A burnt child fears the fire, and a bitten child fears a dog. (Danish)

A dog which has been beaten with a stick is afraid of its shadow. (Roman)

A lofty thing fears being made equal with a lower. (Roman)

A man does not enter a slaughterhouse if he fears blood. (Hausan)

A man may threaten yet be afraid. (French)

A master who fears his servants is lower than a servant. (Roman)

A sword in its scabbard still inspires dread. (Egyptian)

All fear is bondage. (English)

Before the time, great courage; when at the point, great fear. (Spanish)

Do not lose honor through fear. (Spanish)

Do well, and dread no man. (Unknown)

Don't be a thief and you won't fear the king. (Afghani)

Fear a silent man: he has lips like a drum. (Yoruban)

Fear an ignorant man more than a lion. (Kurdish)

Fear and love make everything bigger. (Spanish)

Fear betrays ignoble souls. (Roman)

Fear causes anger to subside. (Roman)

Fear God, beware of men. (Yiddish)

Fear guards the vineyard. (Italian)

Fear has big eyes. (Russian)

Fear increases the danger. (German)

Fear is a bad companion. (Spanish)

Fear is a fine spur; so is rage. (Irish)

Fear is a great inventor. (French)

Fear is no obstacle to death. (West African)

Fear is not a lasting teacher of duty. (Roman)

Fear is worse than fighting. (Irish)

Fear not the man who fears God. (Arabian)

Fear of being caught will guard a vineyard. (Spanish)

Fear of death drives the wretched to prayer. (Roman)

Fear of law gives safety. (Greek)

Fear the goat from the front, the horse from the rear, and man from all sides. (Russian)

Fear the master, not the servant. (Yoruban)
From fear of the porridge he fell into the pot. (Persian)
Grass fears the frost, frost fears the sun. (Chinese)
Great fear is concealed under daring. (Roman)
Greater is the terror of something unknown. (Roman)
Having been bitten by a snake, he's afraid of a rope. (Afghani)
He fears less who fears what is nearer him. (Roman)
He fears the sack who has been in it. (Danish)
He must fear many, whom many fear. (Roman)
He that has been hurt, fears. (Roman)
He who fears every bramble should not go into the woods. (Roman)
He who has much is afraid of many. (Spanish)
He who has tried it, is afraid of it. (Roman)
He who is afraid of leaves must not go into the wood. (Dutch)
He who is feared by many, fears many. (German)
He who is feared gets more than his own. (Spanish)
He who is scared by words, has no heart for deeds. (Danish)
If you wish to fear nothing, think that everything is to be feared. (Roman)
It is the fear of offense that makes men swallow poison. (Nigerian)
It is torture to fear what you cannot overcome. (Roman)
It needs a high wall to keep out fear. (Danish)
Mankind fears an evil man but Heaven does not. (Chinese)
Men stand in greater fear of the gallows than of God himself. (Yiddish)
Of the malady a man fears, he dies. (Spanish)
One ought to fear even the tiniest of creatures. (Roman)
Our fears always outnumber our dangers. (Roman)
The greater the fear the nearer the danger. (Danish)
The one who terrifies others is himself more afraid. (Roman)
There is a limit to grief, but not to fear. (Roman)
There is more to be feared from the doctor than the disease. (Roman)
There is nothing more fearful than a madman and a fool. (Japanese)
To own is to fear. (Spanish)
Where fear is present, wisdom becomes absent. (Roman)
Where there is no fear there is no inhibition. (Spanish)
Who is in fear of every leaf must not go into the wood. (Italian)
Whom men fear, they hate; whom a man hates, he wishes dead. (Roman)

Feast, Feasting
A good feast heats with eating. (French)
Every day cannot be a feast of lanterns. (Chinese)
Everyone speaks of the feast as he finds it. (Portuguese)
Feasting is the doctor's harvest. (German)
Few men and much meat make a feast. (English)
Full feasting breeds ferocity. (Roman)
He who would enjoy the feast should fast on the eve. (Italian)

It is good to feast with friends, but not from the same plate. (Yiddish)
It's good feasting in another's hall. (Dutch)
No feast like a miser's. (French)
One cannot both feast and become rich. (Ashanti)
The company makes the feast. (English)
The delicacy of the feast is the learned guest. (Chinese)
'Tis good feasting in other men's houses. (Italian)

Feather, Feathers
Fair feathers make fair fowls. (French)
Feather by feather the goose is plucked. (French)
Fine feathers make fine birds. (English)

Feet
All feet tread not in one shoe. (Dutch)
Big feet, great luck. (Chinese)
Feet accustomed to go cannot be still. (Portuguese)
Feet that go everywhere are bound to go astray. (Spanish)
Never let your feet run faster than your shoes. (Scottish)
The feet are slow when the head wears snow. (German)
The feet rest but the heart is not at ease. (African)
The feet will not rest where there is no earth. (Hausan)
Your feet will bring you to where your heart is. (Irish)

Female
The female of the species is more deadly than the male. (Sicilian)

Fence
A fence between makes love more keen. (French)
A fence lasts three years, a dog lasts three fences, a horse three dogs, and a man three
    horses. (German)
Build the fence or you will pay for the plunder. (Irish)
Everyone tries to cross the fence where it is lowest. (Danish)
Everyone pushes a falling fence. (Chinese)
Fences make good neighbors. (English)
Make not a fence more expensive or more important than the thing that is fenced.
    (Yiddish)
There is no fence against ill fortune. (English)
Those who cross over fences, acquire new ideas. (Yiddish)

Ferry
The hasty and the tardy wait for the same ferry. (Egyptian)

Festival
It will not always be Saturnalia [i.e., the carnival will not last forever]. (Roman)

Fetters

Fetters of gold are still fetters, and silken cords bind fast. (Roman)
I hate fetters though they be of gold. (Portuguese)
'Tis folly to love fetters, though they be of gold. (Roman)

Feud, Feuds

Old feuds are easily revived. (Unknown)

Fickle

The fickle populace always changes with the prince. (Roman)

Fiction

Fictions meant to please should have as much resemblance as possible to truth. (Roman)

Fiddle, Fiddler

The fiddle sings one tune, the bow another. (German)
The older the fiddle, the sweeter the tune. (Irish)
In a fiddler's house, all are dancers. (French)
They that dance must pay the fiddler. (English)

Fidelity

Fidelity bought with money is overcome by money. (Roman)

Field, Fields

A field becomes exhausted by constant tillage. (Roman)
Fields left fallow recover their fertility. (Roman)
Green is the grass of the least trodden field. (Irish)
Praise the ripe field, not the green corn. (Irish)
The fertile field becomes barren without rest. (Spanish)

Fight

Do not take up the cudgels in another man's affairs. (Roman)
Fight with silver spears, and you will overcome everything. (Roman)
He that would conquer must fight. (Dutch)
He who fights and runs away, may live to fight another day. (English)
If his legs fail him, he fights on his knees. (Chinese)
In the fray the weak are strong. (Italian)
Neither seek nor shun the fight. (Irish)
Never draw your dirk when a dunt [blow] will do. (Scottish)
One man must not fight with two. (Roman)
Only by fighting can the better man be found. (Hausan)
So long as they fight separately, the whole are conquered. (Roman)
When the miller fights with the chimney sweep, the miller gets black and the chimney sweep white. (Yiddish)
When two dogs fight over a bone, a third will take it. (Dutch)

When two elephants fight, it is the grass that gets trampled. (African)
Who cannot fight, wins naught by right. (German)

File

'Tis a good file that cuts iron without making a noise. (Italian)

Fill

When the mouse has had its fill, the meal turns bitter. (Dutch)

Find, Finder

Finders keepers, losers weepers. (American)
He that finds something before it is lost, will die before he is sick. (Dutch)
One lost, two found. (Dutch)
Take heed that you find not what you do not seek. (English)

Finger, Fingers

A dry finger cannot pick up salt. (Chinese)
All the fingers are not alike. (Italian)
Fingers were made before forks. (Danish)
Five fingers are brothers but not equals. (Afghani)
Five fingers hold more than two forks. (German)
Never put your finger between the tree and the bark. (French)
One finger can't lift a pebble. (Native American)
Ten fingers, and none the same size. (Chinese)
The finger that touches rouge becomes red. (French)
The fingers of the man who has lost one are not counted in his presence. (Yoruban)
The fingers of the same hand are not alike. (Portuguese)
The one who points his finger has three pointing back at him. (American)

Fire

A buried fire will flare up. (Korean)
A burnt child dreads the fire. (Irish)
A crooked log makes a good fire. (French)
A fire is difficult to ward off when the next house is in flames. (Roman)
A fire is nourished by its own ashes. (Roman)
A fire today, ashes tomorrow. (Egyptian)
A fire, if neglected, always gathers in strength. (Roman)
A good fire is not always sweet smelling. (Hausan)
A good fire makes a quick cook. (Dutch)
A great fire, unless you feed it, spends its rage in vain. (Roman)
A little fire burns up a great deal of corn. (Yiddish)
A man with grass on his gatto does not help to put out a conflagration. (Hausan)
A person washes only once with fire. (Hausan)
A small fire that warms you, is better than a large one that burns you. (Danish)
Add not fire to fire. (Roman)

Any water will put out fire. (Italian)

By labor fire is got out of a stone. (Dutch)

Charred piles easily catch fire. (Japanese)

Do not light a fire that you cannot yourself put out. (Irish)

Do not stir the fire with a sword. (Roman)

Do not use paper to wrap up fire. (Chinese)

Don't have too many irons in the fire. (English)

Fight fire with fire. (Chinese)

Fire and cotton cannot live in the same place. (Hausan)

Fire and straw are dangerous companions. (German)

Fire and straw soon make a flame. (Danish)

Fire and water are good servants, but bad masters. (German)

Fire is a good servant but a bad master. (German)

Fire is not quenched with fire. (Italian)

Fire straightens a crooked bar. (Greek)

Fuel alone will not light a fire. (Chinese)

He that will have fire must bear with smoke. (Dutch)

He who has a straw tail is always in fear of its catching fire. (Italian)

He who has many irons in the fire, will let some of them burn. (Danish)

He who would enjoy the fire must bear its smoke. (Danish)

If a forest catches fire, both the dry and the wet will burn up. (Afghani)

If you play with fire you'll get burnt. (Spanish)

It is as bad to spit out the fire and be shamed, as it is to swallow it and be burnt. (Danish)

It is bad to be between two fires. (Danish)

It is easier to build two chimneys than to keep a fire in one. (German)

It is easy to poke another man's fire. (Danish)

It is easy to stir the fire with another's hand. (Yiddish)

It is good to warm oneself by another's fire. (Dutch)

Let him who is cold blow the fire. (French)

Little chips kindle fire, and big logs sustain it. (Portuguese)

No fire without smoke. (French)

No one would leave a fire on the roof to go to bed. (Yoruban)

One man's beard is on fire, and another man warms his hands on it. (Indian)

Out of the frying pan and into the fire. (American)

Secret fire is discovered by its smoke. (Catalan)

She is good who is close to the fire and does not burn. (Spanish)

Since the house is on fire, let us warm ourselves at the blaze. (Italian)

The beginning and end of one's life is to draw closer to the fire. (Irish)

The once-burnt child dreads fire. (German)

The fire is welcome within, when icicles hang without. (Danish)

The fire knows well whose cloak burns. (Spanish)

The fire little heeds whose cloak it burns. (Danish)

The fire of reeds is of rapid extinction. (Egyptian)

The fire started by man is called fire; by heaven, a calamity. (Chinese)

The fire you kindle for your enemy often burns yourself more than him. (Chinese)

The more brightly the fire has burnt, the sooner it is extinguished. (Roman)
The same fire which purifies gold consumes straw. (Italian)
Those who play with fire always get burned. (American)
Three removals are as bad as a fire. (English)
When fire is put to the rock, it cracks. (Irish)
When the next house is on fire, it is high time to look to your own. (Nigerian)
When there is a fire in the neighborhood carry water to your own house. (Italian)
When there is a fire, the man wearing a straw loincloth stands back. (Hausan)
When your neighbor's house is on fire, bring water to your own. (Spanish)
When your neighbor's house is on fire, yours is likewise in danger. (Roman)

Fire and Water

Fire purifies, water sanctifies (Greek)
If the fire is greater, the fire wins; if the water is greater, the water wins. (Burmese)
When you flee fire you run into water. (Yiddish)

Fireplace

The fireplace does not burn of its own. (Yoruban)
There is no fireplace like one's own. (Irish)

Firewood

Nobody gathers firewood to roast a thin goat. (Kenyan)

First

As straight trees are first to be chopped down, so a sweet well is drained first. (Chinese)
First come, first served. (English)
First things first. (Japanese)
He who comes first grinds first. (Spanish)
He who is first in time has the prior right. (Roman)
It is better to be whipped first than whipped last. (Korean)
The first bird gets the first grain. (Danish)
The first blow is as good as two. (Italian)
The first comer to the mill grinds first. (French)
The first dish pleases everyone. (Italian)
The first impression makes a lasting impression. (Roman)
There is a class of men who wish to be first in everything, and are not. (Roman)
There's a first time for everything. (American)
'Tis the first step that is difficult. (Unknown)

Fish, Fishing

A fish begins to stink at the head. (Greek)
A fish dies because it opens its mouth. (Spanish)
A fish should swim thrice: in water, in sauce, and in wine. (French)
A fish taken from the water is always fresh. (Persian)
A fish who keeps its mouth shut never gets caught. (Jamaican)

A hook's well lost to catch a salmon. (French)

A rotting fish begins to stink at the head. (Italian)

A small fish has sharp spines. (Korean)

A small fish makes the entire river muddy. (Japanese)

A tiny fish clouds the water of the whole sea. (Korean)

After fish, milk do not wish. (Poor Richard)

All's fish that comes to the net. (Spanish)

Bargain for fish that are still in the water. (Unknown)

Big fish devour the little ones. (Dutch)

Big fish eat little fish. (Spanish)

Big fish spring out of the kettle. (Dutch)

Don't climb a tree to look for fish. (Chinese)

Don't cry fish before they're caught. (German)

Don't eat fish in months with no 'r' [i.e., the hot months]. (Spanish)

Don't make your sauce until you have caught the fish. (Unknown)

Don't stand by the water and long for fish; go home and weave a net. (Chinese)

Every little fish expects to become a whale. (Danish)

Fish do not inhabit clear water. (Japanese)

Fish or cut bait. (American)

Fish swim thrice: in water, batter, and wine. (German)

Fish swim thrice: in water, in hot oil, and in wine. (Spanish)

Great fish are caught in great waters. (German)

Great fish break the net. (Dutch)

Great fish feed on the lesser. (Roman)

He catches the best fish who angles with a golden hook. (Roman)

He fishes on who catches one. (French)

He that lets his fish escape, may cast his net often yet never catch it again. (French)

He that would catch fish, must venture his bait. (Poor Richard)

He who wants to catch fish must not mind getting wet. (Spanish)

If you cannot catch fish, catch shrimps. (Chinese)

If you swear you will catch no fish. (English)

In still water are the largest fish. (Danish)

In the eddies where you least expect it, there will be a fish. (Roman)

In the great sea fish is always to be caught. (Roman)

It is not a fish until it is safely on the bank. (Irish)

It is the fish's death that has brought it to the market. (Yoruban)

It is the worm that lures the fish, not the fisherman or his tackle. (Yiddish)

Large fish do not live in small ponds. (Japanese)

Listen to the sound of the river and you will get a trout. (Irish)

Little fish are sweet. (Danish)

Little fish make the pike big. (German)

Looking for fish? Don't climb a tree. (Chinese)

No fishing like fishing in the sea. (French)

Nothing is so clean as a fish. (Welsh)

One must lose a minnow to catch a salmon. (French)

Put your hand into the creel, and take your choice of flounders. (Irish)
Set a sprat to catch a mackerel. (Spanish)
Skilled hands eat trout. (Spanish)
Small fish mingle with big fish. (Japanese)
The angler eats more than he catches. (Spanish)
The best fish swim nearest the bottom. (English)
The big fish is caught with big bait. (West African)
The fish always stinks from the head downwards. (Russian)
The fish one sees is more difficult to catch. (Spanish)
The fish that can swallow a boat will not live in a runlet. (Japanese)
The fish that has slipped away always seems bigger. (Japanese)
The fishing is good in troubled waters. (German)
The hasty angler loses the fish. (Arabian)
The lost fish always looks bigger. (Korean)
The tender-hearted buys a salted fish and sets it free. (Chinese)
There are finer fish in the sea than have ever been caught. (Irish)
There are plenty more fish in the sea. (English)
They that sleep catch no fish. (English)
To catch the fish, empty the sea. (the Editor)
To catch trout, you must get wet. (Spanish)
Unless the water be deep, fish won't school. (Korean)
Venture a small fish to catch a greater one. (Roman)
Would you teach the fish to swim? (French)
You cannot pull a fish out of the pond without work. (Russian)
You must lose a fly to catch a trout. (Danish)

Fisherman

He who catches one fish is a fisherman. (Spanish)
One fisherman recognizes another from afar. (Russian)
The fisherman could perhaps be bought for less than the fish. (Roman)

Flag

An old flag is an honor to its captain. (Italian)

Flame

The flame is not far from the smoke. (Danish)

Flatter, Flattery

A flatterer has water in one hand and fire in the other. (German)
A flatterer is a secret enemy. (Hungarian)
A flatterer never seems absurd; the flatter'd always take his word. (Poor Richard)
Beware of one who flatters unduly; he will also censure unjustly. (Arabian)
Flatterers are cats that lick before and scratch behind. (German)
Flatterers are the worst kind of enemies. (Roman)
Flattering speech is honey-sweetened poison. (Roman)

Flattery is birdlime. (German)

Flattery is heard with both ears, truth with only half an ear. (Spanish)

Flattery is sickness; reproof is medicine. (Chinese)

Flattery is sweet food for those who can swallow it. (Danish)

Flattery makes friends; truth makes enemies. (Yiddish)

Flattery will get you nowhere. (Yiddish)

Flattery will take you everywhere. (American)

Flattery, which was formerly a vice, is now grown into a custom. (Roman)

He that rewards flattery, begs for more. (French)

If we did not flatter ourselves, nobody else would. (Yiddish)

If you flatter everyone, who will be your enemy? (Chinese)

Many men know how to flatter, few men know how to praise. (Greek)

One must flatter to become rich. (Spanish)

Only inferiors flatter superiors. (Chinese)

Show me a poor man, I will show you a flatterer. (Portuguese)

Tell her she's handsome, and you will turn her head. (Spanish)

The flatterer's throat is an open sepulcher. (Italian)

When flatterers gather to eat, the Devil dines as well. (Spanish)

When the flatterer pipes, the Devil dances. (Spanish)

Who knows not how to flatter knows not how to talk. (Italian)

Flatulence

The fart of a quiet person stinks most. (Japanese)

Flaw

Even jade has its flaws. (Korean)

Flax

Short flax makes long thread. (Danish)

Flea, Fleas

Big fleas have little fleas upon their backs to bite them, and little fleas have lesser fleas, and so on. (Dutch)

Fleas have fleas of their own. (Unknown)

He that lies down with the dogs, will get up with fleas. (Danish)

He who goes to bed with dogs, will wake up with fleas. (German)

If you lie down with the dogs, you will rise up with fleas. (American)

Lie down with dogs, wake up with fleas. (English)

Nothing should be done in haste but catching a flea. (German)

One flea does not hinder sleep. (Italian)

The fatter the flea, the leaner the dog. (German)

The loudest bark rids not a dog of its fleas. (Portuguese)

Flee, Fleeing

A fleeing person is not choosy about his road. (Japanese)

Better to flee than to stand still. (Irish)
By fleeing, men often meet the very fate they seek to avoid. (Roman)
Fleeing from the bull, he fell into the river. (Spanish)
For a fleeing enemy make a silver bridge. (Dutch)
For the fleeing enemy a golden bridge. (Italian)
He that flees may fight another day. (Roman)
In fleeing one enemy you encounter another. (Roman)
It is not all who turn their backs that flee. (Danish)
The hired hand flees from the flock. (Roman)
The one who flees the law confesses his guilt. (Roman)
The one who flees will fight again. (Greek)

Flint
In the coldest flint there is hot fire. (Chinese)

Flirt, Flirtation
He whose mistress squints, thinks she flirts. (German)

Flood, Floods
After high floods come low ebbs. (Dutch)
In an ant colony dew is a flood. (Persian)
The higher flood hath always the lower ebb. (German)
When floods come, it is helpful to know the boatman. (Hausan)

Flour
He who goes to the mill gets covered with flour. (Italian)
Make good flour and you need no trumpet. (Portuguese)
White flour is not got out of a coal-sack. (French)

Flower, Flowers
A country where flowers are priced so as to make them a luxury has yet to learn the first
    principles of civilization. (Chinese)
All that sing in the flowers are not nightingales. (Spanish)
All the flowers of tomorrow are in the seeds of yesterday. (Italian)
Every flower has its scent. (Persian)
Fair flowers do not remain long by the wayside. (German)
Flowers leave a part of their fragrance in the hands that bestow them. (Chinese)
From the same flower the bee extracts honey and the wasp gall. (Italian)
Garden flowers larger, field flowers stronger. (Chinese)
Gather flowers while the morning sun lasts. (Roman)
Gather flowers while you may. (English)
He that paints a flower does not give it perfume. (Italian)
He who paints the flower cannot paint its fragrance. (Roman)
In one day it opens its blossoms, in one day it decays. (Roman)
It is not every flower that smells sweet. (Italian)

Not all flowers are fit for nosegays. (German)
One flower does not a garland make. (French)
Painted flowers have no scent. (Dutch)
Pretty flowers are soon picked. (Unknown)
The fairest flowers will soonest fade. (English)
The prettiest flower does not always have the sweetest smell. (German)
Though we may pluck flowers by the way, we may not sleep among flowers.
    (Portuguese)

Fly, Flies

A fly cannot enter a closed mouth. (Russian)
A fly is little yet it vexes. (Egyptian)
Big flies break the spider's web. (Italian)
Do not make an elephant out of a fly. (Russian)
Even a fly gets angry. (Roman)
Every fly has its shadow. (Portuguese)
Flies are easier caught with honey than with vinegar. (French)
Flies haunt lean horses. (German)
No flies light on a boiling pot. (Spanish)
The busy fly is in every man's dish. (Spanish)
The fly does not kill, but it does spoil. (Yiddish)
The fly knows the face of the milk-seller. (Egyptian)
The fly that bites the tortoise breaks its beak. (Italian)

Fly, Flying

A bird never flew on one wing. (Danish)
Don't fly till your wings are feathered. (German)
It is well to fly low on account of the branches. (French)
No flying without wings. (German)

Foal

Every foal is not like its sire. (Danish)

Foe

A stag at bay is a dangerous foe. (Unknown)
Build golden bridges for the flying foe. (German)
Despise not a petty foe. (English)
Never tell your foe that your foot aches. (English)

Fog

A fog cannot be dispelled by a fan. (Japanese)

Follow, Follower

Follow close on those who go before you. (Roman)
Follow the river and you will reach the sea. (French)

Follow the road and you will reach an inn. (Portuguese)
Follow the road less traveled. (American)
Follow what is worthy of you. (Roman)
He who follows the crowd has many companions. (German)
He who follows two hares loses both. (Roman)
One who walks in another's tracks leaves no footprints. (Italian)
To avoid disfavor, follow the crowd. (Persian)
Wherever you go, do what you see done: when in Rome, do as the Romans do.
    (Spanish)
Who follows others stride for stride is sure to sway from side to side. (Yiddish)

Folly

All folly is afflicted with a disdain of itself. (Roman)
Cent-wisdom and dollar-folly. (Dutch)
Fools multiply folly. (Poor Richard)
Happy is he who knows his follies in his youth. (Danish)
If a man has folly in his sleeve, it will be sure to peep out. (Danish)
If folly were a pain, there would be groaning in every house. (Spanish)
It is folly to die of the fear of death. (Roman)
It is folly to drown on dry land. (Danish)
It is folly to fear what one cannot avoid. (Danish)
It is folly to sing twice to a deaf man. (Danish)
No one should take advantage of another's folly. (Roman)
Nobody so wise but has a little folly to spare. (German)
Not every error is to be called folly. (Roman)
Profit by the folly of others. (Dutch)
The first degree of folly is to conceit one's self wise, the second to profess it, the third to
    despise counsel. (Poor Richard)
The folly of one man is the fortune of another. (German)
The little folk suffer from the follies of the great. (German)
The malady that is most incurable is folly. (Portuguese)
There is no concealing folly except by silence. (Roman)
Though folly succeed, it is still folly. (Yiddish)
Where honor grows a span, folly grows an ell. (German)
You can never catch up with a fool in his folly. (Yiddish)

Food

A bad herring makes a good kipper. (German)
Bad food is always served too hot. (Korean)
Better a salt herring on your own table, than a fresh pike on another man's. (Danish)
Between the hand and the lip the morsel may slip. (Portuguese)
Bread is bread and wine is wine. (Mexican)
Cheese and bread make the cheeks red. (German)
Cheese from the ewe, milk from the goat, butter from the cow. (Spanish)
Chickens and children are always scratching for food. (Spanish)

Death is in the pot. (Dutch)
Everyone bastes the fat hog, while the lean one burns. (German)
Food is a good workhorse. (Irish)
For wolf's flesh, dog sauce. (French)
Fresh pork and new wine kill a man before his time. (English)
God sends us meat, but the Devil sends cooks. (Roman)
He who would relish his food must not see it cooked. (Italian)
It's easy enough to find food, but hard to eat it in peace. (Hausan)
Meats fattens, wine strengthens, bread sustains. (Spanish)
More die by food than famine. (Roman)
More people are slain by supper than by the sword. (Danish)
New dishes beget new appetites. (Danish)
No popular food is delicious. (Japanese)
Of wine the middle, of oil the top, and of honey the bottom is best. (English)
Oil is best at the beginning, honey at the end, and wine in the middle. (Dutch)
One does not like hot, the other does not like cold; make it tepid so that all agree.
    (Madagascan)
Salt and bread make the cheeks red. (Dutch)
The best food is that which makes the belly full. (Egyptian)
The pot cooks but the plate is praised. (Yiddish)
The stomach that is rarely hungry despises common fare. (Roman)
The table kills more than wars. (Spanish)

Fool, Fools

A dead man is mourned seven days, a fool for his lifetime. (Yiddish)
A fair promise binds a fool. (French)
A fool and his money are soon parted. (English)
A fool and water will go the way they are diverted. (Ethiopian)
A fool at forty is a fool indeed. (Ethiopian)
A fool cannot be questioned or explained. (Yiddish)
A fool carves a piece of his heart to everyone that sits near him. (Italian)
A fool finds no pleasure in understanding but delights in airing his own opinions.
    (Italian)
A fool grows without rain. (Yiddish)
A fool is advised by his enemies. (Egyptian)
A fool is always a slave. (Hausan)
A fool is always beginning. (French)
A fool is flogged with his own stick. (Korean)
A fool is his own informer. (Yiddish)
A fool is known by his laugh. (German)
A fool is like all other men as long as he remains silent. (Danish)
A fool is like the big drum that beats fast but does not realize its hollowness. (Malay)
A fool is thirsty in the midst of water. (Ethiopian)
A fool laughs when others laugh. (Danish)
A fool looks for dung where the cow never browsed. (African)

A fool may chance to say a wise thing. (Dutch)

A fool may give a wise man counsel. (Dutch)

A fool may take liberties. (Yiddish)

A fool only wins the first game. (Danish)

A fool puts on airs. (Yiddish)

A fool repays a salve by a stab, and a stab by a salve. (Roman)

A fool talks of folly. (Roman)

A fool who waits for dead men's shoes is barefoot long. (German)

A fool, unless he know Latin, is never a great fool. (Spanish)

A fool's answer is ever on the edge of his tongue. (Egyptian)

A fool's head never whitens. (French)

A fool's heart dances on his lips. (French)

A fool's speech is a bubble of air. (French)

A fool's tongue is long enough to cut his own throat. (French)

A fool's voice is known by a multitude of words. (French)

A fool's wit is an after-wit. (Japanese)

A foolish calf and a foolish servant do not fear the butcher. (Korean)

A foolish man may be known by six things: anger without cause, speech without profit,
    change without progress, inquiry without object, putting trust in a stranger, and
    mistaking foes for friends. (Arabian)

A foolish woman is known by her finery. (French)

A quiet fool is half a sage. (Yiddish)

A whole fool is half a prophet. (Yiddish)

Advice to a fool goes in one ear and out the other. (Danish)

All men are fools, but all fools are not men. (American)

All places are filled with fools. (Roman)

An old fool is worse than a young simpleton. (Danish)

Another's fool is a joke; your own a disgrace. (Yiddish)

Answer a fool according to his folly. (English)

As a dog returns to its vomit, so a fool to his folly. (the Bible)

Bells and fools like to chime. (German)

Better to be a coward than foolhardy. (French)

By much laughter you detect the fool. (Roman)

By the time the fool has learned the game, the players have dispersed. (African)

Do not answer a fool according to his folly, or you will be like him yourself. (Chinese)

Do you want to buy cheap?; then buy of a needy fool. (Spanish)

Don't give cherries to pigs or advice to fools. (Irish)

Enjoy your little while the fool seeks for more. (Spanish)

Entrust trifles to fools. (Roman)

Even a fool may chance to say something wise. (Unknown)

Even a fool may give a wise man counsel. (German)

Even a fool may have one accomplishment – though he won't know what it is.
    (Japanese)

Even a fool may sometimes speak to the point. (Japanese)

Every fool is different. (German)

Every fool is pleased with his bauble. (Spanish)

Every fool is wise when he holds his tongue. (Italian)

Every fool thinks he is clever enough. (Danish)

Every fool wants to give advice. (Italian)

Every man hath a fool in his sleeve. (Italian)

Every man is a fool in some man's opinion. (Spanish)

Everybody loves a fool, but nobody wants him for a son. (African)

Everybody's friend, everybody's fool. (German)

Fools and apes have their mouths agape. (German)

Fools and obstinate men make lawyers rich. (Spanish)

Fools and scissors must be carefully handled. (Japanese)

Fools are thought wise until they speak. (German)

Fools are without number. (German)

Fools delight in their own folly. (German)

Fools go in throngs. (French)

Fools grow without watering. (Italian)

Fools laugh at the Latin language. (Roman)

Fools live poor to die rich. (Italian)

Fools refuse favors. (German)

Fools rush in where angels fear to tread. (English)

Fools' names and fools' faces are always found in public places. (American)

Fools' names stick to the walls (Roman)

Fortune and women are partial to fools. (German)

God alone understands fools. (French)

God and man think him a fool who brags of his own great wisdom. (French)

Great fools must have great bells. (Dutch)

Grind a fool in a mortar, and he says you don't mean to grind him but the pepper.
   (Yiddish)

He has great need of a fool who makes himself one. (French)

He is a fool who boasts of four things: that he has good wine, a good horse, a handsome
   wife, and plenty of money. (Italian)

He is a fool who does not know from what quarter the wind blows. (Italian)

He is a fool who looks for a notch in a saw. (Yiddish)

He is a fool who loses the flight for the leap. (Italian)

He is a fool who makes a mallet of his fist. (French)

He is a fool who makes his physician his heir. (French)

He is a fool who spares the children after having killed the father. (Roman)

He is a fool who thinks that another does not think. (Italian)

He is a great fool who forgets himself. (French)

He is a great simpleton who starves himself to feed another. (Spanish)

He who asks is a fool for five minutes, but he who does not ask remains a fool forever.
   (Chinese)

He who is born a fool is never cured. (African)

He who would make a fool of himself will find many to like him. (Danish)

He's a fool that cannot conceal his wisdom. (Poor Richard)

If a fool could keep silent he would not be a fool. (Swedish)

If every fool wore a crown, we should all be kings. (Welsh)

If fools went not to market, bad wares would not be sold. (Dutch)

If you play with the fool at home, he will play with you abroad. (Danish)

In the abundance of water, the fool is thirsty. (Jamaican)

It is better to deal with a whole fool than half a fool. (German)

It is on the fool's beard that the barber learns to shave. (French)

It needs a cunning hand to shave a fool's head. (Dutch)

Learned fools are the greatest fools. (German)

More people know Tom Fool than Tom Fool knows. (Danish)

Most fools think they are only ignorant. (Poor Richard)

Never challenge a fool to do wrong. (French)

No one is a fool always, everyone sometimes. (Roman)

On the first of April you can send a fool wherever you will. (German)

One fool always finds a greater fool to admire him. (French)

One fool can tell another. (Yiddish)

One fool is enough in a house. (Italian)

One fool makes a hundred. (Spanish)

One fool makes fools of many. (Yiddish)

One fool makes many. (Roman)

One fool praises another. (German)

Only a fool leans upon his own misunderstanding. (Jamaican)

Only fools are glad when governments change. (Rumanian)

Send a fool to close the shutters, and he closes them all over town. (Yiddish)

Send a fool to the market and a fool he will return. (Yiddish)

Sometimes a fool speaks well. (Roman)

Tell an ass by his long ears, a fool by his long tongue. (Yiddish)

The assistance of fools only brings injury. (Roman)

The false shame of fools makes them hide their uncured sores. (Roman)

The fool cuts himself with his own knife. (French)

The fool hunts misfortune. (French)

The fool is always beginning to live. (Roman)

The fool is known by his song. (German)

The fool lives poor to die rich. (Roman)

The fool thinks nothing well done except what he does. (Roman)

The fool with a dirty face scolds his mirror. (Korean)

The fool would sell his inheritance for food.

The fool's world is a paradise. (Yiddish)

The greater the fool, the greater his insolence. (Roman)

The higher the status of fools, the more manifest is their baseness. (Roman)

The learned fool writes his nonsense in better language than the unlearned; but still 'tis nonsense. (Poor Richard)

The more fools, the more laughter. (French)

The more riches a fool hath, the greater a fool he is. (Spanish)

The right answer to a fool is silence. (Afghani)

There is a fool at every feast. (Dutch)
There is no cure for the fool. (Japanese)
There is no fool like a learned fool. (Italian)
There's no fool like an old fool. (English)
'They say' is a fool. (French)
Though the fool waits, the day does not. (French)
To be a fool at the right time is also an art. (Danish)
To every fool his cap. (Dutch)
To reprove a fool is but lost labor. (French)
We have all been fools in our time. (Roman)
Were fools silent they would pass for wise. (Dutch)
When a fool is cursed, he thinks he is being praised. (African)
When fools go to market, peddlers make money. (Dutch)
When the fool has made up his mind the market is over. (Spanish)
When the Lord wants to punish a fool, He inspires him to mouth some piece of
    learning. (Yiddish)
Where there's three, there's always one fool. (German)
Who is born a fool is never cured. (Italian)
Who loves not women, wine, and song, remains a fool his whole life long. (German)
Women, fortune, and gold, favor fools. (German)
You are a fool, doing what has already been done. (Roman)

Foolish
It is foolish not to enjoy what things you have. (Irish)
It is foolish to fear what you cannot avoid. (Roman)
It is foolish to wish to encompass all things. (Roman)
The gold disappears but the foolish woman remains. (Irish)
There are more foolish buyers than foolish sellers. (French)

Foot
Do not have each foot on a different boat. (Chinese)
One foot is better than two crutches. (Rumanian)
One foot is better then two stilts. (French)
The careful foot can walk anywhere. (Chinese)
The foot touches the water before it steps on the sand. (Yoruban)
The man with the boots does not mind where he puts his foot. (Irish)
When one foot stumbles, the other is near falling. (Danish)

Footprints
Footprints do not go backwards. (Roman)

Forbidden
Everything forbidden is sweet. (Egyptian)
Forbidden fruit is sweet. (German)
Forbidden fruit is the sweetest. (English)

Nothing so good as forbidden fruit. (French)
Things forbidden have a secret charm. (Roman)

Force

Contrivance is better than force. (French)
Where force prevails, right perishes. (Spanish)

Foresight

A danger foreseen is half avoided. (German)
A wound foreseen pains the less. (Italian)
Could a man foresee events he would never be poor. (French)
He that considers in prosperity will be less afflicted in adversity. (Turkish)
He that will not look forward must look behind. (Irish)
He who could foresee affairs three days in advance would be rich for thousands of years.
    (Chinese)
He who does not look before lags behind. (Spanish)
If a man knew where he would fall, he would spread straw there first. (Finnish)
One look before is better than two behind. (Irish)
One who does not look ahead remains behind. (Brazilian)
'Tis easy to see, hard to foresee. (Poor Richard)

Forest

Do not call the forest that shelters you a jungle. (West African)
No forest without its bear. (Turkish)
One who enters a forest does not listen to the breaking of the twigs in the brush.
    (African)
Some men go through a forest and see no firewood. (English)
The forest can't be without its jackals. (Georgian)
The forest has ears, the field has eyes. (German)
The forest is the poor man's overcoat. (American)
The forest will answer you in the way you call to it. (Finnish)
The forest will renew the foliage it sheds. (Irish)

Forethought

Forethought is easy, repentance hard. (Chinese)
One good fore-wit is worth two after-wits. (Yiddish)
The afterthought is good, but forethought is better. (Norwegian)

Forever

Forever is a long, long time. (German)
Nothing lasts forever. (American)

Forewarned

A man warned is as good as two. (French)
A man warned is half saved. (German)

Forewarned is forearmed. (English)
A man forewarned is as good as two. (Spanish)

Forget, Forgetful

A forgetful head makes the legs weary. (German)
Forget those who forget their friends. (Spanish)
Forgetting trouble is the way to cure it. (Roman)
Forgotten offenses, healed offenses. (Spanish)
He is lucky who forgets what cannot be mended. (German)
In safety, forget not a dangerous situation; in peace, forget not a rebellious one. (Chinese)
It is impossible to forget what was truly loved. (Spanish)
It is pleasant to forget the calamities of life. (Roman)
It is sometimes expedient to forget what you know. (Roman)
It is sometimes expedient to forget who you are. (Roman)
Thinking of where you are going, you forget whence you came. (Portuguese)
Those who never forget are never at ease. (Spanish)
To know how to forget is to know how to live. (Spanish)
To want to forget something is to remember it. (French)
What one knows is sometimes useful to forget. (German)

Forgive, Forgiven

Forgive and forget. (German)
Forgive and you will be forgiven. (Roman)
Forgive others often, yourself never. (Roman)
Forgiven is not forgotten. (German)
Forgiving the unrepentant is like drawing pictures on water. (Japanese)
He that does you a very ill turn will never forgive you. (Danish)
The Irish forgive their great men when they are safely buried. (Irish)
The offender never forgives. (English)
Transgressions should never be forgiven a third time. (Chinese)
Who knows most, forgives most. (Italian)
'Tis more noble to forgive, and more manly to despise, than to revenge an injury. (Poor Richard)
He who doth the injury never forgives the injured man. (Italian)
Man never tires of sinning, nor God of forgiving. (Spanish)

Forgotten

He who departs is soon forgotten. (Japanese)
Sooner be hated than forgotten. (Spanish)
The dead and the absent are soon forgotten. (Spanish)
There is no worse death than being forgotten. (Spanish)

Fortress

A fortress on its guard is not surprised. (Spanish)
The fortress that parleys soon surrenders. (Italian)

Fortunate

A fortunate man may be anywhere. (Spanish)

Call no man fortunate till he dies. (English)

Don't call me fortunate till you see me buried. (Spanish)

The fortunate man falls into a river and rises with a fish in his mouth. (Egyptian)

To the fortunate, every land is his country. (Roman)

Fortune

A drop of good fortune rather than a cask of wisdom. (Roman)

A good heart breaks bad fortune. (Spanish)

A great fortune is a great slavery. (Roman)

A man may force a livelihood, but cannot force fortune. (Irish)

All the world will beat the man whom fortune buffets. (Portuguese)

An ounce of fortune is worth a pound of forecast. (German)

As fortune is sought, so it is found. (German)

Avoid asking what the future will bring, and every day that Fortune shall grant you, set down as gain. (Roman)

Each person is the architect of his own fortune. (Roman)

Every man is the maker of his own fortune. (Roman)

Everyone should stay within the bounds of his own fortune. (Roman)

Everything may be borne except good fortune. (Italian)

Fortune aids the bold. (Spanish)

Fortune aids the brave. (Roman)

Fortune and flowers do not last forever. (Chinese)

Fortune and glass break soon, alas! (Dutch)

Fortune and misfortune are neighbors. (German)

Fortune and misfortune are two buckets in the same well. (German)

Fortune and the arts assist each other. (Roman)

Fortune can take from us only what she has given us. (French)

Fortune cannot take away what she did not give. (Roman)

Fortune comes to a smiling house. (Japanese)

Fortune comes to him who strives for it. (Italian)

Fortune depends on the virtue of the heart. (Chinese)

Fortune does not change nature. (Roman)

Fortune does not stand waiting at anyone's door. (Dutch)

Fortune enriches or tramples on us at her will. (Roman)

Fortune favors fools. (Roman)

Fortune favors the brave. (Roman)

Fortune favors the bold, but abandons the timid. (Roman)

Fortune favors the young. (Roman)

Fortune finds us friends. (Roman)

Fortune gives many too much, but no one enough. (German)

Fortune gives her hand to a bold man. (German)

Fortune helps a man even against his will. (Roman)

Fortune in brief moments works great changes in our affairs. (Roman)

Fortune is a woman: if you neglect her today, expect not to regain her tomorrow. (French)

Fortune is as fickle as she is fair. (German)

Fortune is blind. (Roman)

Fortune is like glass; when it sparkles, it is broken. (Roman)

Fortune is made of glass. (Rumanian)

Fortune is mother to one, step-mother to another. (Roman)

Fortune is not content to do someone an ill turn only once. (Roman)

Fortune makes a fool of him whom she would ruin. (Roman)

Fortune may steal our wealth, but it cannot take away our courage. (Roman)

Fortune, not wisdom, rules this life. (Roman)

Fortune often knocks at the door, but the fool does not invite her in. (Danish)

Fortune rarely brings good or evil singly. (Danish)

Fortune shields more than it makes safe. (Roman)

Fortune smiles on the brave, and frowns upon the coward. (Roman)

Fortune smiles upon our first effort. (Roman)

Fortune spurns the prayers of cowards. (Roman)

Fortune takes nothing away but what she also gave. (Roman)

Fortune wearies with carrying one and the same man always. (Roman)

Fortune, when she caresses a man too much, makes him a fool. (Roman)

Fortunes are heaven-born gifts. (Italian)

From fortune to misfortune is but a step, from misfortune to fortune is a long way. (Yiddish)

Good fortune smiles on the prosperous. (Korean)

Greater qualities are needed to bear good fortune than bad. (French)

He dances well to whom fortune fiddles. (German)

He who has the fortune brings home the bride. (German)

If bad fortune is in store, let it come at once. (Unknown)

If fortune favors you, do not be elated; if fortune frowns, do not sink in despair. (Roman)

If fortune turns against you, even jelly breaks your teeth. (Persian)

In the greatest fortune lies the least liberty. (Roman)

It is easier to find fortune than to keep hold of it. (Roman)

It is easy to manage when fortune favors. (Danish)

It is when Fortune is most propitious that she is least to be trusted. (Roman)

Make a fortune by honest means, if you can; if not, by any means you can. (Roman)

Man is the architect of his own fortune. (Roman)

Man's fortune and misfortune are like a twisted rope. (Japanese)

May those be happy whose fortunes are already completed! (Roman)

Misfortune and fortune have no door; men themselves incur or win them. (Chinese)

No man has perpetual good fortune. (Roman)

No man knows fortune till he dies. (Dutch)

No one is perfectly satisfied with what fortune allots him. (Roman)

Nothing is worse than being accustomed to good fortune. (Roman)

Once in each man's life fortune smiles. (Roman)

Only he is loved who is the favorite of fortune. (Roman)

Our wisdom is no less at fortune's mercy than our wealth. (Dutch)
Some people make their fortune during times of turmoil. (Mexican)
Something is always wanting to our imperfect fortune. (Roman)
The custody of a large fortune is a wretched business. (Roman)
The footsteps of fortune are slippery. (Roman)
The gifts of fortune do not always benefit us. (Roman)
The good fortunes of life fall to the lot even of the base. (Roman)
The highest spoke in fortune's wheel may soon turn lowest. (Roman)
To a bold man fortune holds out her hand. (French)
To many fortune gives too much, to none does it give enough. (Roman)
We are corrupted by good fortune. (Roman)
What fortune gives today, it takes away tomorrow. (German)
When a man prospers, who does not come?; when fortune falters, who comes?
   (Chinese)
When Fortune calls, offer her a chair. (Yiddish)
When fortune knocks, open the door. (German)
While fortune lasts you will see your friend's face. (Roman)
Whom fortune favors, the world favors. (German)
Wife and children are hostages given to fortune. (English)
Wind and fortune are not lasting. (Portuguese)

Fortune-teller
A fortune–teller cannot tell her own fortune. (Japanese)

Forward
Not to go forward is to go backward. (Roman)

Foul
Foul in the beginning, foul in the end. (Roman)
No harm, no foul. (American)

Foundation
A weak foundation destroys the work upon which it is built. (Roman)
Remove the foundation and the structure falls. (Roman)

Fountain
A fountain is clearest at its source. (German)
At a little fountain one drinks at one's ease. (French)

Fowl
Good is the fowl which another rears. (Spanish)
The disobedient fowl obeys in a pot of soup. (Nigerian)

Fox
A fox is known by its tail. (Roman)

A fox is not caught twice in the same trap. (Roman)

A fox smells its own lair first. (English)

A good fox does not eat its neighbor's fowls. (French)

An old fox does not run twice into the snare. (German)

An old fox is not caught in a snare. (Roman)

At last the foxes all meet at the furrier's. (Italian)

At length the fox loses its teeth. (German)

Bear and bull catch no fox. (German)

Don't sell the skin till you have caught the fox. (Danish)

Even old foxes are caught in the snare. (Italian)

Every fox likes a hen roost. (Italian)

He sets the fox to keep the geese. (English)

It is a poor fox that has but one hole. (German)

It is difficult to trap an old fox. (Danish)

Let every fox take care of its own tail. (Italian)

Many foxes grow gray, but few grow good. (Poor Richard)

Never set the fox as guard over your chickens. (German)

Nothing falls into the mouth of a sleeping fox. (French)

'Our own kin are the worst friends', said the fox, when he saw the dogs after him.
    (Danish)

Set a fox to catch a fox. (Danish)

Take care of your geese when the fox preaches. (Danish)

The fox cannot hide its tail. (German)

The fox does not go twice into the same trap. (Danish)

The fox does not prey near its hole. (German)

The fox is knowing, but more knowing is he who catches him. (Spanish)

The fox knows well with whom it plays tricks. (Spanish)

The fox may grow gray, but never good. (Roman)

The fox may lose its skin, but not its cunning. (Dutch)

The fox never fares better than when it's banned. (Dutch)

The fox never sees its own tail. (Mexican)

The fox sits but once on a thorn. (Armenian)

The fox that sleeps in the morning has not his tongue feathered. (French)

The fox thinks everybody eats poultry like itself. (French)

The fox thrives best when it is most cursed. (French)

The more the fox is cursed, the more prey it catches. (Italian)

The old fox easily smells a trap. (Spanish)

The sleeping fox catches no poultry. (Danish)

When the fox licks its paw, let the farmer check on his geese. (Danish)

When the fox loses the swan, he says he's not hungry. (German)

When you bargain with a fox, beware of tricks. (Roman)

Where there are no dogs the fox is king. (Italian)

With the fox one must play the fox. (Italian)

Foxhole

Never share a foxhole with anyone braver than you are. (French)
There are no atheists in foxholes. (American)

Fragrance

A bit of fragrance always clings to the hand that gives you roses. (Chinese)
Even the sprout of the sandalwood is fragrant. (Japanese)
The more thorns, the greater the fragrance. (Roman)

Fraud

Fraud and deceit are always in haste. (English)
Fraud deals in generalities. (Roman)
Fraud is not fraud, unless craftily planned. (Roman)
It is fraud to conceal fraud. (Roman)
No one can bring suit for his own fraud. (Roman)

Free, Freedom

All are not free who mock their chains. (German)
Better a free bird than a captive king. (Danish)
Better to be free in a foreign land than a serf at home. (German)
Every man's freedom is his own. (German)
Freedom has roots in blood. (Albanian)
Freedom is from God, freedoms from the Devil. (German)
He is not free who drags his chain after him. (Italian)
In a free state there should be freedom of speech and thought. (Roman)
Injurious is the gift that takes away freedom. (Italian)
Nothing in life is free. (American)
Where freedom is, there shall my country be. (Roman)

Frenchman

When the Frenchman sleeps the Devil rocks him. (French)

Friar

The friar who begs for God begs for two. (Spanish)
Where friars abound keep your eyes open. (Spanish)

Friend, Friends

A brother may not be a friend, but a friend will always be a brother. (Poor Richard)
A clear bargain, a dear friend. (Italian)
A fair-weather friend changes with the wind. (Spanish)
A friend at court is worth a penny in one's purse. (Irish)
A friend at one's back is a safe bridge. (Dutch)
A friend by thee is better than a brother far off. (Irish)
A friend in need is a friend indeed. (English)
A friend is better than money in the purse. (Dutch)

A friend is known in time of need. (French)
A friend is not known till he is lost. (Italian)
A friend is one soul in two bodies. (Roman)
A friend is proven in time of necessity. (Roman)
A friend is the solace of life. (Roman)
A friend is to be taken with his faults. (Portuguese)
A friend to all is a friend to none. (German)
A friend to everybody is a friend to nobody. (Spanish)
A friend to my table and wine, is no good neighbor. (French)
A friend, and look to thyself. (Italian)
A friend's dinner is soon dressed. (Dutch)
A friend's eye is a good mirror. (Irish)
A friend's frown is better than a fool's smile. (Danish)
A friend's meat is soon ready. (French)
A good friend is better than silver and gold. (Dutch)
A man's oldest friend is his best. (Roman)
A mile walk with a friend has only one hundred steps. (Russian)
A reconciled friend is a double enemy. (Spanish)
A rock offered by a friend is like an apple. (Sicilian)
A small house will hold a hundred friends. (German)
A stone from the hand of a friend is an apple. (Moroccan)
A table friend is changeable. (French)
A thousand cups of wine do not suffice when true friends meet, but half a sentence is
    too much when there is no meeting of minds. (Chinese)
A true friend is a rare bird. (Roman)
A true friend is a second self. (Roman)
A true friend is certain when certainty is uncertain. (Roman)
A true friend laughs at your stories even when they're not so good, and sympathizes
    with your troubles even when they're not so bad. (Irish)
Admonish your friends secretly, but praise them openly. (Roman)
All are not friends who smile on you. (Dutch)
All things are common among friends. (Roman)
An enemy will agree, but a friend will argue. (Russian)
An old friend met in a far country is like rain after drought. (Chinese)
At the narrow passage there is no brother and no friend. (Arabian)
Avoid a friend who covers you with his wings and destroys you with his beak. (Spanish)
Be on such terms with your friend as if you knew that he might one day become your
    enemy. (Roman)
Be slow in choosing a friend, slower in changing. (Poor Richard)
Beat the churl and he will be your friend. (Italian)
Better a friend than money to spend. (Dutch)
Better a friend's bite than an enemy's caress. (Danish)
Better a good enemy than a bad friend. (Yiddish)
Better an open enemy than a false friend. (Danish)
Better one old friend than two new ones. (Yiddish)

Better to have a friend on the road than gold or silver in your purse. (French)

Better to have friends in the marketplace than money in your coffer. (Portuguese)

Beware of a reconciled friend as of the Devil. (Spanish)

Conceal not your secret from your friend, or you deserve to lose him. (Portuguese)

Do not protect yourself by a fence, but rather by your friends. (Czech)

Do not tell even a true friend your true feelings. (Korean)

Every man's friend is every man's fool. (Danish)

Everybody's friend is true to none. (Norwegian)

Everybody's friend, nobody's friend. (Italian)

Fall sick, and you will see who is your friend – and who not. (Spanish)

Farewell and be hanged; friends must part! (Chinese)

Few there are that will endure a true friend. (Danish)

Forbear a quarrel with a friend: anger breeds hatred; concord sweetens love. (Dutch)

Friends and mules fail in hard trials. (Rumanian)

Friends and wine: the older the better. (Spanish)

Friends are flowers in the garden of life. (Portuguese)

Friends are known in time of need. (Dutch)

Friends are known in times of danger. (Irish)

Friends are like fiddle strings: they must not be screwed too tight. (Italian)

Friends are proved by adversity. (Roman)

Friends are sometimes troublesome. (Roman)

Friends are thieves of time. (English)

Friends are to be regarded from deeds, not words. (Roman)

Friends may meet, but mountains never greet. (Roman)

Friends of our friends are our friends. (French)

Friends should have a high wall between them. (Chinese)

Friends tie their purses with a spider's web. (Italian)

Full of men, vacant of friends. (Roman)

Give as though you have many friends, but know that you have but few. (French)

Go often to the house of a friend; for weeds soon choke up the unused path. (Swedish)

God keep me from my friends, from my enemies I will keep myself. (Italian)

Good accounts make good friends. (Greek)

Good fellow to everyone, good friend to no one. (Yiddish)

Good friends appear in difficulties. (Roman)

Guard against taking sides against your friends. (Irish)

Have but few friends though many acquaintances. (Chinese)

He is my friend that grinds at my mill. (Danish)

He is my friend that succors me, not he that pities me. (Danish)

He is no friend that eats his own by himself, and mine with me. (Portuguese)

He is your friend who gets you out of a fray. (Spanish)

He never was a friend who ceased to be so for a slight cause. (Portuguese)

He that seeks to have many friends never has any. (Italian)

He who is everybody's friend is either very poor or very rich. (Spanish)

He who makes friends of all keeps none. (German)

I am ever my own best friend. (Roman)

If you have a good friend, you don't need a mirror. (German)

In dress, the newest is the finest; in friends, the oldest is the best. (Korean)

In happy times we reckon many friends; but if fortune fails, we will have no friends.
(Roman)

It is as bad to have too many friends as no friends at all. (Roman)

It is easier to visit friends than to live with them. (Chinese)

It is good to have friends but bad to need them. (German)

It is good to have friends even in Hell. (Serbian)

Know well, but take no offense at the manners of a friend. (Roman)

Liberal hands make many friends. (Danish)

Love your friend with her faults. (Italian)

Make a friend when you don't need one. (Jamaican)

Make new friends, but don't forget the old ones. (Yiddish)

Many friends will sit at the same table. (German)

Mind neither storms nor snows for the sake of a friend. (Georgian)

No man can be happy without a friend, or be sure of his friend till he is unhappy.
(Roman)

Of everything else the newest; of friends, the oldest. (Kurdish)

Of oil, wine, and friends, the oldest is the best. (Portuguese)

Old friends and old ways ought not to be disdained. (Danish)

Old friends and old wine are best. (German)

On the road between the homes of friends, grass does not grow. (Norwegian)

Once a friend, always a friend. (Kurdish)

One can care little for man, but we need a friend. (Chinese)

One enemy is too many, a hundred friends is too few. (German)

One God, one wife, but many friends. (Dutch)

One should go invited to a friend in good fortune, and uninvited in misfortune.
(Swedish)

One who looks for a friend without faults will have none. (Yiddish)

Only your real friends will tell you when your face is dirty. (Burmese)

Over the bottle many a friend is found. (Yiddish)

Peel a fig for your friend, a peach for your enemy. (Italian)

Promises may make friends, but performance keeps them. (German)

Save us from our friends. (Italian)

Short reckonings make long friends. (English)

Tell me who's your friend and I'll tell you who you are. (Russian)

Tell your friend a lie; if he keeps it secret, tell him the truth. (Spanish)

The best of friends must part. (English)

The constant friend is never welcome. (Yiddish)

The false friend is like the shadow of a sundial. (French)

The name of friend is common, but a faithful friend is rare. (Roman)

The road to a friend's house is never long. (Danish)

The same man cannot be both friend and flatterer. (Poor Richard)

There is no need like the lack of a friend. (Irish)

There's no living without friends. (Portuguese)

To be intimate with a foolish friend, is like going to bed to a razor. (Poor Richard)

To lose a friend is the greatest of all losses. (Roman)

True friends are tested in adversity. (Roman)

When you know who his friend is, you know who he is. (African)

Where friends, there riches. (German)

Without friends to share it, no good we possess is truly enjoyable. (Roman)

You can hardly make a friend in a year, but you can easily offend one in an hour. (Chinese)

You may be sure that the one who is a friend to himself is a friend to all. (Roman)

Friendship, Friendships

A broken friendship may be mended but never made completely whole. (Yoruban)

A dissimilarity of pursuits dissolves friendship. (Roman)

After a quarrel comes friendship. (Unknown)

After friendship, you should render implicit belief; before friendship, you should exercise judgment. (Roman)

As the yellow gold is tested in the fire, so the faith of friendship can only be known in the time of adversity. (Roman)

Broken friendship may be soldered but can never be made sound. (Portuguese)

Ceremony is the smoke of friendship. (Chinese)

Conviviality reveals secrets. (Roman)

Feigned friendship is to be avoided. (Roman)

Friendship always benefits; love sometimes injures. (Roman)

Friendship broken may be mended, but never made whole. (Spanish)

Friendship is as it is kept. (Irish)

Friendship is but a name; fidelity but an empty name. (Roman)

Friendship is good, but absence from friends is painful. (Irish)

Friendship lasts as long as the pot boils. (Roman)

Friendship with the powerful is pleasant to the inexperienced, but he who has experienced it dreads it. (Roman)

Friendships are cheap when they can be brought by doffing the hat. (Italian)

Friendships know no age. (Spanish)

Friendships should be immortal, enmities should be mortal. (Roman)

Gold is proved in the fire, friendship in need. (Danish)

He takes the greatest ornament from friendship, who takes modesty from it. (Roman)

He that ends a friendship was never a good friend. (German)

In forming new friendships, forget not old friends. (Roman)

Little presents maintain friendship. (French)

Looking too closely at the affairs of a friend spoils the friendship. (Yoruban)

Love is blind, friendship closes its eyes. (Chinese)

Love will enter cloaked in friendship's name. (Roman)

Many pecks of salt must be eaten before the duties of friendship can be discharged. (Roman)

Neglect dissolves many friendships. (Roman)

Of clothing, the newer the better; of friendships, the older the better. (Chinese)

Offer not the right hand of friendship to everyone. (Roman)

Praise paves the way to friendship. (Danish)
Reconciled friendship is like a badly healed wound. (Danish)
Robbing life of friendship is like robbing the world of the sun. (Roman)
Shared friendship is a double friendship. (German)
Spend a new penny on an old friend and share an old pleasure with a new friend.
    (Chinese)
The common crowd seeks friendships for their usefulness. (Roman)
The friendship of a great man is like the shadow of a bush, soon gone. (French)
The friendship of officials is as thin as paper. (Chinese)
The friendship of the great is fraternity with lions. (Italian)
The image of friendship is truth. (Egyptian)
The purse strings are the most common ties of friendship. (English)
There cannot be friendship without virtue. (Roman)
There is no life without friendship. (Roman)
To give counsel, as well as take it, is a feature of true friendship. (Roman)
To preserve friendship one must build walls. (Italian)
True friendship is seen through the heart, not through the eyes. (American)
While the pot boils, friendship blooms. (German)
While you seek new friendships, take care to cultivate the old ones. (Roman)
You cannot knit up a raveled friendship. (Yiddish)

Frog, Frogs
A frog in a well is best off in the well. (Chinese)
Even a frog would bite if it had teeth. (Italian)
If a man falls in love with a frog, he thinks his frog a very goddess. (Roman)
If the father is a frog, the son will be a frog. (Japanese)
Never try to catch two frogs with one hand. (Chinese)
The frog does not jump in the daytime without reason. (Nigerian)
The frog forgets its days as a tadpole. (Korean)
The frog in the well cannot speak of the ocean. (Chinese)
The frog likes water, but not boiling water. (West African)
The frog will jump back into the pool, although it sits on a golden stool. (Dutch)
Though you seat the frog on a golden stool, he'll soon jump off again and into the pool.
    (German)
Where there are no swamps there are no frogs. (German)

Frost
The frost hurts not weeds. (Dutch)
The frost never covers the grass under a great tree. (Chinese)
What God will, no frost can kill. (English)

Frugal, Frugality
Frugality is an estate alone. (Roman)

Fruit

All shall eat the fruit of their actions. (Indian)

Blossoms are the pledge of fruit. (Danish)

Don't show me the palm tree, show me the dates. (Afghani)

Earned fruit tastes good. (German)

Forbidden fruit is sweet. (English)

Good fruit never comes from a bad tree. (Portuguese)

Good tree, good fruit. (Dutch)

He that would eat the fruit must climb the tree. (German)

He who would enjoy the fruit must not spoil the blossoms. (Irish)

Late fruit keeps well. (German)

Little wood, much fruit. (Dutch)

Looking at a tree see its fruit; looking at a man see his deeds. (Russian)

Ripe fruit will fall of its own accord. (German)

Stolen fruit is sweet. (French)

The fruit falls not far from the stem. (Dutch)

The fruit of the earth was created for humanity's use. (Roman)

The hanging fruit is never too heavy for the vine to bear. (Portuguese)

The most attractive fruit is often the most bitter. (German)

The oldest trees often bear the sweetest fruit. (German)

There is no tree but bears some fruit. (German)

There is no worse fruit than that which never ripens. (Italian)

When all fruit falls, welcome haws. (English)

Fuel

Take away fuel, take away flame. (German)

Full

A full bottle won't shake, a half-empty one will. (Chinese)

A full cup must be carried carefully. (English)

A full man is no eater. (Portuguese)

A full moon wanes, a full bloom falls, a full cup runs over, and ripened fruit drops to the ground. (Korean)

A full mouse finds the meal bitter. (German)

A full purse is not so good as an empty purse is bad. (Yiddish)

A full purse never lacks friends. (Chinese)

A full sack pricks up its ears. (Italian)

A full stomach praises Lent. (Danish)

Full cup, steady hand. (Dutch)

Full vessels give the least sound. (German)

Men are like bagpipes: no sound comes from them till they're full. (Irish)

When the measure is full, it runs over. (German)

When the river is full the well is full. (Chinese)

When the sack is full, it pricks up its ears. (German)

Funeral
One funeral makes many. (English)

Funny
There's nothing so funny as folk. (English)

Future
He who has no care for the far future will have sorrow in the near future. (Korean)
It is possible to infer the future from the past. (Roman)
Learn the future by looking at things past. (Indian)
No one lives in the future. (American)
The future is future: live today. (American)
The future is inscrutable. (Roman)

G

Gad, Gadabout
A gadding girl is rarely coy. (Roman)
Women and hens are lost by too much gadding about. (Italian)

Gain, Gains
Gain does not rejoice as much as loss grieves. (Greek)
Gain has a pleasant odor, come whence it will. (Portuguese)
Gain made at the expense of reputation is reckoned loss. (Roman)
Great gains cover many losses. (English)
Light gains make a heavy purse. (Dutch)
Men see the gain, not the danger. (Chinese)
No gain without pain. (English)
No one ought to gain by another person's loss. (Roman)
Sometimes the best gain is to lose. (English)
The earthen pan gains nothing by contact with the copper pot. (Danish)
The hope of gain spurs us on. (Spanish)

Gall, Galling
It is galling to be injured by one against whom you dare not make a complaint. (Roman)
Nothing is more galling than a low man raised to a high position. (Roman)

Gallows
Everyone is a preacher under the gallows. (Dutch)
The gallows takes its own. (Spanish)
The gallows was made for the unlucky. (Spanish)

Gamble, Gambling
Better a son given to gambling than a son given to drink. (Irish)

Gambling sire, gambling son. (Portuguese)

God defend you from the Devil, the eye of a harlot, and the turn of a die. (Spanish)

Hoping to recoup is what ruins the gambler. (Irish)

In gambling, winning money results in losing money. (Chinese)

Keep flax from fire, youth from gaming. (Poor Richard)

Know when to hold 'em, know when to fold 'em. (American)

Like wind blows on egg shells, when a gambler loses his money he feels light [i.e., at ease]. (Chinese)

Losing comes of winning money. (Chinese)

There are two great pleasures in gambling: winning and losing. (French)

Game

At the end of the game we see who wins. (Italian)

It is a bad game where nobody wins. (Italian)

It is well to leave off playing when the game is at its best. (French)

It's not whether you win or lose but how you play the game. (American)

The importance of the game is greater for being lost. (Unknown)

Gamekeeper

An old poacher makes the best gamekeeper. (French)

Gap

Great gaps may be filled with small stones. (Dutch)

Gape

It is useless to gape against an oven. (Danish)

Garbage

Garbage in, garbage out. (American)

Garden, Gardener

A lazy man's garden is full of weeds. (Spanish)

As is the gardener, so is the garden. (German)

Cultivate the garden within. (Roman)

Everyone is nice until the cow gets into the garden. (Irish)

He who plants a garden plants happiness. (German)

In the garden more grows than the gardener sows. (Spanish)

She is fond of greens who kisses the gardener. (Spanish)

Tend to your own garden. (French)

The bad gardener quarrels with his rake. (American)

The gardener's feet do no harm to the garden. (Spanish)

Garland, Garlands

Garlands are not for every brow. (Chinese)

Garlic
Garlic is as good as ten mothers. (Indian)
Garlic makes a man wink, drink, and stink. (English)

Garment
Patching makes a garment last; inattention makes one threadbare. (Yoruban)
The garment, though ragged, answers a very good purpose. (Chinese)

Gate
Don't shut the gate after the horse has bolted. (English)
The gates of tears are never shut. (Yiddish)

Gather, Gathering
Gather and spare can last long. (Norwegian)
One knows not for whom he gathers. (French)
The smaller the gathering the higher the spirits. (Yiddish)

Gaunt
A gaunt brute bites sore. (French)
Fleas haunt a gaunt dog. (the Editor)

Gem
A gem, unless polished, does not glitter. (Japanese)
An uncut gem does not sparkle. (English)
Even a gem has a flaw. (Korean)
Unpolished jade does not make a gem. (Chinese)

Generation
It takes three generations to make a gentleman. (American)
One generation opens the road upon which another generation travels. (Chinese)
One generation plants the trees under whose shade another takes its ease. (Chinese)

Generosity, Generous
A generous man, they say, has never gone to Hell. (Irish)
Generosity is wealth. (African)
Generosity is worth going out to meet. (Irish)
Generous minds are all of kin. (Poor Richard)
Generous with the mouth, stingy with the purse. (German)
God shares with the person who is generous. (Irish)
It is easy to be generous with another man's money. (German)
It is easy to be generous with what is another's. (Roman)
No one is so generous as he who has nothing to give. (French)
The generosity of the poor is the best. (Arabian)

Genius

Genius dies young. (Unknown)

Genius does not have one form and courage another. (Roman)

Genius is an infinite capacity for taking pains. (Dutch)

Genius often goes to waste through misfortune. (Roman)

Genius without education is like silver in the mine. (Poor Richard)

How often does it happen that great genius is hidden in obscurity. (Roman)

The honor accorded to genius is immortal. (Roman)

There has not been any great genius without an element of madness. (Roman)

Gentleman

A true gentleman would rather have his clothes torn than mended. (Spanish)

It takes three generations to make a gentleman. (American)

Gentle, Gentleness

A gentle hand may lead even an elephant by a hair. (Persian)

A gentle word opens an iron gate. (Bulgarian)

All things gently but firmly. (Roman)

Gentleness does more than violence. (French)

Gentleness is the remedy for cruelty. (Roman)

German

German language, hard language. (German)

Get Along

To get along, go along. (American)

Ghost

Call no man ghost until he is dead. (Jamaican)

Even a ghost will listen if you beg. (Korean)

Love, thieves, and fear, make ghosts. (German)

One ought not to wrestle with ghosts. (Roman)

Giant

A giant will keep his size even though he will have stood in a well. (Roman)

He who rides on the giant's shoulders sees further than he who carries him. (French)

Pygmies on a giant's back see more than the giant himself. (Roman)

Surrounding yourself with dwarfs does not make you a giant. (Yiddish)

Gift, Gifts

A gift delayed is not given, but sold dear. (Italian)

A gift with a kind countenance is a double present. (Italian)

A gift with a kind face is a double grace. (German)

A gift, though small, is welcome. (Greek)

Ever receive a present with approval. (Roman)

For a paltry gift, little thanks. (Roman)
Gifts are according to the giver. (German)
Gifts are often losses. (Italian)
Gifts break rock-hard hearts. (Spanish)
Gifts can soften even stone. (Filipino)
Gifts from enemies are dangerous. (Portuguese)
Gifts make friendship lasting. (Danish)
Gifts of enemies are unlucky. (Roman)
Gifts should be handed, not thrown. (Danish)
He gives well and bountifully who accompanies the gift with a pleasing look. (Roman)
He sends his gift with a hook attached. (Roman)
I would know your gift by your graciousness. (Irish)
It doubles the value of a gift to be well-timed. (Roman)
Man has no strength to requite the gifts of Heaven. (Chinese)
Many look with one eye at what they give, but with seven at what they receive.
   (German)
Never look a gift horse in the mouth. (German)
No purchase like a gift. (French)
Old thanks are not for new gifts. (Italian)
Secret gifts are openly rewarded. (Danish)
Small favors conciliate, but great gifts make enemies. (Roman)
Take gifts with a sigh: most men give to be paid. (Irish)
The giver makes the gift precious. (Roman)
The most acceptable gifts owe their value to the giver. (Roman)
Who received should give thanks; who gave should be silent. (German)

Ginger
The older the ginger, the more it bites. (Chinese)

Girl, Girls
A fine girl and a tattered gown always find something to hook them. (French)
A girl draws more than a rope. (Spanish)
A girl in her time is like honey in the comb. (Rumanian)
A girl unemployed is thinking of mischief. (French)
A girl with cotton stockings never sees a mouse. (American)
Boys will be boys and girls will be girls. (English)
Glasses and lasses are brittle ware. (Scottish)
Good girls go to Heaven, bad girls go everywhere. (American)
The girl as she is taught, the flax as it is wrought. (Spanish)
The girl herself is the least part of herself. (Roman)

Give, Giving
A person gives nothing who has nothing. (Roman)
Even the benevolent man reflects upon the cause of giving. (Roman)
Give a grateful man more than he asks. (Portuguese)

Give a little, take a little. (Portuguese)

Give a man some cloth and he'll ask for some lining. (Arabian)

Give a rogue an inch, and he will take an ell. (Danish)

Give a thing, and take a thing, to wear the Devil's gold ring. (Danish)

Give a traitor good words and you make him loyal. (Spanish)

Give an inch, lose a mile. (Unknown)

Give assistance, and receive thanks lighter than a feather; injure a man, and his wrath will be like lead. (Roman)

Give at first asking what you safely can; 'tis certain gain to help an honest man. (Dutch)

Give even an onion graciously. (Afghani)

Give every man his due. (Afghani)

Give him your finger and he will seize your hand. (Dutch)

Give me a seat, and I will make myself room to lie down. (Spanish)

Give one hour for the heart and one for God. (Egyptian)

Give the span, give the inch. (Scottish)

Give to a pig when it grunts, and to a child when it cries, and you will have a fine pig and a bad child. (Danish)

Give to him that has. (Italian)

Give to others and do not regret. (Chinese)

Give to the poor and you will become rich. (Spanish)

Give unto the king what is the king's, and unto God what is God's. (German)

Give willingly all you have to one who can take it all by force. (Spanish)

Givers expect to be getters. (American)

Giving has no bottom. (Roman)

Giving requires good sense. (Roman)

He gives too late who waits to be asked. (Roman)

He gives twice who gives in a thrice. (German)

He gives twice who gives on time. (Roman)

He who gives little gives from his heart; he who gives much gives from his wealth. (Turkish)

He who gives quickly, gives doubly. (German)

He who gives to the poor, lends to the Lord. (German)

He who gives to the public, gives to no one. (Spanish)

He who would take must give. (Spanish)

If you always give, you will always have. (Chinese)

If you continually give, you will continually have. (Chinese)

If you give an inch, he'll take a mile. (American)

If you have much, give of your wealth; if you have little, give of your heart. (Arabian)

If you have, give; if you lack, seek. (Malayan)

If you would take, first give. (Japanese)

In return for a fish, he gives water. (Hausan)

It is better to give than to receive. (Italian)

It is more blessed to give than to receive. (Jesus)

Let the giver be silent and the receiver speak. (Portuguese)

No one can give what he does not have. (Roman)

No one gives without wishing something in return. (the Editor)
One who constantly gives will constantly have wealth and honor. (Chinese)
Sitting you give, standing your receive. (Korean)
Some men give with a spoon and take with a bucket. (German)
The man who gives thinking to receive deserves to be deceived. (Roman)
The one who gives quickly, gives a double benefit to the needy. (Roman)
They that give are ever welcome. (English)
They who give have all things; they who withhold have nothing. (Hindu)
To give and take back is worse that stealing. (German)
To him who can take what you have, give what he asks. (Italian)
What you give away you keep. (Kurdish)
Whatever I have given, I still possess. (Roman)
Whatever we give to the wretched, we lend to fortune. (Roman)
When you give the cow, you give the milk as well. (German)
While you look at what is given, look also at the giver. (Roman)
Who gives to me, teaches me to give. (Dutch)
Who gives, teaches a return. (Italian)

Give and Take
A taker is not a giver. (Yiddish)
All we take with us into the next life is what we have given away. (Indian)
If you would take, first give. (Japanese)
The generous man grows rich in giving, the miser poor in taking. (Danish)
The one who has given today may take away tomorrow. (Roman)
We give and take in turn. (Roman)
What you give, is written in sand; what you take, with an iron hand. (German)

Glass
He who has a glass roof must not throw stones at others. (German)
He whose house is tiled with glass should not throw stones at his neighbor's. (Spanish)
People who live in glass houses shouldn't throw stones. (English)

Glean
One must glean at harvest time. (German)

Globefish
The poison globefish is sweet, but life is sweeter. (Japanese)

Glory
Desire of glory is the last garment that even wise men take off. (Roman)
Glory draws all bound to her shining carriage, low-born and high-born alike. (Roman)
Glory is the fair child of peril. (Unknown)
Glory is the shadow of virtue. (Roman)
Glory paid to the dead comes too late. (Roman)
How difficult is the custody of glory. (Roman)

If glory comes after death, then I am in no hurry. (Roman)

Sudden glory soon fades. (German)

The glory of ancestors should not prevent a man from winning glory for himself. (Serbian)

The love of glory gives an immense stimulus. (Roman)

The one who despises glory will have true glory. (Roman)

When glory comes memory departs. (French)

Glove

A white glove often conceals a dirty hand. (Roman)

Glutton, Gluttony

A bellyful of gluttony will never study willingly. (French)

A fat belly does not produce fine sense. (Italian)

A glutton young, a beggar old. (German)

A small kitchen does not suffice for two gluttons. (Roman)

For a voracious beast pebbles in his feed. (Portuguese)

Glutton: one who digs his grave with his teeth. (French)

Gluttony has killed more than the sword. (French)

Mutton is meat for a glutton. (English)

He who is always drinking and stuffin', will in time become a ragamuffin. (German)

If it rained macaroni, what a fine time for gluttons! (Italian)

Many fall by the sword, but more from gluttony. (Roman)

The glutton becomes a merchant, the lazy man a priest. (Chinese)

Gnat

The gnat trusting itself to the flame is singed. (Roman)

Go, Going

By going gains the mill, and not by standing still. (Portuguese)

Go softly and look afar. (Dutch)

Going beyond is as bad as falling short. (Chinese)

He goes far who never turns. (English)

If you can't go over, you must go under. (Yiddish)

Nowhere invited to come, but go everywhere. (Korean)

One never goes so far as when one knows not where he is going. (French)

The slower you go, the farther you will be. (Russian)

Where everyone goes, the grass never grows. (German)

Who goes slowly goes far. (American)

Who goes softly goes safely, and he that goes safely goes far. (Italian)

Goad

If you strike a goad with your fist, your hand will suffer most. (Roman)

Goal

Before you can score you must first have a goal. (Greek)

Goat

A lame goat will not sleep by day. (Spanish)

Even a goat has its habits. (African)

Feed the goat to fill the pot. (Albanian)

It doesn't take a genius to spot a goat in a flock of sheep. (American)

One goat cannot carry another goat's tail. (Nigerian)

Put silk on a goat and it is still a goat. (Irish)

The chamois climbs high and yet is caught. (German)

The goat must browse where it is tied. (Rumanian)

The goat which has many owners will be left to die in the sun. (Haitian)

God, Gods

A rich man carries God in his pocket, a poor man in his heart. (Yiddish)

All things are possible with God. (Jesus)

Begin to weave and God will give the thread. (German)

Call on God, but row away from the rocks. (Indian)

Dear God: You do such wonderful things for complete strangers; why not for me?
   (Yiddish)

Do not wear the image of God in a ring. (Roman)

Don't burn false incense before a true god. (Chinese)

Each one makes his own dire passion a god. (Roman)

Each person is the image of God in miniature. (Roman)

Even God forgives fools. (Russian)

Every little blade of grass declares the presence of God. (Roman)

Every man for himself, and God for us all. (German)

Everyone sneezes as God pleases. (Spanish)

Everything has an end except God. (Dutch)

Father and mother are kind, but God is kinder. (Danish)

For man plans, but God arranges. (German)

God calls to himself those whom he loves. (Spanish)

God can bring good out of evil. (Spanish)

God chastises those he loves. (Spanish)

God comes at last, when we think he is farthest off. (Danish)

God comes with leaden feet, but strikes with iron hands. (Danish)

God created a world full of little worlds. (Yiddish)

God defends the right. (English)

God delays but doesn't forget. (Spanish)

God does not pay weekly, but pays at the end. (Dutch)

God gave teeth; He will give bread. (Lithuanian)

God gives a cursed one short horns. (Italian)

God gives burdens and shoulders to bear them. (Yiddish)

God gives clothes according to the cold. (Portuguese)

God gives little folks small gifts. (Danish)

God gives the milk, but not the pail. (Rumanian)

God gives wealth to one, happiness to another. (Irish)

God gives, but man must open his hand. (German)

God has his dwelling within every good man. (Roman)

God helps the strongest. (Dutch)

God helps those who help themselves. (American)

God is a good worker but loves to be helped. (Basque)

God is always opening his hand. (Spanish)

God is best known in not knowing him. (Christian)

God is nearer to you than your jugular vein. (Arabian)

God is no man's debtor. (German)

God looks to pure hands, not to full ones. (Roman)

God loves not a lying tongue. (Irish)

God loves the poor and helps the rich. (Yiddish)

God made man because he loves stories. (Yiddish)

God made us, and not we ourselves. (Roman)

God made us, and we admire ourselves. (Spanish)

God may love the poor man, but not the dirty one. (Spanish)

God never hides his face; all who seek will find him. (Spanish)

God never wounds with both hands. (Spanish)

God postpones, he does not overlook. (Turkish)

God promises a safe landing but not a calm passage. (Bulgarian)

God reproves with one hand and blesses with the other. (Yiddish)

God sells knowledge for labor, honor for risk. (Dutch)

God sends corn and the Devil mars the sack. (English)

God sends enough to all. (Roman)

God squeezes but he never chokes. (Mexican)

God stays long his hand but strikes at last. (Unknown)

God takes with one hand, and gives with the other. (Yiddish)

God visits us, but most of the time we are not at home. (French)

God will be present, whether asked or not. (Roman)

God will listen to you whatever cloak you wear. (Spanish)

God writes straight with crooked lines. (Spanish)

God's grace may be slow but it is certain. (Irish)

God's help is nearer than the door. (Irish)

God's mill grinds slow but sure. (German)

God's mill grinds slowly but it grinds fine. (Roman)

God's work is soon done. (French)

He that gave us teeth will give us bread. (Yiddish)

If God bids thee draw, he will find thee a rope; if he bids thee ride, he will find thee a horse. (Danish)

If God gives not bushelfuls, he gives spoonfuls. (Danish)

If God gives us bread, men will give us butter. (Yiddish)

If God be for us, who can be against us? (Christian)

If God so wills it, even a broom can shoot. (Yiddish)

If God wants people to suffer, he sends them too much understanding. (Yiddish)

If God were living on earth, people would break his windows. (Yiddish)

If you want to make God laugh, tell him your plans. (Spanish)

It is expedient that gods exist, and, given it is expedient, let us believe it. (Roman)

It is not good to trifle with the gods. (Roman)

Live among men as if God were watching; speak with God as if men were listening. (Roman)

Man doctors, God heals. (German)

Man drives but God holds the reins. (Yiddish)

Man is dearer to the gods than to himself. (Roman)

Man works and God blesses. (Icelandic)

No image-maker worships the gods. (Chinese)

Not even God above gets all men's love. (English)

Not every wood is fit for a statue of Mercury. (Roman)

Nothing is hidden from God. (Spanish)

Nothing is impossible with God. (Christian)

Nothing is so high and above all danger that is not below and in the power of God. (Roman)

Nothing is void of God; his work everywhere is filled with himself. (Roman)

Often when we are oppressed by one god, another comes to our help. (Roman)

One cannot have God for a father who does not have the Church for a mother. (Christian)

One God, one wife, but many friends. (Dutch)

Only God needs no one. (Spanish)

Piety and holiness of life will propitiate the gods. (Roman)

Put your trust in God, and keep your powder dry. (American)

Take the goods the gods provide. (English)

The deeds of men never escape the gods. (Roman)

The gods are said to aid the stronger. (Roman)

The gods assist the industrious. (Roman)

The gods care about great matters, but they neglect small ones. (Roman)

The gods do not gossip. (Yoruban)

The gods hate unjust men. (Roman)

The gods sell all things to hard labor. (Roman)

The gods send nuts to those without teeth. (Roman)

The gods strike believers and unbelievers alike. (Chinese)

The gods treat us mortals like so many balls to play with. (Roman)

The purse of God is large; let everyone ask him. (Spanish)

The rage of fortune is less directed against the humble, and God strikes more lightly on the low. (Roman)

There is a god within us, and we hold commerce with Heaven. (Roman)

There is nothing that God cannot do. (Roman)

Those whom God loves die young. (Spanish)

'Twas fear that first produced gods in the world. (Roman)

Unless a man is simple, he cannot recognize God. (Bengali)

We must bear what the gods lay on us. (Greek)

When God closes a door, he leaves open a window. (Spanish)

When God closes one door, he opens another. (German)
When God gives light he gives it for all. (Spanish)
When God gives the wound, he also gives the medicine to heal it. (Spanish)
When God gives, he gives to all. (Spanish)
When God will not, the saints cannot. (Spanish)
Where God bestows an office, he provides brains to fill it. (German)
Where God builds a church the Devil will build a chapel. (English)
Where God has his church the Devil will have his chapel. (Spanish)
Where the gods call, there one must go. (Roman)
Whom God blesses, no one can curse. (Jamaican, after the Bible)
Whom God would ruin, he first deprives of reason. (German)
Whom God would sorely vex, he endows with abundant sense. (Yiddish)
Whom Jupiter wishes to destroy, he first dements. (Roman)
Whom the gods would destroy, they first make mad. (Spanish)
Whom the Lord loves, He chastens. (German)
Without divine assistance we can achieve nothing. (Roman)

Godfather
When the child is christened you will have godfathers enough. (French)

Godliness
Peter is so godly that God does not improve his condition. (Spanish)

Gold
A gold key opens every door. (Italian)
A gold ring does not cure a felon. (Italian)
All that glitters is not gold. (Roman)
All that's yellow is not gold, and all white things are not eggs. (Irish)
All the puppets dance for gold. (German)
Better than gold is a tale rightly told. (Irish)
Better whole than patched with gold. (Danish)
Eloquence avails nothing against the voice of gold. (Roman)
Even Buddha Amitabha shines according to the quantity of gold offered. (Japanese)
Even the judgments of Hades may be swayed by gold. (Roman)
Every man thinks his copper is gold. (Danish)
Gold buys silver, but silvers does not buy gold. (Yiddish)
Gold can make a good man bad. (German)
Gold conquers without arms. (Unknown)
Gold does not buy everything. (Italian)
Gold dust blinds all eyes. (German)
Gold glitters in the mud. (Yiddish)
Gold goes in at any gate. (German)
Gold is gold, though it be in a rogue's purse. (Danish)
Gold is proved by fire. (Roman)
Gold is tested by fire, man by gold. (Chinese)

Gold is where you find it. (American)
Gold lies deep in the mountain, dirt on the highway. (German)
Gold makes an honest man an ill man. (English)
Gold may be bought too dear. (German)
Gold opens every door, save Heaven's. (German)
Gold rules all. (Unknown)
Gold rules the world. (Unknown)
Gold's father is dirt, yet it regards itself as noble. (Yiddish)
He that would make a golden gate, must bring a nail to it daily. (Dutch)
Man prates but gold speaks. (Italian)
No gold without dross. (English)
No lock will hold against the power of gold. (French)
Pure gold does not fear the fire. (Chinese)
So it goes in the world: one has the purse, the other has the gold. (German)
The Golden Rule: the one with the gold makes the rules. (American)
There is no lock, if the pick is of gold. (Spanish)
Thousand pieces of gold may not buy you what you like. (Chinese)
Today gold, tomorrow dust. (English)
When gold speaks, not even the least reason avails. (Roman)
When gold talks, every tongue is silent. (Italian)
Where gold avails, argument fails. (German)
Where gold reigns, so reigns vice. (German)
Yellow gold is more plentiful than white-haired friends. (Chinese)
You may speak with your gold and make other tongues silent. (Danish)

Golden

A golden bit makes none the better horse. (Italian)
A golden hammer breaks an iron gate. (German)
A golden key fits every door. (Hungarian)
A golden key opens any door. (Roman)
A golden key opens every door except that of Heaven. (Danish)
Golden dishes will never turn black. (Yiddish)
The golden ass passes everywhere. (Spanish)

Golden Age

The golden age was never the present age. (German)

Golden Rule

Do unto others as you would have done unto you. (English, after Jesus)

Gone

Here today, gone tomorrow. (German)
Thus got, thus gone. (Dutch)
You never know what you've got till it's gone. (English)

Good

All ask if a man be rich, no one if he be good. (English)

All things for the good. (Roman)

As often as we do good, we sacrifice. (Poor Richard)

Associate with the good and you will be one of them. (Spanish)

Be good to the child and he will come to you tomorrow. (Irish)

Better one good thing that is, than two good things that were (Irish)

Good and quickly seldom meet. (Portuguese)

Good finds good. (English)

Good is good if a man does good. (German)

Good is good, but better beats it. (Italian)

Good never comes too often. (Danish)

Good that comes too late, is as good as nothing. (Spanish)

I would rather be called good than well off. (Roman)

If the end is good, all will be good. (Roman)

If you can't be good, be careful. (English)

If you follow the good, you will become good. (Chinese)

It is easy to be good, when all that prevents it is far removed. (Roman)

More good is done without our knowledge than by us intended. (Roman)

No man looks for good when he is well. (Russian)

Nothing is great unless it is good. (Roman)

So good that he is good for nothing. (Italian)

The good die young. (American)

The good is never late. (Irish)

The good is the enemy of the best. (Roman)

The good we do today becomes the happiness of tomorrow. (Indian)

There are only two good men: one is dead and the other unborn. (Chinese)

When you're good to others, you are best to yourself. (Poor Richard)

Where there's no good within, no good comes out. (Dutch)

With the good we become good. (Dutch)

Worldly good is ebb and flow. (Dutch)

Good and Bad

Bad and good are intertwined like rope. (Japanese)

Don't reject the good together with the bad. (Italian)

He begins to grow bad who believes himself good. (Italian)

One man is not bad because another is good. (Danish)

There is good and bad everywhere. (Italian)

There is no hour good for one man that is not bad for another. (Roman)

There's no bad that something good doesn't come from it. (Spanish)

Too good is bad for you. (Yiddish)

We must take the bad with the good. (English)

What is bad for one is good for another. (French)

What's good is often forgotten; what's bad is often hidden. (Norwegian)

Good and Evil

Better a distant good than a near evil. (Portuguese)
Better is the evil that is known than the good yet to be known. (Danish)
Good and evil are interwoven. (Japanese)
Good at a distance is better than evil at hand. (English)
Good comes from evil. (Unknown)
Good is mixed with evil, and evil is mixed with good. (Roman)
Goodness shouts, evil whispers. (Balinese)
Hide the evil, show the good. (Chinese)
In avoiding that which is evil we find that which is good. (Roman)
Manifest the good and punish the evil. (Chinese)
No good or evil lasts forever. (Spanish)
No good thing is failure and no evil thing success. (Italian)
One who stores up evil, though living, is dead; one who stores up goodness, though
    dead, is still living. (Chinese)
Out of a great evil often comes a great good. (Italian)
The good you do to be seen of men is not true goodness; the evil you are afraid to have
    men know is real evil. (Chinese)
Who has not experienced evil cannot appreciate goodness. (Spanish)

Good Deed

Do good and good days will be added to you. (Chinese)
Do good, and then do it again. (English)
Do good and throw it in the sea. (Arabian)
Do good and you shall find evil. (Egyptian)
Do good if you expect to receive it. (Arabian)
Do good in return for evil. (Irish)
Do good to a knave, and pray God he may not do the same to thee. (Danish)
Do good to thy friend to keep him, to thy enemy to gain him. (Poor Richard)
Do good without asking who the recipient will be. (Mexican)
Do good, and care not to whom. (Italian)
If those who do evil succeed and the honest do not, people will soon tire of doing good.
    (Yoruban)
Never weary of doing good. (Roman)

Good Faith

Good faith is a seldom guest, when you have him, hold him fast. (German)
Good faith stole the cow. (German)
If good faith be abolished, all human society is dissolved. (Roman)

Good Humor

Good humor gives good health. (German)

Good Life
A good life defers wrinkles. (Spanish)

Good Man, Good Person
A few good persons can do more than many not so good. (Spanish)
A good man in an evil society seems the greatest villain of all. (English)
A good man is a man of goods. (French)
A good man needs no recommendation. (Yiddish)
A good man's place is beneath the good earth. (Yiddish)
Good men are forever suckers. (German)
Good men are known by their enemies. (Chinese)
Good men are scarce. (Portuguese)
Good men hate to sin out of their love of virtue. (Roman)
Good men must die, but death cannot kill their names. (Spanish)
Good men ought to fear nothing from the rich. (Roman)
Good people live far asunder. (German)
It is part of a good man to love God and country. (Roman)
Of the good man a good pledge, and of the bad neither pledge nor surety. (Portuguese)
The tavern can't corrupt a good man, the synagogue can't reform a bad one. (Yiddish)
Would that Heaven would always produce good men, and that men would always do
     good. (Chinese)
You can't keep a good man down. (American)

Good Name
A good name covers theft. (Spanish)
A good name is a rich inheritance. (German)
A good name is better than a girdle of gold. (French)
A good name is better than fine clothes. (Vietnamese)
A good name is better than riches. (Dutch)
A good name is got by giving, not by wasting. (Irish)
A good name is like sweet-smelling ointment. (Roman)
A good name is more precious than gold. (Irish)
A good name is sooner lost than won. (German)
He is born in a good hour who gets a good name. (English)
How shall he who hath lost his good name gain his living? (Roman)
Take away my good name, take away my life. (French)

Good News
Before good news goes out the door, bad news is known for a thousand miles. (Chinese)
Good news knocks louder than bad. (Spanish)
Good news may be told at any time, but ill in the morning. (English)
He knocks boldly at the door who brings good news. (French)
No news is good news. (English)

Good Sense

Giving requires good sense. (Roman)
Good sense comes only with age. (Irish)
Men are seldom given good fortune and good sense at the same time. (Roman)
Where sense is wanting, every thing is wanting. (Poor Richard)

Good Thing, Good Things

A good thing is esteemed more in its absence than in its enjoyment. (Roman)
A good thing is known when it is lost. (Portuguese)
A good thing lost is a good thing valued. (Spanish)
A good thing lost is valued. (Italian)
All good things are three. (German)
All good things must come to an end. (English)
Cheap things are not good, good things are not cheap. (Chinese)
Do not wait for good things to search for you, but search for them. (Albanian)
Fear less, hope more, eat less, chew more, whine less, breathe more, talk less, say more,
    hate less, love more, and all good things will be yours. (Swedish)
Good things come in small packages. (Portuguese)
Good things come to those who wait. (American)
Good things require time. (Dutch)
Good things soon find a purchaser. (Roman)
You can't have too much of a good thing. (English)

Good Works

The door of good works is hard to open, but when opened it is hard to close. (Chinese)
The good works of this life are consumed in the next life. (Chinese)

Goodness

Concealed goodness is a sort of vice. (Portuguese)
It is not goodness to be better than the worst. (Roman)

Goodwill

The goodwill accompanying the gift is the best portion of it. (Roman)

Goose, Geese

A goose drinks as much as a gander. (Danish)
A wild goose never lays a tame egg. (English)
Geese are plucked as long as they have any feathers. (Dutch)
He that eats the king's geese shall be choked with the feathers. (Spanish)
It is a stupid goose that listens to the fox preach. (French)
Kill not the goose that lays the golden eggs. (English)
The goose goes so often into the kitchen, at last it is stuck on the spit. (Danish)
The goose hisses, but does not bite. (Dutch)
The goose that has a good gander cackles loudly. (Danish)
The goose that has lost its head no longer cackles. (Danish)

The goslings would lead the geese out to grass. (French)

What's good for the goose is good for the gander. (English)

What's sauce for the goose is sauce for the gander. (French)

When one goose drinks, all drink. (German)

Gossip

A gossip's mouth is the Devil's mailbag. (Irish)

A gossiping woman talks of everybody, and everybody of her. (Portuguese)

Do not blab abroad what is said in drink. (Scottish)

From my gossip's bread a large piece for my godson. (Spanish)

Gossip needs no carriage. (Russian)

Gossip when a needle stings, but when a knife it cuts. (Unknown)

He who tells his own secrets will hardly keep those of others. (Spanish)

If the ear does not hear malicious gossip, the heart is not grieved. (Yoruban)

It is merry when gossips meet. (English)

Many a thing whispered into one ear is heard over the whole town. (Danish)

The gossip thinks others gossip about him. (Yoruban)

The gossips fall out and tell each others' truths. (Spanish)

The more sifted, the finer the flour; the more repeated, the rougher the gossip. (Korean)

The mouths of gossips is a mortar, their tongues a pestle. (Unknown)

The one who gossips to you will gossip about you. (Turkish)

The whisperer's tongue is worse than serpent's venom. (Roman)

What is known by three will soon be known by thirty. (German)

What three know, everybody knows. (Spanish)

Whoever gossips to you will gossip about you. (Spanish)

Govern, Government

A community is as those who rule it. (Roman)

A state is regulated by two things: reward and punishment. (Greek)

Govern a horse with a bit, and a shrew with a stick. (Danish)

Govern yourself and you can govern the world. (Chinese)

Government is best which governs least. (American)

Hated governments never last long. (Roman)

No government is safe unless it be fortified by good will. (Roman)

The greatest empire may be lost by the misrule of its governors. (Roman)

Grace

Every flood has an ebb, save the flood of God's grace. (Irish)

Every tide has an ebb, save the tide of grace. (English)

God moves slowly, yet His grace comes. (Irish)

No need of grace before an empty glass. (Serbian)

The grace of God is found between the saddle and the ground. (Irish)

Grain

One grain of wheat does not fill a granary, but it helps. (Spanish)

Grammar
Caesar has no authority over the grammarians. (Roman)

Grandparent
The house with an old grandparent harbors a jewel. (Chinese)

Grape, Grapes
Guards and grape-gatherers eat the best grapes. (Spanish)
One basket of grapes does not make a vintage. (Italian)
The grape is not ripened by the rays of the moon. (Roman)
The sweetest grapes hang highest. (German)

Grasp
Grasp all, lose all. (Swedish)
Grasp no more than thy hand will hold. (Spanish)
He that grasps, loses. (Chinese)
He who grasps all loses all. (Spanish)
He who grasps too much holds on to too little. (Spanish)
He who grasps too much lets much fall. (German)
In grasping for things we need not, we often lose what we have. (English)

Grass
A patch of grass between two fighting buffaloes cannot survive. (Burmese)
Every blade of grass has its share of the dew of heaven. (Chinese)
Grass does not always remain green. (German)
Grass does not grow upon the highway. (German)
Grass is greener in other pastures. (Dutch)
Soft grass follows the wind. (Chinese)
The grass is always greener on the other side of the fence. (English)
The grass which you disregard will injure your eye. (Hausan)
The more you mow the lawn, the faster the grass grows. (Albanian)
The tallest blade of grass is the first to be cut by the scythe. (Russian)
While the grass grows, the steed starves. (English)

Grateful, Gratitude
A grateful dog is better than an ungrateful man. (Persian)
Animals are more grateful of favors than is man. (Chinese)
Don't overload gratitude; if you do, she'll kick. (Poor Richard)
Gratitude is the heart's memory. (French)
Gratitude is the least of virtues, but ingratitude the worst of vices. (French)
Let the grateful man think of repaying a kindness, even while receiving it. (Roman)
Swift gratitude is the sweetest. (Greek)

Grave
All our steps end in the grave. (Spanish)

Better imprisonment than the grave. (Irish)

Clay and lime conceal much evil. (Spanish)

Discard the superfluous honors at the grave. (Roman)

Don't dig your grave with your own knife and fork. (English)

For each man to whom Heaven gives birth, the earth provides a grave. (Chinese)

Graves are of all sizes. (English)

He who digs a grave for another, falls into it himself. (German)

He who lies in the grave, is well lodged. (German)

In war there is hope of peace, in the grave there is no hope of return. (Irish)

Six feet of earth make us all equal. (Italian)

The impartial earth opens alike for the child of the pauper and that of the king. (Roman)

The man digging the grave is burying a corpse; the one weeping is just making noise.
    (Yoruban)

The one who digs a grave for another is first to fall into it. (Sicilian)

There is rest enough in the grave. (German)

When an old man cannot drink, prepare his grave. (Spanish)

Gray Hair

A gray hair can sometimes appear on a young head. (German)

Gray hair is a sign of age, not wisdom. (Greek)

Gray hairs are death's blossoms. (German)

Grease

He who greases his wheels, helps his oxen. (Spanish)

Great

A great man can come from a hut. (Italian)

A great man often steps forth from a humble cottage. (Roman)

A great man's entreaty is a command. (Spanish)

A great oak is not felled by one stroke. (Spanish)

A great position entails great responsibility. (Spanish)

A truly great man will neither trample on a worm, nor sneak to an emperor. (Poor
    Richard)

From little things men go on to great. (Dutch)

Great men know each other. (Japanese)

Great men may joust with saints. (German)

Great men rejoice in adversity just as brave soldiers triumph in war. (Roman)

Great men's requests are commands. (Danish)

Great things are apt to clash. (Roman)

He is not so great who needs a servant. (German)

In order to be great, first be little. (Bengali)

Greater and Lesser

Greater and less do not change the nature of a thing. (Roman)

Who is not greater becomes lesser. (German)

Greatness

Greatness is only achieved through effort. (Hausan)

Greatness will show itself. (African)

It is true greatness to have in one's self the frailty of a man and the security of a god. (Roman)

No mediocrity, no greatness. (Japanese)

Greed, Greedy

A greedy father has thieves for children. (Serbian)

A greedy man God hates. (Serbian)

A greedy mill grinds all kinds of corn. (Danish)

A man can be cured of his lust, but never a fool of his greed. (Roman)

Ants die in sugar. (Malay)

But greed is rich and modesty poor. (Roman)

Greed tears a man's sack. (Mexican)

Greediness to reap helps not the money-heap. (Dutch)

Man's greed is greater than the ocean. (Korean)

The greedy are always needy. (Spanish)

The greedy eagle will rip off its own legs. (Chinese)

The poor lack much, but the greedy more. (Swiss)

Greek

Fear the Greek who comes bearing gifts. (Roman)

When Greek meets Greek, then comes the tug of war. (French)

Greyhound

In the long run, the greyhound kills the hare. (Spanish)

The greyhound that startles many hares kills none. (Portuguese)

Grief, Griefs

A bad branch harms the tree, a foolish son is a grief to his father. (German)

A child cries for attention, an old man because of grief. (Spanish)

Compare your griefs with other men's and they will seem less. (Spanish)

Disputing and borrowing cause grief and sorrowing. (German)

Do not rejoice at my grief, for when mine is old yours will be new. (Spanish)

Drown your grief in pleasure. (Egyptian)

Great grief does not of itself put an end to itself. (Roman)

Great griefs are mute. (Italian)

Grief only brings more loss to your purse. (Persian)

Grief pent up will burst the heart. (Italian)

Grief treads on the confines of gladness. (Roman)

He that conceals his grief finds no remedy for it. (Turkish)

In youth, one has tears without grief; in old age, grief without tears. (French)

Light griefs find utterance, great ones hold silence. (Roman)

New grief awakens the old. (English)

That grief is light which is capable of counsel. (Sicilian)
The most recent grief is the heaviest to bear. (Irish)
We are all afflicted with grief, for which God is the physician. (Egyptian)

Grievance

Do not rake up old grievances. (Rumanian)
One grievance borne, another follows. (Spanish)

Grieve

All men grieve, and if you ask them the reason why, they cannot tell it. (Roman)
Grieve not for that which is irreparably lost. (Roman)
No man grieves long unless by his own fault. (Roman)
No one has the right to feel sorry for himself for a misfortune that strikes everyone.
   (Roman)
One grieves sincerely who grieves unseen. (Roman)
The heart does not grieve for what the eye does not see. (Egyptian)
The one who grieves before it is necessary, grieves more than necessary. (Roman)
Too late to grieve when the chance is past. (French)
What the eye does not see, the heart does not grieve. (Chinese)

Grow, Growing

Be not afraid of growing slowly, be afraid only of standing still. (Chinese)
Three things grow overnight: profits, rents, and girls. (Yiddish)
To grow high, the hop must have a high pole. (German)
Who is not satisfied with himself will grow. (Chinese)

Grumbling

Grumbling fills no bellies. (German)
Grumbling makes the loaf no larger. (German)

Guard

After a house is burnt, they guard against fire. (Japanese)
Be on your guard against a silent dog and still water. (Roman)
Believe nothing and be on your guard against everything. (Roman)
He does not guard himself well who is not always on his guard. (French)
He keeps watch over a good castle who has guarded his own constitution. (Roman)
It is better to be always on our guard than to suffer once. (Roman)
It is more necessary to guard the mouth than the chest. (German)
The guard should watch what he is asked to watch. (Yoruban)
Who shall guard the guards themselves? (Roman)
Yearly, guard against famine; nightly, guard against thieves. (Chinese)

Guest, Guests

A constant guest is never welcome. (German)
A daily guest is a thief in the kitchen. (Spanish)

A frequent guest becomes a burden. (Yiddish)
A guest and a fish stink in three days. (Italian)
A guest for one day can see a long way. (Yiddish)
A guest has not to thank the host, but the host the guest. (Russian)
A guest is like the rain: when he persists, he is a nuisance. (Yiddish)
A guest sees more in an hour than the owner in a year. (German)
A guest should not remain forever a guest. (Roman)
A guest sticks a nail in the wall even if he stays but one night. (Polish)
A guest, like a fish, stinks the third day. (Dutch)
Always pray for good guests. (Yiddish)
An unpleasant guest is as welcome as salt to a sore eye. (Danish)
Fish and guests stink after three days. (Danish)
Guests bring good luck with them. (Kurdish)
Guests only come to a happy house. (Burmese)
It is more disgraceful to turn a guest out than not to admit one. (Roman)
Seven days is the length of a guest's life. (Burmese)
Seven is a banquet, nine a brawl. (Roman)
The guest of two houses dies of hunger. (Indian)
The uninvited guest is ever a pest. (German)
When the guest coughs, he wants a spoon. (Yiddish)
When the guest is in most favor, he will do well to quit. (German)
When the guests have gone the host is at peace. (Chinese)

Guide
One only seeks a guide when one has lost the road. (Hausan)

Guilt, Guilty
An excuse not requested betrays the guilt of him who makes it. (Roman)
An unrequested excuse infers guilt. (Malaysian)
God finds out the guilty. (Roman)
He confesses his guilt who flees from his trial. (Roman)
He declares himself guilty who justifies himself before being accused. (English)
He who flees, proves himself guilty. (Danish)
He who is guilty believes that all men speak ill of him. (Italian)
He who makes excuses accuses himself. (Spanish)
He who takes it to himself, he it is who has done the act. (Roman)
How difficult it is not to betray guilt by our looks. (Roman)
How near to guilt a man may approach without being guilty. (Roman)
Measure your guilt, then stretch your legs. (Arabian)
Refrain from laying the guilt of the few upon the many. (Roman)
The act does not make the person guilty, unless the mind be guilty. (Roman)
The fearful face usually betrays great guilt. (Roman)
The guilt which is committed by many must pass unpunished. (Roman)
The innocent are free from fear; but the guilty have always the dread of punishment
    before their eyes. (Roman)

The receiver is as guilty as the stealer. (German)

Who flees the law admits his guilt. (Spanish)

Gun, Gunpowder

Trust God, but keep your gunpowder dry. (American)

To buy a gun is not as expensive as to buy the gunpowder [i.e., to use it]. (Yoruban)

Gutter

All finds its way to the gutter. (German)

H

Habit, Habits

A bad habit is easily subdued in the beginning, but when it becomes inveterate it gains
   strength. (Roman)

A habit at three years is a habit at eighty. (Korean)

Every man has his peculiar habit. (Roman)

Great is the force of habit. (Roman)

Habit becomes second nature. (Roman)

Habit gives readiness. (Roman)

Habit is a shirt that we wear till death. (Russian)

Habit makes all work easy. (German)

Habits are cobwebs at first, cables at last. (Chinese)

Habits reveal the man. (Spanish)

It is easier to prevent ill habits than to break them. (Dutch)

Men do more things from habit than from reason. (Roman)

Necessity teaches us to bear misfortunes bravely, habit to bear them easily. (Roman)

Old habits die hard. (Danish)

Old habits have deep roots. (Norwegian)

Pursue that course which offers the most advantages and habit will soon make it easy
   and agreeable. (Roman)

Pursuits become habits. (Roman)

So much depends upon habit in the tender years. (Roman)

The habits of our youth accompany us in our old age. (Roman)

What fortune gives, habit soon makes its own. (Roman)

Hair

Curly hair, curly thoughts. (Russian)

Even a hair has its shadow. (Roman)

Every hair casts its shadow. (Spanish)

Fair hair may have foul roots. (German)

Gray hairs are death's blossoms. (English)

Hair does not grow faster by being pulled. (Danish)

How easily a hair gets into the butter. (German)

It's bad combing where there is no hair. (Dutch)
Long on hair, short on wit. (German)
Short hair is soon brushed. (German)
Those who dye their hair fool only themselves. (Spanish)
Why does a man without hair need a comb? (Spanish)

Half

Half and half is not whole. (German)
Half fish half man is neither fish nor man. (German)
He who stops half way is only half in error. (German)
Never do things by halves. (German)
The half is sometimes greater than the whole. (German)
Too clever by half. (English)

Hammer

A golden hammer breaks an iron gate. (German)
If the hammer is light, the nail will bounce it back. (Korean)
The hammer shatters glass but forges steel. (Russian)
The same hammer that breaks the glass forges the steel. (Italian)
When all you have is a hammer, everything looks like a nail. (French)

Hammer and Anvil

A good anvil does not fear the hammer. (Italian)
If you are an anvil, be patient; if you are a hammer, strike hard. (German)
It is better to be the hammer than the anvil. (French)
Once the anvil, now the hammer. (Egyptian)
One must be either anvil or hammer. (French)
The anvil is not afraid of the hammer. (German)
The anvil lasts longer than the hammer. (Italian)
When you are an anvil, bear; when you are a hammer, strike. (Spanish)
When you're an anvil, hold you still; when you're a hammer, strike your fill.
   (Poor Richard)

Hand, Hands

A clean hand needs never washing. (German)
A clean hand moves freely through the land. (Danish)
A cold hand, a warm heart. (German)
A shut fist only gets a closed hand. (Irish)
Arms and money require good hands. (Spanish)
God made hands before knives. (French)
Good hand, good hire. (English)
Hands that give also receive. (Ecuadorian)
He is nearest a thing, who has it in his hands. (Danish)
If you ever need a helping hand you'll find one at the end of your arm. (Yiddish)
It is a bad hand that refuses to guard the head. (Danish)

Kiss the hand you cannot bite. (Roman)

Never let your left hand know what your right hand is doing. (German)

Nothing comes into a closed hand. (Irish)

One hand cannot applaud the other. (the Editor)

One hand finds it hard to applaud. (Chinese)

One hand must wash the other, or both will be dirty. (Danish)

One in hand is worth two in the future. (Mexican)

Only the tent pitched by your own hands will stand. (Arabian)

Scatter with one hand, gather with two. (English)

The hand never loses its way to the mouth. (Roman)

The hand that gives, gathers. (German)

The hand that rocks the cradle rules the world. (German)

The just hand is as precious ointment. (Roman)

The right hand is slave to the left. (Italian)

The right hand toils, the left does little and earns little. (Spanish)

There are more hands than heads. (German)

Though the left hand conquer the right, no advantage is gained. (Chinese)

What man's hands make, man's hands can destroy. (German)

When your hand is in the dog's mouth, withdraw it gently. (Irish)

With one hand he scratches you, and with the other he strikes you. (Roman)

Women, asses, and nuts, require strong hands. (Italian)

Handmaid

Once a handmaid, never a lady. (Roman)

Handsome

A big nose never spoiled a handsome face. (French)

A handsome face is a silent recommendation. (Roman)

A handsome man is not quite poor. (Spanish)

Even the Devil was handsome at eighteen. (Japanese)

Every woman would rather be handsome than good. (German)

Handsome is as handsome does. (German)

Handsome is not what is handsome, but what pleases. (Italian)

Handsome women generally fall to the lot of ugly men. (Italian)

He is handsome that handsome doth. (English)

It is a great affliction to be too handsome a man. (Roman)

Hang, Hanged

Better, 'There he goes', than 'There he hangs'. (German)

He rises early that is hanged before noon. (Roman)

One may as well be hanged for a sheep as for a lamb. (French)

There is no hanging a man for his thoughts. (American)

Hangman

A hangman is a good trade; he doth his work by daylight. (Spanish)

Happen

It happens in a moment, and happens all year long. (Roman)

It happens in an hour, that comes not in an age. (German)

Some people make things happen, some watch things happen, while others wonder
what has happened. (Irish)

That happens in a moment which may not happen in a hundred years. (Italian)

What does not happen in a year may happen in a moment. (Spanish)

What happens in Vegas stays in Vegas. (American)

Whatever happens, happens. (Spanish)

When what you want doesn't happen, learn to want what does. (Arabian)

Happiness

A merchant's happiness hangs upon chance, winds, and waves. (Japanese)

All happiness is in the mind. (English)

Calamities come because of accumulated evil; happiness comes as a blessing to the good.
(Chinese)

Happiness has many friends. (Roman)

Happiness invites envy. (Roman)

Happiness is a warm puppy. (American)

Happiness is founded upon virtue. (Chinese)

Happiness is not a horse that can be harnessed. (Russian)

He is not happy who does not realize his happiness. (Roman)

If you have happiness, don't use it all up. (Chinese)

If you want happiness for a year, inherit a fortune; if you want happiness for a lifetime,
help someone else. (Chinese)

If you want happiness for an hour, take a nap; if you want happiness for a day, go fishing.
(Chinese)

One happiness scatters a thousand sorrows. (Chinese)

The happiness in your pocket: don't spend it all. (Chinese)

The hour of happiness will come, the more welcome when it is not expected. (Roman)

Happy, Happiest

A happy heart is better than a full purse. (Italian)

Call no man happy till he dies. (Italian)

Happy people never count hours as they pass. (Chinese)

He is not happy who knows it not. (Italian)

He spends the happiest life who knows nothing. (Roman)

Make happy those who are near, and those who are far will come. (Chinese)

Men fated to be happy need not hurry. (Chinese)

No one should be called happy before he is dead and buried. (Roman)

Hard Luck

From clogs to clogs is only three generations. (Danish)

From shirtsleeves to shirtsleeves is three generations. (Italian)

Hard Work

Hard work never did anyone any harm. (Italian)

Hardship

A man accustomed to hardships will not mind a little more. (Hausan)

Hare

A hare is like an ass in the length of its ears, yet it is not its son. (West African)

A hare's mouth is too small for a bridle. (Yoruban)

Drumming is not the way to catch a hare. (Roman)

Even a hare will bite when it is cornered. (Chinese)

Even a hare will insult a dead lion. (Roman)

Even hares pull a lion by the beard when it is dead. (Dutch)

Even hares will strike a dead lion. (Roman)

Even the rustling of leaves will alarm the hare. (Roman)

First catch your hare, then cook it. (Dutch)

First the hare, then the hound. (Burmese)

Hares are not caught by the sound of the drum. (French)

In the valley where there is no tiger, the hare is master. (Korean)

The hare does not eat the grass around its burrow. (Chinese)

The hare that escapes had eight legs. (Singhalese)

The one who chases two hares is sure to catch neither. (Roman)

When we least expect it, the hare darts out of the ditch. (Dutch)

Harlot

As brackish water does not become sweet, so a harlot does not change her ways. (Egyptian)

The one who spends money on harlots sells his virtue for disease. (Egyptian)

Harm, Harmed

Better the harm I know than the harm I know not. (English)

Harm no one, neither by word nor by deed. (Roman)

He harms the good who spares the bad. (Roman)

He may be ugly and stupid but he does us no harm. (American)

He who is far from home, is near to harm. (Danish)

No one is harmed but by himself. (Roman)

Not everything that is bad comes to harm us. (Italian)

Occupy yourself, and you will be out of harm's way. (Roman)

The harm we do to others is easily forgotten. (Russian)

To have been silent never does harm, but to have spoken does. (Roman)

We all have power to do harm. (Roman)

Harmony

It is more difficult to restore harmony than sow dissension. (Roman)

The complete harmony of this world consists in discord. (Roman)

With concord small things increase, with discord the greatest things go to ruin. (Roman)

Harp, Harping
All are not harpers, who hold the harp. (Roman)
That person makes himself ridiculous who is ever harping on one string. (Roman)
The harp dispels care. (Roman)

Harvest
Farewell baskets, the harvest is ended. (French)
Fill your barns, harvest lasts not forever. (Roman)
He that has a good harvest must be content with a few thistles. (Spanish)
It is a bitter thing to have sown good deeds and to reap a harvest of evils. (Roman)
No one should speak of the harvest until he has planted the seed. (Unknown)

Haste, Hasty
A hasty man does his work twice over. (Persian)
A hasty man never wants woe. (Chinese)
Allow time and slight delay; haste and violence ruin everything. (Roman)
Food eaten in haste chokes one's gullet. (Korean)
Haste achieves little. (Chinese)
Haste and hurry can only bear children with many regrets along the way. (West African)
Haste burns one's lips. (Unknown)
Haste does not result in prosperity. (Swahili)
Haste is blind and reckless. (Roman)
Haste is from the Devil. (Egyptian)
Haste is good only for catching fleas. (Yiddish)
Haste is next door to panic, delay is nearer to firm courage. (Roman)
Haste makes one late. (Roman)
Haste makes waste and waste makes want. (Swahili)
Haste makes waste. (Poor Richard)
Haste manages all things badly. (Roman)
Haste trips up its own heels. (Roman)
Hasty climbers have sudden falls. (English)
Hasty counsels are followed quickly by repentance. (Roman)
Hasty questions require slow answers. (Dutch)
He that is too much in haste, may stumble on a good road. (French)
He who hastens to be rich will not be without fault. (Roman)
He who hastens too much stumbles and falls. (Roman)
He who makes too much haste gains his end later. (Roman)
He who pours water hastily into a bottle spills more than goes in. (Spanish)
In haste there is error. (Chinese)
Make haste slowly. (Roman)
Make no more haste than good speed. (Yiddish)
Make too much haste and pay the penalty. (Roman)

More haste, less speed. (English)
Nothing in haste but catching fleas. (Dutch)
Rice eaten in haste chokes the throat. (Korean)
The Devil takes a hand in what is done in haste. (Kurdish)
The hasty man was never a traitor. (German)
The more haste, the less speed. (French)
The one who judges in haste repents in haste. (Roman)

Hat

A good head does not want for a hat. (French)
A headstrong man and a fool may wear the same hat. (Danish)
A high hat falls at a single blow. (Egyptian)
Any man can lose his hat in an impish wind. (Irish)
Don't hang your hat higher than you can reach. (Belizean)
He who has a head won't want for a hat. (Italian)
He who has no head wants no hat. (Spanish)
Many a good man is found under a shabby hat. (Chinese)

Hatchet

Throw not thy hatchet at God, lest he turn the sharp edge against thee. (Danish)

Hate, Hatred

As the best wine makes the sharpest vinegar, so the deepest love turns to the deadliest
    hatred. (Spanish)
Do not go forward in your hatred. (Roman)
Great hate follows great love. (Irish)
Hate has no medicine. (African)
Hatred corrodes the vessel in which it is stored. (Chinese)
Hatred is a settled anger. (Roman)
Hatred moves men more than affection. (Yiddish)
Hatred renewed is worse than at first. (Italian)
Hatred unavowed and hidden is to be feared more than when open and declared. (Roman)
Hatred watches while friendship sleeps. (French)
He that fears you present will hate you absent. (Turkish)
Let them hate, so long as they fear. (Roman)
Take care that no one hates you justly. (Roman)
The closer one gets, the harder it is to hate. (the Editor)
The hatred of relatives is the most violent. (Roman)
The hatred of those closest to us is the most bitter. (Roman)
Though hated in life, the same man will be loved after he is dead. (Roman)
We hate the one whom we have wronged. (Roman)
Who hates a priest hates also his stole. (Japanese)

Haughty

Who today is a haughty knight, is tomorrow a penniless wight. (Dutch)

Have

Believe that you have it, and you have it. (Roman)
Better to have than to wish. (German)
Have a thing yourself, or else do without it. (Irish)
'I have' is a better bird than 'If I had'. (German)
To have is better than not to have. (Hausan)
Who has not, cannot. (French)
Who has nothing fears nothing. (Italian)
You can't do anything with it if you don't have it. (Japanese)

Hawk

Hawks will not pick out hawks' eyes. (German)
The hawk is not frightened by the cries of the crane. (Egyptian)
The wise hawk conceals its talons. (Japanese)

Hay, Haystack

Bad grass does not make good hay. (Italian)
Hay is more acceptable to an ass than gold. (Roman)
Hay smells different to lovers and horses. (Roman)
He who was born in a haystack wants to die in it. (Spanish)
Make hay while the sun shines. (English)

Head

A bald head is soon shaven. (German)
A head is not to be cut off because it is scabby. (Danish)
A scabby head fears the comb. (Dutch)
Better to use your head than lose it. (German)
Big head, little wit. (French, German)
He has a head, and so has a pin. (Portuguese)
He that hath a head of butter must not come near the oven.
   (Dutch)
He that hath a head of wax must not approach the fire. (French)
His head in heaven, his tail in water. (Egyptian)
If the head aches all the members languish. (Roman)
It is difficult to get many heads under one hat. (Danish)
Not all heads have a brain. (French)
One head is stronger than a hundred hands. (German)
The bigger the head the worse the headache. (Serbian)
The one without a head needs no hat. (German)
The wiser head gives in. (German)
Thou hast a head and so hath a pin. (Swedish)
Two heads are better than one. (English)
What can the head do that the shoulders cannot? (Yoruban)
What use is a good head if the legs won't carry it? (Yiddish)
When the head is a fool, the whole body is done for. (Yiddish)

When the head is sick the whole body is sick. (Dutch)
Who has a head won't want for a hat. (German)

Headache
A crown is no cure for the headache. (Italian)
When the head aches, all the members suffer with it. (Roman)
When the head hurts, the rest of the body aches. (German)

Heal, Healing
Before healing others, heal yourself. (African)
He that would heal a wound must not handle it. (Italian)
He who hurts in life, heals in death. (Roman)
If you cannot heal the wound, do not tear it open. (Danish)
In nothing are men more like gods than when they heal their fellow men. (Roman)
What stings, heals. (Spanish)

Health, Healthy
A healthy man is a successful man. (French)
A person's health is in his feet. (Irish)
Be not sick too late, nor well too soon. (Poor Richard)
Better to lose a supper than have a hundred physicians. (Spanish)
Eat well, drink in moderation, and sleep sound, in these three good health abound. (Roman)
Feed a cold, starve a fever. (American)
Fond of lawsuits, little wealth; fond of doctors, little health. (Spanish)
He that would be healthy, must eat temperately, and sup early. (Spanish)
He who enjoys good health is rich, though he knows it not. (Italian)
He who has not health has nothing. (French)
Health is better than wealth. (German)
Health without money is a half-malady. (Italian)
If you stand in need of medical advice, let these three things be your physician: a cheerful
    mind, rest, and a moderate diet. (Roman)
If you would live healthy, be old early. (Spanish)
It is better to sweat than to sneeze. (Spanish)
On a hot day muffle yourself more. (Spanish)
One must pay health its tithes [i.e., by suffering little illnesses from time to time]. (Irish)
Rosy cheeks at daybreak may be bone white by eve. (Japanese)
Take care that you keep well. (Roman)
The beginning of health is to know the disease. (Spanish)
The first step to health is to know that we are sick. (English)
The healthy die first. (Italian)
We are usually the best men when in the worst health. (English)
Your health comes first; you can always hang yourself later. (Yiddish)

Heap
Out of many things a great heap will be formed. (Roman)

Hear, Hearing

Bad hearing makes for a second telling. (German)

He that hears much, hears many lies. (Dutch)

He who hath ears to hear, let him hear. (Jesus)

Hear all, say nothing. (Roman)

Hear all, see all, say not. (Roman)

Hear evil with one ear, the good with two, flattery with none. (Spanish)

Hear first, and speak afterwards. (Spanish)

Hear one man before you answer; hear several before you decide. (Danish)

Hear the other side, and believe little. (Italian)

Hear twice before you speak once. (American)

Hearing is never as good as seeing. (Persian)

Hearing one hundred times is not better than seeing once. (Japanese)

It is worth your while to hear. (Roman)

One man's story is no story: hear both sides. (German)

Though the speaker be a fool, let the hearer be wise. (Spanish)

When I did well, I heard it never; when I did ill, I heard it ever. (English)

When one shuts one eye, one does not hear everything. (Swiss)

Who can't hear must feel. (Jamaican)

Hearsay

Hearsay is half lies. (Dutch)

Sight goes before hearsay. (Danish)

Heart

A broken hand works, but not a broken heart. (Persian)

A good heart influences heaven and earth. (Chinese)

A good heart possesses a kingdom. (Roman)

A pure heart has few desires. (Chinese)

A troubled heart is a worm to the bones. (Roman)

As he thinks in his heart, so is he. (German)

Bad mind, bad heart. (Roman)

Cold hands, warm heart. (German)

Easy to know men's faces, not their hearts. (Chinese)

Everyone should carefully observe which way his heart draws him, and then choose that
    way with all his strength. (Chinese)

Faint heart is always in danger. (Portuguese)

Faint heart never won fair lady. (German)

Fire in the heart sends smoke into the head. (German)

For news of the heart, ask the face. (Dutch)

Have a mouth as sharp as a dagger, but a heart as soft as bean curd. (Chinese)

Heart finds a way to heart. (Persian)

If the heart is merry, the foot will be light. (Korean)

If the heart is not dark all laws will be clear. (Chinese)

If there is righteousness in the heart, there will be beauty in character. (Roman)

It's a poor heart that never rejoices. (Dutch)
Many are the roads that lead not to the heart. (Arabian)
No weak heart shall prosper. (Jamaican)
Out of the fullness of the heart the mouth speaks. (German)
Sometimes the mouth laughs when the heart cries. (German)
The heart does not lie. (Dutch)
The heart does not think all that the mouth says. (Italian)
The heart is half a prophet. (Yiddish)
The heart is no traitor. (Spanish)
The heart is willing but the flesh is weak. (Jamaican, after Jesus)
The heart leads whither it goes. (French)
The heart of the wise man is as quiet water. (West African)
The heart remains ever young. (German)
The heart that loves is always young. (Yiddish)
Though stone be changed to gold, the heart of man would not be satisfied. (Chinese)
'Tis a poor heart that never rejoices. (Unknown)
To a young heart everything is sport. (Italian)
We see the faces, we do not know about the hearts. (Spanish)
What comes from the heart, goes to the heart. (German)
What is nearest the heart is nearest the lips. (Irish)
When the heart is full, the tongue runs over. (German)
When the heart speaks, reason sleeps. (German)
When there is room in the heart, there is room in the house. (Danish)
You can see into a man's eyes, but not into a man's heart. (Mexican)

Hearth
A hearth of your own is worth gold. (Danish)
It is hard to make a fire on a cold hearth. (Danish)
See that your own hearth is swept before you lift your neighbor's ashes. (Irish)
The fire burns brightest on one's own hearth. (Danish)
The pot boils best on your own hearth. (Danish)
There is no hearth like one's own. (Irish)
What's done in the corner will come to the hearth. (Irish)

Heat
A quickly heated room quickly cools. (Korean)
Heat belongs to all; cold varies with the clothing. (Chinese)
If you can't take the heat, get out of the kitchen. (American)

Heaven
All things of this world are nothing, unless they have reference to the next. (Spanish)
Crosses are ladders that lead to Heaven. (Unknown)
Do your best and leave the rest to Heaven. (Chinese)
Even one hour of Heaven is worth while. (Yiddish)
He who always looks to heaven will stub his toe. (German)

He who is ripe for Heaven falls not before his day. (Roman)

Heaven has no mouth, and yet it speaks through men's mouths. (Japanese)

Heaven is near and recompense is swift. (Chinese)

Heaven is not indifferent to those whose hearts are earnest. (Chinese)

Heaven knows the deceitful heart. (Chinese)

Heaven knows the good and evil stored in each heart. (Chinese)

Heaven protects children, sailors, and drunken men. (Dutch)

Heaven will make amends for all. (German)

Heaven's eyes are very great, and recompense comes quickly. (Chinese)

Heaven's net is coarse, but catches everything. (Japanese)

Heaven's vengeance is slow but sure. (Unknown)

If Heaven creates a man, there must be some use for him. (Chinese)

If Heaven rained pearls and jade, the cold and hungry could not use them for food or
    clothing. (Chinese)

If Heaven were to drop a date, you must open your mouth. (Chinese)

Man cannot stir one inch without the push of Heaven's finger. (Chinese)

The net of Heaven is large and wide, but it lets nothing through. (Chinese)

The road to Heaven is equally short, wherever we die. (Danish)

The way to Heaven is in everyplace alike. (German)

There is no going to Heaven in a sedan. (German)

There is no Heaven on earth. (American)

There is nothing partial in the ways of Heaven. (Chinese)

When the heavens weep, the earth lives. (Hawaiian)

You can't buy Heaven with money. (Italian)

Heaven and Hell

Better rule in Hell, than serve in Heaven. (Spanish)

Empty the clear path to Heaven, crowded the dark road to Hell. (Chinese)

He who is in Hell knows not what Heaven is. (Italian)

Heaven and Hell are on earth. (Mexican)

Heaven and Hell are within the heart. (Chinese)

Heaven and Hell can be had in this world. (Yiddish)

Heaven has a road but no one travels it; Hell has no gate but men come crashing into it.
    (Chinese)

Hell shared with a sage is better than Paradise with a fool. (Yiddish)

If I cannot bend Heaven then I shall stir up Hell. (Roman)

If you come up in this world, be sure not to go down in the next. (Irish)

It is harder work getting to Hell than to Heaven. (German)

Many a man leaves Heaven for Hell on principle. (Yiddish)

Hedge

Between neighbors' gardens a hedge is not amiss. (German)

One briar does not make a hedge. (Italian)

Where the hedge is lowest, everyone goes over. (Dutch)

Where the hedge is lowest, the Devil leaps over. (German)

Heed

He who heeds not the lost shoe-nail, will soon lose the horse. (German)

Take heed is a good reed. (Irish)

Take heed of an enemy reconciled. (French)

Take heed of an ox before, an ass behind, and a monk on all sides. (French)

Take heed of enemies reconciled, and of meat twice boiled. (English)

Take heed of the vinegar of sweet wine, and the anger of good-nature.
(Poor Richard)

Take heed you do not fall from your high position. (Roman)

Heir, Heirs

A sick man acts foolishly for himself who makes his doctor his heir. (Roman)

A third heir seldom enjoys what is dishonestly acquired. (Roman)

Both good and evil are bequeathed to one's heirs. (Chinese)

He is no great heir that inherits not his ancestor's virtues. (Portuguese)

It is the fool who makes the doctor his heir. (German)

Make your son your heir and not your steward. (Portuguese)

No one is heir of the living. (Roman)

The absent one will not be the heir. (Roman)

The tears of an heir are laughter in disguise. (Roman)

Those in supreme power always suspect and hate their next heir. (Roman)

Walnuts and pears you plant for your heirs. (English)

We sons are heirs no less to diseases than to estates. (Roman)

Hell

A man from Hell is not afraid of hot ashes. (Burmese)

From all sides there is equally a way to Hell. (Greek)

Hell and high water wait for no man. (Unknown)

Hell is filled with the ungrateful. (Roman)

Hell is not so bad as the road to it. (Yiddish)

If there be a Hell, Rome is built over it. (German)

Many are worshipped at the altar who are burning in flames. (Christian)

The descent to hell is easy. (Roman)

The entrance to Hell has a thousand ways, the exit none. (German)

The road to Hell is paved with good intentions. (English)

There are no fans in Hell. (Egyptian)

There is no gate to Hell, but men are determined to enter it. (Chinese)

Help, Helping

A little help is better than a lot of pity. (Irish)

A little help does a great deal. (French)

Even the just has need of help. (Italian)

Eyes too high, hands too low. (Korean)

Give a helping hand to a man in trouble. (Roman)

God helps those who help themselves. (German)

God helps those who obey. (Mexican)

God helps three sorts of people: fools, children, and drunkards. (French)

He who cannot help, may hinder. (German)

He who helps everybody, helps nobody. (Spanish)

Help by actions, not by words. (Roman)

Help comes too late when the fight is over. (Roman)

Help him who is willing to work, not him who shrinks from it. (Roman)

Help is good everywhere, except in the porridge bowl. (Danish)

Help me during the rainy season and I will help you during the dry season. (Yoruban)

Help me to salt, help me to sorrow. (English)

Help thyself and Heaven will help thee. (French)

It is a regal act to aid the fallen. (Roman)

It is easy to help the one willing to be helped. (German)

Many can help one. (German)

Much ado and little help. (English)

One thing needs the help of another. (Roman)

Slow help is no help. (German)

That is poor help that helps you from the feather-bed to the straw. (Danish)

The best place to find a helping hand is at the end of your own arm. (Swedish)

There is help for everything, except death. (Danish)

There is no helping him who will not be advised. (Italian)

Three, helping one another, bear the burden of six. (German)

When the need is highest, the help is nighest. (English)

When need is greatest, help is nearest. (German)

Hen

A bit is too big for a hen's mouth. (Hausan)

A black hen lays a white egg. (French)

A hen is heavy when carried far. (Irish)

Bad hen, bad egg. (Roman)

Even clever hens sometimes lay their eggs among nettles. (Danish)

Had the hen kept silent, it would not have lost its egg. (Spanish)

Hens like to lay when they see an egg. (Dutch)

If the hen had not cackled, we should not know she had laid an egg. (Italian)

It is a bad hen that does not scratch for itself. (Irish)

It is a bad hen that eats at your house and lays at another's. (Spanish)

It is not easy to guard the hen that lays her eggs abroad. (Danish)

It is not the hen which cackles most that lays the most eggs. (Dutch)

Know that hens lay even in nettles. (German)

Old hens make the best soup. (Mexican)

The first hen that cackles is the one that laid the egg. (Chinese)

The hen flies not far unless the cock flies with her. (Danish)

The hen has ruffled feathers until she has reared her brood. (Irish)

The hen that stays at home picks up the crumbs. (Portuguese)

The hen's eyes are with her chicks. (French)

There is little peace in that house where the hen crows and the cock is mute. (Italian)
To get the chicks one must coax the hen. (French)
When the hen scratches the chicks learn. (Indian)

Herb
Like the herb plucked on Sunday, it does neither good nor ill. (Irish)
The herb that can't be got is the one that cures. (Irish)

Hereafter
If matters go on badly at present, they may take a better turn in the hereafter. (Roman)

Hero, Heroism
Heroes know each other. (Japanese)
Heroism consists of hanging on one minute longer. (Norwegian)
No man is a hero to his valet. (French)
Out of rags comes a hero. (Korean)
Out of those clad in rags will rise a hero. (Japanese)
The hero appears only when the tiger is dead. (Burmese)
There is no hero in the eyes of the servant. (Japanese)

Heron
The heron blames the water because he cannot swim. (Danish)

Herring
Every herring must hang by its own gill. (German)

Hesitate
He who hesitates despairs. (Mexican)
He who hesitates is lost. (English)
He who hesitates regrets. (Albanian)

Hid, Hidden, Hide
Do not hide like a fly under the tail of a horse. (Albanian)
Do not hide like the mouse behind the pot. (Albanian)
He that hides can find. (French)
He that hides is no better than he that steals. (Danish)
Hide not the truth from your confessor, your doctor, or your lawyer. (Italian)
Hide not your light under a bushel. (Christian)
Hide the evil; show the good. (Chinese)
It is difficult to hide what everybody knows. (Danish)
It is no use hiding from a friend what is known to an enemy. (Danish)
Love, a cough, and smoke, are hard to hide. (Italian)
Under the sackcloth there is something hid. (Spanish)

High

High birth is a poor dish on the table. (Italian)
High houses are mostly empty in the upper story. (German)
High place, great danger. (Unknown)
High regions are never without storms. (German)
High trees give more shadow than fruit. (Dutch)
High winds blow on high hills. (Dutch)

Hill, Hills

Blue are the hills that are far away. (Italian)
Distant hills are green. (Irish)
Every hill has its valley. (Italian)
If the hill topples, the grass is uprooted. (Burmese)
Praise a hill but keep on the plain. (English)
The higher the hill, the lower the grass. (German)

Hindsight

Hindsight is always 20/20. (English)
When the ship has sunk everyone knows how she might have been saved. (Italian)

Hint

A hint hits harder than the truth. (Yiddish)
Give a hint to the man of sense, and consider the thing done. (Portuguese)
Give the wise man a hint and leave him to act. (Italian)

History

A people without history is like wind on the buffalo grass. (Native American)
Every time history repeats itself the price goes up. (Italian)
Happy is the country which has no history. (Italian)
History is just one damned thing after another. (American)
History is philosophy drawn from examples. (Greek)
History is written by the victor. (Unknown)
History repeats itself. (English)
History, however written, is always a pleasure to read. (Roman)

Hit

One does not always hit what one aims at. (French)

Hoe

The hoe that helped clear the farm slept hungry. (Yoruban)

Hog

A bespattered hog tries to bespatter another. (Spanish)
A hog in armor is still a hog. (German)

Hold

He that holds is no better than he that scourges. (Danish)
He that holds the handle of a frying-pan runs the risk of burning himself.
  (French)
He who hold the thread holds the ball. (French)
He who holds the handle of the frying-pan turns it as he pleases. (French)
What you have, hold. (English)

Hole

A hole is easier to patch than a crack. (Filipino)
Better a patch than a hole. (German)
Carve the peg by looking at the hole. (Korean)
If you find yourself in a hole, the first thing to do is stop digging. (American)
Mend the hole while it is small. (Serbian)
One may see through a wall, if there's a hole in it. (German)
The hole invites the thief. (Spanish)
The hole is more honorable than the patch. (Irish)
There's a peg for every hole. (French)
You can't force a square peg into a round hole. (American)

Holiday

Every day is not a holiday. (Italian)
It will not do to keep holidays before they come. (French)
The holiday will not last forever. (Roman)

Hollow

Hollow objects ring louder than solid ones. (Spanish)
Unplowed fields make hollow bellies; unread books make hollow minds. (Chinese)

Holy Days

'Tis easier to keep holy days than holy commandments. (American)

Home

A peaceful home is a happy home. (German)
Be it ever so humble, there's no place like home. (American)
Better is the smoke of my own house than the fire of another's. (Spanish)
Charity begins at home. (English)
Dry bread at home is better than roast meat abroad. (Roman)
East or West, home is best. (American)
Far from home, near to harm. (German)
He who has no house of his own is everywhere at home. (Spanish)
Home is home though it's never so homely. (Roman)
Home is home, be it ever so humble. (Italian)
Home is where the heart is. (English)
Home is where you hang your hat. (English)
Home, sweet home. (American)

I would rather see smoke from my own chimney than the fire on another's hearth.
  (Danish)
If you stay at home you won't wear out your shoes. (Yiddish)
It is fine any place you go but best at home. (Unknown)
Love begins at home. (German)
My home is my castle. (German)
Over no home can the sign be hung: 'There is no trouble here'. (Roman)
Sooner or later we hasten to one home. (Roman)
The farthest way about is the nearest way home. (German)
There's no place like home. (American)
Those who are happy at home should stay there. (Roman)
Travel east or travel west, a man's own home is still the best. (English)
Where I make my living, there is my home. (Somalian)

Homeland
Anywhere you live is your native land. (Korean)
Each person's homeland is dear to him. (Roman)

Homer
Sometimes even the good Homer nods off. (Roman)

Hometown
Become not a priest in your hometown, nor marry away from it. (Spanish)

Honest, Honesty
A clean mouth and honest hand, will take a man through any land. (German)
A man is not honest simply because he never had a chance to steal. (Yiddish)
An honest face is the best recommendation. (German)
An honest magistrate cannot succeed. (Chinese)
An honest magistrate has lean cheeks. (Chinese)
An honest man does not make himself a dog for the sake of a bone. (Danish)
An honest man is not the worse because a dog barks at him. (Danish)
An honest man will receive neither money nor praise, that is not his due. (Poor Richard)
An honest man's word is as good as the king's. (Portuguese)
An honest man's word is his bond. (German)
Better to take what you can in a straight way than to acquire by crookedness. (Chinese)
He is not an honest man who has burned his tongue and does not tell the company that
    the soup is hot. (Italian)
Honest men fear neither light nor dark. (German)
Honest parents, honest children. (Spanish)
Honesty brings success, dishonesty defeats itself. (Chinese)
Honesty is like an icicle: if once it melts that is the end of it. (American)
Honesty is often goaded to ruin. (Roman)
Honesty is praised and left out to freeze. (Roman)
Honesty is the best policy. (American)

Honesty is true honor. (Roman)
Honesty lasts longest. (German)
Honesty makes one rich, but slowly. (German)
Honesty with poverty is better than ill-gotten wealth. (Roman)
Only those things are good which are honest. (Roman)
The dishonest starve, the honest eat their fruit. (Burmese)
The honest man does not repent. (Roman)
Thrive by honesty or remain poor. (French)

Honey

A drop of honey catches more flies than a hogshead of vinegar. (German)
All the honey a bee gathers during its lifetime doesn't sweeten its sting. (Italian)
As you are fated to eat honey, bees swarm in your beard. (Burmese)
Even honey is bitter if served as a medicine. (Korean)
He is a very bad manager of honey who leaves nothing to lick off his fingers. (French)
He pays dear for honey who licks it off thorns. (French)
He that hath no honey in his pot, let him have it in his mouth. (Dutch)
He that stirs honey will have some of it stick to him. (Spanish)
He who makes himself honey, will be eaten by flies. (German)
He who would gather honey must brave the sting of bees. (Dutch)
Honey catches more flies than vinegar. (Roman)
Honey cloys. (Roman)
Honey is not for asses. (French)
Honey is sweet, but the bee stings. (Dutch)
Honey was not made for the mouth of the ass. (Spanish)
It is costly honey that must be licked off thorns. (German)
It is difficult to spit honey out of a mouth full of gall. (Danish)
More flies are caught with a drop of honey than with a cup of vinegar. (Spanish)
One catches more flies with a spoonful of honey than with twenty casks of vinegar.
    (French)
The honey is sweet, but the bee has a sting. (Poor Richard)
Though honey is sweet, do not lick it off a briar. (Irish)
To reach the honey, sometimes one must break his ax. (Yoruban)
When you taste honey, remember gall. (Poor Richard)
Who divides honey with the bear, will likely get the lesser share. (Italian).

Honor, Honorable

A hole is more honorable than a patch. (Irish)
A seat in the council is honor without profit. (Portuguese)
An honorable death is better than a dishonorable life. (Roman)
An honorable man is honorable even though mishaps befall him. (Egyptian)
Art and knowledge bring bread and honor. (Danish)
Be honorable yourself if you wish to associate with honorable people. (Welsh)
Better poor with honor than rich with shame. (Dutch)
Better to deserve honor and not have it, than have it and not deserve it. (Portuguese)

He who does not honor the lowly is not valued by the great. (German)

He who prizes little things, is worthy of great ones. (German)

Honor a good man that he may honor you, and a bad man that he may not dishonor you. (Portuguese)

Honor and profit will not keep in one sack. (Portuguese)

Honor blossoms on the grave. (French)

Honor buys no meat in the market. (Danish)

Honor has a big shadow. (Swedish)

Honor has its burdens. (Roman)

Honor is better than honors. (Flemish)

Honor is from him who gives it, not in him who gets it. (Yiddish)

Honor is the reward of virtue. (Roman)

Honor lasts beyond the grave. (German)

Honor lies in honest toil. (German)

Honor makes way for honor. (Latvian)

Honor once lost never returns. (Dutch)

Honor pursues him who flees it. (German)

Honor, like life, when once it is lost, is never recovered. (Roman)

If a man speaks of his honor, make him pay cash. (Dutch)

If some men knew who some men were, then some would pay the more honor there. (German)

It is an honorable thing to be accused by those who are open to accusation. (Roman)

It is not honor for an eagle to vanquish a dove. (Italian)

Not all who sit in seats of honor are noble. (Yiddish)

Nothing deters a good man from what honor requires of him. (Roman)

Nowhere is there true honor. (Roman)

One man honored in death is better than a hundred living in shame. (Persian)

Seek honor above money and possessions. (German)

She is good and honored who is dead and buried. (Spanish)

The palm is not obtained without toil. (Roman)

The post of honor is the post of danger. (English)

There is honor among thieves. (Danish)

There is no greater honor than to stay at home. (Yiddish)

What is permissible is not always honorable. (Roman)

When honor is lost the man is dead. (Irish)

Where honor ceases, there knowledge decreases. (German)

Where law lacks, honor should eke it out. (Danish)

Where there is no honor there is no dishonor. (Portuguese)

Who honors his elders honors God. (German)

Who loses honor can lose nothing else. (Roman)

Honors

Don't run after honors and they will come of themselves. (Yiddish)

Honors are enhanced by merit. (Roman)

Honors are the reward of virtue. (Roman)

Honors change manners. (German)

Honors encourage the arts, for all desire fame. (Roman)

Pleasures are transient, honors are immortal. (Greek)

Hope

A good hope is better than a bad possession. (Spanish)

Do not anxiously hope for that which is not yet come; do not vainly regret what is already past. (Chinese)

Do not entertain extravagant hopes. (Irish)

He gains much who loses a vain hope. (Italian)

He that lives in hope dances to an ill tune. (Danish)

He that lives upon hope has but a slender diet. (Danish)

He that lives upon hope will die fasting. (Danish)

He that lives upon hope, dies farting. (Poor Richard)

He who has health has hope; and he who has hope has everything. (Arabian)

He who hopes, despairs. (Roman)

He who lives in hope, breakfasts ill and sups worse. (Spanish)

He who lives with hope, dies singing. (Spanish)

He who travels with hope has poverty for his coachman. (German)

Hope deferred makes the heart sick. (Danish)

Hope delayed hangs the heart upon tenterhooks. (Roman)

Hope for the best, prepare for the worst. (Danish)

Hope gives strength and courage, and saves an otherwise dying man from his grave. (Roman)

Hope is a good breakfast but a bad supper. (Roman)

Hope is an egg of which one man gets the yolk, another the white, and a third the shell. (Danish)

Hope is born of despair. (Persian)

Hope is grief's best medicine. (German)

Hope is our only comfort in adversity. (Roman)

Hope is the diet of fools. (German)

Hope is the dream of the waking. (Danish)

Hope springs eternal. (Danish)

Hope supports men in distress. (Roman)

Hope sustains the farmer. (Roman)

If it were not for hope, the heart would break. (Roman)

In adversity, only the virtuous can entertain hope. (Roman)

Let each be a hope unto himself [i.e., each must rely on himself alone]. (Roman)

Let the wretched live in hope, and the happy be on their guard. (Roman)

Live in hope, and reserve yourselves for more prosperous circumstances. (Roman)

Man lives on hope. (Persian)

Right down to the brink of the grave, a man must still hope and be brave. (Yiddish)

The man who lives only by hope will die with despair. (Italian)

The one who can hope for nothing should despair of nothing. (Roman)

There is hope from the sea, but none from the grave. (Irish)

Those who feed on hope hang on, but they do not live. (Roman)
Where the heart is past hope, the face is past shame. (Spanish)
Where there is life there is hope. (Portuguese)
While there's life, there's hope. (English)

Horn, Horns

'Tis well that wicked cows have short horns. (Dutch)
What has horns will gore. (Dutch)

Horse, Horses

A bad horse eats as much as a good one. (Danish)
A colt you may break, but an old horse you never can. (French)
A fast horse needs no spur. (Spanish)
A fine steed never wears two saddles. (Japanese)
A galled horse will not endure the comb. (French)
A gilded bit does not make for a better horse. (Roman)
A good horse cannot be of a bad color. (Italian)
A good horse is worth its fodder. (Dutch)
A good horse never lacks a saddle. (Italian)
A hired horse and one's own spurs make short miles. (Dutch)
A horse deprived of its food won't work. (Roman)
A horse grown fat kicks. (Italian)
A horse knows its rider. (Unknown)
A horse may stumble, though it has four feet. (Dutch)
A horse of good breed is not dishonored by its saddle. (Arabian)
A horse that will not carry a saddle must have no oats. (Arabian)
A kick from a mare never hurt a horse. (French)
A runaway horse punishes itself. (Italian)
A short horse is soon curried. (Spanish)
A slow horse will still reach the mill. (Scottish)
A young foal and an old horse draw not well together. (Danish)
All lay their loads on a willing horse. (Roman)
An old horse does not change its gait. (Spanish)
Another man's horse and your own whip can do a great deal. (Danish)
Be a horse ever so well shod, it may slip. (French)
Be on a horse when you go in search of a better one. (Chinese)
Be the horse good or bad always wear your spurs. (Italian)
Before you mount, look to the girth. (Dutch)
Better a blind horse than an empty halter. (Dutch)
Better a poor horse than an empty stall. (Danish)
Better an ass that carries me than a horse that throws me. (Portuguese)
Better ride a good horse for a year, than an ass all your life. (Dutch)
A hard bit does not make the better horse. (Danish)
Different courses, different horses. (Unknown)
Don't change horses in midstream. (American)

Don't look a gift horse in the mouth. (Spanish)
Don't put the cart before the horse. (English)
Even a good horse cannot always keep running. (Irish)
Even a good horse cannot wear two saddles. (Chinese)
Even a horse, though it has four feet, stumbles. (Italian)
Even the best horse may stumble. (German)
Have a horse of your own and then you may borrow another's. (Welsh)
He who buys a horse buys care. (Spanish)
He who has a good horse in his stable may go on foot. (Italian)
He who rides behind another does not mount a horse when he will. (Spanish)
Hired horses make short miles. (Dutch)
If two ride a horse, one must ride behind. (English)
If you can't ride two horses at once, you shouldn't be in the circus. (American)
Ill-matched horses draw badly. (Dutch)
It is a good horse that draws its own cart. (Irish)
It is difficult to tie an unborn horse to the manger. (Danish)
It's a very proud horse that will not carry its oats. (Italian)
Judge not a horse by its harness. (American)
Never swap horses while crossing a stream. (American)
No use in beating a dead horse. (German)
Often has a tattered colt grown up to be a splendid horse. (Irish)
One cannot shoe a running horse. (Dutch)
One man can lead a horse to water but twenty cannot make it drink. (Unknown)
Over a long distance, you learn about the strength of your horse. (Chinese)
Ragged colts make the handsomest stallions. (German)
Spur not a willing horse. (German)
The good horse is sold without being taken to market. (Spanish)
The gray mare is the better horse. (Spanish)
The horse is not judged by the saddle it wears. (German)
The horse is not the progeny of the slow-paced ass. (Roman)
The horse that draws most is most whipped. (French)
The horse thinks one thing, the rider another. (Spanish)
The old horse in the stable still wants to run. (Chinese)
The old horse leaves the load on the road. (Albanian)
The slow horse also reaches the mill. (Irish)
The stable wears out a horse more than the road. (French)
The steed does not retain its speed forever. (Irish)
There's nothing so good for the inside of a man as the outside of a horse. (English)
Vicious horses have vicious riders. (Chinese)
When the horse dies, dismount. (German)
When the manger is empty the horses fight. (Danish)
When your horse is on the brink of a precipice, it is too late to pull the reins. (Chinese)
Where there is a braying horse, there is a kicking horse. (Korean)
Who cannot beat the horse let him beat the saddle. (Italian)
Without spur and bridle, which horse can be good? (Spanish)

You can lead a horse to water but you can't make it drink. (English)
You don't need a whip to urge on an obedient horse. (Russian)

Horseshoe
The horseshoe that clatters wants a nail. (Spanish)

Hospitality
Abuse of hospitality breaks the bridge. (African)
Hospitality to the exile, and broken bones to the oppressor! (Irish)

Host
A merry host makes merry guests. (Dutch)
If you are a host to your guest, be also a host to his dog. (Russian)
Who reckons without his host must reckon again. (Dutch)

Hostility
Hostility provokes hostility. (Irish)

Hot
Hot sup, hot swallow. (French)
Soon hot, soon cold. (English)

Hound, Hounds
Many hounds are the death of the hare. (German)

Hour, Hours
An hour in the morning is worth two at night. (Dutch)
An hour may destroy the work of one hundred years. (Chinese)
An hour may destroy what an age has built. (Roman)
Each hour injures, the last one slays. (Roman)
Imperceptibly the hours glide on, and beguile us as they pass. (Roman)
Pleasant hours fly fast. (German)
The hour which gives us life begins to take it away. (Roman)
The passing hour is sometimes a mother, sometimes a stepmother. (Roman)

House
A house filled with guests is eaten up and ill spoken of. (Spanish)
A house without a woman is like a body without a soul. (German)
A house without a cat or a dog is the house of a scoundrel. (Portuguese)
An abandoned house is half in ruins. (Spanish)
An old house is full of leaks and creaks. (Spanish)
Better a little furniture than an empty house. (Danish)
Burn not your house to kill the mice. (English)
Every house has its problems. (German)
Everyone in his own house, and God in all men's. (Spanish)

Half a house is half a hell. (German)
He who buys a house gets many a plank and nail for nothing. (German)
How can one beam support a house? (Chinese)
It fares ill with the house when the distaff commands the sword. (Portuguese)
One house cannot keep two dogs. (Roman)
The house does not rest upon the ground, but upon a woman. (Mexican)
The house of a friend is the best house. (Roman)
The house shows the owner. (German)
Those who live in glass houses shouldn't throw stones. (English)
When the house is swept, everything turns up. (Yiddish)
When you see your house in flames, go warm yourself by it. (Spanish)
Woe to the house where the hen crows and the rooster is still. (Spanish)

Hug
A hug a day keeps the demons at bay. (German)

Human Affairs
As human affairs go, nothing is everlasting. (Roman)
At their summit, human affairs decline. (Roman)
Human affairs are a jest to be wept over. (Roman)

Human Nature
Human nature is the same all the world over. (American)
It is human to err, but diabolical to persevere. (German)
It is human to love, and it is also human to forgive. (Roman)
To err is human, to forgive divine. (English)

Humanity
Forget not that you are a man. (Roman)
Human blood is all of one color. (Danish)
Humanity and justice can turn aside the sword. (Japanese)
Men's skins have many colors, but human blood is always red. (French)
Nothing is too difficult for mortals; we strive to reach Heaven itself in our folly. (Roman)
So long as we live among men, let us cherish humanity. (Roman)
The greater part of humankind is bad. (Greek)

Humble, Humbled
Cap in hand never did any harm. (Italian)
It's hard to be high and humble. (German)
The humble reap advantage; the haughty meet with misfortune. (Chinese)
The more noble, the more humble. (German)
The one who exalts himself will be humbled. (Roman)
To be humble when we need help is manliness. (Egyptian)
To the humble is given happiness, to the proud calamity. (Chinese)
Too humble is half proud. (Yiddish)

Humiliate, Humiliating

Nothing is more humiliating than when a reproach recoils on the head of him who utters it. (Roman)

Humility

A cypher and humility make the other figures & virtues of ten-fold value. (Poor Richard)

Humility brings advantage; arrogance provokes disadvantage. (Chinese)

Humility is the beginning of wisdom. (Unknown)

Humility is the crown of a good disposition. (Egyptian)

Humility makes great men twice honorable. (Poor Richard)

Humor

A sense of humor is the pole that adds balance to our steps as we walk the tightrope of life. (Arabian)

Excess of wit may oftentimes beguile; jests are not always pardon'd by a smile. (Poor Richard)

Humor to a man is like a feather pillow: it is filled with what is easy to get but gives great comfort. (Irish)

Hunchback

The hunchback does not see his own hump, but he sees his neighbor's. (French)

The hunchback never sees his own hump. (German)

Hunger

A light belly, heavy heart. (German)

An empty belly bears no body. (German)

Better hunger than disgrace. (Hausan)

Death strikes some today, but hunger strikes everyone. (Yoruban)

Go not with every hunger to the cupboard, nor with every thirst to the pitcher. (Portuguese)

Hunger drives the wolf from the wood. (French)

Hunger eats through stone walls. (Dutch)

Hunger finds no fault with the cookery. (Dutch)

Hunger gives a relish even to raw beans. (Dutch)

Hunger is a poor advisor. (Mexican)

Hunger is felt by both slave and king. (African)

Hunger is the best cook. (Roman)

Hunger is the best gravy. (English)

Hunger is the best of seasonings. (Roman)

Hunger is the best sauce. (French)

Hunger is the best spice. (English)

Hunger sharpens anger. (Roman)

Hunger sweetens beans. (Roman)

Hunger sweetens everything but itself. (Roman)

Hunger teaches many things. (Greek)

Hunger will change beans into almonds. (Italian)

Hunger will lead a fox out of the forest. (Polish)

If you starve for three days, there is no thought that does not invade your mind. (Korean)

In the land of promise a man may die of hunger. (Dutch)

It is better to buy dearly than to hunger direly. (Danish)

It is better to satisfy our hunger than to be clothed in purple. (Roman)

Sufficiency will render an old man like a boy; hunger will render a boy like an old man. (Hausan)

The one who cannot endure hunger cooks the food for one who can endure hunger. (Yoruban)

Whatever satisfies hunger is good food. (Chinese)

When hunger is appeased we can preach the merits of fasting. (Roman)

Why does man hunger so much after forbidden fruit? (Roman)

Will hunger be satisfied with the first spoonful? (Korean)

Hungry

A hungry bear dances badly. (German)

A hungry belly has no ears. (Japanese)

A hungry belly listens to no one. (Spanish)

A hungry clown is half mad. (French)

A hungry dog and a thirsty horse cannot be goaded. (Danish)

A hungry dog does not fear the stick. (Italian)

A hungry dog will eat dirty pudding. (French)

A hungry horse makes a clean manger. (German)

A hungry man finds more than a hundred lawyers. (Spanish)

A hungry man has no conscience. (German)

A hungry man is an angry man. (Spanish)

A hungry man praises every dish. (Mexican)

A hungry man will listen to nothing. (Roman)

A hungry populace listens not to reason, nor cares for justice, nor is bent by any prayers. (Roman)

A hungry stomach rarely despises common fare. (Roman)

A hungry wolf is not at rest. (Portuguese)

Better to be hungry and have a pure mind than be filled and have an evil mind. (Chinese)

Do not stand in the way of a hungry man. (Roman)

Hungry bellies have no ears. (Polish)

Hungry flies sting sore. (German)

Nothing comes wrong to a hungry man. (Unknown)

There is no burnt rice to a hungry person. (Filipino)

There is no good in preaching to the hungry. (German)

To the hungry, all bread tastes sweet. (German)

You cannot amuse a hungry person. (African)

Hunter, Hunting

A hunter boasts about the game he bought. (Spanish)

All are not hunters that blow the horn. (German)

'An animal chases me' are not fitting words for a hunter. (Yoruban)

Deer hunter, waste not your arrow on the hare. (Chinese)

Every shot does not bring down a bird. (Dutch)

Good hunters track narrowly. (Dutch)

He that hunts others, must run himself. (German)

He that hunts two hares will catch neither. (French)

He who has no falcon, must hunt with owls. (Danish)

He who hunts with cats will catch mice. (Danish)

Hold your dog in readiness before you start the hare. (Danish)

If you would catch a fox you must hunt with geese. (Danish)

In small woods may be caught large hares. (Dutch)

Many a shot goes into the heather. (Irish)

One hunts the hare, and another eats it. (Danish)

Slaughter no more than you can well salt. (German)

The bird hunting a locust is unaware of the hawk hunting him. (Portuguese)

The dog that starts the hare is as good as the one that catches it. (German)

The hunter in pursuit of an elephant does not stop to throw stones at birds.
   (Ugandan)

The hunter never sees the mountain, nor the merchant the sea. (Chinese)

The noisy fowler catches no birds. (English)

The one who hunts deer pays no mind to hares. (Japanese)

There is no hunting but with old hounds. (French)

To scare a bird is not the way to catch it. (French)

Until the lions have their own historians, tales of the hunt shall always glorify the hunter.
   (Nigerian)

What's sport to the hunter is death to the deer. (German)

When its time has arrived, the prey comes to the hunter. (Persian)

When the hares are all caught, the hunter will boil his hound. (Chinese)

When the mantis hunts the locust, he forgets the shrike that's hunting him. (Chinese)

Whoso hunts with cats will catch nothing but rats. (Dutch)

You cannot hunt with a tied dog. (Albanian)

You cannot run with the hare and hunt with the hounds. (English)

Hurry, Hurried

Do not be in a hurry to tie what you cannot untie. (English)

Dress slowly when you are in a hurry. (French)

God did not create hurry. (Finnish)

He who hurries cannot walk with dignity. (Chinese)

Hurried men lack wisdom. (Chinese)

Hurry belongs to the Devil. (Arabian)

Hurry men at work, not at their meals. (Chinese)

Hurry no man's cattle. (German)

Hurrying has no blessing. (Kenyan)
The one in a hurry is always late. (Russian)

Hurt

A man can sleep on every hurt but his own. (Irish)
Everyone complains of his own hurt. (Irish)
No one is hurt by doing the right thing. (Hawaiian)
The least and weakest man can do some hurt. (Cambodian)
'Tis easier to hurt than heal. (German)
Where you hurt, there will you be hit. (Spanish)

Husband

A bad husband is never lost. (Spanish)
A good husband is healthy and absent. (Japanese)
Call your husband cuckold in jest, and he'll never suspect you. (Turkish)
Don't stay long when the husband is not at home. (Japanese)
The husband is always the last to know. (English)
The well-dressed woman draws her husband away from another woman's door.
    (Spanish)
With an old husband's hide one buys a young one. (French)

Husband and Wife

A deaf husband and a blind wife make a happy couple. (French)
A good Jack makes a good Jill. (American)
A good wife makes for a good husband. (English)
A man who's too good for the world is no good to his wife. (Yiddish)
A man without a wife is but half a man. (German)
Husband and wife are a small heaven and earth. (Chinese)
Husband and wife are like birds in the woods: when trouble comes, they flee separately.
    (Chinese)
If the wife sins, the husband is not innocent. (Italian)
If they were not enemies, they would not become husband and wife. (Chinese)
The calmest husbands make the stormiest wives. (English)
When a woman dies, both she and her husband rest in peace. (Spanish)
When the husband earns well the wife spins well. (Dutch)
When the husband sings, the wife follows. (Chinese)
Wisdom in the man, patience in the wife, brings peace to the house, and to both a happy
    life. (Dutch)

Hyena

If the hyena eats the sick man, it will eat the whole one. (Swahili)
When the hyena drinks, the dog can only look on. (Hausan)

Hypocrisy, Hypocrites

Do as I say, not as I do. (Roman)

Do what I say well, and not what I do ill. (Spanish)

Do what the friar says, and not what he does. (Spanish)

Hypocrites are the offspring of vipers. (Roman)

Hypocrites kick with their hind feet while licking with their tongues. (Russian)

I

Ice
Three feet of ice does not result from one day of cold weather. (Chinese)

Idea
A swollen idea can bring ruin. (Burmese)

Idle, Idler
An idle man is the Devil's bolster. (Italian)

An idle man is the Devil's pillow. (Dutch)

An idle mind is the Devil's workshop. (English)

An idle son learns vice. (Spanish)

An idle youth becomes in age a beggar. (Roman)

An idler always alibis. (Korean)

Better to sit idle than work for naught. (Spanish)

Half idle, half dead. (Unknown)

He is too idle to fetch his breath. (Dutch)

I would rather be ill than idle. (Roman)

Idle hands are the Devil's workshop. (American)

It is idle to swallow the cow and choke on the tail. (German)

It is only idle people who can find time for everything. (French)

No god assists the idle. (Roman)

Nobody truly envies the idle. (Spanish)

The busy man is troubled with but one devil, the idle man by a thousand. (Spanish)

The Devil tempts all, but the idle man tempts the Devil. (Italian)

The hardest work is to go idle. (Yiddish)

The idle are always needy. (Roman)

The idle have the least leisure. (Unknown)

To the idle man, the Devil gives wife and child. (Spanish)

With the idle every day is a holiday. (Roman)

Idleness
Evil thoughts often come from idleness. (Irish)

Idleness breeds lust. (Chinese)

Idleness has poverty for wages. (German)

Idleness hopes for good fortune. (Roman)

Idleness is ever the root of indecision. (Roman)

Idleness is hunger's mother. (Dutch)

Idleness is the beginning of all sin. (German)

Idleness is the blight of genius. (Roman)
Idleness is the dead sea, that swallows all virtues. (Poor Richard)
Idleness is the Devil's bolster. (Danish)
Idleness is the root of all evil. (German)
Idleness is the sepulcher of a living man. (German)
Idleness is to be dead at the limbs but alive within. (Fijian)
Idleness ruins the constitution. (Roman)
Poverty is the reward of idleness. (Dutch)

Idolater, Idolatry

A maker of idols is never an idolater. (Chinese)

Ignorance, Ignorant

Ignorance does not excuse the law. (Roman)
Ignorance is bliss. (American)
Ignorance is more troublesome than poverty. (Burmese)
Ignorance is not a sin, nor are ignorant deeds. (Chinese)
Ignorance is the cause of fear. (Roman)
Ignorance is the mother of impudence. (German)
Ignorance is the peace of life. (Kashmiri)
Ignorance lends enchantment to common things. (Unknown)
Ignorance may not kill you, but it does make you sweat a lot. (Haitian)
Ignorance of certain subjects is a great part of wisdom. (Dutch)
Ignorance that supports me is better than wisdom that I must support.
　　(Egyptian)
In extraordinary events ignorance of their causes produces astonishment.
　　(Roman)
It is rash to condemn where you are ignorant. (Roman)
The ignorant is his own enemy. (Arabian)
There is no darkness like ignorance. (Egyptian)
Where ignorance is bliss, 'tis folly to be wise. (English)

Ill, Illness

A lingering illness ends in death. (Irish)
Had he not been visited by sickness, he would have perished utterly. (Roman)
Illness tells us what we are. (Italian)
Mortals must bear many ills. (Roman)
Small ills are the fountains of most of our groans: men trip not on mountains, they
　　stumble on stones. (Chinese)
To the ill, nothing tastes good. (Spanish)

Imitate, Imitation

Do as others do, and few will mock you. (Danish)
Either do as your neighbors do, or move away. (Moroccan)
Emulation begets emulation. (Roman)

Emulation is the whetstone of wit. (Roman)

If I try to be like him, who will be like me? (Yiddish)

If you enter a goat stable, bleat; if you enter a water buffalo stable, bellow. (Indonesian)

If you impersonate a dragon, be like one; if you impersonate a tiger, be like one. (Chinese)

Imitate the snail in deliberation, the bird in execution. (Roman)

Imitation is the sincerest form of flattery. (Roman)

It is destruction to the weak man to attempt to imitate the powerful. (Roman)

Live near a lame man, and you will soon learn to limp. (Roman)

Live with vultures, become a vulture; live with crows, become a crow. (Laotian)

Live with wolves, and you will learn to howl. (Spanish)

We are all easily taught to imitate what is base and depraved. (Roman)

Immature

An immature ear of corn appears first. (Japanese)

Impasse

Even at an impasse, there is a way through. (Chinese)

Impatience

A little impatience spoils great plans. (Chinese)

Impatience does not diminish but augments the evil. (Roman)

Importance

He who gives himself airs of importance, exhibits the credentials of impotence. (Roman)

Impossible

No one is expected to do the impossible. (French)

Nothing is impossible. (Unknown)

The difficult is done at once; the impossible takes a little longer. (American)

To believe a thing impossible is to make it so. (French)

Impression, Impressions

First impressions are the most lasting. (English)

You don't get a second chance to make a first impression. (American)

Improve

He who does not improve today will grow worse tomorrow. (German)

Improve thyself. (Unknown)

It is an easy task to improve upon an invention. (Roman)

Improvident

Light-minded men are improvident of the future. (Roman)

Impunity
Impunity is always an invitation to a greater crime. (English)
Impunity is the parent of ferocity. (Roman)

Inclination
A wolf may lose its teeth but not its inclination. (Spanish)
My inclination first leads me in one direction, then in the opposite. (Roman)

Incompetence
All men rise to the level of their incompetence. (American; the Peter Principle)

Indecision
Indecision is the house of hunger. (African)
Indecision is the key to flexibility. (French)

Indulge, Indulgence
He who requires indulgence for his own offenses should grant it to others. (Roman)
It is delightful to indulge in extravagance on the return of a friend. (Roman)
Little indulgences precede great sorrows. (Yiddish)

Industrious, Industry
An industrious life is the best security for food in old age. (Roman)
Bustle is not industry. (German)
God gives all things to industry. (Poor Richard)
Industry is a recompense to itself. (Roman)
Industry is the parent of fortune. (German)
Industry is the twin brother of prosperity. (Filipino)
When industry goes out of the door, poverty comes in at the window. (Dutch)

Infect
A measly hog infects the whole sty. (Spanish)
One rotten apple in the basket infects the whole. (Dutch)
One scabbed sheep will infect a whole flock. (German)

Infer, Inference
From what has taken place we infer what is about to happen. (Roman)

Infinite
The infinite is in the finite of every instant. (Japanese)

Ingratitude
An ungrateful man is a tub full of holes. (Roman)
If you say that he is guilty of ingratitude, you need say no more. (Roman)
Ingratitude is the daughter of pride. (Spanish)
Ingratitude is the mother of every vice. (French)

Ingratitude is the world's reward. (German)
Ingratitude sickens benevolence. (German)
One ungrateful beggar does injury to all who are wretched. (Roman)
Poor thanks is the way of the world. (Norwegian)
We find much ingratitude, and create more. (Roman)

Inherit, Inheritance

A clever man's inheritance is found in every country. (Danish)
An estate inherited is the less valued. (Portuguese)
Call for the inheritance and you may have to pay for the funeral. (Yiddish)
He who inherits a farthing, is expected to disburse a dollar. (German)
He who pins his hopes on a legacy gives himself up to poverty. (Yoruban)
In the division of inheritance, friendship stands still. (Dutch)
No one knows who will inherit his money. (Mexican)
The right of inheritance never ascends. (Roman)

Inhumane, Inhumanity

Inhumanity is harmful in every age. (Roman)
Jokes directed against the unfortunate are inhumane. (Roman)

Injure, Injury

A blow from a frying-pan blackens, though it may not hurt. (Roman)
A blow with a reed makes a noise but hurts not. (Spanish)
A little injury dismays, and a great one stills. (Portuguese)
Better a leg broken than the neck. (Dutch)
Even to smile at the unfortunate is to do them injury. (Roman)
Favors grow old early, but injuries are life long. (Roman)
He invites future injuries who rewards past ones. (Dutch)
He that courts injury will obtain it. (Danish)
He who does the wrong forgets it, but not he who receives it. (Italian)
He who has received a kindness forgets it; he who has been injured remembers it.
    (Roman)
He who is the offender is never the forgiver. (Italian)
How galling it is to be injured by one against whom you dare not make a complaint!
    (Roman)
If a man does not have the heart to injure others, he will not meet with punishment.
    (Chinese)
Injuries destroy affection. (Roman)
Injuries that are slighted and unnoticed are soon forgotten. (Roman)
Injury is to be measured by malice. (Italian)
It is better to receive than to do an injury. (Roman)
It is better to take many injuries than to give one. (Poor Richard)
Let the injurer not forget. (Italian)
Men are more prone to revenge injuries than to requite kindnesses. (Irish)
No injury can be claimed by a consenting party. (Roman)

No injury is done to a feigned friend. (Roman)
No injury is done to the willing. (Roman)
Recompense injury with justice and kindness with kindness. (Chinese)
Sometimes those who suffer injury find it beneficial. (Roman)
The best remedy for injuries is to forget them. (Roman)
The injured never forgets. (Italian)
The one who is bent on doing an injury has already done it. (Roman)

Injustice

Authority, founded on injustice, does not remain perpetual. (Roman)
Injustice all round is justice. (Persian)

In-law, In-laws

A son-in-law never becomes a son and a daughter-in-law never quite becomes a
   daughter. (Greek)
A son-in-law's friendship is a winter's sun. (Spanish)
As long as I was a daughter-in-law I never had a good mother-in-law, and as long as I
   was a mother-in-law I never had a good daughter-in-law. (Spanish)
Daughter-in-law hates mother-in-law. (German)
If it's the father-in-law you wed, a grizzly bear will share your bed. (Yiddish)
Mother-in-law and daughter-in-law, storm and hail. (Italian)
Never rely on the glory of the morning or the smiles of your mother-in-law. (Japanese)
She is well married who has neither mother-in-law nor sister-in-law. (Portuguese)
The husband's mother is the wife's devil. (German)
The mother-in-law does not remember that she was once a daughter-in-law. (Spanish)
The son-in-law's sack is never full. (Portuguese)
Though my father-in-law is a good man, I do not like a dog with a bell. (Spanish)
To a son-in-law and a hog you need show the way but once. (Spanish)

Inn, Innkeeper

No one would be an innkeeper but for money. (Spanish)
The innkeeper loves the drunkard, but not for a son-in-law. (Yiddish)
The nearer the inn, the longer the road. (German)

Innocence, Innocent

A grim end awaits the innocent. (Roman)
A mind conscious of innocence laughs at the lies of rumor. (Roman)
An innocent heart suspects no guile. (Portuguese)
Children and drunken men are the world's only innocents. (Unknown)
Innocence is no protection. (English)
Innocence itself sometimes hath need of a mask. (Polish)
Innocence plays in the backyard of ignorance. (Polish)
No protection is so sure as that of innocence. (Roman)

Inquire, Inquiry

He who inquires much, learns much. (Danish)
Limit your inquiry after knowledge. (Roman)

Inquisitive

An inquisitive man is always ill-natured. (Roman)

Insane, Insanity

The insane person thinks all others insane. (Spanish)
We have all at one time been insane. (Roman)
Insanity cannot recognize itself any more than blindness can see itself. (Roman)

Insects

Insects do not nest in a busy door-hinge. (Chinese)

Inside

The inside is different from the outside. (Korean)

Insincerity

A forced kindness deserves no thanks. (Italian)
A man without sincerity is like the dross from iron without a bit of steel. (Chinese)
'Yours truly', is not always true. (English)

Inspiration

No man was ever great without some divine inspiration. (Roman)

Instinct

Instinct is stronger than upbringing. (Irish)
Let him make use of instinct who cannot make use of reason. (English)

Instruct, Instruction

Instruction in youth is like engraving in stone. (Moroccan)
Instruction may build skill, but it is practice that makes the master. (German)
The best mode of instruction is to practice what we preach. (Persian)
The things which hurt, instruct. (Poor Richard)

Insult, Insults

A cutting word is worse than a bowstring: a cut may heal, but the cut of the tongue does not. (African)
A public insult requires a public apology. (Hausan)
By submitting to an old insult you invite a new one. (Roman)
Do not tell the man who is carrying you that he stinks. (Sierra Leonean)
He who puts up with insults invites injury. (Yiddish)
Insults follow the afflicted. (Unknown)
It is often better not to see an insult than to avenge it. (Roman)

Integrity

Integrity is true honor. (Roman)

Strict integrity leaves one isolated. (Unknown)

Intellect

No era is closed to great intellects. (Roman)

Intemperance

It is as much intemperance to weep too much, as to laugh too much. (Danish)

Intention, Intentions

A hidden intention is an evil one. (Roman)

Many have good intentions, but something comes across them. (German)

Mere intentions are not to be as esteemed as actions. (Roman)

The consciousness of good intention is the greatest solace of misfortunes. (Roman)

Interpreter

Every man is the best interpreter of his own words. (German)

Intimate

Be on too intimate terms with no one; if your joy be less, so will your grief. (Roman)

Investment

If a little money does not go out, great money will not come in. (Chinese)

'It will come back', said the man, when he gave his sow pork. (Danish)

Iron

Iron does not clang by itself. (Madagascan)

Iron that is not used soon rusts. (Portuguese)

Irritate

It is safer to irritate a dog than an old woman. (Roman)

Island

No man is an island. (English)

No man is an island – but some of us are long peninsulas. (French)

Itch

Let him that itches scratch himself. (French)

J

Jam

Jam tomorrow and jam yesterday, but never jam today. (Chinese)

Jar

The jar will long retain the odor of that which once filled it. (Roman)

Jealous, Jealousy

A neighbor's eye is full of jealousy. (Danish)
Jealousy bites more than fleas. (Spanish)
Jealousy denied is jealousy confirmed. (Spanish)
Jealousy destroys love. (Mexican)
Jealousy is nourished by doubt. (French)
Love expels jealousy. (French)
No jealousy, no love. (German)
The jealousy of a woman sets a whole house aflame. (Roman)
There is no love without jealousy. (Italian)

Jest, Jesting

A bitter jest, when it comes too near the truth, leaves a sharp sting behind it. (Roman)
A jest is half a truth. (Yiddish)
Drop the jest when it is most amusing. (Italian)
Fear not a jest. (Roman)
Good jests bite like lambs, not like dogs. (German)
He makes a foe who makes a jest. (Poor Richard)
He that would jest must take a jest. (Dutch)
It's ill jesting with edged tools. (Dutch)
Jest with your equals. (Danish)
Jesting costs money. (Spanish)
Leave the jest at its best. (Spanish)
Many a true word is spoken in jest. (English)
Play not with a man till you hurt him, nor jest till you shame him. (German)
Said in sport, meant in earnest. (German)
There are limits even to jesting. (English)
When the jest is at its best, 'twill be well to let it rest. (German)

Jew

A Jew's joy is not without fright. (Yiddish)
A wise Jew is very wise; a foolish one is a fool indeed. (Yiddish)

Job

A job is fine, but it interferes with your time. (Yiddish)
Agriculture is best, enterprise is acceptable, but avoid being on a fixed wage. (Indian)
As the job, so the clothes. (German)
Each person at his job is a god. (Albanian)
Each person in his occupation is king. (Mexican)
If you want a job done right, do it yourself. (American)
Never send a boy to do a man's job. (American)
No office so humble but it is better than nothing. (Dutch)

You will not get a big job done from one who does not want to do a small one.
(Albanian)

Join
If you can't beat 'em, join 'em. (American)

Joke, Joking
A joke driven too far brings home hate. (Yiddish)
Even the gods love jokes. (Greek)
He that laughs at his own joke, spoils the fun of it. (Danish)
In jokes, there are truths. (Korean)
Jokes directed against the unfortunate are inhumane. (Roman)
Jokes reveal truths. (Spanish)
Moderation should be used in joking. (Roman)
Never joke in the presence of a prince. (Chinese)
No joke is too small to sting. (Spanish)
Out of a joke comes a truth. (Japanese)
There is no worse joke than a true one. (Italian)

Journey, Journeys
Discreet stops make speedy journeys. (Spanish)
Do not take either a blind guide or a weak advisor. (Greek)
Go further and fare worse. (Persian)
He goes not out of his way that goes to a good inn. (Roman)
He who has left a rogue behind him, has made a good day's journey. (German)
He who is outside the door has already a good part of the journey behind him. (Dutch)
He who stops at every stone never gets to his journey's end. (French)
He who would go further than his horse, must alight and go on foot. (German)
Nothing is lost on a journey by stopping to pray or to feed your horse. (Spanish)
On a long journey even a straw is heavy. (Italian)
One foot is as far as a thousand miles. (Korean)
One may go a long way after one is tired. (French)
Setting out well is a quarter of the journey. (French)
The journey is the reward. (Taoist)
The journey of a thousand miles begins with one step. (Chinese)
You must start by night to arrive by day. (Persian)

Joy, Joyful
A joy that's shared is a joy made double. (English)
A poor man's joy has much alloy. (Danish)
Every inch of joy has an ell of annoy. (German)
Every life has its joy, every joy its law. (Danish)
In the midst of joy do not promise anything; in the midst of anger do not answer anyone.
(Chinese)
Joy creates beauty. (Spanish)

Joy is like the ague: one good day between two bad ones. (Danish)

Let us be joyful, while we are young. (Roman)

No joy comes unmixed; and something of anxiety intervenes with every pleasure. (Roman)

No joy without alloy. (Spanish)

One joy scatters a hundred griefs. (Chinese)

There is no joy without alloy. (Dutch)

Joy and Sorrow

A joyful evening may follow a sorrowful morning. (English)

A joyous evening often leads to a sorrowful morning. (Danish)

At the height of joy, sorrow begins. (Japanese)

Better the cottage where one is merry than the palace where one weeps. (Chinese)

Better to have joy in a cottage than sorrow in a palace. (Spanish)

Heaviness may endure for a night, but joy cometh in the morning. (German)

Joy and sorrow are neighbors. (Unknown)

Joy and sorrow are today and tomorrow. (German)

Joy surfeited turns to sorrow. (Danish)

No one possesses unalloyed pleasure; there is some anxiety mingled with the joy. (Roman)

Some joys are dull, some sorrows are pleasant. (Spanish)

Judge, Judging

A corrupt judge does not carefully search for truth. (Roman)

A foolish judge passes a brief sentence. (French)

A good and faithful judge ever prefers the honorable to the expedient. (Roman)

A good judge is one who prevents litigation. (Roman)

A judge is a speaking law, law a silent judge. (Roman)

Abroad we judge the dress; at home we judge the man. (Chinese)

Do not judge by appearances: a rich heart may be under a poor coat. (Irish)

Do not judge of the ship from the land. (Italian)

Do not judge the dog by its hairs. (Danish)

Do not judge your friend until you stand in his place. (Danish)

Don't judge a man by the words of his mother, listen to the comments of his neighbors. (Yiddish)

Don't judge any man until you have walked two moons in his moccasins. (Native American)

Don't judge hastily of a ragged boy or a shaggy colt. (Irish)

Don't judge of men's wealth or piety, by their Sunday appearances. (Poor Richard)

Empty the glass if you would judge of the drink. (Roman)

From one you may judge of the whole. (Roman)

God help the sheep when the wolf is judge. (Danish)

He cannot be strict in judging who does not wish others to be strict judges of himself. (Roman)

He is no judge who listens to one side only. (Korean)

He who judges between two friends loses one of them. (French)

He who knows little, judges everything by the one thing he knows. (Japanese)

If you would be a good judge, hear what everyone says. (Portuguese)

Judge a man by the reputation of his enemies. (Arabian)

Judge a tree by its fruit, not by its leaves. (Roman)

Judge not of a ship as she lies on the stocks. (Arabian)

Judge not the horse by its saddle. (Chinese)

Judge not the peppercorn by its size: crack it and see how strong it is. (Persian)

Judge not, lest ye be judged. (Jesus)

Judge of the daughter by the mother. (Roman)

Let not the shoemaker judge beyond his last. (Roman)

Measure the corn of others with your own bushel. (Yiddish)

Never judge a book by its cover. (Italian)

No one is a good judge in his own cause. (Portuguese)

No one ought to be judge in his own cause. (Roman)

Tell God the truth, but give the judge money. (Russian)

The good judge condemns the crime, but does not hate the criminal. (Roman)

The judge is condemned when the guilty is acquitted. (Roman)

We judge of the present from the past. (Roman)

When you meet a man, you judge him by his clothes; when you leave, you judge him by his heart. (Russian)

Who judges best of a man, his enemies or himself? (Poor Richard)

Who judges others, condemns himself. (Italian)

Judgment

Imagination gallops, judgment merely walks. (Italian)

Many complain of their memory, few of their judgment. (Poor Richard)

Much memory and little judgment. (French)

Jug

The jug goes to the well until it breaks. (German)

Jump

Jump not before learning to walk. (Korean)

Jupiter

Even Jupiter cannot please everyone, whether he sends rain or fair weather. (Roman)

Far from Jupiter, far from his thunder. (Roman)

Just

A just balance preserves justice. (Roman)

Be just before you're generous. (Chinese)

Just scales and full measure injure no one. (Chinese)

Justice

Everyone likes justice in another's house, none in his own. (Italian)

Favor and gifts disturb justice. (Danish)

He that buys magistracy will sell justice. (English)

Justice and truth are not to be found in this world. (Spanish)

Justice has a waxen nose. (German)

Justice is nothing but the interest of the stronger. (Greek)

Justice is the queen of virtues. (Roman)

Justice is three votes of five. (Spanish)

Justice naturally inhibits men's hearts. (Chinese)

Justice often leans to the side where purse strings pull. (Danish)

Limping justice ne'er will fail to hunt out the longest trail. (Roman)

Money and friendship break the arms of justice. (Italian)

Much law, but little justice. (Portuguese)

No one likes justice brought home to his own door. (Italian)

Nothing can be honorable where justice is absent. (Roman)

Popular agitation leads to justice. (Tamil)

The arm of justice is long. (English)

The fountain of justice is good faith. (Roman)

The highest justice is often the greatest injustice. (Roman)

The millstone of justice grinds slowly, but it grinds sure. (the Editor)

To give everyone his due, that is supreme justice. (Roman)

'Twas fear of injustice that brought justice into being. (Roman)

Who refuses to submit to justice, must not complain of oppression. (German)

Without justice, courage is weak. (Poor Richard)

K

Karma

Karma is the mother, karma is the father. (Burmese)

Keep

It is not easy to keep to yourself what many desire. (Roman)

Keep a thing for seven years and you'll find a use for it. (Irish)

Keep between both extremes. (Roman)

To get is easier than to keep. (Spanish)

Key, Keys

All keys hang not on one girdle. (Danish)

All the keys in the land do not hang from one girdle. (Irish)

Everyone is given the key to the gates of Heaven; but the same key opens the gates of Hell. (Roman)

The key that is used grows bright. (German)

Keyhole

The one who peeps through a keyhole often sees what he does not wish to see.
(German)

Kill

All the hours wound you, but the last one kills you. (Roman)

Don't kill the man at the king's desire. (Spanish)

Even those who have no wish to kill anyone, would like to have the power. (Roman)

Hunger and thirst scarcely kill any, but gluttony and drink kill a great many. (Roman)

I kill the boars, another enjoys their flesh. (Roman)

Kill one to warn a hundred. (Chinese)

Kill the chicken to frighten the monkey. (Chinese)

Kill two birds with one stone. (English)

Never kill a man who says nothing. (Nigerian)

The one who kills the father and leaves the children is a fool. (Roman)

There are many ways of killing a dog without choking him with butter. (Irish)

There are more ways of killing a cat than choking it on cream. (English)

When the tiger kills, the jackal profits. (Afghani)

Kin, Kindred

A man cannot carry all his kin on his back. (Danish)

Everyone is kin to a rich man. (English)

Much kindred, much trouble. (French)

Only in photographs do your kin look nice. (Unknown)

'Our own kin are the worst friends', said the fox, when he saw the dogs after him.
(Danish)

Pass the bridge that your kinsmen have passed. (Georgian)

Rich kin are close kin. (Yiddish)

The nearer the kin, the further in. (German)

Kind, Kindness

A kindness bestowed on the good is never thrown away. (Roman)

Better to be kind at home than burn incense in a far place. (Chinese)

By good nature and kindness even fierce spirits become tractable. (Roman)

Forget injuries, never forget a kindness. (Chinese)

God puts a good root in the little pig's way. (French)

God tempers the wind to the shorn lamb. (Unknown)

How quickly a kindness is forgotten. (Roman)

If a person shave you with a razor, do not shave him with broken glass. (Dutch)

It is no sin to stretch out your hand to the fallen. (Roman)

Kindness begets kindness. (Greek)

Kindness breaks no bones. (German)

Kindness to evil men is as bad as injury to good men. (Persian)

Kindnesses, like grain, increase by sowing. (German)

No gratitude attaches to a kindness long deferred. (Roman)

Nothing grows old sooner than a kindness. (French)

One kindness is the price of another. (Japanese)

Respect for one's superiors, kindness for one's inferiors. (Vietnamese)

The kindness is doubled if what must be given is given willingly. (Roman)

The kindness we show to a hen is not lost; eventually it will make gravy in our mouth. (Yoruban)

The one who sows kindness will reap gratitude. (Arabian)

There is no greater duty than that of repaying a kindness. (Roman)

Wherever there is a human being there is an opportunity for a kindness. (Roman)

Write injuries in the sand, kindnesses in marble. (French)

Kind Words

Kind words are as a physician to an afflicted spirit. (Roman)

Kind words conquer. (Tamil)

Kind words don't wear out the tongue. (Danish)

Kind words heal friendship's wounds. (Danish)

Kind words will unlock an iron door. (Kurdish)

King, Kings

A cork will do for a king, if you need him that badly. (Yiddish)

A good king is better than an old law. (Danish)

A king cannot go as far as he will, only as far as he can. (German)

A king is given for the sake of the kingdom, not the kingdom for the sake of the king. (Roman)

A king is one who fears nothing; a king is one who desires nothing. (Roman)

A king should prefer his country to his children. (Roman)

A king's castle is his home. (Roman)

A king's chaff is worth more than other men's corn. (Roman)

An illiterate king is a crowned ass. (English)

As is the king, so are his people. (Spanish)

Do you not know that kings have long hands? (Roman)

Every monarch is subject to a mightier one. (Roman)

Every person is king in his own home. (Albanian)

It befits the king to be liberal, for he is sure of never falling into poverty. (Portuguese)

Kings have long arms. (Greek)

Kings have many ears and eyes. (Roman)

Kings love the treason, but not the traitor. (Roman)

Kings will find armies, and the world men. (Irish)

Never pray for a new king. (Yiddish)

New king, new laws. (Unknown)

No lapse of time bars the rights of the king. (Roman)

Scratch a king and find a fool. (German)

The greater the king, the greater the people. (German)

The greatest king must at last be laid to rest with a shovel. (French)

The king and the crying child will have their way. (Japanese)

The king can do no wrong. (Roman)
The king cannot rule as he wishes. (German)
The king of the bees has no sting. (Portuguese)
The king's wishes are commands. (German)
The reach of a king is long. (German)
We cannot all be kings. (German)

Kiss, Kisses

A kiss between husband and wife needs no defense. (German)
A kiss without a beard is like an egg without salt. (Dutch)
A kiss without a hug is like a flower without the fragrance. (Maltese)
For sake of the knight the lady kisses the squire. (French)
If you can kiss the mistress, never kiss the maid. (Bulgarian)
Kiss the hand you cannot bite. (Roman)
Kisses are the messengers of love. (Danish)
Kisses that are easily obtained are easily forgotten. (English)
Kissing goes by favor. (English)
Many kiss the child for the mother's sake. (Unknown)
Many kiss the hand they would gladly see cut off. (Spanish)
One kisses the child for the mother's sake, and the mother for the child's sake. (German)
When the gorse is out of bloom, kissing's out of fashion. (Danish)
Who wipes the child's nose, kisses the mother's cheek. (German)

Kitchen

A fat kitchen is next door to poverty. (Italian)
A fat kitchen makes a lean will. (French)
Who frequents the kitchen smells of smoke. (Italian)

Knave

He is no small knave who knows a great one. (Danish)
Once a knave, always a knave. (English)
The hatred of knaves is to be preferred to their company. (Roman)

Knead

It is easy to knead when meal is at hand. (Irish)

Knife

A bad knife cuts one's finger instead of the stick. (Portuguese)
A dull knife cannot sharpen itself. (Korean)
A good knife is not used for scraping. (Chinese)
A knife cannot carve its own handle. (Korean)
One knife keeps another in its sheath. (Italian)
One knife whets another. (German)
The same knife that cut the goat will cut the sheep. (Jamaican)
There was never a good knife made of bad steel. (Poor Richard)

Whether the knife falls on the melon or the melon on the knife, the melon suffers.
    (African)
Would you use a butcher knife to split a pea? (Chinese)

Knot
A hard knot requires a hard wedge. (Roman)

Know, Known
A doctor and a farmer know more than a doctor alone. (German)
All that is known is not told. (Egyptian)
Even though you know a thousand things, ask the man who knows one. (Turkish)
Everyone is least known to himself, and it is very difficult for a man to know himself.
    (Roman)
Everyone wishes to know, but no one is willing to pay the price. (Roman)
Hardly one man in ten knows himself. (Roman)
He that converses not knows nothing. (Turkish)
He who knows himself as well as his opponent will be invincible. (Korean)
He who knows little often repeats it. (English)
He who knows little soon tells it. (Spanish)
He who knows nothing doubts nothing. (Spanish)
He who knows nothing knows enough, if he knows how to be silent. (Italian)
He who knows nothing suspects nothing. (the Editor)
He who knows one knows none. (German)
He who knows the road can ride full trot. (Italian)
If three know it, all know it. (Italian)
It is nothing for you to know a thing unless another knows that you know it. (Roman)
It takes one to know one. (American)
Know not what you know, and see not what you see. (Roman)
Know thyself. (Greek)
Know thyself to know others, for heart beats like heart. (Chinese)
Many know many things, no one everything. (English)
Neither is it permitted to know all things. (Roman)
No man knows whose morrow it will be. (Yiddish)
No one knows what will happen to him before sunset. (Danish)
Not to know is bad; not to wish to know is worse. (Nigerian)
Often it is not even advantageous to know what will be. (Roman)
One is known by his companions. (Roman)
Ten lands are sooner known than one man. (Yiddish)
The afternoon knows what the morning never suspected. (Swedish)
The more one knows, the less one boasts of knowing. (Spanish)
The more one knows, the more one doubts. (Spanish)
The one who knows knows. (Mexican)
The one who knows most says the least. (Italian)
To know a person, you must live with a person. (Irish)
To know all is to forgive all. (French)

To know and to act are one and the same. (Samurai)
To know everything is to know nothing. (Italian)
To know is easier than to do. (German)
To know me is to love me. (American)
To know the road ahead, ask those coming back. (Chinese)
We know what we have, but not what we shall get. (German)
We will be known by the tracks we leave behind. (Native American)
What you don't know can't hurt you. (American)
Who knows most believes least. (Italian)
Who knows most says least. (French)

Knowledge

A little knowledge is a dangerous thing. (Portuguese)
A man of knowledge increases strength. (the Bible)
A man of knowledge like a rich soil feeds, if not a world of corn, then a world of weeds.
   (Poor Richard)
Blind is everyone who lacks knowledge. (Irish)
For knowledge is itself power. (Roman)
He that increases knowledge increases sorrow. (the Bible)
He who has knowledge has power. (Persian)
Knowledge acquired as a child is more lasting than an engraving on stone. (Arabian)
Knowledge brings anxiety in life. (Chinese)
Knowledge comes through practice. (Irish)
Knowledge divorced from justice may be called cunning rather than wisdom. (Roman)
Knowledge is a treasure, but practice is the key to it. (Arabian)
Knowledge is better than money in the bank. (English)
Knowledge is better than riches. (Mexican)
Knowledge is light, ignorance a cloud. (Filipino)
Knowledge is no burden. (German)
Knowledge is not the main thing, but deeds. (Sierra Leonean)
Knowledge itself is power. (English)
Knowledge without wisdom is a load of books on the back of an ass. (Japanese)
Lack of knowledge is darker than night. (Hausan)
Nature has given us the seeds of knowledge, not knowledge itself. (Roman)
Prudent questioning is the half of knowledge. (Roman)
Questioning is the door of knowledge. (Irish)
Search for knowledge though it be in China. (Arabian)
There is a certain wonderful sweetness and delight in gaining knowledge. (Roman)
Ultimate knowledge costs the ultimate price. (Roman)

L

Labor, Laborer

As the labor, so the pay. (German)

Completed labors are pleasant to recall. (Roman)
Copper begets copper, and not the labor of men's bones. (Spanish)
Foolish is the labor that is bestowed on foolish things. (Roman)
Great labor overcomes everything. (Roman)
He who begins and does not finish loses his labor. (French)
It is hard to labor with an empty belly. (Danish)
It is lost labor to sow where there is no soil. (German)
Labor conquers all things. (Roman)
Labor has a bitter root, but a sweet taste. (Danish)
Labor is bitter but the bread it buys is sweet. (Indian)
Labor is in itself a pleasure. (Italian)
Labor is its own reward. (Roman)
Labor is the key to rest. (Indian)
Labor teaches the laborer. (Latvian)
Labor warms, sloth harms. (Dutch)
Life has given nothing great to mortals without labor. (Roman)
Look for a thing until you find it and you'll not lose your labor. (Chinese)
Love makes labor light. (Dutch)
Many a man labors for the day he will never live to see. (Danish)
Rise early, and you will observe; labor, and you will have. (Portuguese)
Smooth hands love the labor of others. (Russian)
Sweet is the memory of past labor. (Greek)
The active should occasionally rest, the inactive should occasionally labor. (Roman)
The laborer is worthy of his hire. (Jesus)
The mountain labored and brought forth a mouse. (Roman)
The remembrance of past labors is pleasant. (Roman)

Ladder
You must climb a ladder step by step. (Persian)

Lady
You a lady and I a lady, who will feed the pigs? (English)
You a lady, I a lady, who is to put the pig outdoors? (Rumanian)

Laggard
The laggard is ever the loser. (Irish)

Lake
Drop by drop the lake is drained. (French)

Lamb
The lamb pays dearly for the friendship between a wolf and the watchdog. (Spanish)
Though lamb may taste good, it cannot be cooked to suit all tastes. (Chinese)
We all like the taste of lamb, but each has a different way of cooking it. (Greek)

Lame

A lame man won't walk with one who is lamer. (French)

In the end, the lame foot overtakes the swift one. (German)

The lame man knows how to dance, only he has no feet. (Yoruban)

The lame man runs if he has to. (Norwegian)

Lamentable

Nothing is lamentable unless you think it so. (Roman)

Lamp, Lamplight

Beneath the lamp it is always dark. (Korean)

By lamplight every country wench seems handsome. (Italian)

If you would have the lamp burn, you must pour oil into it. (German)

Keep oil in your lamps. (Roman)

Light a lamp on the road and thus make the path clear for travelers. (Chinese)

Light your lamp before night overtakes you. (Greek)

No lamp burns till morning. (Persian)

The lamp does not give light to its own base. (Persian)

Land

A lord without land is like a cask without wine. (Danish)

Better a ruined land than a lost land. (French)

Every land has its own trifles. (German)

Every land is home to the wise. (German)

Not every land has all at hand. (German)

On parched land even brackish water is good. (Spanish)

The land a man knows is his mother. (Spanish)

The land is a mother that never dies. (Maori)

Who buys land buys war. (Italian)

Whoever has land has war. (French)

Language

If two languages say the same thing, it is not the same thing. (Roman)

The inhabitants of earth have many tongues, those of Heaven have one. (Roman)

Wherever you go, speak the language of that place. (Chinese)

Who knows the tongues is at home everywhere. (Dutch)

You are as many a person as languages you know. (Armenian)

Lapp

Every Lapp favors his own cap. (German)

Last

Not to hope for things to last forever is what the year teaches, and even the hour which speeds the pleasant day. (Roman)

Nothing lasts forever. (American)

Last Straw
'Tis the last straw that breaks the camel's back. (Unknown)

Late
A late man brings trouble on himself. (Irish)
Better late than never. (English)
Better late than too late. (Irish)
Better never late. (American)
Bones for those who come late. (Roman)
He who always thinks it is too soon is sure to come too late. (German)
It is too late for the bird to shriek when it is caught. (French)
It is too late taking up a shield after being wounded. (Roman)
It is too late to come with water when the house is burnt down. (Italian)
It is too late to cover the well when the child is drowned. (Danish)
It is too late to grieve when chance has passed. (Unknown)
It is too late to lock the stable door after the horse is stolen. (Spanish)
It's too late to shut the stable door after the horse has bolted. (Norwegian)
Long sleep makes hot rowing. (Irish)
The late comer is ill lodged. (German)
The later the evening, the fairer the company. (German)
Who rises late must trot all day. (French)

Laugh
He laughs best who laughs last. (Dutch)
He laughs best who laughs longest. (Swedish)
He laughs ill that laughs himself to death. (German)
He that laughs on Friday may cry on Sunday. (French)
He who laughs alone is recalling his little sins. (Spanish)
He who laughs last laughs best. (German)
He who laughs last laughs longest. (English)
He who laughs much weeps much. (Turkish)
He who laughs overmuch may have an aching heart. (Italian)
He who tickles himself, can laugh when he likes. (German)
If you laugh today, you will cry tomorrow. (Portuguese)
It is better for a man to laugh at life than to lament over it. (Roman)
Laugh with those that laugh. (Roman)
No one becomes a laughing stock who eagerly laughs at himself. (Roman)
One half the world laughs at the other half. (French)
One never wept but another laughed. (Italian)
That day is lost on which one has not laughed. (French)
The laugh is always on the loser. (German)
There is nothing more foolish than a foolish laugh. (Roman)
They will be hushed by a good deed who laugh at a wise speech. (French)
Time spent laughing is time spent with the gods. (Japanese)
Who laughs at others' ills, has his own behind the door. (Italian)

Laughter

Better to die of laughter than of jaundice. (Spanish)

Ill-timed laughter is a dangerous evil. (Greek)

Laughter abounds in the mouth of fools. (Roman)

Laughter cannot bring back what anger has driven away. (Japanese)

Laughter is the best of medicines. (English)

Laughter is the hiccup of a fool. (Japanese)

Laughter makes good blood. (Italian)

Meaningless laughter is a sign of ill-breeding. (Arabian)

Much laughter, little wit. (Portuguese)

The laughter of the cottage is more hearty and sincere than that of the court. (Roman)

Law, Laws

A morally corrupt orator subverts the law. (Roman)

As fast as laws are devised, their evasion is contrived. (German)

Better no law, than no law enforced. (Danish)

Delays in the law are odious. (Roman)

Easy to believe in Heaven's law, but so hard to keep. (Chinese)

Even the gods above are subject to law. (Roman)

Even thieves are said to have laws which they obey. (Roman)

Every land has its own law. (German)

Every land its law, every man his custom. (Unknown)

Extreme law is often extreme wrong. (Roman)

For the upright there are no laws. (German)

From bad morals good laws are produced. (Roman)

From the words of the law there is no departure. (Roman)

God gives the will, necessity gives the law. (Danish)

Good laws grow out of evil acts. (Roman)

Hard cases make bad law. (Roman)

Hard is a new law imposed on old license. (Italian)

He who makes a law should keep it. (Spanish)

How rashly do we sanction an unjust law against ourselves! (Roman)

Ignorance of the law does not excuse breaking it. (Roman)

Ignorance of the law is no excuse. (American)

In the most corrupt state exist the most laws. (Roman)

It injures no one to keep the law. (Roman)

It is better to live unknown to the law. (Irish)

It is but a small matter to be good in the eye of the law. (Roman)

Kings and fools know no law. (German)

Law cannot persuade where it cannot punish. (German)

Law helps the waking, luck may come to the sleeping. (Danish)

Law is a flag and gold is the wind that makes it wave. (Russian)

Laws are made to be broken. (Spanish)

Laws are subservient to custom. (Roman)

Laws catch flies but let hornets go free. (Unknown)

Laws control the lesser man; right conduct controls the greater one. (Chinese)

Laws go the way kings direct. (Spanish)

Laws go where money pleases. (Portuguese)

Laws have been ordained so that the stronger may not have everything their own way. (Roman)

Laws have wax noses. (French)

Laws were made for rogues. (Italian)

Laws, like the spider's webs, catch the flies and let the hawk go free. (Spanish)

Neither make a law nor break one. (Irish)

New laws, new roguery. (German)

No law intends that anyone shall live in poverty or die in anguish. (Roman)

No law is sufficiently convenient to all. (Roman)

Not always the pen, but often the weapon writes the law. (Hungarian)

Not in opinion, but in nature, is law founded. (Roman)

One law for the rich and another for the poor. (Unknown)

Only rogues feel restrained by the law. (Unknown)

Sometimes common error makes law. (Roman)

The construction of the law does injury to no one. (Roman)

The law compels no one to do what is impossible. (Roman)

The law is far, the fist is near. (Korean)

The law is hard, but it is the law. (Roman)

The law is not the same at morning and at night. (English)

The law says what the king pleases. (French)

The law sometimes sleeps, but never dies. (Roman)

The laws are silent in time of war. (Roman)

The laws assist those who watch, not those who sleep. (Roman)

The more by law, the less by right. (Danish)

The more laws, the less justice. (Spanish)

There is always a way around the law. (Spanish)

What good are laws when there are no morals? (Roman)

Where many laws, there little justice. (German)

Where the law is uncertain, there is no law. (Roman)

Where there is law, there is remedy. (Roman)

Where will is right, law is banished. (Danish)

Lawful

It is not lawful to overcome crime by crime. (Roman)

Nothing which is inconvenient is lawful. (Roman)

Where the end is lawful, the means are also lawful. (Roman)

Law Court

He who would not go to Hell, must not go to court. (Danish)

Home is home, as the Devil said when he found himself in the law courts. (Roman)

In a court of fowls, the cockroach never wins its case. (Rwandan)

The court clerk makes more money by what he does not write. (Spanish)

The court is most merciful when the accused is most rich. (Yiddish)
You don't know what a frightful thing it is to go to court. (Roman)

Lawmaker
Lawmakers should not be lawbreakers. (German)

Lawsuit
A bad agreement is better than a good lawsuit. (Italian)
A bad compromise is better than a good lawsuit. (French)
Agree, agree, for the law is costly. (Dutch)
Better a lean agreement than a fat lawsuit. (German)
Do not seek the quarrel, or the suit, of which there is an opportunity of escaping.
    (Roman)
Go to the law for a sheep and lose your cow. (German)
In war and litigation, both sides suffer. (Roman)
No one sues himself. (Roman)
One lawsuit begets another. (Roman)
Sue a beggar and get a louse. (German)
When both litigants are right, justice makes a sorry sight. (Yiddish)

Lawyer, Lawyers
A good lawyer is a bad neighbor. (Spanish)
A lawyer and a wagon wheel must be well greased. (German)
A man who is his own lawyer has a fool for a client. (French)
A peasant between two lawyers is like a fish between two cats. (Spanish)
A wise lawyer never goes to law himself. (Danish)
Fools and the perverse fill the lawyers' purse. (Spanish)
God wanted to chastise mankind, so he sent lawyers. (Russian)
It is better to be a mouse in a cat's mouth than a man in a lawyer's hands. (Spanish)
Lawyers and artists can make black appear white. (German)
Lawyers' houses are built on the heads of fools. (German)
Lawyers' robes are lined with the obstinacy of suitors. (Italian)
No good lawyer ever goes to law himself. (Italian)
Only lawyers and painters can turn white to black. (Japanese)
The better lawyer, the worse Christian. (Dutch)
Where there's a will, there are lawyers (American)
Woe be to him whose lawyer becomes his accuser. (Danish)

Lazy, Laziness
A lazy ass near home trots without the stick. (Portuguese)
A lazy fellow carries a heavy burden on his back [i.e., he tries to carry all at once].
    (Korean)
A lazy messenger finds many excuses. (Yiddish)
A lazy ox is little the better for the goad. (Spanish)
A lazy thief is better than a lazy servant. (Swedish)

A lazy woman excuses herself with her baby. (Korean)
A lazy youth, a lousy age. (Spanish)
A life of leisure, and a life of laziness, are two things. (English)
He who is lazy in spring is envious at harvest time. (Irish)
Laziness is often mistaken for patience. (French)
Laziness is the mother of all bad habits. (Albanian)
Laziness is the mother of poverty. (Filipino)
Laziness travels so slowly, that poverty soon overtakes him. (Poor Richard)
Long sleep makes a bare breech. (Irish)
Merit and fame never crown the lazy. (Chinese)
Offer the lazy an egg, and they'll want you to peel it for them. (Lithuanian)
The door of laziness is the boundary of suffering. (Albanian)
The lazy man busies himself toward evening. (Unknown)
The lazy man is not fed on honey. (Egyptian)
The lazy man who goes to borrow a spade says, 'I hope I will not find one'.
   (Madagascan)
The lazy ox covets the horse's saddle, the slow horse would rather plow. (Roman)
The lazy pig does not eat ripe pears. (Italian)
The lazy servant takes eight steps to avoid one. (Portuguese)
There are lazy minds as well as lazy bodies. (Poor Richard)
To the indolent every day is a holiday. (Roman)
Who is lazy dies from hunger. (Albanian)
Who is lazy today, regrets it later. (Albanian)

Lead, Leader
A good leader makes a good follower. (Roman)
As is the leader, so are his men. (Unknown)
Disasters are wont to reveal the abilities of a leader, good fortune to conceal them.
   (Roman)
Either lead, follow, or get out of the way. (American)
Good leading makes good following. (Dutch)
If people lead, the leaders will follow. (Spanish)
The good leader makes good soldiers. (Roman)
The leader follows in front. (Spanish)

Leaf, Leaves
Leaves enough, but few grapes. (American)
The fall of a leaf is a whisper to the living. (Russian)
The leaves fall before the tree dies. (French)
The more shoots, the more leaves. (Malay)
Though a tree may grow ever higher, the falling leaves return to the ground. (Malayan)

Leak
A gourd that leaks at home will also leak in the field. (Korean)
A small leak will sink a great ship. (German)

Lean, Leaning

A tottering man must lean upon a staff. (Danish)

It is bad to lean against a falling wall. (Danish)

You can only lean against that which resists. (Indian)

You can only lean against that which stands fast. (English)

Lean, Leanness

A goose, a woman, and a goat, are bad things lean. (Portuguese)

A lean calf forgets to skip. (Danish)

A lean horse does not kick. (Italian)

A man that is lean, not from hunger, is harder than brass. (Spanish)

Leap

A great leap gives a great shake. (Spanish)

Everyone leaps over a low dike. (German)

He that takes too great a leap falls into the ditch. (French)

He who would leap far must first take a long run. (Danish)

Learn

A man should learn to sail in all winds. (Italian)

By ignorance we make mistakes, and by mistakes we learn. (Roman)

By inquiring into old things, new things are to be learned. (Japanese)

Either learn, depart, or submit to be flogged. (Roman)

Even while they teach, men learn. (Roman)

First learn, then discern. (English)

From one learn all [i.e., from one sample we judge the rest]. (Roman)

From the old ox the young one learns to plow. (Roman)

He does not do right who unlearns what he has learned. (Roman)

He who does not mix with the crowd learns nothing. (Spanish)

He who goes with wolves learns to howl. (Spanish)

He who is ashamed to ask, is ashamed to learn. (Danish)

He who learns, teaches. (African)

He who lives among wolves learns to howl. (Italian)

If you always live with those who are lame, you yourself will learn to limp. (Roman)

It destroys the craft not to learn it. (Irish)

It is never too late to learn. (Roman)

It is permitted to learn even from an enemy. (Roman)

Learn a lesson from another's failure. (Unknown)

Learn by the peck and use by the bushel. (Korean)

Learn not, know not. (Unknown)

Learn young, learn fair; learn old, learn more. (Scottish)

Let the ignorant learn, and the learned delight in refreshing the memory. (Roman)

Live and learn. (Italian)

No one goes to bed without learning something new. (Spanish)

No one is ever too old to learn. (Roman)

No one learns but by pain or shame. (Dutch)

One learns by failing. (French)

Some people have to learn the hard way. (American)

Tell me and I'll forget; show me, and I may not remember; involve me, and I'll learn. (Native American)

That is never too often repeated which is never sufficiently learned. (Roman)

That which is learned well is never forgotten. (Mexican)

The chick learns in the nest what it already knew in the egg. (German)

Through old things we learn new things. (Chinese)

We learn by teaching. (Italian)

We learn not at school, but in life. (American)

We learn not for school, but for life. (Roman)

What is learned in the cradle is carried to the grave. (English)

What is learned in youth is carved in stone. (Arabian)

What little John hasn't learnt, big John won't know. (American)

What the colt learns in youth continues in old age. (French)

What you learn to your cost you remember long. (Danish)

Whatever is good to know is difficult to learn. (Greek)

Whoever cares to learn will always find a teacher. (German)

You must continue to learn for as long as you do not know, and as long as you continue to live. (Roman)

Learned

A learned man is never alone. (Spanish)

A learned person always has riches within. (Roman)

No one is born learned. (Spanish)

The most learned are not the most wise. (German)

Learning

A good man is always learning. (Roman)

A little learning is a dangerous thing; all flowers are not in one garland. (English)

A man in this world without learning is as a beast of the field. (Indian)

Acquire learning, even if from the mouth of a cow. (Egyptian)

After all else is lost, learning remains. (German)

By learning you will teach, by teaching you will learn. (Roman)

Despise learning and make everyone pay for your ignorance. (Chinese)

Do not confine your children to your own learning, for they were born in another time. (Yiddish)

Don't learn too much, else you must do a great deal. (German)

Even if we study to old age we shall not finish learning. (Chinese)

Gold has its price, but learning is priceless. (Chinese)

If you have learning, you will never lose your way. (Yiddish)

Learning cannot be bequeathed. (Yiddish)

Learning comes through work. (Irish)

Learning does not lead men astray. (Chinese)

Learning has sour roots, but pleasant fruits. (Roman)
Learning is a golden urn that can never be stolen. (Unknown)
Learning is a kind of natural food for the mind. (Roman)
Learning is a weightless treasure that is easily carried. (Chinese)
Learning is like rowing upstream: not to advance is to drop back. (Chinese)
Learning is a treasure no thief can touch. (Chinese)
Learning knows no frontier. (Unknown)
Learning makes people fit company for themselves. (English)
Man is like all creatures except in learning. (Chinese)
Many an ass is disguised under a cloak of learning. (Spanish)
Nothing so much assists learning as writing down what we wish to remember. (Roman)
The man who is afraid of asking is ashamed of learning. (Danish)
The roots of learning are bitter, but the fruit is sweet. (Polish)
There is no royal road to learning. (Greek)
There is no shame in learning. (Turkish)
To know where you can find a thing is the chief part of learning. (Roman)
When house and land are gone and spent, then learning is most excellent. (English)
Without learning life is but the image of death. (Roman)
Youth soon ages, but learning is slow to achieve. (Japanese)

Leave
It is better to leave than to lack. (Italian)
To leave a place is to die a little. (French)

Leaven
A little leaven leavens a great mass. (French)

Lecture
In the forehead and the eye the lecture of the mind doth lie. (French)

Legs
Better walk on wooden legs than be carried on a wooden bier. (Danish)
Everyone stretches his legs according to the length of his coverlet. (Spanish)

Leisure
Great business is good; to sit and sip this glass is better. (Chinese)
He that sits among reeds, cuts pipes when he pleases. (German)
He who knows not how to employ his leisure has more cares than the busiest of men.
    (Roman)
If nothing appears to you delightful without love and sports, then live in love and sports.
    (Roman)
Is any man free except the one who can pass his life as he pleases? (Roman)
Leisure begets vices. (Roman)
Leisure is always a pleasure. (the Editor)
Leisure without literature is death. (Roman)

Our leisure gives us more to do than our business. (Roman)
Seekers of pleasure have no leisure. (the Editor)
The busiest men have the most leisure. (English)
There are as many thousands of different pastimes as there are individuals. (Roman)
There is luck in leisure. (English)
To be entirely at leisure for one day is to be for one day an immortal. (Chinese)
Tranquility is difficult if one has leisure. (Roman)

Lend, Lending
He that lends loses a friend. (German)
He who has but one coat cannot lend it. (Spanish)
He who lends to the poor gets his interest from God. (German)
If you lend money to a friend, you lose both money and a friend. (Korean)
It is good to lend to God and to the soil: they pay good interest. (Danish)
It is safe to lend barley to him who has oats. (Danish)
Lend and lose, so play fools. (English)
Lend to your friend, and ask payment of your enemy. (Danish)
Lend your money and lose your friend. (English)
Lending nurses enmity. (Egyptian)
Lending ruins both borrower and lender. (Egyptian)
Money lent, an enemy made. (Portuguese)
People lend only to the rich. (French)
Who lends to a friend loses doubly. (French)
Who ventures to lend, loses money and friend. (Dutch)
You buy yourself an enemy when you lend a man money. (Yiddish)
You can't force anyone to love you or lend you money. (Yiddish)

Leopard
A leopard cannot change its spots. (Roman)
The rain wets the leopard's spots but does not wash them off. (West African)
When the leopard is at large it will be seen by everybody. (Yoruban)

Leper
Even the leper thinks ill of the syphilitic. (Japanese)

Less
Less is sometimes more. (German)

Letter
A letter does not blush. (Roman)
A letter once written cannot be recalled. (Roman)

Lettuce
Lettuce after wine floats on the acrid stomach. (Roman)

Liar, Liars

A great talker is a great liar. (French)

A liar can go around the world but cannot come back. (Polish)

A liar is not believed, even when he speaks the truth. (Roman)

A liar never believes anyone else. (Yiddish)

He who swears is a liar. (Italian)

How does one know when the liar is telling the truth? (German)

Liars died of old, but nowadays they never catch a cold. (English)

Liars should have good memories. (German)

Once a liar always a liar. (Unknown)

Show me a liar, and I'll show you a thief. (German)

Singers, lovers, and poets are privileged liars. (German)

The liar is soon detected. (Egyptian)

The liar is sooner caught than the cripple. (Spanish)

The liar will pay the penalty for his crime. (Roman)

You may shut your doors against a thief, but not against a liar. (Danish)

Liberality

Liberality is not giving much but giving wisely. (German)

Liberty

Few men desire liberty: the majority are satisfied with a just master. (Roman)

I would rather have a restless liberty than a quiet slavery. (Roman)

Lean liberty is better than fat slavery. (German)

Liberty is a thing of inestimable value. (Roman)

Liberty is given by nature even to mute animals. (Roman)

Liberty is made even more precious by the recollection of servitude. (Roman)

Liberty is never more enjoyable than under a pious king. (Roman)

The approach of liberty makes even an old man brave. (Roman)

The narrower the cage, the sweeter the liberty. (German)

To place yourself under an obligation is to sell your liberty. (Roman)

Woe to him whose liberty is dependent upon a stranger. (Irish)

Library

A library is a storehouse of medicine for the mind. (Greek)

Lice

Starved lice bite the hardest. (Dutch)

Lie, Lies

A half truth is a whole lie. (Yiddish)

A lie can be halfway around the world before the truth gets its boots on. (English)

A lie may take you far, but it will not take you home again. (Yiddish)

A lie prevails until truth arrives. (Mexican)

A necessary lie is harmless. (German)

All that is most ancient is a lie. (Roman)

Ask me no questions, I'll tell you no lies. (English)

Ask no questions and hear no lies. (American)

Better a lie that soothes than a truth that hurts. (Czech)

Even a lie can at times be necessary. (Japanese)

From long journeys long lies. (Spanish)

He that does not lie, does not come of good blood. (Spanish)

He who always tells me a lie never cheats me. (Spanish)

He who comes from afar may lie without fear of contradiction as he is sure to be listened to with the utmost attention. (French)

If lies are to find credence, they must be patched with truth. (Danish)

If lies were Latin, there would be many learned men. (Danish)

If you lie and then tell the truth, the truth will be considered a lie. (Ancient Sumerian)

Lies and gossip have a wretched offspring. (Danish)

Lies and Latin go round the world. (Danish)

Lies have short legs and are soon overtaken. (Spanish)

Lies have short wings. (German)

Lies melt the snow. (German)

Lies that build are better than truths that destroy. (West African)

Never lie to your doctor or lawyer. (German)

Old men and world travelers may lie by authority. (German)

One lie is followed by ten more. (German)

One lie makes many. (Italian)

One man lies, a hundred repeat it as true. (Chinese)

One man's false report sets ten thousand people to believe it. (Chinese)

One who lies for you will also lie against you. (Bosnian)

People spend their lives intermingling truth with lies. (Spanish)

People will pay more for lies than for the truth. (Unknown)

Rabbits and lies easily multiply. (Spanish)

Tell a lie, and you'll hear the truth. (German)

Tell lies, but become not tangled in lies. (Russian)

Ten 'noes' are better then one lie. (Danish)

The one who lies will likewise steal. (German)

They who come from afar are prone to lie. (German)

They who come from afar have leave to lie. (Dutch)

To lie about a far country is easy. (African)

With lies you may go ahead in the world – but you can never go back. (Russian)

You must not lie, but you need not tell the truth. (Yiddish)

Life

A handful of good life is better than seven barrels of learning. (French)

A hard life but a healthy one. (Roman)

A life of peace, purity, and refinement leads to a calm and untroubled old age. (Roman)

A life without a purpose is a rambling one. (Roman)

A long life has many shames. (Japanese)

A long life may not be good enough, but a good life is long enough. (Poor Richard)

A man is lent, not given, to life. (Roman)

A man's life is evaluated only after the coffin is closed. (Korean)

A man's life is twenty years coming, twenty years good, twenty years declining, and twenty years useless. (Irish)

A precipice in front of you, and wolves behind you – that is life. (Roman)

As length of life is denied to us, we should at least do something to show that we have lived. (Roman)

As we live, so we learn. (Yiddish)

Be happy while you're living, for you're a long time dead. (Scottish)

Before one knows his life, it is already half spent. (German)

Better to lose a minute in your life than your life in a minute. (Spanish)

By the yard, life is hard; by the inch, it's a cinch. (American)

Children and fools have merry lives. (French)

Every day of your life is a page of your history. (Arabian)

Everyone's life is dark to himself. (Roman)

From the cradle to the tomb, not all gladness, not all gloom. (Dutch)

Good or bad we must all live. (Italian)

He by whom another does not live does not deserve to live. (Roman)

He is master of another man's life who is indifferent to his own. (Italian)

He is unworthy of life who gives no life to another. (Roman)

He knows enough who knows how to live and keep his own counsel. (French)

He lives long who lives well. (German)

He lives twice who lives well. (Roman)

He lives well who lives industriously. (Roman)

He lives well who lives peacefully. (Roman)

He that at twenty is not, at thirty knows not, and at forty has not, will never be, nor ever know, nor ever have. (Italian)

He who lives a long life must pass through much evil. (Spanish)

Human life is as the morning dew. (Japanese)

If thou wouldst live long, live well; for folly and wickedness shorten Life. (Poor Richard)

It is a misery to be born, a punishment to live, and a trouble to die. (Roman)

It is one life, whether we spend it laughing or weeping. (Japanese)

It's the little things in life that count. (Dutch)

Life begins at forty. (Danish)

Life doesn't end: it goes on and on. (Unknown)

Life hangs by a thread. (Roman)

Life has its ups and downs. (Unknown)

Life is a dream, but don't wake me. (Yiddish)

Life is a road with a lot of signs. (Jamaican)

Life is but a bubble. (Greek)

Life is but a short span. (Unknown)

Life is but an empty dream. (Unknown)

Life is changeable. (Roman)

Life is full of uncertainties. (Unknown)

Life is given to us to be used; it is a loan without interest, and we have no date fixed for repayment. (Roman)

Life is half spent before one knows what life is. (French)

Life is like a passage. (Chinese)

Life is like licking honey from a thorn. (Hungarian)

Life is like this: sometimes sun, sometimes rain. (Fijian)

Life is not a series of pleasant choices, but of problems that call for strength, determination, and hard work. (Indian)

Life is not mere living but the enjoyment of health. (Roman)

Life is short but sweet. (American)

Life is short; the road is long; hurry. (American)

Life is sweet. (Irish)

Life is the greatest bargain: we get it for nothing. (Yiddish)

Life is what you make of it. (German)

Life is worth more than gold. (Jamaican)

Life isn't all beer and skittles. (German)

Life itself is short but evils make it longer. (Roman)

Life with fools consists in drinking; with the wise man living's thinking. (Poor Richard)

Life without effort is like entering a jewel-mine and coming out with empty hands. (Japanese)

Life, if you know how to use it, is long enough. (Roman)

Life's a bitch, then you die. (American)

Life's a gamble: you win or lose. (Unknown)

Life's too short, to worry about life. (the Editor)

Like a brook, life flows away. (Roman)

Love all life. (Chinese)

Man's life is a glittering bubble. (Chinese)

Man's life is a sojourn in a strange land. (Roman)

No man is quick enough to enjoy life to the full. (Spanish)

No matter what happens, life will continue. (Mexican)

Nothing in life is free. (American)

Nothing in life is permanent. (Roman)

Our floating life is like a dream. (Korean)

Our life is like a flame flickering in the wind. (Korean)

Our transient life is like a dream. (Japanese)

Remain hidden in life. (Greek)

The life of a man vanishes like the morning dew. (Japanese)

The part of life which we really live is very short. (Roman)

The simple things in life are best. (American)

To know nothing at all is the happiest life. (Roman)

When the life of a man is at stake, no delay that is afforded can be too long. (Roman)

While life lasts let us enjoy it. (Roman)

While we live, let us live. (German)

You live a true life if you make it your care to be what you seem. (Roman)

You must take life as it happens, but you should try to make it happen the way you want
to take it. (German)

Life and Death
Birth, old age, disease, bitterness and death: who can avoid these? (Chinese)
Fear life, do not fear death. (Russian)
He has not lived ill whose birth and death has passed unnoticed by the world. (Roman)
He is greedy of life who is unwilling to die when the world around him is perishing.
(Roman)
He that lives without account dies without a shroud. (Yiddish)
Insects and ants also covet life and fear death. (Chinese)
Life and death are only separated by the thickness of paper. (Chinese)
Life and death are providential. (Unknown)
Life is not separate from death; it only looks that way. (Native American)
Life is so short, there is no time to seek for death. (Roman)
Live your own life, for you will die your own death. (Roman)
One man's death is another man's life. (Maltese)
Our time runs on like a stream: first fall the leaves and then the tree. (Dutch)
People live with their own idiosyncrasies and die of their own illnesses. (Vietnamese)
Severed living and parted dying, no grief on earth can be so trying. (Chinese)
The whole of life is nothing but a journey to death. (Roman)
To buy a dried fish in order to spare its life is to know no difference between life and
death. (Chinese)

Light
A greater light darkens smaller ones. (German)
A lamp stand gives light to all but itself. (Chinese)
A single light suffices in the darkness. (Roman)
After darkness comes light. (Roman)
Every light hath its shadow. (Danish)
Every light is not the sun. (German)
Hide not your light under a bushel. (Christian)
Light is half a companion. (Italian)
Light is light, though the blind man see it not. (German)
There's light at the end of the tunnel. (Irish)
When the light is crooked, the shadow is crooked. (Yiddish)

Light-hearted
Poor and gay wins the day. (Yiddish)

Lighthouse
A shipwreck on the beach is a lighthouse to the sea. (Dutch)
It is darkest under the lighthouse. (Japanese)

Lightly
Lightly come, lightly go. (German)

Lightning
Lightning does not always strike what it threatens. (German)
Lightning never strikes in the same place twice. (German)

Like
Like father, like son. (Korean)
Like king, like law; like law, like people. (Portuguese)
Like king, like people. (Roman)
Like knows like. (Unknown)
Like likes like. (Roman)
Like master, like servant. (German)
Like mistress, like maid. (Roman)
Like mother, like daughter. (Roman)
Like pot, like cover. (Dutch)
Like priest, like people. (Roman)
Like saint, like offering. (Italian)
Like well, like bucket. (Italian)
No man can like all, or be liked by all. (German)
Since we cannot get what we like, let us like what we can get. (Spanish)
When one has not what one likes, one must like what one has. (French)

Lily
Don't gild the lily. (English)
Even the white lily casts a black shadow. (Hungarian)
Only at high water is a water lily at its best. (Burmese)

Limp
If you live with a lame man you will learn to limp. (Roman)
Never limp before the lame. (French)
No man limps because another is hurt. (Danish)

Linen
Dirty linen is washed at home. (Spanish)
Fine linen often conceals scabby skin. (Danish)
It is at home, not in public, that one washes his dirty linen. (French)

Link
Break one link and the whole chain falls apart. (Yiddish)
Link by link the coat of mail is made. (French)
One link broken, the whole chain is broken. (German)

Lion
A lion may be beholden to a mouse. (Roman)
An old lion is better than a young ass. (Roman)
Be a lion at home and a fox abroad. (Persian)

Destroy the lion while he is but a whelp. (Portuguese)

Do not pluck the beard of a dead lion. (Roman)

Don't wake the sleeping lion. (Jamaican)

Even the lion must defend himself against flies. (German)

Lion skins were never had cheap. (French)

Nourish not a lion's whelp. (Roman)

The lion is known by its claw. (Roman)

The lion is not so fierce as it is painted. (Spanish)

The mane makes the lion a lion [i.e., proves that he is a lion]. (Burmese)

The mouths of lions are handled by their keepers with impunity. (Roman)

The roaring lion kills no game. (African)

Though humbled, a lion will not play with the pig. (Hausan)

To the lion belongs whatever its paw has seized. (Egyptian)

When a lion sleeps, let him sleep. (Yiddish)

When the lion is dead the hares jump upon its carcass. (Italian)

You may know the lion by its claws. (French)

Lips

Loose lips may sink ships. (American)

The poison of asps is under their lips. (Italian)

Listen, Listener

A good listener is a silent flatterer. (Spanish)

A good talker does not equal a good listener. (Chinese)

Eat what is cooked; listen to what is said. (Russian)

Having two ears and one tongue, we should listen twice as much as we speak. (Turkish)

He understands badly who listens badly. (Welsh)

If you do not know how to talk, learn to listen. (Roman)

Listen or your tongue will keep you deaf. (Native American)

Listen to all, plucking a feather from every passing goose – follow after none. (Unknown)

Listen to the one who has four ears [i.e., one who is readier to hear than to speak]. (Roman)

Listen well before your speak. (Spanish)

Stop, look, and listen. (Danish)

Talk little, listen much. (African)

To speak is to sow, to listen is to reap. (Spanish)

Who speaks, sows; who listens, reaps. (French)

Literature

The life of a man without literature is death. (Roman)

Little

A little barrel can give but little meal. (German)

A little bird wants but a little nest. (Arabian)

A little body often harbors a great soul. (Arabian)
A little force will break that which has been cracked already. (Roman)
A little gall embitters much honey. (Spanish)
A little leak will sink a great ship. (Portuguese)
A little man fells a great oak. (French)
A little man sometimes casts a long shadow. (French)
A little pot is soon hot. (Dutch)
A little rain stills a great wind. (French)
A little relationship is worth a lot of charity. (Irish)
A little sheep always seems young. (French)
A little spark kindles a great fire. (German)
A little spark shines in the dark. (French)
A little stone may upset a large cart. (Danish)
A little stream drives a great mill. (Italian)
A little thing often helps. (French)
A little tongue has a long reach. (English)
A little too late is much too late. (German)
A little truth makes the whole lie pass. (Italian)
A little water is a sea to an ant. (Afghani)
Don't use a lot where a little will do. (American)
Every little bit helps. (Dutch)
How great is the virtue of living upon a little. (Roman)
It is better to have too much than too little. (Unknown)
Little and often fill the purse. (Spanish)
Little and often makes a heap in time. (German)
Little by little goes a long way. (Mexican)
Little by little, a little becomes a lot. (Tanzanian)
Little enemies and little wounds must not be despised. (English)
Little grains of sand can raise a mountain; little drops of water can fill a pot. (Unknown)
Little is better than none. (Irish)
Many a little makes a mickle, many small make a great. (Irish)
Many a mickle makes a muckle. (Scottish)
Rejoice in little, shun what is extreme; the ship rides safest in a little stream. (Dutch)

Live
Better to live in a poor hovel than be buried in a rich grave. (German)
He that lives low cannot fall hard. (Dutch)
He that lives too fast, goes to his grave too soon. (English)
If you live long enough, you will live to see everything. (Yiddish)
It matters a great deal with whom you live. (Roman)
Live and let live. (Dutch)
Live as you can since you cannot live as you would. (Roman)
Live every day as if it were your last. (Unknown)
Live for the present; plan for the future. (Unknown)
Live long, suffer much. (Unknown)

Live to live and you will learn to live. (Portuguese)

Live today, forget the past. (Greek)

Live, while you can. (Roman)

Make haste to live, and consider each day a life. (Roman)

Make the night night, and the day day, and you will live pleasantly. (Portuguese)

Neither has he lived ill whose birth and death has passed unnoticed by the world. (Roman)

No one is so old that he does not think it possible to live another year. (Roman)

Not how long, but how well you have lived, is the main thing. (Roman)

One half of the world knows not how the other half lives. (German)

Tell me who you live with, and I will tell you who you are. (Spanish)

They live ill who think they will live forever. (Roman)

To live happily is the same thing as to live in accordance with nature's laws. (Roman)

To live long is to suffer long. (Danish)

To rise at five, dine at nine, sup at five, go to bed at nine, makes a man live to ninety-nine. (French)

Wish not so much to live long as to live well. (Poor Richard)

With art and knavery we live through half the year; with knavery and art we live through the other. (Italian)

Would you live long, be healthy not fat, drink like a dog and eat like a cat. (German)

Would you live with ease, do what you ought, and not what you please. (Poor Richard)

You don't have to do anything in life but live till you die. (Unknown)

Living

He has his life from God and his living from man. (Yiddish)

Men and beasts are alike the living. (Chinese)

Load

It is not the load but the overload that kills. (Spanish)

Light is the load that is cheerfully borne. (Roman)

Loan

Horse, gun, and wife are three things not for loan. (Spanish)

Money taken, freedom forsaken. (German)

Seldom comes a loan laughing home. (English)

Lock

A lock is better than suspicion. (Irish)

A lock is meant only for honest men. (Yiddish)

Locks and keys are not made for honest fingers. (German)

One lock for your purse, two for your mouth. (Spanish)

Log

A crooked log is not to be straightened. (Roman)

One log does not burn long by itself. (German)

Lone
The lone sheep is in danger of the wolf. (Chinese)

Lonely
A lonely person is at home everywhere. (Russian)
'Tis a lonely washing that has no man's shirt in it. (Irish)

Long
Long is not forever. (German)
Long roads test the horse, long dealings the friend. (Chinese)

Look
He who looks a second time loses nothing. (Japanese)
If you look up there are no limits. (Japanese)
Look before, or you'll find yourself behind. (Poor Richard)
Look before you leap. (English)
Look before you leap, for snakes among sweet flowers do creep. (German)
Look down if you would know how high you stand. (Yiddish)
It costs you nothing to take a second look. (Chinese)
The more you look, the less you see. (Jamaican)

Looks
Looks aren't everything. (American)
Many complain of their looks, but none of their brains. (Yiddish)

Lord, Lords
A man is not a lord because he feeds off fine dishes. (Danish)
An insolent lord is not a gentleman. (Roman)
Call someone your lord and he'll sell you in the slave market. (Arabian)
Great lords have long hands, but they do not reach to Heaven. (Danish)
Great lords will have much, and poor folk can give but little. (Danish)
New lords, new laws. (French)

Lose, Loser
A bleating sheep loses a bite. (Ethiopian)
A man may lose his goods for want of demanding them. (Spanish)
A thing easy to get is easy to lose. (Japanese)
Better return half way than lose yourself. (Dutch)
Better to gain in mud than lose in gold. (Portuguese)
Better to lose the anchor than the whole ship. (Danish)
Better to lose the saddle than the horse. (Italian)
Better to lose the wool than the sheep. (French)
Better to lose your labor than your time in idleness. (Dutch)
He chases a wild boar into the mountains but loses his own hogs at home. (Korean)
He loses his way whom blind men guide. (Egyptian)

He who carries nothing loses nothing. (French)
He who does not gain loses. (French)
He who loses is always in fault. (Italian)
He who loses sins. (French)
He who recovers but the tail of his cow does not lose all. (French)
It is better to lose than lose more. (Spanish)
Losers are always in the wrong. (Spanish)
Many seek good nights and lose good days. (Dutch)
The inconsiderate is the first to lose. (Egyptian)
There are occasions when it is certainly better to lose than to gain. (Roman)
We gain and lose by the same means. (Roman)
We lose things certain in pursuing things uncertain. (Roman)
You cannot lose what you never had. (English)
You snooze, you lose. (American)

Loss, Lost

A little loss frightens, a great one tames. (Spanish)
After one loss comes many. (French)
An evil gain equals a loss. (Roman)
Even loss can be a profit. (Persian)
Fortune lost, nothing lost; courage lost, much lost; honor lost, more lost; soul lost,
    all lost. (Dutch)
Four things come not back: the spoken word, the spent arrow, the past life, and the
    neglected opportunity. (Chinese)
He that is not aware of his loss has lost nothing. (Spanish)
He who has lost his oxen is always hearing bells. (Spanish)
If I have lost the ring, I still have the fingers. (Italian)
Large loss for a small gain. (Unknown)
Let what is lost go for God's sake. (Spanish)
Losses make us more cautious. (Roman)
Losses to which we are accustomed affect us little. (Roman)
Lost things are always found in the last place we look for them. (American)
Many things are lost for want of asking. (English)
One man's loss is another man's gain. (Roman)
The first loss is the best. (Spanish)
There's no great loss without some gain. (Italian)
There's no loss without some gain. (English)
We do not know what is good until we have lost it. (Spanish)
We know the worth of a thing when we have lost it. (French)
Your loss is my gain. (American)

Lot in Life

Bloom where you are planted. (English)
Everyone must row with the oars he has. (Dutch)
Everyone sings as he has the gift, and marries as he has the luck. (Portuguese)

Everyone to his own calling, and the ox to the plow. (Italian)
Gnaw the bone which is fallen to your lot. (Italian)
Grow where you are planted. (Roman)

Love, Loved

A boy's love is water in a sieve. (Spanish)
A flower cannot blossom without sunshine nor a garden without love. (Chinese)
A heart in love with beauty never grows old. (Turkish)
A long love, a severe bondage. (German)
A lovelorn cook over-salts the porridge. (German)
A love-marriage is not without problems. (Spanish)
A loving man, a jealous man. (Italian)
A man in love mistakes a pimple for a dimple. (Japanese)
A man in love, though he is hungry, is not hungry. (Roman)
A man is not where he lives, but where he loves. (Roman)
A wall between increases love. (German)
Absence is a foe to love: away from the eyes, away from the heart. (Spanish)
Absence is a foe to love: out of sight out of mind. (Italian)
All ages are submissive to love. (Russian)
All's fair in love and war. (French)
An old man in love is like a flower in winter. (Portuguese)
Anyone who teases you loves you. (Yiddish)
Better a dinner of herbs where love is, than a feast and hatred therewith. (Chinese)
Better to have loved and lost, than not to have loved at all. (Roman)
By beating love decays. (French)
Certainly everyone is blind when maddened by love. (Roman)
Coffee and love are best when they are hot. (German)
Cultivate a heart of love that knows no anger. (Cambodian)
Do not treat your loved one like a swinging door: you are fond of it but you push it back and forth. (Madagascan)
Even a god finds it hard to love and be wise at the same time. (Roman)
Even Jupiter himself cannot be in love and wise at the same time. (Roman)
Follow love and it will flee; flee love and it will follow thee. (German)
For love of the ox the wolf licks the yoke. (Catalan)
For love the wolf eats the sheep. (German)
Forced love does not last. (Dutch)
From love comes anger. (Korean)
Happy is she who is in love with an old dotard. (Italian)
He loves well who does not forget. (Italian)
He saith little that loveth much. (Italian)
He that loves the tree loves the branches.
He who falls in love meets a worse fate than he who leaps from a rock. (Roman)
He who forces love when none is found remains a fool the whole year round. (German)
He who is not impatient is not in love. (Italian)
He who loves much forgives much. (Spanish)

He who loves much suffers much. (Spanish)
He who loves Peter loves his dog. (Spanish)
He who loves waits. (Spanish)
He who loves well is slow to forget. (Spanish)
He who loves well, obeys well. (Spanish)
He who would not be idle, let him fall in love. (Roman)
I say as an expert, no one is faithful in love. (Roman)
If love be timid it is not true. (Spanish)
If there's a will, love finds a way. (the Editor)
If you want to be loved, then love. (Roman)
If you would be loved, love and be loveable. (Poor Richard)
In hunting and in love you begin when you like and leave off when you can. (Spanish)
In love the eyes are our leaders. (Roman)
In love, in delirium. (Roman)
In the war of love, the one who flees conquers. (Italian)
It is best to be off with the old love before you are on with the new. (Danish)
It is better to be loved than feared. (West African)
It is difficult to give up suddenly a long love. (Roman)
It is easy to halve the potato where there's love. (Irish)
It's far better to have loved and lost than never to have loved at all. (English)
Labor is light where love doth pay. (Unknown)
Let enmity stop short, but love linger on. (English)
Love and a cough cannot be hid. (Roman)
Love and blindness are twin sisters. (Russian)
Love and dignity do not dwell together. (Roman)
Love and do what you will. (Roman)
Love and eggs are best when they are fresh. (Russian)
Love and faith are seen in works. (Spanish)
Love and hunger hold the world together. (German)
Love and jealousy are twins. (Spanish)
Love and lordship like no fellowship. (French)
Love and poverty are hard to conceal. (Danish)
Love begets love. (Roman)
Love Bertrand, love his dog. (French)
Love brooks no delay. (Roman)
Love cannot be bought or sold, its only price is love. (German)
Love cannot be cured by herbs. (Roman)
Love conquers all things, let us also yield to love. (Roman)
Love does not rust. (German)
Love does not seek things for itself. (Roman)
Love enters a man through his eyes, a woman through her ears. (Polish)
Love enters through the eyes. (Spanish)
Love for its own sake is true love. (Spanish)
Love for me depends on me. (Korean)
Love for those too easily won does not last long. (Roman)

Love grows with obstacles. (German)
Love has both honey and gall in abundance. (Roman)
Love in his heart, spurs at his heels. (German)
Love is a great leveler. (Spanish)
Love is a kind of warfare. (Roman)
Love is a king who reigns without laws. (Spanish)
Love is a stream that will find its course. (Jamaican)
Love is a thing full of anxious fears. (Roman)
Love is a wound that never heals. (German)
Love is an excuse for its own faults. (Italian)
Love is beyond reflection [i.e., analysis]. (Japanese)
Love is blind. (English)
Love is blind, but not the neighbors. (Mexican)
Love is blind but sees afar. (Italian)
Love is blind to faults and blemishes. (Irish)
Love is like butter, it goes well with bread. (Yiddish)
Love is like dew that falls on both nettles and lilies. (Swedish)
Love is like war, begin when you like and leave off when you can. (French)
Love is master of all arts. (Italian)
Love is more easily quenched than moderated. (Roman)
Love is never without jealousy. (German)
Love is not an impartial judge. (Irish)
Love is one thing, lust another. (Roman)
Love is repaid with love. (Mexican)
Love is a ring, and a ring has no end. (Russian)
Love is a sweet torment. (English)
Love is sweet but tastes best with bread. (Yiddish)
Love is the beginning of sorrow. (German)
Love is the fruit of love. (Roman)
Love is the same in all. (Roman)
Love is the true price at which love is bought. (Italian)
Love is won by affectionate words. (Roman)
Love knows hidden paths. (German)
Love knows no law. (Portuguese)
Love knows not labor. (Italian)
Love lasts as long as the money endures. (Unknown)
Love laughs at locksmiths. (British)
Love lives in palaces as well as in thatched huts. (Japanese)
Love makes sour things sweet. (Unknown)
Love makes the heart to sing. (Portuguese)
Love makes the world go round. (French)
Love makes time pass; time makes love pass. (French)
Love me little, love me long. (French)
Love others as you love yourself and let benevolence abound. (Chinese)
Love received, love returned. (Mexican)

Love rules without law. (Italian)

Love steals on us unseen. (Roman)

Love teaches even asses to dance. (French)

Love tells us many things that are not so. (Ukrainian)

Love that comes late in life bears great interest. (Roman)

Love will change you. (German)

Love will find a way. (English)

Love will find a way; indifference will find an excuse. (Ukrainian)

Love without return is like a question without an answer. (German)

Love would soon perish, were it not nourished by Ceres [food] and Bacchus [wine]. (Roman)

Love, and be loved. (Poor Richard)

Love's anger is fuel to love. (German)

Love's merchandise is jealousy and broken faith. (Italian)

Love's plant must be watered with tears, and tended with care. (Danish)

Love's wounds are cured by love itself. (Roman)

Love's wrath is love's tinder. (German)

Majesty and love do not consort well together, nor do they dwell in the same place. (Roman)

Make love, not war. (American)

Man loves but once. (German)

Money is the sinew of love. (German)

Neither love nor a cough can be hidden. (Roman)

Never love with all your heart, it only ends in breaking. (English)

New love drives out old. (Spanish)

No fate is worse than a life without love. (Mexican)

No herb can remedy the anguish of love. (Roman)

No one in love sees. (Roman)

No one loves another better than himself. (Roman)

Nobody's sweetheart is ugly. (Dutch)

Not all men love the same things. (Roman)

Nothing is hard for one who loves. (Roman)

Of soup and love, the first is the best. (Portuguese)

Old love and old brands kindle at all seasons. (French)

Old love does not rust. (German)

One always returns to his first love. (French)

One cannot love and be wise. (English)

One grows used to love and to fire. (French)

One love drives out another. (Spanish)

Parental love is an ocean, sibling love a trickling stream. (the Editor)

Pleasing manners and a handsome form conciliate love. (Roman)

Separation reveals love. (German)

She who loves an ugly man thinks him handsome. (Spanish)

Sometimes one glance is enough for love to be planted. (Egyptian)

Take hold lightly, let go lightly: this is one of the great secrets of felicity in love. (Spanish)

Tell me whom you love and I'll tell you who you are. (French)

The beautiful is less what one sees than what one dreams. (Belgian)

The body seeks that which has wounded the mind with love. (Roman)

The course of true love never did run smooth. (Roman)

The falling out of lovers is the renewal of love. (German)

The grasshopper is dear to the grasshopper, the ant loves the ant. (Roman)

The greatest love is a mother's, then a dog's, then a sweetheart's. (Polish)

The love of God and our neighbor is the highest happiness. (Roman)

The man in love is no judge of beauty. (German)

The man who does not love a horse cannot love a woman. (Spanish)

The man who loves is easy of belief. (Italian)

The more violent the love, the more violent the anger. (Burmese)

The oaths of one who loves a woman are not to be believed. (Spanish)

The one who loves errs; behold, all men err. (German)

The one who loves well chastises well. (Roman)

The one who loves you will make you weep. (Argentine)

The only victory over love is flight. (French)

The pleasure of love lasts but a moment, but the pain of love lasts a lifetime.
   (French)

The pleasures of love are enhanced by injuries. (Roman)

There are as many pangs in love as shells on the seashore. (Roman)

There are no limits to love. (Japanese)

There is no love greater than a mother's. (Spanish)

There is no teacher for love. (Japanese)

There is no wrong that love will not forgive. (Roman)

Those we think love us, love us only a little. (Yoruban)

Those whom true love has held, it will go on holding. (Roman)

Though there is love downwards, there is no love upwards. (Korean)

'Tis no thief that steals love. (German)

To be loved, be loveable. (Roman)

To be loved, love. (Spanish)

To give is honor, to love is grief. (Spanish)

To love and be wise are two different things. (French)

To love and be wise is impossible. (Spanish)

To love is to choose. (French)

To love living beings is to love oneself. (Chinese)

To understand your parents' love bear your own children. (Chinese)

True love hates, and does not suffer, delay. (Roman)

True love knows no limits [i.e., knows not moderation]. (Roman)

True love never grows old. (Italian)

We are born once, die once, love once. (Spanish)

What is dearly loved is too soon lost. (Spanish)

When love is not madness, it is not love. (Spanish)

When one is in love, a cliff becomes a meadow. (Ethiopian)

When struck by love, love extends even to the crow on your lover's roof. (Japanese)

Where love enters to season a dish, it will please anyone. (Roman)
Where the heart loves, there the legs walk. (Maltese)
Where there is great love there is great pain. (Italian)
Where there is love, there is pain. (Spanish)
Who has love in his heart has spurs in his sides. (Italian)
Who loves well chastises well. (Italian)
Who loves well is slow to forget. (French)
Who loves, believes. (Italian)
Who loves, fears. (Italian)
Who travels for love finds a thousand miles not longer than one. (Dutch)
With soft words must love be fostered. (Roman)
Without bread and wine even love will pine. (French)
You always hurt the one you love. (American)
You can't live on love alone. (Unknown)
You haven't lived if you haven't loved. (Unknown)
You must make a lover angry if you wish him to love. (Roman)
You who seek an end of love, love will yield to business; be busy, and you will be safe.
    (Roman)
You will not be loved if you care for none but yourself. (Spanish)
You will not be loved if you think only of yourself. (Italian)

Love and Hate
A good hater, a good lover. (French)
If you love the boll you cannot hate the branches. (German)
Rarely go where you are loved, and never where you are hated. (Yiddish)
The greatest hate springs from the greatest love. (French)
The lover loves even the crow on his lover's roof; the one who hates hates all things.
    (Chinese)

Lover
A lover should be regarded as a person demented. (Roman)
A lover's anger is short-lived. (Italian)
All the world loves a lover. (Portuguese)
As is the lover so is the beloved. (Italian)
Every lover is a slave: he follows captive at his mistress's heels. (Roman)
Every lover is demented. (Roman)
Every lover is engaged in a war. (Roman)
Every lover makes fair speeches. (Roman)
Let him not be a lover who has not courage. (Italian)
Lovers are lunatics. (Italian)
Lovers remember everything. (Roman)
Lovers think others are blind. (Italian)
Lovers' purses are tied with cobwebs. (Italian)
Lovers' quarrels rekindle love. (Spanish)
Nothing is difficult for the lover. (Roman)

Who can deceive a lover? (Roman)
Jupiter laughs at lovers' deceits. (Roman)

Love-struck
The love-struck talk to trees and stones. (Mexican)
The madman lacks judgment, the love-struck loses it. (Spanish)

Loyalty
Loyalty is more valuable than diamonds. (Filipino)
Loyalty never chose the unfortunate as friends. (Roman)
The best way to keep loyalty in a man's heart is to keep money in his purse. (Irish)

Luck
A blind hen can sometimes find corn. (French)
A blind man may sometimes shoot a crow. (Dutch)
A blind pigeon may sometimes find a grain of wheat. (Danish)
A bold man has luck in his train. (Danish)
A man must keep his mouth open a long while before a roast pigeon flies into it. (Danish)
A person does not seek luck; luck seeks the person. (Turkish)
All is good luck or bad luck in this world. (French)
An ounce of luck is worth a pound of wisdom. (French)
As for luck, wait in your bed. (Japanese)
Better an ounce of luck than a pound of gold. (Yiddish)
Beware good luck: fattening hogs think themselves fortunate. (German)
Even the luckless need their luck. (Yiddish)
Every man makes his own breaks. (German)
God is a father; luck is a stepfather. (Yiddish)
Good luck beats early rising. (Irish)
Good luck comes in slender currents, misfortune in a rolling tide. (Irish)
Good luck does not always repeat itself. (Unknown)
Good luck invites many mishaps. (Japanese)
Good luck is not like a coat that can be taken off and on. (Hausan)
Good luck doesn't last forever. (Roman)
He that changes his place changes his luck – sometimes for the better, sometimes for the worse. (Yiddish)
He that has no bad luck grows weary of good luck. (Spanish)
He that has the luck leads the bride to church. (Dutch)
If good luck comes, who doesn't?; if good luck doesn't come, who does? (Chinese)
If luck comes, let it find your door wide open. (Spanish)
In bad luck, hold out; in good luck, hold in. (German)
It is easier to acquire good luck than to keep hold of it. (Roman)
Knock on wood for luck. (English)
Luck and ill luck are neighbors. (Norwegian)
Luck comes to those who look after it. (Spanish)
Luck has but a slender anchorage. (Danish)

Luck has much for many, but enough for no one. (Danish)

Luck is like having a rice dumpling fly into your mouth. (Japanese)

Luck knocks at the door and inquires whether prudence is within. (Danish)

Luck never gives; it only lends. (Scottish)

Luck sometimes comes without blemish, but never without a catch. (German)

Luck sometimes visits a fool, but never sits down with him. (Danish)

Luck will carry a man across the brook if he is not too lazy to leap. (Danish)

Luck without sense is a bag full of holes. (Yiddish)

Man's life is destined by Heaven but his luck is all his own. (Chinese)

Odd numbers bring luck. (Roman)

One ounce of good luck is better than a ton of smarts. (Slavic)

See a pin and pick it up, all the day you'll have good luck; see a pin and let it lie, bad luck
    you'll have all day. (French)

The Devil's children have the Devil's luck. (English)

The more honest the man, the worse his luck. (German)

There is luck in odd numbers. (Spanish)

There is luck in sharing and luck in spending. (Irish)

There is no luck except where there is discipline. (Irish)

To wait for luck is the same as waiting for death. (Japanese)

When a man has luck, even his ox calves. (Yiddish)

When luck joins in the game, cleverness scores double. (Yiddish)

Where luck is wanting, diligence is useless. (Spanish)

Lucky

A hairy man is a lucky man. (Spanish)

A lucky man is rarer than a white crow. (Roman)

A lucky person is someone who plants pebbles and harvests potatoes. (Greek)

As long as you are lucky, you will have many friends; if cloudy times come, you will be
    alone. (Roman)

Fling a lucky man into the Nile, and he will come up with a fish in his mouth. (Roman)

If you were born lucky, even your rooster will lay eggs. (Russian)

It is better to be born lucky than rich. (Roman)

It wants no wit to be lucky. (Yiddish)

Lucky at cards, unlucky in love. (Danish)

Lucky in love, unlucky at play. (German)

Lucky men need no advice. (German)

Lucky with dames, unlucky at games. (American)

Some people are just born lucky. (American)

The lucky are one in a million. (German)

There is no one luckier than he who thinks himself so. (German)

Throw a lucky man into the sea, and he will come up with a fish in his mouth. (Arabian)

Lunch

There's no such thing as a free lunch. (American)

Lure

He is easy to lure, who is ready to follow. (Danish)

It is hard to lure hawks with empty hands. (Danish)

Lust

Lust is a knife that cuts to the bone. (Chinese)

Lying

A litigious man, a lying man. (French)

If lying were a capital crime, the hangman would work overtime. (Spanish)

Loquacity and lying are cousins. (German)

Lying and gossiping go hand in hand. (Spanish)

Lying is the first step to the gallows. (German)

Lying pays no tax. (Portuguese)

M

Machete

No sane person sharpens his machete to cut a banana tree. (Nigerian)

Mad, Madness

A mad parish, a mad priest. (Italian)

A man of gladness seldom falls into madness. (Roman)

Better to be mad with all the world than wise alone. (French)

It is allowed once in the year to be mad. (Roman)

It is best to profit by the madness of others. (Roman)

The madness of one makes many mad. (Roman)

Madman

A madman is like a man who is absent. (Roman)

A madman is punished by his madness. (Roman)

Every madman thinks all others insane. (Roman)

Make way for a madman and a bull. (Spanish)

Make way for madmen and fools. (Japanese)

The one who claps hands for a madman to dance is himself insane. (Yoruban)

There is a pinch of the madman in every great man. (French)

We are all something of a musician, poet, and madman. (Spanish)

Magic

Don't give in to spells, they won't give in to you. (Irish)

Sleight of hand is no magic. (German)

Magpie

One magpie for sorrow, two for mirth, three for a wedding, four for a birth. (French)

Maiden

Glass and maidens are easily broken. (Korean)

Maidens say no, and mean yes. (German)

You must judge a maiden at the kneading trough, and not in a dance. (Danish)

Make

It is always possible to make something good from something bad. (Mexican)

What man has made, man can destroy. (German)

Malady

Desperate maladies require desperate remedies. (French)

Strong folks have strong ailments. (German)

Malevolent

The malevolent have hidden teeth. (Roman)

Malice

Bear no malice. (Roman)

If you do not have malice within, it will not come from without. (Albanian)

Malice drinks its own poison. (Egyptian)

Many are the ways of malice in men. (Roman)

Though malice may darken truth, it cannot put it out. (Roman)

Mallet

Mallet strikes chisel; chisel splits wood. (Chinese)

Man, Men

A man at five may be a fool at fifteen. (French)

A man at sixteen will prove a child at sixty. (French)

A man can have nothing worse over him than another man. (Yiddish)

A man crows like a rooster when young, works like a burro when he is older, and growls like a pig when aged. (Mexican)

A man dances all the same, though he may dance against his will. (Danish)

A man does not wander far from where his corn is roasting. (Nigerian)

A man if he lives alone is either a god or a demon. (Roman)

A man is a king in his own house. (Roman)

A man is a lion in his own cause. (Scottish)

A man is a lion when single, a peacock when engaged, and a beast of burden when married. (Spanish)

A man is bound by his word, an ox with a strong cord. (Danish)

A man is judged by his clothes. (Roman)

A man is judged by his deeds, not by his words. (Russian)

A man is judged of by his companions. (Roman)

A man is known by the company he keeps. (American)

A man is known by the eye, and the face discovers wisdom. (Irish)

A man is not known till he cometh to honor. (Dutch)
A man is what he is, not what he used to be. (Yiddish)
A man knows no more to any purpose than he practices. (French)
A man lives long in his native place. (Irish)
A man may cause his own dog to bite him. (French)
A man ought to be born either a king or a fool. (Roman)
A man overboard, a mouth the less. (Dutch)
A man takes his own wherever he finds it. (French)
A true man speaks not against his enemies. (Chinese)
A true man, though hungry, will not complain of belly ache. (Chinese)
A wicked man is his own hell. (English)
A young man idle, an old man needy. (Danish)
All men are good-natured until you ask their help. (Chinese)
All men are not cast in the same mold. (American)
All men can't be first. (English)
All men do not admire and love the same things. (Roman)
All men think all men mortal – but themselves. (English)
As the boy, so the man. (English)
Beware the man of two faces. (Dutch)
Different men like different things. (Roman)
Every man has his lot, and a wide world before him. (Danish)
Every man is dearest to himself. (German)
Four things put a man beside himself: women, tobacco, cards, and wine. (Spanish)
He is a man, who acts like a man. (Danish)
How insignificant men are, when I think of it. (Roman)
Man fools himself: he prays for a long life and he fears old age. (Chinese)
Man is a beast to man. (German)
Man is a wolf to his fellow man. (Roman)
Man is Heaven and earth in miniature. (Chinese)
Man is like a banana: when he leaves the bunch, he gets skinned. (American)
Man is the only animal who can be skinned twice. (American)
Man is the soul of all creatures. (Japanese)
Man is the soul of the universe. (Unknown)
Man is to man either a god or a wolf. (German)
Men are the same, except their names. (German)
Mind other men, but mostly yourself. (German)
Once a man, twice a child. (Jamaican)
Ruling men is one thing, entertaining them is another. (Roman)
Silent men are deep and dangerous. (Japanese)
The older the man, the darker the eyes. (Unknown)
The silent man is most trusted. (Danish)
There is more agreement among snakes then among men. (Roman)
Today a man, tomorrow a mouse. (English)
What's in a man will come out of a man. (Yiddish)

Man and Woman

A man of straw is better than a woman of gold. (Portuguese)

A man of straw needs a woman of gold. (Italian)

Man and woman, fire and chaff. (Roman)

Men are as old as they feel, and women as they look. (Italian)

Man is fire, woman is tow, and the Devil comes and blows. (French)

Man without woman, is head without body; woman without man, is body without head. (German)

Thoughts are male, words are female. (Italian)

Who's the man that was never fooled by a woman? (German)

Mankind

All mankind is divided into three classes: those that are immovable, those that are moveable, and those that move. (Arabian)

Manly

He that is not brave at twenty, strong at thirty, rich at forty, or experienced at fifty, will never be brave, strong, rich, or prudent. (Spanish)

Manners

As are the times, so are the manners. (Spanish)

As many places, so many manners. (Unknown)

Better good manners than good looks. (Irish)

Different times, different manners. (Italian)

Evil contact corrupts good manners. (Italian)

Manners make the man. (American)

Manners maketh man. (English)

Similarity of manners is more conducive to friendship than affinity by marriage. (Roman)

The man may be bad whilst his manners are not. (Chinese)

The rough manners of the vulgar are contagious. (Roman)

Mansion

A mansion pulled down is half built up again. (French)

Manure

The foot of the owner is the best manure for his land. (Danish)

Many

Many grains make a heap. (Roman)

Many grains of sand will sink a ship. (Danish)

Many little rivulets make a great river. (Danish)

Many mosquitoes can drive away oxen and sheep. (Japanese)

Many open a door to shut a window. (Dutch)

Many overpower few. (Irish)

So many Hamans and but one Purim. (Yiddish)

So many heads, so many brains. (Italian)
So many heads, so many minds. (Danish)
So many lands, so many customs. (Roman)
So many men, so many fools. (Italian)
So many men, so many opinions. (German)
So many men, so many sentiments: each has his own way. (Roman)
So many mists in March, so many frosts in May. (English)

Mare
The mare's kick does not harm the colt. (Spanish)
The mare's kick caresses the colt. (Portuguese)

Market, Marketplace
Do not seek in the market what you have at home. (Spanish)
Everyone sells his rags in the marketplace. (Egyptian)
Not everyone at the market is there to buy or sell. (Spanish)
Three women and a goose make a market. (Italian)
You must sell as the markets go. (English)

Marriage, Marriages
A marriage of two has God as its author. (Spanish)
Better a dove on the plate than a wood grouse in the mating place. (Russian)
Better a fair pair of heels than a halter. (Russian)
By day they fight, to bed at night. (Yiddish)
Dream of a funeral and you hear of a marriage. (Chinese)
Early marriage, long love. (German)
Far and near is the bond between woman and man. (Korean)
In marriage, choose a man for his courage and a woman for her charm. (Japanese)
It takes two to make a marriage. (German)
Keep your eyes wide open before marriage, half shut afterwards. (Poor Richard)
Like blood, like means, and like age, make the happiest marriage. (German)
Love comes after marriage. (Unknown)
Love does wonders, but money makes marriage. (French)
Marriage: two hearts that beat as one. (American)
Marriage is a battlefield and not a bed of roses. (German)
Marriage is a lottery. (Roman)
Marriage is a strange affinity. (Japanese)
Marriage is heaven and hell. (German)
Marriages are all happy: it's having breakfast together that causes all the trouble. (Irish)
Marriages are made in Heaven. (Unknown)
Marriages are made in Heaven, and spoiled by Hell. (Spanish)
Marriages are not as they are made, but as they turn out. (Italian)
Matches are made by chance. (Japanese)
Mattresses cure marital ills. (Spanish)
No feast without roasting, no marriage without torture. (Irish)

Not all who make love make marriages. (Russian)

One marriage is never celebrated but another grows out of it. (German)

The conjunction of man and woman is of the law of nature. (Roman)

The difference is wide that the sheets will not decide. (English)

The most difficult mountain to cross is the threshold. (Danish)

The only cure for love is marriage. (Irish)

The parents of a handsome daughter can choose a handsome son-in-law. (Korean)

There's more to a marriage than four bare legs in a bed. (English)

There's more to a marriage than husband and wife. (Spanish)

To eat, drink, and sleep together is marriage, methinks. (French)

Where there's marriage without love, there will be love without marriage. (Poor Richard)

Marry, Married

A good man does not get a good wife; and a leper marries a flowering branch. (Chinese)

A maiden marries to please her parents, a widow to please herself. (Chinese)

A married man is a caged bird. (Spanish)

A young man married is a young man marred. (English)

All married women are not wives. (Japanese)

Always say no, and you will never be married. (French)

An old maid who marries becomes a young wife. (Yiddish)

At fifteen I can marry any man I want; at twenty, whom people say; and at thirty, the first to come along. (Spanish)

Before you marry, beware; for it is a hard knot to untie. (Spanish)

Before you marry, have a house to live in, fields to till, and vines to cut. (Spanish)

Before you marry, make sure you know whom you are going to divorce. (Yiddish)

Better it is to marry a man with one eye than with one son. (Spanish)

Better to marry a neighbor than a stranger. (Spanish)

Between promising and giving, a man should marry off his daughter. (French)

Consider well before you marry and before you divorce. (Spanish)

From being married (*casado*) to being tired of it (*cansado*) is but one letter and one step. (Spanish)

Happy is she who marries the son of a dead mother. (Scottish)

He who fain would marry, in choice should not tarry. (Scottish)

He who marries does well, but who remains single does better. (German)

He who marries for love has good nights and bad days. (French)

He who marries ill is long in becoming widowed. (Spanish)

Honest men marry soon, wise men never. (Italian)

How gently glides the married life away, when she who rules still seems but to obey. (English)

If you want to be criticized, marry. (Irish)

If you wish to marry suitably, marry your equal in years. (Roman)

Many a scoundrel marries not for the sheep but for the wool. (Spanish)

Married couples tell each other a thousand things without speech. (Chinese)

Married today, married tomorrow. (French)

Marry a mountain girl and you marry the whole mountain. (Irish)

Marry above thy match, and thou wilt get a master. (Poor Richard)

Marry first for wealth, then for love. (Unknown)

Marry in haste, repent at leisure. (German)

Marry in Lent, live to repent. (English)

Marry in May, you'll rue for aye. (English)

Marry the first time for love, the second time for money. (Unknown)

Marry your equal, and things will work out well for you. (Spanish)

Marry your son when you will, and your daughter when you can. (Spanish)

Marry, and grow tame. (Portuguese)

Marry, marry, sounds well but tastes ill. (Portuguese)

Marrying in the blood is never good. (German)

Marrying is easy, but housekeeping is hard. (German)

Men marry when they please, women when they can. (Spanish)

Never marry for money, but marry where money is. (Roman)

Never marry for money; you can borrow it more cheaply. (Scottish)

No matter her past, when a chambermaid marries a lord she becomes a lady. (Roman)

No woman marries an old man for God's sake. (German)

No woman stays happily married without paying a price for it. (Spanish)

To marry once is a duty; twice a folly; thrice is madness. (Dutch)

When a man's friend marries, all is over between them. (French)

When a widower marries, he honors his first wife. (Unknown)

When young marries old, both are old. (Spanish)

Who dares to marry dares much. (Spanish)

Who marries afar is either deceived or wishes to deceive. (Spanish)

Who marries for a dower loses his power. (German)

Who marries for love has good nights, but sorry days. (German)

Wipe the nose of your neighbor's son, and marry him to your daughter. (Spanish)

You have married a beauty?; so much the worse for you. (Italian)

Young lovers dream, married lovers awaken. (the Editor)

Marsh

The marsh stands aloof as if it were not related to the river. (Yoruban)

Martyr

The blood of the martyrs is the seed of the Church. (Christian)

Marvel

That which is not understood is always a marvel. (Roman)

Those who have seen little marvel much. (Chinese)

Mask

No one can wear a mask for very long. (Roman)

Mason

The mason who strikes often is better than the one who strikes too hard. (Irish)

Masses

Follow not the fickle judgments of the masses. (Unknown)

The masses are asses. (German)

The masses are no asses. (Yiddish)

The masses judge of few things by the truth, of most things by opinion. (Roman)

Master

A good servant makes a good master. (Irish)

As is the master, so is his dog. (Spanish)

Every man is master in his own house. (Dutch)

Everyone has his master. (German)

He must indeed be a good master who never errs. (Dutch)

He who serves two masters must lie to one of them. (Spanish)

He who rides the horse is its master. (Danish)

Master easy, servant slack. (Chinese)

Masters' hints are commands. (Italian)

New master, new hardship. (German)

One eye of the master sees more than four eyes of his servants. (Italian)

One is master, many are servants. (Unknown)

The best feed of a horse is his master's eye. (Spanish)

The best fodder is the master's eye. (Dutch)

The eye of the master does more work than both his hands. (Roman)

The eye of the master fattens the horse. (Italian)

The eye of the master works wonders. (Unknown)

The master of the people is their servant. (Yemeni)

The master sees best in his own affairs. (Roman)

The master should not be graced by the mansion, but the mansion by the master.
   (Roman)

The master's eye has its own effect. (Persian)

The master's eye is the best fertilizer. (Roman)

The student is not above the teacher, nor is the servant above his master. (Jesus)

Matchmaker

Among ten matchmakers only nine will lie. (Chinese)

Mate

Every Jack has his Jill. (Irish)

He who has a mate has a master. (Italian)

There is no beast so savage but plays with its mate. (Spanish)

Maturity

Maturity consists of no longer being taken in by oneself. (French)

Maybe

Every maybe hath a maybe not. (Roman)

Meal

A good meal is worth hanging for. (German)
A good meal ought to begin with hunger. (French)
After dinner rest a while, after supper walk a mile. (English)
After dinner stand a while, or walk nearly half a mile. (German)
At table bashfulness is out of place. (Italian)
Dead songbirds make a sad meal. (Chinese)
Good lunches and hardy dinners drive sorrow away. (Unknown)
Good talk saves the food. (Portuguese)

Means

He who wills the end, wills the means. (Danish)
Live within your means. (Roman)

Measure

As you measure to others, it will be measured back to you. (Chinese)
Better twice measured than once wrong. (Danish)
He who measures oil greases his hands. (Spanish)
Measure for measure. (English)
Measure thrice before you cut once. (Dutch)
You can't measure the whole world with your own yardstick. (Yiddish)

Meat

Beef and pork do not mix well. (German)
Better a mouse in the pot than no meat at all. (Rumanian)
Cheap meat never makes good soup. (Russian)
If flesh is not to be had, then fish must content us. (Roman)
It is a poor roast that gives no drippings. (Danish)
It is not everyday that daddy kills a deer. (Irish)
Leave not the meat to gnaw on the bones, nor break your teeth on worthless stones.
   (German)
Much meat, many maladies. (Portuguese)
No man will feed on herbs when meat is to be had. (Roman)
Not all meat can be eaten. (German)
One man's meat is another man's poison. (English)
Strangers' meat is the greatest treat. (Danish)
Sweet meat requires sour sauce. (Italian)
The best meat is at another's expense. (German)
The man with meat seeks fire. (Hausan)
The nearer the bone, the sweeter the meat. (English)

Meddle

Meddle not in things you do not understand. (Roman)

Meddle with dirt and some of it will stick to you. (Danish)

Who is always meddling into other men's affairs, leads a dangerous life. (Spanish)

Mediator

The go-between wears out a thousand sandals. (Japanese)

Medicine

A medicine cannot stay in the bottle and be effective. (Yoruban)

An expensive physic always does good, if not to the patient at least to the apothecary.
  (German)

He who lives by medical treatment lives a wretched existence. (Roman)

Medicine sometimes destroys health, sometimes restores it. (Roman)

People are man's medicine. (West African)

Physicians rarely take medicine. (Danish)

Mediocrity

Mediocrity is climbing molehills without sweating. (Icelandic)

To the mediocre, mediocrity appears great. (Indian)

Medley

Gray and green make the worst medley. (French)

Meek

The meek shall inherit the earth. (Jesus)

Meet, Meeting

Meeting is the beginning of parting. (Japanese)

Men may meet but mountains never greet. (Irish)

Merry meet, merry part. (English)

People meet but hills and mountains never greet. (English)

Those who meet must part. (Korean)

Though separation be hard, two never meet but must part. (Irish)

We never meet but we part. (English)

Memory

Memory is the treasure of the mind. (English)

Memory is the treasury and guardian of all things. (Roman)

The best memory is not so firm as faded ink. (Chinese)

The best memory is that which forgets nothing but injuries. (Persian)

The event is past, the memory remains. (Roman)

The life of the dead is placed in the memory of the living. (Roman)

The memory of a benefit vanishes, but that of an injury sticks fast in the heart.
  (Roman)

The memory of happiness makes misery woeful. (Roman)
Your power of memory will diminish unless you exercise it. (Roman)

Mend

Get the coffin ready and watch the man mend. (Chinese)
He that resolves to mend hereafter, resolves not to mend now. (Poor Richard)
In the end, things will mend. (French)
It is never too late to mend. (Roman)
Least said, soonest mended. (English)
Men take more pains to mask than mend. (Poor Richard)
When things seem at their end, everything is sure to mend. (German)
Who errs and mends, to God himself commends. (German)

Merchant

He is no merchant who always gains. (Dutch)

Mercy

Fire, water, and government know nothing of mercy. (Roman)
Mercy often inflicts death. (Roman)

Merit

Assume the proud place your merits have won. (Roman)
If you wish your merit to be known, acknowledge that of others. (Chinese)
It is better to gather merit than riches; for merit brings goodness, riches misfortune.
   (Chinese)
Let him bear the prize, who has deserved it. (Roman)
Men are equal by birth; merit alone makes the difference. (Roman)
Merit consists in action. (Roman)
Merit is often belied by the countenance. (Roman)
The test of merit is success. (Roman)

Merry

A merry heart makes a long life. (English)
A merry host makes merry guests. (Dutch)
A merry life forgets father and mother. (French)
All are not merry that dance. (English)

Message, Messenger

A slow messenger is the better for your going to meet him. (Irish)
Be sure to send a lazy messenger for the Angel of Death. (Yiddish)
He knocks boldly who brings a welcome message. (Danish)

Mettle

Mettle is dangerous in a blind horse. (Roman)

Method

There is a method in all things. (Roman)

There's a method even to madness. (Unknown)

Mice

Burn not your house to kill the mice. (English)

It takes a good many mice to kill a cat. (Danish)

Mice care not to play with kittens. (Roman)

Walls have mice and mice have ears. (Persian)

Middle

Blessed are they who have kept a middle course. (Roman)

Take the middle of the way and thou wilt not fall. (Spanish)

The middle path is the safe path. (Roman)

Might, Mighty

A handful of might is better than a sackful of right. (German)

Might is two-thirds of right. (Irish)

Might knows no right. (French)

Might makes right. (Roman)

Might maketh not right. (Unknown)

Might overcomes right. (French)

The pleasures of the mighty are the tears of the poor. (Roman)

Where might is master, justice is servant. (German)

Where might is right, right has no might. (German)

Mile, Miles

The miles are longer at night. (German)

Milk

Black cows give white milk. (German)

Don't cry over spilt milk. (English)

He who has scalded himself on milk, weeps when he sees a cow. (Spanish)

His mouth still smells of his mother's milk. (Korean)

It is no use crying over spilt milk. (Italian)

Milk on wine is poison, wine on milk is welcome. (English)

Of what use is it that the cow gives plenty of milk, if it upsets the pail? (German)

Why buy a cow when milk is so cheap? (English)

Why buy the cow when you can drink the milk for free? (American)

You can endure a few kicks, if the cow gives you milk. (Hindi)

You cannot swallow hot milk, nor can you throw it away. (Portuguese)

Mill

A mill cannot grind with the water that is past. (Italian)

All is grist that comes to the mill. (Unknown)

Every miller draws the water to his own mill. (French)
He who has come to the mill first does not grind last. (Roman)
He who remains in the mill grinds, not he who goes to and fro. (Spanish)
No mill, no meal. (German)
The corn that is taken to a bad mill will be badly ground. (Danish)
The miller does not see everything that floats by his mill. (Roman)
The mills of God grind slowly, but they grind finely. (Irish)
The mills of the gods grind slowly, yet they grind exceedingly small. (Greek)
Water past will not turn the mill. (Spanish)

Millstone
A millstone gathers no moss. (German)

Mind, Minds
A closed mind is like a closed book: just a block of wood. (Chinese)
A good mind possesses a kingdom. (Roman)
A great mind becomes a great fortune. (Roman)
A mind enlightened is like the halls of Heaven; a mind in darkness is like the realm of
    Hell. (Chinese)
A sound and vigorous mind is the highest possession. (Roman)
A vacant mind is open to all suggestions, as a hollow mountain returns all sounds.
    (Chinese)
Be master of mind rather than mastered by mind. (Japanese)
Conversation is the image of the mind: as the man, so his speech. (Roman)
Great minds think alike. (German)
It is the mark of a great mind to despise injuries. (Roman)
Like minds, happy for life; unlike minds, always out of mind. (Burmese)
Little minds are caught by little things. (Roman)
Little things please little minds. (Dutch)
Man's mind cannot be foretold. (Japanese)
Man's mind changes morning through evening. (Korean)
Man's mind is a watch that needs winding daily. (Welsh)
Many heads, many minds. (Greek)
May we have a sound mind in a sound body. (Roman)
Men's minds are as different as their faces. (Japanese)
Men's minds are more deeply disturbed by what they do not see. (Roman)
Minds that are ill at ease are agitated both with hope and fear. (Roman)
Minds that are too much elated ought to be kept in check. (Roman)
Minds together, bodies apart. (Burmese)
Much bending breaks the bow; much unbending the mind. (Roman)
Put your mind under lock and key. (Japanese)
Rage and anger hurry the mind. (Roman)
Rusty mind, blighted genius. (Roman)
See with your mind, hear with your heart. (Kurdish)
Straining breaks the bow, and relaxation the mind. (Italian)

The body builds up with work, the mind with study. (Albanian)
The eye sees, but it is the mind that understands. (Hausan)
The mind alone cannot be exiled. (Roman)
The mind attracted by what is false refuses better things. (Roman)
The mind, conscious of integrity, scorns the lies of rumor. (Roman)
The mind is formed by reading deep rather than reading wide. (Roman)
The mind is playful when unburdened. (Roman)
The mind is the true self. (Roman)
The mind of man is uncertain. (Chinese)
The mind rules the body. (Chinese)
We know men's faces, not their minds. (Chinese)
When the mind is ill at ease, the body is affected. (Roman)

Miner
Miners find more rocks than gold. (German)

Minute
Take hold of a good minute. (Spanish)

Miracle
Let the miracle be wrought, though it be by the Devil. (Spanish)
The age of miracles is past. (English)

Mire
The more you stir the mire, the more it stinks. (German)

Mirror
Deprive a mirror of its silver and even the czar won't see his face. (Russian)
Everyone sees his best friend in the mirror. (Yiddish)
Objects in the mirror are closer than they appear. (American)
The best mirror is an old friend. (English)

Mirth
A pennyworth of mirth is worth a pound of sorrow. (English)

Mischief
A little neglect may breed great mischief. (Unknown)
He that hatches mischief, catches mischief. (Unknown)
Many a one is good because he can do no mischief. (French)
Mischief comes soon enough. (Danish)
Mischief has swift wings. (English)
The mother of mischief is no bigger than a midge's wig. (Scottish)
The person with nothing to do thinks about the mischief he will do. (Mexican)

Miser

A miser and a liar bargain quickly. (Greek)

A miser does nothing right except when he dies. (Roman)

A miser is ever in want. (Greek)

A miserly father makes a prodigal child. (French)

Do not be like a miser who saves for those who will bury him. (Madagascan)

Misers' money goes twice to market. (Spanish)

No one calls on a miser. (Yoruban)

The generous man grows rich in giving, the miser poor in taking. (Danish)

The miser and the pig are of no use till dead. (French)

The miser cooks lunch after his guests have left. (Korean)

The miser is as much in want of that which he has, as of that which he has not. (Roman)

The miser is ever on the search, yet fears to use what he has acquired. (Roman)

The miser is his own stepmother. (German)

The miser pays dearer and the sluggard walks farther. (Yiddish)

The miser sells his own soul. (German)

The miser's bag is never full. (Danish)

The poor man wants much, the miser everything. (Danish)

To beg of the miser is to dig a trench in the sea. (Turkish)

Misery, Miserable

A person in misery is a sacred matter. (Roman)

From the miseries of others he fears for his own position. (Roman)

He is miserable indeed that must lock up his miseries. (Italian)

He is miserable once, who feels it; but twice, who fears it before it comes. (Italian)

Is there any thing men take more pains about than to render themselves unhappy?
   (Poor Richard)

Misery acquaints a man with strange bedfellows. (English)

Misery loves company. (Roman)

The recollection of past miseries is pleasant. (Roman)

Misfit

You are pressing a round peg into a square hole. (American)

Misfortune, Misfortunes

A great fortune in the hands of a fool is a great misfortune. (French)

A misfortune and a friar seldom go alone. (Italian)

An unlucky man falls on his back and breaks his nose. (French)

Another's misfortune does not cure my pain. (Portuguese)

Another's misfortune is only a dream. (French)

Blessed is the misfortune that comes alone. (Italian)

Even in misfortune, there is blessing. (Japanese)

Grieving for misfortunes is adding gall to wormwood. (Roman)

He falls out of the frying pan and into the fire. (Unknown)

He who cannot bear misfortune is truly unfortunate. (Greek)

He who is born to misfortunate stumbles as he goes, and though he fall on his back will fracture his nose. (German)

He who is the cause of his own misfortune may bewail it himself. (Italian)

Ignorance of one's misfortunes is clear gain. (Greek)

In misfortune we need help, not pity. (Roman)

It is a great art to laugh at your own misfortune. (Danish)

It is good to see in the misfortune of another what we should shun ourselves. (Roman)

It is joy to the unhappy to have companions in misfortune. (Roman)

Kings have long arms, but misfortune longer. (Poor Richard)

Misfortune comes from the mouth. (Japanese)

Misfortune comes on horseback and goes away on foot. (French)

Misfortune is a second master. (Roman)

Misfortune is not that which can be avoided, but that which cannot. (Chinese)

Misfortune may turn out to be blessing. (Korean)

Misfortune never comes alone. (Spanish)

Misfortune teaches us to pray. (English)

Misfortune will sooner or later find the one whom it has passed by. (Roman)

Misfortunes are always at hand. (Roman)

Misfortunes benefit the good man. (Roman)

Misfortunes cannot be avoided but they can be sweetened. (Dutch)

Misfortunes come but not all the time. (Irish)

Misfortunes come not as single spies but as battalions. (English)

Misfortunes come unsought. (Roman)

Misfortunes make friends. (Roman)

Misfortunes make happiness more sweet when it comes. (Roman)

Misfortunes never come singly. (Italian)

Misfortunes often stir up genius. (Roman)

Misfortunes watch by the door and slip in at the first opportunity. (Spanish)

Misfortunes, when asleep, are not to be awakened. (Italian)

Most of man's misfortunes are due to man. (Roman)

Not to feel one's misfortunes is not human, not to bear them is not manly. (Roman)

One has always strength enough to bear the misfortunes of one's friends. (French)

One misfortune brings on another. (Dutch)

One misfortune is followed closely by another. (Roman)

Stay far away from an unfortunate person. (Roman)

The misfortune of the foolish is a warning to the wise. (Roman)

The misfortunes of some people are advantages to others. (Egyptian)

The misfortunes to which we are accustomed affect us less deeply. (Roman)

The road to misfortune is short. (Russian)

There is no greater misfortune than not to be able to endure misfortune. (Roman)

We are the authors of our own misfortune. (Roman)

When misfortune comes in at the door, love flies out of the window. (German)

When misfortune sleeps, let no one wake her. (Spanish)

Wise from the misfortune but not rich. (Finnish)

Miss
A good marksman may sometimes miss. (Unknown)
A miss is as good as a mile. (English)
An inch in a miss is as good as a mile. (American)
No one so sure but he may miss. (Dutch)

Mistake
A mistake is no fraud. (German)
A mistake is no reckoning. (French)
Do not mistake a goat's beard for a fine stallion's tail. (Irish)
If you don't make mistakes, you don't make anything. (German)
Only he who does nothing makes a mistake. (French)

Mistress
As the mistress, so the maid. (German)

Mob
Nothing is so valueless as the sentiments of the mob. (Roman)

Mock, Mockery
Do not laugh at a deformed person today; you may be him tomorrow.
   (Yoruban)
He who made fun of the old man, laughed at first and cried afterwards. (Spanish)
Mock not the fallen, for slippery is the road ahead of you. (Russian)
Mockery is the fume of little hearts. (English)

Moderate, Moderation
Blessed are they who have kept a middle course. (Roman)
He that never eats too much, will never be lazy. (Poor Richard)
In everything the middle course is best: all things in excess bring trouble to men.
   (Roman)
It is a sign of a great mind to despise greatness, and to prefer things in measure to things
   in excess. (Roman)
Late hours and love and wine lead not to moderation in anything. (Roman)
Make moderate use of possessions. (Roman)
Moderate measures succeed best. (Roman)
Moderation is medicine, excess is peril. (Burmese)
Moderation is the mark of a great heart. (Roman)
Safety is in going the middle course. (Roman)
Seek moderation in all things. (Roman)

Modest, Modesty
A modest dog seldom grows fat. (Danish)
A modest friar never was a prior. (Italian)
Great modesty often hides great merit. (Poor Richard)

He is never likely to have a good thing cheap that is afraid to ask a price. (Danish)
He who takes his rank lightly raises his own dignity. (Yiddish)
It becomes a young man to be modest. (Roman)
Modesty forbids what the law does not. (Roman)
Modesty is inborn, it cannot be learned. (Roman)
So rare is the union of beauty with modesty. (Roman)
When modesty goes, she goes forever. (Roman)

Monarch
The greatest monarch on the proudest throne, is oblig'd to sit upon his own arse.
　(Poor Richard)

Money
A friend who borrows money soon becomes your enemy. (Spanish)
A glimpse of money makes even the blind to see. (Chinese)
A little, often, leaves wrinkles in the purse. (Irish)
Above all is he admired who is not moved by money. (Roman)
Abundance of money is a trial for a man. (Moroccan)
All fall silent before money. (Spanish)
All things are obedient to money. (Roman)
An abundance of money ruins youth. (English)
As cheese attracts mice, so money the thief. (Spanish)
Bad money always comes back. (German)
Bad money drives out good. (American)
Bad money follows good. (Unknown)
Beauty is potent, but money is omnipotent. (Dutch)
Better a steady dime than a rare dollar. (Yiddish)
Dirty hands make money clean. (German)
Disclose not your hoarded money to anybody. (Spanish)
Do not lend your money to a great man. (French)
Don't marry for money, you can borrow it cheaper. (Scottish)
Don't take any wooden nickels. (American)
Ducats are clipped, pence are not. (German)
Even the blind open their eyes to money. (German)
Everything in this world depends on money. (Japanese)
Fair money can cover much that's foul. (Dutch)
Follow the money. (American)
Getting money is like digging with a needle; spending it is like water soaking into the
　sand. (Japanese)
Good management is better than good income. (Portuguese)
Good manners and plenty of money will make my son a gentlemen. (Portuguese)
He that has no money in his purse, should have fair words on his lips. (Danish)
He that has not money in his purse should have honey in his mouth. (French)
He that shows his money shows his judgment. (Italian)
He who builds a house, or marries, is left with a slender purse. (Spanish)

He who has money can eat sherbet in Hell. (Lebanese)
He who has money has capers. (French)
He who throws away money with his hands will seek it with his feet. (Italian)
'Here's your money' will bring even a fetus rushing out of the womb. (Korean)
If money be not thy servant, it will be thy master. (Japanese)
If you don't know the value of money, then go and borrow some. (German)
If you have money, take a seat; it you have none, take to your feet. (German)
If you think you know what a dollar is worth, try to borrow one. (American)
If you want to know what a man is really like, notice how he acts when he loses money.
   (Spanish)
In for a penny, in for a pound. (English)
It costs money to make money. (American)
It is easier to make money than to hold onto it. (Yiddish)
Love does much, money everything. (French)
Making money selling manure is better than losing money selling musk. (Egyptian)
Money and mice hide at the slightest noise. (Spanish)
Money attracts money. (Mexican)
Money borrowed is soon sorrowed. (French)
Money brings power. (German)
Money burns many. (French)
Money buys everything but good sense. (Yiddish)
Money can move even the gods. (Chinese)
Money can't buy happiness. (American)
Money can't buy happiness, but it can sure buy a lot of other things. (American)
Money does not choose the people. (Albanian)
Money doesn't grow on trees. (Yiddish)
Money first, virtue later. (Italian)
Money goes to one place, suspicion to a thousand. (Persian)
Money grows on the tree of persistence. (Japanese)
Money has no smell. (Japanese)
Money has wings. (Korean)
Money hides a thousand deformities. (Chinese)
Money in the purse dispels melancholy. (German)
Money is a good servant but a bad master. (French)
Money is the root of all evil. (Unknown)
Money is bewailed with a greater tumult than death. (Roman)
Money is both blood and life to mortal men. (Roman)
Money is either our master or our slave. (Roman)
Money is king, money is queen, money is everything. (American)
Money is lost only for want of money. (French)
Money is money's brother. (Italian)
Money is more eloquent that a dozen members of parliament. (Danish)
Money is not gained by losing time. (Portuguese)
Money is power. (Unknown)
Money is round, and rolls. (Italian)

Money is sweet balm. (Egyptian)

Money is the key that opens every door. (Unknown)

Money is the measure of all things. (Portuguese)

Money is truthful. (Dutch)

Money isn't everything. (Dutch)

Money isn't everything, but it's way ahead of whatever's in second place.
  (American)

Money makes dogs dance. (French)

Money makes even the cats to dance and the dogs to sing. (Spanish)

Money makes even the fool a master. (English)

Money makes friends strangers. (Japanese)

Money makes money. (French)

Money makes the man. (Portuguese)

Money makes the mare to trot. (French)

Money makes the world go 'round. (American)

Money makes the wretched seem virtuous. (Unknown)

Money never goes out of fashion. (German)

Money rules the world. (German)

Money smells good no matter its source. (Roman)

Money soothes more than a gentleman's words. (Spanish)

Money speaks in a language all nations understand. (Unknown)

Money talks. (English)

Money turns bad into good. (Spanish)

Money will do more than my lord's letter. (Spanish)

Money will make even the gods your servants. (Korean)

Money wins the battle, not the long arm. (Portuguese)

Money, like a queen, bestows both rank and beauty. (Roman)

Much coin, much care. (Portuguese)

Much money moves the gods. (Chinese)

Much money, many friends. (German)

Muck and money go together. (English)

Nothing is so strongly fortified that it cannot be taken by money. (Roman)

Nothing stings more deeply than the loss of money. (Roman)

One bag of money is stronger than two bags of truth. (Danish)

One hand full of money is stronger than two hands full of truth. (Danish)

One penny is better on land than ten on the sea. (Danish)

Public money is like holy water: everyone helps himself to it. (Italian)

Put your money where your mouth is. (American)

Ready money can buy whatever is in stock. (Chinese)

Ready money is ready medicine. (Roman)

Ready money works great cures. (French)

Sooner ask a man for his life, than for his money. (Yiddish)

Take care of your pennies and your dollars will take care of your widow's next husband.
  (American)

Take care of your pennies and your pounds will take care of themselves. (Scottish)

Take care of your pennies and your pounds will take care of your heirs and barristers.
  (English)
That which is stamped a penny will never be a pound. (Danish)
That's but an empty purse which is full of other men's money. (Danish)
The art is not in making money, but in keeping it. (Dutch)
The loss of money is bewailed with true tears. (Roman)
The love of money increases as wealth itself increases. (Roman)
The love of money is a root to all kinds of evil. (Christian)
The money-maker is never tired. (Irish)
The more money, the more debt. (Unknown)
Those who despise money will eventually sponge on their friends. (Chinese)
To despise money on occasion sometimes leads to very great gain. (Roman)
To have money is a fear, not to have is a grief. (Unknown)
Transactions in Hell also depend upon money. (Japanese)
Unwise are the elderly who have no money. (Yoruban)
When money talks, it is usually saying goodbye. (English)
When money talks, the truth is silent. (Russian)
Where money, there friends. (German)
Where there are two friends with one purse, one sings, the other weeps. (Spanish)
Where there's money, there is the Devil; but where there's none, a greater evil.
  (German)
Where there's muck there's money. (German)
Who has no money in his purse must have honey in his mouth. (Italian)
Who has no money must have no wishes. (Italian)
With money in your pocket, you are wise and you are handsome – and you sing well
  too. (Yiddish)
With money one may command devils; without it, one cannot even summon a man.
  (Chinese)
With money you are a dragon; without it you are a worm. (Chinese)
With money you can build a road in the sea. (Maltese)
With money you would not know yourself, without money nobody would know you.
  (Spanish)
Without money all is vain. (Roman)
Without money, both birth and virtue are as worthless as seaweed. (Roman)

Monk, Monks
A monk cannot shave his own head. (Korean)
A monk has no concern with a comb. (Burmese)
A monk in his cloister, a fish in the water, a thief in the gallows. (German)
A runaway monk never speaks well of his convent. (Dutch)
If wood-hewing were an order, there would be fewer monks. (German)
Never was a hood so holy but the Devil could get his head into it. (Dutch)
Not all monks practice what they preach. (German)
The abbey does not fail for want of one monk. (French)
The cowl does not make the monk. (Roman)

The food of the monk is the food of the temple. (Korean)
The monk that begs for God's sake begs for two. (French)

Monkey

A monkey is not to be caught in a trap. (Roman)
A monkey remains a monkey, though dressed in silk. (Spanish)
By trying often, the monkey learns to jump from the tree. (West African)
Do chattering monkeys mimic men, or we, turned apes, out-monkey them? (Roman)
Even a monkey has a position to uphold. (Korean)
Even a monkey may sometimes fall from the tree. (Japanese)
Monkey see, monkey do. (American)
The higher the monkey climbs the more it shows its tail. (German)
The higher the monkey climbs, the more one sees of its behind. (Jamaican)
The monkey knows the tree it climbs. (Puerto Rican)
The monkey, so base a creature, how like ourselves! (Roman)
The old monkey is caught last. (Roman)
When the monkey reigns, dance before him. (Egyptian)

Month

If one month is long, another month is short. (Korean)

Monument

A monument is an unnecessary expense; our memory will endure if we have earned it
  by our life. (Roman)

Moon

Does the moon on high concern itself with the barking of a dog? (Roman)
God saves the moon from the wolves. (French)
If the moon is with you, care not about the stars. (Egyptian)
If you do not agree with the phases of the moon, get a ladder and repair it. (Hausan)
The light of all the stars is not equal to the moon. (Chinese)
The moon does not heed the baying of dogs. (Italian)
The moon is not seen because of great stature. (Hausan)
The moon ripens no fruit. (German)
The moon shines but does not warm. (Russian)
The older the moon, the brighter it shines. (Jamaican)
When the moon is full, it begins to wane. (Unknown)
Wolves have howled at the moon for centuries, yet it is still there. (Italian)

Moonlight

The loveliest of faces are to be seen by moonlight, when one sees half with the eye and
  half with the fancy. (Persian)

Moose

If you give a moose a muffin it will ask for butter and jam. (American)

Morals

Bad company corrupts good morals. (Christian)

Can you expect that the mother will teach good morals or ones other than her own? (Roman)

Do not think any vice trivial so as to do it; do not think any virtue trivial so as to neglect it. (Chinese)

It is a hard thing not to surrender morals for riches. (Roman)

The one who is proficient in learning and deficient in morals is more deficient than proficient. (Roman)

More

More in possibility than in actuality. (Roman)

The more the merrier. (English)

Morning

The morning hour has gold in its mouth. (German)

The morning is wiser than the evening. (Russian)

Morsel

Let him eat the tough morsel who would eat the tender. (Portuguese)

One good morsel and a hundred vexations. (Italian)

Mortal

Thou too art mortal. (Roman)

Mortar

Even a stone mortar will lose its bottom someday. (Korean)

Moth

The moth flutters about the candle till at last it gets burnt. (Dutch)

Mother

A bad mother wishes for good children. (Spanish)

A bustling mother makes a slothful daughter. (Portuguese)

A child's fingers are not scalded by a piece of hot yam which her mother puts into her palm. (African)

A lover loves one day, a mother all her life. (Spanish)

A tender-hearted mother makes a disagreeable daughter. (French)

All mothers are daughters of Mother Eve. (Yiddish)

An ounce of mother is worth a pound of priests. (Spanish)

Every beetle is a gazelle in the eyes of its mother. (African)

God could not be everywhere and therefore he made mothers. (Yiddish)

If mama ain't happy, ain't nobody happy. (American)

Mother and child are reunited, and love returns to the earth. (Irish)

Mother knows best. (German)

Mother's love is ever in its spring. (French)

Mother's truth keeps constant youth. (German)

One good mother is worth a hundred school teachers. (Unknown)

The beetle is a beauty in the eyes of its mother. (Egyptian)

The mother must have a large apron to cover the faults of her children (Yiddish)

The mother who spoils her child, fattens a serpent. (Spanish)

To a mother a bad son does not exist. (Mexican)

Who takes the child by the hand takes the mother by the heart. (German)

Motion

Motion drawing to its end is swifter. (Roman)

Motive

Take away the motive, and the sin is taken away. (Spanish)

Mountain

Behind every mountain lies a vale. (Dutch)

Beyond the mountain is another mountain. (Haitian)

Don't make a mountain out of a molehill. (English)

Every mountain has its wolves. (German)

In a flat country a hillock thinks itself a mountain. (Kurdish)

Mountains never unite. (Roman)

The higher the mountain the deeper the valley. (Korean)

The higher the mountain, the greener the grass. (Jamaican)

The man who removes a mountain begins by carrying away small stones. (Chinese)

The mountains shake but do not fall. (Albanian)

There are many paths to the top of the mountain, but the view is always the same. (Chinese)

Though the wind blows, the mountains are unmoved. (Japanese)

You must scale the mountains if you would view the plain. (Chinese)

Mourn

Men mourn for those who leave fortunes behind. (Chinese)

Men never mourn over the opportunities lost to do good, only the opportunities lost to do evil. (Greek)

None mourn with more affection of sorrow than those who inwardly rejoice. (Roman)

Mouse

A mouse does not rely on just one hole. (Roman)

A mouse in time may bite a cable in two. (Roman)

A mouse may help a lion. (Roman)

A mouse will put the finishing stroke to a castle wall. (Roman)

A mouse will scare a thief. (Italian)

Do not throw a stone at the mouse and so break the precious vase. (Spanish)

Don't stop the plow to catch a mouse. (German)

It is a bold mouse that makes its nest in the cat's ear. (Danish)
It is a clever mouse that can nest in sight of the cat. (German)
It is a poor mouse that has but one hole. (Dutch)
Not the mouse is the thief, but the hole in the wall. (Yiddish)
Pour not water on a drowned mouse. (Spanish)
The mouse perishes by betraying itself. (Roman)
The mouse that hath but one hole is soon caught. (Dutch)
Though an owl has big eyes, it cannot see as well as a mouse. (Japanese)
What honor is there in killing a mouse? (American)
When the mouse laughs at the cat, there is a hole nearby. (Nigerian)
Who plays the mouse shall be eaten by the cat. (German)
Why use a steamroller to kill a mouse? (American)

Mouth, Mouthful

A closed mouth and open eyes never did anyone harm. (German)
A closed mouth catches no flies. (Italian)
A foul mouth must be provided with a strong back. (Danish)
A mouth cannot be so dirty that the owner cannot eat with it. (Yoruban)
A shut mouth keeps one out of strife. (Portuguese)
A wise head makes a closed mouth. (Irish)
All mischief comes from much opening of the mouth. (Chinese)
Big mouthfuls often choke. (Italian)
Buy one lock for your purse and two for your mouth. (Spanish)
Close your mouth as you would close a bottle; guard your thoughts as you would a city.
    (Chinese)
Close your mouth, open your eyes. (Roman)
Don't make use of another's mouth unless it has been lent to you. (Belgian)
Even a fish wouldn't get into trouble if it kept its mouth shut. (Korean)
Even the shelled egg won't leap into your mouth. (Yiddish)
He must gape wide who would gape against an oven. (Dutch)
He that would stop everybody's mouth needs plenty of flour. (German)
He who would close another man's mouth, should first tie up his own. (Danish)
I have a mouth which I feed, it must speak what I please. (Dutch)
If his mouth were silent another part of him would speak. (Egyptian)
If you keep your mouth shut, you won't put your foot in it. (English)
If your mouth becomes a knife, it will cut off your lips. (African)
Illness goes in at the mouth, calamity comes out of the mouth. (Japanese)
Keep your ears wider and your mouth narrower. (Russian)
Keep your mouth, and keep your friend. (Danish)
Let not him that has a mouth ask another to blow. (Portuguese)
Most illnesses enter through the mouth. (Spanish)
Mouth of honey, heart of gall. (Portuguese)
No pear falls into a shut mouth. (Italian)
Out of the mouth, a word goes around the world. (Japanese)
Out of the mouths of babes come gems. (English)

Out of the same mouth comes blessing and cursing. (Christian)
Roasted pigeons will not fly into one's mouth. (Dutch)
Shut your mouth and you'll catch no flies. (Portuguese)
Sweet is the sound of the silent mouth. (Irish)
The mouth expresses what the heart feels. (Spanish)
The mouth is right but the heart is wrong. (Chinese)
The mouth is the gate of evil and misfortune. (Japanese)
The mouth of the one who cries 'fire' is not burnt. (Egyptian)
The mouth of the wicked is sweet but the heart is bitter. (Chinese)
The mouth often utters that which the head must answer for. (Danish)
The mouth, though small, can consume house and hall. (German)
The pocket pays for the indiscretions of the mouth. (Spanish)
The sweeter the mouth the more venomous the heart. (Chinese)
Though your mouth is bent, speak straight. (Korean)
To stop the mouths of people is more difficult than to stop the current of a stream.
    (Korean)
What you don't see with your eyes, don't invent with your mouth. (Yiddish)

Much

Much never cost little. (Spanish)
Much would have more. (German)
Much would have more, and lost all. (French)
To him who hath much, much will be given; to him who hath not, even that will be
    taken away. (Jesus)
Who has much has much to use. (German)

Mud, Muddy

He who is in the mud likes to get another into it. (Spanish)
Mud chokes no eels. (German)
Muddy springs will have muddy streams. (French)
Muddy water won't do for a mirror. (Italian)
The mud of one country is the medicine of another. (Albanian)
Throw mud against a wall; even if it doesn't stick it will surely leave a mark. (Egyptian)

Muhammad

If the mountain will not go to Muhammad, let Muhammad go to the mountain.
    (English)

Mule

Cutting off a mule's ears doesn't make it a horse. (American)
He who rides the mule shoes it. (French)
He who wants a mule without faults must walk on foot. (Spanish)
Mules make a great fuss about their ancestors having been horses. (German)
The mule keeps a kick in reserve for its master. (French)

Murder

Murder can be forgiven, but justice cannot let it pass. (Chinese)

Murder will out. (English)

Never murder a man who is about to commit suicide. (German)

Music, Musician

A cough assists a musician when he hesitates. (Roman)

All flute players are mad: when once they begin to blow, away goes reason. (Roman)

Even the fear of death is dispelled by music. (Roman)

It is the tone that makes the music. (French)

Move your neck according to the music. (Ethiopian)

Music hath charms to soothe the savage breast. (English)

Music is the best cure for a sorrowing mind. (Roman)

Music is the handmaid of divinity. (Roman)

Music provokes love. (Roman)

Musicians are brothers. (Welsh)

Not all who own a lyre are lyre-players. (Roman)

Poor is the church without music. (Irish)

The diseases of the mind are either caused or cured by the power of music. (Roman)

Why should the Devil have all the best tunes? (English)

Must

Must is a hard nut. (German)

Myrtle

A myrtle among thorns is a myrtle still. (Unknown)

N

Nail

A nail secures the horseshoe, the shoe the horse, the horse the man, the man the castle, and the castle the whole land. (German)

Do not hang all on one nail. (German)

Drive not a second nail till the first be clinched. (German)

Drive the nail that will go. (Danish)

He takes out a nail and puts in a pin. (Italian)

It takes a heap of licks to strike a nail in the dark. (American)

Leave no nail unclenched. (Italian)

One man knocks in the nail, and another hangs his hat on it. (German)

One nail drives out another. (German)

One stroke on the nail and a hundred on the horseshoe. (Spanish)

The nail that sticks up will be hammered down. (Japanese)

Naked

Anything will fit a naked man. (Irish)

It is as well to be naked as to have no covering. (Danish)

Naked came we into the world, naked shall we depart. (English)

No naked person ever lost anything. (Japanese)

People despise a naked man until they need mud for a wall. (Hausan)

The more a man exposes his nakedness the colder he is. (French)

The naked do not fear robbery. (Russian)

There is no stripping a naked man. (German)

You cannot strip the garment off a naked man. (Roman)

Name, Names

A name doesn't harm the man, if the man doesn't harm the name. (Estonian)

A person with a bad name is already half hanged. (English)

Be mindful, even though you lose your wealth, not to lose your name. (Irish)

Everybody has a name, but not always the same luck with it. (Roman)

Get a name for rising early, and you may lie in bed all day. (Spanish)

He who has a bad name is half hanged. (Italian)

One has a good name, another the worth. (Greek)

Sticks and stones may break my bones, but words will never hurt me. (American)

Though a man dies, he leaves his name. (Korean)

Tigers die and leave their skins; people die and leave their names. (Japanese)

Nature

Nature abhors a vacuum. (Roman)

Nature and nature's laws lay hid in night. (Poor Richard)

Nature draws stronger then seven oxen. (German)

Nature gives what no man can take away. (English)

Nature has granted man no better gift than the brevity of life. (Roman)

Nature herself makes the wise man wealthy. (Roman)

Nature is a good mother. (Unknown)

Nature is better than a middling doctor. (Chinese)

Nature is our mother. (Roman)

Nature never says one thing and wisdom another. (Roman)

Nature teaches one duty. (Roman)

Nature trumps nurture. (American)

Nature will come through the claws, and the hound will follow the hare. (Irish)

Self-preservation is the first law of nature. (English)

The greatest force is that of nature. (Roman)

There is a nature in all things. (American)

We cannot command nature except by obeying her. (English)

You may drive out nature with a pitchfork, but she will keep coming back. (Roman)

Naught

Naught is good for the eyes, but not for the stomach. (German)

Naught is never in danger. (German)
Naught is that muse that finds no excuse. (English)
Naught needs no hiding-place. (German)

Near, Nearest
Everyone is nearest to himself. (Roman)
Near is my shirt, but nearer is my skin. (English)
The nearest, the dearest. (German)

Necessity
Make a virtue of necessity. (Roman)
Necessity becomes will. (Italian)
Necessity breaks iron. (German)
Necessity gives law without itself accepting one. (Roman)
Necessity is a good teacher. (Mexican)
Necessity is a powerful weapon. (Roman)
Necessity is the last and strongest weapon. (Roman)
Necessity is the mother of invention. (English)
Necessity is the mother of the arts. (Roman)
Necessity knows no holiday. (Roman)
Necessity knows no law. (Roman)
Necessity makes sour sweet. (Norwegian)
Necessity never made a good bargain. (Poor Richard)
Necessity requires no decision. (Roman)
Necessity seeks bread where it is to be found. (German)
Necessity teaches arts. (German)
Necessity teaches even the lame to dance. (German)
Necessity teaches us to bear misfortunes bravely, habit to bear them easily. (Roman)
Necessity unites hearts. (German)
No burden is really heavy to a man which necessity lays on him. (Roman)
You cannot escape necessity, but you can overcome it. (Roman)

Neck
However long the neck, the head is above it. (Hausan)
Move your neck according to the music. (Ethiopian)
Where there is a neck there will be a yoke. (Russian)

Need, Needs
Do not tell your needs to those who cannot help you. (Spanish)
He that desires but little has no need of much. (Danish)
Need makes greed. (Scottish)
Need makes the old woman trot. (French)
Need teaches a plan. (Irish)
Need will have its course. (Unknown)
One often has need of a lesser than oneself. (French)

What you do not need is costly at a penny. (Roman)
When the need is highest, the help is nighest. (English)

Needle
He looks for a needle in a haystack. (Unknown)
If a needle can pierce it, don't chop it with an axe. (Burmese)
It takes a needle to get a thorn out of one's foot. (Persian)
The needle clothes, yet it is naked. (Egyptian)

Negation
Negation proves nothing. (Roman)

Neglect, Negligence
He who neglects the little, loses the greater. (Roman)
If two men feed a horse, it will be thin; if two men mend a boat, it will leak. (Chinese)
Neglect will heal an injury sooner than revenge. (Roman)
Neglected things flourish. (Roman)
Negligence always has misfortune for a companion. (Roman)
Negligence is the great enemy. (Japanese)

Neighbor
A good neighbor adds value to your house. (German)
A good neighbor is a found treasure. (Chinese)
A good neighbor is a good friend. (Mexican)
A good neighbor is better than a brother far off. (Danish)
An enemy and an envious man carefully watches over his neighbor. (Roman)
Ask about your neighbors, then buy the house. (Yiddish)
Be patient with a bad neighbor: he may move or face misfortune. (Egyptian)
Better a bad harvest than a bad neighbor. (Serbian)
Better a near neighbor than a distant cousin. (Italian)
Close neighbors are better than distant relatives. (Japanese)
Do not wrong or hate your neighbor for it is not he that you wrong but yourself.
   (Native American)
For a wife and a horse go to your neighbor. (Italian)
He who can give has many a good neighbor. (French)
He who has good neighbors, gets a 'good morning'. (German)
I am ever my nearest neighbor. (Roman)
If a man would know what he is, let him anger his neighbors. (German)
If your neighbor dislikes you, change the gate of your house. (Egyptian)
Keep well with your neighbors, whether right or wrong. (German)
Love thy neighbor as thyself. (Jesus)
Love thy neighbor, but do not pull down thy hedge. (German)
Love your neighbor, but put up a fence. (Russian)
Many a man is a good friend but a bad neighbor. (Danish)
Mix with the neighbors, and you learn what's doing in your own house. (Yiddish)

Neighbor once over the hedge, neighbor over it again. (German)
Neighbors watch more closely than foxes. (Greek)
No one is rich enough to do without his neighbor. (Danish)
One's neighbors are one's brothers and sisters. (Yoruban)
Our neighbors' children are always the worst. (German)
The bad neighbor sees only what enters the house, not what goes out. (Egyptian)
There are three bad neighbors: great rivers, great lords, and great roads. (Danish)
To have a good neighbor is to find something precious. (Chinese)
Woe to him who gives preference to one neighbor over another. (Irish)
Woe to him whose example is a warning to his neighbor. (Irish)
You too are in danger when your neighbor's house is on fire. (Roman)
Your close neighbor is better than your faraway brother. (Arabian)
Your neighbor's apples are the sweetest. (Yiddish)

Nest

Build but one nest in one tree. (Roman)
By slow degrees the bird builds its nest. (Dutch)
In the broken nest there are no whole eggs. (Chinese)
Little bird, little nest. (Spanish)
Little by little the bird builds its nest. (Spanish)
Prepare a nest for the hen and it will lay eggs for you. (Portuguese)
Though the bird may fly over your head, let it not make its nest in your hair. (Danish)
'Tis an ill bird that soils its own nest. (French)
To every bird its own nest seems fair. (French)

Net, Nets

A net will catch more than a pole. (Russian)
A new net won't catch an old bird. (Italian)
All is not fish that comes to the net. (Dutch)
Cast your empty net only as far as you can draw it back full. (Irish)
If the net be spread too widely, the bird avoids the snare. (Roman)
The net misses the fish that can swallow a boat. (Japanese)
The net of the sleeper catches fish. (Greek)
There is a day to cast your nets and a day to dry your nets. (Chinese)
Weaving a net is better than praying for fish at the edge of the water. (Chinese)

Nettle

I bought the nettle, sowed the nettle, and then the nettle stung me. (Kashmiri)
If you gently touch a nettle, it'll sting you for your pains; if you grasp it like a lad of
    mettle, as soft as silk it remains. (English)
The nettle stings with all its body. (Yoruban)
The stinging nettle is often next to the rose. (Roman)

Never

A hundred years is not much, but never is a long while. (French)

Better once than never. (Italian)
Never is a long time. (Italian)
Never say never. (Jamaican)
Never say, of this water I will not drink, of this bread I will not eat. (Portuguese)
Never seek the wind in the field. It is useless to try to find what is gone. (Polish)

New

Always something new, seldom something good. (German)
Everything is pretty when it is new. (English)
Everything new is beautiful. (Italian)
New churches and new taverns are seldom empty. (German)
New things are most looked at. (Danish)
Nothing is so new as what has long been forgotten. (German)
Nothing is so new but it has happened before. (Danish)
The newest is not always the truest. (English)
What is new cannot be true. (American)

New and Old

Everything new is pleasing, and everything old is distasteful. (Irish)
The new antler towers over the old horns. (Korean)
The new is always liked, though the old is often better. (Danish)
With a new dress on the wall, the old is no disgrace at all. (Yiddish)

News

Before good news goes out the door, bad news is known for a thousand miles. (Chinese)
Do not fret for news, it will grow old and you will know it. (Spanish)
Go abroad and you'll hear news of home. (Italian)
Good news knocks louder than bad. (Spanish)
Good news may be told at any time, but ill in the morning. (English)
He knocks boldly at the door who brings good news. (French)
News does not have wings, yet it can cross the seven seas. (West African)
No news is good news. (English)
The news we hear about the market makes us frequent the market. (Yoruban)

Night

At night, all cats are gray. (German)
Even after the coldest night day breaks. (Swedish)
Night brings counsel. (Spanish)
Night does not know the man of honor. (Yoruban)
Night has no friend. (French)
Night is the mother of councils. (French)
Night is the time for counsel, day for arms. (Roman)
The longer the night lasts, the more our dreams will be. (Chinese)
The night is a cloak for sinners. (German)
Wait until it is night before saying that it has been a fine day. (French)

Nip

Nip the briar in the bud. (French)

Nip the briar in the bud or you will have to use an ax. (Japanese)

No

No is a good answer when given in time. (Danish)

No makes no man poor. (American)

Noble, Nobility

A noble heart is often hid under a tattered cloak. (Danish)

A noble mind accepts even the most painful injuries. (Roman)

A noble prince never has a coin to bless himself. (French)

A nobleman, though drowning, would never dog-paddle. (Korean)

A nobleman's calf does not know how a butcher kills. (Korean)

Adam got a hoe, and Eve got a spinning-wheel, and thence come all our nobles.
    (Danish)

He is noble who performs noble deeds. (Dutch)

He loses all nobility whose only merit is noble birth. (Roman)

It is easier to make a lady of a peasant-girl than a peasant-girl of a lady. (Dutch)

It is not a hallway filled with dusty portraits that makes a man noble. (Roman)

Nobility imposes obligations. (French)

Nobility is nothing but ancient riches, and money is the world's idol. (French)

Nobility without wealth is seaweed left by the tide. (Roman)

Piety, prudence, wit, and civility, are the elements of true nobility. (German)

The more noble, the more humble. (English)

There were never fewer nobles than when all would be so. (Danish)

Nobody

A nobody today, a prince tomorrow. (Roman)

Nod

A nod is as good as a wink to a blind horse. (Irish)

Noise

Pigs in the cold and men in drink make a great noise. (Portuguese)

Nonsense

As charms are nonsense, nonsense is a charm. (Poor Richard)

He who speaks much is sure to speak nonsense. (Greek)

Nose

Don't cut off your nose to spite your face. (English)

He must have clean fingers who would blow another's nose. (Danish)

It is better to leave the child's nose dirty than wring it off. (French)

Keep your nose to the grindstone. (Danish)

Who blows his nose too hard makes it bleed. (French)

Nostalgia
Many a one leaves the roast who afterwards longs for the smoke of it. (Italian)

Nothing
He who has nothing fears nothing. (French)
He who makes himself nothing, is nothing. (German)
Man brings nothing at birth and at death he takes nothing away. (Chinese)
Nothing can be created of nothing. (Roman)
Nothing comes of nothing. (Greek)
Nothing for nothing. (English)
Nothing from nothing leaves nothing. (American)
Nothing happens for nothing. (French)
Nothing is had for nothing. (French)
Out of nothing, nothing comes. (Roman)

Novelty
Every innovation startles us more by its novelty than it benefits us by its utility. (Roman)
He something out of nothing makes, and paints feet upon his snakes. (Chinese)
Human nature is greedy of novelty. (Roman)
In all things novelty is what we prize most. (Roman)
It is in human nature to hunt for novelty. (Italian)
Novelty always appears handsome. (Roman)
Novelty in all things is charming. (Roman)
The novelty of noon is out of date by night. (Unknown)

Nuisance
A whistling woman and a crowing hen are neither fit for God nor men. (Roman)

Nut
He that would eat the kernel must crack the nut. (French)
It doesn't take a hammer to crack a nut. (American)

O

Oak, Oaks
An oak is not felled at one stroke. (Spanish)
From little acorns mighty oaks do grow. (American)
Great oaks from little acorns grow. (German)
It is not easy to straighten in the oak the crook that grew in the sapling. (Danish)
Little strokes fell great oaks. (Dutch)
The oak lives on, but the hand that had planted it is gone. (Irish)
The repeated stroke will fell the oak. (German)

Oaths

Eggs and oaths are easily broken. (Japanese)

Vain oaths are the Devil's own language. (German)

Obedience, Obey

He that cannot obey, cannot command. (Poor Richard)

He who will not obey father, will have to obey step-father. (Danish)

It is the raised stick that makes the dog obey. (Danish)

Learn to obey before you command. (Greek)

Let thy child's first lesson be obedience, and the second may be what thou wilt.
   (Poor Richard)

Obedience is better than respect. (Chinese)

Obedience is the mother of happiness. (Roman)

To obey is better than sacrifice. (the Bible)

Obligation, Obligations

Be not unmindful of obligations conferred. (Roman)

Excess of obligation may lose a friend. (Roman)

Obscurity

Out of a ditch a dragon may rise [i.e., out of obscurity, a great man may arise].
   (Korean)

Obstruct

One may obstruct many. (Chinese)

Occasion

Use the occasion, for it passes swiftly by. (Roman)

Ocean

Little drops of water make a mighty ocean. (Roman)

Offend, Offense

He who offends against Heaven has none to whom he can pray. (Chinese)

If the truth so offends, be offended. (the Editor)

Nothing is ill-said if it is not ill-taken. (Italian)

Who offends writes on sand; who is offended, on marble. (Italian)

Nothing is more offensive than a low-bred man in a high station. (Roman)

Offer

Never refuse a good offer. (Roman)

Office

Office tests the man. (Roman)

Office without pay makes thieves. (German)

The office shows the man. (Roman)
The office teaches the man. (German)

Offspring

No one is presumed to have preferred another's offspring to his own. (Roman)

Often

See it often, it looks smaller; smell it often, it loses its scent. (Burmese)

Oil

He that measures oil shall anoint his fingers. (English)
One sesame seed will not make oil. (Burmese)

Old

A man is as old as his feet. (American)
All wish to live long, but none wish to be called old. (Danish)
All would live long, but none would be old. (Poor Richard)
An old horse knows the way, an old ox makes a straight furrow. (German)
Be old early that you may be old long. (Roman)
Be old when young, if you would be young when old. (Roman)
Better old debts than old sores. (Irish)
Flowers bloom and wither year by year, but the old do not grow young again. (Chinese)
In old houses many mice, in old furs many lice. (German)
It is not the years that make a person old, but the cares. (Spanish)
Let old things recede. (Roman)
Men are as old as they feel, women as old as they look. (Italian)
Old swine have hard snouts, old oxen hard horns. (Danish)
The old have always a tale to tell. (Unknown)
The old see best in the distance. (German)
You're only as old as you feel. (American)

Old Age

A restful old age is the reward for a youth well spent. (Spanish)
A sensuous and intemperate youth transfers to old age a worn-out body. (Roman)
Childhood is a crown of roses, old age a crown of thorns. (Yiddish)
Fear old age, for it does not come alone. (Greek)
He that would avoid old age must hang himself in youth. (Yiddish)
How incessant and great are the ills with which a prolonged old age is replete. (Roman)
I owe it to old age, that my desire for conversation is so increased. (Roman)
Laugh not at a man because he is old, for age will also come to you. (Chinese)
Many are the discomforts that gather around old age. (Roman)
Milk and eggs make old men young. (Spanish)
Old age comes with friends. (Albanian)
Old age does not announce itself. (Zulu)
Old age is a heavy burden. (German)
Old age is a hundred disorders. (Welsh)

Old age is a second childhood. (Spanish)
Old age is an incurable disease. (Roman)
Old age is itself a sickness. (Roman)
Old age is not a blessing. (Russian)
Old age is not a joy, but death is not a gain. (Russian)
Old age is ripeness. (American)
Old age serves as medicine. (Japanese)
Old age will not come alone. (Welsh)
Our temples do not conceal our age. (Roman)
Poor is he who does not think of old age. (Albanian)
The crown of old age is authority. (Roman)
We do not perceive old age, seeing it creeps on us apace. (Roman)
When spring comes, withered trees can burst forth into blossoms, but old men cannot
    be young again. (Chinese)
You become milder and better as old age advances. (Roman)
You must become an old man soon if you would be an old man long. (Roman)

Old and New
Out with the old, in with the new. (French)
They love the old that do not know the new. (German)
Through old things we learn new things. (Korean)
What is new soon becomes what is old. (the Editor)

Old and Young
As the gourd collects sediment from water, so an elder suffers insults from the younger.
    (Yoruban)
Honor the old, teach the young. (Danish)
Old boys have their playthings as well as young ones; the difference is only in the price.
    (Poor Richard)
The old direct, the young effect. (German)
The old for want of ability, and the young for want of knowledge, let things be lost.
    (Spanish)
The old forget, the young don't know. (German)
The old ones sing, the young ones pipe. (Dutch)

Old Man, Old Men
A child comes, a young man stays, an old man goes. (Spanish)
An old man is there to talk. (Nigerian)
An old man is twice a boy. (Roman)
An old man loved is a winter with flowers. (German)
An old man never lacks a tale to tell. (German)
An old man's sayings are seldom untrue. (Danish)
Old men are twice children. (Italian)
The sea will run out of fish sooner than an old man his stories. (Spanish)
When old, a man becomes a child. (Korean)

Omelet
You cannot make an omelet without breaking a few eggs. (French)

Omen, Omens
A mute bird makes no omen. (Spanish)
He that follows omens, omens will follow him. (Roman)
There is something in omens. (Roman)

One, Once
One day at a time. (American)
Once is never. (German)
One thing at a time. (German)
We are born once, die once, love once. (Spanish)

One-eyed
A man who has but one eye must take good care of it. (French)
A man with one eye is always rubbing it. (Unknown)
Blessed is the one-eyed person in the country of the blind. (Roman)
Sometimes, the one-eyed see better than the two-eyed. (Spanish)
The one-eyed man is a king in the country of the blind. (Spanish)
The one-eyed only thanks Allah for his one eye when he sees a blind man.
    (Hausan)

Onion
An onion will not produce a rose. (Roman)

Onlooker
An onlooker sees more of the game than a player. (Spanish)
He who looks on has two-thirds of the game. (Italian)
Onlookers see most of the game. (Italian)
To the onlooker no work is too hard. (German)

Open
Open hand makes open hand. (German)
Open your purse, and I will open my mouth. (Portuguese)

Opera
The opera isn't over till the fat lady sings. (American)

Opinion, Opinions
A man's own opinion is never wrong. (Italian)
Differences of opinion make horse races and lawsuits. (German)
Do not give an opinion until it is asked for. (Roman)
Do not seek out the opinion of another beside yourself. (Roman)
Even a flea has an opinion. (Korean)

No sensible person ever charged someone with inconstancy who had merely changed his opinion. (Roman)

Opinions founded on prejudice are always sustained with the greatest violence. (Yiddish)

The opinions of men are fallible. (Roman)

The person who has no opinion will seldom be wrong. (French)

Three Spaniards, four opinions. (Spanish)

Various are the opinions of men. (Roman)

Whilst standing he holds one opinion, whilst sitting another. (Roman)

Woe to him who deems his opinion a certainty. (Irish)

Opportunity, Opportunities

A good opportunity is seldom presented, and is easily lost. (Roman)

An opportunity is often lost through deliberation. (Roman)

Get bait while the tide is out. (Irish)

Grind wheat with every wind. (Roman)

Intelligence consists in recognizing opportunity. (Chinese)

Let nothing pass that will give you advantage; hairy in front, opportunity is bald behind. (Roman)

Let us snatch our opportunity from the passing day. (Roman)

Make bread while the oven is hot. (Persian)

Opportunities neglected are lost. (German)

Opportunities, like eggs, come one at a time. (American)

Opportunity makes desire. (Dutch)

Opportunity makes the thief. (Roman)

Opportunity never knocks twice at any man's door. (Roman)

Opportunity knocks but once. (Roman)

Seize the opportunity. (Roman)

Seize opportunity by the beard, for it is bald behind. (Bulgarian)

Seize the opportunity that is offered. (Roman)

The first occasion offered quickly take, lest thou repine at what thou didst forsake. (Dutch)

Time and opportunity are in no man's sleeve. (German)

You may always find an opportunity in your sleeve, if you like. (Danish)

Opposite, Opposites

Opposite cures opposite. (Roman)

Opposites attract. (English)

Oppressed, Oppression

A house established by oppression cannot long enjoy its prosperity. (Chinese)

Oppression causes rebellion. (Roman)

Optimism

All's for the best in the best of all possible worlds. (German)

Orders
In uncertain cases it is best to follow orders. (Roman)

Origin
Everything reverts to its origin. (Persian)

Orphan
A motherless son is a fish in low water. (Burmese)

Other
Other times, other counsels. (Portuguese)
Other times, other folk. (Danish)
Other times, other manners. (French)
Other towns, other lasses. (German)

Oven
An old oven is easier to heat than a new one. (French)
If the mother had never been in the oven, she would not have looked for her daughter
    there. (Roman)

Overflow
Everything that is superfluous overflows from the full bosom. (Roman)

Owe, Owes
He who owes is always in the wrong. (Roman)
He who owes nothing fears not the sheriff's officer. (Roman)

Owl
When the owl comes, so too calamity. (Chinese)

Own
To everyone his own is not too much. (German)
You may call that your own which no one can take from you. (Danish)
What's not your own, that let alone. (German)

Owner
The owner's watchful eye fattens the horse.

Ox, Oxen
An obstinate ox wastes its strength. (German)
An ox with long horns, even if he does not butt, will be accused of butting. (Malaysian)
At the right time, the thin ox will kick. (Burmese)
Do not muzzle the ox that plows. (the Bible)
God gives short horns to the cruel ox. (Roman)
He who plows with young oxen, makes crooked furrows. (German)

However strong, can an ox be a king? (Korean)
If you cannot drive an ox, drive a donkey. (Roman)
In straightening the horn he kills the ox. (Japanese)
Old oxen have stiff horns. (Danish)
Old oxen tread hard. (German)
The old ox plows a straight furrow. (English)
The ox comes to the yoke at the call of his feeder. (Spanish)
The ox halts before the slaughter-house door. (Korean)
The ox plows the field and the horse eats the grains. (Chinese)
The ox when most weary is most sure-footed. (Roman)
The village ox does not feed on village grass. (Burmese)
What more can you expect from an ox than beef? (Yiddish)
When the ox stumbles, all whet their knives. (Yiddish)
Where shall the ox go, and not have to plow? (Portuguese)

P

Pace

If a wren tries to keep step with a stork, its legs will be torn apart. (Korean)
It is the pace that kills. (French)
Pace yourself and you will live longer. (Mexican)

Pain

Even pain has its joy. (Russian)
Great pain and little gain make one soon weary. (German)
He who lives long knows what pain is. (French)
Hope of gain lessens pain. (Poor Richard)
No pain, no gain. (English)
No pains, no gains. (German)
Pain is an excellent instructor. (Unknown)
Pain is forgotten where gain follows. (English)
Pain makes even the innocent man a liar. (Roman)
Pain mingles with pleasure. (Roman)
Pain of mind is worse than pain of body. (Roman)
Pain past is a pleasure. (Roman)
The hand travels often to the part where the pain is. (Roman)
The pain of the little finger is felt by the whole body. (Filipino)
True pain cannot be concealed. (Serbian)
Two blows on the head cause pain. (Egyptian)
When the wound is healed the pain is forgotten. (Danish)
When you are dressing a wound, pain is pain's medicine. (Roman)
Where a man feels pain, there he lays his hand. (Dutch)
Where gain comes, pain is forgotten. (American)

Paint

He who cannot paint must mix the colors. (German)

Palace

For the sake of your palace shall we demolish our huts? (Egyptian)

Panic

Panic is contagious. (German)

Paper

Even a sheet of paper has two sides. (Japanese)

Paper can't wrap up a fire. (Chinese)

Paper is patient. (German)

Paradise

One would not be alone in paradise. (Italian)

Self-exaltation is the fool's paradise. (Italian)

Taking the first step with the good thought, the second with the good word, and the
    third with the good deed, I enter Paradise. (Persian)

This world is the unbeliever's paradise. (Turkish)

Parasite

A parasite cannot live alone. (African)

The parasite has no roots – all trees are its relations. (Yoruban)

Pardon

Never ask pardon before you are accused. (Spanish)

Offenders never pardon. (German)

Pardoning the bad is injuring the good. (Poor Richard)

The one who needs pardon should readily grant it. (Roman)

Parent, Parents

A bad parent will lead the child astray. (Korean)

A parent who excuses his child's ways makes him a thief. (Yoruban)

Children hold cheap the life of parents who would rather be feared than respected.
    (Roman)

From the father comes honor, from the mother comfort. (Dutch)

Good parents, happy marriages; good children, fine funerals. (Chinese)

Honor thy father and mother, both during their life and after their death. (Unknown)

In prosperity a father, in adversity a mother. (Indian)

Let the parents punish the child. (African)

One parent maintains ten children better than ten children one parent. (German)

Our parents nourished us when we were young, we must care for them when they are
    old. (Chinese)

Parents are known by their children. (Spanish)

Parents are the first teachers of children. (Burmese)

Parents can give us everything but common sense. (Yiddish)

Parents can provide a dowry, but not good luck. (Yiddish)

Parents who are afraid to put their foot down usually have children who step on their toes. (Chinese)

Revere your parents. (Roman)

Serve your parents as you would serve Heaven. (Chinese)

Paris

Paris was not built in a day. (French)

Parrot

It's not the fault of the parrot, but of the one who teaches it to talk. (Guatemalan)

Parsley

Parsley seed goes nine times to the Devil. (French)

Parting

Parting is such sweet sorrow. (English)

Partner

A partner in evil will also be a partner in punishment. (Roman)

Partridge

The partridge loves peas, but not those that go into the pot with it. (West African)

Pass

This, too, shall pass. (African)

Passion, Passions

A man in a passion rides a horse that runs away with him. (Roman)

A man in a passion rides a mad horse. (Poor Richard)

Govern your passions, or they will govern you. (Roman)

He is a governor that governs his passions, and he a servant that serves them. (Poor Richard)

He's a wise man that leads passion by the bridle. (Italian)

Hot passion easily cools. (Japanese)

It is not the greatest beauties that inspire the most profound passion. (French)

Let him be guided by his passions, who can make no sense of his reason. (Roman)

Passion is the master. (Yiddish)

Passion will master you if you do not master your passion. (English)

Time and reflection temper a moment's passion. (Spanish)

To passion, even haste is slow. (Roman)

When passion enters at the foregate, wisdom goes out of the postern. (English)

Past

Consider the past and you will know the future. (Chinese)
Each one suffers from the spirits of his own past. (Roman)
Everything in the past dies yesterday; everything in the future was born today. (Chinese)
He that praises the past blames the present. (Finnish)
In the great uncertainty of events, nothing is certain except the past. (Roman)
The past teaches many lessons. (Unknown)
There is no appeal from time past. (Italian)
Things past cannot be recalled. (Roman)

Patch

Better a patch than a hole. (German)
Disgrace is a patch, dishonor a hole. (Unknown)
There is no better patch than one off the same cloth. (Spanish)

Path

A well-beaten path does not always make the right road. (Roman)
Every path has its puddle. (English)
Follow the path less traveled. (American)
Follow the path that lies before thee. (Unknown)
No grass grows on a beaten path. (French)
Take the path of least resistance. (German)
The beaten path is the safest path. (Roman)
The middle path is the safe path. (Roman)
The trodden path is the safest. (German)
Why take the crooked path when there is a straight road? (Mexican)

Patience, Patient

A handful of patience is worth a bushel of brains. (Dutch)
A patient mind is the best remedy for trouble. (Roman)
All things come to those who wait. (English)
At the bottom of patience is Heaven. (Chinese)
Awaiting brings a sweet day. (Japanese)
Be patient with a friend or you might lose him. (Egyptian)
Be patient with the faults of others. (German)
Bear and forbear. (English)
Easy to declare, hard to bear. (Yiddish)
Every misfortune is to be subdued by patience. (Roman)
Everyone ought to bear patiently with what is done after his own example. (Roman)
He is prudent who has patience. (Roman)
He that can be patient finds his foe at his feet. (Dutch)
If you are patient in one moment of anger, you will escape a hundred days of sorrow.
  (Chinese)
If you do not have patience you cannot make beer. (African)
If you lack patience in small things, you will confound great plans. (Chinese)

In difficulty, win by patience. (Roman)
Let patience grow in your garden. (English)
Nothing is so full of victory as patience. (Madagascan)
One minute of patience, ten years of peace. (Greek)
Patience abused becomes fury. (Roman)
Patience conquers destiny. (Irish)
Patience in anger and forgiveness of men will cause calamities to cease. (Chinese)
Patience is a bitter plant, but it has sweet fruit. (Chinese)
Patience is a plaster for every wound. (Irish)
Patience is a virtue. (English)
Patience is beautiful. (Arabian)
Patience is bitter but its fruit is sweet. (Persian)
Patience is like kindling, it's quickly used up. (Hausan)
Patience is power: with time and patience the mulberry becomes silk. (Japanese)
Patience is the key to paradise. (Turkish)
Patience is the virtue of asses. (French)
Patience kills the game. (German)
Patience makes more tolerable that which it is impossible to correct. (Roman)
Patience masters all chances. (Roman)
Patience surpasses learning. (Dutch)
Patience, when too often offended, is turned into rage. (Roman)
Take time: much may be gained by patience. (Roman)
The herb patience does not grow in every man's garden. (Danish)
The patient man gets more than enough. (Hausan)
The secret of patience is doing something else in the meantime. (Spanish)
With patience and time the mulberry leaf becomes a silk gown. (Chinese)

Patient

An ill-mannered patient makes the physician cruel. (Roman)
Every patient is a doctor after his cure. (Irish)

Patriotism

Everyone praises his own land. (Irish)

Pauper

No one is so hard upon the poor as the pauper who has come into power. (Danish)
Nobody will give a pauper bread, but everybody will give him advice. (Armenian)
The pauper hungers without noticing it. (Yiddish)

Pay, Payment

He who pays is fairly entitled to speak his mind. (French)
He who pays last never pays twice. (English)
He who pays well is master of another man's purse. (Dutch)
He who pays well is well served. (French)
If we pay for the music we will take part in the dance. (German)
If you pay peanuts, you get monkeys. (Chinese)

If you pay what you owe, what you're worth you'll know. (Spanish)

It is better to pay the cook than the doctor or the undertaker. (German)

It pays to advertise. (American)

Misreckoning is no payment. (German)

Pay in like coin. (German)

Pay what you owe, and be cured of your complaint. (Spanish)

Pay what you owe, you will get well of your malady. (Portuguese)

Pay your money, take your choice. (American)

Pay-day comes every day. (German)

Paying beforehand was never well served. (Italian)

The one who pays the piper calls the tune. (German)

You get what you pay for. (American)

Paymaster

A good paymaster does not hesitate to give good security. (Italian)

A good paymaster is keeper of other men's purses. (Spanish)

A good paymaster needs no security. (Spanish)

Peace, Peaceful

A cake eaten in peace is worth two in trouble. (French)

A good sword is the one left in its scabbard. (Japanese)

A more severe war lurks under the guise of peace. (Roman)

All look for peace, but not where it is found. (Spanish)

Arms are the supports of peace. (Roman)

Better a bad peace than a good war. (Yiddish)

Better a lean peace than a fat war. (English)

Better a little in peace and with right, than much with anxiety and strife. (Danish)

Better an egg in peace, than an ox in war. (Portuguese)

Better an unjust peace than a just war. (German)

Better and safer is the certainty of peace than the hope of victory. (Roman)

Better to keep peace than make peace. (Dutch)

Do not look to the peaceful man for a weapon. (Irish)

Eternal peace lasts only until the next war. (Russian)

He who would prosper in peace must suffer in silence. (German)

Hear, see, and say nothing if you would live in peace. (French)

If a man would live in peace he should be blind, deaf, and dumb. (Persian)

If you desire peace be ever prepared for war. (Roman)

It is madness for a sheep to talk of peace with a wolf. (French)

Love is the token of peace. (Roman)

No one can have peace longer than his neighbor pleases. (Dutch)

No one has paid so much for peace as the one who is without it. (Irish)

Nor is Heaven always at peace. (Roman)

Peace and a well-built house cannot be bought too dearly. (Danish)

Peace and tranquility are a thousand gold pieces. (Chinese)

Peace gains value from discord. (Roman)

Peace is costly but it is worth the expense. (African)

Peace is preferable to war. (Roman)

Peace is produced by war. (Roman)

Peace is the well from which the stream of joy runs. (Irish)

Peace lasts as long as one holds it. (Unknown)

Peace lasts until the army comes, and the army lasts until peace comes. (Russian)

Peace makes plenty. (German)

Peace must be bought even at a high price. (Danish)

The lion and the lamb shall lie down together, but the lamb won't get much sleep.
 (Italian)

The peace of nations cannot be maintained without arms. (Roman)

When they make a desolation they call it peace. (Roman)

Where there is peace there is plenty. (Danish)

White-robed peace becomes men, savage anger wild beasts. (Roman)

You cannot have peace longer than your neighbor chooses. (Danish)

Peacemaker

No matter who comes off well, the peacemaker is sure to come off ill. (Irish)

The peacemaker does not go free. (Irish)

Peacock

A peacock has too little in its head, too much in its tail. (Swedish)

Pearl, Pearls

He who searches for pearls should not sleep. (Libyan)

Neither cast your pearls before swine. (Jesus)

Peasant

A peasant will stand on the top of a hill for a very long time with his mouth open before
 a roast duck will fly in. (Spanish)

An ennobled peasant does not know his own father. (Dutch)

Every peasant is proud of the pond in his village because from it he measures the sea.
 (Russian)

Set a peasant on horseback, and he forgets both God and man. (Spanish)

The peasant knows not the worth of spurs. (French)

The peasant will not cross himself before it begins to thunder. (Russian)

Pebble

You are not the only pebble on the beach. (German)

Peddler

A peddler who cannot pass off mouse droppings for pepper has not learned his trade.
 (German)

A little pack serves a little peddler. (French)

A small pack becomes a small peddler. (Portuguese)

Every peddler praises his own needles. (Portuguese)
He praises his wares who wishes to palm them off upon another. (Roman)
Let every peddler carry his own pack. (German)

Pedigree
Ask not after a good man's pedigree. (Spanish)
Of what use are pedigrees? (Roman)

Peg
Carve the peg by looking at the hole. (Korean)
You can't force a square peg into a round hole. (American)

Pen
From swords flow blood, from pens malice. (Egyptian)
The pen is less inhibited in speaking than the tongue. (Spanish)
The pen is mightier than the sword. (English)
The pen stings worse than the arrow. (Yiddish)

Penance
We do penance in old age for the follies of our youth. (Roman)

Penniless
A penniless man will pick the largest cake. (Korean)
The penniless man has nothing to lose. (Roman)

Penny, Pennies
A bad penny always turns up. (German)
A bad penny never gets lost. (Yiddish)
A penny for an ox, and you haven't got a penny! (Yiddish)
A penny in the purse is better than a friend at court. (English)
A penny in time is as good as a dollar. (Danish)
A penny is a lot of money – if you haven't got a penny. (Yiddish)
A penny is sometimes better spent than spared. (Yiddish)
A penny saved is a penny earned. (English)
A penny spared is twice got. (English)
Every penny counts. (Yiddish)
Penny and penny laid up will be many. (Italian)
Penny is penny's brother. (German)
Penny wise, pound foolish. (English)
Save your pennies for a rainy day. (English)
That which is stamped a penny will never be a pound. (Danish)
The unrighteous penny consumes the righteous dollar. (German)

People
Famine, pestilence, and war are the destruction of a people. (Roman)
Sometimes the common people see what is right, at other times they err. (Roman)

Pepper

Beware asking the person with pepper in his mouth to blow dust out of your eye.
  (Yoruban)
Pepper has a beautiful face with an ugly temper. (African)
Though small, pepper is very strong. (Korean)

Perfect, Perfected

Man without trials remains unperfected. (Chinese)
Nobody's perfect. (English)
The gem cannot be polished without friction, nor a man perfected without trials.
  (Chinese)

Perfection

No man acquires perfection all at once. (Roman)
Nothing is invented and brought to perfection all at once. (English)
Of every perfection there is a decline. (Turkish)
One without trials cannot reach perfection. (Chinese)

Perfume

The one who uses perfume has good reasons for using it. (Roman)

Peril

Sleep not in time of peril. (Roman)

Perish

Nor is there any law more just, than that those seeking to harm should perish by their
  own devices. (Roman)
The best things are the first to perish. (Roman)
We perish by permitted things. (Roman)

Persevere, Perseverance

By perseverance the Greeks reached Troy. (Roman)
Perseverance brings success. (Dutch)
Perseverance is the key to success. (Unknown)
Perseverance kills the game. (Spanish)
Persevere and never fear. (Swedish)
Without perseverance, talent is a barren bed. (Welsh)

Persistent, Persistence

A bar of iron, continually ground, becomes a needle. (Chinese)
A constant drip hollows a stone. (Roman)
A great estate is not gotten in a few hours. (French)
A persistent beggar never sleeps on an empty stomach. (Spanish)
By diligence and patience, the mouse bit in two the cable. (Poor Richard)
Constant dripping wears away stone. (Italian)

Constant dripping will pierce through stone. (Chinese)
Fall seven times, stand up eight. (Japanese)
Persistence pays. (English)
Persistence pays off. (German)

Persuade
Would you persuade, speak of interest, not of reason. (Poor Richard)
Better to be convinced by words than by blows. (Danish)

Pheasant
Had the pheasant not called, it would not have been caught. (Japanese)
Pheasants are fools if they invite the hawk to dinner. (Danish)

Philanthropy
If charity cost no money and benevolence caused no heartache, the world would be
    filled with philanthropists. (Yiddish)

Philosopher, Philosophy
It dishonors a philosopher to be disheartened. (Roman)
Keep quiet and people will think you a philosopher. (Roman)
Many talk like philosophers and live like fools. (English)
Philosophy as well as foppery often changes fashion. (Poor Richard)
Philosophy bakes no bread. (Danish)
Philosophy can be feigned, eloquence cannot. (Roman)
Philosophy is the true medicine of the mind. (Roman)
Pursuit of the Philosopher's Stone will turn a man's gold into lead. (Poor Richard)
The beard does not make the philosopher. (Italian)
There is nothing so absurd but it may be said by a philosopher. (Roman)

Phoenix
Among a thousand chickens there is but one phoenix. (Korean)

Physician
A physician is careless of his own health. (Japanese)
A physician may cure disease, but he cannot heal fate. (Chinese)
A physician to others, while you yourself are full of ulcers. (Roman)
Feed sparingly and defy the physician. (American)
God cures and the physician takes the fee. (English)
Honor physicians for the sake of necessity. (Roman)
If you have a friend who is a physician, send him to your enemy's house.
    (Portuguese)
Nature, time, and patience are three great physicians. (English)
No man is a good physician who has never been sick. (Arabian)
Physician, heal thyself. (Jesus)
Physicians kill more than they cure. (English)

The blunders of physicians are covered by the earth. (Portuguese)
The earth covers the errors of the physician. (Italian)
Where the philosopher ends, there the physician begins. (Greek)

Pick

Pick and choose, and take the worst. (French)
Pick your inn before the dark, your road before the dawn. (Chinese)

Picture

A picture is a silent poem. (Roman)
A picture is worth a thousand words. (English)
Every picture tells a story. (English)

Piety

A man can hide much under a saintly cloak. (Spanish)
There is no piety but among the poor. (German)

Pig

A clean pig makes lean bacon. (Serbian)
A pig may whistle, though it has a bad mouth for it. (English)
A pig used to dirt turns its nose up at rice. (Japanese)
A pig's tail will never make a good arrow. (Spanish)
Child's pig, father's pork. (Portuguese)
He that has but one pig easily fattens it. (Italian)
If you catch a pig, catch it by the leg. (Irish)
If you pull one pig by the tail all the rest will squeal. (Dutch)
Old pigs have hard snouts. (German)
Providence often puts a large potato in a little pig's way. (Unknown)
The best pears fall into pigs' mouths. (Italian)
The life of a pig is short and sweet. (French)
The worst pig often gets the best pear. (Italian)
To sheer a pig is to cause a great commotion over very little wool. (Irish)
To wash a pig is to waste both water and soap. (American)
What can you expect from a pig but a grunt? (Swedish)
When the pig has had a bellyful it upsets the trough. (Dutch)
Whether you ignore a pig or worship that pig from afar, to the pig it's all the same.
   (Spanish)

Pilgrim, Pilgrimage

Pilgrims seldom come home saints. (German)

Pilot

A good pilot is not known when the sea is calm and the weather fair. (Danish)
The best pilots are ashore. (Dutch)

Pine

A pine is an evergreen only in winter. (Korean)

Pint

A pint is a pound the world over. (American)

Pipe

Every reed will not make a pipe. (Italian)
Not every wood will make a pipe. (German)
One may live without one's friends, but not without one's pipe. (Irish)
The old pipe gives the sweetest smoke. (Irish)

Piper

Those who dance must pay the piper. (German)
Who pays the piper calls the tune. (French)

Pirate

Corsairs against corsairs, there is nothing to win but empty casks. (Italian)
When the pirate prays, there is great danger. (Dutch)
Where there is a sea there are pirates. (Greek)

Pit

He falls into the pit which he himself made. (Roman)
He who digs a pit for others falls into it himself. (German)

Pitch

He who handles pitch, besmears himself. (German)

Pitcher

A pitcher long taken to the well at last becomes broken. (Irish)
A useless pitcher does not get broken. (Roman)
Little pitchers have large ears. (Dutch)
Little pitchers have long ears. (French)
Often a pitcher goes to the well, but at last it comes home broken. (English)
Whether the pitcher strikes the stone, or the stone the pitcher, woe be to the pitcher.
   (Spanish)

Pity

Better to be envied than pitied. (Italian)
Foolish pity ruins a city. (German)
He that pities another remembers himself. (English)
If anyone pities the dead, he must also pity those who have not been born. (Roman)
Nothing is more deserving of pity as a poor man who has seen better days. (Roman)
Pitiable is the life of those who prefer being feared to being loved. (Roman)
Pity has pure intentions. (Yiddish)

Pity is a poor plaster. (English)
Pity is akin to love. (English)
Pity the son whose father went to Heaven. (Portuguese)
Pity those that get the worst of it. (Roman)
Those who suffer from the same illness pity each other. (Japanese)

Place

A place for everything, and everything in its place. (Italian)
Give place to your betters. (Roman)
He is in no place who is everywhere. (Italian)
He who quits his place loses it. (French)
One cannot be in two places at once. (French)

Plague

A pestilence follows a famine. (Roman)
A Sunday's child never dies of the plague. (French)
Running water carries no plague. (Italian)

Plan, Plans

A good plan today is better than a perfect plan tomorrow. (Danish)
Any plan is bad that cannot be changed. (Italian)
Bad mind, bad designs. (Roman)
Even a cat can cross your plans. (Yiddish)
Failing to plan is planning to fail. (Chinese)
Good plans are ruined through bad execution. (German)
He who does not look ahead, must take misfortune for his earnings. (Danish)
It's an ill plan that cannot be changed. (Roman)
Man has a thousand plans, Heaven but one. (Chinese)
Man proposes, but God disposes. (German)
Men's plans should be regulated by the circumstances, not circumstances by the plans.
    (Roman)
Plan your year in the spring, your day at dawn. (Chinese)
When a man plans a thousand-year future, he will provoke the Devil's derision.
    (Chinese)

Plant, Plants

A man must put grain in the ground before he can cut the harvest. (Unknown)
He plants trees to benefit another generation. (Roman)
He who plants fruit trees, must not count upon the fruit. (Dutch)
He who plants thorns must never expect to gather roses. (Arabian)
If you are planning for a year, sow rice; if you are planning for a decade, plant trees; if you
    are planning for a lifetime, educate people. (Chinese)
It doesn't bud if you don't seed. (Japanese)
No one plants pebbles in hope of potatoes. (Irish)
One man plants the tree, another man eats the fruit. (German)

One seed for the mouse, one seed for the crow, one seed to rot, one seed to grow.
  (English)
One year's seeding makes seven years' weeding. (Portuguese)
Plant melons and you will gather melons; plant plums and you will gather plums.
  (Chinese)
Plant the crab-tree where you will but it will never bear pippins. (Chinese)
Plant the good and the good will come forth. (Chinese)
Plants oft moved never thrive. (German)
The best time to plant a tree was twenty years ago; the second best time is today.
  (Chinese)
The diligent farmer plants trees, of which he himself will never see the fruit. (Roman)
The industrious husbandman plants trees, not one berry of which he will ever see.
  (Roman)
The man who plants 100 yams and calls them 200 will eat 100 yams and 100 lies.
  (Yoruban)
The one who plants the tree is not the one who will enjoy its shade. (Chinese)
The person who plants corn should like to eat corn. (Mexican)
The seeds of the day are best planted in the first hour. (Dutch)
When eating a fruit, think of him who planted the tree. (Vietnamese)
When eating bamboo sprouts, remember the man who planted them. (Chinese)

Play

A child's play does not last long. (African)
An hour of play discovers more than a year of conversation. (Portuguese)
Fair play is good play. (English)
It is best to play with equals. (Danish)
It is pleasant at times to play the madman. (Roman)
Leave off while play is good. (English)
Like plays best with like. (Danish)
Manual play, clown's play. (Spanish)
Play may conceive a baby. (Korean)
Play with an ass and he will slap his tail in your face. (Spanish)
Play with fire and you're apt to get burnt. (German)
Play with the fool at home, and he will play with you abroad. (Spanish)
Play's good, while it is play. (Spanish)
There is no shame in having sported, but in not having broken off play. (Roman)
Those who have free seats at the play hiss first. (Chinese)
Turnabout is fair play. (English)

Pleasantries

There is room for more pleasantries. (Roman)

Please

Do not care how many, but whom, you please. (Roman)
Eat to please thyself, but dress to please others. (Poor Richard)

Eat whatever you fancy, but dress as others do. (Egyptian)
Even Jupiter cannot please everyone. (Roman)
He has much to do who would please everybody. (Spanish)
He is not yet born who can please everybody. (Danish)
He labors in vain who tries to please everybody. (Roman)
He must rise early who would please everybody. (Dutch)
He that would please all, and himself too, undertakes what he cannot do. (Dutch)
It is hard to please everyone. (Dutch)
No dish pleases all palates alike. (French)
Nothing is ever long that never ceases to please. (Roman)
One cannot please everybody and one's father. (French)
Please the eye, and pick the purse. (Spanish)
Please your eye and plague your heart. (English)
That which pleases is twice repeated. (Roman)
That you may please others you must be forgetful of yourself. (Roman)
Trying to please costs you dear. (Yiddish)
What pleases, nourishes. (Roman)
You can't please everyone. (English)
You can't please everyone, but you can please yourself. (American)

Pleasure, Pleasures
Consider not the pleasures as they come, but as they go. (English)
Despise pleasure: pleasure bought by pain is injurious. (Roman)
Enjoy your present pleasures, so as not to injure those which are to come. (Roman)
Even pleasure itself is a toil. (Roman)
Everyone takes his pleasure where he finds it. (French)
From short pleasure long repentance. (French)
In the midst of our pleasures there is always some wrong that arises to vex us. (Roman)
Many a man thinks he is buying pleasure, when he is really selling himself a slave to it.
   (Poor Richard)
Men are transformed by pleasures. (Roman)
Moderate pleasure relaxes the spirit, and moderates it. (Roman)
One should be just as careful in choosing one's pleasures as in avoiding calamities.
   (Chinese)
Our pleasures are shallow, our sorrows are deep. (Chinese)
Pleasure arises out of labor. (Roman)
Pleasure begins to live when life itself is departing. (Roman)
Pleasure has a sting in its tail. (Unknown)
Pleasure is the bait of evil. (Roman)
Pleasure is the greatest incentive to vice. (Greek)
Pleasure is the seed of trouble. (Indian)
Pleasure requires company. (Mexican)
Pleasures rarely used are greatly enjoyed. (Roman)
Pleasures steal away the mind. (Dutch)
Pleasures, while they flatter, sting. (Dutch)

Seek pleasures while you may. (English)
Seekers of pleasure have no leisure. (the Editor)
Short pleasure often brings long repentance. (Danish)
The enlightened find pleasure in water; the benevolent, in mountains. (Chinese)
The greatest pleasures are only narrowly separated from disgust. (Roman)
The pleasures we enjoy are lost by coveting more. (Roman)
There is no small pleasure in sweet water. (Roman)
Whatever is God's pleasure should be man's pleasure. (Roman)
When pleasure interferes with business, give up business. (American)
Where pleasure prevails, all the greatest virtues fail. (Roman)
Why be miserable for the sake of pleasure? (Indian)

Pleasure and Pain

For one pleasure a thousand pains. (French)
In hawks, hounds, arms, and love, for one pleasure a thousand pains. (French)
In war, hunting, and love, for one pleasure a hundred pains. (Portuguese)
Nothing brings more pain than too much pleasure; nothing more bondage than too
    much liberty. (Poor Richard)
Pleasure and pain succeed each other. (Roman)
Pleasure bought with pain is injurious. (Roman)
Pleasure is sweeter after pain. (Unknown)
Pleasure is the source of pain; pain is the source of pleasure. (Japanese)
Pleasure often comes from pain. (Roman)
Short-lived pleasure is the parent of pain. (Roman)
We forget our pleasures, we remember our pains. (Roman)

Pledge

Beware of a pledge that eats. (Portuguese)

Plenty

He who has plenty of butter, may put some in his cabbage. (Danish)
He who has plenty of peas may put more in the pot. (Roman)
He who has plenty of pepper may season his food as he likes. (Roman)
Plentiness makes daintiness. (American)
Plenty brings pride. (German)
Plenty knows good ale, but not much after that. (English)

Plot

The downcast head plots a thousand mischiefs. (Egyptian)
The one who plots the downfall of another does not do so in his presence. (Yoruban)
Those who plot the destruction of others very often fall victim themselves. (Roman)

Plow

A man must plow with the oxen he has. (Chinese)
Don't yoke the plow before the horses. (Dutch)

Drive not too many plows at once, some will make foul work. (Danish)

He plows the land of others, and leaves his own untilled. (Roman)

Many can drive an ox; few can plow. (Roman)

Plow deep and you will have plenty of corn to keep. (Portuguese)

Plow deep whilst sluggards sleep, and you shall have corn to sell and corn to keep. (Spanish)

Plow or not plow, you must pay your rent. (Spanish)

Plow wet or dry, and you will not have to kiss your neighbor's breech. (Spanish)

Take care of your plow, and your plow will take care of you. (German)

The bad plowman quarrels with his ox. (Korean)

The used plow shines, standing water stinks. (Danish)

You'll never plow a field by turning it over in your mind. (Irish)

Pluck

Pluck the magpie, and don't make it scream. (Italian)

Pluck the rose and leave the thorns. (Italian)

Plumber

The plumber's house always leaks. (Turkish)

Plum

A black plum is as sweet as a white one. (English)

Pocket

'Tis too late to spare when the pocket is bare. (German)

Poem, Poet

A poet is born, not made. (Roman)

Even if nature denies power, indignation makes verse. (Roman)

Every old poem is sacred. (Roman)

Horses and poets should be fed, not pampered. (French)

Indignation gives inspiration to verse. (English)

Leave poets free to perish as they will. (Roman)

No man writes, whose verses no one reads. (Roman)

No poet thinks another better than himself. (Roman)

Poetry is the wine of demons. (Roman)

Poets wish either to profit or to please. (Roman)

The dog may be wonderful prose, but only the cat is poetry. (French)

We are born poets, we become orators. (Roman)

Poison

A poison embitters much sweetness. (English)

Another man's poison is not necessarily yours. (English)

Control poison with poison. (Japanese)

Deadly poisons are concealed under sweet honey. (Roman)

Do not drink poison to quench a thirst. (Arabian)

Good wine and a pretty wife are two sweet poisons to a man. (Rumanian)

He eats arsenic to poison the tiger. (Chinese)

'I am a judge of cresses', said the peasant, as he was eating hemlock. (Danish)

If you have to take poison, lick even the plate. (Japanese)

No poison is drunk out of earthenware [i.e., the poor and powerless need not fear being poisoned]. (Roman)

One poison is cured by another. (Roman)

Poison drives out poison. (Italian)

Poison is drunk from a gold cup. (Roman)

Take not the antidote before the poison. (Roman)

The one who stirs poison will taste it. (Egyptian)

There is no poison in a poor man's house. (German)

What does not poison, fattens. (Italian)

What's one man's meat is another man's poison. (German)

When the bee sucks, it makes honey, when the spider, poison. (Spanish)

Polish

Elbow grease is the best polish. (English)

Politeness

Great politeness usually means 'I want something'. (Chinese)

Learn politeness from the impolite. (Egyptian)

More than polite is rude. (Japanese)

Politeness costs nothing and gains everything. (German)

Politeness costs us nothing. (English)

Politeness is what warmth is to wax. (German)

Politeness pleases even a cat. (Czech)

Politeness travels on short fares. (German)

Politeness wins the confidence of princes. (Chinese)

Politics

Democracy is the best and the worst type of government. (American)

Democrats will do anything for the poor – except make them rich. (American)

Faith and piety are rare among the men who follow the camp [either political or military]. (Roman)

Far from court, far from care. (English)

For lack of good men, they made my father mayor. (Spanish)

Former magistrates will always be thought the best. (Korean)

He who would succeed at court, must lie sometimes low, sometimes high. (German)

In politics, a man must learn to rise above principle. (American)

In rivers and bad governments, the lightest things swim at top. (Poor Richard)

Let not your own, but the public wishes, motivate you. (Roman)

Politics has no religion. (French)

Politics makes strange bedfellows. (American)

serves the public, serves a fickle master. (Dutch)
serves the public, serves no one. (Italian)

Ponder
Ponder long before you act. (Roman)
Ponder over many things by night. (Roman)

Pool, Pools
Standing pools gather filth. (German)

Poor
A hut is a palace to the poor man. (Irish)
A man without money is like a ship without sails. (Dutch)
A moneyless man goes fast through the market. (Danish)
A north wind has no corn, and a poor man no friend. (Spanish)
A poor man has few acquaintances. (Danish)
A poor man is all schemes. (Spanish)
A poor man is always behind. (American)
A poor man is glad for whatever he gets. (Irish)
A poor man is hungry after eating. (Portuguese)
A poor man sings folk songs. (Chinese)
A poor man who shouts is like a barking dog. (Yoruban)
A poor person isn't he who has little, but he who needs a lot. (German)
A threadbare coat is armor-proof against highwaymen. (Turkish)
Better poor on land than rich at sea. (Dutch)
Better to die ten years early than live ten years poor. (Chinese)
Better to go to Heaven in rags than to Hell in silks. (Chinese)
Deep draughts, and long morning slumbers, soon make a man poor. (Danish)
Dice, wine, and women, these three have made me poor. (Roman)
Dogs show no aversion to the poor. (Chinese)
Don't make yourself poor to one who won't make you rich. (Portuguese)
Even a little pleases a poor man. (Irish)
Everywhere the poor man is despised. (Roman)
'Had I known' is a poor man. (German)
Having been poor is no shame, but being ashamed of it is. (Poor Richard)
He is not poor that hath not much, but he that craves much. (Italian)
'I have had' is a poor man. (German)
If a poor man ate it, they would say it was because of his stupidity. (Arabian)
If a poor man gives to you, he expects more in return. (Portuguese)
If poor, act with caution. (Roman)
If you would grow poor without perceiving it, employ workmen and go to sleep.
    (Portuguese)
It is a bad thing to be poor, and seem poor. (Italian)
It is no shame to be poor. (German)
It's the poor who say that money doesn't buy happiness. (American)

Much wisdom is smothered in a poor man's head. (Dutch)

Much wit is lost in a poor man's purse. (German)

No means, no market. (Kurdish)

No one fears the poor. (Unknown)

No one heeds the poor. (Unknown)

No one is poor but he who thinks himself so. (Portuguese)

No one is so poor in life as he was at birth. (Roman)

Pity the poor man who does evil. (Irish)

Poor people entertain with the heart. (Haitian)

Prison and Lent were made for the poor. (Spanish)

The poor are glad of pottage. (Irish)

The poor man eats at double cost. (Portuguese)

The poor man meets many devils. (Chinese)

The poor sleep soundly. (Japanese)

The strong break the pots but the poor pay for them. (Egyptian)

When the sea turned into honey, the poor man lost his spoon. (Bulgarian)

Poorhouse

The poorhouses are filled with honest people. (Spanish)

Pope

After one pope another is made. (Italian)

He who wishes to live at Rome must not quarrel with the pope. (French)

The pope eats peasants, gulps gentlemen, and voids monks. (German)

Popularity

Do not aim at too much popularity. (Roman)

Popularity is the small change of glory. (French)

Porcupine

A porcupine speaking to its baby says, 'O my child of velvet'. (Afghani)

One should never rub butts with a porcupine. (West African)

Pork

Pork has many different flavors, all of them good. (Spanish)

Port

Any port in a storm. (Italian)

Possess, Possessions

A bird in the hand is worth two in the bush. (English)

A sparrow in hand is worth a pheasant that flies by. (French)

A sparrow in the hand is better than a pigeon on the roof. (German)

A thousand cranes in the air are not worth the one sparrow in the fist. (Egyptian)

A trout in the pot is better than a salmon in the sea. (Irish)

Better a bird in the hand than ten in the air. (Dutch)
Better mine than yours. (Portuguese)
Get what you can, and what you get, hold. (Poor Richard)
Possession is as good as a title. (French)
Possession is nine points of the law. (English)
Possession is the grave of pleasure. (French)
Possessions satisfy, even when unused. (Irish)
What we possess is always beautiful. (Roman)

Posterity
Posterity gives to everyone what is his due. (Roman)

Postpone
A thing postponed is a thing lost. (Spanish)
By the street of 'By-and-By' one arrives at the house of 'Never'. (Spanish)
By-and-by has no end. (Italian)
Never do today what you can put off until tomorrow. (American)
Never put off till tomorrow what you can do today. (English)

Pot, Potter
A watched pot never boils. (Welsh)
Better an old pot than a new potsherd. (Yiddish)
Do not put your spoon into the pot which does not boil for you. (Rumanian)
Don't scuffle with the potter, for he makes money by the damage. (Spanish)
Every pot has two handles. (Dutch)
Every potter praises his own wares. (German)
Every potter praises his pot, especially if cracked. (Spanish)
Little by little, a pot is emptied. (Unknown)
Little pots soon run over. (German)
Pots touch, ropes tangle. (Burmese)
The bottom of a pot calls the bottom of a kettle black. (Korean)
The day is never so holy that the pot refuses to boil. (Danish)
The flawed pot lasts longest. (French)
The pot that goes too often to the well, comes home broken at last. (English)
The potter drinks water from a broken pot. (Persian)
The white porridge comes from a blackened pot. (Yoruban)
There is no pot so ugly but it finds its cover. (Spanish)
When the pot boils over it cools itself. (Dutch)

Potato
One potato, two potato, three potato, four; five potato, six potato, seven potato, more.
    (American)

Potential
'It hasn't' doesn't mean 'it won't'. (German)

Poverty

A dog won't forsake its master because of poverty. (Chinese)

An advantage of poverty: your relatives gain nothing by your death. (Yiddish)

Hard is the path from poverty to renown. (Roman)

Honest poverty is thinly sown. (French)

If poverty be your lot, knock only at large gates. (Egyptian)

Kin or no kin, woe to him who has nothing. (Italian)

Large desire is endless poverty. (Indian)

No harsher masters than poverty and want. (Dutch)

Nothing to be got without pains but poverty. (French)

Painless poverty is better than embittered wealth. (Greek)

Patiently bear the burden of poverty. (Roman)

Poverty and anger do not agree. (Egyptian)

Poverty and hunger have many learned disciples. (German)

Poverty and misfortune travel hand in hand. (Mexican)

Poverty dulls the wits. (Japanese)

Poverty follows the poor. (Yiddish)

Poverty has no kin. (Italian)

Poverty hides wisdom. (Yiddish)

Poverty hinders the greatest talents from advancing. (Roman)

Poverty is a daughter of vice. (French)

Poverty is a sort of leprosy. (French)

Poverty is cunning: it catches even a fox. (German)

Poverty is death in another form. (Roman)

Poverty is no crime. (Spanish)

Poverty is no disgrace, but it is a great inconvenience. (Roman)

Poverty is no disgrace, but no honor either. (Yiddish)

Poverty is no sin. (Italian)

Poverty is no sin, but it is a branch of immorality. (Spanish)

Poverty is not possessing few things, but lacking many things. (Roman)

Poverty is shunned and treated as a crime throughout the world. (Roman)

Poverty is the sixth sense. (German)

Poverty makes a man mean. (Roman)

Poverty makes quarrels. (Korean)

Poverty makes sadness. (Irish)

Poverty makes strange bedfellows. (English)

Poverty never sped well in love. (Portuguese)

Poverty parts friends. (Portuguese)

Poverty parts good company. (Irish)

Poverty shows itself first in the face. (Yiddish)

Poverty shows us who are our friends and who our enemies. (Roman)

Poverty tries friends. (Roman)

Poverty won't allow him to lift up his head; dignity won't allow him to bow it down. (Madagascan)

Poverty, that deep disgrace, bids us to do or suffer anything. (Roman)

Those who are silent about their poverty fare better than those who beg. (Roman)
When industry goes out of the door, poverty comes in at the window. (Dutch)
When poverty comes in the door, love flies out the window. (English)

Power, Powerful
A man has his powers and a woman has hers. (Chinese)
All power is impatient of a partner. (Roman)
He is the most powerful who has himself in his power. (Roman)
He who has great power should use it lightly. (Roman)
His tongue says little, but powerful is his right arm. (Roman)
In seasons of tumult and discord, the worst men have the greatest power. (Roman)
In the greatest power exists the least exercise of power. (Roman)
In the struggle between those seeking power there is no middle course. (Roman)
Lust of power is the strongest of all passions. (Roman)
No one ever held power long by violence. (Roman)
No power is strong enough to last. (Unknown)
Power always passes from inferior to superior. (Unknown)
Power corrupts; absolute power corrupts absolutely. (English)
Power is easily retained by those arts through which it was first acquired. (Roman)
Power is more safely retained by cautious than by severe counsels. (Roman)
Power is strengthened by union. (Roman)
Power often goes before talent. (Danish)
Terrifying are the weaknesses of power. (Greek)
The less power a man has, the more he likes to use it. (Chinese)
The one who is all powerful still aims at possessing greater power. (Roman)
To someone seeking power, the poorest man is the most useful. (Roman)
Unless a serpent devour a serpent, it will not become a dragon [i.e., unless one power
    absorbs another, it will not become a great power]. (German)
Use power to curb power. (Chinese)

Practice
An ounce of practice is worth a pound of precept. (Dutch)
Constant practice often outdoes both intelligence and skill. (Roman)
Difficult things become easier with practice. (Roman)
Practice gives skill. (Roman)
Practice is better than theory. (Roman)
Practice is the best teacher. (Roman)
Practice makes perfect. (English)
Practice not your art, and 'twill soon depart. (Roman)
Practice produces the master. (Mexican)

Praise, Praised
A puff of wind and popular praise weigh alike. (Hungarian)
As great the love of praise, so great the anxiety for victory. (Roman)
Do not praise a dish before you taste it. (Spanish)

Even too much praise is a burden. (Turkish)

Every man likes his own praise best. (Danish)

Everyone praises his own saint. (Italian)

Faint praise is akin to abuse. (Danish)

From praise, as from a shadow, a man is neither bigger nor smaller. (Danish)

He that refuses praise the first time does it because he would have it the second. (French)

He who receives the offerings let him ring the bells. (Spanish)

If one man praises you, a thousand will repeat the praise. (Japanese)

If the student is good then the master is praised. (Yiddish)

If you would reap praise you must sow the seeds, gentle words and useful deeds. (Poor Richard)

It is a disgrace to be praised by those undeserving of praise. (Roman)

It is pleasing to be praised by a man of praise. (Roman)

Let another man praise thee, not thine own mouth. (Danish)

May you receive pudding while alive and praise after death. (Poor Richard)

One has only to die to be praised. (German)

Praise a fair day at night. (Roman)

Praise a fool, and you may make him useful. (Danish)

Praise borrowed from ancestors is but very sorry praise. (Danish)

Praise does not pay the bills. (German)

Praise in public, admonish in private. (Spanish)

Praise is ever the attendant on great wealth. (Roman)

Praise is not pudding. (Danish)

Praise little, dispraise less. (Poor Richard)

Praise makes a bad man worse. (American)

Praise the child, and you touch the heart of the mother. (Danish)

Praise the fine day in the evening. (Irish)

Praise the young and they will blossom. (Yiddish)

Praise without profit puts little in the pocket. (Irish)

Praise without profit puts little in the pot. (English)

Praising is not loving. (German)

The father in praising the son extols himself. (Chinese)

The praise got by a lie lasts only till the truth comes out. (Roman)

The praise of fools is censure in disguise. (Dutch)

The praise of the honorable is worth more than that of the multitude. (Roman)

'Tis better to receive a thimbleful of pudding than a cupful of praise. (Poor Richard)

To be praised by those worthy of praise is the greatest possible praise. (Roman)

To have won the approval of important people is not the last degree of praise. (Roman)

True praise is an honor, false praise a rebuke. (Roman)

Who knows how to praise knows also how to lie. (Albanian)

Who praises his wife wishes to be rid of her. (German)

Women and maidens must be praised, whether truly or falsely. (German)

Pray, Prayer

A short prayer reaches Heaven. (English)

Better to pray for oneself than curse another. (Yiddish)
Cease to hope that the decrees of the gods can bend to prayer. (Roman)
He that cannot pay, let him pray. (Yiddish)
He that would learn to pray should go to sea. (Spanish)
He who does not speak, God does not hear. (Spanish)
He who prays and then sins evens the score. (Spanish)
Hussars pray for war, and doctors for fever. (German)
If a dog's prayers were answered, bones would rain from the skies. (German)
If a man would learn to pray let him go often to sea. (French)
Lose not the time that offers itself by praying. (Roman)
Nothing costs so much as what is bought by prayers. (Roman)
Pray earnestly, but beware of telling God what you want. (French)
Pray for a good harvest, but keep on hoeing. (Slavic)
Pray to God, but continue to row to the shore. (Russian)
Pray to God, but hammer away. (Spanish)
Pray to the saint until you have passed the slough. (Portuguese)
Prayer is food for the soul. (Unknown)
Prayer is best heard at night. (Yiddish)
Prayers ascend and blessings descend. (Yiddish)
Praying kneads no dough. (Russian)
Some pray to God with one hand and slap their fellow man with the other.
   (Mexican)
The family that prays together stays together. (American)
The fewer the words, the better the prayer. (German)
The man who prays for rain gets a flood. (Hausan)
The one who prays for his neighbor will be heard for himself. (Yiddish)
To have prayed well is to have striven well. (Roman)
To pray is to work, to work is to pray. (Roman)
When the hand ceases to scatter, the heart ceases to pray. (Irish)
Who knows not how to pray let him go sail the sea. (Italian)

Preach, Preacher

A young preacher, a new hell. (Danish)
He preaches well who lives well. (Italian)
He who has his purse full preaches to the poor man. (French)
It is easy to preach fasting with a full belly. (Italian)
Practice what you preach. (American)
There are many preachers who don't hear themselves. (German)

Precaution

After victory, tighten your helmet cord. (Japanese)
Better safe than sorry. (English)
Death foreseen never comes. (Italian)
Even in crossing a stone bridge, tap it before you do. (Japanese)
Lock your door rather than accuse your neighbor. (Lebanese)

Precaution said, 'Good friend, this counsel keep: strip not yourself until you're laid to sleep'. (Dutch)

Precedent
Every bad precedent originated as a justifiable measure. (Roman)

Precious
Precious ointments are put in small boxes. (French)

Prefer, Preference
Everything goes by kinship and favor. (French)
Some prefer carrots while others like cabbage. (Chinese)

Prepare, Prepared
Have your hook always baited; in the pool where you least think it, there will be a fish. (Roman)
He who is well prepared has won the battle. (Portuguese)
Hope for the best, prepare for the worst. (Danish)
Prepare for the worst; the best can take care of itself. (Yiddish)
The better prepared, the more secure. (Roman)
The one who is not prepared today will be less prepared tomorrow. (Roman)
When one is prepared, difficulties do not come. (Ethiopian)

Presage
Certain signs precede certain events. (Roman)
Coming events cast their shadows before. (Spanish)

Presence, Present
Present to the eye, present to the mind. (Chinese)

Presents
His presents conceal a baited hook. (Roman)
Presents can be more burdensome than profitable. (Roman)
Presents from an enemy must be received with suspicion. (Roman)
Presents keep friendship warm. (German)

Preserve
Carry on and preserve yourselves for better times. (Roman)
Preserve the old, but know the new. (Chinese)

Presumption
Presumption first blinds a man, and then sets him to running. (Roman)

Pretend, Pretense
A bad man, when he pretends to be a good man, is the worst man of all. (Roman)

Affectation is a greater injury to the face than smallpox. (German)
Many desire the tree who pretend to refuse the fruit. (Italian)

Pretty, Prettiness
Little things are pretty. (Dutch)
Prettiness makes not pottage. (Irish)
Pretty is as pretty does. (American)

Prevention
An ounce of prevention is worth a pound of cure. (English)
Keeping from falling is better then helping up. (Italian)
Prevention is better than cure. (English)

Price, Prices
Every man has his price. (English)
Everything has its price. (American)
When prices go down buy; when prices go up sell. (American)

Pride, Proud
A little dog, a cow without horns, and a short man, are generally proud. (Danish)
A man gains nothing by pride but contempt and hatred. (Spanish)
A man well mounted is always proud. (French)
A man who prides himself on his ancestry is like the potato plant, the best part of which is underground. (Spanish)
A proud pauper and a rich miser are contemptible beings. (Italian)
As pride increases, fortune declines. (Poor Richard)
As sore places meet most rubs, proud folks meet most affronts. (Poor Richard)
Better badly mounted than proud on foot. (German)
Don't carry your head too high, the door is low. (German)
Every cock is proud on its own dunghill. (Spanish)
Half a fall causes a person to lose half his pride. (Mexican)
He that stands upon his pride has starvation by his side. (Yiddish)
If a man be great, even his dog will wear a proud look. (Japanese)
If pride were an art, how many doctors we should have. (Italian)
In pride, a man shakes even his tail. (Unknown)
No pride like that of an enriched beggar. (German)
Pride and grace never dwell in one place. (English)
Pride and poverty often live together. (Unknown)
Pride blossoms, but bears no fruit. (Spanish)
Pride brings loss, humility brings increase. (Chinese)
Pride dines upon vanity, sups on contempt. (Poor Richard)
Pride feels no pain. (Egyptian)
Pride goes before a fall. (German)
Pride goes before destruction, and a haughty spirit before a fall. (the Bible)
Pride invites calamity, humility reaps its harvest. (Japanese)

Pride is innate in beauty, and haughtiness is the companion of the fair. (Roman)
Pride is the fitting companion of fortune. (Roman)
Pride is the mask of one's own faults. (Yiddish)
Pride joined with many virtues chokes them all. (Yiddish)
Pride stands atop a dunghill. (Unknown)
Pride that dined with vanity supped with poverty. (Yiddish)
Pride went out on horseback, and returned on foot. (Italian)
The best manners are stained by the addition of pride. (Roman)
The man whom the new day sees standing proud is by its close seen prostrate. (Roman)
The nobler the blood, the less the pride. (Danish)
The proud hate pride – in others. (Poor Richard)
There is no pride like that of a beggar grown rich. (French)
Though you walk proud of your money, yet fortune has not changed your birth. (Roman)
Unless what we do is useful, our pride is foolish. (Roman)
When a proud man hears another praised, he feels himself injured. (English)
Where pride leads, shame follows. (Welsh)

Priest, Priests

A priest's pocket is not easily filled. (Danish)
Once a priest, always a priest. (English)
Priests bless themselves first. (German)
Priests pay each other no tithes. (German)
Priests return to the temple, merchants to the shop. (Chinese)
Priests, friars, nuns, and chickens never have enough. (Italian)
That priest is a fool who decries his relics. (Italian)
The priest to his book, the peasant to his plow. (Danish)

Prince, Princes

A prince should be slow to punish, and swift to reward. (Roman)
All are not princes who ride with the emperor. (Dutch)
As princes fiddle, subjects must dance. (German)
If the prince wants an apple, his servants take the tree. (German)
In the presence of princes the cleverest jester is mute. (Chinese)
It is the greatest merit of a prince to know his subjects. (Roman)
Princes are mortal, the republic eternal. (Roman)
Princes become wise by associating with the wise. (Greek)
Princes have long arms. (Italian)
Princes have long hands and many ears. (German)
Princes keep good reckoning, they never lose anything. (French)
Princes use men as the husbandman uses bees. (French)
Princes will not be served on conditions. (French)
Punctuality is the politeness of princes. (French)
Put not your trust in princes. (Dutch)
To criticize princes is perilous, to praise them tenuous. (Italian)
Whosoever draws his sword against the prince must throw the scabbard away. (French)

Privilege
Not everyone is permitted to go to Corinth [i.e., we cannot all be wealthy or have the same opportunities]. (Roman)
Privilege is private law. (Roman)
The magistrate's son gets out of every scrape. (Spanish)

Problem
If you're not part of the solution, you're part of the problem. (American)

Procession
One cannot ring the bells and walk in the procession. (Spanish)

Procrastination
Procrastination is the thief of time. (English)

Profane
Give not that which is holy to the dogs, neither cast your pearls before swine. (Jesus)

Profit
A bucket shop profits when wind blows. (Japanese)
Be diligent and God will send profit. (Egyptian)
He catches carp with shrimp bait. (Korean)
He who takes the profit ought also to take the labor. (Roman)
Love pursues profit. (Irish)
Profit is better than fame. (Danish)
Profit is profit even in Mecca. (Nigerian)
There is no profit without another's loss. (Roman)

Progress
The one who does not make progress loses ground. (Roman)

Promise, Promises
A man's word is his honor. (Danish)
A promise is a cloud; fulfillment is rain. (Arabian)
A promise is a debt. (Irish)
A promise makes you a debtor. (Hungarian)
A promise must be kept not merely in the letter, but in the spirit. (Roman)
A thing promised is a thing due. (Spanish)
All promises, and nothing on the plate. (French)
Better to deny at once, than to promise long. (Danish)
Every promise is a debt. (Italian)
Fair promises bind fools. (Italian)
Great say-masters, bad pay-masters. (German)
He ruins himself in promises, and clears himself by giving nothing. (French)
He who promises for others pays for himself. (Italian)
It is easier to make a promise than to keep it. (Persian)

Many promises weaken faith. (Roman)

Men apt to promise are apt to forget. (American)

Never make a promise if you don't intend to keep it. (American)

No one gives greater promises than the one who has nothing to give. (Dutch)

Nothing weighs lighter than a promise. (German)

One of these days is none of these days. (German)

Promise is a comfort to a fool. (Jamaican)

Promise little, do much. (Yiddish)

Promises and undressed cloth are apt to shrink. (Danish)

Promises are like the full moon: if they are not kept at once they diminish day by day. (German)

Promises do not put food on the table. (Spanish)

Promises don't fill the belly. (German)

Promises make debts. (German)

Promises make debts, and debts make promises. (Dutch)

Promises must not fill the place of gifts. (Roman)

Promises, like pie-crust, are made to be broken. (English)

Promising is not giving, but serves to content fools. (Portuguese)

Promising is one thing, performing is quite another. (German)

Put up or shut up. (American)

There is no virtue in a promise unless it be kept. (Danish)

Who makes no promises, has none to perform. (German)

Proof

Assertion is no proof. (German)

'For example' is no proof. (Yiddish)

The proof of the pudding is in the eating. (English)

Property

Property ill-got is property ill-spent. (Roman)

Property is robbery. (Roman)

Prophecy, Prophet

A prophet is not without honor save in his own country. (German)

Children and fools are prophets. (French)

He who guesses well prophesies well. (Italian)

Hold him the best prophet who forms the best conjectures. (Roman)

No man is a prophet in his own country. (French)

Propriety

Among those who stand, do not sit; among those who sit, do not stand; among those who laugh, do not weep; among those who weep, do not laugh. (Yiddish)

Clothing and food before propriety and justice. (Chinese)

He is deserving of praise who considers not what he may do, but what it becomes him to do. (Roman)

Propriety cannot be separated from what is honorable. (Roman)
Propriety governs the superior man; law, the inferior. (Chinese)

Prosper, Prospering

A prospering man should remain at home. (Roman)
He that spares to speak spares to prosper. (Irish)
He who will not prosper in his sleep will not prosper when awake. (Danish)
He who would prosper must follow the Church, the sea, or the king's service.
   (Spanish)
Ill-gotten goods seldom prosper. (German)
In a prosperous house, even an eggplant bears melons. (Korean)
May God not so prosper our friends that they forget us. (Spanish)
When the sister prospers, the brother rides high; when the brother prospers, the sister is
   in the kitchen. (Burmese)

Prosperity

Do not rejoice too much in prosperity. (Roman)
Do not trust prosperity too much. (Roman)
Great and sudden prosperity has a deadening effect on the human mind. (Roman)
How greatly does prosperity overspread the mind with darkness. (Roman)
In prosperity caution, in adversity patience. (Dutch)
In prosperity look out for squalls. (Roman)
In prosperity no altars smoke. (Italian)
In prosperity you may count on many friends; if the sky becomes overcast you will be
   alone. (Roman)
In prosperity, think of adversity; in adversity never think of prosperity. (Chinese)
In the hour of prosperity even the best leaders become haughty and insolent. (Roman)
In time of prosperity consider how you will bear adversity. (Roman)
In times of prosperity friends will be plenty, in times of adversity, not one in twenty.
   (English)
It is not easy to bear prosperity unruffled. (Roman)
It shows a weak mind not to bear prosperity as well as adversity with moderation.
   (Roman)
Our hearts run riot in prosperity. (Roman)
Prosperity asks for fidelity; adversity exacts it. (Roman)
Prosperity comes through vigilance, energy, and wise counsel. (Roman)
Prosperity discovers vice, adversity virtue. (Poor Richard)
Prosperity finds the lucky man, but an unlucky man gives a blind leap. (Irish)
Prosperity forgets father and mother. (Spanish)
Prosperity has many friends. (Roman)
Prosperity is never friendless. (Greek)
Prosperity is the nurse of an angry disposition. (Roman)
Prosperity proves the fortunate, adversity the great. (Roman)
Prosperity rests with Heaven. (Chinese)
Prosperity tries the soul with sharper temptations. (Roman)

When prosperity smiles, beware of her guiles. (Dutch)
Whom prosperity has charmed too much, adversity will shatter. (Roman)

Protest

Protest long enough that you are right, and you will be wrong. (Yiddish)

Prove

He who proves too much proves nothing. (Roman)

Proverb, Proverbs

A country can be judged by the quality of its proverbs. (German)
A proverb is a short sentence based on long experience. (Spanish)
A proverb is the child of experience. (French)
A proverb is to speech what salt is to food. (Arabian)
A proverb says what man thinks. (Swedish)
Don't quote your proverb 'til you bring your ship to port. (Irish)
Proverbs are like butterflies: some are caught and some fly away. (German)
Proverbs are the children of experience. (English)
Proverbs are the daughter of daily experience. (Dutch)
Proverbs are the lamp of speech. (Arabian)
Proverbs bear age, and he who would do well may view himself in them as in a mirror.
  (Italian)
Proverbs beautify speech. (Russian)
The maxims of men disclose their hearts. (French)

Providence

Bold resolution gains the favor of Providence. (Roman)
Do your best and leave the rest to Providence. (Irish)
God never sends mouths but he sends meat. (Danish)
God will provide: if only God would provide until he provides. (Yiddish)
Providence assists not the idle. (Roman)
Providence crushes pride. (Roman)
Providence has not entirely deserted us. (Roman)
Providence is always on the side of big battalions. (English)
Providence may delay, but punishment will come at length. (Roman)
Providence often puts a large potato in a little pig's way. (Unknown)
Providence provides but short horns for the fierce ox. (Roman)
Providence tempers the wind to the shorn lamb. (Roman)

Prudence, Prudent

A fool shows his annoyance at once, but a prudent man overlooks an insult.
  (Yiddish)
A prudent man does not make the goat his gardener. (Hungarian)
A prudent man may, on occasion, change his opinion, but a fool changes as often as the
  moon. (Roman)

A prudent man will observe the indications of character which nature reveals in others. (Roman)

An ounce of prudence is worth a pound of gold. (English)

Colts by falling, and lads by losing, grow prudent. (Spanish)

Good nature without prudence is foolishness. (French)

I prefer silent prudence to loquacious folly. (Roman)

Know how to save and know how to spend. (Korean)

Prudence avails more than strength. (Roman)

Prudence is the charioteer of all virtues. (Roman)

Prudence is the first thing to forsake the wretched. (Roman)

Prudence keeps one safe. (German)

Prudence looks before as well as behind. (American)

Prudence must not be expected from a man who is never sober. (Roman)

Prudent people are ever ready to profit from the experiences of others. (Roman)

The anger of the prudent never shows. (Burmese)

The most prudent yields to the strongest. (Italian)

Those who have no prudence will soon be overtaken by misery. (Chinese)

We accomplish more by prudence than by force. (Roman)

Where there is prudence, a protecting deity is not far away. (Roman)

You will conquer more surely by prudence than by passion. (Roman)

Public Good
A surrender of glory and fame must be made for the public good. (Roman)

Public Opinion
A wise man makes his own decisions, an ignorant man follows public opinion. (Chinese)

Publicity
Any publicity is good publicity. (American)

Pull
A long pull and a strong pull and a pull altogether. (Russian)

If all pulled in one direction, the world would keel over. (Yiddish)

Pull if it does not work when you push. (Japanese)

When one pulls the other slackens. (Mexican)

Punish, Punishment
A man does not punish a crab by throwing it into the sea. (German)

A punishment always appears far more severe when it is inflicted by a merciful man. (Roman)

A sleepless night is the worst punishment. (Yiddish)

Criminals are punished, that others may be amended. (Italian)

Death punished him, but so also the earth that pressed over him. (Egyptian)

Do not pursue, with a weighty scourge, the person who deserves only a slight whip. (Roman)

Everyone takes his flogging in his own way. (French)
For punishment even a shadow is pursued. (Roman)
God does not smite with both hands. (Spanish)
It is less to suffer punishment than to deserve it. (Roman)
Let no one be punished for the fault of another. (Roman)
Let the punishment equal the crime. (Roman)
Let those who have deserved their punishment, bear it patiently. (Roman)
Man punishes the action, but God the intention. (Spanish)
No one should be punished twice for the same crime. (Roman)
Rarely does punishment, even at a slow pace, fail to overtake the criminal in his flight.
    (Roman)
Strange sins, strange punishments. (Roman)
That fear may reach all, punish but a few. (Roman)
The best way to avoid punishment is to fear it. (Chinese)
The first and greatest punishment of sinners is the conscience of sin. (Roman)
The prince who does not punish informers encourages them. (Roman)
The time that precedes punishment is the severest part of it. (Roman)
Those acting and those consenting ought to bear equal punishment. (Roman)
Who does not punish the guilty is himself guilty. (German)
Who punishes one threatens a hundred. (French)

Puppy, Puppies
A puppy fears not the lion. (English)
Pigs and puppies have a very different smell. (Roman)
The bitch in her haste brings forth blind puppies. (Roman)

Pure, Purify
Fire purifies, water sanctifies. (Greek)
This world is purified by three means: by plague, by war, and by monastic seclusion.
    (Roman)
To the pure, all things are pure. (Christian)

Purpose
Everything exists for its own reason. (Unknown)
Everything is good for something. (Italian)
Seek a useful purpose. (Roman)

Purse
A full purse makes the mouth run over. (English)
A happy heart is better than a full purse. (Italian)
A heavy purse makes a light heart. (English)
A light purse makes a heavy heart. (English)
Ask your purse what you should buy. (Arabian)
Better an empty purse than an empty head. (German)
Gold is gold, though it be in a rogue's purse. (Danish)

Grief only brings more loss to your purse. (Persian)
Keep your purse and your mouth closed. (English)
Light gains make a heavy purse. (Dutch)
That's but an empty purse which is full of other men's money. (Danish)
The purse of God is large; let everyone ask him. (Spanish)
You cannot make a silk purse from a sow's ear. (German)

Pursue, Pursuit

He who pursues two hares at once catches neither. (Japanese)
A person engaged in various pursuits, minds none well. (Roman)

Q

Quarrel, Quarrelsome

A bad plowman quarrels with his ox. (Korean)
A bad worker quarrels with his tools. (Chinese)
A quarrel due to envy is not settled with the passage of time. (Yoruban)
A quarrel is like buttermilk: once it's out of the churn, the more you shake it, the more
    sour it grows. (Irish)
A quarrelsome man has no good neighbors. (Poor Richard)
An old quarrel is easily renewed. (Italian)
Better to quarrel than to be lonesome. (Irish)
Children and princes will quarrel for trifles. (Poor Richard)
Do not lengthen the quarrel while there is an opportunity of escaping. (Roman)
In a quarrel, leave room for reconciliation. (Russian)
Interfere not in the quarrels of others. (Roman)
It is easier to keep out of a quarrel than to get out of one. (Roman)
It takes two to make a quarrel. (English)
It's not one person's fault if two people quarrel. (Swedish)
Most bitter are the quarrels of brothers. (Roman)
Never fall out with your bread and butter. (English)
No one wins a quarrel by quarreling. (German)
One must not quarrel with one's bread and butter. (German)
Quarrels end, but words once spoken never die. (African)
Quarrels enhance the pleasures of love. (Roman)
Quarrels never could last long, if on one side only lay the wrong. (Poor Richard)
Quarrelsome dogs come limping home. (Swedish)
The coroner and the lawyer grow fat on the quarrels of fools. (Irish)
The first quarrel is the best quarrel. (Yiddish)
The quarrel of lovers is the renewal of love. (Roman)
The quarrels of children become the quarrels of parents. (Korean)
Those who in quarrels interpose, must often wipe a bloody nose. (Poor Richard)
Though the man quarrels with the storm, it still passes over his house. (Yoruban)
Tired folks are quarrelsome. (French)

To quarrel with a drunk is to dispute with a man who is not there. (Roman)
When kingfisher and clam quarrel, the fisherman profits. (Japanese)
When one will not, two cannot quarrel. (Roman)
When shepherds quarrel, the wolf has a winning game. (German)
When the cook and the steward fall out we hear who stole the butter. (Dutch)
When the cook and waiter quarrel, we hear who has imbibed the wine. (German)
When two quarrel both are in the wrong. (Dutch)

Question, Questions

As the question, so the answer. (Swedish)
Ask a silly question and you get a silly answer. (Russian)
Ask no questions, get no lies. (American)
Hasty questions require slow answers. (Dutch)
He that inquires much, learns much. (Danish)
One fool can ask more questions than ten sages can answer. (Yiddish)
One fool may ask more questions than seven wise men can answer. (German)
Tear off the veil of doubt by questions. (Egyptian)
There are two sides to every question. (Greek)
To a hasty question a leisurely answer. (Portuguese)
To a quick question give a slow reply. (Italian)
To every answer you can find a new question. (Yiddish)

Quick, Quickly

Quick and well seldom go together. (Danish)
Quick believers need broad shoulders. (German)
Quick enough, if but good enough. (German)
Quick enough, if safe enough. (Roman)
Quickly come, quickly go. (Roman)
What is done quickly, perishes quickly. (Roman)

Quid Pro Quo

Cook a little spit for me, and I'll cook one for you. (Irish)
Scratch my back and I'll scratch yours. (American)

Quiet, Quietness

It is the quiet pig that eats the meal. (Irish)
Quiet people are well able to look after themselves. (Irish)
Quietness is worth the price. (Irish)

Quotation

A fine quotation is a diamond on the finger of a man of wit, and a pebble in the hand of
   a fool. (French)

R

Rabbit

A sly rabbit will have three openings to its den. (Chinese)

Rabble

Most of the happy rabble hate the evil deed they come to see. (Roman)
The rabble is not influenced by reason, but blind impulse. (Roman)

Race

Slow and steady wins the race. (American)

Rage

Rage avails less than courage. (French)

Ragged

A ragged coat finds little credit. (Italian)
A ragged colt may make a good horse. (Irish)
A ragged colt often makes a powerful horse. (Irish)
A ragged sack holds no grain, and a poor man is not taken into counsel. (Italian)

Rags

If you must be in rags, then let your rags be tidy. (Irish)

Rain

A heavy rain is good for the fields but bad for the roads. (Yiddish)
A heavy shower is soon over. (Italian)
A rainy morn oft brings a pleasant day. (Italian)
A small rain can lay down a great dust. (German)
After great droughts come great rains. (Dutch)
After rainfall the ground becomes harder. (Japanese)
Don't empty the water jar until the rain falls. (Filipino)
Drop by drop rain fills the pot. (African)
He who is under cover when it rains is a great fool if he moves. (Italian)
In a drizzle, a person does not realize that his clothes are getting wet. (Korean)
Into every life a little rain must fall. (Roman)
It never rains but it pours. (English)
It never thunders but it rains. (Italian)
It's pleasant to look on the rain, when one stands dry. (Dutch)
Nobody knows from which cloud the rain will fall. (Korean)
Rain beats a leopard's skin but does not wash off the spots. (Ashanti)
Rain before seven, fine before eleven. (English)
Rain cannot wash away beauty. (Yoruban)
Rain does not fall on one roof alone. (West African)
Rain falls on the good and evil alike. (Jamaican, after Jesus)

The rain is not a friend to anyone, whether rich or poor, good or evil. (Yoruban)

When it rains, it pours. (American)

Raindrops

Raindrops come heavy on a house unthatched. (Irish)

Raindrops will hollow a stone. (Korean)

Raindrops will pierce through stone. (Japanese)

Rare

Rich gamblers and old trumpeters are rare. (German)

Rash, Rashness

A rash man, a skin of good wine, and a glass vessel, do not last long. (Portuguese)

Rashness is a characteristic of youth, prudence of old age. (Roman)

Rashness is not always fortunate. (Roman)

Rashness is not valor. (English)

Rat, Rats

A cornered rat may dare to bite a cat. (Chinese)

A rat who gnaws at a cat's tail invites destruction. (Chinese)

An old rat easily finds a hole. (Dutch)

An old rat is a brave rat. (French)

An old rat won't go into the trap. (Dutch)

Careless rat chewing on a cat's tail: beware lightning! (Japanese)

Drive a rat into a corner, and it'll jump at you. (German)

Rats desert a sinking ship. (French)

Rats gnaw through leather by degrees. (Yoruban)

Rats know the way of rats. (Chinese)

Seeing the jar, one cannot throw a stone at a rat. (Korean)

The rat does not leave the cat's house with a bellyful. (Portuguese)

When the time comes, even a rat becomes a tiger. (Japanese)

Wise rats run from a falling house. (Dutch)

Rather

Rather a husband with one eye than with one son. (Portuguese)

Rather a little correctly than much incorrectly. (Norwegian)

Rather a single grape for me than a pair of figs for thee. (French)

Rather an ass that carries than a horse that throws. (Italian)

Rather free in a foreign place than a slave back home. (Norwegian)

Rather go rob with good men than pray with bad. (Portuguese)

Rather hat in hand than hand in purse. (Italian)

Rather have a little one for your friend, than a great one for your enemy. (Italian)

Rather lose the wool than the sheep. (Portuguese)

Rather once cry your heart out than always sigh. (Chinese)

Rather the egg today than the hen tomorrow. (Danish)

Raven

Bring up a raven, and it will peck out your eyes. (German)
If bad be the raven, his company is no better. (Irish)
One raven does not peck out another's eyes. (Danish)
The raven is fair when the rook is not by. (Danish)
The raven thinks its own chick is fair. (Irish)

Razor

A razor may be sharper than an ax, but it cannot cut wood. (African)

Reach

If you wish to reach the highest, begin at the lowest. (Roman)
Things beyond our reach are not worth our consideration. (Roman)

Read, Reading

After three days without reading, talk becomes flavorless. (Chinese)
Read the whole if you wish to know the whole. (Roman)
Reading makes a full man, meditation a profound man, discourse a clear man.
    (Poor Richard)
What is not read is not believed. (Roman)
Whilst I read, I give assent. (Roman)

Reap, Reaper

A bad reaper never gets a good sickle. (Irish)
Better reap two days early than one day late. (Dutch)
Everyone reaps as he sows. (Portuguese)
If they call you reaper, then whet your scythe. (Egyptian)
Some sow, others reap. (Roman)

Reason

Against reason no sword will prevail. (Japanese)
Every why has a wherefore, every rhyme a reason. (English)
For an honest man half his wits are enough; the whole is too little for a knave. (Italian)
If you will not hear reason, she will surely rap your knuckles. (Russian)
If you wish to subject everything to yourself, subject yourself to reason. (Roman)
Reason can generally effect more than blind force. (Roman)
Reason does not come before years. (German)
Reason is a slowpoke. (Yiddish)
Reason is absent when impulse rules. (Roman)
Reason is the guide and light of life. (Roman)
Reason is the spirit and soul of the law. (Roman)
Reason lies between bridle and spur. (Italian)
Reason not with the great, 'tis a perilous gate. (French)

Rebel, Rebellion

To rebel in season is not to rebel. (Greek)

Twelve highlanders and a bagpipe make a rebellion. (Scottish)

Rebuke, Rebukes

A profitable rebuke does not smart. (Egyptian)

A sharp rebuke makes a quick payment. (German)

Rebuke a wise man and he will like you. (Sudanese)

Rebukes ought not to have a grain more of salt than of sugar. (French)

Recall

It is to live twice, when you can enjoy recalling your former life. (Roman)

Time and words can't be recalled, even if it was only yesterday. (Yiddish)

Reckless

Reckless youth makes rueful age. (French)

Reckon

The mother reckons well, but the child reckons better. (Spanish)

Reconciliation

Nothing is preferable to reconciliation. (Irish)

Recover

Not to wish to recover is a mortal symptom. (Spanish)

Rectify

Until you have rectified yourself, you cannot rectify others. (Chinese)

Red

He who mixes with vermilion becomes red. (Japanese)

Reflection

No one can see their reflection in running water; it is only in still water that we can see.
   (Taoist)

Reform

He who reforms, God assists. (Spanish)

Refuge

He who seeks refuge under a tree may be crushed; it is safer to take refuge under a man.
   (Burmese)

Refuse

A civil denial is better than a rude grant. (French)

He that will not when he can, cannot when he will. (Spanish)

He that will not when he may, when he will he shall have nay. (English)
It is better to refuse with a smile than to grant with a grunt. (Spanish)

Regard
Things are not as they are, but as they are regarded. (Italian)

Regret
A hundred years of regret pays not a farthing of debt. (German)
A man is not old until his regrets take the place of his dreams. (Yiddish)
A thousand regrets do not pay one debt. (Turkish)
Better to be safe than sorry. (Irish)
Regret always comes too late. (Unknown)
Regret magnifies the loss. (Unknown)
Regret never precedes the event. (Japanese)
Regret nothing. (American)

Reign
A short reign brings no respite to the masses. (Roman)
Who knows not how to dissemble knows not how to reign. (Italian)

Rein
Rein in the horse at the edge of the cliff. (Chinese)

Rejoice
If an onion causes rejoicing, what then of sugar? (Egyptian)
Rejoice with those who rejoice. (St Paul)

Relations, Relatives
No relation is poor. (Spanish)
Poor relations have little honor. (Danish)
The day your horse dies and your money's lost, your relatives become strangers. (Chinese)
A man's arms are his relatives. (Yoruban)
All people are your relatives, therefore expect only trouble from them. (Chinese)
Eat and drink with your relatives; do business with strangers. (Greek)
Even the emperor has straw-sandaled relatives. (Chinese)
Go to friends for advice; to women for pity; to strangers for charity; to relatives for
    nothing. (Spanish)
He will never be disagreeable to others who makes himself agreeable to his own
    relations. (Roman)
Love your relations, but live not near them. (English)

Religion
A baptized Jew is a circumcised Christian. (German)
A convert is not a Jew and not a Gentile. (Yiddish)
A man devoid of religion is like a horse without a bridle. (Roman)

A man should be religious, not superstitious. (Roman)
All women are good Lutherans: they would rather preach than hear mass. (Danish)
Before all things reverence the gods. (Roman)
Every sect has its truth, every truth has its sect. (Chinese)
He who carves the Buddha never worships him. (Chinese)
He will never worship the image on the altar who knew it when it was a piece of wood in the garden. (Spanish)
If the heart is orthodox it does not fear heresy. (Chinese)
If the thunder is not loud, the peasant forgets to cross himself. (Russian)
If there were no gods or demons in the world, man would do all kinds of things. (Chinese)
If you willingly bear the Cross it will bear you. (German)
Many have quarreled about religion, that never practiced it. (Poor Richard)
Many who scruple to spit in church defile the altar. (Italian)
Men who have no religion, have no honor. (Roman)
Men's ignorance makes the pot boil for priests. (French)
Nature teaches us to love our friends, but religion our enemies. (German)
No penny, no Paternoster. (German)
Religion has two children: love and hatred. (Russian)
Religion is not abolished by abolishing superstition. (Roman)
Religious contention is the Devil's harvest. (French)
The discharge of our duty towards God is called religion; towards our parents, piety. (Roman)
To how many evils does not religion persuade! (Roman)
We do not destroy religion by destroying superstition. (Roman)
Whether the Buddha will be fat or lean depends on the stone cutter. (Korean)

Relish
What one relishes, nourishes. (Poor Richard)

Remedy, Remedies
Adapt the remedy to the disease. (Chinese)
Early, not late remedies, are the most effective. (Roman)
For extreme ills extreme remedies. (Italian)
For great evils strong remedies. (Dutch)
If there be no remedy, why worry? (Spanish)
No one tries extreme remedies at first. (Roman)
Remedies are slower in their operation than diseases. (Roman)
Some remedies are worse than the disease. (Roman)
The same remedies do not suit every patient. (Roman)
There are a thousand forms of evil; there will be a thousand remedies. (Roman)
There is a remedy for all things save death. (Dutch)

Remember
Better twice remembered than once forgotten. (Dutch)
Remember that you are a man. (Roman)

That is pleasant to remember which was hard to endure. (Italian)
Who will remember you after you are dead? (German)

Renounce
One who casts aside the world obtains great clearness of perception and understanding.
  (Chinese)
The more a person denies himself, the more will he receive from the gods. (Roman)

Renown
Renown is denied to the living. (Roman)
Renown is more lasting than life. (Irish)

Rent
Rent and taxes never sleep. (German)
Rent to the lord is like food to a child. (Irish)

Repair
Better to repair the gutter than the whole house. (Portuguese)
He that repairs not a part, builds all. (French)
He who does not repair his gutter has a whole house to repair. (Spanish)
If it ain't broke don't fix it. (American)
Rotten wood cannot be carved and mud walls cannot be plastered. (Chinese)

Repeat, Repetition
Once gets a cheer, twice a deaf ear, thrice a kick in the rear. (Yiddish)
Repetition is the mother of learning. (Russian)
Repetition is the mother of study. (Roman)

Repel
Drive not away what never came near you. (Danish)

Repent, Repentance
Amendment is repentance. (German)
He repents in thorns that sleeps in beds of roses. (English)
Late repentance is rarely sincere. (Roman)
Rejoiced in youth, repented in age. (German)
Repentance always comes too late. (Korean)
Repentance costs dear. (French)
Repentance for silence is better than repentance for speaking. (Moroccan)
Repentance is the heart's medicine. (German)
Repentance never comes ahead. (Japanese)
Sinning is the best part of repentance. (Arabian)
Sudden trust brings sudden repentance. (German)
Take nothing in hand that may bring repentance. (Dutch)
The end of passion is the beginning of repentance. (Poor Richard)
The end of wrath is the beginning of repentance. (German)
The one who repents of having sinned is almost innocent. (Roman)

Report

The truest report comes last. (German)

Reproach

The sting of a reproach, is the truth of it. (Poor Richard)

Reproof

A smart reproof is better than a smooth deceit. (German)
Reproof bears fruit. (Dutch)

Republic

A republic cannot be well conducted under the command of many. (Roman)

Repute, Reputation

A bad wound may be cured, bad repute kills. (Spanish)
A good reputation is hard to establish, but reports of evil deeds easily circulate. (Chinese)
Develop a reputation and then relax. (Mexican)
Don't consider your reputation and you may do anything you like. (Chinese)
Get a good name and go to sleep. (Italian)
Glass, china, and reputation, are easily crack'd, and never well mended. (Poor Richard)
Good repute is better than a golden belt. (French)
Good repute is like the cypress: once cut, it never puts forth leaf again. (Italian)
He buys a name and fishes for a reputation. (Chinese)
He loses repute who compares himself with unworthy people. (Roman)
He who has lost his reputation is a dead man among the living. (Spanish)
It is a hard thing to prop up a falling reputation. (English)
It is not the height but the presence of the man that gives him his reputation. (Chinese)
Of a dead leopard we keep the skin, of man his reputation. (Chinese)
One who has the reputation of an early riser may safely lie in bed until noon. (Yiddish)
Repute hangs a man. (French)
The damage done to reputation is greater than can be possibly estimated. (Roman)
Try to deserve the reputation you enjoy. (Roman)
When a door opens not to your knock, consider your reputation. (Arabian)

Resent, Resentment

Large demands on oneself and little demands on others keep resentment at bay.
   (Chinese)
Resent not the water with which you wash your face. (Roman)
Resentment which is concealed is dangerous; hatred avowed loses its opportunity for
   vengeance. (Roman)

Resolve, Resolute

A resolute heart endures no counsel. (Portuguese)
Be resolved and the thing is done. (Chinese)
Keep your foot firm till death. (Portuguese)

Never say die. (American)
Put a stout heart to a steep hill. (Scottish)

Resources
Lack of resources has hanged many a person. (Irish)

Respect, Respectful
Antiquity is entitled to respect. (Roman)
Do not have greater respect for money than for man. (Vietnamese)
He who respects his parents never dies. (Greek)
If you want to be respected, you must respect yourself. (Spanish)
No one in a shabby coat is treated with respect. (Roman)
No strength within, no respect without. (Kashmiri)
Respect for one's superiors, kindness for one's inferiors. (Vietnamese)
Respect for parents should be the fountain of all actions. (Chinese)
Respect is given to wealth, not to men. (Lebanese)
Respect is greater at a distance. (Roman)
Respect the rights of others and you will have peace. (Mexican)
Respect yourself and others will respect you. (Chinese)

Response
There is no wise response to a foolish remark. (Roman)

Responsibility
A child's back must be bent early. (Danish)
Man has responsibility, not power. (Native American)

Rest
A short rest is always good. (Danish)
I rest, therefore I rust. (German)
Nothing can exist long without occasional rest. (Roman)
Rest comes from unrest, and unrest from rest. (German)
Rest is good after the work is done. (Danish)
Rest is sweet after hard toil. (German)
Rest makes rust. (Dutch)
Sometimes we must rest. (Roman)
Take rest: a field that has rested gives a bountiful crop. (Roman)

Retreat
A good retreat is better than a poor defense. (Irish)
The one who retreats fifty paces derides the one who retreated one hundred. (Japanese)

Retribution
An eye for an eye and a tooth for a tooth. (the Bible)

Revenge

A man need never revenge himself; the body of his enemy will be brought to his own
　　door. (Chinese)

Because a man has injured your goat, do not go out and kill his bull. (Kenyan)

Blood will have blood. (Afghani)

Don't get mad, get even. (German)

From a bad paymaster take even straw. (Italian)

He who cannot revenge himself is weak, he who will not is contemptible. (Italian)

He who seeks revenge should remember to dig two graves. (Chinese)

He who would seek revenge must be on his own guard. (Danish)

In revenge, haste is criminal. (Roman)

In taking revenge, a man is equal with his enemy; but in passing it over he is superior.
　　(Danish)

It is best to stand aside and allow God to take revenge. (Yoruban)

No one rejoices more in revenge than a woman. (Roman)

No revenge is more honorable than the one not taken. (Spanish)

Revenge a hundred years old has still its baby teeth. (Italian)

Revenge converts a little right into a great wrong. (German)

Revenge does not long remain unavenged. (German)

Revenge in cold blood is the Devil's own act and deed. (German)

Revenge is a confession of pain. (Roman)

Revenge is a dish that is best served cold. (English)

Revenge is always the delight of a little and narrow mind. (Roman)

Revenge is an inhuman word. (Roman)

Revenge is new wrong. (German)

Revenge is sweet. (English)

Revenge postponed is not forgotten. (Icelandic)

Shameful deeds bring on revenge. (Norwegian)

The best kind of revenge is success. (American)

The revenge of an idiot is without mercy. (Roman)

To forget a wrong is the best revenge. (Spanish)

Who has patience sees his revenge. (Italian)

Who holds his peace and gathers stones, will find a time to throw them. (Portuguese)

Revenue

Economy is a great revenue. (Roman)

Reverence

Our reverence is ever due to those who have passed on. (Roman)

Reverence ceases once blood is spilt. (Irish)

Reverse

The reverse side also has a reverse side. (Japanese)

Revolution
Revolutions are not made with rose water. (Roman)

Reward, Rewards
Great praise is the reward of children who respect the wishes of their parents. (Roman)
He is the best gentleman, who is the son of his own deserts. (Roman)
Men do not value a good deed unless it brings a reward. (Roman)
Reward sweetens labor. (Dutch)
Rewards stimulate goodness, punishments repress evil. (Chinese)
The reward for bitter toil is sweet. (Chinese)
The reward of a thing rightly done is to have done it. (Roman)
The reward of silence is certain. (Roman)
The reward of virtue and vice is like shadow following substance. (Chinese)
The rewards of good deeds endure. (Roman)

Rhinoceros
Do not speak of a rhinoceros if there is no tree nearby. (Zulu)
The rhinoceros never turns away defeated from the enemy. (Roman)

Rice
Can a spoonful of rice fill the empty stomach? (Korean)
It is not the sticky rice that is sticking, but the rough rice. (Burmese)
Without rice, even the cleverest housewife cannot cook. (Chinese)

Rich
A rich man and a spittoon get dirtier as they accumulate. (Japanese)
A rich man has no need of character. (Yiddish)
A rich man is either a scoundrel or the heir of a scoundrel. (Spanish)
A rich man is either an unjust man or the heir of one. (Roman)
A rich man is never ugly in the eyes of a girl. (French)
Everyone is kin to the rich man. (English)
Get what you can and keep what you have; that's the way to get rich. (Scottish)
He is rich enough who does not want. (Italian)
He is rich who owes nothing. (Italian)
He is richest who is poorest in his desires. (Roman)
He who would be rich in a year gets hanged in six months. (Italian)
I never saw a silent rich man. (French)
If a rich man ate a snake, they would say it was because of his wisdom. (Portuguese)
If there is a rich man in the area three villages are ruined. (Korean)
In a rich house hens always have plenty to peck at. (Spanish)
In the rich woman's house she always commands; he never. (Spanish)
No just man ever became suddenly rich. (Roman)
Not only are rich men rich, but their checks are good. (Yiddish)
Rich is the one who wishes no more than he has. (Roman)
Rich people are everywhere at home. (German)

The one who desires to become rich, desires to become rich quickly. (Roman)

The rich don't fight. (Japanese)

The rich eat without any fuss. (Yoruban)

The rich have many friends. (Dutch)

The rich man has more relations than he knows. (French)

The rich never have to seek out their relatives. (Italian)

The rich of the earth have already enjoyed their heaven. (Spanish)

The richest man carries nothing away with him but a shroud. (French)

The truly rich are those who enjoy what they have. (Yiddish)

The upright never grow rich in a hurry. (Danish)

There is nothing more insufferable than a rich woman. (Roman)

To be rich is not everything, but it certainly helps. (Yiddish)

To grow rich one has only to turn his back on God. (French)

To the rich, all money is theirs. (Unknown)

Were it not for 'if' and 'but', we should all be rich. (French)

When a man is rich, he begins to save. (German)

When a peasant gets rich, he knows neither relations nor friends. (Spanish)

Rich and Poor

A rich child often sits in a poor mother's lap. (Danish)

Avarice is rich, while modesty is poor. (Roman)

Be rich to yourself, poor to your friends (Roman)

Better a poor man's son than a rich man's slave. (Rumanian)

If life is a thing money could buy, then the rich would live and the poor would die.
    (American)

If the rich could hire others to die for them, the poor could make a wonderful living.
    (Yiddish)

If the servant grows rich and the master poor, they are both good for nothing.
    (German)

If you live according to nature, you will never be poor; if according to the notions of
    men, you will never be rich. (Roman)

It is no credit to be rich and no disgrace to be poor. (Roman)

It's as difficult to be rich without bragging as it is to be poor without complaining.
    (Chinese)

Never promise a poor person, and never owe a rich one. (Brazilian)

Poor men do penance for rich men's sins. (Italian)

Poor men take to the sea, rich men to the mountains. (Irish)

Rich man down and poor man up – they're still not even. (Yiddish)

Rich men accumulate money, the poor accumulate years. (Chinese)

Riches run after the rich, poverty after the poor. (French)

Sometimes poor, sometimes rich. (Burmese)

The poor enjoy the grace of the rich; the rich enjoy the grace of Heaven. (Chinese)

The poor is hated by his neighbor, but the rich have many friends. (Italian)

The poor man has few enemies, the rich man fewer friends. (Yiddish)

The poor man seeks for food, the rich man for appetite. (Danish)

The poor man who enters into partnership with a rich man makes a risky venture. (Roman)

The poor man's labor is the rich man's wealth. (German)

The poor must dance as the rich pipe. (German)

The pride of the rich makes the labors of the poor. (English)

The rich devour the poor and the Devil devours the rich, and so both are devoured. (Dutch)

The rich have relatives, the poor are orphaned. (Yoruban)

The rich have their ice in the summer, the poor have theirs in winter. (English)

The rich man plans for tomorrow, the poor man for today. (Chinese)

The rich man transgresses the law, and the poor man is punished. (Spanish)

The rich man who is stingy is the worst pauper. (Yiddish)

The rich worry over their money, the poor over their bread. (Vietnamese)

The rich would have to eat money if the poor did not provide food. (Russian)

The richer the man, the poorer the soul. (Spanish)

To the rich the meat, to the poor the broth. (Burmese)

We give to the rich, and take from the poor. (German)

When poor, liberal; when rich, stingy. (Spanish)

Wishing does not make a poor man rich. (Arabian)

Riches

He who multiplies riches multiplies cares. (Poor Richard)

Many a man would have been worse, if his estate had been better. (Poor Richard)

Riches abuse them who know not how to use them. (German)

Riches allow one to be foolish. (Roman)

Riches and fame are but dreams among men. (Chinese)

Riches and favor go before wisdom and art. (Danish)

Riches and honor are providential. (Japanese)

Riches are a dream in the night, fame a gull floating on water. (Chinese)

Riches are desired to bring about our pleasures. (Roman)

Riches are not the only wealth. (Icelandic)

Riches are often abused, but never refused. (Danish)

Riches breed care, poverty is safe. (Danish)

Riches cause arrogance; poverty, meekness. (German)

Riches fall not always to the lot of the most deserving. (Roman)

Riches serve a wise man, but command a fool. (French)

Riches, the incentives to evil, are dug out of the earth. (Roman)

The generous man is never satisfied with riches. (Egyptian)

The riches that are in the heart cannot be stolen. (Russian)

We should seek riches so that we may give to the deserving. (Roman)

Ride, Riding

He who rides slow, must saddle early. (German)

More belongs to riding than a pair of boots. (German)

Ride an ox until you can ride a horse. (Japanese)

Ride on, but look before you. (Dutch)
You cannot ride two horses with one behind. (Russian)

Ridicule, Ridiculous

From the sublime to the ridiculous there is but one step. (French)
Ridicule is the test of truth. (Dutch)
Ridicule is the weapon of the ignorant. (the Editor)

Right

By dint of going wrong all will come right. (French)
Extreme right is extreme wrong (German)
He is always right who suspects that he makes mistakes. (Spanish)
He that is always right is always wrong. (Italian)
If inwardly right, don't worry. (Roman)
Many love to praise right and do wrong. (Danish)
No one is always right. (Portuguese)
Once right does not make always right. (the Editor)
Right is with the strongest. (German)
Right overstrained turns to wrong. (Spanish)
The right man comes at the right time. (Italian)
There is no right way to do a wrong thing. (Turkish)
To know the right as right and the wrong as wrong is true knowledge. (Chinese)
Two blacks don't make a white, two wrongs don't make a right. (English)

Right, Rights

A right is said to have its beginning from possession. (Roman)
A man may lose what are his clearest rights by not demanding them. (Roman)
A right sometimes sleeps, but never dies. (English)
If a person is away, his right is away. (Spanish)
It is from disuse that rights are lost. (Roman)

Righteous

The righteous man pays for the sinner. (Portuguese)

Ring

Don't put too tight a ring on your finger. (Italian)
When they offer you a ring, hold out your finger. (Spanish)

Ripe, Ripen

Early ripe, early rotten. (Japanese)
Soon ripe, soon rotten. (Roman)
The monkeys eat the ripest fruit and leave the seeds. (Indian)
The riper the grain the lower it hangs its head. (Korean)
The ripest fruit will not fall into your mouth. (Portuguese)
What ripens fast does not last. (German)

When ripe, fruit will drop of itself. (Chinese)
When the pear is ripe, it falls. (German)
You can tell ripe corn by its look. (African)

Rise and Fall
See how he has risen from a mayor to a hangman. (Spanish)
Speedy rise, speedy fall. (German)
The higher the rise the greater the fall. (French)

Risk
A turtle makes progress when it sticks its neck out. (Spanish)
Better to risk a little than lose the whole. (American)
Better to stretch your hand than your neck. (Dutch)
Don't risk a gold coin for something worth a copper coin. (Spanish)
Great estates may venture more. (Poor Richard)
Great profits, great risks. (German)
He that ventures not fails not. (French)
He who doesn't risk never gets to drink champagne. (Russian)
He who risks nothing can gain nothing. (Italian)
If the profits are great, the risks are great. (Chinese)
If you don't speculate, you can't accumulate. (Chinese)
Naught venture, naught have. (French)
Nothing ventured, nothing gained. (English)
The greater the risk, the greater the gain. (Spanish)
Who ventures nothing has no luck. (Spanish)
With houses and gold, men are rarely bold. (German)

Rival, Rivalry
A concubine cannot bear the sight of another concubine. (Korean)
Rivals do not agree. (Hausan)
The man of your own trade is your enemy. (Portuguese)
Bear patiently with a rival. (Roman)
Rivalry is the whetstone of talent. (Roman)
Rivalry of scholars advances wisdom. (Yiddish)

River
A river is not contaminated by having a dog drink from it. (Afghani)
A thousand years hence the river will run as it did. (Turkish)
At a great river be the last to pass. (Italian)
Deep rivers move in silence; shallow brooks are noisy. (Danish)
Do not push the river, it will flow by itself. (Polish)
Don't just cross a river, but cross it bearing fire. (Indian)
Even a great river's glory ends at the sea. (Russian)
Every river has its own course. (Yiddish)
Every river runs to the sea. (Jamaican)
From great rivers come great fish. (Portuguese)

He who is brought up near the river will die in the river. (Japanese)

If the river makes noise, it is because it carries water. (Mexican)

If thou canst not see the bottom, wade not. (English)

If you saw what the river carried, you would never drink the water. (Jamaican)

In an old river, water never gets dry. (Japanese)

It's a long river whose source can't be found. (Irish)

No matter how full the river, it still wants to grow. (African)

No one tests the depth of the river with both feet. (African)

Strong currents one moment, still water the next. (Burmese)

Take stock of the river before you plunge into the current. (Irish)

The bigger the river the bigger the fish. (Spanish)

The course of a river is not to be altered. (Roman)

The deepest rivers flow with the least noise. (Roman)

The great river refuses no streamlet. (Korean)

The river does not swell with clear water. (Italian)

The river is never so full as to cover the eyes of the fish. (Yoruban)

Where the river flows calmly, there is it perchance the deepest. (Roman)

You can never enter the same river twice. (Greek)

You can often find in a river what you cannot find in the ocean. (Indian)

Road, Roads

A shady lane breeds mud. (English)

All roads lead to Rome. (French)

Don't leave the high road for a short cut. (Portuguese)

Every road has two directions. (Russian)

Every road leads somewhere. (Filipino)

He who takes the wrong road must make his journey twice over. (Spanish)

If there is no road, don't go. (Korean)

It is a long road that has no turning. (Irish)

Long and weary is the road with no milestones. (the Editor)

Many are the roads that lead a man nowhere. (the Editor)

No matter how far you have gone on the wrong road, turn back. (Turkish)

No one knows where the road goes. (German)

Not all roads lead to Rome. (Russian)

Where the road is straight, don't look for a short cut. (Russian)

Rob, Robber

Even a robber fastens his door. (Japanese)

It is easy robbing when the dog is quieted. (Italian)

Robbers are plundered by thieves. (Chinese)

To rob a robber is not robbing. (French)

Rogue

A sly rogue is often in good dress. (Irish)

It is easier to fill a rogue's belly than his eye. (Danish)

Little rogues easily become great ones. (Poor Richard)
No rogue like the godly rogue. (Spanish)

Roll
From the roof of a house a melon may roll either of two ways. (Chinese)

Romance
Every suitor is not a heartbreaker. (Roman)
Remove leisure, and the bow of Cupid will lose its effect. (Roman)
The faded rose, no suitor knows. (Roman)
The he-goat goes a-seeking the she-goat and he returns with child. (Hausan)
To win the mistress, flatter the maid. (Unknown)
Where the cobwebs grow, the beaux don't go. (German)
Who the daughter would win, with her mother must begin. (German)

Rome
All roads lead to Rome. (French)
Not all roads lead to Rome. (Russian)
Rome wasn't built in a day. (English)
The farther from Rome the nearer to God. (German)
When in Rome do as the Romans do. (English)
When you are at Rome, live after the Roman fashion. (Roman)

Rooster
Roosters are the clock of the fields. (Spanish)
The country rooster does not crow in the town. (Swahili)
The rooster of a lucky man lays eggs for him. (Spanish)

Root
When the root is worthless, so is the tree. (German)

Rope
A triple rope is not easily broken. (Roman)
Don't talk about rope in a hanged man's home. (Spanish)
Even a rotten rope can be put to use. (Japanese)
Give a man a rope and he will surely hang himself. (American)
Give a man enough rope and he will hang himself. (English)
He who would hang himself is sure to find a rope. (Danish)
Pull gently at a weak rope. (Dutch)
Put a rope around your neck and many will be happy to drag you along. (Egyptian)
You can't push on a rope. (Persian)
You cannot pull hard with a broken rope. (Danish)

Rosary
Rosary in hand, devil at heart. (Portuguese)

Rose, Roses

A rose by any other name would smell as sweet. (English)

A rose is a rose is a rose. (Roman)

A rose issues from thorns. (Egyptian)

Every rose has its thorn. (Italian)

He who wants the rose must respect the thorn. (Persian)

He who would gather roses, must not fear thorns. (Dutch)

Instead of complaining that the rosebush is full of thorns, be happy that the thorn bush has roses. (German)

Not everyone may pluck roses. (German)

Seek not the rose which is once lost. (Roman)

Stop and smell the roses. (Danish)

Stop looking for the place where a late rose may yet linger. (Roman)

The rose has thorns only for those who would gather it. (Chinese)

The rose that many people smell is bound to lose some of its fragrance. (Spanish)

Row, Rowing

It is not the nodding of heads that does the rowing. (Irish)

Let him take the oars who has learned to row. (Roman)

Nodding the head does not row the boat. (English)

Royal Court

A courtier should be without feeling and without honor. (French)

At court there are many hands, but few hearts. (German)

At court they sell a good deal of smoke without fire. (Danish)

At the king's court, everyone for himself. (French)

Be not an esquire where you were a page. (Spanish)

Courts grant not their favors as men are good and deserving. (Roman)

He that would rise at court, must begin by creeping. (Poor Richard)

If you care for the court, the court will bring cares for you. (Roman)

Life at court is often a shortcut to Hell. (Danish)

The court official in one life has seven rebirths as a beggar. (Chinese)

The courts of kings are full of men, empty of friends. (Roman)

The steps at court are slippery. (Danish)

Ruin

By what slight means are great affairs brought to ruin! (Roman)

He will be ruined who tries to ruin others. (Burmese)

I suffer ruin worthy of mine own invention. (Roman)

The road to ruin is paved with good intentions. (German)

Rule, Ruler

He who would rule must hear and be deaf, see and be blind. (German)

He would have been universally deemed fit for empire, if he had never reigned. (Roman)

It is absurd that he should rule others, who knows not how to rule himself. (Roman)

It is easy to rule over the good. (Roman)
Neither are there two suns, neither two rulers over the people. (Chinese)
No one can rule who cannot also submit to authority. (Roman)
Only with a new ruler do you realize the value of the old one. (Burmese)
The desire to rule is the most ardent of all the affections of the mind. (Roman)
The first art to be learned by a ruler is to endure envy. (Roman)
The one who knows not how to dissemble, knows not how to rule. (Roman)
To rule the mountains is to rule the river. (French)
When a ruler makes a mistake, all the people suffer. (Chinese)
Who holds the purse rules the house. (Unknown)

Rule, Rules

Every rule has its exception. (English)
Rules are made to be broken. (English)
Submit to the rule you have yourself laid down. (Roman)
There is an exception to every rule. (German)
Three things without rule: a woman, a pig, and a mule. (Irish)

Rumor

A false report rides post. (Chinese)
A rumor goes in one ear and out of many mouths. (Chinese)
All is not false which is publicly reported. (Roman)
Idle talk by one is believed when picked up and spoken by many. (Chinese)
Innate to all persons is a natural desire to spread rumors. (Roman)
Nothing is swifter than rumor. (Roman)
Rumor grows as it goes. (Roman)
Rumor is a great traveler. (Unknown)
Rumor makes the wolf bigger than he is. (German)
Rumor never reports things in their true light. (Roman)
Rumor runs away. (Roman)
There is no evil swifter than a rumor. (Roman)
What children hear at home soon flies abroad. (German)
What children hear by the fireside they repeat in the highway. (Spanish)

Run, Runs

Don't run too far, you will have to return the same distance. (French)
Easy to run downhill, much puffing to run up. (Chinese)
He runs far who never turns. (Italian)
He runs from a shower and enters a downpour. (Hausan)
He runs heavily who is forced to run. (Danish)
He that runs fast will not run long. (French)
If you run from fire, you run into water. (Yiddish)
It is better to run back than to run on the wrong way. (Roman)
To run away is not glorious, but very healthy. (Russian)
Who runs is followed. (Dutch)

Russian

Scratch a Russian and you find a Tartar. (French)

One Russian is a drunk; two Russians a chess game; three Russians a revolution; four Russians a string quartet. (French)

Rust

Better to wear out than rust out. (French)

'If I rest, I rust', says the key. (German)

Rust wastes more than use. (French)

S

Sack

A sack is best tied before it is full. (French)

A sack was never so full but that it would hold another grain. (Italian)

Bad is the sack that will not bear patching. (Italian)

Let every man carry his own sack to the mill. (Danish)

Nothing can come out of a sack but what is in it. (Italian)

Sacred

Do not give that which is sacred to dogs. (Jesus)

Sacrifice

Personal affections must be sacrificed for the greater cause. (Chinese)

The sacrifice of an ox will not bring us all we want. (Roman)

To obey is better than sacrifice. (the Bible)

Sad

The sad detest the cheerful, and the cheerful the sad. (Roman)

Saddle

A saddle fits more backs than one. (Italian)

Better to lose the saddle than the horse. (Italian)

We have not saddled and yet we are riding. (Portuguese)

Sadness

It is difficult to feign wit when one is in a sad mood. (Roman)

Sadness and gladness succeed each other. (French)

Safe, Safely

A beaten track is a safe one. (Roman)

A middle course is the safest. (Roman)

Be afraid and you will be safe. (Irish)

Be busy and you will be safe. (Roman)

Cheap things are safe from harm. (Roman)
He goes safely who has nothing. (French)
He may lie safely who comes from afar. (Italian)
He that keeps out of harm's way will gather goodly riches. (Danish)
It is best to be on the safe side, it saves trouble in the end. (Danish)
It is better to be safe than sorry. (American)
Keep to the common road, and thou wilt be safe. (Roman)
Safely bound, safely found. (English)
The way to be safe is never to feel secure. (Czech)
Things locked up are safe. (Roman)
Things lost are safe. (Roman)

Safeguard

From smooth water God preserve me, from rough I will preserve myself. (Spanish)
From those I trust God guard me, from those I mistrust I will guard myself.
    (Italian)

Safety

A strong shield is the safety of leaders. (Roman)
A subject faithful to his king is the safety of the kingdom. (Roman)
He is in safety who rings the tocsin. (Spanish)
He most values safety who experiences danger. (Persian)
Safety must sometimes be bought with money. (Roman)
There is safety in many advisors. (Roman)
There is safety in numbers. (Italian)

Sages

The gods and demons revere the words of the sages. (Chinese)
After a thousand years, the words of the sages still pertain. (Chinese)

Said

Nothing is said now that has not been said before. (Roman)
Sooner said than done. (English)
That which is unsaid, may be spoken; that which is said, cannot be unsaid. (Danish)
The less said the sooner mended. (Dutch)
The more said the less done. (English)

Sail, Sailor

A smooth sea never made a skilled sailor. (English)
Hoist your sail according to the fair wind. (Japanese)
It is good rowing with set sail. (Dutch)
It is good sailing with wind and tide. (Dutch)
It is safest sailing within reach of the shore. (Dutch)
One should learn to sail in all winds. (Italian)
Raise your sail one foot and you get ten feet of wind. (Chinese)

Sail while the breeze blows: wind and tide wait for no man. (Danish)

Set your sail according to the fair wind. (French)

Too many sailors sink the ship. (Egyptian)

You are not a sailor until your boat has been under full sail. (Irish)

You cannot sail as you would, but as the wind blows. (Danish)

Saint

All are not saints who go to church. (Italian)

All saints do not work miracles. (Italian)

Don't believe him a saint until you have seen his miracles. (Spanish)

Every saint has his festival. (Italian)

Little saints also perform miracles. (Danish)

Saint cannot if God will not. (French)

Saints appear to fools. (Portuguese)

Saints don't fill the belly. (Portuguese)

Saints fly only in the eyes of their disciples. (Indian)

The father of a saint, the son of a sinner. (Spanish)

The saint who works no cures has few pilgrims at his shrine. (French)

To every saint his candle. (French)

We pray to God to give us saints, but not too many. (Spanish)

Satiety

Satiety causes disgust. (German)

Satiety has killed more men than hunger. (Roman)

Salt

Salt never calls itself sweet. (Jamaican)

Salt seasons everything. (Roman)

Salt seasons tainted meat, but what if the salt is tainted? (Persian)

Salt spilt is never all gathered. (Spanish)

Salvation

He that will not be saved needs no preacher. (German)

No sin, no salvation. (Russian)

Save and lift up those in sorrow and difficulties. (Chinese)

The first step toward salvation is the recognition of sin. (Roman)

Who cannot work out his salvation by heart will not do it by book. (French)

Salve

There is a salve for everything. (German)

There's a salve for every sore. (English)

Sandpiper

Every sandpiper praises its own swamp. (Russian)

Sap
No sap from a dry tree. (Unknown)

Sarcasm
Praise undeserved is sarcasm in disguise. (Irish)

Satan
Ol' Satan couldn't get along without plenty of help. (American)

Satisfy, Satisfaction
He is rich that is satisfied. (French)
I being satisfied, the world is satisfied. (Italian)
No one is satisfied with his lot. (Roman)
Satisfaction is natural wealth. (Japanese)

Sauce
It is the sauce that makes the fish edible. (French)
What's sauce for the goose is sauce for the gander. (French)

Save, Saving
A penny saved is a penny earned. (English)
For age and want save while you may, no morning sun lasts all day. (American)
Better to save than to spend. (Irish)
Give nine, save ten. (Kurdish)
He that does not save pennies, will never have pounds. (English)
He who eats and puts by, has sufficient for two meals. (Spanish)
He who saves in little things, can be liberal in great ones. (German)
He who saves, finds. (Spanish)
He who would save, should begin with the mouth. (Danish)
If you eat it up at supper, you cannot have it for breakfast. (Spanish)
Look after the pennies and the pounds will look after themselves. (English)
Mind the pence and save a pound. (English)
Money saved is as good as money gained. (Danish)
Put by for a rainy day. (Egyptian)
Save while your sack is full. (Croatian)
Saving is a greater art than gaining. (German)
Saving is getting. (French)
Who saves when he gets has when he needs. (Finnish)

Say, Saying
Beware what you say, when and to whom. (Roman)
Everybody says it, nobody knows it. (Danish)
He acts wisely who says little. (Roman)
He that says what he should not, will hear what he would not. (Danish)
He who says nothing never lies. (Italian)

It is better to say nothing than not enough. (Roman)
It is difficult to say what is common in a distinct way. (Roman)
Nothing can be said that has not been said before. (Roman)
Of what does not concern you say nothing, good or bad. (Italian)
Say before they say. (Spanish)
Say but little, and say it well. (Irish)
Say it tomorrow if you have something to say. (Japanese)
Say little and listen much. (Greek)
Saying is one thing, doing another. (Italian)
Tell it well, or say nothing. (Spanish)
The one who says much is likely to say too much. (Yoruban)
The one who says what he likes will hear what he does not like. (Roman)
There can be nothing said now that has not been said before. (Roman)
There is much distance between saying and doing. (Mexican)
When you say one thing, the clever person understands three. (Chinese)
Who says little has little to answer for. (German)

Sayings
All old sayings have something in them. (Icelandic)

Scald
When you're scalded by the hot, you blow on the cold. (Yiddish)

Scales
Good scales bring good customers. (Greek)
Just scales and full measure injure no man. (Chinese)

Scandal
Scandal is like an egg: when it hatches it has wings. (African)

Scar
He laughs at scars who never felt a wound. (German)
He who scratches a scar is twice wounded. (Russian)

Scarce
Scarce things are prized. (Roman)

Scatter, Scattering
If the cattle are scattered the tiger seizes them. (Burmese)
Scattering is easier than gathering. (Irish)
Strike the shepherd and scatter the sheep. (the Bible)
What one gathers, another scatters. (German)

Scent
An empty cask retains the scent of the wine that filled it. (Irish)

Scheme, Scheming

The best-laid schemes o' mice an' men gang aft a-gley [or, oft go awry]. (English)

Scheming seldom has success. (American)

Schlemiel (an unlucky person)

The schlemiel kills a rooster and still it hops; he winds up a clock and at once it stops.
   (Yiddish)

The schlemiel lands on his back and bruises his nose. (Yiddish)

Scholar, Scholars

A nation's treasure: scholars. (Chinese)

A scholar's ink lasts longer than a martyr's blood. (Irish)

A table is not blessed if it has fed no scholars. (Yiddish)

Great scholars are not the shrewdest men. (French)

It is a sacrilege for scholars to malign scholars. (Roman)

Poverty is the common fate of scholars. (Chinese)

Rivalry of scholars advances wisdom. (Yiddish)

The greatest scholars are not the wisest men. (Roman)

School

Despise school and remain a fool. (Roman)

In school, we learn not the lessons of life, but of school. (Roman)

John has been to school to learn to be a fool. (English)

No more pencils, no more books, no more teachers' dirty looks. (American)

Tell no tales out of school. (German)

Science

Every form of nonsense is promoted under the name of science. (Spanish)

Half of science is putting forth the right questions. (English)

Scoffer

The scoffer's own house is often on fire. (Danish)

Scold

He scolds most that can hurt the least. (Danish)

Score, Scores

Man only ever scores nine out of ten. (Hausan)

Scorpion

Every stone conceals a lurking scorpion. (Roman)

Nature, not spite, give the scorpion its sting. (Persian)

Scratch

Scratch me and I'll scratch thee. (English)

Scratch people where they itch. (German)
You scratch my back and I'll scratch yours. (American)

Scylla and Charybdis
In avoiding Charybdis, he falls into Scylla. (Roman)

Sea
A great sea comes not through a narrow strait. (Irish)
Being on sea, sail; being on land, settle. (Roman)
Better on the heath with an old cart that at sea in a new ship. (Dutch)
Drops that gather one by one finally become a sea. (Persian)
Even the sea, great as it is, grows calm. (Italian)
He ought not to complain of the sea who returns to it a second time. (Italian)
He that is once at sea, must either sail or sink. (Danish)
He that would go to sea for pleasure would go to Hell for a pastime. (French)
He who is at sea does not direct the winds. (French)
In a calm sea, every man is a pilot. (German)
Praise the sea, and keep on land. (Italian)
Smooth seas do not make skillful sailors. (African)
Ten thousand rivers flow into the sea, but the sea is never full. (Chinese)
The one who knows not his way to the sea should seek the river for his companion.
    (Roman)
The roughest seas are far from land. (Roman)
The sea has an enormous thirst and an insatiable appetite. (French)
The sea refuses no river. (French)
Those who go to sea are only a plank's thickness from death. (Unknown)
Where the sea goes let the sands go. (Spanish)

Seagull
The seagull that flies highest sees farthest. (French)

Seaman
The good seaman is known in bad weather. (Italian)

Search
No man looks for another in a sack, unless he has been there himself. (Danish)
Search not too curiously lest you find trouble. (English)
The fun is in the search, not in the finding. (German)

Season
Everything is good in its season. (Italian)
There is a season for all things. (Roman)
To everything there is a season, and a time to every purpose under Heaven. (the Bible)

The Seasons (Winter, Spring, Summer, Fall)

A cold April the barn will fill. (English)

A dripping June sets all in tune. (German)

A good year is determined by its spring. (Portuguese)

A green Yule makes a fat churchyard. (Danish)

A leap year is never a good sheep year. (English)

A load of March dust is worth a ducat. (German)

A peck of March dust is worth a king's ransom. (Spanish)

A swarm in May is worth a load of hay; a swarm in June is worth a silver spoon; but a
     swarm in July is not worth a fly. (Roman)

A warm January, a cold May. (Welsh)

April showers brings May flowers. (English)

Barnaby bright, Barnaby bright, the longest day and the shortest night. (English)

Buy a fan in December and firewood in July. (Spanish)

By a single fallen leaf, the whole world knows that autumn has come. (Korean)

Christmas comes but once a year. (Italian)

Consider how long the winter will last. (Roman)

Every spring has an autumn and every road an ending. (Persian)

Everything in its season, and turnips in Advent. (Spanish)

He who passes a winter's day passes one of his mortal enemies. (French)

If Saint Paul's day be fair and clear, it will betide a happy year. (English)

It is a hard winter when dogs eat dogs. (English)

It is not spring until you can plant your foot upon twelve daisies. (Italian)

It is the season, not the soil, that brings the crop. (Roman)

It will not always be summer. (Greek)

March comes in like a lion and goes out like a lamb. (English)

May and December never agree. (French)

May chickens come cheeping. (French)

Ne'er cast a clout till May be out. (English)

One crow does not make a winter. (Dutch)

One lark does not make it spring. (French)

One swallow does not make it spring. (Greek)

One swallow doesn't make a summer. (English)

September blow soft, till the fruit's in the loft. (English)

Spring has come when you can put your foot on three daisies. (English)

Spring is when you feel like whistling even with a shoe full of slush. (English)

Summer will not last forever. (Roman)

The blossoms in the spring are the fruit in autumn. (Roman)

The summer works for the winter. (Georgian)

The summer's heat or winter's cold is only until the equinox. (Japanese)

When it rains in August, it rains honey and wine. (Spanish)

When it rains in February, it will be temperate all the year. (Spanish)

When the summer is winter, and the winter is summer, it is a sorry year. (Spanish)

Winter comes fast on the lazy. (Irish)

Winter either bites with its teeth or lashes with its tail. (Slavic)

Winter finds out what summer lays up. (Slavic)

Winter is summer's heir. (Roman)

Seat, Seated

A seat in the council is honor without profit. (Portuguese)

He has command of the sack who is seated on it. (Danish)

The highest seat does not hold two. (Roman)

Those who have free seats at the play hiss first. (Chinese)

Who is well-seated should not budge. (German)

Secrecy

Secrecy is the beginning of tyranny. (Italian)

Secret, Secrets

A secret imparted is no longer a secret. (Italian)

A secret is like a dove: when it leaves my hand it takes wing. (Arabian)

Do not tell your secrets behind a wall or a hedge. (Spanish)

Don't tell a secret to anybody, unless you want the whole world to know it. (Roman)

External actions indicate internal secrets. (Roman)

Give up the smallest part of a secret, and the rest is no longer in your power. (German)

He who keeps his own secret avoids much mischief. (Spanish)

He who reveals his secret makes himself a slave. (Greek)

If you would keep your secret from an enemy, tell it not to a friend. (Poor Richard)

It is wise not to seek a secret, and honest not to reveal it. (Poor Richard)

Keep no secrets of thyself from thyself. (Greek)

Love, a cough, and money cannot keep a secret. (Spanish)

Love, grief, and money cannot be kept secret. (Spanish)

My chest locked, my soul safe. (Portuguese)

No secret but will come to light. (Japanese)

Nothing is so burdensome as a secret. (French)

Part with your head, but not with your secret. (Kurdish)

Tell your friend your secret, and he will set his foot on your neck. (Spanish)

The only way to keep a secret is to say nothing. (French)

The secret of two is God's secret, the secret of three is everybody's secret. (French)

There is no house without its secrets. (Spanish)

Three may keep a secret, if two of them are dead. (English)

Time and chance reveal all secrets. (English)

To be in on a secret is no blessing. (Yiddish)

Where you tell your secret you surrender your freedom. (Portuguese)

Wine in, secret out. (Yiddish)

Your friend has a friend; don't tell him your secret. (Yiddish)

Security

A house with two doors is difficult to guard. (Spanish)

False security is the great foe. (Unknown)

He that is too secure is not safe. (French)
Security is nowhere safe. (German)
Security is the first cause of misfortune. (German)

See

A priest sees people at their best, a lawyer at their worst, but a doctor sees them as they
    really are. (Belgian)
All rush to see a wedding or a fire. (Spanish)
Believe what you see and lay aside what you hear. (Arabian)
Better to see the face than to hear the name. (Japanese)
Distracted by what is far away, he does not see his nose. (Madagascan)
Drink nothing without seeing it, sign nothing without reading it. (Spanish)
He who does not open his eyes must open his purse. (German)
If the eyes do not want to see, neither light nor glasses will help. (German)
Many see more with one eye than others with two. (German)
Old people see best in the distance. (German)
One may have good eyes and see nothing. (Italian)
Seldom seen soon forgotten. (Italian)
They that live longest, see most. (Scottish)
To see is not to obtain. (Hausan)
What is not often seen is often neglected. (Welsh)
What you see in yourself is what you see in the world. (Afghani)
What you see is what you get; and you ain't seen nothin' yet. (American)
When you see a palm tree, the palm tree has seen you. (West African)
Who lives will see. (French)

Seed

A good seed, planted even in poor soil, will bear rich fruit by its own nature. (Roman)
Every seed knows its time. (Russian)
Good seed makes a good crop. (English)
If all the seeds that fall were to grow, then no one could follow the path under the trees.
    (West African)
The person who scatters seed on poor soil will not even recover his seed. (Mexican)
Unsown seed will not sprout. (Japanese)

Seeing

Seeing is believing. (English)
Seeing is better than hearing. (Hausan)
Seeing is different than being told. (African)
Seeing the bark you know the tree; seeing his face you know his character. (Burmese)
Seeing the eye does not prevent one from eating the head. (Hausan)

Seek, Sought

He that seeks, finds – and sometimes what he would rather not. (Italian)
He who seeks, finds. (Spanish)

Nothing sought, nothing found. (Unknown)
Seek and ye shall find. (Jesus)
Seek rather to make a man blush for his guilt than to shed his blood. (Roman)
Those seeking for one thing will find another. (Irish)
What is sought is found, what is neglected evades us. (Greek)
Who seeks more than he needs hinders himself from enjoying what he has. (Yiddish)
Who seeks what he should not, finds what he would not. (English)

Seem
Never seemed prison fair, or mistress foul. (French)
Things are not always what they seem. (American)
What you would seem to be, be really. (Poor Richard)

Self
Free me from that bad fellow, myself. (Roman)
It is more difficult to contend with oneself than with the world. (Kurdish)
It is not a little thing to know oneself. (Roman)
Let everyone look to himself, and no one will be lost. (Dutch)
Live with yourself: get to know how poorly furnished you are. (Roman)
Neither blame nor applaud yourself. (Roman)
Seek not yourself from outside yourself. (Roman)
To thine own self be true. (English)
Wherever you go, you can't get rid of yourself. (Polish)

Self-Control
He conquers twice who conquers himself. (Roman)
He is indeed a conqueror who conquers himself. (Italian)

Self-Defense
Self-defense is no crime. (German)

Self-Interest
All wish matters to be better with themselves than with others. (Roman)
Every miller draws the water to his own mill. (French)
Everyone for himself. (Hausan)
Everyone is eloquent in his own cause. (Roman)
Everyone rakes the fire under his own pot. (Chinese)
Love others well, but love thyself the most; give good for good, but not to your own cost.
   (Dutch)
Men often mistake themselves, seldom forget themselves. (Poor Richard)

Selfish, Selfishness
A dog with a bone knows no friends. (Dutch)
A morsel eaten selfishly gains no friends. (Spanish)
All had rather it were well for themselves than for another. (German)

Self-Love

He who is in love with himself need fear no rival. (Roman)
He who loves himself lacks love of neighbors. (German)
Many will hate you, if you love yourself. (Roman)
Self-love is a mote in every man's eye. (Roman)
Self-love is bad, and makes the eyes sad. (German)
Self-love is blind. (Dutch)
Self-love lacks love from others. (German)

Self-Praise

He who praises himself befouls himself. (Italian)
He who praises himself takes away praise from himself. (Mexican)
Self-praise is base. (Roman)
Self-praise is no praise at all. (English)
Self-praise is no recommendation. (American)
Self-praise is odious. (Roman)
Self-praise stinks. (German)
The praise one bestows upon oneself is of little value. (Roman)
You cannot propel yourself forward by patting yourself on the back. (Chinese)

Self-Reliance

Every man should support himself, and not hang upon another. (Spanish)
Love many, trust few and always paddle your own canoe. (American)

Self-Sacrifice

A man will die for one who recognizes his ability. (Japanese)

Sell, Seller

Beat your drum and sell your wares. (German)
Beat your gong and sell your candles. (Chinese)
Better to sell cheap than for credit. (Hausan)
Every seller praises his wares. (Yiddish)
He that sells upon trust, loses many friends, and always wants money. (Poor Richard)
He who hangs out a branch wants to sell his wine. (Spanish)
Never sell the bearskin till you have killed the bear. (French)
No melon-peddler cries: Bitter melons!; no wine-dealer says: Sour wine! (Chinese)
Pleasing ware is half sold. (German)
Seldom does anyone sell a good horse. (Mexican)
Sell as the markets go. (German)
Sell me dear, and measure me fair. (Italian)
Sell not virtue to purchase wealth, nor liberty to purchase power. (Poor Richard)
When you sell the cow, you sell the milk as well. (Dutch)

Senile

No sooner wise than senile. (Unknown)

Sermon

A lengthy sermon is intolerable. (Roman)
Funeral sermon, lying sermon. (German)
Long sermon, little attention. (Unknown)
Preach a sermon according to your listeners. (Japanese)

Serpent

A serpent, though put in a bamboo tube, cannot crawl straight. (Korean)
As many cherish the serpent, so many will it bite (Kashmiri).
If a serpent loves you, wear it as a necklace. (Egyptian)
The serpent brings forth nothing but little serpents. (Egyptian)

Servant

A servant and a cock must be kept but one year. (Portuguese)
A true servant speaks no ill of his former master. (Chinese)
Do not employ handsome servants. (Chinese)
Do not stuff your servant with bread, and he won't ask for cheese. (Spanish)
Every great house is full of haughty servants. (Roman)
Great men's servants don't think little of themselves. (German)
He that would be ill served should keep plenty of servants. (Italian)
He who has servants has unavoidable enemies. (Spanish)
He who makes himself a servant is expected to remain a servant. (Italian)
If you pay not the servant, he will pay himself. (German)
In the master there is the servant, in the servant there is the master. (Roman)
It is bad to have a servant, but worse to have a master. (Portuguese)
Let no man be the servant of another, who can be his own master. (Roman)
Play with a servant and he will insult you. (Egyptian)
Servants to the rich are the most abject. (Roman)
The more servants, the worse service. (Dutch)
The tongue is the worst part of a bad servant. (Roman)
Who has many servants has many thieves. (Dutch)

Serve

He who serves is not free. (Spanish)
He who serves many masters must neglect some of them. (Spanish)
He who serves small masters is himself one of them. (German)
He who serves the people has a bad master. (German)
He who serves two masters must lie to one of them. (Italian)
He who will not serve one master must needs serve many. (Italian)
He who would serve everybody gets thanks from nobody. (Danish)
If you want to be served, serve yourself. (Portuguese)
Lions and leopards do not serve. (Yoruban)
No man can serve two masters. (Jesus)
Serve a lord, and you will know what it is to be vexed. (Portuguese)
To serve the ungrateful is an offense to the gods. (Roman)

Who serves well and says nothing makes claim enough. (Italian)
Who serves well asks enough. (French)
You cannot serve God and mammon. (Jesus)
You cannot serve or satisfy two masters. (Irish)

Service, Services

A service done to the unwilling is no service. (Roman)
Be first, that you may be of service. (Roman)
Service is greatness. (Kashmiri)
Service is not inheritance. (Italian)
Services unrequired go unrequited. (German)
Unwilling service earns no thanks. (Danish)

Servitude

Servitude, the cage of the soul. (Roman)

Seven

As one is at seven, so one is at seventy. (Yiddish)
Seven is company, nine a brawl. (American)
Seven trades but no luck. (Arabian)
Seven will not wait for one. (Russian)

Sexual Relations

After sexual intercourse, every animal is sad. (Roman)
Below the navel there is neither religion nor truth. (Italian)
The body is excited by infrequent coitus, by frequent it relaxes. (Roman)

Shade

Do not cut down the tree that gives you shade. (Egyptian)
Fruit ripens not well in the shade. (Roman)
He waits in the sun for the shade to come. (Burmese)
No tree so small but it can give shade. (German)
When the tree falls there is no shade. (Chinese)

Shadow

A crooked stick will have a crooked shadow. (French)
A hair casts its shadow on the ground. (Spanish)
A man cannot jump over his own shadow. (Yiddish)
A shadow is a feeble thing, but no sun can drive it away. (Swedish)
Even the shadow of a disagreeable man is deformed. (Singhalese)
Grasp not at the shadow and so lose the substance. (Korean)
If you are standing upright, don't worry if your shadow is crooked. (Chinese)
No man sees his shadow who faces the sun. (Danish)
No sunshine but hath some shadow. (English)
Nobody can rest in his own shadow. (Hungarian)

One's shadow grows larger than life when admired by the light of the moon. (Chinese)
The hill's shadow is not cast upon the mountain. (German)

Shake

All that shakes falls not. (German)
Don't shake the tree when the pears fall off themselves. (Slavic)
The one who tries to shake a tree stump only shakes himself. (Yoruban)

Shallow

Shallow brooks are noisy. (English)
Shallow waters make a great noise. (Irish)

Shame, Shamed

A bad haircut is two people's shame. (Danish)
A long life has many shames. (Japanese)
A shamefaced man seldom acquires wealth. (Irish)
He who tells lies to gain honor will be shamed. (Yoruban)
Many a one would like to lay his own shame on another man's back. (Danish)
Natural things are without shame. (Roman)
Shame comes to no man unless he himself helps it on the way. (Danish)
Shame forbids what the law does not. (Roman)
Shame lasts longer than poverty. (Dutch)
Some thinking to avenge their shame increase it. (French)
The beginning of shame is baring the body in public. (Roman)
The longer the life, the more the shame. (Japanese)
There is no shame in not knowing but in not wanting to know. (Unknown)
Three ailments without shame: love, an itch, and thirst. (Irish)
What is no sin, is no shame. (German)
Whate'er's begun in anger ends in shame. (Poor Richard)
Who fears no shame comes to no honor. (Dutch)
Who has no shame all the world is his own. (Italian)
Who is not shamed by his sins, sins double. (German)

Share, Shared

A candle loses nothing by lighting another candle. (Italian)
He who shares honey with the bear, hath the least part of it. (Roman)
Share and share alike. (German)
Share not your pears with your master, either in earnest or in jest. (Unknown)
Shared joy is a double joy; shared sorrow is half a sorrow. (Swedish)
Shared sorrow is half sorrow. (Danish)
We can enjoy nothing without someone to share the pleasure. (Roman)
What we share with another ceases to be our own. (Roman)
Who would share in the meal must also share in the work. (German)

Sharp, Sharpen

Jade and men, both are sharpened by hard tools. (Chinese)

Man must be sharpened on man, like knife on stone. (Chinese)

Too keen an edge does not cut, too fine a point does not pierce. (French)

Shave, Shaven

A beard once washed is half shaven. (Portuguese)

A beard well lathered is half shaved. (Spanish)

Shear

Shear the sheep but don't flay them. (Dutch)

When the sheep are sheared, the lambs tremble. (Yiddish)

Sheath

The blade wears out the sheath. (French)

Sheep

A good sheep bleats little and gives much wool. (English)

A lazy sheep thinks its wool heavy. (English)

All the sheep are not for the wolf. (Italian)

Better to give the wool than the sheep. (Italian)

Do not allow the sheep to die for a halfpenny of tar. (Chinese)

Even counted sheep are eaten by the wolf. (German)

Every sheep is suspended by its own heels. (Egyptian)

Every time the sheep bleats it loses a mouthful. (Italian)

He who has sheep has fleeces. (Spanish)

It is a bad sheep that is too lazy to carry its own fleece. (Danish)

It's a foolish sheep that makes the wolf its confessor. (Italian)

It's a poor sheep that cannot carry its own wool. (German)

Make yourself a sheep and the wolf will eat you. (French)

No sheep runs into the mouth of a sleeping wolf. (Dutch)

One mangy sheep spoils a whole flock. (Danish)

One sheep follows another. (Unknown)

Paired sheep drown one another. (Dutch)

Silly sheep: where one goes, all go. (Spanish)

The deceived sheep went for wool and came back shorn. (Spanish)

The scabbier the sheep the harder it bleats. (Dutch)

The sheep that bleat the most give the least milk. (Danish)

The sheep which moves in the company of dogs will eat excrement. (Yoruban)

There is a black sheep in every flock. (Roman)

There's a black sheep in every family. (American)

When one sheep is over the dam, the rest follow. (Dutch)

Where one sheep goes, all the others follow behind. (Spanish)

Shepherd

A lazy shepherd is a wolf's friend. (Welsh)

A poor shepherd makes the wolf void wool. (French)

Red sky in the morning, shepherds take warning. (German)

Straying shepherd, straying sheep. (German)

Strike the shepherd and scatter the sheep. (the Bible)

The good shepherd shears, not flays. (Italian)

The more shepherds, the less care. (Danish)

The shepherd smells of sheep, even when he becomes a nobleman. (Greek)

Without a shepherd, the sheep are not a flock. (Russian)

Shine

Even a tin knocker will shine on a dirty floor. (Irish)

Ship

A great ship is often lost because of one man. (Irish)

A great ship must have deep water. (Dutch)

A ship and a woman are ever repairing. (English)

A ship and a woman ever require mending. (Roman)

Do not ship all in one bottom. (German)

Don't build a new ship out of old wood. (Chinese)

Don't spoil the ship for a halfpenny-worth of tar. (English)

Last ship, best ship. (English)

Often has a ship been lost close to the harbor. (Irish)

The ship that has two captains will sink. (Arabian)

When a large ship has opened a way, it is easy for a small one to follow. (Chinese)

Shipwreck

A shipwreck may occur near the beach. (Japanese)

A shipwreck on the beach is a lighthouse to the sea. (Dutch)

A common shipwreck is a consolation to all. (Roman)

Let another's shipwreck be your sea-mark. (Danish)

No one can complain of the sea who twice suffers shipwreck. (German)

The man who has suffered shipwreck shudders even at a calm sea. (Roman)

The one who suffers shipwreck twice is unjust to blame Neptune. (Roman)

Shirt

Even a silk shirt only clothes a naked body. (German)

Let not your shirt know all your thoughts. (Italian)

My shirt is nearer than my cloak. (Dutch)

Shoe, Shoes

A buckle is a great addition to an old shoe. (Irish)

A great shoe fits not a little foot. (English)

A handsome shoe often pinches the foot. (French)

Don't throw away your own shoes till you have got new ones. (Dutch)
Everybody knows best where his own shoe pinches. (German)
If the shoe fits, wear it. (English)
If you have one pair of good soles it is better than two pairs of good uppers. (Irish)
It is of no use making shoes for geese. (Danish)
No one knows where another's shoe pinches. (Dutch)
Not every shoe fits every foot. (German)
Not every wood will make wooden shoes. (Danish)
One shoe will not fit every foot. (German)
Shoes too large trip one up. (German)
The same shoe does not fit every foot. (Roman)
The shoe knows whether the sock has holes. (German)
When you buy shoes, measure your feet. (Chinese)

Shoemaker
A shoemaker's wife and a smith's mare are always the worst shod. (Spanish)
No shoemaker is well shod. (Spanish)
Shoemakers go to mass and pray that sheep may die. (Spanish)
The shoemaker speaks of his last and the sailor of his mast. (Yiddish)
The shoemaker's son always goes barefoot. (English)

Shoot, Shooting
He must shoot well who always hits the mark. (Dutch)
He who shoots often, hits at last. (German)

Shop
Every shop has its trick. (Italian)

Shore
Keep close to the shore; let others venture into the deep. (Roman)

Shorn
Many a sheep goes out woolly and comes home shorn. (Danish)
Many who go out for wool come back shorn. (Unknown)

Short Cut
A short cut is often a wrong cut. (Danish)
Short cuts are roundabouts. (Roman)
Where the road is straight, don't look for a short cut. (Russian)

Shoulder
Bare is the shoulder that has no kinsman near. (Irish)
Who lets another sit on his shoulder, will soon have him on his head. (German)

Show

He who does not show himself, is overlooked. (Spanish)

The show must go on. (American)

Shrew

A shrew gets her wish but suffers in the getting. (Irish)

A shrew of a wife may yet be in the right. (Yiddish)

A shrew will get her wish though her soul will not get mercy. (Scottish)

Shrewdness

By application a docile shrewdness conquers every difficulty. (Roman)

Shrimp

Better the tail of a shrimp than the head of a sardine. (Japanese)

Shrimps may dance but they do not leave the river. (Japanese)

The sleeping shrimp is carried away by the current. (Mexican)

Though they jump around, shrimps cannot leave the river. (Chinese)

Shroud, Shrouds

Shrouds are made without pockets. (Yiddish)

Shun

Many shun the brook, and fall into the river. (German)

Many shun the sword, and come to the gallows. (German)

Shun a he-goat's front, a horse's hind, and a fool's every side. (Yiddish)

Shun evil company. (Irish)

Shy, Shyness

Do not be shy of those who are not shy. (Albanian)

He that wants should not be bashful. (Italian)

Who is shy dies from hunger. (Albanian)

Sick, Sickly

A sick mind cannot endure any harshness. (Roman)

Sick people are like kings. (Madagascan)

Sickly body, sickly mind. (German)

The sick man is free to say all. (Italian)

The sick man sleeps when the debtor cannot. (Italian)

To the sick, while there is life there is hope. (Roman)

Sickle

Take not your sickle to another man's corn. (Danish)

Sickness

A king, a master, a parent, a judge, may fail to frighten us; but sickness coming brings
 with it successful reproof. (Roman)

In time of sickness man is ever on his best behavior. (Roman)
Sickness comes at a gallop but departs at a slow trot. (Spanish)
Sickness comes in haste, and goes at leisure. (Danish)
Sickness comes on horseback and departs on foot. (Dutch)
Sickness comes uninvited – no need to bespeak it. (Danish)
Sickness is every man's master. (Danish)
Sickness shows us what we are. (Roman)
Sickness soaks the purse. (German)

Sides
There are two sides to everything. (German)

Sieve
Everyone who buys a sieve knows that it cannot hold water. (Hausan)

Sight
Better squinting than blind. (Dutch)
Out of sight, out of mind. (American)
Sight goes before hearsay. (Danish)
The keenest of all our senses is the sense of sight. (Roman)
Who is lost from sight is lost from the heart. (Persian)

Sign, Signs
All signs are misleading. (Yiddish)
Old signs do not deceive. (Danish)

Silence
Better eloquent silence than eloquent speech. (Yiddish)
Even silence speaks. (Hausan)
He who cannot keep silence cannot speak. (Swedish)
I grew up among wise men and found that there is nothing better for man than silence.
   (West African)
If a word be worth a shekel, then silence is worth two. (Yiddish)
No one betrays himself by silence. (German)
No one is hanged for keeping silence. (Spanish)
No wisdom like silence. (Chinese)
Silence and reflection cause no dejection. (German)
Silence answers much. (Dutch)
Silence gives consent. (Spanish)
Silence is a fence around wisdom. (Yiddish)
Silence is a fine jewel for a woman, but it is little worn. (Yiddish)
Silence is a woman's best garment. (Greek)
Silence is also speech. (Yiddish)
Silence is an attribute of the dead: he who is alive speaks. (Yoruban)
Silence is golden. (English)

Silence is golden, speech is silver. (American)
Silence is learned by the many misfortunes of life. (Roman)
Silence is more eloquent than words. (German)
Silence is not always a sign of wisdom, but babbling is ever a mark of folly.
     (Poor Richard)
Silence is the best answer to the stupid. (Egyptian)
Silence is the door of consent. (African)
Silence is the greatest ornament in a woman. (Roman)
Silence is the voice of complicity. (Roman)
Silence is wisdom and gets a man friends. (Roman)
Silence is worth a thousand pieces of silver. (Burmese)
Silence is worth more than excessive talking. (Mexican)
Silence keeps birds and men safe. (Japanese)
Silence keeps the flies out (Arabian)
Silence surpasses speech. (Japanese)
Silence was never written down. (Italian)
Some things are better praised by silence than by remark. (Roman)
Speaking comes by nature, silence by understanding. (German)
Speaking is silver, silence is gold. (Dutch)
Speaking silence is better than senseless speech. (Danish)
Speech is often repented, silence never. (Danish)
Speech is silvern but silence is golden. (Swiss)
The fruit of silence is tranquility. (Arabian)
The silence of the people is a warning for the king. (French)
There is no reply to the ignorant like keeping silence. (Turkish)
Though silence is not necessarily an admission, neither is it a denial. (Roman)
We must have reasons for speech but we need none for silence. (French)

Silent

A silent man is seldom ridiculed for his thoughts. (German)
A silent man's words are not brought into court. (Danish)
A silent mouth is sweet to hear. (Irish)
A silent pig digs the deepest root. (Lithuanian)
A silent woman is always more admired than a noisy one. (Roman)
Be silent and you will pass for a philosopher. (Roman)
Be silent, or say something better than silence. (German)
Better to be silent than speak ill. (Portuguese)
Deliver us from a silent man, and a dog that does not bark. (Spanish)
Even a fool is thought wise if he keeps silent, and discerning if he holds his tongue.
     (Italian)
He who is silent gains store. (Spanish)
It is best to be silent in a bad cause. (Roman)
It is better to be silent in a bad situation. (Hausan)
It is but a small merit to observe silence, but a grave fault to speak of matters on which
     we should be silent. (Roman)

It is well for one to know more than he says. (Roman)
It is well to know how to be silent till it is time to speak. (Portuguese)
Never miss a good chance to shut up. (American)
The one who is silent is seen to consent. (Roman)
The silent dog is the first to bite. (German)
The silent find peace in everything. (Spanish)
The silent man is most trusted. (Danish)
The silent sin not, nor tells lies. (Spanish)

Silk
The finest silk is soon stained. (German)

Silly
It is sweet to be silly in places. (Roman)

Silver
A silver hammer breaks an iron door. (French)
He that has no silver in his purse, should have silver on his tongue. (Chinese)
Silver has no shine while it is hidden in the earth. (Roman)
Silver has no splendor of its own, unless it shines by temperate use. (Roman)

Simile
No simile runs on all fours [i.e., applicable in every case]. (Roman)

Simplicity
Simplicity is nowadays very rare. (Roman)

Sin, Sins
A man may know his Holy Writ and yet may grievous sins commit. (Yiddish)
A secret sin is half forgiven. (Spanish)
Adam ate the apple, and our teeth still ache. (Hungarian)
All sins cast long shadows. (Irish)
Better the world should know you as a sinner than God know you as a hypocrite.
   (Danish)
Each man must suffer for his own sin. (Chinese)
Every man's sin falls on his own head. (Roman)
Everyone finds sin sweet and repentance bitter. (Danish)
Everyone thinks himself without sin because he has not those of others. (Italian)
Few are unwilling to sin, all know how. (Roman)
For the wages of sin is death. (St Paul)
Habit in sinning takes away the sense of sin. (Roman)
He sins as much who holds the bag as he who puts into it. (French)
He who sins when drunk will have to atone for it when sober. (Roman)
In his sleep it isn't the man who sins but his dreams. (Yiddish)

In men every mortal sin is venial, in women every venial sin is mortal. (Italian)

It costs little to sin, but much to make amends. (Spanish)

It is better to avoid sin than to flee from death. (German)

It is no excuse for sin if we have sinned for the sake of a friend. (Roman)

It is more wicked to love a sin than to commit one. (Roman)

It is not a sin to sell dear, but it is to make ill measure. (Irish)

It's a sin to steal a pin. (English)

Keep yourself from temptations and God will keep you from sins. (Italian)

Little sins make room for great ones. (German)

Many sin like King David, but few repent like him. (Yiddish)

Nip sin in the bud. (French)

No man suffers for another's sins – he has enough of his own. (Yiddish)

No one has license to sin. (Roman)

No one leaves this world without paying for his sins. (Mexican)

No sin stands alone. (Spanish)

Not to be ashamed of sin is double sin. (German)

Old sins cast long shadows. (English)

One man sins, the other is punished. (Roman)

One sin draws a hundred after it. (Welsh)

Sin is cheap, making amends costly. (Spanish)

Sin is the root of sorrow. (Chinese)

Sins of omission are seldom fun. (Arabian)

That which comes with sin, goes with sorrow. (Danish)

The bad refrain from sin for fear of punishment. (Roman)

The fruit of sin is bitter. (Roman)

The greater part of mankind is angry with the sinner and not with the sin. (Roman)

The green burns for the dry, and the righteous pay for sinners. (Spanish)

The knowledge of sin is the beginning of salvation. (Roman)

The one who denies his sins does not atone for them. (Roman)

The sins of the fathers are visited upon the children. (Unknown)

To see life perishing, and not save it, is one of the greatest of sins. (Chinese)

Where a chest lies open, a righteous man may sin. (Chinese)

Who avoids small sins, does not fall into great ones. (German)

With a good name one may easily sin. (Dutch)

Without knowledge, without sin. (German)

Sincere, Sincerity

A sincere thought can influence heaven and earth. (Chinese)

Be truly what you would be thought to be. (French)

No one can succeed without sincerity. (Chinese)

Sincerity embodies the virtues. (Chinese)

Sincerity gives wings to power. (Roman)

Sincerity will meet with doubts; faithfulness will suffer slander. (Chinese)

There is honor in sincerity. (Roman)

To act sincerely with the insincere is dangerous. (Chinese)

Sing, Singing

Every bird sings as it is beaked. (Dutch)
He that sings to himself is the best pleased. (Danish)
He who sings drives away sorrow. (Italian)
I can't sing a note but I know all about it. (Yiddish)
I sing the song of the person whose bread I eat. (French)
It is not for the swan to teach eaglets to sing. (Danish)
Let every bird sing its own note. (Danish)
Loving and singing are not to be forced. (German)
Martha sings well when she has had her fill. (Portuguese)
Sing before breakfast, cry before night. (Roman)
Singing lightens sorrows. (Spanish)
Singing makes the heart merry. (Mexican)
Some sing who are not merry. (Italian)
The Italians cry, the Germans bawl, and the French sing. (French)
Those who wish to sing can always find a song. (Swedish)

Singer

Every singer is a drinker. (Spanish)
The worst singers sing the loudest. (Spanish)

Single

A single arrow is easily broken, but not ten in a bundle. (Japanese)
A single beam cannot support a great house. (Chinese)
A single blow does not fell a mighty oak, but many blows will bring it down.
   (Spanish)
A single conversation with a wise man is better than ten years of study. (Chinese)
A single day grants what a whole year denies. (Dutch)
A single penny fairly got is worth a thousand that are not. (German)
A single rose does not mean it's spring. (Persian)
A single stick may smoke, but it will not burn. (Ethiopian)
A single stroke fell not the oak. (German)

Sinner

The greater the sinner, the greater the saint. (English)

Sit

All sit in front for a wedding, in back for a wake. (the Editor)
Don't budge, if you sit at ease. (German)
He sits well who can rise without help. (Danish)
One who sits between two chairs may easily fall down. (Rumanian)
Sit a while and go a mile. (Unknown)
Sit atop the mountain and watch the tigers fight. (Chinese)

Size

No man is so tall that he need never stretch, and none so small that he need never stoop. (Danish)

Size matters. (American)

Skeleton

There's a skeleton in every house. (Roman)

Skeptic, Skeptical

Better to be too credulous than too skeptical. (Chinese)

Skeptics are never deceived. (French)

Skill, Skilled

A good skill has a golden foundation. (Danish)

A skilled worker holds a key to a pantry. (Spanish)

Even from skillful hands, water may sometimes leak. (Japanese)

Every skilled man is to be trusted in his own art. (Roman)

Give a man a fish and you feed him for a day; teach a man to fish and you feed him for a lifetime. (English)

Having mastered the lesser difficulties, you will more safely venture on to greater achievements. (Roman)

He that makes one basket can make a hundred. (Spanish)

Skill will enable us to succeed in that which sheer force could not accomplish. (Roman)

'Tis skill, not strength, that guides the ship. (German)

Skin

The skin is nearer than the shirt. (French)

Sky

If the sky falls, hold up your hands. (Spanish)

If the sky falls, there will be broken pots. (Spanish)

If the sky should fall, we shall catch larks. (German)

Red sky in the morning, sailor take warning; red sky at night, sailor take delight. (English)

Red sky in the morning, shepherds take warning. (German)

The sky is not the less blue because the blind man does not see it. (Danish)

The sky's the limit. (American)

Slander, Slanderer

He who slanders his neighbor makes a rod for himself. (Dutch)

Slander cannot destroy an honest man: when the flood recedes the rock is there. (Chinese)

Slander expires at a good woman's door. (Danish)

Slander flies gently, but wounds deeply. (Roman)

Slander leaves a score behind it. (Danish)

Slander slays three persons: the speaker, the spoken to, and the spoken of. (Yiddish)
Slander, slander, some of it will stick. (French)
There is no remedy against the bite of a secret slanderer. (Roman)
Slanderers are the Devil's bellows, to blow up contention. (French)

Slap
Get a box on the ear and you get an enemy for good measure. (Yiddish)
The father slaps his son; the son slaps the dog; the dog slaps its own tail. (Unknown)

Slave, Slavery
A slave does not choose his master. (African)
A slave yesterday, today a freedman. (Roman)
Better a poor man's son than a rich man's slave. (Rumanian)
Better an old man's darling than a young man's slave. (French)
He who has been a slave from childhood knows not the value of rebellion. (Yoruban)
He will always be a slave, because he knows not how to live upon little. (Roman)
If to you the slaves belong, you are master and never wrong. (Yiddish)
The kind-hearted becomes a slave. (Burmese)
The most severe slavery is to be a slave to oneself. (Roman)
The slave rides in the same chariot as the master. (Roman)

Sleep, Sleeping
A sick man sleeps, but not a debtor. (Spanish)
All who snore are not asleep. (Danish)
Better straw, than nothing. (Portuguese)
He sleeps securely who has nothing to lose. (French)
He sleeps well, who is not conscious that he sleeps ill. (Roman)
He who sleeps catches no fish. (Italian)
He who sleeps forgets his hunger. (English)
He who sleeps much, learns little. (Spanish)
He who sleeps well does not feel the fleas. (Italian)
In sleep, all is forgotten. (Yiddish)
Long sleep makes a bare breech. (Irish)
One hour's sleep before midnight is worth two hours after. (English)
One sleeps tranquilly on the hurt of another. (Irish)
Seven hours of sleep is enough for both young and old. (Roman)
Six hours' sleep for a man, seven for a woman, eight for a fool. (English)
Sleep has no master. (Jamaican)
Sleep is a thief that steals half one's life. (German)
Sleep is the best cure for waking troubles. (Spanish)
Sleep is the best doctor. (Yiddish)
Sleep is the brother of death. (Irish)
Sleep is the image of death. (Roman)
Sleep on it, and you will come to a resolution. (Spanish)
Sleep without supping, and you'll rise without owing for it. (Poor Richard)

Sleeping people can't fall down. (Japanese)
The beginning of health is sleep. (Irish)
The child who will not let his mother sleep will not himself sleep. (Yoruban)
The more one sleeps, the less one lives. (Polish)
The more you sleep, the less you sin. (Russian)
The person who is tired will find time to sleep. (English)
When there is too much to be done, one goes to sleep. (Yiddish)
Who sleeps warmly, feels even cold. (Albanian)
Without sleep, without health. (English)
You roll seven times and wake up eight times. (Japanese)
You sleep only as well as your bed is laid. (American)

Slice

A slice off a cut loaf isn't missed. (Roman)

Slip

One slip may bring a lifetime of regret. (Chinese)
One slip of the foot involves a thousand ages of remorse. (Chinese)
The body pays for a slip of the foot, and gold pays for a slip of the tongue. (Malaysian)
There's many a slip 'twixt cup and lip. (English)
'Twixt the spoon and the lip, the morsel may slip. (Dutch)

Sloth, Slothful

A slothful man never has time. (Italian)
At evening the slothful man is busy. (German)
For the diligent, a week has seven days; for the slothful, seven tomorrows. (German)
Sloth is the beginning of vice. (Dutch)
Sloth is the mother of poverty. (German)
You must avoid that wicked siren Sloth. (Roman)

Slow

Slow and sure. (English)
Slow but sure. (German)

Small

A small body can hold a big soul. (Spanish)
A small bolt to hold the house is better than none at all. (Danish)
A small cloud may hide both sun and moon. (Danish)
A small competence is best. (Roman)
A small family is soon provided for. (English)
A small gift is better than a great promise. (German)
A small gift, but well-timed. (Roman)
A small hatchet fells a great oak. (Portuguese)
Alexander the Great was but of small stature. (Roman)
Every great thing is composed of many things that are small. (Roman)

From small beginnings come great things. (Dutch)
From small things a great heap is made. (Roman)
From trifling causes great results arise. (Roman)
In small boxes the best spice. (Dutch)
It is a small thing that outlives the man. (Irish)
Many a small make a great. (German)
Small handfuls make a load. (Irish)
Small is beautiful. (English)
Small men think they are small; great men never know they are great. (Chinese)
Small minds are captivated by trifles. (Roman)
Small profits and often are better than large profits and seldom. (German)
Small profits are sweet. (Danish)
Small rain lays great dust. (Italian)
Small saints also work miracles. (German)
Small showers fill the stream. (Hausan)
Small things become the small. (Roman)
Small things have their own peculiar charm. (Roman)
Small things will make a large pile. (Roman)
Small undertakings give great comfort. (German)
Small winnings make a heavy purse. (Chinese)

Smart
He that is too smart is surely done for. (Yiddish)

Smell
A clean stablehand smells of manure. (Spanish)
A dead man and an uninvited guest smell after three days. (Mexican)
If you will stir up the mire, you must bear the smell. (Danish)
Pigs and puppies have a very different smell. (Roman)
They that smell least, smell best. (Scottish)

Smile, Smiling
A smile will gain you ten more years of life. (Chinese)
A smiling face is half the meal. (Latvian)
One who smiles rather than rages is always the stronger. (Japanese)
There is no enemy against a smiling face. (Japanese)

Smith
A smith becomes a smith by working at the forge. (Roman)
Between smith and smith no money passes. (Spanish)
He is a bad smith who cannot bear smoke. (German)
He is a poor smith who is afraid of sparks. (Danish)
In a silversmith's house the knives are wooden. (Spanish)

Smoke

If you burn a house, can you conceal the smoke? (Unknown)
Much smoke, and little roast. (Italian)
No smoke without fire. (German)
Smoke follows the fairest face. (German)
The smoke of my land is brighter than the fire of another. (Spanish)
There is no fire without smoke. (Danish)
They who shun the smoke often fall into the fire. (Italian)
Where there's smoke, there's fire. (English)

Snail

The snail climbs the tree slowly and carefully. (Yoruban)

Snake

A snake deserves no pity. (Yiddish)
A snake lies hid in the grass. (Roman)
Because we focused on the snake, we missed the scorpion. (Egyptian)
Don't trouble a quiet snake. (Greek)
If you strike a snake without killing it, it will turn and bite you. (Chinese)
The snake bites a man only once. (Yoruban)
The snake moves and erases its tracks. (Albanian)
The snake must be straight to enter the hole. (Persian)
When the snake is old the frog will tease him. (Persian)
Whether small or large, a snake cannot be used as a belt. (Yoruban)

Snare

Always be on your guard: there are many snares for the good. (Roman)
In the snare laid for others is taken your own foot. (Roman)

Snow

From snow, whether baked or boiled, you will get nothing but water. (Spanish)
Year of snow, fruit will grow. (English)

Soap

It is a loss of soap to wash the ass's head. (Spanish)
One does not argue at the stream whether his soap will lather. (Yoruban)

Society

Reason and speech are the bond of society. (Roman)

Soft

Soft and fair goes far. (Spanish)

Soil

Cultivate not a barren soil. (Roman)

Every soil does not bear the same fruit. (Roman)
If one finger touches oil it will soil the others. (Nigerian)

Soldier, Soldiers

All are not soldiers who go to war. (Spanish)
At once a good general and a stout soldier. (Roman)
Old soldiers never die. (Danish)
Old soldiers never die, they simply fade away. (American)
Soldiers must be well paid, and well hanged. (German)
The best soldiers are not warlike. (Chinese)
The common soldier's blood makes the general great. (Italian)
The soldier's blood commends the captain. (Italian)
The soldiers fight, and the kings are heroes. (Yiddish)

Solitary, Solitude

A solitary man is either a brute or an angel. (Italian)
Solitude is the nest of thought. (Kurdish)
Solitude is the nurse of wisdom. (German)
Who hears music feels his solitude. (French)

Something

Better aught than naught. (German)
Remember that everyone you meet is afraid of something, loves something, and has lost
    something. (French)
Something is better than nothing. (Spanish)
You don't get something for nothing. (American)

Son, Sons

A son is the bone of hard times. (African)
A son should begin where his father has left off. (American)
Better a son given to gambling than a son given to drink. (Irish)
Good sons are born to good parents. (Korean)
He to whom God gives no sons, the Devil gives nephews. (Spanish)
It is a wise son that knows his own father. (Spanish)
It is easier to rule a nation than a son. (Chinese)
No son is as good as his father. (Korean)
One worthy son, one valuable gem. (Burmese)
Runaway son, a shining jewel; runaway daughter, tarnished. (Chinese)
The good son a good father makes. (Mexican)
The son thinks that he is one month older than his father. (Burmese)
The unruly son who marries is soon tamed. (Spanish)
Your son is your son until he marries, but your daughter is your daughter until you die.
    (Irish)

Song, Songs
A silly song may be sung in many ways. (Danish)
A sweet song has betrayed many. (German)
Black care will be soothed by song. (Roman)
Even a sweet song, sung too long, becomes disagreeable. (Korean)
Every new song can be sung to an old tune. (Yiddish)
Everybody thinks his own cuckoo sings better than another's nightingale. (German)
He who pitches too high won't get through his song. (German)
It's the melody that makes the song. (French)
New songs are eagerly sung. (German)
New songs are liked the best. (Danish)
No song can give pleasure for long, that is written by drinkers of water. (Roman)
No song, no supper. (German)
There are two sides to every story and twelve versions of every song. (Irish)
Water drinkers do not write songs. (Greek)
You will hate a beautiful song if you sing it too often. (Korean)

Soon
Better too soon than too late. (American)
Soon enough is well enough. (French)
Soon fire, soon ashes. (Dutch)
Soon gained, soon squandered. (French)
Soon grass, soon hay. (Dutch)
Soon hot, soon cold. (German)
Soon ripe, soon rotten. (Roman)
What flares up fast, extinguishes soon. (Turkish)

Soot
One who handles soot soon blackens his hands. (German)

Sorcerer
The sorcerer cannot exorcise his own demons. (Korean)

Sore, Sores
One always knocks oneself in the sore place. (French)
Different sores must have different salves. (English)

Sorrow, Sorrows
A child's sorrow is short-lived. (Danish)
A day of sorrow is longer than a month of joy. (Chinese)
A glad heart seldom sighs, but a sorrowful mouth often laughs. (Danish)
After joy, sorrow follows. (Chinese)
Don't let your sorrow come higher than your knees. (Portuguese)
Give wine to them that are in sorrow. (Roman)
He gains enough who loses sorrow. (French)

He who loves sorrow will always find something to mourn over. (Danish)

If sorrow would not talk it would die. (Serbian)

If the eyes don't see, the heart won't break. (Spanish)

Let each recall his own woes. (Roman)

Little sorrows are loud, great ones silent. (Danish)

Man is himself the author of every sorrow he endures. (Roman)

Our pleasures are shallow, our sorrows are deep. (Chinese)

Sorrow and ill weather come unsent for. (Roman)

Sorrow brings on premature old age. (Roman)

Sorrow dwells on the confines of pleasure. (Roman)

Sorrow follows pleasure. (Roman)

Sorrow for the death of a father lasts six months; sorrow for a mother, a year; sorrow for a wife, until another wife; sorrow for a child, forever. (Indian)

Sorrow is born of excessive joy. (Chinese)

Sorrow is like rice in an attic: you use a little every day and at the end it is all gone. (Madagascan)

Sorrow is the child of too much joy. (Chinese)

Sorrow is to the soul what the worm is to wood. (Turkish)

Sorrow seldom comes alone. (Danish)

Sorrow will pay no debts. (Irish)

Sorrows come after joy. (Roman)

Sorrows come uninvited. (Roman)

To die is not much sorrow, but to suffer pain is the real sorrow. (Korean)

The end of mirth is the beginning of sorrow. (Dutch)

The more sorrow one encounters, the more joy one can contain. (Malay)

The remembrance of past pleasures adds to present sorrows. (Roman)

There is no day without sorrow. (Roman)

When sorrow is asleep wake it not. (German)

When the ear does not listen, the heart escapes sorrow. (Chinese)

With you in counsel, without you in sorrow. (Danish)

You cannot prevent the birds of sorrow from flying over your head, but you can prevent them from building nests in your hair. (Chinese)

Youth never comes twice, but sorrow comes twice a night. (Irish)

Soul

Be master of your soul, lest your untamed nature bring forth deceit and disgrace. (Roman)

Cultivation is as necessary to the soul as food is to the body. (Roman)

Excellence and greatness of soul are most conspicuously displayed in contempt of riches. (Roman)

From whence comes the word, comes the soul. (Albanian)

Great souls have wills; feeble ones have only wishes. (Chinese)

Nobility of soul is more honorable than nobility of birth. (Dutch)

The body is not the abode of the soul but its enemy. (Roman)

When the soul hungers, even bitter things taste sweet. (Roman)

Your soul to God, your body to dust, your land to your relatives, 'tis written thus.
(Italian)

Soup

Between the hand and the lip the soup may be spilt. (German)
One cannot make soup out of beauty. (Estonian)
Soup is a luxury to those who cannot afford meat. (Irish)
Where there are too many cooks the soup will be too salty. (Italian)

Sour

After the sour comes the sweet. (Dutch)
He deserves not sweet who will not taste of sour. (German)

Sour Grapes

Sour grapes will ne'er make sweet wine. (Roman)
The fox who cannot reach the grapes says they are sour. (French)
The grapes one cannot reach are always sour. (German)

Sow, Sown

After a bad crop, immediately begin to sow. (Roman)
As you have sown, so also shall you reap. (Jesus)
Do not abstain from sowing for fear of the pigeons. (French)
He who sows brambles must not go barefoot. (Spanish)
He who sows courtesy reaps friendship, and he who plants kindness gathers love.
(Spanish)
He who sows hatred shall gather rue. (Danish)
He who sows inequity shall reap shame. (Danish)
He who sows little, reaps little. (Danish)
He who sows money, will reap poverty. (Danish)
He who sows peas along the highway does not get all the pods into his barn. (Danish)
He who sows thistles reaps thorns. (French)
He who sows virtue reaps fame. (French)
He who sows well, reaps well. (Spanish)
If you do not sow in the spring you will not reap in the fall. (Irish)
If you do not sow, you will have nothing to reap. (Albanian)
Nobody sows a thing that will not sell. (Spanish)
Sow beans, reap beans. (Korean)
Sow much, reap much; sow little, reap little. (Spanish)
Sow not money on the sea, lest it sink. (Dutch)
Sow with one hand, reap with both. (Albanian)
Sown corn is not lost. (German)
They that sow sparingly shall reap sparingly. (the Bible)
We must sow even after a bad harvest. (Danish)
Who sows ill reaps ill. (Italian)
You sow for yourself, you reap for yourself. (Roman)

Sow

A barren sow is never kind to pigs. (Danish)
A sow may whistle, though it has an ill mouth for it. (Danish)
A sow prefers bran to roses. (French)
A still sow eats up all the draff [i.e., dregs]. (Dutch)
'Every little helps', said the sow, when she snapped at a gnat. (Danish)
'Great cry and little wool', said the Devil, when he sheared the sow. (Irish)
The sow prefers the mire. (Danish)

Sow's Ear

You cannot make a silk purse from a sow's ear. (German)

Spare

Better spare at the brim that at the bottom. (Danish)
He that spares something today will have something tomorrow. (Dutch)
He who spares the rod hates his son. (Roman)
He who spares vice wrongs virtue. (French)
Lavish with others yet sparing at home. (Irish)
Spare and have is better than spend and crave. (Poor Richard)
Spare the paper which is fated to perish. (Roman)
Spare the rod and spoil the child. (the Bible)
Spare to speak and spare to prosper. (French)
Spare well and have to spend. (English)

Spark, Sparks

A small spark has often kindled a great fire. (Scottish)
A spark can start a fire that burns the entire village. (Chinese)
A spark may raise an awful blaze. (French)
Even the smallest spark shines brightly in darkness. (Roman)
From a small spark a great house is burnt. (Dutch)
He who blows in the fire will get sparks in his eyes. (German)

Sparrow

Sparrows should not dance with cranes. (Danish)
The lowly sparrow lays many more eggs than the majestic eagle. (Korean)

Speak, Speaker

A bad speaker makes a long speech. (Unknown)
A good speaker makes a good liar. (German)
A good thing can be twice, nay, even thrice spoken. (French)
A man has two ears and one mouth that he hear much and speak little. (German)
Anger and drunkenness speak truly. (Irish)
Better to be ill-spoken of by one before all than by all before one. (Scottish)
Better to speak and be condemned than remain silent and be damned. (the Editor)
Do you wish people to think well of you? Don't speak. (French)
Don't speak to the man at the helm. (French)

Don't speak unless you can improve on the silence. (Spanish)

Everyone speaks as he is. (Portuguese)

Examine what is said, not him who speaks. (Egyptian)

For a common man to mutter what he thinks is a risky venture. (Roman)

He is a fool that praises himself, and he a madman that speaks ill of himself. (Danish)

He that speaks much, is much mistaken. (Poor Richard)

He that speaks truth must have one foot in the stirrup. (Turkish)

He that speaks without care shall remember with sorrow. (Turkish)

He that speaks, sows; he that hears, reaps. (Turkish)

He who speaks ill of himself is praised by no one. (Danish)

He who speaks ill of his country offends his mother. (Spanish)

He who speaks makes mistakes. (Spanish)

He who would speak well should well consider his subject beforehand. (Roman)

In speaking with friends, let your words be faithful. (Chinese)

It is good speaking that improves good silence. (Dutch)

It's ill speaking between a full man and a fasting man. (Dutch)

Lay your hand on your bosom and you will not speak ill of another. (Portuguese)

Listen a hundred times, ponder a thousand times, speak once. (Kurdish)

Lords and fools speak freely. (Danish)

Many speak much who cannot speak well. (American)

Neither speak against the sun nor dispute what is obvious. (Roman)

Never speak ill of the dead. (Arabian)

Never speak in a hurry. (Roman)

No one can speak well, unless he thoroughly understands his subject. (Roman)

No sooner have you spoken than what you have said becomes the property of another.
    (Indian)

One should speak little with others and much with oneself. (Danish)

Speak little and well: they will think you somebody. (Portuguese)

Speak little of your ill luck, and boast not of your good luck. (Danish)

Speak not against the dead. (Roman)

Speak not ill of the year until it is past. (Italian)

Speak not of my debts unless you mean to pay them. (English)

Speak of the Devil and he appears. (Italian)

Speak the truth, but leave immediately after. (Slavic)

Speak well of your friend; of your enemy, neither well nor ill. (Italian)

Speak when you are spoken to. (Italian)

Speaking without thought is like shooting without taking aim. (Spanish)

The eyes speak as much as the mouth does. (Japanese)

The inarticulate speak longest. (Japanese)

The less one thinks, the more one speaks. (French)

The person who speaks little makes few mistakes. (Mexican)

Those who know do not speak, those who speak do not know. (Japanese)

Those who speak well do not always think well. (the Editor)

To speak kindly does not hurt the tongue. (Roman)

When silent men speak, they speak to the purpose. (German)

When you speak at night look below, when you speak in the day look behind.
   (Burmese)
While you live you dare not speak; when you die you cannot. (Yiddish)
Who speaks ill of others to you will speak ill of you to others. (German)
Who speaks much, errs much. (Spanish)

Speech

A grand eloquence, little conscience. (Spanish)
A man never becomes an orator if he has something to say. (American)
A man's speech mirrors his thoughts. (Chinese)
An unguarded speech reveals the truth. (Roman)
As is the bird, so is its song; as is the man, so is his manner of speech. (Roman)
As the man is, so is his speech. (Danish)
As was his speech so was his life. (Roman)
Eloquence is difficult. (Roman)
Many an injury comes from a fool's speech. (Roman)
Soft speeches injure not the mouth of the speaker. (Roman)
Speech both conceals and reveals the thoughts of men. (Roman)
Speech is an indicator of thought. (Roman)
Speech is the messenger of the heart. (Yiddish)
The good speech of an ass is better than the bad word of a prophet. (Irish)
The greatest virtue of speech is clarity. (Roman)

Spend, Spender

As won, so spent. (German)
Got with the fife, spent with the drum. (German)
Great spenders are bad lenders. (Poor Richard)
He who buys and sells does not feel what he spends. (Spanish)
He who has four coins and spends five needs no purse. (Spanish)
He who spends more than he should shall not have to spend when he would. (Danish)
How many a hand weak in gaining is profligate in spending. (Egyptian)
If you know how to spend less than you get, you have the Philosopher's Stone.
   (Poor Richard)
Ill-gotten, ill-spent. (Roman)
Let not your spending exceed your income. (Roman)
Many estates are spent in the getting. (Poor Richard)
Many spend a pound to earn a farthing. (English)
Spend and God will send. (English)
Spend not, where you may save; spare not, where you must spend. (German)
Spending is quick, earning is slow. (Russian)
Spending your money with many a guest, empties the kitchen, the cellar, and chest.
   (German)
Through not spending enough we spend too much. (Spanish)
To spend much and gain little is the sure road to ruin. (German)

Spice
If you beat spice it will smell the sweeter. (Chinese)
The best spices are in small bags. (Italian)
Variety is the spice of life. (American)

Spider
If you want to live and thrive, let the spider run alive. (Spanish)
Spiders are born to spin, men to work. (Spanish)
The spider weaves not its web for one fly. (Russian)
The spider lives by deception. (the Editor)

Spill
Fear to let fall a drop and you will spill a lot. (Malaysian)
He is most likely to spill who holds the vessel in his hand. (Danish)

Spirit
A broken spirit is hard to heal. (Yiddish)
For the letter kills, but the spirit gives life. (St Paul)
Rule your spirit well or it will rule over you. (Roman)
The spirit is willing but the flesh is weak. (Jesus)
The spirit of a child lasts a hundred years. (Japanese)
The spirit of the rich man will carry nothing to the shades below. (Roman)

Spit
Don't spit into the wind. (English)
He who spits above himself will have it fall on his face. (Spanish)
Spit in a whore's face, and she will say it is raining. (Yiddish)
Spit into the sky, it'll fall into your eye. (Jamaican)
Spit not in the well, you may have to drink its water. (French)
Who spits against Heaven, gets wet. (French)
Who spits against the wind, spits in his own face. (French)

Spoil
One bad apple spoils the bushel. (American)
One rotten egg spoils the whole pudding. (German)
One speck of rat dung spoils a whole pot of rice. (Chinese)
Too little and too much spoils everything. (Danish)

Spoils
Do not divide the spoils till the victory is won. (German)

Spoon
Better no spoons than no broth. (German)
One needs no cellar where a spoon suffices. (German)
The spoon knows the contents of the pot. (Mexican)

Sports, Sportsmanship
Begin and end shaking hands. (German)
Stopping at third base adds no more to the score than striking out. (American)

Spot
A spot shows most on the finest cloth. (Spanish)

Spouse
To know how to choose a good spouse is to know a lot. (Spanish)

Spring
Do not defile a spring that once quenched your thirst. (Hindi)
From a pure spring pure water flows. (Roman)

Spur
One's own spurs and another's horse make the miles short. (Italian)
Spur not a willing horse. (French)

Squander
He who has once squandered his own ought not to be trusted with another's. (Roman)

Squat
Don't squat with your spurs on. (American)

Staff
Leave not your staff at home. (Roman)

Stain
A common blot is held no stain. (Roman)

Stairs
Stairs are climbed step by step. (Kurdish)
The stairs are swept downwards, not upwards. (Rumanian)

Stand
He who stands high is seen from afar. (Danish)
He who stands near the woodcutter is likely to catch a splinter. (Danish)
If you don't stand for something, you will fall for anything. (African)
What stands firmest cannot be overthrown. (Roman)

Star, Stars
Even a small star shines in the darkness. (Danish)
Except for the night, we could never know the stars. (German)

Starlings
Starlings are lean because they go in flocks. (Italian)

Start
Do not start what you cannot finish. (Spanish)

Status
Do not take for yourself the seat of honor. (Jesus)
It is good to be neither high nor low. (Chinese)
Seat yourself in your place and you will not be made to quit it. (Spanish)

Starve
Play in summer, starve in winter. (English)

Stay
Stay a while, and lose a mile. (Dutch)

Steal, Stealing
Cover the ears when stealing the bells. (Chinese)
Do not steal a loaf from him that kneads and bakes. (Spanish)
He that will steal an egg will steal an ox. (English)
He who steals a calf will steal a cow. (German)
He who steals a needle will steal an ox. (Korean)
He who steals once is never trusted. (Spanish)
He who would steal honey must not be afraid of bees. (Danish)
It is hard to steal where the host is a thief. (Dutch)
It is not easy to steal in thieves' houses. (Italian)
It is not enough to know how to steal, one must know also how to conceal. (Italian)
One who steals a prawn will not be satisfied to eat only one. (Yoruban)
The one who conceals is as bad as the one who steals. (German)
There is no choicer morsel than that which is stolen. (Spanish)
Who steals chickens in the daytime will steal cows at night. (Chinese)
Who steals needles when young will steal gold when old. (Chinese)

Steel
Steel whets steel. (Spanish)

Steer
Any man can steer in a calm sea. (Roman)

Stench
No one admits the stench of his own excrement. (Korean)
The whole boat will stink of a single carp. (Burmese)

Step
It is the first step that is difficult. (Nigerian)
Every step leads to death. (Filipino)
One step at a time. (English)

Step by step one goes far. (Dutch)
Step by step one goes to Rome. (Italian)
Step on a crack, break your mother's back. (American)
Step on a dog's tail and it will yelp. (German)
The first step binds one to the second. (French)
The greatest step is out of doors. (German)
The hardest step is the one over the threshold. (Chinese)

Stew
Bad beef never made good stew. (Greek)
The stew mixed by many is ill-seasoned and worse cooked. (Spanish)

Stick, Sticks
A stick has two ends. (Persian)
A stick is a peacemaker. (French)
It is easy to find a stick to beat a dog. (Italian)
Sticks and stones may break my bones, but names cannot hurt me. (English)

Stick, Sticky
Lay it on thick and some of it will stick. (Italian)

Sting
He who has been stung by the scorpion is frightened at its shadow. (Spanish)

Stingy
A rich man who is stingy is the worst of paupers. (Yiddish)
A stingy man is always poor. (French)
Many take by the bushel, and give with the spoon. (German)

Stitch
A stitch in time saves nine. (English)
The stitch is lost unless the thread be knotted. (Italian)

Stocks
Both legs in the stocks or only one, 'tis all the same. (German)

Stomach
A dainty stomach empties the purse. (German)
A good stomach can digest everything. (German)
Bargain on a full stomach. (Korean)
Better a light stomach than a heavy conscience. (Greek)
It proves a dainty stomach to taste of many things. (Roman)
Let your head be more than a funnel to your stomach. (German)
The first spoonful cannot fill the stomach. (English)
The full stomach has little sympathy for the empty one. (Irish)

The stomach is a god. (Greek)
The stomach is easier filled than the eye. (German)
The way to a man's heart is through his stomach. (English)
There is no idol as demanding as the stomach, which everyday receives its offerings.
    (Yoruban)
When the stomach is full the heart is glad. (Dutch)

Stone, Stones

A bird's beak cannot break a stone. (Yoruban)
A drop hollows out a stone. (Russian)
A little stone may upset a large cart. (Danish)
A rolling stone gathers no moss. (Roman)
Constant dripping wears away stone. (Italian)
No stone without a tale to tell. (Roman)
Rolling stones often cross paths. (Mexican)
The drop hollows the stone, not by force but by constant dripping. (Roman)
The stone that everyone spits upon will be wet at the last. (Danish)
The stone the builders have rejected has become the cornerstone. (the Bible)
You are trying to get water from a stone. (Roman)
You cannot get blood from a stone. (English)
You may get something off a bone, but nothing off a stone. (Danish)

Stonemason

He is not a good mason who refuses any stone. (Italian)

Stool

Between two stools one falls to the ground. (Spanish)

Storm

A calm portends a storm. (Italian)
After a storm comes a calm. (French)
Stoop, and let it pass; the storm will have its way. (Danish)
Storms make oaks take deeper root. (Unknown)
The more violent the storm, the sooner it is over. (Roman)
The person who does not like storms should not become a sailor. (Mexican)
There's always a calm before the storm. (English)

Story

A false story has seven endings. (African)
Half the story has never been told. (Jamaican)
If it's not true, it's a good story. (Italian)
The one who comes with a story will leave with two. (Irish)
There are three sides to every story: your side, my side, and the truth. (Jamaican)
There are two tellings to every story. (Irish)

Stranger

A stranger has big eyes but sees nothing. (African)

An eye is blind in another man's corner. (Irish)

Truth is often stranger than fiction. (American)

Woe to the stranger when trouble comes, for there will be no friend to take his part.
(Irish)

Straw

A straw can show which way the winds blow. (American)

Even a straw becomes heavy if you carry it far enough. (Roman)

Every straw is a thorn at night. (Irish)

Much straw and little corn. (Portuguese)

'Tis the last straw that breaks the camel's back. (French)

You cannot make bricks without straw. (English)

Stray

Deviate an inch, lose a thousand miles. (Chinese)

When the shepherd strays, the sheep stray. (Dutch)

Stream

A stream cannot rise about its source. (Unknown)

Believe not that the stream is shallow because its surface is smooth. (Roman)

Cross the stream where it is the shallowest. (English)

'Tis hard to swim against the stream. (German)

Wade the shallow stream as though it were deep. (Korean)

When you want to test the depths of a stream, don't use both feet. (Chinese)

Where the stream is shallowest, greatest is its noise. (Irish)

Strength

Attempt nothing beyond your strength. (Roman)

Dwell not upon your weariness, your strength shall be according to the measure of your
desire. (Arabian)

Loss of strength is more frequently due to faults of youth than old age. (Roman)

Strength, lacking judgment, collapses by its own weight. (Roman)

Union gives strength to the humblest of aids. (Roman)

Union is strength. (Japanese)

Stretch

If you draw out the inch it becomes a span. (English)

Only stretch your foot to the length of your blanket. (Afghani)

Stretch your arm no further than your sleeve will reach. (English)

Stretch your legs according to your coverlet. (German)

Strife

Happy is the man who keeps out of strife. (Roman)

When you can avoid it, never seek strife. (Roman)
Who would avoid all strife should be a bachelor. (Roman)

Strike
He who strikes another on the neck does not strike far from the head. (Danish)
If you are a peg, endure the knocking; if you are a mallet, strike. (Moroccan)
Strike the innocent, that the guilty may confess. (Egyptian)
Strike the shepherd and scatter the sheep. (the Bible)
Strike while the iron is hot. (English)

String
If a string has one end, then it has another end. (Chinese)

Strive
He that will not strive in this world should not have come into it. (Italian)

Stroke, Strokes
Different strokes for different folks. (Roman)
If strokes are good to give, they are good to receive. (Serbian)

Strong, Stronger
Man is stronger than iron and weaker than a fly. (Yiddish)
Only the strong will survive. (Jamaican)
The stronger always succeeds. (Roman)
The strongest is always in the right. (Italian)
The strongest rules. (American)
The strongest sometimes yields to the smallest. (Roman)
Would you be strong, conquer yourself. (German)
You must be strong to pull a rope against a stronger. (Danish)

Struggle
That which arises from struggle often goes beyond the mark. (Roman)

Stubborn, Stubbornness
A hard head makes a soft behind. (Jamaican)
For a stubborn ass, a stubborn driver. (French)
He is the more obstinate for being advised. (French)

Student
A student who doubts nothing learns nothing. (Spanish)
First student, then master. (German)
It is only the students who become masters. (Indian)
Many a student has gained more wealth than his master. (Greek)
Sore hand and head are student's excuses. (Unknown)
The most disorderly students make the most pious preachers. (German)

413

Study

Study invites study, idleness produces idleness. (Roman)
Study the past if you would know the future. (Chinese)
The early morn favors study. (Roman)
We can study until old age and still not finish. (Chinese)

Stumble

A stumble is not a fall. (Haitian)
A stumble may prevent a fall. (English)
Better to stumble once than be always tottering. (French)
He who stumbles and does not fall mends his pace. (Spanish)
He who stumbles twice over one stone deserves to break his shins.
   (Spanish)
Many who leap over a block stumble over straw. (German)

Stupid, Stupidity

It is shrewd to feign stupidity. (Spanish)
It is sometimes prudent to feign stupidity. (Roman)
Stupid is as stupid does. (Roman)
There is no cure for stupidity. (German)

Succeed, Success

All things which the mind conceives do not always succeed. (Roman)
Attempt not, or accomplish. (Roman)
Behind an able man there are always other able men. (Chinese)
Boldly ventured is half won. (Roman)
Earnestness and sport go well together. (Danish)
Haste and speed seldom succeed. (the Editor)
Half success is better than whole failure. (Irish)
He puts up with small annoyances to gain great results. (Roman)
He who succeeds is reputed wise. (Italian)
He who undertakes too much seldom succeeds. (Dutch)
If at first you don't succeed, try, try, again. (American)
If you like things easy, you'll have difficulties; if you like problems, you'll succeed.
   (Laotian)
If you would succeed, you must not be too good. (Italian)
Nothing succeeds like success. (English)
Success alters our manners. (Roman)
Success and rest don't sleep together. (Russian)
Success consecrates the foulest crimes. (Russian)
Success doesn't come overnight. (Jamaican)
Success has a thousand fathers. (American)
Success has many fathers, while failure is an orphan. (Russian)
Success has many friends. (Greek)
Success has ruined many a man. (Poor Richard)

Success intoxicates without wine. (Yiddish)

Success is doing what you like and making a living at it. (American)

Success is its own reward. (American)

Success isn't how far you have gotten, but the distance you have traveled from where you started. (Greek)

Success leads to insolence. (Roman)

Success makes a fool seem wise. (Roman)

Success makes some crimes honorable. (Roman)

Success mine, failure yours. (Unknown)

Success renders a man bold. (Egyptian)

The door to success is marked 'push' and 'pull'. (Yiddish)

Those who succeed are apt to forget friends and favors. (Spanish)

When you get to the top, don't look back. (Yiddish)

Such

Such a beginning, such an end. (German)

Such as the man is, such will his discourse be. (German)

Sucker

Never give a sucker an even break. (American)

There's a sucker born every minute. (American)

Suckle

The gentle calf suckles any cow. (Portuguese)

The gentle lamb suckles any ewe; the surly lamb suckles neither its mother or another. (Spanish)

Suffer, Suffering

A sparrow suffers as much when it breaks its leg as does a Flanders horse. (Danish)

Better to suffer ill than to do ill. (English)

Great sufferings have neither tears not laments. (Spanish)

He that bears the Cross, blesses himself first. (Danish)

He who fears to suffer, suffers from fear. (French)

How great the sufferings we men endure! (Roman)

It is better to suffer once than always to be cautious. (Roman)

Keep within your compass and you may be sure, that you will not suffer what others endure. (German)

Many a one suffers for what he can't help. (French)

Men suffer much – and forget much suffering – in the course of a day. (German)

'O what we must suffer for the sake of God's church!', said the abbot, when the roast fowl burned his fingers. (German)

Present sufferings seem far greater to men than those they merely dread. (Roman)

Suffering follows those who flee. (Roman)

We have suffered lightly, if we have suffered what we should weep for. (Roman)

Who does not know how to suffer, knows not how to rule. (Spanish)

Who lives long may suffer much. (German)
With suffering comes benefit. (Burmese)

Sufficient

That man is not poor who has what is sufficient for all his wants. (Roman)
We have what is sufficient, when we have what nature requires. (Roman)

Sugar

Even sugar itself may spoil a good dish. (Hausan)
Where there is sugar, there are bound to be ants. (Malay)

Suit, Suitable

All things are not equally fit for all men. (Roman)
Like to like, and Joan for John. (English)
Like to like, Jack to Jill, a penny a pair. (Dutch)
Suit yourself to the times. (German)
What you can't get is just what suits you. (French)

Sultan

The sultan is reviled only in his absence. (Egyptian)

Sun, Sunshine

After clouds sunshine. (Roman)
Every sun has to set. (Arabian)
If you count the sunny and the cloudy days of the whole year, you will find that
    sunshine predominates. (Roman)
Let the sun shine on me, for I care not for the moon. (Spanish)
Make use of the sun while it shines. (Danish)
More do homage to the rising sun than to the setting one. (Roman)
No matter how tall the mountain, it cannot block out the sun. (Chinese)
No morning sun lasts a whole day. (Poor Richard)
No one turns toward the setting sun. (Spanish)
No sunshine but hath some shadow. (English)
Sunshine all the time makes a desert. (Arabian)
Sunshine follows gloom. (Irish)
The eye of the sun cannot be hidden. (Egyptian)
The same sun bleaches linens and blackens the field hand. (Yiddish)
The setting sun doubles the increasing shadows. (Roman)
The sun loses nothing by shining into a puddle. (English)
The sun may yet shine into a rat's hole. (Korean)
The sun of all days has not yet set. (Roman)
The sun shines even on the wicked. (Roman)
The sun shines even when it is cloudy. (Albanian)
The sun shines for all the world. (French)
The sun shines onto dung but is not tainted. (Greek)

The sun spreads its rays even into the sewer and is not stained. (Roman)
The sun will bring to light what lay under the snow. (German)
There is nothing new under the sun. (the Bible)
Turn your face to the sun and the shadows fall behind you. (Maori)
When the sun shines on you, you need not care for the moon. (Italian)
Who would dare to call the sun a liar? (Roman)

Sundial
The sundial counts only the bright hours. (German)

Supper
A light supper is beneficial. (Roman)
By suppers more have been killed than Galen ever cured. (Roman)
If you go to bed without supper, you will rise without having slept. (Yiddish)

Support
A man's greatest support is not the gods but his own two arms. (Yoruban)

Surety
The one who is surety for another is never sure himself. (German)

Surgeon
A good surgeon has an eagle's eye, a lion's heart, and a lady's hand. (English)
A good surgeon must have soft words and a firm hand. (Spanish)
Call not a surgeon before you are wounded. (Italian)

Surpass
No one likes to be surpassed by those of his own level. (Roman)

Surrender
A starved town is soon forced to surrender. (Italian)
Hunger and cold surrender a man to his enemy. (Portuguese)
Surrender to one wrong and soon another will follow. (Portuguese)

Suspect, Suspicion
A slight suspicion may destroy a good reputation. (Danish)
A suspicious mind sees everything on the dark side. (Roman)
Avoid suspicion: when you're walking through your neighbor's melon patch, don't tie
    your shoe. (Chinese)
Caesar's wife should be above suspicion. (Roman)
If you suspect a man, don't employ him; if you employ a man, don't suspect him.
    (Chinese)
One is quick to suspect where one has suffered harm before. (Roman)
Suspicion breeds phantoms. (Japanese)
Suspicion conjures up black devils. (Chinese)

Suspicion is the poison of friendship. (French)
Suspicion may be no fault, but showing it may be a great one. (Poor Richard)
The better the man is, the harder it is for him to suspect dishonesty in others. (Roman)
The losing side is full of suspicion. (Roman)
The suspicious mind sees many demons. (Chinese)
When suspicions enter, love departs. (Danish)

Swan

Every man thinks his own geese swans. (German)
The swan sings when death comes. (French)
When the crows are silent the swans begin to sing. (Danish)

Swear

To swear is to call God to witness. (Roman)

Sweat

No sweet without sweat. (Kashmiri)
Nothing is sweet without sweat. (American)
Sweat makes good mortar. (German)

Sweep

Let everyone sweep before his own door. (German)
Sweep before your own door before you look after your neighbor's. (Dutch)
Were everyone to sweep before his own house, every street would be clean. (Dutch)
When you sweep the stairs, you start at the top. (German)

Sweet, Sweetness

After the sour comes the sweet. (Dutch)
Don't be too sweet lest you be eaten up; don't be too bitter lest you be spewed out.
   (Yiddish)
He deserves not sweet who will not taste of sour. (German)
No sweet without sweat. (Kashmiri)
Some of the sweetest berries grow among the sharpest thorns. (Irish)
Sugar cane is sweet always, man only sometimes. (Burmese)
Sweet things come after bitter things. (Roman)
Sweetness brings satisfaction. (Roman)
That which is sweet to some is bitter to others. (Roman)
There is always room for something sweet. (Yiddish)
Things sweet to the mouth do not always nourish the belly. (Japanese)
What is sweet in the mouth is not always good in the stomach. (Danish)
You can't expect both ends of a sugar cane to be as sweet. (Chinese)

Swift

The swift are overtaken by the slow. (Roman)

Swim, Swimmer

A good swimmer is known only after the boat sinks. (Chinese)
A good swimmer is not safe against drowning. (French)
Don't jump in the water if you can't swim. (Jamaican)
Either you sink or you swim. (Spanish)
Good swimmers are drowned at last. (Italian)
He may swim boldly who is held up by the chin. (French)
It is easy to swim downstream. (Spanish)
Never venture out of your depth till you can swim. (Unknown)
The best swimmer is the first to drown himself. (Italian)
'Tis hard to swim against the stream. (German)

Swine

He who lies down in the wash will be eaten by swine. (Danish)
He who mixes himself with the slops will be eaten by the swine. (Dutch)
Neither cast your pearls before swine. (Jesus)
Still swine eat all the dregs. (Irish)

Sword

A good sword is the one left in its scabbard. (Japanese)
Good sword has often been in poor scabbard. (Irish)
He who plays with a sword plays with the Devil. (Rumanian)
Let not your sword be drawn at any man's bidding. (Roman)
Never give a child a sword. (Roman)
One sword keeps another in the sheath. (German)
The sword does not recognize the smith who made it. (Yoruban)
Those who live by the sword shall die by the sword. (Jesus)
Who carries the sword, carries peace. (Unknown)

Swordsman

A good swordsman is never quarrelsome. (French)

Sympathy

Give no sympathy to the Devil. (American)
Sympathy without relief is like mustard without beef. (English)

T

Table

At a round table there is no dispute about place. (Italian)
Spread the table and contention will cease. (English)

Tail

A dog's tail can never be straightened. (Indian)

A short tail won't keep off flies. (Italian)
Even wicked dogs wag their tails. (Italian)
If the tail is too long, the cow will trample on it. (Korean)
In the tail lies the venom. (French)
It is not till the cow has lost her tail that she discovers its value. (German)
Leave a bit of the tail to whisk off flies. (Chinese)
Let everyone keep off the flies with his own tail. (Italian)
Long tails get trampled upon. (Korean)
Take care lest your tail be caught in the door. (Italian)
The ass does not know the worth of its tail till it is lost. (Italian)
The dog wags its tail not for you, but for your bread. (Italian)
The dog wags its tail not for you, but for your meat. (Spanish)
The horse may run quickly, but it can't escape its own tail. (Russian)
The tail is always the hardest part to flay. (Italian)
The sting is in the tail. (Italian)

Tailor

Dull scissors make crooked-mouthed tailors. (Danish)
Nine tailors make a man. (English)

Take

A hand accustomed to taking is far from giving. (Egyptian)
'An egg is an egg', said the vicar, but he took the goose egg. (German)
If the eyes didn't see then the hands wouldn't take. (Yiddish)
If they give to you – take; if they take from you – yell! (Yiddish)
If you can't get it in bushels, take it in spoonfuls. (German)
Let him take who can. (Roman)
Let people take and dogs bark. (German)
Of this world each man has as much as he takes. (Italian)
Take all you want; eat all you take. (German)
Take what you can get, and pay what you can. (Irish)
Taking out without putting in, soon comes to the bottom. (Portuguese)
You can't take it with you. (American)

Tale, Tales

A good tale ill told is marred in the telling. (English)
A good tale is none the worse for being twice told. (French)
A tale never loses in the telling. (Scottish)
A tale twice told is cabbage twice sold. (English)
Change but the name, and the tale is told of you. (Roman)
Do not ask questions of fairy tales. (Yiddish)
Never tell tales out of school. (English)
One tale is good till another is told. (German)
The gadabout has many a tale to tell. (Unknown)

Talent, Talents
Great talents mature late. (Japanese)
Immortal glory waits on talent. (Roman)
There is talent for everything except for dying. (Mexican)
The greatest talents are often hidden from sight. (Roman)

Talk, Talkative
A talkative bird will not build a nest. (West African)
Beware of the dog that does not bark and the man who does not talk. (Spanish)
By talking people understand each other. (Mexican)
Don't talk unless you can improve the silence. (American)
Fore-talk spares after-talk. (German)
He that keeps his mouth shut keeps his life; but he that opens wide his lips shall have
     destruction. (Italian)
He who knows does not talk; he who talks does not know. (Chinese)
He who talks much, lies much. (German)
He who talks incessantly, talks nonsense. (African)
He who talks much is sometimes right. (Spanish)
He who talks to himself talks to a fool. (English)
Little folks are fond of talking about what great folks do. (German)
Long talk makes short days. (French)
Much chatter, little wit. (Portuguese)
Much talk brings trouble, much food indigestion. (Chinese)
Much talk, little work. (Dutch)
Talk is cheap. (English)
Talk is cheap, but it takes money to buy whiskey. (American)
Talk is easy, action difficult. (Spanish)
Talk little and well, and you will be looked upon as somebody. (Spanish)
Talk much, err much. (Spanish)
Talk of a man and his shadow will turn up. (Japanese)
Talk of the Devil and he is bound to appear. (English)
Talk of the Devil and you hear his bones rattle. (Dutch)
Talk of the wolf and behold its skin. (Portuguese)
Talk of the wolf and its tail appears. (Dutch)
Talk too much and you talk about yourself. (Yiddish)
Talking is easier than doing, and promising than performing. (German)
Talking is tax free. (American)
The same person will not both talk much and to the purpose. (Roman)
They talk like philosophers and live like fools. (Unknown)
To talk good is not to do good. (Chinese)
When you talk on the road, remember there may be men in the grass.
     (Chinese)

Talker
A talker neither listens nor learns. (German)

Great talkers are commonly liars. (German)
Great talkers are not great doers. (French)

Tall
No need to be tall to be great. (Yiddish)
Tall branches are apt to be broken. (Korean)
Tall men make good soldiers, short men scholars. (Unknown)
Tall trees catch much wind. (Dutch)

Tame, Tamed
The fierce ox becomes tame on strange ground. (Spanish)
The savage ox grows tame on strange ground. (Portuguese)
The unruly son who marries is soon tamed. (Spanish)

Tango
It takes two to tango. (American)

Task
Accept tasks that bring you praise as well as profit. (Roman)
He that performs his own errand saves the messenger's hire. (Danish)
He that would have a thing done quickly and well must do it himself. (Italian)
The harder the task the easier God's help. (Yiddish)

Taste, Tastes
A different man, a different taste. (Greek)
A lordly taste make a beggar's purse. (German)
All tastes are tastes. (Italian)
Every man has his liking. (Danish)
Every man to his taste. (French)
He who tastes of every man's broth, often burns his mouth. (Danish)
More of good taste than expense. (Roman)
Much taste, much waste. (German)
Tastes differ. (Dutch)
There's no accounting for taste. (English)
There's no disputing about tastes. (Italian)

Tattler
A tattler is worse than a thief. (African)
A tattler will die first. (Korean)

Tavern
When a tavern keeper treats you, it is with your own money. (Spanish)
Whoever frequents a tavern supports two houses. (Spanish)

Tax, Taxes
Free man, free goods. (German)

Free ships, free goods. (American)

Talking is tax free. (American)

Taxes: the more you make, the more they take. (the Editor)

Taxes are the sinews of the republic. (Roman)

Taxes are the sinews of war. (Greek)

There is no tax upon lying. (Spanish)

Tea

If man has no tea in him, he is incapable of understanding truth and beauty. (Japanese)

Teach, Taught

He who can does, he who cannot teaches. (German)

He who is not taught by God is taught by man. (Irish)

He who teaches children learns more than they do. (German)

He who teaches me for one day is my father for life. (Chinese)

It is hard to teach old dogs to bark. (German)

Not only is there an art in knowing a thing, but also a certain art in teaching it. (Roman)

Shall the gosling teach the goose to swim? (Arabian)

Teaching others teaches the teacher. (English)

Teaching others teaches yourself. (Chinese)

That which hurts teaches. (Roman)

The one who falls in a ditch teaches others to be careful. (Yoruban)

The one who teaches himself has a fool for a student. (German)

The one who teaches learns. (Roman)

Those that can, do; those that can't, teach. (American)

To teach is also to learn. (Japanese)

Whatever you teach, be brief. (Roman)

Whoever teaches his son teaches not only his son but also his son's son, and so on to the end of generations. (Yiddish)

You can't teach an old dog new tricks. (American)

Teacher

A library of books does not equal one good teacher. (Chinese)

A teacher is better than two books. (German)

A teacher will not teach us to do evil if there is no evil inside us. (Yoruban)

A young man respects and looks up to his teachers. (Roman)

Every teacher has been a pupil. (Spanish)

He who is his own teacher has a fool for his pupil. (German)

Looking for a pupil he finds a teacher. (Burmese)

Teachers open the door; you enter by yourself. (Chinese)

Use is the best teacher. (Roman)

Where the pupil is willing; the teacher will appear. (Italian)

Tear, Tears

A tear, when shed for the misfortunes of others, is quickly dried. (Roman)

Nothing dries sooner than a tear. (Roman)
Our tears will fail before we cease to have cause for grief. (Roman)
A child's tear rends the heavens. (Yiddish)
A small tear relieves a great sorrow. (Portuguese)
A woman's tears and a dog's limping are not real. (Spanish)
A woman's weapons are her tears. (French)
Behind every smile lies two hundred tears. (Persian)
Even tears at times have the weight of speech. (Roman)
He wastes his tears who weeps before the judge. (Italian)
Ready tears are a sign of treachery, not of grief. (Roman)
Tears are the charity of the poor. (Egyptian)
Tears are the nature of things, the mind touched by human mortality. (Roman)
The fewer the years, the fewer the tears. (Unknown)
The nose-drop laughs at the tear-drop. (English)
Two barrows of tears will not heal a bruise. (Chinese)
When a woman weeps, she is setting traps with her tears. (Roman)
Women's tears are a fountain of craft. (Italian)

Tear, Torn
Wide will wear but tight will tear. (English)

Tease, Teasing
Teasing eventually turns to a quarrel. (Burmese)

Teeth
Do not show your teeth until you can bite. (Irish)
Don't show your teeth if you can't bite. (French)
Eat coconuts while you have teeth. (Singhalese)
God gives almonds to one who has no teeth. (Spanish)
He who has teeth has no bread, and he who has bread has no teeth. (Italian)
Hot things, sharp things, sweet things, cold things all rot the teeth, and make them look
    like old things. (Poor Richard)
If you had teeth of steel, you could eat iron coconuts. (Singhalese)
In a hundred years our teeth will no longer hurt. (German)
My teeth are nearer than my kindred. (Spanish)
Some men dig their graves with their teeth. (English)
The tongue is soft and remains; the teeth are hard and fall out. (Chinese)
To hard bread and a hard nut belong sharper teeth. (German)
You can't chew with somebody else's teeth. (Yiddish)

Tell
Tell no one what you want no one to know. (Spanish)
Tell not all you know, nor judge of all you see, if you would live in peace. (Spanish)
Tell not all you know; believe not all you hear; do not all you are able. (German)
Tell not thy mind to thy foolish friend, nor to thy wise enemy. (Irish)

Tell nothing to thy friend which thy enemy may not know. (Danish)

Tell your affairs in the marketplace, and one will call them black and another white. (Spanish)

Tell your own story first. (Spanish)

Temper

A quick temper does not bring quick success. (Japanese)

Control your temper. (Roman)

He who loses his temper is in the wrong. (French)

Temperance

Temperance in drinking saves the mind from confusion; restraint of passion preserves fortunes unimpaired. (Chinese)

Temperance is the best medicine. (Italian)

Temple

Those near the temple make fun of the gods. (Chinese)

Tempt, Temptation

All temptations are found either in hope or fear. (English)

An open box tempts an honest man. (Portuguese)

An open door tempts even a saint. (Spanish)

Constant occupation prevents temptation. (German)

He that is busy is tempted but by one devil; he that is idle by a legion. (Italian)

He who avoids the temptation avoids the sin. (Spanish)

Never spread your corn to dry before the door of a saintly man. (Spanish)

Temptation wrings integrity even as the thumbscrew twists a man's fingers. (Chinese)

The Devil tempts all, but the idle man tempts the Devil. (Kurdish)

Tender

Who is tender in everything is a fool in everything. (Catalan)

Termite

A termite can do nothing to a stone but lick it. (Sudanese)

Terror

If you are a terror to many, then beware of many. (Roman)

Why should a terror seize the limbs before the trumpet sounds? (Roman)

Testimony, Testimonies

Testimonies are to be weighed, not counted. (Roman)

The testimony of the heart is stronger than a hundred witnesses. (Turkish)

Thankful

A thankful heart is not only the greatest virtue, but the parent of all the other virtues. (Roman)

Thankless
A thankless man never does a thankful deed. (Danish)

Thanks
Old thanks will not pay a new debt. (English)
Thanks are justly due for things we do not pay for. (Roman)
Who gives not thanks to men gives not thanks to God. (Egyptian)

Theft
A good name covers theft. (Spanish)
Careless concealment invites theft. (Chinese)

Thief, Thieves
A fair booty makes a fair thief. (English)
A hundred bakers, a hundred millers, and a hundred tailors, are three hundred thieves.
    (Dutch)
A hundred tailors, a hundred millers, and a hundred weavers, are three hundred thieves.
    (Spanish)
A postern door makes a thief. (Spanish)
A thief and darkness are friends. (African)
A thief does not willingly see another carry a basket. (Danish)
A thief is a king till he's caught. (Persian)
A thief is always tearful, and a swindler devout. (Russian)
A thief knows a thief as a wolf knows a wolf. (Persian)
A thief makes opportunity. (Dutch)
A thief passes for a gentleman when stealing has made him rich. (Dutch)
A thief seldom grows rich by thieving. (German)
A thief thinks every man steals. (Danish)
All are not thieves that dogs bark at. (English)
An egg thief becomes a camel thief. (Persian)
As there are mice in the house, so are there thieves in the countryside. (Korean)
Entertain a thief and he will steal your clothes. (Egyptian)
Even a thief takes ten years to learn his trade. (Japanese)
Everyone is a thief in his own craft. (Dutch)
Great thieves always have their sleeves full of gags. (French)
Great thieves hang little thieves. (Dutch)
Hang a thief when he's young and he won't steal when he's old. (French)
Hang the young thief, and the old one will not steal. (Danish)
He is a thief indeed who robs a thief. (French)
He who cheats a cheat and robs a thief, earns a dispensation for 100 years. (German)
He who holds the ladder is as bad as the thief. (German)
If there were no recipients, there would be no thieves. (English)
If you would make a thief honest, trust him. (Spanish)
It is not the thief who is hanged, but the one who was caught stealing. (Czech)
It takes a thief to catch a thief. (American)

Little thieves are hanged by the neck, great ones by the purse. (Italian)
Little thieves are hanged, but great ones go free. (Italian)
Little thieves have iron chains, and great thieves gold ones. (Dutch)
Look upon thieves not as eating stolen meat, but look upon them as suffering
    punishment. (Chinese)
Nothing for his friends but something for the thief. (Korean)
On a thief, the hat's on fire. (Polish)
Once a thief, always a thief. (German)
People regard all that a thief has as stolen. (Unknown)
Poor thieves in fetters we behold; and great thieves wear their chains of gold. (English)
Save a thief from the gallows and he will cut your throat. (German)
Save a thief from the gallows and he will see you hanged. (Italian)
Set a thief to catch a thief. (German)
Sometimes even the thief gets robbed. (Japanese)
The hole invites the thief. (Spanish)
The open door invites the thief. (Dutch)
The thief does not steal in his own corner of town. (Egyptian)
The thief is frightened even by a mouse. (Italian)
The thief is king over the wealth of others. (Hindi)
The thief is no danger to the beggar. (Irish)
The thief is sorry he is to be hanged, not that he is a thief. (Irish)
The thief proceeds from a needle to gold, and from gold to the gallows. (Portuguese)
The thief sells cheaply what he stole. (Yoruban)
The thief thinks that all are like himself. (Spanish)
The thief who stole the king's bugle cannot use it. (Yoruban)
The thief's wife does not always laugh. (Italian)
There are more thieves than are hanged. (Dutch)
There is no thief without a receiver. (Spanish)
Thief knows thief, and wolf knows wolf. (Roman)
Though the poor have nothing for relief, they have something for the thief. (Korean)
Time and place make the thief. (German)
Time betrays and hangs the thief. (German)
We hang little thieves, and applaud great ones. (German)
We hang little thieves, and let great ones escape. (Dutch)
What's left from the thief is spent on the fortune teller. (Yiddish)
When a thief kisses you, count your teeth. (Yiddish)
When thieves fall out the peasant recovers his goods. (Danish)
When thieves fall out the thefts come to light. (Spanish)
When two thieves quarrel the farmer gets his cow back. (Finnish)
Whoredom and thieving are never long concealed. (Spanish)

Thin
Being thin is not dying. (Hausan)

Think, Thinking

As a man thinketh, so is he. (the Bible)

If you were in my place, you would think differently. (Roman)

People think of others what is truest of themselves. (Unknown)

Think much, speak little, write less. (Spanish)

Think of three things: whence you came, where you are going, and to whom you must give account. (Poor Richard)

Think well of all men. (English)

Think with the wise, but talk with the vulgar. (Greek)

Thinking is not knowing. (Portuguese)

What you think of yourself is much more important than what others think of you. (Roman)

Who has never done thinking never begins doing. (Italian)

Third

The third time pays for all. (Portuguese)

The third time's the charm. (American)

Thirst, Thirsty

A brook may quench thirst as well as a great river. (German)

A thirsty fellow digs a well. (Korean)

A thirsty man falls into a well. (Burmese)

Even the fountains complain of thirst. (Roman)

He spits into the well but comes back when he's thirsty. (Korean)

It is a wretched business to be digging a well just as thirst is mastering you. (Roman)

Thirst comes from drinking. (Italian)

When you're thirsty it's too late to think about digging a well. (Japanese)

Who has no thirst has no business at the fountain. (Dutch)

Thistles

Gather thistles, expect prickles. (Roman)

He who sows thistles reaps thorns. (French)

Thorn

A thorn comes into the world point first. (French)

A thorn defends the rose harming only those who would steal the blossom. (Chinese)

A thorn pierces young skin more quickly than old. (Serbian)

Among thorns grow roses. (Italian)

Beware asking the person with thorns in his hands to rub your back. (Yoruban)

Does a sharpened stick surpass a thorn in sharpness? (Hausan)

Even the smallest thorn festers. (Irish)

From a thorn comes a rose, and from a rose comes a thorn. (Greek)

He knows well where the thorn pricks him. (Italian)

It early pricks that will be a thorn. (Roman)

No rose without a thorn. (Italian)

Often the prickly thorn produces tender roses. (Roman)
The point of the thorn is small, but he who has felt it does not forget it. (Italian)
The roses fall, the thorns remain. (Italian)
The youngest thorn is the sharpest. (Irish)
Who sows thorns should not go barefoot. (French)

Thought, Thoughts

A pleasant thought never comes too soon. (Danish)
Be slow in thought but quick in action. (Spanish)
Bodily fatigue affects the mind less than intense thought. (Roman)
Dark thoughts lead to dark deeds. (American)
Darkness and night are mothers of thought. (Dutch)
Everyone thinks that all the bells echo his own thoughts. (German)
If thoughts were legal witnesses, many an honest man would be proved a rogue. (Danish)
No one deserves punishment for a thought. (Roman)
Our thoughts are free. (Roman)
Out of one thousand thoughts, one may make a slip. (Korean)
Second thoughts are wiser thoughts. (Greek)
Take your thoughts to bed with you, for the morning is wiser than the evening.
    (Russian)
Thought breaks the heart. (African)
Thought is free. (English)
Thoughts are toll-free, but not hell-free. (German)

Thoughtless

The thoughtless leave the road to Heaven and descend to Hell. (Korean)

Thread, Threads

All things human hang by a slender thread. (Roman)
As you have arranged the thread so must you weave it. (Roman)
By the thread we unwind the skein. (Spanish)
It is not the fine, but the coarse and ill-spun thread that breaks. (Spanish)
One has woven the thread, another has drawn it forth. (Roman)
The thread must follow the needle. (Korean)
Threads do not break for being fine, but for being ill-spun. (Portuguese)
Where the thread is weakest it breaks. (French)

Threat, Threaten

A threatened beating is never well given. (Italian)
A threatened man lives long, if he can get bread. (Danish)
All those that threaten do not fight. (Dutch)
He can do but little who cannot threaten another. (Spanish)
He threatens the innocent who spares the guilty. (English)
He who threatens is afraid. (French)
He who threatens to strike, and does not, is afraid. (Spanish)

It is easy to threaten a bull from a window. (Italian)
Many a one threatens and yet is afraid. (Italian)
Men do not die of threats. (Dutch)
More are threatened than are struck. (German)
The one who threatens sometimes gets a beating. (French)
The person who injures one threatens many. (Roman)
Threatened men live long. (English)
Threats are arms for the threatened. (Italian)
Threats don't kill. (Dutch)
Who threatens, warns. (German)

Thrift, Thrifty

After a thrifty father, a prodigal son. (Spanish)
Look after the pennies and the pounds will look after themselves. (English)
The art of getting riches consists very much in thrift. (Poor Richard)
Thrift is a great revenue. (Roman)
Thrift is too late when you are at the bottom of your purse. (Roman)
Thrift makes one a slave. (Burmese)

Thrive

He that would thrive must first ask his wife. (English)
To hope and strive is the way to thrive. (Danish)

Throw

He who throws a stone at the sky, gets hit on the head. (Italian)

Thunder

A bolt does not always fall when it thunders. (German)
Big thunder, little rain. (English)
Loud thunder, little rain. (Chinese)
Thunder clouds do not always give rain. (Armenian)
Thunder without rain is like words without deeds. (Burmese)
When the thunder rumbles once, all the world under heaven immediately knows.
   (Chinese)

Tickle

Those who tickle themselves may laugh whenever they please. (German)

Tide

A rising tide lifts all boats. (Roman)
Boats sail with the tide. (Korean)
Every tide has its ebb. (Irish)
The greater the tide, the greater the ebb. (Welsh)
The tide will fetch away what the ebb brings. (Spanish)
Time and tide wait for no one. (Irish)
What is written on the sand is washed out by the tide. (Filipino)

Tie

He that ties well, unties well. (Spanish)

Tiger

A tiger does not have to proclaim its tigritude. (Nigerian)
A tiger will not eat its own cubs. (Malaysian)
As the doe gives birth to the fawn, the tiger eats it. (Burmese)
Court not companionship with tigers. (Roman)
He who rides a tiger is afraid to dismount. (Japanese)
It takes two to collar a tiger. (the Editor)
The bleating of the lamb merely arouses the tiger. (French)
The child of a tiger is a tiger. (Haitian)
The one who rears a tiger courts danger. (Japanese)
'Tis hard to hold a tiger by the tail. (English)
Unless you enter the tiger's den, you won't catch her cubs. (Japanese)
Vicious as a tigress can be, she never eats her own cubs. (Chinese)
When tigers transform themselves into men, their tails do not change. (Chinese)
Who rides a tiger cannot dismount. (Chinese)

Time

A man with a watch knows what time it is; a man with two watches is never sure.
   (French)
A stitch in time saves nine. (English)
All comes right in time. (German)
All things grow with time, except grief. (Yiddish)
All times are good when old. (Polish)
An ounce of gold will not buy an inch of time. (Chinese)
Better to take your time. (Roman)
But meanwhile it is flying, irretrievable time is flying. (Roman)
Employ thy time well, if thou meanest to gain leisure. (Poor Richard)
Every moment is golden. (English)
Everything becomes mellower with time. (Roman)
Everything has its time. (Portuguese)
From tomorrow till tomorrow time goes a long journey. (French)
Give time time. (Italian)
He that gives time to resolve, gives time to deny, and warning to prevent. (Roman)
He that has time has life. (English)
He that neglects time, time will neglect. (Spanish)
Hour by hour time departs. (Italian)
If you don't have time to do it right, you must have time to do it over. (Russian)
In time a mouse will gnaw through a cable. (Dutch)
In time the bull is brought to wear the yoke. (Roman)
In time the unmanageable young oxen come to the plow; in time the horses are taught
   to endure the restraining bit. (Roman)
In time, even a bear can be taught to dance. (Yiddish)

In time, little and often make a heap. (Unknown)

It is never too late to ask what time it is. (Roman)

It is not that we have so little time, but that we have lost so much. (Roman)

Length of time rots a stone. (Roman)

Let us redeem the time for the days are evil. (St Paul)

Lost time is never found again. (Poor Richard)

Make good use of your time, for it flies fast. (Roman)

No time to waste like the present. (English)

Once upon a time, was no time. (German)

Only time will tell. (American)

Redeem the time. (Christian)

Take time when time is, for time will slip away. (Russian)

The happier the moments, the shorter the time. (Italian)

The happier the time, the more quickly it passes. (Roman)

The one who loses Monday loses the week. (Russian)

The right time comes but once. (Italian)

The third time's the charm. (American)

There is a time and place for everything. (Roman)

There is a time to speak and a time to be silent. (English)

There's always a first time. (American)

There's no time like the present. (American)

Those who have the most to do will find the most time. (English)

Time and the hour are not to be tied with a rope. (Unknown)

Time and tide wait for no one. (Irish)

Time brings roses. (English)

Time covers and discovers everything. (German)

Time cures our griefs. (Roman)

Time destroys all things. (Dutch)

Time enough, always proves little enough. (Poor Richard)

Time erases the comments of opinion, but it confirms the judgments of nature.
   (Roman)

Time flies. (Roman)

Time flies like an arrow. (Japanese)

Time flies with hasty step. (Roman)

Time gained, much gained. (Dutch)

Time gives good advice. (Maltese)

Time heals all wounds. (American)

Time heals old pain, while it creates new ones. (Yiddish)

Time is a broom that sweeps us into our graves. (Spanish)

Time is a great healer. (Yiddish)

Time is a great storyteller. (Irish)

Time is an herb that cures all diseases. (Poor Richard)

Time is an inaudible file. (Italian)

Time is anger's medicine. (German)

Time is gold. (Mexican)

Time is medicine. (Korean)
Time is money. (English)
Time is not tied to a post, like a horse to the manger. (Danish)
Time is the best of the healing arts. (Roman)
Time is the best preacher. (German)
Time is the field where I sow. (Spanish)
Time is the greatest innovator. (Roman)
Time is the herald of truth. (German)
Time is the rider that breaks youth. (English)
Time lost cannot be won again. (Unknown)
Time marches on. (American)
Time never stands still. (Unknown)
Time passes like the wind. (Portuguese)
Time past never returns. (Dutch)
Time reveals the truth. (Roman)
Time rolls on steadily, and eludes us as it steals past. (Roman)
Time softens animosity. (Roman)
Time tries all things. (Japanese)
Time waits for no man. (German)
Time will tell. (Jamaican)
Time works wonders. (English)
Wasting time is robbing oneself. (Estonian)
What greater crime than loss of time? (German)
What is there that corroding time does not damage? (Roman)
While I am speaking, time flies. (Roman)
You don't need a watch to know when it's time to die. (Yiddish)

Times

As are the times, so are the manners. (Spanish)
Like times, like men. (Yiddish)
One must move with the times. (Roman)
Other times, other manners. (French)
Suit yourself to the times. (German)
The times are changing, and we too are changing with them. (Roman)

Timid, Timidity

A timid dog barks more violently than it bites. (Roman)
A timid love is not a true love. (Spanish)
A timid man has little chance. (Danish)
A timid man is far from danger. (Irish)
A timid sparrow was hit by a stone before. (Burmese)
Bold in design, but timid in execution. (Roman)
The fruit of timidity is neither loss nor gain. (Arabian)
The mother of a timid man seldom has reason to weep. (Roman)

Timing

Timing has a lot to do with the outcome of a rain dance. (American)

Tinker

In mending one hole, the bad tinker makes three. (Spanish)

Tire, Tired

He who does not tire, achieves. (Spanish)
The tired mare goes willingly to pasture. (Portuguese)
The tired ox plants its foot more firmly. (Roman)

Tit for Tat

Claw me and I'll claw thee. (German)
Strife engenders strife, and injury likewise engenders injury. (Roman)
You break my pot, I break your bowl. (Burmese)
For kindness, return kindness; for evil, return evil. (Japanese)
Hit with a fist, be hit with a club. (Korean)
Hit with a stick, be hit with a club. (Japanese)

Today

Let us live today, forgetting the cares that are past. (Greek)
Today is another day. (Mexican)
Today is yesterday's pupil. (German)

Today and Tomorrow

A bar of candy today is sweeter than a bowl of honey tomorrow. (Korean)
For tomorrow belongs to the people who prepare for it today. (African)
It is because of tomorrow than one cleans up today. (Hausan)
Never do today what you can put off until tomorrow. (American)
One hour today is worth two tomorrow. (Roman)
One today is worth two tomorrows. (German)
Prefer fifty today than a hundred tomorrow. (Japanese)
Rooster today, feather duster tomorrow. (Russian)
Today does not secure tomorrow's affairs; going to bed does not ensure one's rising
    again. (Chinese)
Today in finery, tomorrow in filth. (German)
Today is senior to tomorrow. (Yoruban)
Today looks forward, but tomorrow looks back. (the Editor)
Today stately and brave, tomorrow in the grave. (Dutch)
Today's daring paves the way for tomorrow's regret. (Spanish)
Today's egg is better than tomorrow's hen. (Turkish)
Tomorrow is today. (Mexican)
Tomorrow will not likely be like today. (Yoruban)
Tomorrow's remedy will not ward off today's evil. (Spanish)
What is lost today is regained tomorrow. (Mexican)

What you sow today is what you will reap tomorrow. (Yoruban)
When God says Today, the Devil says Tomorrow. (German)

Toe

The toe of the star-gazer is often stubbed. (Russian)

Toil

Don't make a toil of pleasure. (Yiddish)

Toilet

Crap or get off the pot. (American)

Tomb

Men walk out of jail but never from the tomb. (Mexican)

Tomorrow

It is not permitted to man to know what tomorrow may bring forth. (Roman)
Let us think of tomorrow when tomorrow comes. (Persian)
No one can lock the door on tomorrow. (Unknown)
No one has seen tomorrow. (Portuguese)
No one knows what tomorrow will bring. (Yiddish)
Take off your hat to your yesterdays; take off your coat for your tomorrows. (Dutch)
Tomorrow is another day. (English)
Tomorrow is often the busiest day of the week. (Spanish)
Tomorrow never comes. (American)
Tomorrow will take care of itself. (Jesus)
Tomorrow your horse may be lame. (Yiddish)
Tomorrow's winds will blow tomorrow. (Japanese)

Tongue

A brain is worth little without a tongue. (French)
A bridle for the tongue is a necessary piece of furniture. (Chinese)
A honey tongue, a heart of gall. (German)
A long tongue betokens a short hand. (Spanish)
A long tongue is the staircase by which misfortunes ascend. (Chinese)
A man's ruin lies in his tongue. (Egyptian)
A nasty tongue is worse than a wicked hand. (Yiddish)
A quiet tongue shows a wise head. (Irish)
A slip of the foot you may soon recover, but a slip of the tongue you may never get over. (Poor Richard)
A slip of the tongue ought not to be rashly punished. (Roman)
A smooth tongue is better than smooth locks. (Danish)
A soft tongue may strike hard. (Poor Richard)
A still tongue makes a wise head. (English)
A thousand gold pieces in debt may be settled with a silver tongue. (Korean)

A woman's tongue is her sword, and she does not let it rust. (French)

An evil tongue is the proof of an evil mind. (Roman)

Better a slip of the foot than a slip of the tongue. (Spanish)

Bind your tongue or your tongue will have you bound. (Roman)

Dogs have so many friends because they wag their tails, not their tongues. (Chinese)

Fear the quick tongue more than the sword. (Japanese)

For evil tongues, scissors. (Spanish)

Four horses cannot overtake the tongue. (Chinese)

God gave us teeth to hold back our tongue. (Greek)

He loses least in a quarrel who keeps his tongue in check. (Danish)

He who guards his tongue guards his property. (Spanish)

He who has a bad tongue should have good loins. (Italian)

He who has a tongue, may go to Rome. (Italian)

He who holds his tongue does not commit himself. (French)

In the tongue there lurks a dragon; no blood is seen and yet it murders many. (Chinese)

It is more difficult to bridle the tongue than to conquer an army. (Roman)

Keep not two tongues in one mouth. (Danish)

Keep the tongue in your mouth a prisoner. (Turkish)

Let him who is well off hold his tongue. (German)

Let not the tongue utter what the head must pay for. (Spanish)

Let not your tongue cut your own throat. (Jamaican)

Let the poor man mind his tongue. (Roman)

Many a man's own tongue gives evidence against his understanding. (Poor Richard)

Nature has given us two ears, two eyes, and but one tongue. (German)

No one ever repented of having held his tongue. (Italian)

Nothing looks more like a man of sense than a fool who holds his tongue. (German)

Obey the tongue and you will later repent. (Egyptian)

One man uses his tongue, another his teeth. (Roman)

One should beware of the double-tongued. (Roman)

See, hear, and hold your tongue. (Spanish)

Teach thy tongue to say, 'I do not know.' (Yiddish)

The entire world rests on the tip of the tongue. (Yiddish)

The one without silver must have silk on his tongue. (German)

The pen of the tongue should be dipped in the ink of the heart. (Chinese)

The silent tongue receives nothing. (German)

The strength of a woman is in her tongue. (Hausan)

The tongue bites sharper than the teeth. (Spanish)

The tongue can raise you, and it can behead you. (Indian)

The tongue has no bones yet it can break bones. (Greek)

The tongue is ever turning to the aching tooth. (Poor Richard)

The tongue is like a sharp knife: it kills without drawing blood. (Chinese)

The tongue is more to be feared than the sword. (Japanese)

The tongue is not steel, yet it cuts. (Unknown)

The tongue is the neck's worst enemy. (Egyptian)

The tongue of a bad friend cuts more than a knife. (Spanish)

The tongue of the wise is in his heart, the heart of the fool is in his mouth.
  (Egyptian)
The tongue offends, and the ears get the cuffing. (Poor Richard)
The tongue wounds more than a lance. (French)
There is an ax hidden below the tongue. (Korean)
Thistles and thorns prick sore, but evil tongues prick more. (Dutch)
Though the tongue has no bone, it breaks many a head. (Irish)
To make another person hold his tongue, be first silent. (Roman)
To restrain the tongue is not the least of the virtues. (Roman)
Turn your tongue seven times before speaking. (French)
Use your ears and eyes, but hold your tongue, if you would live in peace. (Roman)
What the heart thinks the tongue speaks. (Irish)
Whatever is in the heart will come out on the tongue. (Persian)
When tongues move, the hands rest. (Spanish)
Where the tongue slips it speaks the truth. (Irish)
Wide ears and short tongue are the best. (English)
Wounds from the knife are healed, but not those from the tongue. (Spanish)

Too Many

Too many bricklayers make a lopsided house. (Chinese)
Too many captains will sink the ship. (Danish)
Too many cooks oversalt the porridge. (Dutch)
Too many cooks spoil the broth. (English)
Too many doctors and the son dies. (Burmese)
Too many irons, too little heat. (the Editor)
Too many sacks are the death of the ass. (German)
Too many sailors will sink a ship. (Egyptian)

Too Much

Better there should be too much than too little. (Spanish)
Too much bed makes a dull head. (German)
Too much breaks the bag. (Spanish)
Too much care does more harm than good. (Roman)
Too much carp makes the curry insipid. (Burmese)
Too much effort may injure rather than improve your work. (Roman)
Too much familiarity breeds contempt. (Portuguese)
Too much fruit bursts the bag. (German)
Too much honor is half a shame. (Yiddish)
Too much humility is pride. (German)
Too much is not enough. (German)
Too much luck is bad luck. (German)
Too much medicine may poison the body. (Japanese)
Too much mothering can be downright smothering. (the Editor)
Too much of anything is a bad thing. (Roman)
Too much of anything is too much. (Unknown)

Too much of one thing is good for nothing. (German)
Too much talk will incur errors. (Burmese)
Too much water drowned the miller. (French)
Too much wisdom is folly. (German)
Too much zeal spoils all. (French)
Who undertakes too much, succeeds but little. (Dutch)

Tool
It's no delay to stop to sharpen the tool. (Irish)
Man is greater than the tools he invents. (American)

Tooth
Better a tooth out than one always aching. (German)
The tooth often bites the tongue, and yet they keep together. (Danish)

Top
The climb may be steep, but it's good to be at the top. (American)
There's always room at the top. (English)

Torch
The more light a torch gives, the shorter it lasts. (German)

Torment, Tormentor
He who torments others does not sleep well. (French)
The tormentor forgets that there is tomorrow. (Yoruban)

Tortoise
The tortoise carries his house with him. (Yoruban)

Tough
Things are tough all over. (American)
Tough times don't last but tough people do. (French)
When the going gets tough, the tough get going. (American)

Tower, Towers
Lofty towers fall with a heavier crash. (Roman)
Towers are measured by the shadows they cast. (Spanish)

Town
Don't live in a town where there are no doctors. (Yiddish)
God made the country, man made the town. (Spanish)
If everyone swept in front of his house, the whole town would be clean. (Polish)
The town that parleys is half surrendered. (French)

Trade

A good trade will carry farther than a thousand florins. (German)

A handful of trade, a handful of gold. (Dutch)

A jack of all trades is master of none. (English)

A trade not properly learned is an enemy. (Irish)

Another man's trade costs money. (Portuguese)

Every man has a good wife and a bad trade. (Italian)

Every man to his trade. (Portuguese)

He who has a trade may travel throughout the world. (Spanish)

Seven trades but no luck. (Arabian)

There are tricks in every trade. (English)

Trade follows the flag. (English)

Trade knows neither friends nor kindred. (French)

Two of a trade can never agree. (English)

Train, Trained

Branches may be trained; not the trunk. (Roman)

Traitor

Even among the apostles there was a Judas. (Italian)

No wise man ever thought that a traitor should be trusted. (Roman)

The loyal man lives no longer than the traitor pleases. (Spanish)

Translation

Translation is at best an echo. (German)

Trap

Everyone is glad to see a knave caught in his own trap. (German)

If the trap does not catch the rat, the bait is returned to the owner. (Yoruban)

Subtlety set a trap and caught itself. (Roman)

Trash

One man's trash is another man's treasure. (American)

Travel, Traveled

A man travels as far in a day as a snail in a hundred years. (French)

Abroad one has a hundred eyes, at home not one. (German)

Abroad to see wonders the traveler goes, and neglects the fine things which lie under his nose. (German)

Even at six feet a day, the city will be reached. (Burmese)

Go as far as you can see, and when you get there you'll see further. (Persian)

He that would travel much, should eat little. (Poor Richard)

He travels fastest who travels alone. (Roman)

He who goes abroad by day has no need of a lantern. (French)

He who goes everywhere gains everywhere. (French)

He who goes softly, goes safely; he who goes safely, goes far. (Italian)

He who wants to travel far takes care of his beast. (French)

He who would travel through the land, must go with open purse in hand. (Dutch)

If a worthless fellow travel with you, don't let him go; else a worse fellow may join you.
    (Egyptian)

If you stop every time a dog barks, your road will never end. (Arabian)

It is better to travel hopefully than to arrive. (Spanish)

Little by little one goes far. (Spanish)

Only he that has traveled the road knows where the potholes lie. (Chinese)

Some roads aren't meant to be traveled alone. (Chinese)

Travel broadens the mind. (English)

Travel ripens a man. (Persian)

When you travel by boat be prepared to swim. (Chinese)

Where a man never goes, there his head will never be washed. (Danish)

Who loves to roam may lose his home. (Italian)

Who wishes to travel far spares his steed. (French)

Traveler

A traveler to distant places should make no enemies. (Nigerian)

Often has luck attended a slow traveler. (Scottish)

The penniless traveler sings before the robber. (Roman)

The traveler has tales to tell. (Irish)

Treachery

He covers me with his wings, and bites me with his bill. (Dutch)

Honeyed speech often conceals poison and gall. (Danish)

If a man secretly betrays his friends, evil things will secretly happen to him.
    (Yoruban)

In the end, treachery will betray even itself. (Roman)

It is not becoming to play the fox, or to play upon both sides. (Roman)

No one can guard against treachery. (German)

Treachery is admired, but not the one who commits it. (Spanish)

Treachery lurks in honeyed words. (Danish)

Treachery returns. (Irish)

Trust makes way for treachery. (Arabian)

Tread, Trodden

He who lies on the ground must expect to be trodden upon. (German)

He who treads on eggs, must tread lightly. (German)

Treason

The treason is loved, the traitor hated. (German)

Treasure, Treasures

All the treasures of earth cannot bring back one lost moment. (French)

The richest treasures are the deepest buried. (Spanish)
There are no better treasures than children. (Japanese)

Treat
People treat you as they perceive you. (Mexican)

Tree, Trees
A bad tree does not yield good apples. (Danish)
A fallen tree provides plenty of kindling. (Armenian)
A tree does not move unless there is wind. (Nigerian)
A tree is best measured when it's down. (Nigerian)
A tree is known by its fruit. (Roman)
A tree makes progress when transplanted. (Roman)
A tree must be bent while it is young. (Japanese)
A tree often transplanted does not thrive. (Roman)
A tree that grows crooked can never straighten its limbs. (Mexican)
A well-regarded tree may have dry rot. (Korean)
A young tree bends, an old one hardens and breaks. (Spanish)
Apples do not fall far from the apple tree. (Slavic)
As a tree falls, so shall it lie. (the Bible)
As bends the sapling, so grows the tree. (German)
As the tree, so the fruit; as the mistress, so the maid. (German)
As the twig is bent, so is the tree inclined. (German)
Bend the tree while it is young. (Italian)
Do not cut the bough you are sitting on. (Rumanian)
Does a woodsman tap a withered tree? (Unknown)
Don't trim the tree that gives you shade. (Hungarian)
Even the goats will jump on a slanted tree. (Polish)
Everyone gets wood from a fallen tree. (Spanish)
Great trees are envied by the wind. (Japanese)
Great trees give more shade than fruit. (German)
Honor the tree that gives you shelter. (Danish)
If you lean upon a good tree you will be protected by a good shadow. (Spanish)
It is easy to stride a tree when it is down. (Danish)
It is only at the tree loaded with fruit that people throw stones. (French)
It is soon known which trees will bear fruit. (Roman)
Not all trees have birds' nests. (Japanese)
Old trees are not to be bent. (German)
On a big tree, there are always dead branches. (Chinese)
One tree won't hold two robins. (Roman)
Rivers have sources, trees have roots. (German)
The banana tree is free from the knife of the carver. (Yoruban)
The bigger the tree the harder it falls. (Jamaican)
The fig tree splits huge blocks of marble. (Roman)
The highest tree hath the greatest fall. (Roman)

The leaves don't fall too far from the tree. (Jamaican)
The nobler the tree, the more pliant the twig. (Dutch)
The older the tree the more weight it bears. (German)
The one who cares for the tree must also care for its branches. (Mexican)
The root of a tree that grew up in wind is strong. (Japanese)
The tallest tree has but its measure. (German)
The tallest tree is rooted in the ground. (Russian)
The tree does not fall at the first stroke. (Italian)
To dig up a tree you must begin with the root. (Chinese)
Trees often transplanted seldom prosper. (Dutch)
When the tree dies, the grass underneath withers. (Chinese)
Where the tree falls, there shall it lie. (Jamaican)
Who stays under the tree, eats the fruits. (Albanian)
You cannot transplant an old tree without its dying. (Danish)

Trial
He goes safely to trial whose father is a judge. (Spanish)

Trick, Trickery
A trick is clever only once. (Yiddish)
One trick is met by another. (Spanish)
Trickery comes back to its master. (French)

Trifle
A trifle may incur murdering. (Korean)
Do not trifle with fire or women. (Spanish)

Triumph
Do not celebrate your triumph before you have conquered. (Roman)
Old age and treachery will triumph over youth and skill. (Greek)

Trojans
The Trojans were wise too late. (Italian)

Trouble, Troubled
A trouble shared is a trouble halved. (English)
Bygone troubles are good to tell. (Yiddish)
Do not meet troubles half-way. (Yiddish)
Don't make waves. (Belgian)
Everyone bears his own cross. (French)
He that seeks trouble always finds it. (English)
He that will have no trouble in this world must not be born in it. (Dutch)
He who has a white horse and a fair wife is seldom without trouble. (Danish)
If it's not one thing, it's another. (Italian)
If severe, short; if long, light. (Roman)

If you go looking for trouble, trouble will find you. (Jamaican)

In time of test, family is best. (Burmese)

Never trouble trouble until trouble troubles you. (English)

No one gets into trouble without his own help. (Danish)

One man's good is another man's trouble. (German)

The day sees many troubles. (German)

The way out of trouble is never as easy as the way in. (American)

They who have nothing to be troubled at, will be troubled at nothing. (Poor Richard)

Trouble hangs around the neck of the living. (Yoruban)

Trouble is to man what rust is to iron. (Yiddish)

Troubles come at a gallop and go away at a snail's pace. (Spanish)

When in trouble one remembers Allah. (Hausan)

Who troubles others has no rest himself. (Italian)

True

Not everything that is true is to be discussed. (Spanish)

Speak little, speak truth; spend little, spend true. (German)

That is true which all men say. (Danish)

What everybody says must be true. (Roman)

Trump

With someone holding nothing but trumps it is impossible to play cards. (German)

Trust

A betrayed trust is a mortal thrust. (Burmese)

Do not trust the emir if his vizier should cheat you. (Egyptian)

Don't rely on the label of the bag. (French)

Faith in a lord, a cap for the fool. (Italian)

He that trusts a faithless friend has a good witness against him. (Spanish)

He who looks demurely, trust him not with your money. (Spanish)

He who trusts a woman and leads an ass will never be free from plague. (French)

If you trust before you try, you will repent before you die. (Burmese)

In God we trust – all others pay cash. (American)

It is an equal failing to trust everybody and to trust nobody. (English)

It is better to trust our eyes than our ears. (Roman)

It is equally an error to trust in all and in none. (Roman)

It is wise not to trust too hastily. (Roman)

More die by trust than caution. (Spanish)

Never trust an alliance with the powerful. (Roman)

Never trust the man who tells you all his troubles but keeps from you all his joys. (Yiddish)

Never trust to another what you should do yourself. (German)

Respect all, but trust few. (Spanish)

Trust and God will provide. (German)

Trust everybody, but thyself most. (Danish)

Trust God and keep your powder dry. (American)

Trust in Allah, but tie your camel. (Persian)
Trust in God but lock your doors. (Russian)
Trust is the mother of deceit. (English)
Trust makes way for treachery. (Arabian)
Trust neither a cow's horn, a dog's tooth, nor a horse's hoof. (English)
Trust neither a dog's tooth, a horse's hoof, nor a baby's bottom. (French)
Trust no man till you have eaten a peck of salt with him. (Roman)
Trust not a dog that limps. (Portuguese)
Trust not a new friend or an old enemy. (Portuguese)
Trust not a spiteful man. (Irish)
Trust not still water nor a silent man. (Danish)
Trust not the man who always smiles. (Spanish)
Trust not the words of the base and immoral. (Roman)
Trust not too much in a beautiful complexion. (Roman)
Trust only heavenly saints. (Spanish)
Trust was a good man; Trust-not was a better. (Italian)
Trust Well rides away with the horse. (German)
Trust, but beware whom. (German)
Trust, but be careful in whom. (Roman)
Trust, but not too much. (German)
We should trust more to our eyes than to our ears. (Roman)
Woe to the goose that trusts the fox. (Danish)

Truth, Truths

A document does not blush. (Roman)
A known mistake is better than an unknown truth. (Arabian)
A thing is never much talked of but there is some truth in it. (Italian)
A thousand probabilities do not make one truth. (Italian)
A truth that hurts is preferable to a lie that flatters. (Spanish)
A truth-teller finds the doors closed against him. (Danish)
A truth-telling woman has few friends. (Danish)
All the truth should not be told. (Scottish)
All truths are not good to be uttered. (French)
Anyone can tell a lie, but the truth reveals itself. (Jamaican)
Better to suffer for truth than prosper by falsehood. (Danish)
Between wrangling and disputing truth is lost. (German)
By way of doubting we arrive at the truth. (Roman)
Children and drunkards always tell the truth. (Mexican)
Children and fools tell the truth. (German)
Craftiness must have clothes, but truth loves to go naked. (English)
Do not conceal the truth from confessors, doctors, or lawyers. (French)
Even the truth may be bitter. (Irish)
Half the truth is a whole lie. (Yiddish)
Half the truth is often a great lie. (Poor Richard)
He must keep a sharp look-out who would speak the truth. (Danish)

He who does not speak the whole truth is a traitor to it. (Roman)

How many will listen to the truth when you tell them? (Yiddish)

If everybody says so, there must be some truth to it. (Yiddish)

If the truth so offends, be offended. (the Editor)

In everything truth surpasses its imitation. (Roman)

It is best not to tell every truth. (Italian)

It is good to know the truth, but it is better to speak of palm trees. (Arabian)

It is said that truth is often eclipsed but never extinguished. (Roman)

It is truth that makes many angry. (Italian)

Nature has planted in our minds an insatiable desire to seek the truth. (Roman)

Not all that is true is to be spoken. (Portuguese)

Nothing is loftier than the love of truth. (Roman)

Obsequiousness brings us friends, the truth brings forth enemies. (Roman)

Out of falsehood comes truth. (Japanese)

Plato is my friend, but truth is more my friend. (Roman)

Seeing is believing, but feeling's the truth. (German)

Seek the truth from a child. (Persian)

Sooner or later the truth comes to light. (Dutch)

Tell the truth and run. (Slavic)

Tell the truth and shame the Devil. (English)

Tell the truth and you ask for a beating. (Yiddish)

The greater the truth, the greater the libel. (English)

The language of truth is simple. (Roman)

The path of truth leads to God. (Yiddish)

The truth can be told, even in jest. (Turkish)

The truth is an offense, but not a sin. (Jamaican)

The truth is not always what we want to hear. (Yiddish)

The voice of truth is easily known. (African)

Though a lie be swift, truth overtakes it. (Italian)

To withhold truth is to bury gold. (Danish)

Truth becomes disagreeable only to the fool. (Egyptian)

Truth begets hatred. (Roman)

Truth, by whomever it is spoken, comes from God. (Roman)

Truth came to the market and could not be sold; we buy lies with ready cash. (Yoruban)

Truth conquers all things. (Roman)

Truth fears nothing but concealment. (Roman)

Truth gives a short answer, lies go round about. (German)

Truth has but one face, a lie has one hundred. (Spanish)

Truth hates delays. (Roman)

Truth ill-timed is as bad as a lie. (German)

Truth is better than friendship. (Indian)

Truth is bitter, lies are sweet. (the Editor)

Truth is God's daughter. (Danish)

Truth is great and will prevail. (Roman)

Truth is indeed an attribute of wine. (Roman)

Truth is lame, but it forges ahead. (Maltese)
Truth is lost with too much debating. (Roman)
Truth is often stranger than fiction. (English)
Truth is the safest lie. (Yiddish)
Truth lies at the bottom of a well. (Roman)
Truth lies wrapped up and hidden in the depths. (Roman)
Truth, like oil, always comes to the surface. (Spanish)
Truth may be kept down, but not crushed. (Roman)
Truth may be suppressed, but not strangled. (Roman)
Truth may suffer but it will never die. (Spanish)
Truth may walk through the world unarmed. (Arabian)
Truth must be seasoned to make it palatable. (Danish)
Truth never dies, but it lives a wretched life. (Yiddish)
Truth rests with God alone, and a little with me. (Yiddish)
Truth shines in the dark. (Welsh)
Truth should not always be revealed. (German)
Truth sits upon the lips of a dying man. (Unknown)
Truth will out. (English)
We are often misled by the appearance of truth. (Roman)
When you tell the truth, have one foot in the stirrup. (Turkish)
Whoever tells the truth is chased out of nine villages. (African)
Women always speak the truth, but not the whole truth. (Italian)

Try
Nothing beats a failure but a try. (Jamaican)
There's nothing like trying. (German)
To try and to fail is not laziness. (African)

Tub
Every tub must stand on its own bottom. (English)

Tune
There's many a good tune played on an old fiddle. (English)

Turkey
A turkey never voted for an early Christmas. (Irish)

Turn, Turns
Everything comes and goes by turns. (Unknown)
It is an ill turn that does good to no one. (Danish)
Mine today, yours tomorrow. (German)
One good turn deserves another. (English)

Turnabout
Turnabout is fair play. (English)

Turnip

You cannot get blood from a turnip. (German)

Turtle

When you see a turtle on top of a fence post, you know it had some help. (African)

Twig

A tender twig is easiest to twist. (Scottish)

A twig is difficult to bend after becoming a tree. (Irish)

Bend the twig while it is green. (Scottish)

Twine

Even the biggest ball of twine unwinds. (Yiddish)

Two

It is always good to have two strings to your bow. (Italian)

It is best to trust to two anchors. (Danish)

It takes two to tango. (American)

One man can do nothing, two can do much. (Roman)

Two birds disputed about a kernel, when a third swooped down and carried it off. (African)

Two captains will sink the ship. (Turkish)

Two cats and one mouse, two women in one house, two dogs to one bone, will not agree long. (German)

Two cocks in one house, a cat and a mouse, an old man and young wife, are always in strife. (Dutch)

Two cocks in one yard do not agree. (Italian)

Two dogs fight for a bone and a third runs away with it. (Italian)

Two dogs seldom agree over one bone. (Dutch)

Two donkeys together will act and smell like asses. (Persian)

Two dry sticks will burn a green one. (Poor Richard)

Two eyes can see more than one. (Roman)

Two eyes, two ears, only one mouth. (German)

Two good talkers are not worth one good listener. (Chinese)

Two heads are better than one. (English)

Two heroes cannot brook rivalry. (Japanese)

Two in distress makes sorrow the less. (German)

Two may lie so as to hang a third. (Danish)

Two men may meet, but never two mountains. (French)

Two needles cannot hurt each other. (Mexican)

Two of a trade can never agree. (English)

Two pieces of meat confuse the mind of the fly. (Hausan)

Two pigs will not go into one bag. (English)

Two shorten the road. (Irish)

Two things are a burden: a fool among wise men, and a wise man among fools. (Yiddish)

Two things prolong your life: a quiet heart and a loving wife. (English)

Two watermelons cannot be held under one arm. (Turkish)

Two who sleep in the same bed will soon dance to the same tune. (Spanish)

Two wrongs don't make a right. (English)

Two's company but three's a crowd. (American)

Two's company, three's trumpery [i.e., deception]. (English)

Where two fall out, the third wins. (German)

Tyrant

It is time to fear when tyrants seem to kiss. (English)

The tyrant is only the slave turned inside out. (Egyptian)

The wealth of a tyrant is the poverty of his subjects. (Roman)

What is more violent than the ear of a tyrant? (Roman)

U

Understand, Understanding

If you understand everything, you must be misinformed. (Japanese)

If you would understand men, study women. (French)

In chatter a river, in understanding but a single drop. (Roman)

It is afterwards that events are understood. (Irish)

The less a man understands, the better off he is. (Yiddish)

A thing is not bad if well understood. (German)

Be not disturbed at being misunderstood; be disturbed at not understanding. (Chinese)

Unexpected

The day I did not sweep the house was the day there came someone I did not expect.
   (Spanish)

The unexpected always happens. (German)

Unforeseen

Unlooked-for often comes. (German)

Unfortunate

The unfortunate rejoiced at the rising of the Nile, and were drowned. (Egyptian)

Ungrateful

A donkey always says thank you with a kick. (Kenyan)

He is an ungrateful man who is unwilling to acknowledge his obligation before others.
   (Roman)

If you pronounce a man ungrateful you say all that can be said against him. (Roman)

The earth produces nothing worse than an ungrateful man. (Roman)

The ungrateful return evil for good. (Japanese)

Uninvited

Come uninvited, sit unserved. (German)

He who comes uninvited goes away unthanked. (Dutch)

Union

All for one and one for all. (Roman)

In union is strength, in discord destruction. (Spanish)

Union gives strength to the humblest of aids. (Roman)

Union is strength. (Japanese)

United, Unity

A common danger begets unity. (Roman)

There is no strength without unity. (Irish)

United we stand, divided we fall. (American)

When spiders unite, they can tie down a lion. (Ethiopian)

Unkind

He that is unkind to his own will not be kind to others. (Rumanian)

Unknown

Everything unknown is thought to be magnificent. (Roman)

The unknown is always great. (American)

The unknown is ever imagined. (Greek)

Unlikely

Often has the likely failed and the unlikely prospered. (Irish)

Unlucky

The day dawns after an unlucky man leaps. (Unknown)

The unlucky man fell on his back and broke his nose. (Korean)

Unseemly

What is unseemly is unsafe. (Roman)

Uneducated

An uneducated boy is like an untamed colt. (Spanish)

An uneducated person is like an unpolished mirror. (German)

Unwilling

Nothing is easy to the unwilling. (French)

Up and Down

Dive down till you reach the bottom; climb up till you reach the top. (Burmese)

What goes down usually comes up. (German)

What goes up must come down. (American)

449

Upbringing

Better than birth is upbringing. (Japanese)
Between age ten and thirteen, bend the twig while it be green. (Scottish)
Birth is much, but breeding is more. (Unknown)
Every child is as it is brought up. (Irish)
Everything a man says was learned in the nursery. (German)
He is not well-bred, that cannot bear ill-breeding in others. (Poor Richard)

Uphill

Every uphill has its downhill. (Yiddish)

Upright

If you are standing upright, don't worry if your shadow is crooked. (Chinese)

Use, Used, Useful

A spade used often will not rust. (Japanese)
A used plow shines, standing water stinks. (German)
As a thing is used, so it brightens. (German)
By constant use an iron ring is worn away. (Roman)
From misuse one sometimes learns the correct use. (German)
He who is of no use to himself is of no use to anyone else. (German)
More than we use is more than we want. (English)
That which is despised is often most useful. (Roman)
Things break with repeated use. (French)
Use not today what tomorrow you may want. (English)
What is in use, wants no excuse. (Spanish)
What is useful is valuable. (Roman)

V

Vagrant

Take away the danger, remove the restraint, and vagrant nature bounds forth free.
   (Roman)

Vain

Gold is vain, silver is vain; you, the dead, cannot them retain. (Chinese)
It is in vain for a man to rise early who has the repute of lying in bed all the morning.
   (French)
It is in vain to cast nets in a river where there are no fish. (Spanish)
It is in vain to lay a net in sight of the birds. (Italian)
It is in vain to lead the ox to the water if it is not thirsty. (French)
It is in vain to fish without a hook. (Italian)

Valley

He that stays in the valley will not get over the hill. (French)

Valor

Hidden valor is as bad as cowardice. (Roman)
Valor becomes feeble without an opponent. (Roman)
Valor even in an enemy is worthy of praise. (Roman)
Valor will give, care will keep. (Roman)
Valor would fight, but discretion would run away. (English)

Value, Valued

A man is valued according to his own estimate of himself. (French)
A thing too much seen is little prized. (French)
An indispensable thing never has much value. (Russian)
Every man has his value. (French)
Everyone counts for as much as he has. (German)
If you would know the value of money, try to borrow some. (English)
The value of each man consists in what he does well. (Egyptian)
Who would wish to be valued must make himself scarce. (German)
You will be of as much value to others as you have been to yourself. (Roman)

Vanity

A vain beauty breaks her mirrors when old. (Korean)
Levity is inborn, but vanity is instilled. (Roman)
Vanity has no greater foe than vanity. (French)

Variety

Nothing is pleasant to which variety does not give relish. (Roman)
Variety is delighting. (Roman)
Variety is the spice of life. (American)
Variety seasons the stew. (German)

Vengeance

A woman's vengeance knows no bounds. (German)
The noblest vengeance is to forgive. (Dutch)
The smallest vengeance poisons the soul. (Yiddish)
Vengeance follows after vice. (Unknown)
Vengeance is slow, but stern. (Roman)

Vessel

A vessel holds only its fill. (Irish)
A worthless vessel is seldom broken. (Roman)
An ugly vessel never falls from the hand. (Spanish)
The greatest vessel hath but its measure. (Unknown)
Unless the vessel is clean, everything you pour into it turns sour. (Roman)

Vice, Vices

After one vice a greater follows. (Spanish)

Every vice ever stands on a precipice. (Roman)

Everyone has his own vices. (Roman)

Excess in anything becomes a vice. (Roman)

Gambling is akin to robbery; adultery is next door to murder. (Chinese)

Great men's vices are accounted sacred. (German)

In fleeing one vice we are sometimes caught by another. (Roman)

Let thy vices die before thee. (Poor Richard)

Maintain peace with men, war with their vices. (Roman)

Men aren't enticed by vice, they entice themselves. (Chinese)

Neither can we endure our vices nor the remedies for them. (Roman)

The one who hates vice, hates humanity. (Roman)

Vice is learnt without a schoolmaster. (Danish)

Vice is nourished by concealment. (Roman)

Vice knows she's ugly, so puts on her mask. (Poor Richard)

Vice rules where gold reigns. (English)

Where vice, there vengeance. (Unknown)

Victor

Often the victor triumphs but to fall. (Unknown)

Victory

A man surprised is half beaten. (German)

Do not exult too much in your victory. (Unknown)

Do not triumph before the victory. (English)

Don't divide the spoil before the victory is won. (German)

Even after victory, tighten your helmet strap. (Japanese)

Even the fiercest are overcome. (Roman)

Give way to him with whom you contend; by doing so you will gain the victory. (Roman)

He who has victory, has right. (German)

He who knows how to yield knows how to win. (Spanish)

Not by force but by virtue, not with arms but with art, is victory won. (Roman)

On the day of victory no fatigue is felt. (Egyptian)

Sing not of triumph before the victory. (Roman)

The greatest victory is victory over self. (Unknown)

The harder the fight the sweeter the victory. (Jamaican)

The race is not always to the swift, nor the battle to the strong. (the Bible)

This is how it is with human affairs: in victory even cowards boast, whereas in defeat even the brave are discredited. (Roman)

Victory has a hundred fathers but defeat is an orphan. (Chinese)

Victory lies in the hands of God. (Unknown)

Victory will carry itself. (German)

Winning battles is easier than securing victory. (Chinese)

Viewpoint
If no one is willing to accept your point of view, try to see his point of view. (Syrian)

Vigilance
Vigilance prevents misfortune. (Italian)

Village
It is better that a village should fall than a custom. (Albanian)
It takes a village to raise a child. (Nigerian)
The village that is in sight needs no guide. (Turkish)
The whole village is mother to the motherless. (Indian)

Villain
Anoint a villain and he will prick you, prick a villain and he will anoint you. (French)
No villain like the conscientious villain. (German)

Vine
Every vine must have its stake. (Italian)

Vinegar
Neither every wine nor every life turns to vinegar with age. (Roman)
Strong is the vinegar of sweet wine. (Italian)
The sweetest wine makes the sharpest vinegar. (German)

Violence, Violent
It is natural to man to resist violence. (Roman)
That which is violent never lasts long. (Roman)
If man's heart is violent, Heaven's heart will be violent. (Chinese)

Viper
No viper so little but hath its venom. (German)
Vipers breed vipers. (Danish)

Virgins
Glasses and virgins are in constant danger. (German)

Virtue, Virtuous
As gold is worth more than silver, so is virtue worth more than gold. (Roman)
Be like your father in virtue, unlike him in fortune. (Roman)
Better poverty than a home without virtue. (Chinese)
Does training produce virtue, or does nature bestow it? (Roman)
Fewer possess virtue than those who feign it. (Roman)
For who would embrace virtue itself if you took away its reward? (Roman)
From our ancestors come our names, but from our virtues our honors. (Roman)
He that sows virtue shall reap fame. (English)

If a man is evil, men fear him but Heaven does not; if a man is virtuous, men oppress him
    but Heaven does not. (Chinese)
If all men were just, there would be no need of virtue. (Greek)
In the ascent to virtue there are many steps. (Roman)
It is a little thing to starve to death, a great thing to lose one's virtue. (Chinese)
Let them recognize virtue and rot for having left it behind. (Roman)
Man ponders upon punishment but not on virtue. (Chinese)
Mankind scorns a virtuous man, but Heaven does not. (Chinese)
Men are more prone to pleasure than to virtue. (Roman)
No one can be happy without virtue. (Roman)
No possession is greater than virtue. (Roman)
One who is evil and not destroyed is sure to have hidden virtue. (Chinese)
Only one path in this life leads to tranquility: the path of virtue. (Roman)
Poverty does not destroy virtue, nor does wealth bestow it. (Spanish)
Praise is bestowed on virtue but vanishes more quickly than frost in the Spring.
    (Roman)
Praise is the hire of virtue. (Danish)
Remove severe restraints, and what will become of virtue? (Roman)
Riches adorn the house, virtue the person. (Chinese)
Straitened circumstances at home obstruct the path of virtue. (Roman)
The door of virtue is hard to open. (Chinese)
The fortune of the household stands by its virtue. (Roman)
The one who dies for virtue does not perish. (Roman)
There must ever be a place for virtue. (Roman)
Things sprung from virtue rarely perish. (Roman)
To wicked men the virtue of others is always a matter of dread. (Roman)
True virtue shines with unstained honors. (Roman)
Virtue and happiness are mother and daughter. (Unknown)
Virtue becomes a wife, beauty a concubine. (Chinese)
Virtue commands respect. (Roman)
Virtue flourishes in misfortune. (German)
Virtue is all the fairer when it comes in a beautiful body. (Roman)
Virtue is its own reward. (Roman)
Virtue is not inherited. (Mexican)
Virtue is not knowing but doing. (Japanese)
Virtue is not left to stand alone. (Chinese)
Virtue is praised and left out to freeze. (Roman)
Virtue is the best inheritance. (German)
Virtue lives beyond the grave. (Roman)
Virtue never dies. (German)
Virtue smells sweet after death. (Roman)
Virtue when concealed is a worthless thing. (Roman)
Virtue, not pedigree, is the mark of nobility. (Roman)
Virtue, which parleys, is near a surrender. (Roman)
Virtuous men are a kingdom's treasure. (Chinese)

We measure great men by their virtue, not their fortune. (Roman)
Where there is shame, there is virtue. (German)

Virtue and Vice
Every virtue is but halfway between two vices. (Roman)
Following virtue is like ascending a steep mountain; following vice is a landslide down a
    precipice. (Chinese)
Great abilities produce great vices as well as virtues. (Greek)
If vices were profitable, the virtuous man would be the sinner. (Roman)
It is easier to run from virtue to vice than from vice to virtue. (Roman)
Never lose virtue or promote vice. (Chinese)
Practice no vice because it's trivial; neglect no virtue because it's so. (Chinese)
Search others for their virtues, thyself for thy vices. (Poor Richard)
Some rise by sin and some by virtue fall. (Unknown)
To flee vice is the beginning of virtue. (Roman)
Vice is most dangerous when it puts on the garb of virtue. (Danish)
Vice makes virtue shine. (Unknown)
Vice that is powerless is called virtue. (Roman)
Vices steal upon us under the name of virtues. (Roman)
Virtue is the foundation of happiness; vice the presage of misery. (Chinese)

Vision
Vision without action is a daydream; action without vision is a nightmare. (Japanese)

Visit, Visits
God bless him who pays visits – short ones. (Egyptian)
He who never visits your home does not want you to visit his. (Mexican)
Short visits make long friendships. (English)
Visit rarely, and you will be more loved. (Arabian)
Visits always give pleasure; if not the arrival, then the departure. (Portuguese)

Visitor
A visitor comes with ten blessings, eats one, and leaves nine. (Kurdish)
Visitors' footfalls are like medicine: they heal the sick. (African)

Voice, Voices
One voice, no voice. (Italian)
The voice of the people, the voice of God. (Roman)
The voice of the people is the voice of Heaven. (Japanese)
Two voices cannot enter one ear. (Yiddish)

Volunteer
A volunteer is worth twenty pressed men. (Italian)
One volunteer is worth ten conscripted men. (Hausan)
One volunteer is worth two pressed men. (English)

Vow, Vows

Vows made in storms are forgotten in calms. (English)

Vulgar, Vulgarity

No medicine can cure a vulgar man. (Chinese)

Never descend to vulgarity even in joking. (Roman)

Vulture

As soon as the market breaks up, the vulture begins to drink up the blood. (Hausan)

The vulture does not come here for no reason. (Unknown)

Where the carcass is, there shall the vultures be gathered. (English)

Why do people find fault with the vulture, which eats not sown seeds? (Hausan)

W

Wade

Do not wade where you see no bottom. (Danish)

Wage, Wages

Good wages, good work. (German)

He cannot lead a good life who serves without wages. (Italian)

Wager

A wager is a fool's argument. (Scottish)

Don't bet more than you can afford to lose. (Spanish)

Wagon

A loaded wagon creaks; an empty one rattles. (German)

Wait, Waiting

All things come to those who wait. (English)

For a good dinner and a gentle wife you can afford to wait. (Danish)

He who can wait obtains what he wishes. (Italian)

He who waits for another's platter has a cold meal. (Catalan)

He who waits for dead men's shoes, may have to go long barefoot. (Danish)

He who waits till an opportunity occurs may wait forever. (Roman)

If he waits long enough the world will be his own. (Dutch)

One who is waiting thinks the time long. (Irish)

The waiting is the hardest part. (American)

Tide and time wait for no man. (Roman)

Time and tide wait for no one. (Irish)

To one who waits, a moment seems a year. (Chinese)

You never wait too long, when you wait for something good. (Swedish)

Walk, Walking
Better to walk alone than to walk in bad company. (Mexican)
Better to walk before a hen than behind an ox. (French)
He that walks straight will not stumble. (Yiddish)
He that walks too hastily, often stumbles in plain way. (French)
If you let everyone walk over you, you become a carpet. (Bulgarian)
If you take big paces you leave big spaces. (Burmese)
Learn to walk before you run. (American)
One step at a time is good walking. (Chinese)
The one who does not yet know how to walk cannot climb a ladder. (Ethiopian)
Tiger and deer do not walk together. (Chinese)
Walk softly and carry a big stick. (Roman)
We do not walk on our legs, but on our will. (Turkish)

Wall, Walls
A wall is made of stones both large and small. (Irish)
A white wall is the fool's paper. (Italian)
Better to plaster an old wall than build a new one. (Hausan)
Do not tear down the east wall to repair the west. (Chinese)
Hard and hard do not make a wall [i.e., brick against brick, without mortar]. (Roman)
If you see a high wall leaning toward you, run from under it. (Egyptian)
One family builds a wall, two families enjoy it. (Chinese)
Walls have mice and mice have ears. (Persian)
Walls sink and dunghills rise. (Spanish)
You have not built a wall until your have rounded the corner. (Irish)

Walnuts
Among walnuts only the empty one speaks. (Moroccan)

Want, Wants
A man who wants bread is ready for anything. (French)
Always to be sparing is always to be in want. (Danish)
Bad is want which is born of plenty. (Roman)
For want of a nail the shoe is lost; for want of a shoe, the horse is lost; for want of a horse the rider is lost. (Poor Richard)
God's beloved are in want of nothing. (Roman)
He is nearest to God who has the fewest wants. (Danish)
Mills and wives are ever wanting. (German)
The more men have, the more they want. (Roman)
The more one has, the more one wants. (Spanish)
Those who long for much are in want of much. (Roman)
Want is the whetstone of wit. (English)
Want makes strife 'tween husband and wife. (English)
Want makes wit. (English)
We are born naked, and soon we want everything. (Spanish)

We lessen our wants by lessening our desires. (Roman)

When want comes in at the door, love flies out at the window. (Dutch)

Women and wine, game and deceit, make the wealth small, and the wants great. (Poor Richard)

War

A dead man does not make war. (Italian)

A headless army fights badly. (Danish)

A petty war may lead to a great upheaval. (Yiddish)

Advantage is a better soldier than rashness. (English)

After donning the helmet, it is too late to repent of war. (Roman)

An old horse for a young soldier. (Italian)

At the wars as they do at the wars. (French)

Both soldier and surgeon pray for war. (German)

Councils of war never fight. (German)

Equal parties do not start wars. (German)

Even war has its laws. (Roman)

Every bullet has its billet. (English)

God is on the side of the strongest battalions. (French)

Had it not been for the horse, I would have gladly gone to war. (Hausan)

He who has a handsome wife, a castle on the frontier, or a vineyard on the roadside, is never without war. (Spanish)

He who has land has war. (Spanish)

If there is a strong general there will be no weak soldiers. (Chinese)

In a moment comes either sudden death or joyful victory. (Roman)

In time of war, the Devil makes more room in Hell. (German)

In time of war, the laws are silent. (Roman)

In time of war, there is pay for every horse. (Italian)

It becomes a wise man to try all methods before having recourse to arms. (Roman)

It is not permitted to err twice in war. (Roman)

Leave war to others. (Roman)

Let him who does not know what war is go to war. (Chinese)

Many return from the war who cannot give an account of the battle. (Italian)

Money is the sinews of war. (Dutch)

No war is more bitter than a war of friends – but it does not last long. (Irish)

Not all who go to war are soldiers. (Spanish)

Of war all can prattle, away from the battle. (German)

Soldiers and surgeons pray for war. (German)

Stratagem is better than brute force. (African)

The battlefield judges justly. (Irish)

The conquered dare not open their mouths. (Roman)

The conqueror weeps, the conquered is ruined. (Roman)

The conquerors are kings, the conquered bandits. (Chinese)

The fear of war is worse than war itself. (Italian)

The fidelity of barbarians depends on fortune. (Roman)

The fires of war have often been kindled by one word. (Egyptian)

The results of war are uncertain. (Roman)

To win a war quickly takes long preparation. (Roman)

Truth is the first casualty of war. (American)

Under a great general there is no feeble soldier. (Korean)

War appears pleasant to those who have never experienced it. (Roman)

War begun, Hell unchained. (Italian)

War brings scars. (German)

War ends nothing. (African)

War gives no opportunity for repeating a mistake. (Italian)

War is always easy to start, but very hard to end. (Roman)

War is death's feast. (English)

War is delightful to the inexperienced. (Italian)

War is hell. (American)

War is much too serious a matter to be entrusted to the military. (French)

War is pleasant to those who have never tried it. (German)

War is sweet to him who does not go to it. (Portuguese)

War ought neither to be dreaded nor provoked. (Roman)

Wars are fought by the young, not by the old. (Yoruban)

When the general falls, the army flees. (Irish)

War and Peace

A bad peace is better than a good war. (Russian)

An unhappy peace may be profitably exchanged for war. (Roman)

He comes with incense in one hand, in the other a spear. (Chinese)

He that keeps not his arms in time of peace will have none in time of war. (Irish)

He who sweats more in peace, bleeds less in war. (Italian)

I prefer the most unjust peace to the most just war. (Roman)

If we wish to enjoy peace, prepare for war; if we shrink from war, we shall never enjoy
    peace. (Roman)

If you want peace, prepare for war. (Roman)

In peace they are lions, in battle they are deer. (Roman)

In times of peace we should think of war. (Roman)

Let arms yield to the toga, laurels to paeans. (Roman)

No ruler can be so confident of peace as not to prepare for war. (Roman)

Peace feeds, war wastes; peace breeds, war consumes. (Danish)

Peace with a cudgel in hand is war. (Portuguese)

Scarcely is there any peace so unjust that it is better than even the fairest war. (German)

The same laws hold for peace as for war. (Roman)

War at the beginning is better than peace at the end. (Persian)

War makes thieves, and peace hangs them. (French)

War with all the world, and peace with England. (Spanish)

Water in peace is better than wine in war. (German)

You need only a show of war to have peace. (Roman)

Wares
Rare commodities are worth more than good ones. (Chinese)

Warm
He that is warm thinks all so. (English)
Some who mean only to warm, burn themselves. (French)
The head and feet keep warm, the rest will take no harm. (English)
A cold hand, a warm heart. (German)

Warning
A shipwreck on the beach is a lighthouse to the sea. (Dutch)
Happy he who can take warning from the mishaps of others. (Danish)
He was slain that had warning, not he that took it. (French)
Others' dangers are our warnings. (Roman)

Warp and Woof
Neither laughter nor reproof can change the world's warp and woof. (Yiddish)

Wash, Washes
Do not wash your dirty linens in public. (French)
It will all come out in the wash. (Spanish)
One hand washes the other. (Roman)
One hand washes the other, and both the face. (Spanish)
When both hands wash each other, they will be clean. (Yoruban)

Wasp
Don't pick a wasp out of a cream-jug. (Yiddish)
The wasp makes not honey. (Turkish)
Wasps haunt the honey pot. (English)

Waste
Better to burst the belly than spoil good food. (Dutch)
Don't waste good iron for nails or good men for soldiers. (Chinese)
Don't waste too many stones on one bird. (Chinese)
He who has money to throw away, let him employ workmen, and not stand by. (Italian)
Though you live near a forest, do not waste your firewood. (Chinese)
Waste makes want. (Indian)
Waste not, want not. (English)
Willful waste makes woeful want. (Scottish)

Watch
A dog cannot watch two gates. (English)
A girl, a vineyard, an orchard, and a cornfield, are hard to watch. (Portuguese)
It takes little effort to watch a man carry a load. (Chinese)
To him who watches, everything reveals itself. (Italian)

Watch even the road that is known to you. (Korean)
Watch the faces of those who bow low. (Polish)
Who watches not catches not. (Dutch)

Water, Waters

A drop of water breaks a stone. (Italian)
All water runs to the sea. (Italian)
As the water flows, so is the dam raised. (Burmese)
Cast your bread upon the waters, and it will return to you. (the Bible)
Dirty water does not wash clean. (Italian)
Dirty water will quench fire. (Italian)
Don't cast out the old water until you have the clean water in. (Irish)
Don't cross the water unless you see the bottom. (Italian)
Dripping water makes the rock hollow, not by its force but by constant action. (Roman)
Each draws water to his own mill. (Irish)
Even water gets stale if it stays in one place. (Albanian)
Far water cannot quench near fire. (Japanese)
Foul water will quench fire. (English)
He knows the water best who has waded through it. (Danish)
He who would have clear water should go to the fountain head. (Italian)
If you want clear water, draw it from the spring. (Portuguese)
In calm water every ship has a good captain. (French)
Let God's waters run over God's acres. (Dutch)
Let water flow that you do not intend to drink. (Mexican)
Much water passes by the mill that the miller perceives not. (Italian)
Rippling water shows lack of depth. (Indonesian)
Silent water is dangerous water. (Spanish)
Soft water constantly striking the hard stone wears it at last. (Portuguese)
Spilt water can never be gathered up again. (Chinese)
Still water breeds vermin. (Italian)
Still waters become stagnant. (Persian)
Still waters run deep. (Roman)
Stolen waters are the sweetest. (Roman)
Store water while it rains. (Burmese)
The water runs while the miller sleeps. (Danish)
The water that bears the ship is the same that engulfs it. (Chinese)
The water that does not flow is not fit to drink. (Albanian)
There is no worse water than still water. (French)
Water always finds its own level. (Hausan)
Water can support a ship, and water can upset it. (Chinese)
Water comes where water has been. (Swedish)
Water does not get bitter without a cause. (Hausan)
Water does not rise above its source. (Filipino)
Water does not run uphill. (Jamaican)
Water flows to low ground. (Burmese)

461

Water is not drunk from the gourd that dug the well. (Hausan)
Water is the strongest drink: it drives mills. (German)
Water poured on the head goes down to the heels. (Korean)
Water washes everything. (Portuguese)
Waters have their source; trees their roots. (Chinese)
Waves will rise on silent water. (Irish)
What water gives, water takes away. (Portuguese)
When fire and water are at war, it is the fire that loses. (Spanish)
When water covers the head, a hundred fathoms are as one. (Persian)
When you drink water, think of its source. (Chinese)
Whenever the water rises, the boat will rise too. (Chinese)
Where the water recedes, there is a crocodile. (African)
Where water has been, water will come again. (German)
You don't miss the water until the well runs dry. (Jamaican)

Wax
Wax will show the quality of the gold. (Burmese)

Wax and Wane
Wax and wane is the world's way. (Japanese)

Way
Each to his own way. (German)
He knows the way best who went there last. (Norwegian)
It is often better to go the circuitous way than the direct one. (Roman)
Many will show you the way once your cart has overturned. (Kurdish)
The longest way round is the shortest way home. (English)
The Russian knows the way, yet he asks for directions. (German)
The smoothest way is full of stones. (Yiddish)
The way to Heaven is not strewn with roses. (Spanish)

Weak, Weakest
A chain is only as strong as its weakest link. (Roman)
The strong prey upon the weak. (Japanese)
The weakest goes to the wall. (English)
The weakest must hold the candle. (French)

Wealth, Wealthy
A heavy purse makes a light heart. (Yiddish)
A man with wealth will always get a servant. (African)
A man's wealth is his enemy. (English)
A wealthy man can err with impunity. (Roman)
A wealthy man who was once a pauper has a heart as hard as copper. (Spanish)
All claim kindred with the prosperous. (Roman)
By labor comes wealth. (Yoruban)

Command your wealth, else it will command you. (Spanish)

Great wealth is from Heaven; little wealth from diligence. (Chinese)

Great wealth, great care. (Dutch)

He is most loved in the world who hath the most bags. (Dutch)

He most enjoys wealth who least desires wealth. (Roman)

He should possess wealth, who knows how to use it. (Roman)

He who is not stingy is not wealthy. (Chinese)

If worldly goods cannot save me from death, they ought not to hinder me of eternal life. (Poor Richard)

If you share a man's wealth, try to lessen his misfortune. (Chinese)

Inherited wealth has no blessing. (African)

Just as ants never bend their way to visit empty storehouses, so no friend will visit departed wealth. (Roman)

Little wealth, little care. (Unknown)

Men make wealth, and women preserve it. (Italian)

Much wealth brings many enemies. (African)

No man inquires how you obtained your wealth; but it is necessary to possess it. (Roman)

Nothing prevails against wealth. (Roman)

Now I've a sheep and a cow, every body bids me good morrow. (Poor Richard)

Only a beggar can count his wealth. (Serbian)

Real wealth consists not in having, but in not wanting. (Roman)

Silver and gold are all men's dears. (Danish)

Slippery are the flagstones of the mansion door. (Irish)

Small gains bring great wealth. (Dutch)

The best wealth is health. (Welsh)

The one who has acquired wealth in time, unless he saves it in time, will come to starvation in time. (Roman)

The shortest way to wealth lies in the contempt of wealth. (Roman)

The wealth which you give away will ever be your own. (Roman)

The wealthy are neither fat nor ugly. (Mexican)

The wealthy have many worries. (Japanese)

The wealthy have short memories. (Chinese)

The wealthy man never sleeps. (Indian)

Unless you take pains you will never acquire wealth. (Persian)

Wealth conquered Rome after Rome had conquered the world. (Italian)

Wealth has many friends, poverty none. (Unknown)

Wealth is both an enemy and a friend. (Nepalese)

Wealth is but manure, useful only when spread around. (Chinese)

Wealth is like snow in March. (Yiddish)

Wealth is not his that has it, but his that enjoys it. (Poor Richard)

Wealth is the greatest danger to health. (German)

Wealth is the mother of idleness, and the grandmother of poverty. (Spanish)

Wealth lightens not the heart and care of man. (Roman)

Wealth makes the fool a master. (Japanese)

When the light of the lamp flickers, you will obtain wealth. (Chinese)
Where there is wealth, friends abound. (Roman)

Weapon

A weapon is an enemy even to its owner. (Turkish)
A weapon is silenced by a weapon. (Indian)

Weary

If the knitter is weary, the baby will have no new bonnet. (Irish)
To the weary the bare ground is a bed. (Roman)

Weather

After clouds comes clear weather. (German)
After rain comes fair weather. (Dutch)
Evening red and morning gray help the traveler on his way; evening gray and morning
    red bring down rain upon his head. (Italian)
Everyone can navigate in fine weather. (Italian)
If the weather is fine, put on your cloak; if it rains, do as you please. (French)
Some are weather-wise, some are otherwise. (Poor Richard)
The farmer hopes for rain, the traveler for fine weather. (Chinese)
The weather determines the clothes. (German)

Weave

Do not put in more warp than you can weave. (Danish)

Web

For a web begun God sends thread. (French)

Wed, Wedlock

Age and wedlock bring a man to his nightcap. (English)
Age and wedlock tame man and beast. (English)
Wedlock is a padlock. (Chinese)
Who weds a sot to get his cot, will lose the cot and keep the sot. (Dutch)

Wedding

Do not stand like the bride at a wedding. (Albanian)
One wedding brings another. (English)
The most dangerous food is a wedding cake. (American)
The woman cries before the wedding and the man after. (Polish)
Weddings beget weddings. (Spanish)

Wedge

One wedge drives another. (German)

Weed, Weeds

A bad weed never dies. (Mexican)

He that neglects to weed will surely come to need. (American)

Ill weeds are not hurt by frost. (Spanish)

Ill weeds grow apace. (Roman)

Ill weeds grow the fastest and last the longest. (Danish)

One ill weed mars a whole pot of pottage. (Danish)

Weeds never die. (German)

Weep, Wept

A man may chance to bring home with him what makes him weep. (Spanish)

I wept when I was born, and every day shows why. (German)

It is better to weep with wise men than to laugh with fools. (Spanish)

Laugh and the world laughs with you; weep and you weep alone. (Danish)

There is a certain pleasure in weeping: pain is soothed and alleviated by tears.
　　(Roman)

Weeping hath a voice. (Roman)

Weeping makes the heart grow lighter. (Yiddish)

When you live next to the cemetery, you cannot weep for everyone. (African)

Weigh, Weight

First weigh, then venture. (German)

Give ear and weigh the matter well. (Roman)

Good weight and measure is Heaven's treasure. (English)

Great weights may hang on thin wires. (Dutch)

Little posts cannot support heavy weights. (Chinese)

Man must be so weighed as though there were a god within him. (Roman)

Welcome

A hearty welcome is the best cheer. (German)

Harsh is the voice that would dismiss us, but sweet is the sound of welcome. (Roman)

He who brings is always welcome. (German)

Welcome brings the best cheer. (Danish)

What you cannot avoid, welcome. (Chinese)

When you go, leave a welcome behind you. (German)

Who comes seldom, is welcome. (Italian)

Well

A well is not filled with dew. (Egyptian)

A well which is drawn from is improved. (Roman)

Cast no dirt into the well that gives you water. (Korean)

Dig a well before you are thirsty. (Chinese)

Do not throw a stone in the well from which you drink. (Egyptian)

Don't spit into the well – you might drink from it later. (Yiddish)

Drawn wells are seldom dry. (German)

Drawn wells have the sweetest water. (Persian)
It is a bad well into which one must put water. (German)
It is not necessary to fall into a well to know its depth. (Spanish)
It's difficult to draw pure water from a dirty well. (Irish)
One who sits by the well will never go thirsty. (Malayan)
Sink a well together, draw water alone. (Korean)
The more the well is used, the more water it yields. (German)
We never know the worth of water till the well is dry. (French)
Why would a man go to another's well for water? (Spanish)
You never miss the water till the well runs dry. (English)

Well-bred

Well-born good, well-bred better. (Japanese)
Well-fed, well-bred. (Unknown)

Well-fed

The well-fed does not perceive the hungry. (Irish)
The well-fed have no religion. (Kashmiri)

Well-wisher

A well-wisher sees from afar. (Spanish)

Wheel

A fifth wheel to a cart is but a hindrance. (Spanish)
A wheel not greased will creak. (Roman)
It's the squeaky wheel that gets the grease. (English)
The squeaky wheel gets the grease. (American)
The wheel comes full circle. (American)
The wheel turns round. (Yiddish)
The worse the wheel, the more it creaks. (Dutch)
To make the cart go you must grease the wheels. (Italian)
You must grease the wheels if you would have the carriage run. (Italian)

Wheelbarrow

Old wheelbarrows creak. (German)

Whine

A whining dog becomes thin. (Korean)

Whip

An old coachman loves the crack of the whip. (German)
Often has a man cut a switch to whip himself. (Irish)

Whirlwind

They that sow the wind shall reap the whirlwind. (the Bible)

Whisper

A whisper is a spoken word. (African)
A whisper is heard louder than a shout. (the Editor)
He who whispers, lies. (Danish)
The whisper of a pretty girl can be heard further than the roar of a lion.
    (Arabian)
What is whispered in your ear is often heard a hundred miles off. (Chinese)

Whistle

'I am hungry' is not expressed by whistling. (Yoruban)
Who cannot sing, may whistle. (German)
You cannot drink and whistle at the same time. (Danish)

Whole

In the whole the part is also contained. (Roman)

Whore, Whoredom

A whore in a fine dress is like a dirty house with a clean door. (Scottish)
A young whore, an old saint. (English)
Once a whore, always a whore. (English)
Whoredom and grace dwelt never in one place. (Scottish)
Whoredom and thieving are never long concealed. (Spanish)

Why

Every why has its wherefore. (English)

Wicked, Wickedness

A wicked book cannot repent. (Chinese)
A wicked companion invites us all to Hell. (Chinese)
A wicked dog must be tied short. (French)
A wicked man's gift hath a touch of his master. (French)
As the tree is known by its fruit, so is the wicked man by his deeds. (Roman)
Disaster awaits the wicked on every side. (Roman)
God permits the wicked – but not forever. (Danish)
No one becomes extremely wicked all at once. (Roman)
No one is wicked enough to wish to appear wicked. (Roman)
No time is too short for the wicked to injure their neighbors. (Roman)
The one who aids the wicked, suffers in the end. (Roman)
The wicked even hate vice in others. (Italian)
The wicked shun the light as the Devil does the Cross. (Dutch)
There's no rest for the wicked. (German)
We never profit by the gifts of the wicked. (Roman)
Why should the wickedness of a few be laid to the account of all? (Roman)
Wickedness and malice only require an opportunity. (Roman)
Wickedness may be safe, but never secure. (Roman)

Wickedness takes the shorter road, and virtue the longer. (Roman)
Wickedness with beauty is the Devil's hook baited. (Roman)

Widow, Widower

A buxom widow must be married, buried, or cloistered. (Spanish)
A rich widow weeps with one eye and signals with the other. (Portuguese)
A young widow is not long a widow. (Spanish)
Do not trust a widow three times married. (Spanish)
He who marries a widow lives also with her late husband. (Spanish)
He who marries a widow with three children, marries four thieves. (Danish)
Short a bride, short a widow. (Unknown)
Only a widow can grieve with a widow. (Korean)
The grief of a widower is sharp but short. (Spanish)
The rich widow weeps with one eye and beckons suitors with the other.
 (Spanish)
The rich widow's tears soon dry. (Danish)
The woman who marries a widower has a rival in the other world. (Spanish)
When a widower remarries, he honors his first wife. (the Editor)

Wife

A bad wife drinks a big share of her bad buttermilk. (Irish)
A bad wife is a lifelong death. (Unknown)
A bad wife is sixty years of a bad harvest. (Japanese)
A bad wife will lead her family to downfall. (Korean)
A bad wife wishes her husband's heel turned homewards, and not his toe.
 (Danish)
A brilliant daughter make a brittle wife. (Dutch)
A cheerful wife is the joy of life. (German)
A faithless wife is shipwreck to a house. (Roman)
A good wife and health is a man's best wealth. (English)
A good wife is half of life. (Irish)
A man's second wife is treated like an equal. (Mexican)
A mill and a wife are always in want of something. (Italian)
A rich wife is a source of quarrel. (Danish)
A virtuous wife saves her husband from evil ways. (Chinese)
A virtuous wife will lessen the misfortunes of her husband. (Chinese)
A wife gives beauty to a house. (Indian)
A wife is a household treasure. (Japanese)
A wife is a little dove and a little devil. (Yiddish)
A wife is not a pot, she will not break so easily. (Russian)
A wife is sought for her virtue, a concubine for her beauty. (Chinese)
A wife who has no children makes a dear and delightful friend to her husband's heirs.
 (Roman)
'All freight lightens', said the skipper, when he threw his wife overboard. (German)
An undutiful daughter, will prove an unmanageable wife. (Poor Richard)

As you would have a daughter so choose a wife. (Italian)

Choose a wife from among your equals. (Roman)

Curse your wife at evening, sleep alone at night. (Chinese)

Happy is the man who has a handsome wife close to an abbey. (French)

He drives a good wagonful into his farm who gets a good wife. (Danish)

He that has not got a wife, is not yet a compleat Man. (Poor Richard)

He that hath a wife hath strife. (English)

He that takes a wife, takes care. (Poor Richard)

He that tells his wife news is but lately married. (French)

He that would have a beautiful wife should choose her on a Saturday. (Spanish)

He who does not honor his wife, dishonors himself. (Spanish)

He who does not pick up a pin cares nothing for his wife. (Spanish)

He who has a good wife can bear any evil. (Spanish)

He who has a wife has everything he needs. (Spanish)

He who has no wife, is for thrashing her daily; but he that has one, takes care of her.
(Spanish)

He who takes a wife takes a master. (French)

If your wife is beautiful, she will cheat you; if ugly, she will tire you; if poor, she will ruin
you; and if rich, she will command you. (Spanish)

If your wife wants to throw you off the roof, try to find a low one. (Spanish)

It is a good horse that never stumbles, and a good wife that never grumbles. (Italian)

One should choose a wife with the ears, rather than with the eyes. (French)

Prudent men choose frugal wives. (German)

Seek a wife in your own sphere. (Roman)

Smoke, floods, and a troublesome wife, are enough to drive a man out of his life.
(French)

The first wife is a broom, and the second a lady. (Spanish)

The first wife saves, the second wife spends. (Unknown)

The old wife, if she does not serve for a pot, serves for a cover. (Spanish)

The wife and the king rule by Heaven. (German)

The wife of a devil becomes a devil. (Japanese)

The wife who is given in marriage to a man against her will becomes his enemy.
(Roman)

The wife who tricks her husband wrecks the home. (German)

When a man loves his wife deeply, he will bow even to the stakes of his father-in-law's
house. (Korean)

Who has a bad wife, his hell begins on earth. (Dutch)

Whoso is tired of happy days, let him take a wife. (Dutch)

You cannot pluck roses without fear of thorns, nor enjoy a fair wife without danger of
horns. (Poor Richard)

Wile, Wiles

Wiles can sometimes do what force cannot. (English)

Wiles help weak folk. (German)

Will, Willed

Easier to bend the body than the will. (Chinese)

He that complies against his will is of his own opinion still. (Dutch)

He that will, does more than he that can. (Portuguese)

In great things, it is enough even to have willed. (Roman)

Take the will for the deed. (Spanish)

The will cannot be forced. (Roman)

Though strength may be lacking, yet the will is to be praised. (Roman)

When the will is prompt the legs are nimble. (Italian)

When you will, they won't; when you won't, they will. (Roman)

Where there is no want of will, there will be no want of opportunity. (Spanish)

Where there's a will there's a way. (English)

Who will not when he can, can't when he will. (Portuguese)

Will is the cause of woe. (English)

Will is power. (French)

Willful

A willful fault has no excuse, and deserves no pardon. (Welsh)

A willful man must have his way. (English)

He who does what he wills, does not what he ought. (Spanish)

Willing, Willingly

A willing heart makes feet light. (German)

A willing helper does not wait until he is asked. (Danish)

All things are easy that are done willingly. (Roman)

Nothing is difficult to a willing mind. (Italian)

Nothing is impossible to a willing mind. (French)

To be willing is to be able. (French)

Willow, Willows

Bend the willow while it is young. (Roman)

Willows are weak, but they bind the faggot. (Poor Richard)

Win, Winning

He plays well that wins. (French)

Let them that win laugh. (Roman)

The better man may win, but he cannot fail to be the worse for his victory. (Roman)

Win by persuasion not by force. (Roman)

Winning isn't everything, it's the only thing. (American)

You can't win 'em all. (American)

Win and Lose

Sometimes you win, sometimes you lose. (Jamaican)

The first winner is the last loser. (Yiddish)

Win at first, lose at last. (German)

Win your lawsuit and lose your money. (Chinese)
You win a few, you lose a few (American)
You win some, you lose some. (American)

Wind, Windy

A little wind kindles a fire, too much will put it out. (English)
A reed before the wind lives on, while mighty oaks do fall. (English)
As the wind, so the sail. (French)
Be in readiness for favorable winds. (Chinese)
Every wind does not shake down the nut. (Italian)
Every wind is against a leaky ship. (Danish)
From the straws in the air we judge of the wind. (Portuguese)
Horses and cows face the wind differently. (Chinese)
If the wind will not serve, take to the oars. (Roman)
If there is a wave there must be a wind. (Japanese)
If wind comes from an empty cave, it's not without a reason. (Chinese)
It is hard to sail without wind, and to grind without water. (Danish)
No wind can serve him who steers for no port. (French)
No wind, no waves. (Chinese)
Straws tell which way the wind blows. (Danish)
The wind gathers the clouds, and it is also the wind that scatters the clouds. (Rumanian)
The wind that comes in through a crack is cold. (Japanese)
The wind will fell an oak, but it cannot break a reed. (Hungarian)
The windy day is not the day for thatching. (Irish)
'Tis an ill wind that blows no one any good. (Roman)
We cannot direct the wind, but we can adjust the sails. (German)
What is brought by the wind will be carried away by the wind. (Persian)
When the wind is in the east, 'tis neither good for man nor beast. (English)
When there is no wind every man is a pilot. (French)
When there is wind in the clouds there are waves on the river. (Chinese)
Winds call forth no response in horses or cattle. (Chinese)
You can't know which way the wind will blow. (American)

Window

Windows break all on their own. (German)

Wine

A cup of wine is medicine, a gallon of wine is ruin. (Korean)
A meal without wine is like a day without sunshine. (Italian)
A restive morsel needs a spur of wine. (French)
Above all, avoid quarrels excited by wine. (Roman)
After stuffing pears within, drink old wine until they swim. (Spanish)
Bacchus hath drowned more men than Neptune. (Roman)
Don't put new wine into old bottles. (Russian)
Drink wine and let water go to the mill. (Italian)

Drink wine upon figs. (Spanish)

Eat bread at pleasure, drink wine by measure. (French)

Fire tests metal, wine tests men. (Japanese)

First man drinks wine, then wine drinks wine, then wine drinks man. (Japanese)

From the sweetest wine, the sharpest vinegar. (English)

Gold is tested by fire, men by wine. (Japanese)

Good wine gladdens the eye, cleans the teeth, and heals the stomach. (Spanish)

Good wine is milk for the aged. (German)

Good wine makes good blood. (Italian)

Good wine makes men's hearts rejoice. (Roman)

Good wine makes the horse go. (French)

Good wine needs no bush. (Italian)

Good wine needs no crier. (Spanish)

Good wine needs no sign. (French)

Good wine praises itself. (Dutch)

Good wine ruins the purse, and makes the stomach bad. (German)

Good wine sells itself. (German)

Half a cup of wine brings tears, a full cup laughter. (Korean)

He who likes drinking is always talking of wine. (Italian)

He who works, drinks water; he who works not, drinks wine. (Spanish)

If the landlady is fair, the wine is fair. (German)

If the sea were wine, everyone would be a sailor. (Spanish)

In the mirror we see our form, in wine the heart. (German)

In wine there is truth. (Roman)

It has passed into a proverb, that wisdom is overshadowed by wine. (Roman)

Medicine can cure a false disease; wine cannot dispel real sorrow. (Chinese)

Not wine – men intoxicate themselves; not vice – men entice themselves. (Chinese)

Prudent men abstain from wine. (Roman)

Since the wine is drawn it must be drunk. (French)

Sometimes the lees are better than the wine. (Italian)

Sweet is the wine but sour is the payment. (Irish)

Sweet wine makes sour vinegar. (German)

The best wine has its lees. (French)

Truth and folly dwell in the wine-cask. (Danish)

Water for fish, wine for men. (Spanish)

Water for oxen, wine for kings. (Spanish)

What I have in my heart is brought out by the wine. (Albanian)

When the wine enters, out goes the truth. (Poor Richard)

When the wine is in the man, the wit is in the can. (Dutch)

When wine enters, modesty departs. (Italian)

When wine flows in, the wits flow out. (English)

When wine flows the wits go. (American)

When wine sinks, words swim. (Italian)

Where the best grapes grow, the worst wine is drunk. (German)

Where the hostess is handsome the wine is good. (French)

Wine and women make fools of everybody. (German)
Wine and women make the prince a pauper. (German)
Wine begins with a ceremony and ends in a riot. (Japanese)
Wine brings forth the truth. (Spanish)
Wine can throw man's nature into disorder. (Chinese)
Wine carries no rudder. (Roman)
Wine diffuses the bite of cares. (Roman)
Wine gladdens the heart of man. (Roman)
Wine hath drowned more men than the sea. (German)
Wine held in a jar is yours, but wine held in the stomach is its own. (Spanish)
Wine in, secret out. (Yiddish)
Wine in the bottle does not quench thirst. (Roman)
Wine is a cunning wrestler: it trips up the feet. (Roman)
Wine is first a friend, then an enemy. (Unknown)
Wine is given to bring mirth not drunkenness. (Roman)
Wine is one thing, drunkenness another. (Roman)
Wine is the key of all evil. (Moroccan)
Wine is the mirror of the mind. (Roman)
Wine mars beauty and destroys the freshness of youth. (Roman)
Wine opens the seals of the heart. (Roman)
Wine reveals the words of one's inner mind. (Chinese)
Wine tastes best when shared with a friend. (Spanish)
Wine wears no mask. (Spanish)
Wine will not keep in a foul vessel. (French)
Without wine, without guests. (Chinese)

Wing, Wings
According to his pinions the bird flies. (Danish)
There is no flying without wings. (French)

Wipe
Wipe your sore eye with your elbow. (Portuguese)

Wisdom
A child's wisdom is also wisdom. (Yiddish)
A poor man's wisdom goes for little. (Dutch)
Bought wisdom is best. (German)
By committing foolish acts, one learns wisdom. (Singhalese)
Continual cheerfulness is a sign of wisdom. (Irish)
Enough of eloquence, but little of wisdom. (Roman)
Even from a foe a man may learn wisdom. (Greek)
He gets his wisdom cheaply who gets it at another's cost. (Roman)
He who rises early will gather wisdom. (Danish)
In every head is some wisdom. (Egyptian)
It is best to learn wisdom from the follies of others. (Roman)

473

Much wisdom is lost in poor men's mouths. (German)

Not to speak is the flower of wisdom. (Japanese)

Once I had strength but no wisdom; now I have wisdom but no strength. (Persian)

Rarely are beauty and wisdom found together. (Roman)

Ripeness is in wisdom, not in years. (Unknown)

Speech is given to all, wisdom to few. (Roman)

Talking comes by nature, silence by wisdom. (Yiddish)

The arts are the servants of life, wisdom its master. (Roman)

The beginning of wisdom is to call things by their right names. (Chinese)

The doors of wisdom are never shut. (Poor Richard)

The fear of God is the beginning of wisdom. (the Bible)

The first step toward wisdom is to distinguish what is false. (Roman)

Thinking is the essence of wisdom. (Persian)

'Tis altogether vain to learn wisdom, and yet live foolishly. (Dutch)

'Tis wisdom sometimes to seem a fool. (Roman)

To fear the master is the beginning of wisdom. (Roman)

To feign stupidity is, in certain situations, the highest wisdom. (Roman)

Up to seventy we learn wisdom – and die fools. (Yiddish)

What use is wisdom when folly reigns? (Yiddish)

Wisdom and virtue are like the two wheels of a cart. (Japanese)

Wisdom does not consist in dress. (Roman)

Wisdom grows by study. (Roman)

Wisdom is a birth of nature, not of years. (Roman)

Wisdom is a good purchase, though we pay dear for it. (Dutch)

Wisdom is better than gold and silver. (Jamaican)

Wisdom is found even under a tattered coat. (Roman)

Wisdom is in the head and not in the beard. (Swedish)

Wisdom is learned through the wisdom of others. (Yoruban)

Wisdom is not attained with years, but by ability. (Roman)

Wisdom is the least burdensome traveling pack. (Danish)

Wisdom rides upon the ruins of folly. (Danish)

With how little wisdom the world is governed! (Roman)

Wise, Wiser

A change of fortune hurts a wise man no more than a change of the moon.
   (Poor Richard)

A fall into a ditch makes you wiser. (Chinese)

A rich man's foolish sayings pass for wise ones. (Yiddish)

A thing we are looking for is always wiser than ourselves. (Yoruban)

A wise man does nothing against his will, nothing from sorrow, nothing under coercion.
   (Roman)

A wise man hears one word and understands two. (Yiddish)

A wise man is better than a strong one. (Roman)

A wise man is known by what he does not say. (Spanish)

A wise man may learn from a fool. (French)

A wise man should never give his wife too much rein. (Roman)

A wise man turns chance into good fortune. (Roman)

A wise man whose wisdom does not serve him, is wise in vain. (Roman)

A wise man will make more opportunities than he finds. (Roman)

A wise man will make tools of what comes to hand. (Roman)

A wise man, a strong man. (German)

A wise man's trouble is his own secret. (German)

Adversity and loss make a man wise. (Welsh)

All children are clever when they are small, but most of them grow no wiser. (Yiddish)

All wise men think the same; every fool has his own opinion. (Indian)

Dare to be wise, begin at once. (Roman)

Everyone is wise for his own profit. (Portuguese)

Everyone is wise when the mischief is done. (Spanish)

Everybody is wise after the fact. (American)

Everyone is wise until he speaks. (Irish)

For every wise man there is one still wiser. (Kurdish)

From the faults of another a wise man will correct his own. (Roman)

Half a word to the wise is enough. (Dutch)

He dies before he is old who is wise before his day. (Roman)

He is happily wise who is wise at the expense of another. (Roman)

He is not a wise man who cannot play the fool on occasions. (Italian)

He is not wise who will not be instructed. (Irish)

He is the wisest man who does not think himself so. (French)

He is wise to no purpose who is not wise regarding himself. (Roman)

He is wise who does not long persist in folly. (Roman)

He is wise who suits himself to the occasion. (Roman)

He is wise who watches. (Roman)

He who considers himself wise, has an ass near at hand. (German)

He would be wise who knew all things beforehand. (Dutch)

If everyone were wise, a fool would be the prize. (German)

It is not always good to be wise. (German)

It's easy to be wise after the event. (English)

Men are wise as far as their beards. (Roman)

No one is at all times wise. (Roman)

No one alone is sufficiently wise. (Roman)

No one is born wise. (German)

No one is wise in his own affairs. (Dutch)

No one was ever wise by chance. (Roman)

Older is not always wiser. (Unknown)

Older than you by a day, wiser than you by a year. (Arabian)

Some are wise and some are otherwise. (English)

The believer is happy; the doubter is wise. (Hungarian)

The one who is wise looks ahead. (Roman)

The wise are ever learning. (German)

The wise man has long ears and a short tongue. (German)

The wise man seeks honor, not profit, as the reward of virtue. (Roman)

The wise man sits on the hole in his carpet. (Persian)

The wise wage war for the sake of peace, and endure toil in the hope of leisure. (Roman)

Those who have white hair are old enough to be wise. (Roman)

Walk with the wise and you shall become wise. (Jamaican)

We become wiser as we grow older. (Roman)

Wise is the person who talks little. (Roman)

Wise men learn from their foes. (German)

Wise and Foolish

A fool finds pleasure in evil conduct, but a man of understanding delights in wisdom. (Italian)

A fool gives full vent to his anger, but a wise man keeps himself under control. (Italian)

A fool may meet with good fortune, but only the wise profits by it. (Dutch)

A fool says what he knows, and a wise man knows what he says. (Yiddish)

A fool takes two steps where a wise man takes none. (Yiddish)

A fool throws a stone into a well, and it requires a hundred wise men to get it out again. (Italian)

A fool who can keep silent is counted among the wise. (Yiddish)

A fool will ask more questions than the wisest man can answer. (Unknown)

A nod for a wise man, and a rod for a fool. (Roman)

A wise man and a fool together, know more than a wise man alone. (Italian)

A wise man changes his mind, a fool never. (Spanish)

A wise man does at first what a fool must do at last. (Italian)

A wise man hides his wisdom, a fool reveals his folly. (Yiddish)

Better a blow from a wise man than a kiss from a fool. (Yiddish)

Better to lose with a wise man than win with a fool. (Yiddish)

Fools build houses and wise men live in them. (German)

Fools look to tomorrow, wise men use today. (Scottish)

The enmity of the wise is better than the friendship of fools. (Egyptian)

The fool inherits, the wise acquires. (German)

The fool speaks, the wise man listens. (African)

The fool wanders, the wise man travels. (Unknown)

The fool who is silent passes for wise. (French)

The wise follow their own decisions; the foolish follow public opinion. (Chinese)

The wise man draws more advantage from his enemies, than the fool from his friends. (Poor Richard)

The wise man knows that he knows nothing, the fool thinks he knows all. (German)

The wise man lays plans, but so does the fool. (Yiddish)

The wise man, even when he holds his tongue, says more than the fool when he speaks. (Yiddish)

There are no wise men without fools. (English)

Those who wish to appear learned to fools will appear fools to the learned. (Roman)

Were there no fools there would be no wise men. (Japanese)

What saddens the wise man gladdens the fool. (Yiddish)

What the fool does at last the wise man does at first. (Spanish)
When a fool is silent, he too is counted among the wise. (Yiddish)
Where there are no fools, there would be no wise men. (German)
Wise lads and old fools were never good for anything. (Italian)
Wise men learn by other men's mistakes, fools by their own. (Italian)
With a wink the wise understands, the fool with a kick. (Egyptian)
Women are wise impromptu, fools upon reflection. (Italian)

Wish, Wishes

Don't wish upon someone else's star. (African)
If man could have half his wishes, he would double his troubles. (Poor Richard)
If things are not as you wish, wish them as they are. (Yiddish)
If wishes were horses, beggars would ride. (Scottish)
If wishes were true, shepherds would be kings. (French)
Men willingly believe that which they wish for. (Roman)
The wish is father to the thought. (English)
The wish is the father of the deed. (American)
What we wish is good, what we please is sacred. (English)
What you wish you readily believe. (Hungarian)
Wishes are the echo of a lazy will. (Dutch)
Wishes never filled the bag. (French)
Wishes won't wash dishes. (American)
With wishing comes grieving. (Italian)
You cannot have all you wish for. (Roman)

Wit, Wits

A dram of mother's wit is better than a pound of school smarts. (English)
A handful of mother wit is worth a bushel of learning. (Spanish)
An ounce of mother-wit is worth a pound of school-wit. (German)
An ounce of wit that is bought, is worth a pound that is taught. (Poor Richard)
As many heads, as many wits. (Spanish)
Better wit than wealth. (English)
Might and courage require wit in their suite. (Danish)
One cannot live by another's wits. (Yiddish)
Pen and ink is wit's plow. (English)
The wit one lacks spoils what one has. (French)
There is nothing more telling than wit. (Roman)
Ushered in according to your clothes, ushered out according to your wit. (Yiddish)
Where there is no wit within no wit will come out. (Danish)
Wit without discretion is a sword in the hand of a fool. (Spanish)

Witness, Witnesses

A dark night has no witnesses. (Serbian)
Better one eyewitness than ten hearsay witnesses. (Dutch)
No man should be a witness in his own cause. (Roman)

One witness, no witness. (Roman)
One witness, one liar; more witnesses, all liars. (Greek)
The eyewitness observes what the absent doesn't see. (Egyptian)

Woe, Woes
There is no want of woe. (English)
By telling our woes we often assuage them. (French)

Wolf, Wolves
A bad watchman often feeds the wolf. (French)
A wolf hankers after sheep even at its last gasp. (Dutch)
A wolf is accused whether it is guilty or not. (Greek)
A wolf may lose its teeth but not its inclination. (Spanish)
A wolf often lies concealed in the skin of a lamb. (Roman)
An old wolf is not scared by loud cries. (Danish)
At the front door the tiger was checked, but a wolf entered from the back door.
    (Chinese)
Do not leave the wolf to protect the sheep. (Mexican)
He that lives with wolves, must howl with wolves. (Dutch)
He who stands godfather to a wolf should have a dog under his cloak. (German)
If the wolf had stayed in the wood there would have been no hue and cry after him.
    (German)
If you call for one wolf, you invite the pack. (Bulgarian)
It is easy to cut the tail off a dead wolf. (Albanian)
On every small pretext the wolf seizes the sheep. (Italian)
One wolf does not kill another. (Portuguese)
The cautious wolf fears the snare. (Roman)
The wolf bemoans the sheep, and then eats it. (Italian)
The wolf changes its coat, but not its disposition. (Roman)
The wolf is always said to be bigger than it is. (Italian)
The wolf is not afraid of the dog, but is vexed by its bark. (Yiddish)
The wolf is not scared by the number of the sheep. (Roman)
The wolf loses its teeth but not its ways. (English)
Though you teach a wolf the Paternoster, it will say 'Lamb! Lamb!' (Danish)
'Tis a hard winter when one wolf eats another. (Russian)
What a fine shepherd a wolf must be. (Roman)
When the wolf grows old the crows ride him. (Dutch)
When you see the wolf, do not look for its track. (Italian)
Where the wolf gets one lamb it looks for another. (Italian)
Wolves are often hidden under sheep's clothing. (Danish)
Wolves don't eat wolves. (Italian)
You must howl with wolves if you wish to be one of their pack. (Roman)

Woman, Women
A beautiful woman is a beautiful trouble. (Jamaican)
A drunken woman is lost to shame. (Irish)

A man works from sun to sun but a woman's work is never done. (English)

A mule and a woman do what is expected of them. (Spanish)

A pig is bolder than a goat, but a woman surpasses the Devil. (Irish)

A sack full of fleas is easier to watch than a woman. (German)

A ship and a woman are ever repairing. (English)

A ship and a woman ever require mending. (Roman)

A woman and a glass are always in danger. (Spanish)

A woman and a hen are soon lost through gadding. (Portuguese)

A woman and a melon are hard to choose. (French)

A woman conceals only what she does not know. (French)

A woman for a general, and the soldiers will be women. (Roman)

A woman hath nine lives like a cat. (Roman)

A woman is mightier than pen or sword. (Spanish)

A woman is to be from her house three times: when she is christened, married and
 buried. (Italian)

A woman keeps secret only what she does not know. (German)

A woman laughs when she can, and weeps when she pleases. (French)

A woman smells sweetest when she smells not at all. (Roman)

A woman turned witch is worse than a born witch. (Yiddish)

A woman who accepts, sells herself; a woman who gives, surrenders. (French)

A woman who has lost her rival has no sorrow. (African)

A woman without a man is like a fish without a bicycle. (American)

A woman without husband is like fire without wood. (Spanish)

A woman, a dog, and a walnut tree, the more you beat them the better they be. (German)

A woman, when she either loves or hates, will dare anything. (Roman)

A woman's answer is never to seek. (Italian)

A woman's first counsel is the best. (Danish)

A woman's in pain, a woman's in woe, a woman is ill, when she likes to be so. (Italian)

A woman's mind and a winter wind oft change. (Unknown)

A woman's work is never done. (English)

All women may be won. (Danish)

An ill-tempered woman is the Devil's door-nail. (Danish)

An old woman dancing raises a great dust. (Roman)

Being but a woman, raise not the sword. (Roman)

Between a woman's 'Yes' and 'No' there is no room for the point of a needle. (German)

Beware of a bad woman, and put no trust in a good one. (Spanish)

But what a woman says to her lover it is best to write in the wind and the swiftly flowing
 water. (Roman)

Choose not a woman nor linen by candlelight. (English)

Empty and cold is a house without a woman. (Irish)

Even a beautiful woman is not without a blemish. (African)

Every expensive thing is the wish of a woman. (Irish)

Every woman would rather be handsome than good. (German)

Fair, good, rich, and wise, is a woman four stories high. (French)

Far-fetched and dear-bought is good fitting for ladies. (Dutch)

Hell hath no fury like a woman scorned. (Italian)

In darkness, it matters not whether a woman is blonde or brunette. (Spanish)

Kind words and few are a woman's ornament. (Danish)

Long and lazy, little and loud; fat and fulsome, pretty and proud. (English)

Many women, many words. (Kurdish)

Melons and women are difficult to judge. (Spanish)

Neither all your love nor all your money should be given to a woman. (Mexican)

No woman is ugly when she is dressed. (Spanish)

Of two evils choose the lesser; of two women, the third. (Yiddish)

Put out the light, and all women are alike. (German)

The best women are the most silent. (German)

The fox loves cunning, the wolf covets the lamb, and a woman longs for praise. (Roman)

The happiest women, like the happiest nations, have no history. (Unknown)

The laughter, the tears, and the song of a woman are equally deceptive. (Roman)

The moment they see a woman alone in the street, they cry scandal. (Roman)

The prettiest woman can only give what she has. (French)

The thoughts of a woman when alone tend to mischief. (Roman)

There is hardly a bad cause in which a woman has not been a prime mover. (Roman)

What a woman wills, God wills. (French)

When woman gets off the wagon, horses have easier work. (American)

When women reign, the Devil governs. (German)

Woman is a torment, but let no home be without torment. (Persian)

Woman is ever fickle and changeable. (Roman)

Women and their wills are dangerous ills. (English)

Women are as fickle as April weather. (German)

Women are as wavering as the wind. (German)

Women are necessary evils. (German)

Women are watches that keep bad time. (German)

Women rouge that they may not blush. (Italian)

Women, money, and wine have their balm and their harm. (French)

Women, when offended, are not easily appeased. (Roman)

Women: can't live with them, can't live without them. (American)

Women and Men

A hundred men may make an encampment, but it takes a woman to make a home. (Chinese)

A woman's appetite is twice that of a man's; her sexual desire, four times; her intelligence, eight times. (Indian)

God created woman from man's side, that she should be near his heart. (Yiddish)

Man works from sun to sun, but a woman's work is never done. (American)

Water, smoke, and a vicious woman, drive men out of the house. (Italian)

Woman decides at once; man, upon reflection. (Italian)

Women surpass men at scheming evil. (Roman)

Words are for women, actions for men. (Italian)

Words are women, actions are men. (German)

Wonder, Wonders

A wonder lasts but nine days in a town. (Scottish)
No wonder lasts more than three days. (Italian)
Wonder at nothing. (Greek)
Wonder is the beginning of wisdom. (Greek)
Wonders will never cease. (English)

Wood

A chip on the shoulder indicates wood higher up. (Yiddish)
Chop, and you will have splinters. (Danish)
Crooked wood burns just as well as straight. (German)
Dry wood makes a quick fire. (Danish)
Green wood makes a hot fire. (English)
He that picks up all sorts of wood, soon gets an armful. (German)
If fortune favors, knock on wood. (Unknown)
Little sticks kindle a fire, great ones put it out. (Danish)
One chops the wood, the other does the grunting. (Yiddish)
Rotten wood cannot be carved. (Chinese)
The wood for a temple does not come from one tree. (Chinese)
Wood already touched by fire is not hard to set alight. (African)
Young wood makes a hot fire. (Greek)

Woods

Do not halloo until you are out of the woods. (English)

Wool

All the wool is hair, more or less. (Portuguese)
Bad is the wool that cannot be dyed. (Italian)
'Great cry and little wool', said the fool, when he sheared a pig. (German)
He who goes to collect wool may come back shorn. (French)
Much bleating for little wool. (Spanish)
Never give the sheep when you can pay with the wool. (German)
Some card the wool, others take the credit. (Spanish)
The wool seller knows the wool buyer. (Yiddish)
Who lets the rams graze gets the wool. (Albanian)
Would you shear a donkey for wool? (Roman)

Word

A bad word whispered will echo a hundred miles. (Chinese)
A bad wound heals but a bad word doesn't. (Persian)
A good word quenches more than a cauldron of water. (Portuguese)
A kind word can attract even the snake from its nest. (Arabian)
A kind word is better than alms. (Yiddish)
A kind word is like a Spring day. (Russian)
A kind word never broke anyone's mouth. (Irish)

A kind word is never lost. (American)

A man's word is his bond. (Spanish)

A true word needs no oath. (Turkish)

A tune is more lasting than the song of the birds, and a word is more lasting than the wealth of the world. (Irish)

A word and a stone once thrown cannot be recalled. (Spanish)

A word and an arrow in this are alike: they both quickly find their targets. (Yiddish)

A word before is worth two after. (Unknown)

A word once out flies everywhere. (French)

A word once spoken can never be recalled. (Roman)

A word once let out, flies quickly away. (Italian)

A word spoken in season is like an apple of gold set in pitchers of silver. (Unknown)

A word spoken is past recalling. (English)

A word to the good is enough, but even a stick won't help the bad. (Yiddish)

A word to the wise is sufficient. (Roman)

A word, once let loose, cannot be caught even by four galloping horses. (Japanese)

Among men of honor a word is a bond. (Italian)

Avoid a strange and unfamiliar word as you would a dangerous reef. (Roman)

Better one living word than a hundred dead ones. (German)

Even the fool says a wise word sometimes. (Italian)

If one word does not succeed, ten thousand are of no avail. (Chinese)

Many a true word is spoken in jest. (English)

No word is ill-spoken, that is not ill-taken. (Portuguese)

One good word quenches more fire than a bucket of water. (Italian)

One ill word asks for another. (Italian)

One kind word can warm three winter months. (Japanese)

One word beforehand is better than ten afterwards. (Danish)

One word brings on another. (Italian)

One word spoken may last for a lifetime. (Burmese)

One written word is worth a thousand pieces of gold. (Japanese)

Say not a word, bitter or sweet. (Korean)

Take a horse by its bridle and a man by his word. (Dutch)

Take an ox by its horn, a man by his word. (French)

The best word has not yet been said. (Spanish)

The smart of a blow subsides, the sting of a word abides. (Yiddish)

The swiftest horse cannot overtake the word once spoken. (Chinese)

The voice that is heard perishes, the word that is written remains. (Roman)

The written word remains, what is spoken perishes. (Roman)

There would be no ill word were words not ill-taken. (Spanish)

Though footless, a word can travel a thousand miles. (Korean)

To a kind word given, a kind word is returned. (Korean)

When the word is out, it belongs to another. (German)

Words

A man of words and not of deeds is like a garden full of weeds. (Italian)

A round egg can be made square according to how you cut it; words would be harsh according to how you speak them. (Japanese)

As a person is, so are his words. (Spanish)

Big words seldom go with good deeds. (Danish)

Don't discredit your words by your looks. (Roman)

Don't use words too big for your mouth. (Persian)

Evil words corrupt good manners. (Dutch)

Fair words don't fill the pocket. (German)

Fair words please the fool, and sometimes the wise. (Danish)

Fair words won't fill the sack. (Dutch)

Fair words, but look to your purse. (Italian)

Few words are best. (Danish)

Fine words butter no parsnips. (Roman)

Fine words do not produce food. (Nigerian)

Fine words don't fill the belly. (Dutch)

Fine words without deeds go not far. (Danish)

Food becomes shorter and words become longer the farther they go. (Korean)

Give your ears to words but do not give your words to ears. (Indian)

Good fists do not fight nor do good words curse. (Chinese)

Good words and no deeds are rushes and reeds. (Spanish)

Good words fill not a sack. (Spanish)

Hard words break no bones. (Italian)

If you wish to know the mind of a man, listen to his words. (Chinese)

Ill words are bellows to a slackening fire. (Roman)

In a multitude of words, there will certainly be a mistake. (Chinese)

It is bitter fare to eat one's own words. (Danish)

It takes many words to fill a sack. (Danish)

Let the words spoken in the jungle disappear in the jungle. (Burmese)

Many books do not use up words; many words do not use up thoughts. (Chinese)

Many words do not fill a basket. (Yoruban)

Many words, little credit. (Roman)

Mere words do not feed the friars. (Irish)

More is done with words than with hands. (German)

Of words and feathers, it takes many to make a pound. (German)

One sentence may spoil a man's case; one sentence may improve it. (Yoruban)

One who speaks fair words feeds you with an empty spoon. (Italian)

Peaceful words bring a cola nut from the pocket, but hard words bring an arrow from the quiver. (Yoruban)

Plenty of words when the cause is lost. (Italian)

Poor people's words go many to a sack-full. (German)

Smooth words do not flay the tongue. (Italian)

Smooth words make for smooth ways. (Italian)

Soft words break no bones. (Irish)

Soft words butter no parsnips, but they won't harden the heart of the cabbage either. (Irish)

Soft words do not cut the tongue. (French)
Soft words will get the snake out of its hole. (Persian)
Soft words win hard hearts. (Unknown)
Sugared words generally prove bitter. (Spanish)
Sweet words please fools. (Japanese)
The same words conceal and declare the thoughts of men. (Roman)
Though you may fear the words of others, fear first your own. (Unknown)
To rude words deaf ears. (French)
To the understanding, few words suffice. (Roman)
Under fair words beware of fraud. (Portuguese)
Under the fair words of a bad man there lurks some treachery. (Roman)
Use soft words and hard arguments. (English)
Water and words are easy to pour but impossible to recover. (Chinese)
Whose life is as lightning, his words are as thunder. (Roman)
Words are but sands; 'tis money buys lands. (French)
Words are female, deeds are male. (Italian)
Words are good, but fowls lay eggs. (German)
Words are like eggs: when they are hatched they have wings. (Madagascan)
Words are like spears: once they leave your lips they can never come back. (Yoruban)
Words are man's cud. (Persian)
Words are the voice of the heart. (Chinese)
Words become seeds. (Korean)
Words bind men, cords the horns of a bull. (Roman)
Words have no wings but they can fly a thousand miles. (Korean)
Words may either conceal character or reveal it. (Roman)
Words often do more than blows. (German)
Words on paper do not blush. (Italian)
Words once spoken cannot be taken back. (Chinese)
Words once uttered cannot be overtaken, even by a four-horse coach. (Korean)
Words pay no debts. (Roman)
Words should be weighed, not counted. (Yiddish)
Words spoken fly, words written remain. (Roman)
Words will not fail when the matter is well considered. (Roman)
Words without thought are merely wind. (Spanish)
Wounds heal, but not ill words. (Spanish)
You may gain by fair words what may fail you by angry ones. (Danish)

Work, Works, Working
A good rest is half the work. (Slavic)
A woman's work is never done. (English)
A plow that works, shines, but still water stinks. (Dutch)
All work and no play makes Jack a dull boy. (English)
As a man eats, so he works. (German)
As the master, so the work. (German)
Business before pleasure, work before leisure. (English)

By the hands of many a great work is made light. (Roman)

Every work stands in awe of the master. (Estonian)

First the work, then the rest. (German)

He does a good day's work who rids himself of a fool. (French)

He has enough to do who holds the handle of a frying pan. (French)

He is deserving who is industrious. (Roman)

He never did a good day's work who went sullenly about it. (French)

He who does not work should not partake. (Mexican)

He who works on the highway will have many advisors. (Spanish)

He who would rest must work. (Italian)

If I sleep, I sleep for myself; if I work, I know not for whom. (Italian)

If the hours are long enough and the pay is short enough, someone will say it's women's
    work. (Italian)

If work were good for you, the rich would leave none for the poor. (Haitian)

If you would have your work ill done, pay beforehand. (Italian)

It is better to work without pay than to live idly. (Spanish)

It is not the big oxen that do the best day's work. (French)

It is not the long day, but the heart that does the work. (Italian)

Like box makers, more noise than work. (French)

Many hands make work light. (Roman)

Many hands make work quick. (German)

More hands mean more work. (Greek)

Never let fools see half-finished work. (Danish)

Never was a good work done without much trouble. (Chinese)

Nothing can be done without work. (Unknown)

One plows, another sows; who will reap?, no one knows. (Danish)

One who works hard arouses enmity in a lazy man. (Yoruban)

Only fools and horses work. (Maltese)

Only the young are patient under hard work. (Hausan)

Shirk work and you will want bread. (Roman)

The hardest work is to do nothing. (American)

The man who works like a slave eats like a king. (Indian)

The one who does no work, shall not eat. (St Paul)

The work praises the workman. (German)

The way one eats is the way one works. (Czech)

The work of the youth is the blanket of the old. (Albanian)

To get work from a man, you have to stoke the fire. (German)

To the spectator no work is too hard. (German)

Two-thirds of the work is the semblance. (Irish)

Weighty work must be done with few words. (Danish)

When it comes to work, two boys are half a boy, and three boys are no boy at all. (English)

Who does not work is a burden to the earth. (Albanian)

Who loves his work and knows to spare, may live and flourish anywhere. (German)

Whoever invented work must not have had anything to do. (German)

Without work you won't get any cakes. (Unknown)

Work and you will be strong; sit and you will stink. (Moroccan)

Work as if you were to live 100 years, pray as if you were to die tomorrow. (Poor Richard)

Work done expects money. (Portuguese)

Work expands to fill the time. (American; Parkinson's law)

Work for a single grain and reckon up the profits of him who does nothing. (Egyptian)

Work gives dignity and vigor; idleness weakens and degrades. (Spanish)

Work ill done is twice done. (German)

Work is a good appetizer. (Irish)

Work is a pleasure in itself. (Roman)

Work is sacred: don't touch it! (Spanish)

Work is the best of relishes [i.e., work stimulates one's appetite]. (Roman)

Work is the medicine for poverty. (Yoruban)

Work like an ox, eat like a mouse. (Korean)

Work makes one free. (German)

Work summons forth the best men. (Roman)

Work without end is a housewife's lot. (Irish)

Work, even for a little, then sit idle for nothing. (Egyptian)

Working overruns poverty. (Japanese)

Working slowly produces fine goods. (Chinese)

Works have a stronger voice than words. (Roman)

You do the work, another takes the credit. (English)

You must judge a man by the work of his hands. (African)

You tell a man by the work, not by the clothes. (Albanian)

Your hand is never the worse for doing its own work. (Welsh)

Worker, Workman

At the end of the work you may judge of the workman. (Italian)

He is a bad workman who cannot talk of work. (German)

It's a poor workman who complains about his tools. (Spanish)

Not to oversee workmen, is to leave them your purse open. (Poor Richard)

The bad workman blames his tools. (American)

The money paid, the worker's arm is broken. (French)

The work praises the workman. (German)

The work tests the workman. (Roman)

The workman is known by his labor. (French)

We become workmen by working. (Roman)

Where there are too many workmen, there is little work. (German)

Work makes the workman. (Roman)

Workmen are easier found than masters. (German)

World

A fair world, a radiant world – but for whom? (Yiddish)

Ancient times were the youth of the world. (English)

Better one day in this world than one thousand in the other. (Japanese)

Eat and drink, and let the world go to ruin. (Egyptian)
Half the world knows not how the other half lives. (English)
Half the world supports that other half. (Spanish)
He is the world's master who despises it, its slave who prizes it. (Italian)
He that best understands the world, least likes it. (Poor Richard)
It is a wicked world, and we make part of it. (English)
It takes all sorts to make a world. (English)
Take the world as it is, not as it ought to be. (German)
That corner of the world smiles for me more than anywhere else. (Roman)
The gown is hers that wears it; and the world is his who enjoys it. (French)
The whole world isn't crazy. (Yiddish)
The world befriends the elephant and tramples on the ant. (Indian)
The world is a mirror – view and be viewed. (Egyptian)
The world is an ocean – learn to swim. (Yoruban)
The world is changed by arms not arguments. (Unknown)
The world is governed with little brains. (Italian)
The world is like a staircase: some go up, others go down. (Italian)
The world is not for the timid and quiet. (Spanish)
The world is the living image of God. (Italian)
The world laughs at those who fall. (German)
The world's a stage: each plays his part, and takes his share. (Dutch)
This world is the world of everyone in turn. (Irish)
Treat everything of this world as mere vanity. (Roman)

Worm

Even a worm will turn. (English)
Every worm has its hole. (Yiddish)
Silent worms bore holes in the wall. (Japanese)
Tread on a worm, and it will turn. (French)

Worry, Worries

A hundred years of fretting will not pay a cent of debt. (French)
A man's life is scarcely a hundred years, yet he worries enough for a thousand.
    (Chinese)
A pretty basket does not prevent worries. (African)
Do not worry about tomorrow, because you do not even know what may happen to
    you today. (Yiddish)
Don't worry about tomorrow. (Korean)
First worry, then rejoice. (Chinese)
He who does as he likes has no worry. (Italian)
It is not the work that kills, but the worry. (African)
People worry, and God smiles. (Yiddish)
'Tis not work that kills, but worry. (English)
Worries go down better with soup than without. (Yiddish)
Worry changes a person's character. (Mexican)

Worry often gives a small thing a big shadow. (Swedish)
Worrying never did anybody any good. (Swedish)

Worse
If things don't get better, depend on it, they will get worse. (Yiddish)

Worship
Men worship the rising, not the setting sun. (Roman)

Worth
If it is worth taking, it is worth asking for. (Irish)
One never gets more than one's money's worth of anything. (French)
Surely the worth of a man lies in two of his smallest parts – his heart and his tongue. (Egyptian)
The worth of a thing is what it will bring. (Dutch)
Three things in the world worth having: courage, good sense, caution. (Hausan)
What is worth receiving is worth returning. (French)

Worthless
Worthless things cause us the most problems. (Mexican)

Wound, Wounds
A knife wound heals; a wound caused by words does not. (Turkish)
A wound never heals so well that the scar cannot be seen. (Danish)
A wound, when fresh, shrinks from the touch. (Roman)
A wounded spirit is hard to heal. (Yiddish)
Old age and poverty are wounds that can't be healed. (Greek)
Old wounds easily bleed. (German)
Reopen not a wound once healed. (Roman)
The evil wound is cured but not the evil name. (German)
The wound of words is worse than the wound of swords. (Arabian)
Unbending the bow does not heal the wound. (Italian)

Wrath
A soft answer turns away wrath. (the Bible)
Can wrath so great dwell in heavenly minds? (Roman)
The wrath of brothers is the wrath of devils. (Spanish)
The wrath of kings is always severe. (Roman)
Wrath often consumes what God gives husbands. (Icelandic)

Wreath
Wreaths are for the dead. (Mexican)

Wreck
The wreck of a ship is a beacon at sea. (English)

Wrestle, Wrestler

He that is thrown would still wrestle. (French)

If I wrestle with a filthy thing, win or lose, I shall be defiled. (Roman)

If you wrestle with a coalminer you will be blackened. (French)

A defeated wrestler is not tired of wrestling. (Turkish)

Wretched

Nothing else is necessary to make you wretched than to believe you are so. (Roman)

Write

Learned and unlearned, we all write. (Roman)

The one who writes reads twice. (Roman)

To write is to act. (Roman)

Where you have nothing to write, write and say so. (Roman)

Write kindness in marble and write injuries in the dust. (Persian)

Write quickly and you will never write well; write well, and you will soon write quickly. (Roman)

Write the bad things that are done to you in sand, but write the good things that happen to you on marble. (Arabian)

Write with the learned, pronounce with the vulgar. (Poor Richard)

Writer

A fine writer chooses his brushes carefully. (Korean)

A good writer is not choosy about his brushes. (Korean)

Even the best ink-brush does not make one a fine writer. (Korean)

Even the best writer has to erase. (Spanish)

One quill is better in the hand than seven geese upon the strand. (Dutch)

The poor writer blames the pen. (Spanish)

Writing, Writings

A goose quill is more dangerous than a lion's claw. (English)

By writing one learns to write. (Roman)

Knowledge is the fountain and source of good writing. (Roman)

Learn to handle a writing-brush and you'll never handle a begging-bowl. (Chinese)

Many have an incurable itch for writing – which takes full possession of their disordered faculties. (Roman)

Writings should not be published readily. (Roman)

Wrong

No one can take advantage of a wrong committed by himself. (Roman)

Nowadays those are rewarded who make right appear wrong. (Roman)

One wrong does not justify another. (Roman)

Revenge a wrong by forgiving it. (English)

Truly it is much better to suffer wrong than to do wrong. (American)

Two wrongs don't make a right. (English)

With a little wrong a man comes by his right. (Spanish)
Wrong cannot rest, nor ill deeds stand. (Irish)

Y

Yawn

As the bird goes from tree to tree, the yawn goes from man to man. (Irish)
One man yawning makes another yawn too. (Roman)

Year, Years

A cherry year, a merry year; a plum year, a dumb year. (West African)
A cow-year, a sad year; a bull-year, a glad year. (Dutch)
As the years pass, they rob us of one thing after another. (Roman)
It will be all the same a hundred years hence. (American)
Nothing is swifter than the years. (Roman)
The years are gravediggers of our joys and sorrows. (Finnish)
The year has a wide mouth and a big belly. (Danish)
The years glide swiftly by. (Roman)
The years lead to the grave. (German)
The years roll on and on. (Italian)
What does not happen in a year may happen in a moment. (Spanish)
Years and months are like flowing water. (Japanese)
Years and sins are always more than owned. (Italian)
Years know more than books. (Italian)

Yearn

He who has, worries; he who has not, longs. (Burmese)
One is never too old to yearn. (Italian)

Yelp

One dog yelping at nothing will set a thousand straining at their collars. (Japanese)

Yes

Half a yes is better than complete refusal. (Irish)
The burden of saying 'yes' does not press down on one's neck. (Yoruban)
Yes is surrender. (English)

Yes and No

Better a friendly no than an unwilling yes. (German)
No is a wall, yes an open gate. (the Editor)
Out of yes and no comes all dispute. (French)
It will not do to say yes to a man's face and no behind his back. (Chinese)

Yesterday

No man can call back yesterday. (Roman)

Yesterday a cowherd, today a cavalier. (Spanish)

Yesterday cannot last into today. (German)

Yesterday is but a dream, tomorrow but a vision. But today well lived makes every
 yesterday a dream of happiness, and every tomorrow a vision of hope. (Indian)

Yesterday will not return. (Japanese)

Yesterday's fruit is but today's dream. (Japanese)

Yield, Yielding

Yield not to misfortunes, but rather go more boldly to meet them. (Roman)

Yield to divine power. (Roman)

Yielding is sometimes the best way of succeeding. (Italian)

Yielding stays war. (German)

Yoke

An ox and an ass don't yoke well to the same plow. (Dutch)

Unequal yoke, uneven furrow. (German)

Yorkshire

Yorkshire born and Yorkshire bred, strong in arm and weak in head. (English)

Young, Younger

A young branch takes on all the bends that one gives it. (Chinese)

A young pheasant flaps its wings and is startled by the wind it makes. (Korean)

A young puppy does not fear the tiger. (Korean)

Let us be joyful, while we are young. (Roman)

The heart and eyes are always young. (Spanish)

We shall never be younger. (Roman)

Who would be young in age, must in youth become a sage. (German)

You're only young once. (American)

Young and Old

A man as he manages himself may die old at thirty, or young at eighty. (Roman)

A young prodigal, an old beggar. (English)

Age but tastes, youth devours. (Spanish)

An intemperate youth transfers to old age a worn-out body. (Roman)

Honor the old, teach the young. (Danish)

If young men had wit and old men strength everything might be well done. (Italian)

Old age is heavy, but youth is easily borne. (German)

The aged forget, but the young know nothing. (Japanese)

The aged in council, the young in action. (Danish)

The aged talk, the young act. (Unknown)

The doctor should be old, the lawyer should be young. (Burmese)

The work of the youth is the blanket of the old. (Albanian)

The young cannot teach tradition to the old. (Yoruban)

The young cock crows as he hears the old one. (Yoruban)

The young fight the battles of the old. (the Editor)

The young have strength, the old have knowledge. (Albanian)

The young know little, the old forget. (Unknown)

The young may die, but the old must die. (English)

The young pig grunts like the old sow. (German)

The young ravens are beaked like the old. (Dutch)

The young rely on their fathers, the old on their children. (Vietnamese)

We pay when old for the excesses of our youth. (Roman)

What one is accustomed to in youth, one does in old age. (German)

What the young one begs for, the grown-up one throws away. (Russian)

What you break in youth you feel in old age. (English)

What youth acquires, old age wastes. (German)

What youth learns, age does not forget. (Danish)

What youth practices, age remembers. (German)

What youth wastes, old age wants. (Spanish)

Where old age is evil, youth can learn no good. (English)

Where the elder comes to stop, the younger man catches up. (Yoruban)

You cannot put an old head on young shoulders. (English)

Young folk, silly folk; old folk, cold folk. (Dutch)

Young fools think that the old are dotards, but the old have forgotten more than the young fools know. (Dutch)

Young gambler, old beggar. (German)

Young men act, old men advise. (Spanish)

Young men may die, but old men must die. (German)

Young men think old men fools, but old men know the young to be so. (German)

Young men's knocks old men feel. (German)

Young people don't know what age is, and old people forget what youth was. (English)

Young people must be taught, old ones honored. (Danish)

Young people tell what they are doing, old people what they have done, and fools what they wish to do. (French)

Young pigs grunt as old pigs grunted before them. (Danish)

Young saint, old devil. (German)

Young soldiers, old beggars. (German)

Young birds seek the old nest. (Chinese)

Young twigs may be bent, but not old trees. (Dutch)

Young, a donkey; old, an ass. (Yiddish)

Youth has a beautiful face, old age a beautiful soul. (Swedish)

Youth is green, age is sturdy. (Russian)

Youth lives on hope, old age on remembrance. (French)

Youth seek, the old use. (Roman)

Youth

A beardless man has a woman's face. (Spanish)

A fledgling pigeon cannot fly over a mountain. (Korean)

A growing youth has a wolf in his belly. (German)

From boys men, from girls brides. (German)

If youth but had the knowledge and old age the strength, everything would be done well. (French)

If youth knew what age would crave, it would both get and save. (English)

In the boy you can see the man; in the girl, the woman. (Chinese)

It is the fault of youth that it cannot govern its own impulses. (Roman)

The beardless cannot be trusted to do anything well. (Chinese)

The greatest consideration is due to the innocence of youth. (Roman)

The vigor of youth passes away like a spring flower. (Roman)

Youth and lost time do not return. (German)

Youth and white paper take any impression. (German)

Youth and wine are like a whip to a galloping horse. (Japanese)

Youth cannot be stored for the winter. (German)

Youth comes but once. (Korean)

Youth does not mind where it sets its foot. (Irish)

Youth foresees not poverty, nor the fool his mischief. (Irish)

Youth has a small head. (Irish)

Youth is the time to sow. (German)

Youth is unduly busy pampering the outer man. (Roman)

Youth is wasted on the young. (Irish)

Youth is without virtue. (German)

Youth itself is beauty. (the Editor)

Youth likes to wander. (Irish)

Youth likes to flit away, and fools are fond of removing. (Irish)

Youth may stray afar yet return at last. (French)

Youth must be served. (English)

Youth sheds many skins. (Irish)

Youth slips away as water from a sandy shore. (Irish)

Z

Zeal

Zeal is a bad servant. (Unknown)

Zeal is fit only for wise men but is found mostly in fools. (Ancient Sumerian)

Zeal without knowledge is like fire without light. (English)

Zeal without knowledge is the sister of folly. (English)

Zeal without prudence is frenzy. (English)

SUBJECT INDEX

Related titles from Routledge

The New Partridge Dictionary of Slang and Unconventional English

Edited by Tom Dalzell and Terry Victor

First published in 1937, Eric Partridge's brilliant magnum opus, *The Dictionary of Slang and Unconventional English*, set new standards in the spirited and intelligent appraisal of slang.

Containing over 60,000 entries, this two-volume *The New Partridge Dictionary of Slang and Unconventional English* takes up the mantle to present a definitive record of the slang of the last sixty years.

Alongside US and British English slang, the dictionary also boasts entries from Australia, New Zealand, Canada, India, South Africa, Ireland and the Caribbean. Entries are given a published source and, where possible, an early or significant example of the term's use in print.

Like its forebear, *The New Partridge Dictionary of Slang and Unconventional English* is a monumental piece of work infused with humour and learning – a prize for anyone with a love of, and a fascination with, language.

ISBN10: 0–415–21258–8 (hbk)
ISBN13: 978–0–415–21258–8 (hbk)

Available at all good bookshops
For ordering and further information please visit:
www.routledge.com

Related titles from Routledge

The Routledge Dictionary of Gods, Goddesses, Devils and Demons

Manfred Lurker

From classical Greek and Roman mythology to the gods of Eastern Europe and Mesopotamia; from Nordic giants to Islamic jinns and Egyptian monsters, this classic dictionary is packed with descriptions of the figures most worshipped and feared around the world and across time. Fully cross-referenced and with over 100 illustrations, it also features two handy appendices listing the functions and attributes shared by these deities and demons.

Covering over 1800 of the most important gods and demons from around the world, this is the essential resource for anyone interested in comparative religion and the mythology of the ancient and contemporary worlds.

ISBN10: 0–415–34018–7 (pbk)
ISBN13: 978–0–415–34018–2 (pbk)

Available at all good bookshops
For ordering and further information please visit:
www.routledge.com

Related titles from Routledge

Complete Fairy Tales
Brothers Grimm

'Among the few indispensable common-property books upon which Western culture can be founded ... it is hardly too much to say that these tales rank next to the Bible in importance.' – *W. H. Auden*

Many of Jacob and Wilhelm Grimm's stories are gruesome tales of gore and violence. Contrary to today's sanitized children's stories they are outrageously savage. Then again, these tales were never intended to be read predominantly by, or to, children. These were the stories kept alive by German peasants of the time, told around the fireplace to entranced listeners, young and old.

ISBN10: 0–415–28595–X (hbk)
ISBN10: 0–415–28596–8 (pbk)

ISBN13: 978–0–415–28595–7 (hbk)
ISBN13: 978–0–415–28596–4 (pbk)

Available at all good bookshops
For ordering and further information please visit:
www.routledge.com

Related titles from Routledge

The Bible in Western Culture

Dee Dyas and Esther Hughes

The influence of the Bible in Western culture is immeasurable. *The Bible in Western Culture* is the essential guide for those wishing to find out more about the Bible and its impact on the world around us.

It offers concise and accessible introductions to the Bible's most important characters, stories and themes, enabling better understanding, study and analysis of the Christian element in Western culture.

With no prior biblical knowledge required, the volume offers a framework of understanding for those studying Western literature, art, historical events, or for those just wanting to improve their general knowledge.

It provides:

- edited extracts from the Bible
- explanations of the context and beliefs of each passage
- links to related biblical texts
- examples of related key works of art and literature
- brief biographies of key figures
- a comprehensive glossary defining specialist terms
- chronology
- suggested further reading.

This book enables readers to encounter key Bible stories directly, while also providing background information on issues of content, context and influence.

ISBN10: 0–415–32617–6 (hbk)
ISBN10: 0–415–32618–4 (pbk)

ISBN13: 978–0–415–32617–9 (hbk)
ISBN13: 978–0–415–32618–6 (pbk)

Available at all good bookshops
For ordering and further information please visit:

www.routledge.com

Related titles from Routledge

The Concise Encyclopedia of
Western Philosophy
Edited by Jonathan Rée

On its first appearance in 1960, the *Concise Encyclopedia of Western Philosophy* established itself as a classic; this third edition builds on its original strengths but brings it completely up to date. The *Concise Encyclopedia* offers a lively, readable, comprehensive and authoritative treatment of Western philosophy as a whole, incorporating scintillating articles by many leading philosophical authors. It serves not only as a convenient reference work, but also as an engaging introduction to philosophy.

ISBN10: 0–415–32923–X (hbk)
ISBN10: 0–415–32924–8 (pbk)

ISBN13: 978–0–415–329323–1 (hbk)
ISBN13: 978–0–415–32924–8 (pbk)

Available at all good bookshops
For ordering and further information please visit:
www.routledge.com

Made in the USA
Las Vegas, NV
13 May 2022

48863260R00299